fundamental principles of law and economics

This textbook places the relationship between law and economics in its international context, explaining the fundamentals of this increasingly important area of teaching and research in an accessible and straightforward manner. In presenting the subject, Alan Devlin draws on the neo-classical tradition of economic analysis of law while also showcasing cutting-edge developments, such as the rise of behavioural economic theories of law.

Key features of this innovative book include:

- case law, directives, regulations, and statistics from EU, UK, and US jurisdictions are presented clearly and contextualised for law students, showing how law and economics theory can be understood in practice;
- succinct end-of-chapter summaries highlight the essential points in each chapter to focus student learning;
- further reading is provided at the end of each chapter to guide independent research.

Making use of tables and diagrams throughout to facilitate understanding, this text provides a comprehensive overview of law and economics that is ideal for those new to the subject and for use as a course text for law and economics modules.

Alan Devlin is an antitrust lawyer with the San Francisco office of Latham & Watkins LLP, and has taught courses on law and economics, antitrust, and intellectual property as an adjunct member of the law faculties of the University of Chicago, DePaul University, Trinity College Dublin, University College Dublin, and most recently UC Hastings College of Law.

fundamental principles
of law and economics

Alan Devlin

Routledge
Taylor & Francis Group

LONDON AND NEW YORK

First published 2015
by Routledge
2 Park Square, Milton Park, Abingdon, Oxon, OX14 4RN

and by Routledge
711 Third Avenue, New York, NY 10017

Routledge is an imprint of the Taylor & Francis Group, an informa business

British Library Cataloguing in Publication Data
A catalogue record for this book is available from the British Library

Library of Congress Cataloging-in-Publication Data
Devlin, Alan (Alan James)
   Principles of law and economics / Alan Devlin.
      pages cm
   ISBN 978-1-138-80601-6 (hbk) — ISBN 978-1-138-80602-3 (pbk) —
   ISBN 978-1-315-75188-7 (ebk)   1. Law and economics.
   2. Law—Economic aspects.   3. Public policy (Law)   I. Title.
   K487.E3D49 2015
   340'.11—dc23   2014017372

ISBN: 978-1-138-80601-6 (hbk)
ISBN: 978-1-138-80602-3 (pbk)
ISBN: 978-1-315-75188-7 (ebk)

Typeset in Joanna
by RefineCatch Limited, Bungay, Suffolk

Printed and bound in Great Britain by
TJ International Ltd, Padstow, Cornwall

Outline Contents

Introduction   1

PART 1   **ECONOMIC THEORY, LAW, AND MORALITY**
1   Background Principles in Microeconomics   11
2   Essential Concepts in the Law and Economics Literature   28
3   Utilitarianism, Neoclassical Welfare Economics, and the Ethics of Markets   43

PART 2   **THE LAW OF TORT**
1   The Economics of Liability Rules and Accidents   65
2   An Economic Account of Tort Doctrine   88

PART 3   **CRIMINAL LAW**
1   An Economic Account of Criminal Behaviour   105
2   Optimal Criminal Sanctions   112
3   Problems in Criminal Law   127

PART 4   **PROPERTY**
1   The Economic Role of Property Rights   147
2   Protecting Entitlements   160

PART 5   **THE LAW OF CONTRACT**
1   An Economic Theory of Contract Law   175
2   The Economics of Contractual Remedies   197

PART 6   **LITIGATION**
1   An Economic Theory of Litigation   209

PART 7   **INNOVATION POLICY**
1   Innovation Policy   235
2   The Patent System   251
3   Copyright Law   283

PART 8   **COMPETITION LAW AND NATURAL MONOPOLY REGULATION**
1   Antitrust and The Regulation of Business Strategy   303
2   Antitrust Limits on Contract   334
3   Monopolisation   348
4   The Regulation of Natural Monopoly   370

PART 9   BEHAVIOURAL LAW AND ECONOMICS
1   Behavioural Law and Economics   395

Conclusion   413

Index   417

Detailed Contents

Introduction   1
   A.   The Economic Analysis of Law   2
   B.   Essential Insights   4
       References and Further Reading   8

PART 1   ECONOMIC THEORY, LAW, AND MORALITY
1   Background Principles in Microeconomics   11
   A.   Utility and the Distribution of Scarce Resources   12
   B.   Consumer Choice and the Law of Demand   13
   C.   Firm Behaviour and the Law of Supply   18
   D.   Market Equilibrium, and an Illustrative Application to Criminal Law   20
   E.   Game Theory   23
       Key Points   27
       References and Further Reading   27

2   Essential Concepts in the Law and Economics Literature   28
   A.   The Coase Theorem   29
   B.   Efficiency and Appetite for Risk   31
   C.   Rationality   34
   D.   Decision Making in the Presence of Risk: Expected Value and Expected Utility   37
   E.   Decision Making under Uncertainty   39
       Key Points   40
       References and Further Reading   41

3   Utilitarianism, Neoclassical Welfare Economics, and the Ethics of Markets   43
   A.   Utilitarianism   44
   B.   Neoclassical Welfare Economics as Applied to Law   50
   C.   The Ethics of Markets   53
       Key Points   59
       References and Further Reading   60

PART 2   THE LAW OF TORT
1   The Economics of Liability Rules and Accidents   65
   A.   Introduction   66
   B.   Which Liability Rule?   68
   C.   Unilateral-Care Scenarios with Fixed Activity Levels   68
   D.   Bilateral-Care Scenarios with Fixed Activity Levels   71

E.   Unilateral-Care Scenarios with Variable Activity Levels   76
F.   Bilateral-Care Scenarios with Variable Activity Levels   78
G.   Tort Law, Risk Aversion, Insurance, and Moral Hazard   82
H.   Is Law and Economics Theory Realistic about Optimal Remedies?   84
        Key Points   86
        References and Further Reading   87

2   An Economic Account of Tort Doctrine   88
A.   Introduction   89
B.   The Injury Requirement   90
C.   Foreseeability, Proximity, and Causation   90
D.   Problems in the Determination of Liability   94
E.   Defective Products   96
F.   Intentional Torts   100
        Key Points   101
        References and Further Reading   102

PART 3   CRIMINAL LAW
1   An Economic Account of Criminal Behaviour   105
A.   Introduction   106
B.   Categorically Inefficient Crime   106
C.   Potentially Desirable Crime   108
        Key Points   111
        References and Further Reading   111

2   Optimal Criminal Sanctions   112
A.   Introduction   113
B.   Regulating the Crime Level   113
C.   Driving Output to Zero: Minimising Inefficient Crime at the Lowest Cost 123
        Key Points   125
        References and Further Reading   126

3   Problems in Criminal Law   127
A.   Introduction   128
B.   Why Is Intent a Necessary Element of Most Crimes?   128
C.   Why Punish Unsuccessful Attempts?   130
D.   Price Discrimination   130
E.   Irrationality and the Realism of the Law and Economics Account of Crime 132
F.   Do Criminals Respond to Incentives?: The Empirical Literature   132
G.   Drug Policy   137
        Key Points   143
        References and Further Reading   143

PART 4   PROPERTY
1   The Economic Role of Property Rights   147
A.   Introduction   148
B.   Ownership Rights and the Efficient Utilisation of Resources   149
C.   The Coase Theorem and Allocation of Scarce Resources   151

	D.	Problems in the Creation of Property Rights	154
	E.	Conclusion	158
		Key Points	158
		References and Further Reading	159

2	**Protecting Entitlements**		160
	A.	Introduction	161
	B.	Protecting Ownership Rights in Zero-Transaction-Cost Environments	162
	C.	Supporting Entitlements Where Transaction Costs are Positive but not Preclusive	165
	D.	Proprietary Interests in High-Transaction-Cost Settings	169
		Key Points	170
		References and Further Reading	170

PART 5	**THE LAW OF CONTRACT**		
1	**An Economic Theory of Contract Law**		175
	A.	Contracts and the Coase Theorem	176
	B.	Frustration, Impracticability, and Impossibility	179
	C.	Mistake, Duress, Undue Influence, and Misrepresentation	184
	D.	Problems in Interpretation	188
	E.	Limits on Autonomy: Unconscionable Agreements	190
	F.	Third-Party Effects and Inefficient Accords: Contracts Against Public Policy	194
		Key Points	194
		References and Further Reading	196

2	**The Economics of Contractual Remedies**		197
	A.	Introduction: Efficient Breach and Optimal Reliance	198
	B.	The Effect of Damages on Breach and Reliance Decisions	199
	C.	Consequential Damages	204
		Key Points	205
		References and Further Reading	205

PART 6	**LITIGATION**		
1	**An Economic Theory of Litigation**		209
	A.	Introduction	210
	B.	Explaining the Litigation Process	211
	C.	Negative-Value Lawsuits	217
	D.	English and American Rules Compared	222
	E.	The Optimal Level of Litigation	226
	F.	Conclusion	229
		Key Points	230
		References and Further Reading	231

PART 7	**INNOVATION POLICY**		
1	**Innovation Policy**		235
	A.	Introduction	236
	B.	Building a Platform for Technological Progress	236

C.   Conclusion   249
Key Points   249
References and Further Reading   250

2   The Patent System   251
A.   Public-Goods Theory and the Economics of Innovation   252
B.   A Primer on Patent Law and Economics   258
C.   Incentives to Invent Independent of the Patent System   266
D.   Industry-Specific Innovation Profiles   269
E.   Alternatives to Patents: Prizes, Buy-Outs, and Regulatory Exclusivity   276
F.   Conclusion   280
Key Points   280
References and Further Reading   282

3   Copyright Law   283
A.   Introduction   284
B.   Copyright Law and the Incentive to Create Expressive Works   285
C.   The Optimal Scope of Copyright Protection   290
D.   The Efficient Copyright Term   294
E.   Piracy Wars: File-Sharing, DRM, and ISP Injunctions   295
F.   Conclusion   297
Key Points   298
References and Further Reading   298

PART 8   COMPETITION LAW AND NATURAL MONOPOLY REGULATION
1   Antitrust and The Regulation of Business Strategy   303
A.   Introduction: The Economic Role of Competition Policy   304
B.   The Evolving Schools of Antitrust Economics   305
C.   The Economics of Competition and Monopoly   309
D.   Industrial Organisation: Imperfectly Competitive Markets   314
E.   The Role of the Market: Definition, Power, and Self-Correction   323
Key Points   330
References and Further Reading   332

2   Antitrust Limits on Contract   334
A.   Introduction   335
B.   Horizontal Restraints on Competition   336
C.   Vertical Restraints on Competition   342
D.   Conclusion   344
Key Points   345
References and Further Reading   346

3   Monopolisation   348
A.   Monopoly as an Elusive Prize: The Dilemma for Competition Regulators   349
B.   Product Tying   352
C.   Anticompetitive Pricing   355
D.   Refusals to Deal   359
E.   Loyalty Rebates   361
F.   Vertical Integration   362

G.   Anticompetitive Mergers: Unilateral and Coordinated Effects   364
      Key Points   367
      References and Further Reading   368

4   **The Regulation of Natural Monopoly**   370
A.   The Economics of Natural Monopoly   371
B.   Containing Monopoly Power: Regulation of Price and Entry   373
C.   Restoring Competition: The Deregulatory Movement   381
D.   The Limits of Competition: The Case of the Financial Services Industry   389
E.   Conclusion   390
      Key Points   391
      References and Further Reading   392

PART 9   **BEHAVIOURAL LAW AND ECONOMICS**
1   **Behavioural Law and Economics**   395
A.   Introduction   396
B.   Revisiting Expected-Value Theory: Cognitive Psychology, Systemic Biases, and
      Prospect Theory   397
C.   Behavioural Law and Economics: Applications   404
D.   Normative Dimensions to Rationality: Paternalism and Behavioural Economics   407
E.   The Continuing Importance of Neoclassical Law and Economics   409
      Key Points   411
      References and Further Reading   412

Conclusion   413

Index   417

Introduction

Chapter Contents

A.   The Economic Analysis of Law   2

B.   Essential Insights   4

References and Further Reading   8

A. The Economic Analysis of Law

Law and conduct are intertwined. As enough people take heed of its call, the law influences social behaviour, allowing policymakers to craft rules to effect desired outcomes. Thus, liberal democracies enforce property rights, proscribe criminality, impose liability in tort, and grant damages for breach of contract to promote certain goals. They believe that people respond to positive incentives, such as promised rewards, and to negative ones, such as threatened punishment. Society recognises that law can affect the rate of accidents, crime, innovation, competition, and other matters of public importance.

If legislatures pass laws to spur particular goals, then they must understand how rules shape conduct. Economics is the study of incentives, and thus provides the requisite understanding. It predicts how rules will affect behaviour, enabling lawmakers embracing a forward-looking theory of justice to mould doctrine to achieve desired results. Especially since the 1970s, economic research has explored how law affects incentives, thus informing the law's theory, content, and practice to this day. Such has been its influence that commentators variously describe law and economics as, "by almost any measure, the most dominant school of legal thought in the last half a century"[1] and as "the most influential development in legal thought since the demise of legal realism in the early 1940s".[2] The discipline is the predominant methodology for understanding law in the United States, and is growing in influence elsewhere.

This book introduces the field of law and economics, presenting the subject as a powerful analytic tool. It extrapolates the central tenets of law-and-economics theory, and reveals how those principles shed light on countless legal questions. It focuses on the economic analysis of tort, crime, contracts, property, litigation, innovation, competition, and regulation.

This introductory section orientates the uninitiated reader to the field, explaining some threshold concepts useful for understanding law and economics. Those topics include distinguishing positive and normative analysis, explaining the "efficiency" or wealth-maximisation criterion that economists sometimes use to define optimal laws, and noting the value of interdisciplinary legal study. It concludes with representative insights that economics has made into legal doctrine, theory, and practice.

1. Positive and normative analysis

Law and economics has two components: positive study and normative evaluation. These consist of predicting the effect of laws and advocating rules, respectively. Positive law and economics uses simplified models of decision making – typically, game theory and neoclassical price theory – to predict how individuals would act when subject to a given rule. This theory can generate testable hypotheses about how proposed legislation or a particular judicial interpretation of law would impact market-level behaviour. This analysis can illuminate proposed laws' likely effects, thus helping legislators and judges to make determinations informed as to the probable consequences of their decisions.

The normative branch, by contrast, recommends what the law should be. One cannot formulate a prescriptive theory of law without implicating morality-laden principles of justice, on which subject people routinely disagree. Law and economics takes a distinctive view on this subject, embracing "efficiency" as the pertinent lodestar. The normative weight of law and economics thus depends on whether one's sense of justice aligns with efficiency. It is thus important to explain the meaning of that concept, which is where we begin.

---

1 Grant M. Hayden and Stephen E. Ellis, 'Law and economics after behavioral economics' (2007) 55 Kansas L Rev 629, 629.
2 Eli Salzberger, 'The economic analysis of law – The dominant methodology for legal research?!' (2008) 4 Haifa Law Review 207.

2. Efficiency

In its neoclassical formulation, law and economics first identifies people's revealed preferences and then classifies as "efficient" an outcome that satisfies at least one person's preference without violating another's. This conception of efficiency – known as a "Pareto improvement" – is, of course, narrow as many changes in law or behaviour negatively affect at least some third parties. When conflicts arise, the economic problem is one of incompatible preferences, which condition applies across the spectrum from tort and crime to innovation and competition. To resolve such disputes, the prescriptive wing of law and economics appeals to a hypothetical bargain that would have taken place between the parties in the absence of transaction costs. The "efficient" result is one that achieves a net increase in welfare: i.e., an outcome that allows the benefited parties to compensate those negatively affected, while still being better off themselves *ex post*.

This analysis is rooted in law and economics' most important concept: the Coase Theorem. This theorem provides that, when bargaining is free, the market will efficiently allocate resources regardless of their initial assignment. The reason is that, when transaction costs are absent, stakeholders will contract with one another such that owned resources will move to their highest value uses.

It would be remarkable if any field of study could rise to such ascendancy without attracting criticism, and the economic analysis of law is no exception. Those who are hostile to the field raise a number of objections. Against the positive arm of law and economics, some critics question the realism of predictions premised on neoclassical conceptions of rationality. Normative economic analysis is more controversial, as some commentators decry the idea that efficiency or wealth maximisation is an appropriate criterion for justice. These objections, and the defences that economists have mounted against them, are crucial to an informed understanding of both law and economics and the larger field of legal study. This book introduces these and other issues in the discipline.

Although there is more to law than economics alone, the author hopes that the reader will appreciate the many rich insights that economic analysis bestows upon legal problems.

3. The value of interdisciplinary study

The economic analysis of law is an interdisciplinary subject. Unfortunately, not everyone agrees that lawyers should concern themselves with non-legal fields. Such scepticism may arise from the perception that law is self-enclosed. Countless students have learned to love the intellectual richness of the common law, which rarely takes the promotion of efficiency as its explicit goal. In reasoning from first principles, solemnly deferring to precedent, and drawing nuanced distinctions in both law and fact, students grow to appreciate the acuity of legal thinking. No doubt, the common law displays an attractive internal structure and, although it is not blind to the circumstances in which it operates, it does display a certain form of autonomy. For some students, it is an easy leap to conclude that the law is a closed system that rests apart from other fields of study.

This view of the law, however, is seriously incomplete. The law's purview is the entire domain of human activity, such that law ignorant of other fields of study would be incoherent, ill-informed, and ultimately impoverished. A rich legal education exposes students not only to statutes, regulations, law, and the nature of legal reasoning, but to a variety of ancillary fields that, beyond economics, include philosophy, history, political science, accounting, finance, sociology, psychology, engineering, science, and more. For that reason, law is inherently interdisciplinary. Only by understanding the context in which legal rules and standards operate can one identify the optimal constitution of the law. In this respect, the characteristics of an effective education mirror those of an excellent lawyer, who, in addition to displaying the sharpness of mind that a rigorous legal education instils, can both empathise with her clients and quickly become adept with the workings of exotic issues, industries, and technologies. Thus, understanding the law at an academic level and employing it in practice require more than mere mastery of legal doctrine. To develop a full understanding, one must appreciate how ancillary fields of knowledge inform the theory and real-life application of law. The economic principles explored in this book can significantly add to students' understanding of law.

B. Essential Insights

Law students, like lawyers, are beset with difficult questions. Should the courts hold injurers strictly liable for harms they innocently cause or should negligence be a requisite of liability? When is increased cost in performing a contractual duty sufficient to discharge a promisor's obligation? Should the law require a breaching party to pay restitution, reliance, or expectation damages? Is an owner entitled to an injunction requiring the return of her property, or should the law merely award her damages? What is an appropriate sanction for a criminal offence?

To be sure, charged questions concerning morality, individual autonomy, and the role of the state weigh on such legal issues. Nevertheless, economics provides a framework for analysing these and countless other questions. This is not to say, of course, that the economic method always yields an objectively "right" answer to which no other mode of analysis can reply. Jurisprudential problems are too thorny to be resolved in such absolutist fashion. Nevertheless, a student with a grasp of economics can coherently analyse almost any legal problem by focusing on the incentive effects of proposed laws. In elucidating those consequences, one may not only reach an internally satisfactory resolution, but may highlight insights that others miss, making consensus more likely.

This Introduction concludes with economic insights into torts, crime, property, and contract, which subjects are, of course, staples of the first-year curriculum. The chapters that follow delve into economic theory and substantive law in greater detail. The following synopsis, however, should help the reader to understand how economics informs the substance and practice of law.

1. Crime

Deterrence is a major goal of criminal law. To dissuade someone, of course, one must understand incentives, which is where economics comes in. It illuminates the incentive effects of the various punishments and policing strategies that governments can employ to address the problem of crime. Among other things, it can reveal unforeseen side-effects of well-intentioned policies.

Imagine that an upsurge in burglaries causes a public outcry, leading the government to devote extra police resources to those crimes and to increase sentences for those convicted of committing them. The economic effect of both such measures would be to increase the "price" (i.e. the expected cost to an offender) of committing a burglary. One would expect such a policy to make burglaries less attractive, and hence to reduce their number, but is it that simple? Economists would say: no. Criminals, like all actors, choose between alternatives, and there are close substitutes for burglaries. Prospective burglars may be almost as satisfied with other forms of property crime, such as robberies. If so, sharply increasing the price for burglary may simply increase robberies by an off-setting amount. The proposed solution would be no solution at all. A lawyer versed in economics would realise that a viable solution requires increasing the price of all illegal substitutes without raising the price of lawful substitutes.

Another economic insight goes to tailoring punishment to deter a specific crime. The essential point is simple: to deter an offence, the punishment must exceed the expected benefit of the crime to the offender. Yet, moulding the sanction is not straightforward. For one thing, an uniformed judge or legislator may think that a 20-year sentence imposes twice the cost of a 10-year term. It does not. For a person with a 10% discount rate – a measure of how much an individual values the present over the future – the former term is less than 1.4 times as unpleasant as the latter. Worse, many of those predisposed to criminality – like those given to poor judgment generally – place a greater premium on present satisfactions than law-abiding types do. For those living by the mantra "future consequences be damned", deterring present conduct based on the threat of future consequences is difficult, and may require imposing draconian or unjust sentences.

This suggests that it may be a mistake to ramp prison terms up and up to achieve ever-greater deterrence. The marginal increase in deterrence is apt to be modest vis-à-vis the social cost of imprisonment. Illustratively, the average cost of incarcerating a person for a year in England and Wales is in the realm of £41,000, which excludes the suffering caused to the family and friends of loved ones who are locked up, and the contribution that the detainee would otherwise have made to the economy. For that reason, punishments imposed in the near term are more likely to be effective and cost-justified. Economists thus favour fines in lieu of imprisonment when it is possible to deter by threat of pecuniary sanction alone.

Economic analysis may also show that ostensibly promising laws are foolhardy. For example, suppose that the death penalty is off the table, and that a 40-year sentence without the possibility of parole is the most severe penalty available, no matter how egregious the crime. The government looks to a variety of terrible crimes – for the purpose of this example, assume them to be particularly appalling sexual offences – and decides that it must do everything possible to stop them from occurring. As a result, it amends the law to hold that a person convicted of those crimes will automatically receive a 40-year jail term. So far, so good, one might imagine. Economists, however, would see a problem. For those predisposed to commit such crimes, why would a potential 40-year sentence stop them, knowing that, regardless of what they do next, they will receive the harshest possible punishment under the law? Their self-interested, rational (though most assuredly immoral) reaction would be to minimise the likelihood of being caught. That may entail murdering their victims so that there are no witnesses to testify against them. Even if they are caught for murder, the criminal punishment would be no worse than it would have been otherwise. This example demonstrates economists' practice of thinking at the margin. The literature on the economics of crime recommends solving this problem by maintaining marginal deterrence, which means structuring the price (i.e., punishment) schedule so that each more-serious crime punishes the offender more than the last.

As a final illustration of the economic contribution to criminal law, consider what the law should and should not criminalise. The normative wing of law and economics focuses on individual autonomy, allowing people to choose their preferences for themselves. An "efficient" outcome is one that satisfies at least one person's preference without harming those of any other. Prescriptive law and economics thus relates to John Stuart Mill's harm principle, which holds that the government can legitimately exercise power over an individual against his will only if doing so prevents harm to others. To those who find this view appealing, economic analysis can provide a window into the legitimacy of criminal proscriptions. For example, it faults contemporary prohibition on soft-drug use, and applauds criminal laws that prohibit the taking of others' property without permission. In such cases, the economic focus is on directing people toward voluntary – and thus presumptively efficient – transactions, and away from coercive ones.

2. Tort

The tort system allows certain accident victims to recover for injuries they sustain at the hands of others. Its economic function is to induce people to take cost-justified precautions and to regulate how much they engage in risky behaviour. In short, we make negligent injurers liable for the harm they cause in the belief that the promise of such punishment encourages people to behave responsibly.

How can economics elucidate the law of tort? One answer is that it reveals trade-offs that may not be immediately obvious to policymakers. Suppose, for example, that a wave of financial accounting scandals reminiscent of Enron, WorldCom, and Tyco of the early 2000s occurs. In response, the legislator seeks to impose the greatest possible incentive on auditors to unearth fraud. Reasoning that strict liability will cause the accountancy profession to be as assiduous as possible in reviewing their clients' accounts, the legislature passes a law holding auditors liable for any harm that investors suffer due to undisclosed fraud, regardless of whether a reasonable auditor would have uncovered it. Economic analysis, however, would show that such a law would not impart the desired incentives. Counter-intuitively, strict liability imparts precisely the same incentive to take care as negligence, at least if the law defines negligence as a failure to take the precautions that minimise the combined costs of expected accidents and care.

Now imagine that another legislature deems strict liability to be unfair because it holds injurers liable even if they could not have avoided accidents at reasonable cost. The legislature thus eliminates strict liability from tort law. The problem now is that negligence fails to induce those engaged in high-risk activities to consider reducing or eliminating their participation in favour of alternative conduct. People owning potentially dangerous pets next door to children, for example, would not be liable if they took reasonable precautions, even if an unexpected series of events resulted in a mauling. Strict liability, by contrast, would encourage such neighbours to consider getting a more placid animal instead. Under a negligence regime, companies transporting hazardous materials through residential neighbourhoods would have no incentive under the law to re-route via less-populated areas.

As a final example, suppose that a government decides to impose strict liability on all drivers and motorcycle riders to cause them both to take care and to consider using the roads less often. This would be economically sound insofar as inducing those behind the wheel to act efficiently, but it would cause a different problem: it would cause cyclists and pedestrians to take less than optimal care because they know that, even if they act negligently, drivers will pay for at least some of the harm. Thus, economists could tell the legislature that it ought to introduce contributory or comparative negligence to incentivise victims, as well as tortfeasors, to take precautions.

Ultimately, the economic problem in tort law is how best to reconcile the conflicting preferences of potential injurers to engage in valued behaviour and of possible accident victims to avoid being hurt. Economics provides a framework for resolving this problem in consequentialist terms. With economics, law students can distinguish the effects of different tort remedies, and the impact of various approaches to foreseeability, implied consent, and other limitations on recovery.

3. Contract

Some people perceive a contract as an unbreakable, solemn bond, such that a promisor having agreed to perform must do so. Should he seek to renege on his commitment, specific performance is the appropriate remedy. Economists look at contracts differently. Absent negative third-party effects, voluntary agreements effect Pareto improvements and are thus efficient, because they satisfy the contracting parties' preferences without harming those of any other. Nevertheless, not all contracts are equally valuable. For that reason, making specific performance the default remedy may have unintended consequences, holding parties to a losing deal while a superior one goes by the wayside. Economists thus embrace the concept of "efficient breach".

"Efficient breach" does not imply that a promisor should be off the hook just because he discovers a better deal shortly after committing himself to another. Rather, the law should compensate the promisee with the monetary equivalent of her contracted-for performance, while leaving the promisor free to go where his performance is more valuable. Economists have studied the incentive effects of expectation, reliance, and restitution damages and have concluded that the first alone spurs promisors to breach only when it is efficient do so. They have also shown, however, that expectation damages – which give the disappointed promisee a sum equal to the subjective value of receiving performance – encourage promisees to spend excessively on reliance in anticipation of performance. The reason is that this damages remedy effectively insures them against the possibility of breach. Where undue reliance would be problematic, economics shows that a restitution damages award can deter it. These are just a modest subset of the insights that economic analysis provides into the law of contract.

4. Property

Property rights lie at the heart of the economy because they coordinate economic activity. Individuals know more about their own wants than any central planner ever could. Market exchanges harness this private information, which is one reason why western societies infuse property rights with the force of law. Recognising ownership interests also encourages people to improve scarce resources. If the government declined to enforce property rights, free-rider problems would hobble investment. Moreover, without an exchange-based economy founded on respect for property rights, there would be no basis to assume that resource distribution would become more efficient over time.

For these reasons, economics places a special premium on ownership. Indeed, law and economics' most fundamental concept, the Coase Theorem, provides that the creation of property rights will itself solve the problem of inconsistent preferences when all parties can bargain together freely. That principle has fruitful applications across the law.

Economics explains why problems emerge when the law defines property rights in imprecise terms or creates an exclusive right that is too narrow. Unclear exclusive rights impair the coordination of economic activity. When people fight over who owns a resource and what rights are subsumed within that ownership right, property fails to facilitate the efficient alienation of scarce resources. Difficulties also emerge when the law creates too-narrow an exclusive right. Fragmented ownership of complementary rights, which must be combined to create an end product, can stymie economic activity. This problem is increasingly clear in the information technology field, where myriad patents of vague scope reading on narrow discrete technologies combine to frustrate, rather than to promote, innovation. Economic analysis likewise explains why the government properly exercises eminent domain – or compulsory-purchase – powers. An owner who waits until the government has invested in a motorway project that implicates her property, for example, can command a monopoly price based not on the standalone value of her lot, but on the cost to the state of abandoning the project.

An important question concerns how the law protects ownership rights. When someone invades a property owner's right, a court can award an injunction or damages. At first blush, it might seem as if the law should always order the return of taken property. Indeed, that is often the appropriate rule, as when an uninvited person moves onto your land without your permission. Yet, there are many cases in which it is better to provide an owner with a monetary award only. Economics explains when it is best to protect ownership rights with property, liability, or inalienability rules. A general rule of thumb, subject to many qualifications, is that damages awards (i.e. a liability rule) are preferable when transaction costs are high (i.e. where it was not feasible for the owner and taker to bargain for permission). In that setting, a court can set a price upon which the parties would have agreed had it been hypothetically possible to contract. When voluntary trade is feasible, however, an injunction (i.e. a property rule) is likely to be better as the parties will probably have superior information than the court.

With this background in place, we proceed to study law and economics in detail. Our discussion begins with basic principles of economics, followed by the relationship between economic analysis of law and legal theory. As with every chapter in this book, this one ends with a list of sources that the interested reader can use to explore relevant topics in greater detail. The next chapter points to introductory materials suitable for students wishing to appreciate the basic tenets of law and economics.

References and Further Reading

Books
Friedman, David, *Law's Order: What Economics has to do with Law and Why It Matters* Chs. 1–4 (2000).
Katz, Avery Weiner, *Foundations of the Economic Approach to Law* (1998).
Mercuro, Nicholas and Medema, Steven, *Economics and the Law: From Posner To Post-Modernism and Beyond*, 2nd edn (2006).
Posner, Richard A., *Economic Analysis of Law*, 8th edn (2011) Ch. 2.
Ulen, Thomas and Cooter, Robert D., *Law and Economics*, 6th edn (2011) Ch. 1.

Articles
Baker, Edwin C. 'Starting points in economic analysis of law' (1980) 8 Hofstra L Rev 939.
Calabresi, Guido 'Some thoughts on risk distribution and the Law of Torts' (1961) 70 Yale LJ 499.
Coase, Ronald H. 'The problem of social cost' (1960) 3 JL & Econ 1.
Hovenkamp, Herbert 'Law and economics in the United States: A brief historical overview' (1995) 19 Cambridge J Econ 331.

Part 1

Economic Theory, Law, and Morality

1	Background Principles in Microeconomics	11
2	Essential Concepts in the Law and Economics Literature	28
3	Utilitarianism, Neoclassical Welfare Economics, and the Ethics of Markets	43

Chapter 1

Background Principles in Microeconomics

Chapter Contents

A.	Utility and the Distribution of Scarce Resources	12
B.	Consumer Choice and the Law of Demand	13
C.	Firm Behaviour and the Law of Supply	18
D.	Market Equilibrium, and an Illustrative Application to Criminal Law	20
E.	Game Theory	23
Key Points		27
References and Further Reading		27

Understanding the economic contribution to law requires some familiarity with the "dismal science". This chapter introduces the basic elements of microeconomic theory, including the laws of supply and demand, price theory, and the concept of equilibrium. These basic pillars of economics yield insights into broad swathes of law.

A. Utility and the Distribution of Scarce Resources

We begin with the most basic question – what is economics? Broadly defined, it is the study of how society allocates scarce resources. Whenever people value a good (or service) but there is an insufficient quantity available to satisfy everyone, a dilemma arises: who should get the desired items? This may be a question of moral desert, but can we articulate a coherent rule of decision? A promising answer might be to rank consumers based on inter-personal comparisons of the happiness that each person would experience in obtaining the good. The concept of "utility" captures the magnitude of an individual's satisfaction. Allocating scarce, but valuable, goods to consumers who would benefit the most from them makes sense. To distribute scarce resources justly, society could rank consumers according to their respective utilities, and allot the products accordingly.

Nevertheless, such an approach would face formidable obstacles. Inter-personal comparisons of utility are notoriously difficult to conduct. Extreme differences in circumstance may make optimal allocation of a scare product clear – for example, a life-saving drug would presumably confer more utility on a person who is suffering from the relevant medical condition than on one who merely fears contracting it. Nevertheless, in most cases, distinctions between consumers' utilities would be unclear and thus incommensurate. To complicate matters further, a declarant's assertion that he values the good more than others is not credible. Every consumer would have reason to say so, regardless of whether it is true.

Furthermore, the availability of a desirable resource is not fixed. Society can often produce more goods, thus satisfying more demand. Maximising utility would require expanding production until the cost of building an additional unit equals the utility that that extra unit would yield. Yet, how can the government know the right quantity to produce, and how can it spur private actors to produce it?

Market economies solve this dilemma through property rights. Since people have unique information concerning their tastes, they can trade with one another to their mutual benefit. The market process relies on prices, as proxies for value, to coordinate economic activity. We have said that ranking consumers by utility would enable society to distribute scarce products, but such an approach is unworkable because governments cannot make inter-person utility comparisons. The economic solution is to equate willingness and ability to pay with preference, which may itself be a rough proxy for one's utility. In other words, one can infer utility from a person's voluntary market choices, which demonstrate "revealed preferences". From this view, if two people wish to consume a good, but only one is available, the person who offers a higher price should receive it.

In addition to facilitating the efficient distribution of resources – "efficient" meaning that the person willing to pay the most for a scarce resource obtains it – a price-based market incentivises manufacturers to expand production, thus further enhancing welfare. Additional benefits ensue. Producers' profits attract competition, which forces output even higher and causes price to fall toward manufacturers' marginal cost of production and distribution. This leads to economically desirable conditions of allocative and productive efficiency.[1]

---

1 Allocative efficiency refers to the condition in which the price that consumers pay for a product equals the marginal cost of producing that good. As price increases beyond marginal cost, some consumers who value the product at or beyond the cost to society of producing it cannot buy it. For this reason, above-marginal-cost prices – otherwise known as supracompetitive or, in a looser sense, "monopoly" prices – do more than transfer wealth from consumers to sellers. They destroy social value, thus causing "deadweight loss". Productive efficiency exists when firms produce goods at the lowest average total cost of production (i.e., using the lowest possible number of inputs).

A key principle of economics is that the amount of wealth in a society is not set. Resources are more valuable in some people's hands than in others, and so the law can do more than distribute income: it can help to create wealth where none existed before. As but one example, in 2010, the US Chamber of Commerce tied 75% of post-World War II growth in the US economy to innovation.[2] The economy did not find that value; it created it.

Some people can use a resource more productively than others. Similarly, some derive different satisfaction than others in consuming a good. In either situation, if a person who does not value the relevant good the most currently owns it, assigning that resource to a higher-value user will increase social welfare. This gives rise to a crucial insight: agreements into which informed, competent, parties consensually enter advance welfare by satisfying the preferences of the contracting parties as long as the relevant arrangement carries no harmful third-party effects. Thus, in recognising property rights and enforcing contracts, the law facilitates voluntary exchanges that enhance value.

Armed with a basic understanding of preferences and the role of price in rationing scarce resources accordingly, we can proceed further. First, we need to say more about how markets operate, both in terms of how consumers make preference-satisfying decisions and how supply and demand interact to determine the price of a good and its associated output.

For the uninitiated reader, this discussion may appear alien to the nature and operation of law. After all, we do not typically think of law, and much of the behaviour that it seeks to regulate, in terms of markets. Yet, economists can fruitfully study almost all aspects of the legal system using price theory. For instance, one can understand tort law as spurring both an efficient level of risk-bearing behaviour and optimal precautions. It does so by imposing a price (a "Pigouvian tax") through the tort system that equals the negative externality that the potentially negligent behaviour creates.[3]

B. Consumer Choice and the Law of Demand

Consumer behaviour is complex. People are idiosyncratic, buffeted by motivations and pressures that differ from one individual to the next. Out of this morass of influences, neoclassical economists focus on core incentives, devising formal models of decision making that predict consumer choice. Rationality is the organising principle. By assuming that consumers rationally maximise their utility, economic models can generate hypotheses about future behaviour. The relevance of this methodology to law becomes clear when one realises that "consumers" within the realm of legal analysis include people engaging in risky conduct (tortfeasors), promisors considering whether to breach their contracts, litigants, innovators, and – yes – even criminals.

The assumptions underlying such neoclassical models are simplified and unrealistic when applied to individual consumers, who often behave irrationally. Nevertheless, these assumptions are critical, as without them it would be impossible to devise a model of choice sufficiently workable to enable researchers to study key determinants of behaviour. By devising simplified models of decision making, social scientists sacrifice descriptive realism for predictability and feasibility.

1. Rationality as an organising principle

The core neoclassical hypothesis is that individuals are rational maximisers who choose the optimal combination, or "bundle," of goods and services that satisfy their preferences. The only constraints

---

2 US Department of Commerce, Patent Reform: Unleashing Innovation, Promoting Economic Growth, and Producing High Paying Jobs (13 April 2010). Available at: www.commerce.gov.

3 A "negative externality" is the cost that an action creates, but that the actor does not himself experience. Negative externalities cause people to do too much of the activity that yields the negative third-party effects. A classic example is pollution, as much of its cost falls not on the polluting factory but on society.

on people's consumption decisions are budgetary limitations and the cost of acquiring and processing information with which to inform their decision making.

For the time being, accept that each consumer has a preference ordering regarding the various goods (or services) that are available for her consumption. A "utility function" encapsulates which products are attractive to a particular person and to what degree. Assume that consumers' preferences are complete and internally consistent ("transitive"), and thus give rise to an ordinal ranking.[4] Furthermore, if a product is attractive to an individual then, other things being equal, she would rather have more of the good than less of it (this is the quality of "strong monotonicity").

In weighing the available mix of products that he might purchase, a consumer will be indifferent between particular combinations of goods. In other words, he will not prefer one such bundle over another. One can display this phenomenon graphically using an "indifference curve". If one such curve is above another then, by the assumption of preferring more desirable goods over less, a rational person would rather consume any chosen combination of products on the higher curve than on the lower one. In this world of choice, our consumer's problem is one of constrained optimisation. To make a rational consumption decision, he would choose the bundle of goods that provides the maximum possible utility given the limited amount of money that he has available.

In the diagram below, a consumer must choose how much of two different kinds of goods, A and B, to purchase. Assume that our prospective purchaser can assign an ordinal ranking to her consumption options, that her preferences are consistent and that, other things being equal, she always prefers more of a good to less. Each indifference curve represents the A–B combinations with which she is equally satisfied. Notice that these curves are not straight, but are convex from the origin, which demonstrates that A and B are not perfect substitutes. When the consumer has many of A, she would be willing to give up more than one of A to get one of B. The "marginal rate of substitution" between two goods measures the number of one kind of product that is necessary to remedy the loss to a consumer of a single other product. It declines because a consumer will give up increasingly less of A to get one more of B, and vice versa. The marginal rate of substitution measures the slope of the indifference curve.

As our consumer values more of both A and B, she prefers any indifference curve that is higher than another. Thus, she prefers I_3 over I_2 over I_1. She would, of course, prefer indifference curves that are further from the origin than I_3, but she faces what economists call a "constraint". In this case, as in many cases in life, she can only afford to purchase so much. "B" represents an inviolable budgetary constraint.

The consumer acts rationally by maximising her utility, which she does by choosing the A:B product mix on the highest indifference curve that is still within her budget. This point is where her indifference curve farthest from the origin is tangential to her budget constraint, marked as "X_*" (see Figure 1.1).

A person's consumption choice depends on many factors. It depends most obviously on the individual's utility function. That function, in turn, is not set in stone. Parenting, friends, education, religion, and culture all instil norms. The law, too, plays some role in shaping preferences and hence in informing the constitution of consumers' utility functions. Law and economics analysis, however, generally assumes that consumers' preferences are "exogenous" – in other words, it assumes that external factors, rather than the economic models under consideration, determine preferences. It also treats such preferences as "immutable", which is to say unchangeable.

This feature of law and economics is simultaneously attractive and problematic. It is attractive because it takes a non-judgmental view on people's desires, leaving each individual to decide for

---

4 An ordinal ranking ascribes a specific position in a numbered series. So, for example, a consumer presented with a choice between chicken, beef, and fish for dinner could provide such a ranking if she prefers fish over chicken, and chicken over beef: 1. fish; 2. chicken; 3. beef.

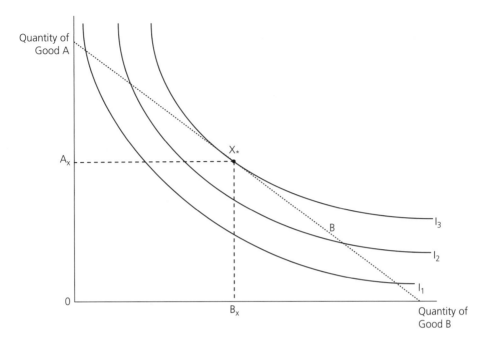

Figure 1.1

herself what she wants. It is problematic for much the same reason – it views as sacrosanct preferences that some people possess, but that most people would regard as distasteful or immoral. In appropriate settings, we shall discuss the possibility of relaxing these particular assumptions and explore how this might affect analysis.

2. The price effect

With the prior assumptions in place, the relative price of the goods in a person's consumption bundle determines that individual's consumption decision. What happens when the price of one good increases relative to that of another? Answering this question is important to the economic analysis of law, which views the legal system as a price-setting mechanism that induces people to substitute away from undesirable behaviour towards more-efficient conduct by increasing the cost of the former relative to the latter. The law performs this function through *ex post* liability, punitive sanctions, and injunctive decrees.

What is the effect of increasing the price of just one good in a consumption bundle? If a person considers two products, A and B, a rise in A's price will have two consequences. First, there will be a "substitution effect". Product A will now be worth less to the consumer at a given price and this will make interchangeable goods, in this example product B, more attractive. The marginal rate of substitution between goods A and B determines the magnitude of the substitution effect.

Second, a "wealth effect" will occur. The increase in the price of A will reduce our consumer's wealth. Now less well off, an individual may view the goods available for her consumption differently. The larger the fraction of her wealth represented by the now-more-expensive good, the more significant the price effect will be. In tracing the impact of an elevated price on relative demand, economists draw a distinction between superior, normal, and inferior goods. Reduced wealth increases a person's demand for inferior goods, reduces demand for normal goods proportionately with the reduction in wealth, and disproportionately lessens demand for superior goods. Superior and inferior goods probably include luxury sports cars and public transportation, respectively. The qualification is necessary because the nature of superiority, normality, and inferiority is not inherent in a product, but specific to the individual and to her specific tastes.

Applied to our example, if good A is superior relative to good B, the wealth effect will magnify the substitution effect toward good B. If good A is inferior relative to good B, however, then the wealth effect will have the opposite effect than the substitution effect. The net effect of the substitution and wealth effects is the price effect. This is the effect that typically concerns economists studying the legal system. If the law increases the cost of taking another's property, breaching a contract, or filing a lawsuit, what will be the ultimate price effect (i.e. the change in behaviour)?

Could the wealth effect outweigh the substitution effect? If so, increasing the price of a product could magnify its demand. Applied to law and economics, this would mean that increasing the expected cost of committing a crime or acting negligently would *increase* the amount of crime or negligence – an odd result, to be sure. Economists describe goods for which this phenomenon is true as "Giffen goods". These products violate the law of demand, such that demand curves for Giffen goods slope upward. In reality, though, no such good may exist.

Thus far, we have seen how consumers make purchase decisions and react to changes in the price of a good in their consumption bundle. The allocation of products in that bundle will change according to the relevant price effect, which is the combination of the substitution and income (wealth) effects. Whether the substitution and income effects reinforce one another depends on whether the product the price of which has increased is a superior, normal, or inferior good. The following graph illustrates the effect of an increase in the price of one good (product "B") when the price for the other good (product "A") remains unchanged. Together those goods comprise the relevant bundle (products A and B):

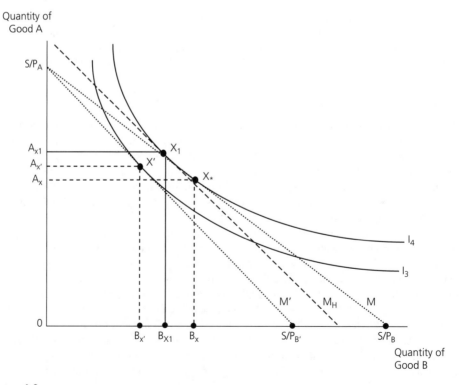

Figure 1.2

X_* represents the optimal consumption bundle before the price change. The ensuing increase in the price of B, however, reduces the amount of B that the consumer can afford to buy. The maximum such amount is the consumer's savings, "S", divided by the price of B, and so the maximum quantity falls from S/P_B to $S/P_{B'}$. Thus, the horizontal intercept for the new monetary constraint, M', shifts inward, though the vertical intercept remains the same (the consumer can still buy the same amount of A given her budget).

To determine the substitution effect, one can draw a hypothetical budget constraint (M_H) that is parallel to the new budgetary constraint (M') and that is tangential to the indifference curve on which the pre-price-change consumption bundle lay. The reason for doing this is that, by measuring the effect of the price change while holding real income fixed, we can isolate the substitution effect. Point X_1 thus represents the A:B input combination that the consumer would purchase in light of the price change if she were given sufficient extra income to compensate for her loss in wealth. Looking at the graph, we can see that the substitution effect results in a decrease in the quantity of the now-more-expensive B, from B_X to B_{X1}, and an increase in the quantity of A, from A_X to A_{X1}.

Yet, the substitution effect does not account for the full impact of B's higher price. By constructing an imaginary budget constraint tangential to the original indifference curve, we effectively compensated the consumer for the loss in income occasioned by B's becoming more expensive. Absent such compensation, however, the heightened price of B will reduce the consumer's wealth, which will, in turn, affect her demand for various goods. If B is an inferior good, the effect will be consistent with the model shown above. The "income effect" on B is the difference between $B_{X'}$ and B_{X1}. The combined impact of the substitution and income effects is the difference between $B_{X'}$ and B_X, which economists refer to as the "price effect".

3. Demand

The preceding discussion represents a basic theory of consumer choice. To extend our analysis from the individual to the larger market, however, we need to tie the question of individual decision making to economic activity at the market level. Economists accomplish this by deriving individual supply and demand curves, which they can aggregate to form market-level supply and demand curves. As a theoretical matter, it is straightforward to determine a person's demand curve for a product. One can simply track the quantity of the good demanded by that person as the price changes. The following diagram illustrates how one may graph D_B, the demand curve (specifically, the "Marshallian" or "uncompensated" demand curve[5]) for product B (see Figure 1.3).

The demand curve for product B slopes downward, revealing that consumers desire less of the good as its price increases. This downward slope represents "the law of demand". The economic analysis conducted below assumes that that law applies not only to commercial products sold in industry, but to people's desire to breach contracts, to commit torts, to appropriate another's property, to innovate, and to carry out a crime. In all such cases, theory suggests that increasing the price that the law imposes on such activities will lead to a reduction in demand for them.

We are now ready to consider the other side of the market – namely, the producers of the goods or services that are available for consumption. The interrelation between consumers and producers leads to the interplay of supply and demand; together these determine the market price and output of a particular commodity.

---

5 Marshallian demand reflects both substitution and income effects, while "Hicksian" or "compensated" demand is composed solely of substitution effects.

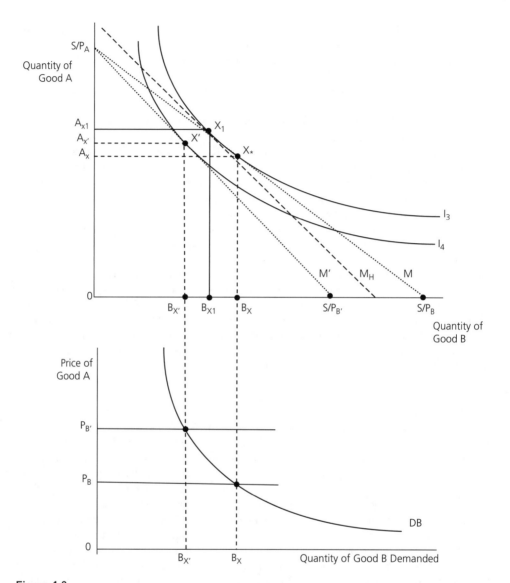

Figure 1.3

C. Firm Behaviour and the Law of Supply

Just as neoclassical economists assume that consumers act rationally to maximise their utility, they assume that manufacturers and sellers optimise their own welfare. While consumers choose an optimal bundle of goods subject to their budgetary and informational constraints, suppliers determine the quantity of products that they should manufacture and sell to maximise their utility. While consumers make the purchase decisions that best satisfy their preferences, purveyors of goods make price and output decisions to maximise their profit.

Consider rational behaviour on the production side of the economy. How many units of a good will a producer decide to make? Economists always think at the margin, so the pertinent question is to ask: when will a firm produce one more unit? We can begin by answering this question negatively: a company will not manufacture another good if the price that it can obtain for the product is less than its average variable cost. This cost represents total variable cost – those costs that change depending on the firm's output and which are to be distinguished from fixed expenses, which do not vary according to the number of products sold – divided by the firm's output (or total number of goods produced). This leads to a first conclusion: no producer will supply an additional product if the available price is less than the average *variable* cost of manufacturing that good.[6]

Would a rational manufacturer sell an additional product for less than the company's average *total* cost? The answer is yes, in the short term, as long as the relevant price meets or exceeds average variable cost. This may seem like an odd result, as any sale at a price less than average total cost involves a company's failing to break even. The mystery disappears when one recognises that, in the short term, fixed costs are sunk, such that a company cannot recover them by exiting the market. If an available price exceeds average variable cost, but is less than average total cost, then the firm would rationally sell an additional unit at that price because, in doing so, it would reclaim its non-sunk costs.

Thus, we know that, in the short term, a producer will manufacture and sell a product if, and only if, the price it can command exceeds its average variable cost. A company's average-variable-cost curve thus constitutes a floor, such that supply at prices below this curve will be zero.

This insight, however, does not explain how many units a rational company will decide to produce. The answer lies in the important concepts of marginal cost and marginal revenue. The former term constitutes the expense involved in selling one more unit. It is distinct from variable costs because marginal cost represents the increment in total cost involved in manufacturing one-more product, and can thus include both fixed and variable costs. Marginal revenue represents the income that the company realises in selling the additional product.

Other than in strategic situations, such as certain oligopolistic markets in which a company must factor into its price/output decision the anticipated actions of its rivals, a firm with market power maximises profit by adjusting its output until its marginal cost of production equals its marginal revenue. Intuitively, if the revenue achieved in selling one extra product exceeds the expense of making that product, then the company can increase profit by selling that additional good. It will keep selling more goods until marginal cost and marginal revenue coincide. Any further sales past that point would reduce the firm's profit. It is worth noting that at least two factors limit the profit-maximising level of output. First, most companies' marginal cost of production eventually increases with rising output, which ensures that there will be a point where marginal revenue no longer exceeds marginal cost. Second, marginal revenue will eventually decrease with sufficiently high prices because borderline consumers will abandon the higher-priced good in favour of substitutes at an accelerating rate.

Combining these insights, and under perfect competition which forces price to marginal cost, a firm's short-term supply curve is the company's marginal-cost curve above its average-variable-cost curve (the dashed portion below). This supply curve, given the relevant market price, determines the quantity of a good that a profit-maximising company operating in a perfectly competitive market would produce in the short term.

The short-term supply curve, unlike the demand curve, will slope upwards. There are two reasons for this. First, a higher price results in greater marginal revenue to the firm, which creates an incentive for it to increase production. Second, successive increases in output eventually lead to elevated costs, which mean that a rational company will require a higher price to increase output further. A standard supply curve for a given product, A, might therefore look like this:

---

6 An exception could lie in strategic reasons, such as predatory pricing or breaking into a network market (see discussion in Part 8). In such cases, a rational company might sell for less-than-average variable cost.

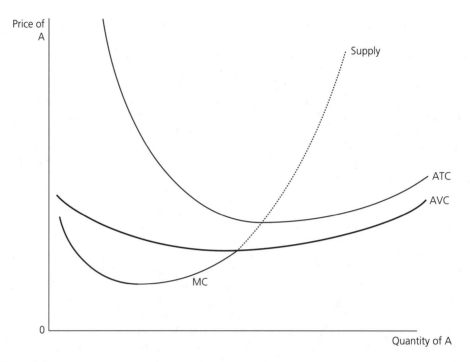

Figure 1.4

D. Market Equilibrium, and an Illustrative Application to Criminal Law

The summation of demand and supply curves gives rise to the industry demand and supply curves, respectively. Consistent with above, short-term industry demand and supply curves will generally slope downward and upward, respectively.[7] The intersection of the industry demand and supply curves represents a point of equilibrium.

An important aspect of economic analysis of markets concerns the effect of a change in industry conditions. Exogenous changes – like an adjustment in the cost of an input in the production process or an alteration in consumer wealth – lead to endogenous changes in industry supply or demand, which will, in turn, translate into a different market price and hence output. Tracing the market impact of any such event requires analysing both short- and long-term effects, as equilibrium reestablishes itself.

To place this discussion in a context befitting a book on law and economics, consider an unlikely example: a shadow market for crime, say robbery. This is not a market in the sense of how non-economists would usually construe the term: robbers and their victims do not engage in voluntary transactions. Nor do they exchange and purchase goods, or otherwise act within a

---

7 In the long term, however, the slope of the industry supply curve will be less steep, and may conceivably approach horizontality or "perfectly elasticity". This phenomenon occurs because, in the long term, even fixed costs are variable due to the possibility of industry entry and exit.

cognisable industry. Nevertheless, one can fruitfully conceive of robbery as an economic activity. The ensuing analysis applies not only to commercial market transactions but to all manner of behaviour, including litigation, contracts, torts, property investment, and so on.

First, the market output is the number of robberies that criminals carry out in a particular geographical location in a relevant period (e.g. in one year). Second, the market price – the price that an individual pays for carrying out a robbery – is the expected cost to the prospective robber of carrying out his chosen crime. That cost largely comprises the state-imposed criminal sanction, discounted to present value and by the probability of non-detection and non-successful prosecution. The price, however, also may reflect other punishments, such as reduced employment prospects and social stigma for violating communal norms. Of course, depending on one's peers, the reputational effects of committing a particular crime may benefit an actor, in which case stigma reduces the price.

Third, the industry demand curve reflects the quantity of robberies that criminals would demand at different hypothetical prices that society could impose. This curve slopes downward because the greater the sanction under the criminal laws and the larger the other private costs experienced by one who commits robbery, the more attractive substitutable activities, both lawful and unlawful, will become to prospective robbers. The income effect of the higher price, however, may decrease the degree of the downward slope of the demand curve if robbery is an inferior good of which people demand proportionately more as their wealth decreases. Finally, the supply curve represents the number of potential victims whom criminals can rob.

To give this analysis a more concrete foundation, consider an informal, but theoretically instructive, example: the possible effect that a severe recession in Ireland in 2008 and 2009 (an external shock) may have had on robberies. This economic upset led to a precipitous drop in employment – the unemployment rate increased from 4.6% in 2007 to 11.8% in 2009. It also led gross national product per capita to decrease from € 37,661 to € 29,653 over the same time frame.[8]

Any such large rise in unemployment and loss of wealth will have multitudinous effects, and predicting the net impact of such an event is an intricate endeavour. The myriad factors that influence behaviour form a complex, interconnected web, such that events appearing to have discrete impact invariably initiate larger ripple effects throughout the economy. Interestingly, although some people expect recessions to cause higher levels of crime, the empirical literature does not reveal a statistically significant relationship between the overall crime rate (the dependent variable) and changes in the unemployment rate (the explanatory variable).[9] There is, however, a positive correlation between changes in that explanatory variable and in property crimes.[10]

To simplify for ease of exposition, a drop in income and employment prospects of the kind that occurred in Ireland in 2008 and 2009 could increase short-term demand for robbery (a property crime). Assuming such a change in demand, consider the following graph, which reflects the impact of a hypothetical increase in the demand for robbery in light of a change in the exogenous factor discussed above (see Figure 1.5).

P_R represents the expected cost that a person experiences in committing a robbery, which remains unchanged immediately after the shock. D_1 represents the industry demand curve before the onset of the recession, and D_2 signifies the demand curve after this event. D_2 shifts outward on account of the fact that, due to a recession-created deprivation of wealth, stealing others' property

---

8 See www.cso.ie/statistics/nationalingp.htm.
9 See, e.g., Steven Raphael and Rudolf Winter-Ebmer, 'Identifying the effect of unemployment on crime' (2001) 44 JL & Econ 259; Steven Levitt, 'The effect of prison population size on crime rates: evidence from prison overcrowding litigation' (1996) 111 QJ Econ 319.
10 Ibid.

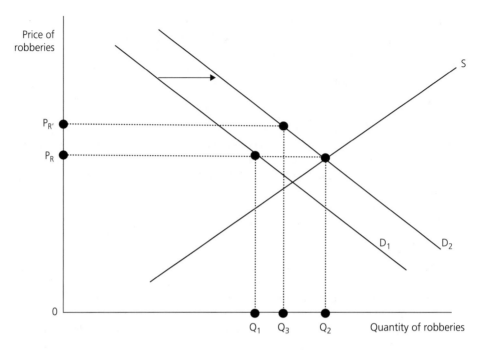

Figure 1.5

becomes more attractive to at least some prospective robbers. Q_1 and Q_2 represent the pre- and post-recession amount of robberies.

In the short term, the recession-induced shift in the demand curve to the right results in a new equilibrium between supply and demand at price P_R, which leads to a greater number of robberies, Q_2. Consistent with this informal model, the number of robberies in Ireland in 2010 had increased by 54% over 2007.[11]

In a commercial market in which trading takes place, a shift in the demand curve away from the origin would, holding other factors constant, cause prices to increase, thus leading the market to readjust to a new equilibrium. In markets for non-traded activity, however, there is no explicit price mechanism. Instead, society uses the legal system to impose a shadow price. The government can manipulate this process to adjust market output. Thus, society might react to the spike in output in the market for robberies by increasing the number of police on the street and by enhancing the severity of the criminal sanction imposed on those convicted of the offence. Both such actions would increase the shadow price for committing robberies – here, from P_R to $P_{R'}$ – thus leading to a new market equilibrium in which output drops from Q_2 to Q_3.

Of course, myriad factors influence supply and demand of different kinds of crime, and a change in any of these may affect the equilibrium quantity of criminal behaviour. Demand curves reflect such diverse background conditions as education, social-welfare assistance (which increases

---

11 *See* www.cso.ie/Quicktables/GetQuickTables.aspx?FileName=cja01c15.asp&TableName=Robbery+,+extortion+and+hijacking+ offences&StatisticalProduct=DB_CJ.

the opportunity cost of crime), social norms governing acceptable behaviour, family structure, and so on. The point for now is that one can chart non-explicit-market phenomena through the lens of price theory.

E. Game Theory

Neglecting the burgeoning field of game theory would do an injustice to this chapter's introductory discussion of economics. Initially developed by John Nash in the first half of the twentieth century, game theory departs significantly from the neoclassical analysis referenced thus far. Both concepts rely on rationality, but the defining feature of game theory is its focus on the strategic interrelationships that can exist between decision makers and that influence their optimal choices. Game theory has revolutionised economic analysis. Within the realm of law, it has especially influenced the economics of competition policy, though it has a range of applications to legal problems generally.

1. Single-shot (static) games

The classic game-theory problem is the prisoners' dilemma. This refers to the strategic predicament facing two suspects whom the police have apprehended for committing a crime.

The officers lack sufficient evidence to charge either arrestee with the more serious offence, which carries a maximum punishment of ten years. In the absence of an admission from one or both of the suspects, the police could only obtain convictions for a relatively minor transgression, which carries no more than a one-year jail term. How might the police elicit confessions from either or both of the arrestees? They could do so, as follows.

Having placed each suspect in separate interview rooms, the detectives could offer each of them the same deal: (1) Admit your culpability and testify against your accomplice, in which case you shall either (a) go free if your accomplice denies committing the crime; or (b) receive an eight-year sentence if he similarly admits to carrying out the offence. (2) Deny the charges, in which case (c) you will receive a ten-year sentence if your co-accused admits his guilt and implicates you; or (d) you will get a one-year stretch if your co-arrestee also denies guilt. If each arrestee cares about his own freedom more than his accomplice's liberty, each person will have an incentive to confess and to testify against his partner in crime.

This quandary entails a classic tension between collective and individual interest. Obviously, the two arrestees are collectively better off if they both deny the charges and receive one-year sentences, as that path yields them an aggregate cost of two years. Again, taking a combined view of the two suspects' welfare, the worst outcome is for them both to confess, as this will result in their collectively receiving 16 years in jail. Were the accomplices free to enter into a binding contract with one another, they would agree to keep quiet.

Locked up away from one another, however, each suspect will reason as follows: if my counterpart confesses, I can either confess, and get an eight-year sentence or I can deny the charges and get a ten-year sentence. Clearly, in that eventuality, I should confess. However, what if my accomplice does not confess? In that case, I should still confess because doing so would result in my going free, while if I deny responsibility, I would receive a one-year sentence. No matter what my co-arrestee does, I am better off admitting what I did.

In the parlance of game theory, each suspect's "dominant strategy" in this scenario is to confess because that strategy yields a greater payoff than any other choice, regardless of any other player's decision. As each suspect will reason the same way, both criminals will receive eight-year sentences, which is contrary to their aggregate welfare. The following payoff matrix represents the scenario in typical game-theory manner:

		Criminal 2	
		Remain silent	Confess
Criminal 1	Remain silent	1,1	10,0
	Confess	0,10	8,8

Figure 1.6

The prisoners' dilemma is well-worn territory. By changing this payoff matrix slightly, however, we can recreate a game that featured centrally in the 2008 film, *The Dark Knight*. There, the Joker secretly rigged two ships with explosives, placed the detonator for each boat on the other ship, and then told the passengers on both vessels that he would spare the first boat to blow up the other, but that, if neither ship blew up its counterpart within 15 minutes, he would destroy them both.

A crucial factor of the game-theory analysis of this problem concerns the nature of the payoff to both parties (for simplicity, we shall momentarily treat all the occupants of one boat as a single entity). If the players concern themselves solely with their own survival, then they necessarily prefer "life" to "death" in the following payoff matrix and the solution to the game is straight-forward:

		Boat 2	
		Press the trigger	Don't press the trigger
Boat 1	Press the trigger	live if first, live if first	live, die
	Don't press the trigger	die, live	die, die

Figure 1.7

On these facts, each party will race to be the first to press the detonator. Each side would reason: "If the other boat does not press the detonator, I can either (a) blow up the other vessel and live or (b) not press the detonator, in which case the Joker will destroy both my ferry and the other one. The optimal strategy given the other ship's decision not to press the detonator is obviously to destroy the other boat. Conversely, if the other boat presses the detonator, I die if I do not press my detonator first."

In this situation, economists would say that pressing the detonator "weakly dominates" not pressing it because even though choosing to destroy the other boat does not always yield a better result than choosing not to do so, it may yield a superior outcome and in no circumstances will it produce a worse result. Thus, on the assumptions that the players are self-interested and prefer living to dying, game theory would predict a race between both ships to blow up the other.

Those readers familiar with *The Dark Knight*, of course, will recall that this was not the result, as the passengers on each vessel refused to kill those on the other. Their refusal to do so, of course, reflected the altruism of the people on board the two boats, which was the moral point that the incident contributed to the plot of the film. Within the terminology of economics, the occupants' utility functions would seem to have incorporated the preferences of third parties.

One can still not explain the film's outcome on this basis, however, because declining to press the detonator would cause the Joker to blow up both ships at the end of 15 minutes. Thus, even if each passenger cared about her counterparts on both ships as much as she did about herself, this would not be a basis to refuse to blow up either boat: not pressing the detonator would ultimately result in a worse result than blowing up one of the vessels.

It is possible that the passengers could not identify which boat would yield the lesser harm in destroying. Faced with two identical ships and the same number of occupants on each one, the passengers might be indifferent between destroying one over the other. Could this equivalence lead to indecision and inaction? The possibility brings to mind the tale of a hyper-rational donkey placed in a position that was precisely equidistant between two sources of food. Lacking a rational basis for choosing the food in one direction over the other, the donkey starved, whereas a less rational creature would have lived. Might the same phenomenon explain the passengers' refusal to destroy one of the boats?

The filmmakers were clever here because they established that the occupants of one ferry were law-abiding, while those on the other were convicts serving custodial sentences. That fact could facilitate a consequentialist determination that the death of those on the criminal-bearing ferry would be less terrible than those on the other boat. Thus, the rational choice might be for the law-abiding citizens to blow up the other vessel, were the cost of destroying neither the assured destruction of both. If this were true, and still assuming (a) perfect altruism toward others, and (b) that the probability of the Joker's fulfilling his promise to destroy both vessels after 15 minutes if both then remained unscathed was 100%, the following conclusion would hold. The dominant strategy for the criminals was not to trigger the detonator, while the dominant strategy for the law-abiding people was to blow up the other ferry. Consistent with this, the convicts in the film threw the detonator overboard and the non-criminals on the other boat reached a majority decision to destroy the other boat.

Yet, when push came to shove, none of the law-abiding citizens could press the detonator switch. How might we explain this? It is not easy to do within the confines of law-and-economics theory. The fact that we see the players' refusal to kill those on the other boat as virtuous reflects the moral distinction between positive actions and omissions (non-actions). This distinction looms large in our moral intuition, even though it is difficult to reconcile with consequentialism.

Applied to the case presented in The Dark Knight – and ignoring the possibility of a hero coming to the rescue – recognising a categorical imperative not to kill another person would result in the demise of all, while killing another would bring about the death of only half. In this respect, one might characterise the law-abiding citizens' decision as myopic. However, many people would perceive a moral distinction between (1) killing with your own hand, and (2) holding your hand, even if you know that the result will be a wicked person's killing more. This quagmire draws the deontological and utilitarian theories of morality into conflict. The following chapter addresses the ethical implications, benefits, and limitations of law-and-economics theory in more detail.

1. Dynamic games

The preceding discussion concerned what economists refer to as simultaneous move (or static) games. Many legal problems, however, concern multi-step games in which players move sequentially and which play out over a period of time. The dynamic feature of these games makes representation more straightforward through a tree (extensive form) rather than payoff matrices (normal form) of the kind considered in the previous section. A further distinction between static and dynamic games is that, in the latter setting, the first non-mover knows the other player's preceding decision.

Begin with a commercial example, in which a monopolist ("M") currently enjoys an entire market to itself. A potential competitor ("C") contemplates whether to enter the market to seek a share of the supracompetitive profits. The decision whether to enter or not is strategic, depending on the anticipated reaction of the monopolist. The payoffs are as follows. If the prospective rival chooses not to enter, the incumbent will continue to enjoy monopoly profits of 100. If the potential entrant enters the market, however, the monopolist can either accommodate the entrant by sharing profits (50/50) or it can cut prices below cost, causing both companies to suffer losses (−90/−10). The monopolist would suffer greater losses because, in carrying out its below-cost campaign, it would make loss-making sales on a larger volume of output. What is the potential competitor's rational entry decision? The extensive-form representation of this game is as follows:

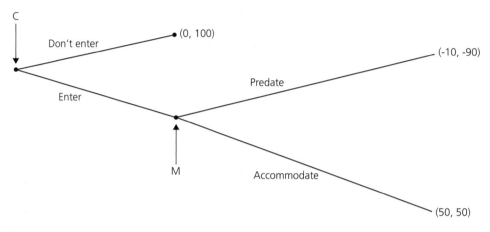

Figure 1.8

The "root node" is the very left node, which depicts the choice facing C, the first mover in the game. C can either decline to enter the market, in which case it will earn a return of 0, while M enjoys a profit of 100. Conversely, if C enters, the parties' respective payoffs depend on M's ensuing decision. The relevant payoffs are as described and illustrated above. Recall that, by convention, the first figure within each payoff parenthesis refers to the first player (here, C) while the second refers to the second player (M).

The key to solving dynamic games lies in so-called backward induction. Looking to the right at M's choice whether to predate or to accommodate, the option is between a positive return of 50 or a loss of 90. If M is rational, it would rather earn 50 and so it will accommodate if confronted with C's entry. Moving backward to consider the root node, C thus faces a choice between earning 0 if it does not enter and 50 if it does enter. C will therefore choose to enter. Enter, accommodate is thus the Nash equilibrium in this game because neither player can derive a better private result given the choice of the other player. In this example it is the only Nash equilibrium (though the reader should be aware that some games have multiple Nash equilibria, while some others have none).

On account of this basic model, one might conclude – as some economists have – that predatory pricing is generally an irrational strategy and that an incumbent's threats of such action to dissuade entry are non-credible. As Part 8 explains in detail, however, more complex game theory models of predatory pricing suggest that the exclusionary strategy could be rational in certain settings. Game theory makes frequent appearance throughout this book, reflecting the centrality of this analytic approach to modern economic analysis of law.

The last chapter of Part 1 explains the utilitarian backdrop to law and economics, which will provide the reader with a deeper understanding of the normative principles underlying economic analysis of law, as well as an appreciation for both the attractive qualities and the ethical limitations of the field. The discussion examines some of the commonly articulated objections to the law-and-economics paradigm, and argues that these concerns are misplaced if one appropriately defines the contours of what the economic analysis of law does, and does not, seek to accomplish.

Before exploring that subject matter, however, we need to address the field's core concepts, which is the subject of the next chapter.

Key Points

- Economics is the study of how society allocates scarce resources.
- Neoclassical welfare economics evaluates the efficiency of resource allocations. It does not seek to compute and compare utilities, such as by quantifying people's happiness under different outcomes, and thus does not recommend distributing scarce resources based on a utility ranking. Instead, it concludes that society should allocate goods according to people's willingness and ability to pay, which is an imperfect but workable proxy for utility.
- Demand curves slope downward, meaning that people consume less of a good as it becomes more expensive. The reason is that a higher price causes a substitution effect toward interchangeable but more affordable products. Although a higher price can increase demand for an inferior good (the wealth effect), that effect is most unlikely to outweigh the substitution effect.
- Supply curves slope upward, meaning that a higher price induces producers to supply greater quantities of the relevant good.
- Market equilibrium exists at the point where demand meets supply. Exogenous changes (i.e. those occurring due to factors that are not in the economic model) can upset that equilibrium. In active markets the price will change so that demand once again meets supply.
- One can analyse many legal phenomena using price theory, even though they do not involve explicit markets. The law can perform a market function by adjusting the price to calibrate output, thus effecting public policy. Thus, the law can affect the quantity of negligence, crime, breach of contract, innovation, litigation, and more besides. That is the focus of many of the chapters that follow.

 ## References and Further Reading

Baird, Douglas G., Gernter, Robert H., and Picker, Randal C., *Game Theory and the Law* (1998).
Georgakopoulos, Nicholas L., *Principles and Methods of Law and Economics: Basic Tools for Normative Reasoning* (2005).
Jackson, Howell E., *Analytical Methods for Lawyers* (2003).
Ippolito, Richard A., *Economics for Lawyers* (2005).
Mankiw, N. Gregory, *Principles of Economics*, 6th edn (2011) Chs. 1–3, 4, 6–7, 10.
McEachern, William A., *Microeconomics: A Contemporary Introduction* (2010) Chs. 1, 4–6.
Miceli, Thomas J., *The Economic Approach to Law*, 2nd edn (2004) Appendix Ch. 1.
Posner, Richard A., *Economic Analysis of Law*, 8th edn (2011) §§ 1.1–1.2.
Seidenfeld, Mark, *Microeconomic Predicates to Law and Economics* (1996).
Ulen, Thomas and Cooter, Robert D., *Law and Economics*, 6th edn (2011) Chs. 1–2.

Chapter 2

Essential Concepts in the Law and Economics Literature

Chapter Contents

A.	The Coase Theorem	29
B.	Efficiency and Appetite for Risk	31
C.	Rationality	34
D.	Decision Making in the Presence of Risk: Expected Value and Expected Utility	37
E.	Decision Making under Uncertainty	39
Key Points		40
References and Further Reading		41

Several concepts pervade law and economics. These include the Coase Theorem; rationality; Pareto and Kaldor-Hicks benchmarks of efficiency; shadow markets and prices; game theory, dominant strategies and Nash equilibria; and appetite for risk. Nominally complex and admittedly framed in intimidating terms, these principles are straightforward. They are also fundamental to the economic analysis of tort, crime, property, contract, and myriad legal subjects beyond. Thus, by explaining these key principles, this chapter facilitates more-comfortable analysis of the specific legal subjects that follow.

A. The Coase Theorem

The Coase Theorem is the economic analysis of law's most fundamental concept. Introduced in Ronald Coase's famous 1960 article, *The Problem of Social Cost*, the theorem provides that all property assignments are efficient in zero-transaction cost settings. More specifically, without bargaining costs and income effects, the market efficiently allocates resources regardless of the initial assignment of the relevant property rights.[1]

In this form, the Coase Theorem is tautological (i.e. necessarily true) because it provides that, if it is in the mutual interest of parties to bargain with one another, they will do so. Nevertheless, it bears important applications, as we shall now explain.

1. A numerical example

Consider a lively pub that sits next to a residential building. Noise from the bar, though commensurate with the patrons' enjoyment, annoys neighbours. Whose interests should give way? Residents relish quiet use of their property, including a good night's sleep, but the owners of the bar wish to run their business by offering a service that their customers value. Traditional analysis would recognise a property right in the party whom the externality "harmed". Since the racket comes from the bar, the residents next door should have the right to enjoin it.

The Coase Theorem, however, makes two points. First, if the bar owners and the residents can bargain freely, it does not matter who gets the property right. Suppose that the publicans profit £10,000 per week in running the bar, and that their neighbours value a lack of noise at £7,000 per week. If the government gives the property right to the residents, they will sell that right for an amount between £10,000 and £7,000. If the state vests the ownership right in the publicans, however, the property right will stay where it is. The outcome will be efficient either way.

Second, if the parties cannot negotiate freely, the traditional "Pigouvian tax" solution may be mistaken.[2] In our example, it is inefficient for the bar to close its doors because its owners derive greater value from operating it than the neighbours would enjoy in having it closed. Yet, if the state allowed the residents to enjoin the bar's operations and if transaction costs exceeded the £3,000 co-operative surplus that the parties could realise by striking a bargain, the outcome will be undesirable.

To dispel a recurring mistruth, the Coase Theorem does not suggest that the market will always or typically solve externalities, or that free markets ensure efficient outcomes. On the contrary, it provides that markets will efficiently allocate resources only in the unrealistic case where all stakeholders can bargain at zero cost. Instead, the theorem gives policymakers a structured way in which

---

1 There are several definitions of the Coase Theorem, which differ in subtle but material ways. The competing explanations attached to the theorem reflect, in large part, disagreement over the role played by such complications as income effects, discussed below.

2 See Arthur Pigou, *The Economics of Welfare* (1920). A Pigouvian tax is a fee that society charges an actor, where that fee equals the net third-party effects of his behaviour. The idea is that such taxes cause entities to internalise the costs and benefits of their actions, thus making decisions consistent with society's best interests.

to analyse the problem of inconsistent preferences. It suggests that the law can improve efficiency by defining property rights to minimise transaction costs, and by giving property rights to those most likely to purchase them in the market. It also focuses attention away from the misleading question of who "causes" the harm.

2. The Coase Theorem and externalities

Externalities are a recurring market failure. They arise when an actor does not experience the full benefits or costs of his behaviour. Positive externalities occur when actors do not enjoy the full social value of their conduct, while negative ones take place when entities do not suffer the full costs of their behaviour. Positive externalities result in not enough externality-generating conduct's taking place, while negative externalities have the opposite effect.

Examples of both kinds abound. Free markets underproduce inventions, ideas, artistic expression, and other so-called "public goods". As the creators of such goods cannot prevent third-party appropriation, positive externalities result, thus justifying intellectual property laws. Conversely, negative externalities arise in situations running the gamut from negligent behaviour to criminal conduct, where actors do not internalise the harm of their behaviour on others. The law steps in to "tax" such behaviour, forcing people to consider others' interests, as well as their own.

The traditional public policy response to negative externalities was to impose a Pigouvian tax − a fee equal to the externality. In the criminal setting, the punishment would equal the social harm of the crime. With respect to pollution, the tax would reflect the cost of the pollution. Similarly, to solve the positive-externalities problem in innovation, society could award an inventor with a Pigouvian subsidy. That sum would equal the social value of the invention that others appropriated. In all such cases, a Pigouvian tax causes the actor to experience both the desirable and undesirable consequences of her conduct, thus leading her to act efficiently.

The Coase Theorem exposes two significant, albeit related, defects underlying the use of Pigouvian taxes. First, the concept of a Pigouvian tax assumes that the taxed actor is the lowest cost avoider of the relevant harm (or benefit in the case of positive externalities). In fact, multiple actors are often involved in harmful situations. In tort, potential accident victims can take care to avoid being injured, and can steer clear of dangerous conduct altogether. With respect to nuisance, a factory's emission of a pollutant would not harm residents had they not chosen to live by the factory. In these and countless other examples, someone other than the harm-causing actor may either be the lowest cost avoider or optimally placed to solve the externality problem.

Second, a Pigouvian tax is unnecessary if the government creates and recognises a property right and if transaction costs are zero. If these conditions are satisfied, then the parties will bargain to the efficient outcome. If transaction costs preclude agreement, then public policy would more fruitfully understand the problem as a bargaining failure rather than externalities as externalities disappear in the absence of transaction costs. This insight feeds back into the first problem with Pigouvian taxes discussed above, which is that the taxed individual may not be the lowest cost avoider.

In reality, some transaction costs invariably exist. What does this mean for the Coase Theorem? The answer is four-fold. First, the Theorem should approximate reality when the benefits to the parties of reaching agreement exceed the search and bargaining costs involved in doing so. Second, in positive-transaction-cost environments, the government should define property rights to minimise the costs of contracting to a potentially superior solution. Third, it is a mistake to think that the person "causing" harm is necessarily the person against whom the law should establish a right. Finally, even in cases of significant transaction costs, it does not follow that government regulation is superior to private-contract solutions. Government action is also imperfect, and so the question is which approach is better. Coase himself holds the view that markets, even where imperfect, display a flexibility in response to inefficient allotments of rights that regulators would be unlikely to share.

3. Strong and weak versions of the Coase Theorem

A final note on the Coase Theorem is necessary. Two variants exist in the literature. The "strong version" or "invariance principle" contends that, without transaction costs, the ultimate locus of an entitlement is invariant to the initial assignment of the property right. The "weak version" or "efficiency hypothesis" states that, in the absence of bargaining costs, the allocation of an entitlement will be efficient regardless of the initial assignment. The difference between the two variants is that, under the strong version, the same party will always end up with the property right.

The strong version of the Coase Theorem ignores potential income or wealth effects that the initial allocation of a property right creates. To understand those effects, consider a simple example. Imagine that A owns land upon which he wishes to build a structure that would block light from reaching the land of his neighbour, B. The problem involves the nature of the relevant property rights. May A build whatever shadow-casting building he wants on his land as an incident of his ownership rights, or does B have the right to enjoy access to light as a constituent element of her ownership of land? Assuming no transaction costs, the Coase Theorem tells us that the answer does not matter as long as the government establishes a property right in some direction.

Yet, the question whether A or B enjoys the pertinent right certainly matters as to the distribution of income between them. If A values the right to build the structure at £50,000, and if B would pay up to £40,000 to maintain her access to light, there are two possible outcomes. First, the government could give B the right to enjoy access to light, in which case A would pay B an amount between £40,000 and £50,000. Second, the law could grant A the right to build the structure, regardless of the light it blocks, in which case there would be no agreement between the parties (A would not part with his right for less than £50,000, and yet B would not willing to pay more than £40,000). A is at least £40,000 worse off in the first case than in the second, while the opposite is true of B.

Thus, the initial allocation of a property right affects the distribution of income. Unless all parties' preferences are invariant (i.e. unless parties' marginal utility of income is constant), assignment-induced changes in wealth will alter the parties' relative demand, thus altering their consumption decisions. If a property assignment renders a consumer better off, we would expect his demand for superior and inferior goods to increase and diminish, respectively.

Income effects also arise because a person's budgetary constraint limits his ability to purchase an entitlement, while no such constraint limits his ability to sell. This phenomenon can create a disconnect between an individual's maximum purchase and minimum sell prices. That is most likely when a resource constitutes a significant amount of a person's utility. Suppose that two critically ill patients need a transplant, but only one organ is available. There, the initial assignment would be final. The person receiving the right would not sell it, even if the other patient placed a higher subjective utility on receiving the organ. This example violates the strong, but not the weak, version of the Coase Theorem. As law and economics measures a person's preference by her willingness and ability to pay, the government's allocating the right to the organ on either patient is efficient. This demonstrates that "efficiency" can describe a spectrum, rather than a point.

Ultimately, the problem of externalities – or, more accurately, bargaining failures – is a recurring feature of law and economics. As the following chapters explain, law-and-economics theory seeks to induce actors to internalise the costs and benefits of their actions, such that the social-welfare optimum guides their decisions. The Coase Theorem lies at the heart of this normative principle.

B. Efficiency and Appetite for Risk

1. Efficiency

Efficiency matters. One doubting that proposition need merely appeal to common experience. Anyone who has ever waited in an ever-growing queue at an airport in the presence of idle security personnel and unused lanes knows the visceral annoyance of inefficiency. Most people have encountered poorly run organisations that offer dilatory service or inferior products at excessive prices. In a world of limited resources, and valuable time, efficiency is important.

This is all well and good, but how does efficiency relate to law? Questions of justice seem far removed from productive efficiency, which involves manufacturing at the lowest possible per-unit cost, and allocative efficiency, which entails distributing goods to all those who value them at or above their marginal cost of production. In short, efficiency may matter, but why does it matter to law?

In fact, efficiency plays a critical role in the legal system for reasons that are variously apparent and subtle. At the more obvious end of the spectrum, efficiency requires the provision of services at prices approaching the incremental costs of their production. Applied to the courts, few things are more antithetical to justice than inefficiency, as supracompetitive pricing renders legal proceedings unaffordable. Conversely, an efficient bar that facilitates cost-effective access to the legal system allows people to vindicate their rights regardless of, or perhaps in a manner less contingent on, their affluence. If low prices are an indispensable component of an efficient legal system, so too are efficient procedures, as protracted and wasteful litigation processes cause proceedings to languish for years. The maxim that "justice delayed is justice denied" has a strong basis in efficiency.

As economists employ the term in analysing law, however, efficiency carries a distinct meaning, one going beyond the cost and duration of legal proceedings. Neoclassical economists determine efficiency by reference to the satisfaction of people's preferences.

The principal criterion for measuring efficiency is the concept of a "Pareto improvement". The concept is simple: given a pre-existing resource distribution, an exchange effects a Pareto improvement if it satisfies at least one person's preference without making any other individual worse off. An example would be a mutually beneficial contract that lacks any negative third-party effects. Since it is hard to fault an arrangement that renders some people better off without harming anyone else, reallocations effecting a Pareto improvement are seldom, in themselves, controversial. This benchmark of efficiency emphasises individual consent, as any reallocation that runs roughshod over even a single person's interests cannot be a Pareto improvement.

The condition of "Pareto superiority" or "Pareto optimality" represents an important benchmark of efficiency. It refers to a situation in which no further adjustment of rights can move a person to a preferred position without rendering any other person worse off. A system is therefore Pareto optimal if no further reallocation constituting a Pareto improvement is possible. Given any initial rights allocation, then, achieving Pareto superiority is desirable. This is not the same as saying, however, that Pareto-optimal outcomes are ethically sound, as their appeal is inextricably linked to the initial resource allocation. Imagine a world in which one person owns the vast majority of the wealth, and seven billion others live an identical, penurious existence. This distribution would be unjust, but it would also be Pareto superior if it is not possible to move any of the seven billion unfortunates to any of their preferred positions without making the rich person worse off.

For that reason, the benchmark of efficiency in the law and economics literature, though important, is not morally ironclad. Economists do not deny that distributive justice matters, but they generally argue that taxation systems are superior mechanisms of wealth redistribution than the law. They argue that courts and legislators should interpret and create law to maximise wealth, which the government can then divvy up as it sees fit.

One can expect competitive markets to tend toward Pareto optimality. The reason is that, consistent with the Coase Theorem, parties bargain to effect Pareto improvements. Indeed, under assumptions of perfect competition, the first welfare theorem holds that competitive equilibria are Pareto efficient. Restrictive and unrealistic conditions, however, underlie the economic model of perfect competition. Those traits include perfect information, productive efficiency, homogeneous goods, atomistic sellers and purchasers, and no externalities. Thus, the view that competition produces Pareto-superior equilibria is a theoretical abstraction. In real life, the panoply of ever-present market imperfections means that few, if any, market outcomes will be Pareto optimal.

Nevertheless, private contracts constitute Pareto improvements in the absence of negative third-party effects, and market mechanisms generally produce allocations closer to Pareto optimality than did the underlying, initial distribution. Furthermore, Pareto improvements remain useful for assessing a proposed law, arrangement, or policy.

Of course, many arrangements yield some negative third-party effects. Almost any policy question of note involves conflicting claims of right, such that a resolution necessarily makes someone worse off. Furthermore, many easy resource reallocations – those benefiting some, and harming none – will have taken place already. Stakeholder opposition, coupled with transaction costs, are likely to stymie many efficient reallocations that have yet to take place. As a result, Pareto optimality is more an academic aspiration than it is a practical benchmark by which to determine the normativity of various laws.

There is, however, a more workable, though potentially less robust, form of efficiency. "Kaldor-Hicks efficiency" – otherwise known as a "potential Pareto improvement" – arises when an action increases the net welfare of society, but harms at least one person. In such circumstances, the parties benefiting from the arrangement could compensate the injured people and still be better off themselves *ex post* than they were *ex ante*. Most public-policy questions bear negative consequences for at least some stakeholders, regardless of how the government resolves the issue. Kaldor-Hicks efficiency is therefore important for tackling legal problems that involve incompatible claims. It entails carrying out a cost–benefit analysis.

The problem is that Kaldor-Hicks efficiency abandons the principle of explicit consent upon which Pareto improvements and optimality depend. If a contract benefits two parties by more than it injures a third, who is to say that the third party would consent to the arrangement in the absence of perfect compensation? An answer lies in the Coase Theorem. Economists appeal to a hypothetical bargain in which parties negotiate in a setting of zero transaction costs. The idea is that, when bargaining is free, all affected parties would have agreed upon the value-maximising outcome and would compensate the disadvantaged entity, thus giving rise to a Pareto improvement. Yet, a difficulty with hypothetical consent lies in interpersonal comparisons. How to tell whether the gains from a contract, for instance, outweigh the losses, such that its effectuation constitutes a Kaldor-Hicks efficient outcome? The answer, as we shall see, lies in crafting rules of decision that capitalise on parties' private information, thus creating an incentive toward Kaldor-Hicks efficient behaviour.

2. Risk

We need to say more about utility and its relationship to wealth. Individuals generally experience diminishing marginal utility of income. This concept reflects the idea that extra income is worth less to a person the more money that person already possesses. Taken to its extreme, this presumption might justify large-scale wealth redistribution throughout society. Whether diminishing marginal utility of income is universally true, however, is less clear. It is doubtless true when large wealth differences exist. Giving Warren Buffet an additional £1,000 would not confer the same utility (subjective happiness) upon him as it would a welfare recipient. Within more modest wealth ranges, however, the principle is not obviously valid.

Diminishing marginal utility of income implicates a person's appetite for risk, which features prominently in law and economics. An individual is risk neutral when he is indifferent between the expected value of a risky action and a guaranteed return of the same value. For instance, a person would be risk neutral if he were indifferent between a 100% probability of receiving £100 and a 10% chance of obtaining £1,000. If he would prefer the definite £100, he would be risk averse, while if he would prefer a 10% probability of £1,000, he would prefer risk. One can compute the extent of a person's appetite for risk by identifying the certain benefit or cost that would render her indifferent between the sure thing and the gamble. For example, a person who would be indifferent between definitely having to *pay* £101 and a 10% chance of having to pay £1,000 would be mildly risk averse, while a person indifferent between paying £50 and a 10% chance of paying £1,000 would be more strongly risk preferring.

As the money at stake rises relative to the decision maker's total wealth, the likelihood that that person will be averse to risk increases. Risk-averse individuals would rather smooth their income over time, and would thus pay a premium to convert a probabilistic cost or benefit into a certain one. This phenomenon explains the role of insurance contracts, though, as we shall see, an important component of economic analysis of law is how best to use legal rules to shift risk from risk-averse to risk-neutral (or, better yet, to risk-preferring) individuals. Generally, we would expect companies and individuals with diversified investment portfolios to tend towards risk neutrality.

C. Rationality

Rationality is simultaneously fundamental to law and economics, and obscure. Neoclassical economists typically assume that people act "rationally", which is to say that they formulate consistent preferences and make decisions calculated in light of the environment in which they find themselves to satisfy those preferences.

1. Rationality as an elusive concept

"Rationality" may have a different meaning depending on whether one uses it in a descriptive or predictive function. Economists often wish to predict how people will react to a change in the law. Neoclassical economists construct models incorporating (what they expect to be) important explanatory variables affecting choice. To "solve" the model (i.e. to generate a specific prediction) one needs an organising principle. One answer lies in rational-choice theory, which assumes that actors maximise their utility through informed decisions. The necessary assumptions are often unrealistic at the individual level, but allow economists to use mathematical techniques of constrained optimisation. The model can usefully predict the behaviour of large populations, where deviations from rational choice will cancel one another out in the absence of systemic biases. Thus, it is not troublesome that assumed rational behaviour is unrealistic. Only the accuracy of the ensuing prediction matters, which is why empirical testing is so important. The next section "Rationality in Price Theory" explores what "rational choice" entails in neoclassical models.

A descriptive function, however, may require a different definition of rationality. No one would behave "rationally" if doing so meant always electing the single best private-welfare-maximising path. Few act pursuant to a fully informed cost–benefit analysis, incorporating all laws and facts, no matter how obscure that information may be or how difficult it may be to procure. In our complex world, information is costly. Due to the effort involved and the opportunity cost of our time, processing that knowledge is also expensive. To act rationally, then, one would only assimilate such information into the decision calculus as is cost justified. This phenomenon explains our ubiquitous use of heuristics – mental shortcuts that economise on the time involved in processing information.

From a descriptive perspective, one must consider the cost of obtaining and processing information to define rational behaviour in satisfactory fashion. Yet, this detail raises problems of its own, not least because it threatens to swallow the definition. Specifically, the opportunity cost of people's time, and (relatedly) the expense of learning one's options, is individual specific: what may be rational for one person may not be for another. Indeed, one could explain many irrational decisions by the seemingly anomalous actor's cost of processing information or attitude to risk. For instance, if a person wishes to but a suit for an interview in a week's time, is it rational for that individual to pay £1,000 for a brand suit at his local shop when an extended search of the city would have revealed the same suit available for £800? The answer, of course, would depend on whether the cost of the interviewee's search exceeds £200. Whether it does, or not, however, will be specific to the individual.

A further complication concerns the nature of a person's welfare over time. Cost–benefit analyses typically weigh present and future consequences. The outcome of that weighing process depends on the relevant individual's discount rate, which measures how strongly she favours today over tomorrow. When a person embraces an immediate pleasure at grave long-term cost, many observers are quick to label the actor's conduct irrational. Examples may include trying significant doses of an addictive and destructive drug, or robbing a bank in circumstances where one is likely to be caught. Yet, if one accepts a person's strong bias in favour of immediate experiences in lieu of eventual ones as a legitimate preference, her acting pursuant to short-term gratification is rational. The problem is that such a person's course of conduct is not, according to most people's judgment, sensible. This is one reason why it is hard to cleanse the concept of rationality of all moral implication and to employ the term in a purely objective manner. When one speaks of rationality, the conversation often implies a determination as to how one ought to behave.

2. Rationality in price theory

Despite these difficulties, economists generate predictions using rational-choice theory and test them using empirical methods. They have done so by making certain assumptions concerning rational behaviour.

First, rationality implies decision making consistent with a cost–benefit inquiry. This need not entail an explicit weighting of the pros and cons of available options. It is enough if a person implicitly considers the relative virtues of alternatives and chooses the one that best satisfies her preferences. This need not even entail conscious deliberation. From this perspective, a person chooses to engage in negligent conduct, to breach a contract, or to commit a crime if the perceived private benefits of doing so exceed the private costs. That is why the law can spur more desirable behaviour, principally by altering the private cost, and hence relative demand for, certain courses of conduct.

Second, a rational actor's preferences are "complete" and "transitive". Completeness means that an individual can ordinally rank her consumption options.[3] This assumption allows a person to be indifferent between two or more alternatives. The quality of transitivity means that preferences are consistent, such that if a person prefers good B to good A, and would rather consume good C than B, it necessarily follows that that individual would prefer good C to good A. This assumption features in the theory of consumer choice, specifically with respect to the existence of non-overlapping indifference curves. If his preferences were intransitive, a consumer would be unable to make a utility maximising consumption decision. A simple example of intransitivity would entail a choice between rock, paper, and scissors in the well-known children's game.

There is reason to believe that the assumptions of completeness and transitivity hold in at least some circumstances. The reason is that people violating these assumptions would suffer losses as a result. For instance, assume that a person prefers an Audi A6 to a Lexus IS250, prefers a BMW 535i to an Audi A6, but yet prefers the IS250 over the BMW. Suppose that he currently owns the Lexus IS250 but willingly parts with it and pays an additional premium to get the Audi. Having done so, however, he would still prefer the BMW. So, he gives up the Audi and pays a further premium for the BMW. Of course, given the intransitive preferences just described, this person would then trade in the BMW for the Lexus, obviously losing money along the way. The result is that he ends up where he started, except that he is poorer.

---

3 An ordinal ranking is an ordering of preferred outcomes, such as: first, second, third, and so on. Cardinal rankings, in contrast, assign numbers to each outcome that have consistent meanings and that are thus comparable. Examples of the latter include weight, height, age, and income. All cardinal rankings are also ordinal, but not all ordinal rankings can be assigned cardinal rankings.

More generally, if people learn over time, one would expect irrational behaviour to be ephemeral. The same principle should apply to the selling side of the market, as companies that consistently fail to act rationally and maximise profit will ultimately find themselves subject to insolvency, takeover, or shareholder challenge. This is particularly likely to be true in competitive markets.

Third, economists generally assume that rational actors' preferences display "strong monotonicity". This term captures the idea that more is better, and thus assumes a lack of satiation. Companies will always seek to make more profit than less. If a consumer likes a product, he will necessarily prefer a greater quantity of the good. Under this simplifying assumption, rational consumers will always maximise their consumption set subject only to their budget constraints. This implies that consumers will spend all of their income, such that the rational consumption choice lies on the budget line. This assumption permits economists to create models that they can solve as constrained optimisation problems.

Fourth, a rational person treats "sunk costs" as irrelevant. The fact that she may have spent considerable amounts of money on a project, or have devoted considerable effort to it, does not impede her eschewing that project should an alternative path subsequently promise to be more fruitful. Bygones are bygones. For example, the fact that a person may have invested several years and much capital in pursuing an education in medicine should have no impact on his decision to abandon his course of study if he realises that another professional avenue would yield greater rewards, comprising both pecuniary and non-monetary satisfaction.

Fifth, in choosing between alternatives that offer probabilistic outcomes, a risk-neutral, rational actor will rank those alternatives by the "expected value" of each.[4] Thus, for example, if option A would provide a 10% chance of receiving £500, while option B would yield a 20% chance of £400, a risk-neutral rational actor would choose option B because its expected value of £80 exceeds that of option A (£50).

Sixth, for simplicity, many neoclassical models assume that rational individuals maximise their financial well-being independent of perceived issues of fairness. On this view, an economically rational decision maximises profit. A well-known example involves the "ultimatum game" in which two people are given a sum of money (say £100) on the condition that they agree on how to divide it. One party will make an offer dividing the sum in any way she sees fit (e.g. £50/£50, £20/£80, £0.01/£99.99, etc.), which the other party can either accept or not. There is no negotiation. If the offeree accepts, the parties get the money on the offered terms. If the offeree rejects, neither party gets anything. Neoclassical-economics theory predicts that the offeror would suggest a division of £0.01/£99.99, which the offeree would accept because he would be better off with one penny than with no money at all. Note, however, that this aspect of rationality assumes that fairness and altruism do not form part of the relevant actor's utility function. One can relax this assumption as part of the neoclassical model of rational choice, though doing so complicates analysis.

Some take issue with characterising human behaviour by reference to the formal calculation of costs and benefits. This discomfort emanates in part from the fact that few people explicitly tally quantitative benefits and disadvantages in choosing between substitutable forms of conduct. People for whom the rational choice feature of law and economics seems unpalatable may take comfort in the field of behavioural law and economics. This field of economic analysis draws on cognitive psychology to enrich the assumptions underlying economic models, thus generating models giving rise to more-accurate predictions. This book introduces behavioural economics in Part 9.

---

4 "Expected value" is the mean or average of a random variable. One can calculate this value by multiplying each possible outcome by the likelihood of its occurrence, and then by adding all of the resulting values. For instance, a bet in which a person rolls a dice and gets £10 for a 6, £8 for a 5, and £0 for any of a 1 to 4 possesses an expected value of £3 (£10*[1/6] + £8[1/6] + £0[4/6]).

Yet, much scepticism of rational-choice theory flows from inadequate understanding. Neoclassical economics does not purport to describe the manner in which individuals make decisions. Rather, it is a theory of behaviour, designed to *predict* market-level conduct. Law and economics does not provide a descriptive account of the mental process by which individual people elect to act as they do. The theory does not seek to capture every independent variable that influences a person's choice. Instead, it provides a simplified model of human behaviour, which enables economists to demarcate theoretically implied explanatory variables. Economists can, in turn, run regressions using empirical data to determine whether a statistically significant relationship exists between the independent variable being considered and the dependent variable (typically, behaviour). Having identified such a relationship, law-and-economics theory can then inform the legislature and judiciary as to the consequential effects of the law.

Finally, it is worth noting that law and economics, with its focus on rational responses to incentives, is least controversial in the setting of explicit market phenomena. These include the fields of competition and regulation, discussed in Part 8. Rationality is more divisive, however, when applied to settings in which regular market transactions involving tangible goods or services do not occur. The idea of a person's engaging in a cost–benefit calculus in deciding whether to commit a crime, to marry, or to drive recklessly strikes some observers as implausible.

Yet, it is no requisite of an effective theory that it accurately characterise the manner in which people make decisions. Instead – and this is the crucial point – the relevant question is whether the theory yields useful predictions concerning the manner in which a relevant population reacts to incentives. Law-and-economics theory predicts, and with few exceptions empirical literature confirms, that people respond to incentives. If society increases the relative price of a crime, neoclassical economics would predict that marginal consumers (in this example, criminals who are on the fence as whether to commit the prohibited act) will substitute the relevant crime for what are now more attractive activities. Empirical research bears out this hypothesis, which is, in turn, a vindication of theory.

Of course, the theory does not provide a perfect account of market-level behaviour. The "R^2", which is a measure of the correlation between the explanatory variables of a model and observed data, is less than one because the correlation is imperfect. In Part 9, we will consider whether a behavioural account of law and economics can lead to systemically superior predictions. We will see that the answer is a qualified yes, though the behavioural law and economics literature does not yet enjoy a comprehensive theoretical foundation.

D. Decision Making in the Presence of Risk: Expected Value and Expected Utility

Circumstances often require us to choose between options bearing non-guaranteed outcomes. Economists use the concept of "risk" to refer to situations in which a variety of results are possible and where one can ascribe a probability to each such specific consequence. This issue is of some importance, as few choices in life lend themselves to definite outcomes. To understand rational behaviour when it comes to decision making in the presence of risk, economists appeal to the concept of "expected value" or "expected return".

The expected value of a particular choice, such as an investment decision, is the average of the probability distribution of all potential returns. For instance, imagine that a person, Kate, must decide whether to enter into a contract requiring the promisor, Robert, to manufacture a machine that Kate would use to expand her business in the next year. The value of that machine depends on whether, and by how much, demand increases for the product that Kate sells. If demand does not rise at all, the contracted for machine would be worthless to Kate; if demand increases by 5%, the machine would be worth £10,000; and, if demand rises by 10%, the machine would be worth

£30,000. There is a 20% chance that demand will not increase next year, a 30% chance that it will rise by 5%, and a 50% chance that it will increase by 10%. The cost of the machine is £16,000. Should Kate enter into the contract?

The answer depends on comparing the price of the machine to Kate's expected return in purchasing it. The expected return is £0*0.2 + £10,000*0.3 + £30,000*0.5 = £18,000. As this return exceeds the purchase price of £16,000, the rational choice for Kate, assuming that she is risk neutral, is to buy the machine.

Risk neutrality, however, is a key assumption if one is to equate rational choice in the presence of risk with the decision that maximises expected value. Where complete diversification of risk is not feasible, and especially if the relevant investment decision implicates a significant amount of a person's overall wealth, the decision maker will probably be risk averse. Depending on the degree of risk aversion, a rational individual may make decisions at odds with the expected value criterion.

For instance, imagine a small business owner who encounters the following investment option: Invest £100,000 in researching a new technology, which has a 1% chance of yielding a successful new product that would garner £25 million, but has a 99% chance of hitting a dead end. The expected return of this research project would be £150,000. If the £100,000 investment constitutes a significant amount of his present wealth, the owner may prefer to hold onto that amount with a 100% certainty instead of losing all of that money with a 99% probability. Such a decision is rational in light of the business owner's risk aversion. The fact that people regularly do not maximise expected value, however, raises the question whether there is a more robust theory of choice in the presence of risk.

Theoretical problems with decision making based on expected value magnify the need for a better theory. For instance, the St Petersburg paradox refers to the odd result when one calculates the expected return of a coin-toss game in which the player wins £2^n in the event of the coin's landing tails, where "n" represents the number of throws before the coin lands tails. Thus, if a player gets tails on his first throw, he would receive £2. If he took three throws to get tails, he would obtain £8. If he took 10 throws, he would get £1,024, and so on. How much would a rational person pay to earn the right to play such a game?

The expected payoff of each throw is £1 because, for any given throw, the available prize is the inverse of the probability of landing tails. For instance, the odds of a person's landing tails for the first time on the fifth throw is 1 out of 32. The payoff for the same is £32, so the expected payout is £1. What is the expected return of playing the game? This requires one to aggregate all the expected payouts of all possible outcomes, which results in an expected return of infinity! This implies that an expected value-maximising gambler would pay any amount less than infinity to enter the game, which is obviously implausible. It would seem to be obviously irrational to pay, for example, £10 million to enter a game that provides a 50% chance of winning £2, a 25% chance of winning £4, a one-eighth chance of winning £8, and so on. If so, there is something wrong with expected-value theory.

The larger difficulty involved in equating rational choice with maximising expected return is that the marginal utility of income is not constant. Winning £1 million may confer twice the purchasing power on the winner as £0.5 million, but it does not bestow twice the utility. By decoupling income and utility in considering probabilistic payoffs, we can derive a more accurate account of rational decision making in situations of risk.

Economists use expected-utility theory to accomplish this task. In doing so, they seek to construct formal models of choice that take account of diminishing marginal utility of income. Once a specific utility can be computed for each possible outcome, one can assign each such possible return a specific probability and, from there, calculate the expected utility of a particular decision. Depending on the extent of risk aversion, the resulting choice may differ significantly from the expected-value computation.

Nevertheless, expected value is an important component of decision making in the presence of risk, especially where the actor is risk neutral. Such neutrality is especially likely when an actor's decision relates to one of many diversified choices the independent risk profiles of which do not correlate with one another.

Finally, even at this early juncture, it is worth making preliminary reference to a more modern theory of choice in the presence of risk, known as prospect theory. This approach to decision making is descriptive, trying more accurately to account people actually choose for how in such environments. The key to understanding prospect theory is to focus on the concept of a reference point, by which people judge the desirability of an outcome. Unlike expected-utility theory, which depends on absolute wealth, prospect theory depends on wealth relative to a fixed point against which a person measures perceived gains and losses. Part 9 on behavioural law and economics, which applies cognitive psychology to the economic analysis of legal problems, explores prospect theory in greater depth.

E. Decision Making under Uncertainty

"Knightian uncertainty" refers to an incalculable risk (i.e. a possible outcome to which decision makers cannot ascribe a probability). This phenomenon creates considerable problems for rational choice and economic analysis generally. Many contingencies are not amenable to calculation, which frustrates the calculation of expected value. For instance, it would have been difficult, *ex ante*, to attach a percentage probability to the occurrence of a global banking and credit crisis of the kind that rocked the world economy in 2008; nor could one have precisely calculated the likelihood that a nuclear reactor at the Fukushima power plant would suffer a meltdown in 2011 as the result of an earthquake and ensuing tsunami. On a more quotidian basis, few decisions that we face are amenable to calculation in a manner comparable to those accompanying a game of roulette. Might such consequential ambiguity render rational decisions indeterminate?

The answer is yes, but a word of caution is first appropriate. Even the most common choices implicate possible outcomes to which a decision maker cannot attach a specific probability. It does not follow, however, that expected return and expected utility theories lose their validity in such circumstances. One can often estimate the probability of possible outcomes, even if it is not possible to define those probabilities in precise terms. For instance, envision a person who is deciding whether to study law, finance, or drama in a particular college. It is not possible to attach an exact likelihood to the various possible outcomes of the prospective student's choosing any one field of study. It is difficult to predict the exact odds of her finishing at various levels of her class. Nor is it possible to foresee with absolute confidence the state of the labour market four years hence. Nevertheless, by accessing employment information concerning the median and mean salaries of recent graduating classes, researching the relevant industries, and making other pertinent inquiries, the individual could attach meaningful probabilities to the possible payoffs under each available choice.

In such settings, the rational-choice model explored above provides ready means by which to define a narrow range of rational behaviour. To reiterate, however, rational-choice theory does not posit that decision makers, in practice, sit down and mathematically calculate expected returns before making a choice. It is, instead, a model – an artificial abstraction from reality – that economists employ to capture the important variables underlying decisions. It seems fair to postulate that people make implicit determinations in cost–benefit terms, and the perceived probabilities of various outcomes will doubtless factor into that calculus.

Problems do arise, however, where uncertainty becomes sufficiently serious that the probabilities which decision makers attach to relevant outcomes become arbitrary. In such circumstances, the band of "rational" choices that people could make within the confines of the relevant model may be so broad as not to yield a meaningful basis for predicting behaviour. This result flows from "uncertainty" in the sense of how Frank Knight employed the term.[5]

This problem raises the question how economists might expect rational actors to react to conditions of uncertainty, as opposed to risk. One possibility comes from decision theory, which suggests that decision makers should consider the relative harm of Type I and Type II errors. For instance, if an antitrust regulator must decide whether to impose liability on a dominant company for its refusal to cooperate with its rivals, it may lack sufficient information to make an informed decision concerning the merits of liability. If the regulator commits a Type I error, or "false positive", it will find the company liable in circumstances where it should not. If the regulator errs in the opposite direction, committing a Type II error, or "false negative", it will find that the wrong-doing company did no wrong. In situations of uncertainty, these possibilities may seem like a wash. The long-term consequences of Type I errors, however, may be worse than Type II mistakes. If this is the case, a rational regulator would properly err on the side of letting more guilty companies go free.

Another possibility is that rational individuals should react to uncertain outcomes by assigning a specific probability to each conceivable return based on their best guess. Once this is accomplished, decision makers can rely on a traditional analysis based on expected value or expected utility. While this approach enables economists to analyse choice under uncertainty within the confines of formal models, it is vulnerable to actors' estimate of outcomes. Should those estimates depart significantly from the actual, though unobservable, probabilities, analysis based on expected value or expected utility will display serious flaws.

A potentially more fruitful view, though one less susceptible to formal economic analysis, is that people do not make decisions based on utility calculations in uncertain environments. Instead, they do what they do as the result of a compulsion to act rather than do nothing. This is the phenomenon of people's "animal spirits", which Keynes famously described in his groundbreaking work, *The General Theory of Employment, Interest and Money*:

> [A] large proportion of our positive activities depend on spontaneous optimism rather than mathematical expectations, whether moral or hedonistic or economic. Most, probably, of our decisions to do something positive, the full consequences of which will be drawn out over many days to come, can only be taken as the result of animal spirits – a spontaneous urge to action rather than inaction, and not as the outcome of a weighted average of quantitative benefits multiplied by quantitative probabilities.

Recent work suggests that an uncertain business environment impeded economic recovery after the 2008–2009 banking crisis, as unclear government policies and unpredictable macroeconomic conditions stifled investment and business expansion.[6]

Key Points

- The Coase Theorem holds that, freed of transaction costs, the market will efficiently allocate property rights regardless of how the government first assigns them.

    o   The strong version posits that the final assignment of a property right is invariant to the initial allocation.

---

5 Frank Knight, *Risk, Uncertainty, and Profit* (1921).
6 *See, e.g.,* Gary S. Becker, Steven J. Davis and Kevin M. Murphy, 'Uncertainty and the slow recovery' (2010) *Wall St Journal*, 4 January.

o   The weak version says that the final assignment will always be efficient, but its location may change depending on the initial allocation, which affects the parties' relative wealth and hence demand.

● A Pigouvian tax is a price that an actor must pay equal to the externality that he creates. The Coase Theorem shows that the person "causing" an externality may not be its lowest cost avoider. Furthermore, positive transaction costs, rather than externalities, are why markets fail to allocate entitlements efficienty.

● Efficiency is a metric that economists use variously to describe and prescribe laws.

o   A Pareto improvement exists when a resource reallocation makes at least one entity better off (i.e. it satisfies his preference) without making anyone else worse off.

o   Where no further reallocation is possible without making at least one stakeholder worse off, the condition of Pareto optimality or superiority exists.

● There are several theories of rational choice. The most simple is expected-value theory.

o   Expected-value theory predicts that a rational actor weighs a choice by summing each possible outcome discounted by the chance of each one's occurrence. So, for example, if a gamble carries a 20% chance of generating a £100 return, a 50% probability of producing a £200 return, a 10% likelihood of a £500 return, and a 20% chance of no return, its expected value is £170. A rational actor would thus choose another gamble if it bore an expected value greater than £170—for instance, he would prefer a gamble bearing a 1% chance of £18,000 and a 99% probability of nothing (an expected value of £180).

o   People will follow expected-value theory only if they are risk neutral. Appetite for risk thus informs a person's rational choice. Most people are risk averse, meaning that they would prefer a choice bearing relatively low expected value but little variance in outcome.

o   Expected-utility theory incorporates diminishing marginal utility of income in quantifying outcomes, thus seeking to account (in part) for risk aversion. It is more complicated than expected-value theory, though neoclassical economists use it widely in price-theoretic models.

o   Another theory of rational choice is prospect theory, which is a major contribution of behavioural economics. Part 9 discusses prospect theory.

● It is difficult to model rational choice using expected utility or expected value under Knightian uncertainty, where outcome probabilities are unknown.

 ## References and Further Reading

Books
Finkelstein, Michael O., *Basic Concepts of Probability and Statistics in the Law* (2009).
Miceli, Thomas J., *The Economic Approach to Law*, 2nd edn (2004) Ch. 1.
Polinsky, Mitchell A., *An Introduction to Law and Economics*, 4th edn (2011) Ch. 3.
Posner, Richard A., *Economic Analysis of Law*, 8th edn (2011) Ch. 1.
Posner, Richard A., 'Values and consequences: An introduction to economic analysis of law', in *Chicago Lectures in Law and Economics*, Eric Posner (ed.) (2000) pp. 189–201.
Ulen, Thomas and Cooter, Robert D., *Law and Economics*, 6th edn (2011) Ch. 2.

Articles
Aivazian, Varouj A. and Callen, Jeffrey L., 'The Coase Theorem and the empty core' (1981) 24 JL & Econ 175.
Coase, Ronald H., 'The problem of social cost' (1960) 3 JL & Econ 1.

Coase, Ronald H., 'The Coase Theorem and the empty core: a comment' (1981) 24 JL & Econ 183.

Cooter, Robert D., 'The cost of Coase' (1982) 11 J Legal Stud 1.

Dahlman, Carl J., 'The problem of externality' (1979) 22 JL & Econ 141.

Farnsworth, Ward, 'Do parties to nuisance bargain after judgment? A glimpse inside the cathedral' (1998) 66 U Chi L Rev 373.

Farrell, Joseph, 'Information and the Coase Theorem' (1987) 1 J Econ Persp 113.

Hoffman, Elizabeth and Spitzer, Matthew L., 'The Coase Theorem: Some experimental tests' (1982) 25 JL & Econ 73.

Hovenkamp, Herbert J., 'Marginal utility and the Coase Theorem' (1990) 75 Cornell L Rev 783.

Kahneman, Daniel et al., 'Experimental tests of the endowment effect and the Coase Theorem' (1990) 98 J Political Econ 1325.

Medema, Steven G., 'The myth of two Coases: what Coase is really saying' (1994) 28 J Econ Issues 208.

Regan, Donald H., 'The problem of social cost revisited' (1972) 14 JL & Econ 427.

Stigler, George J., 'Two notes on the Coase Theorem' (1989) 99 Yale LJ 631.

Chapter 3

Utilitarianism, Neoclassical Welfare Economics, and the Ethics of Markets

Chapter Contents

A.	Utilitarianism	44
B.	Neoclassical Welfare Economics as Applied to Law	50
C.	The Ethics of Markets	53
Key Points		59
References and Further Reading		60

In regulating behaviour, the law implicates questions of morality and justice. Economic analysis of law thus implicates the same questions. This chapter explores the ethical dimensions of law and economics, introducing the relationship between economic analysis and legal theory.

Not all applications of law and economics are laden with moral concerns. The positive arm, for example, may be ethically neutral. This application of law and economics predicts consequences to which others can ascribe appropriate ethical weight. Economists can provide factual answers to non-evaluative questions, even if the motivation underlying those questions and the aim to which policymakers will use pertinent answers have ethical dimensions. One might think of positive economic analysis as serving a neutral function within a larger framework of policy making, which, taken as a whole, is interwoven with ethical concerns. The economist's role in answering a consequentialist enquiry as to the likely effect of a proposed law may be independent of morality.

Still, even in undertaking positive analysis, economists can benefit from a philosophy, which allows them better to understand the rationale underlying the research that others have asked them to do. More importantly, positive law and economics is more narrow than may first appear. This is because many questions that policymakers put to economists, particularly in the legal sphere, have an evaluative character to which one cannot ascribe a value-independent response. The line between normative and positive questions is not always clear, and when those questions blur it is no answer to say that economics offers a scientific or neutral view of the legal system. Indeed, the field's core concept of rationality, including the assumption of non-altruistic wealth maximisation, has ethical dimensions. As a result, someone using economics to inform legal analysis should have some appreciation for its philosophical implications. This chapter provides some exposure to these issues.

Neoclassical welfare economics, which derives from utilitarianism, lies at the heart of mainstream law and economics. This chapter therefore begins with utilitarian moral philosophy, and then addresses some differences between classical utilitarianism and the premises underlying neoclassical welfare economics. It concludes with a simple examination of the ethical dimensions of market processes, which lie at the core of the Coase Theorem and the larger field of economic analysis of law.

A. Utilitarianism

Utilitarianism is a consequentialist moral theory holding that an act or policy is desirable if it enhances the amount of pleasure, happiness, or "utility" in society. It is therefore teleological, taking as its goal (or "telos") the maximisation of utility, against which metric society must judge the morality of all questions. The approach is bold in that it reduces seemingly complex moral dilemmas to a cost–benefit analysis that weighs the gains occasioned by an action against the costs with the aim, as its founder Jeremy Bentham famously put it, of yielding "the greatest good to the greatest number". In its classic expression, this approach lends itself to a hedonic calculus, which quantifies people's satisfaction or dissatisfaction with various outcomes and weighs them against one another to identify the best course.

Utilitarianism displays an attractive simplicity, and it is likely the dominant method of public-policy analysis. The theory has an intuitive quality in that it comports with much of our daily decision making, which is couched, albeit implicitly, in cost–benefit terms. In deciding whether to act, and if so in what manner, we invariably rely on intuition, if not rough mental calculation, as to which course will best serve our ends. More often than not, our preferred ends are those that make us most happy.

One of utilitarianism's principal virtues is that it provides a theoretical framework with which to resolve conflicting claims of right. Contested issues, of course, invariably surround any notable policy decision. Related to this point, utilitarian theory counters the phenomenon of regulatory capture that public-choice theorists predict with some accuracy. Certain policies can benefit a small subset of society whilst diffusing disproportionately large costs over a greater number of citizens. Interest groups consistently lobby for the adoption of laws that are antithetical to the welfare of society as a whole. Such groups act rationally in advocating policies that inure to their benefit, and so may the administrative and legislative arms of the state act in passing such rules into law, for the political gains of doing so may be significant.

This is an externality problem. Individual incentives will not align with the social-welfare optimum whenever a gulf arises between the private gains and costs to an actor and those that society experiences. A utilitarian view on public policy would insist that lawmakers and regulators justify their decisions by reference to the well-being of the collective (i.e. the aggregate welfare of all those who comprise society). Such a requirement bridges the gap between private and social cost that spurs the public choice problem in the first place.

Despite these benefits, there are at least two broad problems with utilitarianism, which we shall now consider in turn.

1. Objection 1: Quantifying and Comparing Utility

The first objection to utilitarianism is the theory's supposition that one can determine the pleasure or displeasure associated with any outcome, quantify it on a common scale, and thus cardinally rank the results.[1] In other words, it presupposes a workable hedonic calculus. Determining and comparing the utility that one derives from disparate experiences is far from straightforward however, and in some cases can lead to absurdities.

This measurement issue creates special problems when one defines utility in monetary terms. Assigning a specific value to every relevant experience in a person's life is difficult, maybe even impossible. What is the disutility, in pecuniary terms, to one person's losing his little finger on his non-writing hand? What is the comparative utility of watching *Family Guy* or reading *Ulysses*? To how many cups of tea is a beautiful sunset equivalent? These experiences, like many in life, appear to be at least somewhat incommensurate.[2] Even if we could construct a coherent ranking of preferences at the individual level, and in doing so ascribe a specific numerical value to each experience, it does not obviously follow that we could reliably compare respective values across different persons. William Jevons famously remarked: "Every mind is inscrutable to every other mind, and no common denominator of feeling seems to be possible."[3]

These objections, troubling as they may be, are potentially surmountable. Economists acknowledge that directly measuring people's utilities is impractical, and so they appeal to revealed preferences. From this perspective, the lower cap on the "utility" that a person derives from a good is the amount that he pays to obtain it. Law and economics thus abandons the pursuit of cardinal rankings, and instead focuses on ordinal rankings. It may not be possible to conclude that the disutility to a person of losing his leg is (for example) £500,000, while the disutility of losing his hand is £450,000, but it may indeed be possible to determine that this person would rather lose his hand than his leg. More generally, markets reveal individual preferences through the prices at which

---

1 A cardinal ranking is based on a scale that permits one to compare by magnitude. For example, the difference between 120 kph and 100 kph is the same as that between 60 kph and 40 kph. Cardinal rankings allow one meaningfully to compare one number with another.

2 Indeed, social scientists have performed experiments to determine the monetary value that people place on diverse experiences. For instance, Michael Sander points to the outcome of a 1937 survey study by Edward Thorndike in which people negatively valued these experiences as follows: moving to Kansas ($300,000), choking a stray cat to death ($10,000), losing a pinky toe ($57,000), eating a six-inch worm ($100,000), and to have an upper front tooth pulled out ($4,500). *See* Michael Sander, *Justice: What's the Right Thing to Do?* (2009). The bizarre nature of these valuations suggests that the relevant experiences are not (easily, at least) quantifiable and commensurate.

3 William Stanley Jevons, *The Theory of Political Economy* (3rd edn) 14.

different people are willing to buy and sell, so one can determine whether a transaction satisfies people's preferences. This holds true even though market prices do not allow economists to determine the magnitude of the utility gain that such a transaction achieves. Furthermore, even if direct inter-personal comparisons of utility are impossible, economists can infer that voluntary, informed transactions make all of the contracting parties better off.

Yet, does satisfying a person's preference necessarily enhance that individual's "utility"? Generally, we would expect the answer to be yes. If a person would rather have good A than good B, satisfying that preference would presumably make her happier. Indeed, who could be a superior judge of a person's well-being than the person himself? Although this is surely true as a general matter, it is not so as a universal matter. Meeting an immediate preference does not always advance the person's welfare. A drug addict may prefer another score over a rehab clinic, but he would be much better off with the latter.

A special problem concerns the value of human life. Public-policy problems routinely implicate matters of life and limb, making hard questions unavoidable. The tempting answer is that life is priceless. Although appealing, this view is unworkable as a policy matter. If a person's life were of infinite value, governments would do everything possible to minimise the risk of death. They would forbid driving, unhealthy food, alcohol, contact sports, employment in hazardous work environments, and all manner of everyday, but risky, conduct. Governments would never go to war, at least offensively. The fact that we do not observe laws banning (and government policies at all costs avoiding) dangerous conduct demonstrates that society values human life finitely.

This observation is unremarkable. The more controversial issue concerns assigning specific monetary value to life. Few people would knowingly accept certain and immediate death for anything less than an infinite amount. Revealed preferences, however, allow economists to calculate the compensation that people require for exposing themselves to a heightened risk of death. From that information, they can derive the implied value that people place on their lives. Representative calculations include the US Environmental Protection Agency's valuation of a life at $9.1 million and the US Food and Drug Administration's figure of $7.9 million.[4] In the United Kingdom, the National Institute for Health and Clinical Excellence, relying on the concept of quality-adjusted life years (QALYs), purportedly places a cap of approximately £30,000 per QALY.[5]

Such valuations receive a hostile reception in some quarters, but ethical objections do not solve an unavoidable government problem: how should society enact laws and pursue policies that must weigh benefits against risks to human life? Utilitarianism could provide the means by which to address these questions, but only if the government can specify the relevant values. Even a simple example clarifies the point: Many western countries undertake a utilitarian calculus in determining which potentially life-saving drugs and treatments to purchase and to allot to patients. The United States, for instance, has measured the value of a QALY at $50,000 to measure cost-effectiveness, though economic studies have suggested that this figure is significantly too low.[6]

As governments must weigh human life to resolve many public-policy questions, why is valuation so fraught with controversy? Perhaps the debate concerns the magnitude of the value on life. If that is true, however, the dispute is not one of principle, but of detail.

Consider the infamous Ford Pinto case, which resulted in near-universal condemnation of the company and punitive damages of $125 million, which a court subsequently lowered to $3.5

---

4 Binyamin Appelbaum, 'As U.S. Agencies Put More Value on a Life, Businesses Fret', NY Times (16 February 2011); see also http://news.bbc.co.uk/2/hi/uk_news/magazine/8633484.stm.

5 See www.nice.org.uk/newsroom/features/CitizensCouncilReport.jsp.

6 See R. Scott Braithwaite et al., 'What does the value of modern medicine say about the $50,000 per Quality-Adjusted Life-Year Decision Rule?' (2008) 46 Medical Care 349; see also Kathleen Kingsbury, 'The Value of Human Life: $129,000', Time, 20 May 2008.

million. Ford, placing a $200,000 value on each human life, declined to recall its defective Pinto cars, which were liable to explode when hit from behind. It refused because the cost of recalling the cars exceeded its expected liability for loss of human life.

The analytic difficulty lies in the unavoidability of trade-offs. Every car manufacturer must design its new vehicles balancing safety with the cost of production and ensuing price to the consumer. Fundamentally, the case was about a social contract. In zero-transaction cost settings, all stakeholders would have been privy to Ford's design decisions, ensuring that risks and cost were efficiently allocated. In the real world of preclusive bargaining costs and information asymmetry, however, the law must do what the market cannot by imposing a sufficiently high price.

The real problem, then, was two-fold. First, the liability regime that created an expected cost of $200,000 per victim undervalued human life – a shortcoming that the jury sought to rectify.[7] Second, the company limited its decision making to bottom-line profit maximisation – it did not value its customers' lives independently of anticipated liability verdicts. Neoclassical price theory hypothesises profit maximisation because it allows economists to construct models using mathematical methods of constrained optimisation, and hence to predict behaviour. But nothing in law and economics holds that it is ethically proper to value others' lives only to the degree society makes you pay for them. To the contrary, the field envisions a social contract in which each actor fully internalises third-party effects. The role of the courts in high-transaction cost environments is to impose such liability as would incentivise conduct consistent with such a contract.

Ultimately, people experience disproportionately greater disutility from the risk of death as that probability increases. Value-of-life estimates derive from acceptance of limited risk rather than acceptance of definite or near-certain death. The distinction between low- and high-probability risks of harm is important for the legal responses to tortious and criminal behaviour involving the possibility of death (or other serious injuries) and its valuation. In the setting of tort, the appropriate question concerns how much money potential victims would require willingly to undertake the risk of being injured. Only with knowledge of that figure can society determine the optimal amount of risky behaviour. Conversely, and putting aside the cost of utilising the legal system, the efficient "output" of crimes involving deliberate violent injury or death is zero. This is precisely because there is no amount that specific potential victims would have been willing to pay in a low-transaction cost environment to agree to the criminal act.

Yet, there is a further limitation to how people construe value-of-life estimates. This shortcoming concerns the perceived, but erroneous, distinction between probabilities and certainties. People fail to understand that statistical probabilities equate to certainties over a sufficiently large number of repeat plays. For example, the government will likely (and rightly) spend millions of pounds to rescue a trapped miner, and yet refuse to spend a lesser sum on reducing the risk of a future mining accident, even though, over time, the latter expenditure would save many more lives. This phenomenon may be the result of cognitive shortcomings. For better or for worse, though, people perceive *ex ante* probabilities and *ex post* actualities differently, even if, over time, the distinction evaporates as a matter of statistical fact.

2. Objection 2: Utilitarianism as a flawed theory of morality

A second objection is that utilitarianism does not comport with important intuitions about morality. A feature of utilitarian theory is that a choice can potentially be moral even if its consequences are terrible. This result holds if the consequences of all other available choices are even worse.

---

7 Interestingly, the company did not derive this figure on its own, but adopted it from a government study.

Unfortunately, events occasionally force people to choose among unpalatable options. In medical emergencies where the number of injured overwhelms a hospital's resources, doctors must decide whom to treat first. If only one organ is available for a life-saving transplant, to whom should the hospital give it? If terrorists appear to have hijacked an airliner and are flying towards a city, should the government shoot down the plane? In all such cases, utilitarian theory offers a quantitative solution. Utilitarianism's ability to answer such questions makes it useful for resolving public policy questions.

Yet, such cold cost–benefit calculus sits uncomfortably with many people, and can lead to prescriptions that contradict our moral intuitions. Consider the following classic example:[8] Imagine that you drive a trolley on San Francisco's famous steep hills. While proceeding down a particularly sharp incline, the brakes fail. As your vehicle hurtles downhill, you notice that two people, who are unaware of the danger and will be killed if struck by the trolley, are standing on the track at the bottom of the hill. There is, however, a separate track that the tram could follow if you pulled a lever. At the end of that track, unfortunately, stands a single person, who is similarly oblivious to the looming danger. Hence, the moral dilemma: should you pull the lever and kill one person or do nothing and kill two?

The utilitarian answer is straightforward: pull the lever because one person's death is better than that of two. This follows if each potential victim's life is of equal worth or if there is no way to tell otherwise. That choice comports with most people's moral intuition. There is no happy outcome from the hypothetical, so all anyone can do is minimise the loss. Consider, however, the following situation. Once more, a trolley is running out of control down a hill, but this time you are an onlooker who observes that, unless someone can stop the tram, two people at the bottom of the track will die. You know that you are too small to stop the trolley by jumping in front of it, but, as it happens, a large gentleman is standing next to the track. Pushing him in front of the speeding trolley would kill him, but would save the two pedestrians at the bottom of the track. What should you do?

The classic utilitarian answer is, once more, that you should kill one person to save two. This response, however, would strike most people as decidedly immoral. What dissimilarity explains the divergence? Both cases involve a choice between one person's dying and two people's doing so. A plausible explanation is that the second case involves using a person as a means to an end, rather than as an end in himself. In the first case, the relevant action involved pulling the lever – it was not the actor's intention to kill the person, even if that naturally resulted from his action. In the second case, however, the actor arguably intended to kill the large man, with the larger aim of saving two others. From this perspective, the second hypothetical is objectionable for the same reason that it would be wrong for a doctor to kill one healthy person, harvest his organs, and use them to save several others. Using an autonomous being in an instrumentalist fashion is wrong. Every person has a right not to be used as a means for achieving another's goal.

Utilitarianism conflicts with many people's moral distinction between actions and omissions. Generally, consequentialism draws no distinction between action and inaction. This makes utilitarianism a demanding theory of morality because it draws little ethical distinction between, for example, one person failing to save another and that person's deliberately killing the victim.

A further feature of Benthamite utilitarianism that undermines the field's moral integrity is that the normative quality of an act is necessarily contingent. This contingency depends on how people at any one time happen to perceive the relevant act. As an extreme example, it is theoretically possible that throwing Christians to lions in the Roman Coliseum instilled such excitement and

---

8 *See* Judith Jarvis Thomson, 'The trolley problem' (1985) 94 Yale LJ 1395.

passion in a large number of spectators that their utility outweighed the (severe) disutility that the victims experienced. Yet, as sensibilities change over time and empathy grows, the moral pendulum would swing away from the propriety of the Coliseum even though the scrutinised actions remain identical. The fact of contingency need not always be problematic – circumstances can affect an action's consequences, and it may be dogmatic to insist that the moral quality of an act is necessarily invariant to the facts of a given case – but when consequences depends on perception alone, this fact introduces a troubling vagary to the question of morality. This does not mean that utilitarianism is invalid as a moral theory, but it does reveal that this branch of philosophy conceives of morality differently than many people's intuitions do. Our discomfort may emanate from our wish to view morality as an objective truth independent of subjective judgment, rather than as a relative concept.

Consistent with this concern, some people find the utilitarian view that morality is consequence specific to be unsettling. Of course, a utilitarian might defend her philosophy in the Coliseum example by pointing out the improbability that the onlookers' happiness could ever outweigh the suffering that such extreme cruelty inflicts. For those taking issue with utilitarianism, however, this defence misses the point. The idea that the morality of such an act depends on the outcome of a calculus strikes some observers as repugnant as, in their view, one can define the morality of actions based on their innate nature. Throwing a person to hungry lions is wrong regardless of the consequences. Deontologists, who embrace rule-based conceptions of morality that apply without reference to case-specific repercussions, are among such critics of utilitarianism.

It does not necessarily follow, however, that the consequentialist nature of utilitarianism is inconsistent with hard rules that are invariant to circumstance. In fact, some utilitarian philosophers advocate behavioural rules that apply without regard to whether a specific action fulfils the utilitarian criterion. All that matters is that, taken as a whole, adhering to the ethical principle advances net utility more than error-prone, case-specific determinations of utility would do. On this view, the Coliseum example need not undermine utilitarianism, for society would properly ban all such cases under a utility-derived prohibition on killing or battery. Even if killing or battery occasionally enhanced utility, such cases would be so rare as to warrant banning all of them.

This rule-based, as opposed to act-based, perspective on utilitarianism enjoys some support, though it does not state an irrefutable case. The problem is that, if, as Bentham said, the standards of right and wrong are fastened to the throne of pain and pleasure, then utility always defines the moral quality of an act. A rule-centred approach to utilitarianism is therefore vulnerable, for if a person could definitively demonstrate that, contrary to the relevant rule, a particular action promoted well being in a specific case, utility would justify violating the rule. If this were possible, however, then any derived rule would presumably degrade over time until exceptions fatally compromised it. Over time, a rule-based approach may be indiscernible from act-based utilitarianism.

John Stuart Mill had a solution to the extreme implications of Bentham's utilitarianism. Specifically, he distinguished higher and lower pleasures, arguing that only the former were worthy of inclusion in the social-welfare calculus. From that perspective, the pleasure of those viewing the bloody spectacle in the Coliseum would be entitled to little or zero weight, so throwing Christians to the lions would have been unambiguously immoral. Mill explained:

> Human beings have faculties more elevated than the animal appetites, and when once made conscious of them, do not regard anything as happiness which does not include their gratification . . . [T]here is no known Epicurean theory of life which does not assign to the pleasures of the intellect, of the feelings and imagination, and of the moral sentiments, a much higher value as pleasures than to those of mere sensation.[9]

---

9 John Stuart Mill, *Utilitarianism* (1861) Ch. 2.

On Mill's account, it is improper to think of utilitarianism as a philosophy blindly attached to the hedonistic maximisation of base pleasures. People differ from beasts in their cognitive capacities, which allow humans to appreciate the worth of more sophisticated pleasures that flow from a higher order of thinking. That satisfying the intellect is superior than blindly pursuing sensual pleasures is clear because those who have experienced both know that the utilitarian case for the former is compelling. As Mill opined:

> [f]ew human creatures would consent to be changed into any of the lower animals for a promise of the fullest allowance of a beast's pleasures; no intelligent human being would consent to be a fool, no instructed person would be an ignoramus[.][10]

Mill's approach strengthens the moral legitimacy of utilitarianism and solves, to some degree, the problem of incommensurability. Yet, it raises the difficult task of distinguishing good from bad utility when people differ on the distinction. The fact that someone must decide whose welfare considerations count deprives utilitarianism of part of its logical purity, and raises moral problems of its own. Mill recognised that people will differ on whether one action bestows greater utility than another, but he left no doubt as to his view on the legitimacy of such a debate: "It is better to be a human dissatisfied than a pig satisfied; better to be Socrates dissatisfied than a fool satisfied. And if the fool, or the pig, are of a different opinion, it is because they only know their own side of the question."[11]

Of course, even if one accepts Mill's distinction between higher and lower pleasures, it is not obvious how utilitarian philosophers could articulate a workable rule of decision as to how properly to incorporate certain utilities in, and omit others from, the social-welfare calculus. In any event, Bentham's and Mill's respective accounts of utilitarianism both yield important insights for the economic analysis of law. Although neoclassical economists typically eschew subjective utility in their models, the idea that a policy is desirable if it renders society as a whole better off is central to law and economics. If we trust that people reliably judge their own welfare, then economic policies aimed at satisfying individual preferences are consistent with utilitarianism. Thus, Benthamite utilitarianism provides useful insights into the economic analysis of such subjects as tort, property, contract, and competition law, in which one can usefully conceive of a social-welfare calculus comprised of each actor's well being. Yet, in other situations, such as with respect to criminal law and intentional torts, crediting the preferences of all actors may be problematic. To resolve the public-policy issues raised in these circumstances, one might distinguish legitimate and illegitimate preferences, which mirrors Mill's distinction of higher and lower pleasures.

The following section discusses how neoclassical welfare economics, which informs traditional law-and-economics theory, differs from utilitarian moral philosophy.

B. Neoclassical Welfare Economics as Applied to Law

This section centres on *normative* law and economics. It explains what economists mean when they recommend a particular law on the ground that it is "efficient", and explores the extent to which economic analysis of law escapes the problems that afflict classical utilitarianism. The discussion will enable readers to decide for themselves how to weigh the values underlying the efficiency metric.

---

10 *Ibid.*
11 *Ibid.*

Law and economics does not simply apply utilitarian moral theory to legal problems. Economists understand the deficiencies underlying this branch of philosophy, and have devised their own approach to resolving conflicting claims of right. First, they do not try to estimate people's utility. By jettisoning cardinal measures of utility, economists avoid calculating which policy would maximise the amount of pleasure in the world. Instead, law and economics focuses on hypothetical consent, and on satisfying individual preferences, which approach reflects personal autonomy. Thus, when studying law, economists typically use the term "utility" in the sense of "ordinal utility". In other words, they embrace the notion that a person has a stable and consistent preference for one item over another, as measured by that individual's paying more for one product than for the other. Economists will not attempt to specify cardinal values.

A recurring feature of law-and-economics theory is that rules can induce people to behave efficiently (i.e. in a manner consistent with what all stakeholders would have collectively agreed to *ex ante* in a hypothetical setting of no transaction cost). Yet, the economic analysis of law can do more than induce efficient behaviour. Consistent with that hypothetical bargain, the economic approach can achieve equity by remedying dissatisfied preferences through compensation. Law and economics thus attempts to achieve Pareto improvements, where possible.

What happens when people's preferences conflict, as they often do? The most extreme case is where one person wants another to suffer. In the vocabulary of economics, one person's disutility constitutes a positive element of another person's utility function. More generally, individual preferences conflict when a policy or action negatively afflicts some people, whilst benefiting others. The harm in this second case is an incident, rather than an object, of the relevant policy. Law and economics solves incompatible preferences as follows: it makes consent the measure and requisite of efficiency.

Consider the case where harm is the ancillary side effect of an action. Countless public-policy questions implicate the well-being of stakeholders in variously negative and positive fashions. When conflicting preferences accompany a policy decision, what should be the pertinent rule of decision? The answer, from the perspective of law and economics, is to appeal to the Coase Theorem and to ask how the parties, in a world without transaction costs, would have agreed to resolve the issue. A foundational premise underlying law and economics is that such stakeholders would have agreed on the path that maximises their collective well being, even if that outcome would appear to render some of them potentially worse off *ex post*. They would so agree because the benefitted parties could compensate the people whom the policy decision negatively afflicted and yet still be better off than they were *ex ante*. Such compensation would effect a Pareto improvement, such that adopting the more efficient course increases the total welfare of society without leaving anyone worse off.

The reader may question the assumption that those bargaining over the resolution of a policy issue would agree, *ex ante*, to maximise their combined welfare. Some people, after all, concern themselves only with their own utility, as opposed to that of other stakeholders. Why would non-altruistic types make collective well-being, rather than their own, the object of their desire, when their and society's interests may be in conflict?

John Rawls famously argued that, negotiating behind a "veil of ignorance", people would maximise equality. According to Rawls, each person would reason that he could not know where he will lie on the social ladder in the future state of the world. If he agreed to an unequal society, he might end up on the bottom. For that reason, he and other members of society would seek *ex ante* to minimise the impact of their potential misfortune *ex post*. Morality justifies departures from equality, Rawls argued, only insofar as they satisfy "the difference principle" – specifically, such departures must benefit those who are least well off.

If Rawls is right, might economists be wrong to think that parties would negotiate *ex ante* to the wealth-maximising outcome? Of course, that is a matter of debate. Still, Rawls's thesis is not iron clad. The members of his hypothetical collective are highly risk averse. In fact, each of them is infinitely risk averse, maximising not expected value, but the minimum value that each could obtain in the world. This can lead to absurdities. John Harsanyi observed, for example, that Rawls's "maximin" principle would cause people always to avoid the worst possible outcome, even if the probability of that event were almost vanishingly small.[12] Thus, a person would not accept a dream job in a desirable city because flying there would entail a non-zero chance of dying in a plane crash. No one would cross a street; no one would get married; and so on.

Further, the assumptions underlying Coasean hypothetical bargaining and the Rawlsian veil of ignorance are different. In the latter setting, probabilities are unknown, while they are under the Coase Theorem. Under the assumption of zero-transaction-cost bargaining where probabilities can be assigned to possible outcomes, expected-utility theory has force. This makes the efficiency metric a legitimate basis for policy recommendations about tortious conduct, breach of contract, property rights, and more besides.

Now consider the problem of the so-called "utility monster". Economic analysis of law would reject the following argument: efficiency justified a person in hurting another because the pleasure that the actor derived from injuring his victim exceeded the latter's trauma. In any such case, be it murder, rape, battery, burglary, robbery, larceny, or any other serious crime, transaction costs would not be so high as to foreclose *ex ante* agreement between the criminal and the victim. In the case of any of the crimes just mentioned, the guilty party could have sought permission from the victim *ex ante*, but did not. Where bargaining costs are low, economics will not entertain claims of efficiency when the wrongdoing party bypassed the market (i.e. where he did not seek the injured party's consent). For instance, it would not credit an argument that a stolen car is worth more to the robber than to the owner.

This discussion might strike the reader as an odd way to address the wrongfulness of crime. Is something of moral significance lacking if one analyses serious offences by reference to foregone market transactions and without regard to the innate wrongness of the conduct? In fact, law and economics captures this quality of wrongness – it merely expresses it in a different way. The reality of serious crime is that there is no amount of money that a criminal would pay and that a potential victim would accept to undergo the relevant experience. The price that a person would demand in exchange for permitting another to kill him would be, absent euthanasia concerns or some outlandish scenario, infinite. This approach to crime recognises the right of the individual to consent to a chosen course. If a person would not agree to it, the criminal who nevertheless takes what he wants should be subject to the full condemnation of the law.

Notice that, even if transaction costs were high such that bargain was not feasible, one could safely condemn the criminal act were it clear that the victim would not have consented to the relevant behaviour even if negotiations had been possible. This insight distinguishes two sorts of potentially criminal behaviour: that which society should, and should not, abolish entirely. An illuminative way to apply the defence of necessity, for instance, is to ask whether the parties would have agreed to the conduct *ex ante* had transaction costs not been prohibitive. As explored in Part 3, however, if one excludes cases of necessity and the costs of employing the criminal-law system, the optimal level of much criminal activity (i.e. the efficient output in the market for crime) is zero.

The preceding account defines welfare through the satisfaction of preferences, which economists assume to be fixed and exogenous. By adopting neoclassical theory, normative law and economics provides policy prescriptions aimed at promoting this vision of welfare. This perspective celebrates individual autonomy, thus respecting the ends that different people choose for themselves. In this sense, law and economics theory displays a libertarian quality.

---

12 John C. Harsanyi, 'Can the maximin principle serve as a basis for morality? A critique of John Rawls's theory' (1975) 69 Am Pol'y Sci Rev 594.

As with any normative theory, however, economic analysis of law has limitations. These occur when paternalistic considerations come to the fore, most obviously when people make decisions that hurt their interests. Imagine a person whose preferences are antithetical to her well being. Law and economics would applaud an arrangement that satisfies those preferences, even though they inure to her ruin. An extreme, though illuminative, example involves a bizarre case of consensual cannibalism in Germany. An individual by the name of Armin Meiwes sought online a volunteer for the once-in-a-lifetime experience of being killed and eaten. As unlikely as it was, someone actually agreed to the offer. Meiwes was ultimately convicted of murder – in many ways, an unremarkable result. If the individuals involved, however, were both informed and competent (a fantastical assumption, perhaps) then an arrangement that satisfied the preferences of all contracting parties is efficient and therefore desirable within the confines of neoclassical welfare economics.

Yet, outlier cases may not be the best metric by which to judge theories. In many, if not most, circumstances, people can determine their welfare better than third parties can. For those who believe that a person should decide his wants for himself, normative law and economics may be attractive.

This section closes with a word of caution. In analysing public-policy questions, economists can often identify efficient solutions. That function is valuable because efficiency is important. Yet, that goal is but a component of justice. Although the two concepts may sometimes be coterminous, resolving some policy questions may involve goals that conflict with efficiency. Law and economics still plays an important role in these situations, however, in quantifying the cost of policy decisions that depart from efficiency. Legislatures, in making difficult determinations, should have all available information in front of them, so that they may make informed conclusions.

For example, consider whether a state should implement a "three-strikes law". California is a jurisdiction that imposes mandatory life sentences on criminals whom it convicts of a third felony. Such laws can involve grave disparities between the wrong (it may be non-violent) and the severity of the ensuing punishment. This gulf between crime and punishment offends many people's sense of justice, which requires proportionality between the offending act and corresponding penalty. Yet, a prediction that the "three-strikes" law would reduce crime surely weighs on whether to enact such legislation. It remains true, of course, that a legislature may properly refuse to pass draconian laws, but its decision is more informed if it has all relevant information, including that supplied by economic analysis.

The point, in short, is that efficiency need not be controversial, especially when one realises that efficiency is but a component of the larger concept of justice. Law and economics is a powerful tool of policy analysis, but it is by no means the exclusive means by which to understand legal problems.

C. The Ethics of Markets

1. Introduction: contracts, market transactions, and efficiency

Voluntary transactions play a celebrated role within law and economics. To recognise the legitimacy of private contract is to pay homage to individual liberty. From a neoclassical perspective, voluntary agreements generate benefits by mutually satisfying contracting parties' preferences, at least if one respects adults as competent determinants of their own well-being. Such satiation renders contracting parties "better off", at least if one accepts the premise that fulfilling an individual's wish without violating that of another person advances welfare.

Binding arrangements can still benefit informed, competent parties even if some promisors ultimately regret their contractual obligations. People contract because doing so yields net expected benefits *ex ante*. Most agreements allocate risk, promoting each contracting party's welfare *ex ante*. Nevertheless, the person for whom the embraced risk comes to pass may be worse off *ex post*. While relieving him of contractual responsibility would benefit that party in the short term, doing so would undo the long-term value of contracts for all.

By advancing individual well being at the micro level, contracts generate macro-level benefits. Private deals reallocate scarce resources from lower- to higher-value uses, thus efficiently distributing scarce resources throughout the economy. No government can hope unilaterally to perform a comparable function. Stymied by information constraints, buffeted by interest groups, handicapped by regulatory lag, and inhibited by inadequate resources, the government cannot effectively dictate and continually monitor the optimal path of economic activity. Market-based economies, in contrast, harness private information to coordinate the efficient utilisation of scarce resources. Individual contracting, which lies at the heart of this process, creates a decentralised price mechanism that synchronises the extrication, transformation, and ultimate consumption of limited resources. The failure of centrally managed economies, such as that of the former Soviet Union, to achieve sustained levels of economic growth comparable to capitalist countries evidences this fact, as does China's extraordinary growth since its hybrid adoption of market mechanisms.

Of course, pointing out that those voluntary transactions foster efficiency does not amount to an unreserved defence of the market. Markets can and do fail, and understanding the circumstances in which they do is an imperative element of the study of economics. Markets fail in settings beyond dramatic implosions of the kind that crippled the world economy in 2008. Part 8, for example, discusses network industries, the regulation of which derives from the failure of natural monopolies to achieve efficiency absent public intervention. Similarly, much of Part 8's examination of innovation policy concerns the manner in which markets under-produce certain inventions absent government action in the form of intellectual-property laws, prize mechanisms, or regulatory exclusivity rules.

This section seeks to accomplish a distinct goal, which is to address some of the potential ethical implications of market processes and the private contracting that underlies them. This issue is distinct from the question whether markets allocate resources to their optimal uses. Instead, it asks whether the manner in which free exchange operates is just. Such criticism implicates the question whether "efficient" outcomes are necessarily desirable. These questions are profound, and warrant far-greater treatment than is possible within the confines of this book. Nevertheless, the study of law and economics, which addresses the role of law in fostering efficiency through its interaction with market processes, would be incomplete without considering the ethical qualities of those mechanisms.

2. Objection 1: Wealth distribution

Efficiency treats the pre-existing distribution of resources in society as given (i.e. as exogenous). The wealth and opportunities that partially determine people's tastes are therefore factors for which economists generally do not account in their work.

Why does this matter? When economists commend a scrutinised market arrangement because it effects a Pareto improvement, it is because the outcome fulfils the contracting individuals' preferences without violating those of any other. The ensuing reallocation of rights is desirable because it improves the pre-contract state of the world. This analysis is powerful, for it demonstrates that free exchange between competent and informed entities renders all of them better off. It follows that a law interfering with freedom of contract between capable parties reduces welfare if the relevant agreements lack negative third-party effects.

Nevertheless, this conclusion presupposes that people's preferences are sufficiently creditable that their satisfaction actually enhances social welfare. Yet, preferences are contingent on the stations in life in which people happen to find themselves. It follows that, although Pareto improvements (ultimately leading to Pareto optimality under ideal conditions) are the preferred outcome from the perspective of efficiency, distinct Pareto-optimal points exist for different *ex ante* resource distributions. This fact implicates the ethical quality of prescriptive law and economics analysis.

This issue is significant. Nevertheless, it may not be as weighty as might first appear. Normative law and economics takes the world as it finds it. This focus on preferences reflects a practical concern. One could not formulate workable models while trying simultaneously to account for the infinite amalgam of factors that are collectively responsible for the state of the world in which the behaviour of interest takes place. The fact that efficiency analysis takes the *ex ante* distribution of wealth as given limits, rather than indicts, normative law and economics theory. Thus, economists' treating pre-existing wealth distribution as a neutral fact ought to remind us that the normative conclusions emanating from economic analysis come subject to that qualification.

So viewed, price theory's informing the optimal constitution of law should not be controversial, for the theory's perspective – properly understood – contributes rather than controls. Indeed, the tenets of prescriptive economic analysis are likely to be authoritative only when applied to explicit market-based legal issues. Broad consensus exists in that setting that economic efficiency is the principal criterion of interest. Competition law and the regulation of natural monopoly are the prime examples, which the book addresses in Part 7 below.

Nevertheless, if one conflates normative welfare economics with morality, treating these concepts as coterminous, one enters divisive territory. If a person believes that the contemporary distribution of wealth, influence, talent, and other sources of privilege is just, then treating that division of opportunity as exogenous to an economic model is to be applauded. If one views this initial distribution as questionable or arbitrary, however, the fact that normative claims of efficiency derive from a particular wealth allocation may be an important qualification. Ultimately, it is for the reader to reflect on the justice of the resource distribution that feeds individual preferences underlying the efficiency metric by which economists study market transactions.

3. Objection 2: The fairness of market prices

The key benefit of a decentralised price mechanism is that private actors possess superior information than the government. Yet, consider two related objections. First, market resource allocations may be simultaneously efficient and objectionable because willingness to pay departs sharply from subjective need. As a result, some people may be unjustly priced out of the market. Second, markets may sometimes produce unconscionable prices. We shall now consider each criticism in turn.

(a) The relationship between utility and willingness to pay

Economists ignore subjective utility in measuring efficiency. Instead, they compare people's competing preferences for a given resource based on their respective willingness to pay. By that metric, efficiency requires that a person, A, obtain a good if A is willing and able to pay more for it than person B. If claims of normativity founded on efficiency are to carry persuasive force, however, a connection must exist between willingness to pay and some form of welfare or moral desert. If there is no such nexus, prescriptive law and economics enjoys little independent force as a tool for guiding public policy.

Although such a nexus does exist, a claim that market-generated prices are conclusively fair is dubious. The relationship between utility and willingness to pay does not approach mathematical identity, for departures between a person's ability to pay and need do occur. Some people are priced out of markets, which raises questions of fairness. These problems notwithstanding, a person's willingness to pay is at least a workable, and sometimes a close, proxy for welfare. Other things being equal, the more that a person desires a good, the more that she will pay to acquire it. We should therefore expect willingness to pay to correlate with subjective desire and need. Furthermore, tying efficiency to price has a further benefit. A person's budgetary constraint is rarely fixed over time. If a person places great subjective value on an item that he cannot now afford, he has an incentive to enhance his income and hence his purchasing power.

An individual's desire to expand purchasing power generates important incentives toward enhanced economic activity. Working harder, being more industrious, taking entrepreneurial risks, and furthering one's education significantly enhance one's expected lifetime income, thus making otherwise-unaffordable luxury items attainable. Crucially, this process of achieving private gains occasions positive spillover effects. When a person devotes himself to working more assiduously, to achieving his innate potential in his chosen profession, and to imparting the greatest possible value on his clients or customers, he makes himself better off as a direct result of making others better off.

In sum, if a person's willingness to pay correlates with her subjective need and if market economies generate desirable incentives, market prices operate in a legitimate, even if not ethically unassailable, manner. This point becomes all the more compelling when one realises that the relevant policy question is not whether contemporary capitalism works perfectly, but whether it works better than other available systems.

(b) Unconscionable prices

Within limits, markets generally work well in stable economies, yielding prices that distribute scarce goods among those who are willing to part with the most to get them. Such prices incentivise enhanced production and judicious consumption in times of growing demand or limited supply, and produce opposite effects in situations of excess capacity. When markets operate smoothly, they do not obviously conflict with moral intuition.

Smooth operation, however, is a loaded characterisation. In considering whether market-determined prices are inherently just, consider exogenous events that yield sudden price changes. In some such cases, claims of unconscionability may accompany demanded prices. In response to this perceived problem, some jurisdictions have enacted laws prohibiting price gouging. Is "unconscionability" a meaningful concept, however, if the criticised price is one upon which contracting parties voluntarily agree?

Market prices fluctuate all the time, of course, and such movement is an important component of efficient market processes. Any time the demand for a product or service grows without a simultaneous, off-setting rise in supply, the market-clearing price will increase. For example, the scheduling of prominent international sporting events typically causes the prices of hotels in, and flights to, the relevant city on the pertinent date to rise, and has the same effect on prices of consumables such as food and alcohol close to the relevant stadium. This phenomenon may annoy consumers, particularly when the price increase does not appear to reflect any increase in underlying cost justifying the price rise. Nevertheless, this price-adjusting feature carries three easily overlooked benefits.

First, when demand suddenly increases relative to supply, it necessarily follows that, in the short run, not all those who want the product or service will be able to get it. Prices allocate scarce goods to those who value them most, where of course "value" refers to a person's willingness to pay. If vendors declined to increase their prices in such settings, the result would be queues. The process of waiting in line is itself a price. Instead of directly parting with their money, people pay the opportunity cost of their time.

A second benefit is that higher prices encourage people to be judicious in their consumption of goods that are now in greater demand. Of course, frugality in such circumstances is precisely what efficiency requires. Third, higher prices spur enhanced supply. When demand rises, the higher resulting prices translate into greater premia for sellers. The prospect of extra profit induces existing sellers to increase output and spurs third-party manufacturers or service providers to enter the market. The resulting increase in production translates into a greater quantity of goods and services, thus lowering prices and ultimately reaching a new equilibrium.

These justifications, however, are not as convincing if the shock to the market is severe. When events of sufficient magnitude upset normal market operations, price demands may ensue that some perceive to be extortionate. A good example involves the aftermath of natural disasters. After Hurricane Katrina, for instance, prices of many essential items skyrocketed. Rental rates for hotels and prices for bottled water, ice, petrol, and basic food stuffs increased, in some instances, to many multiples of the pre-hurricane market price level.

How should one characterise the ethics of such pricing? To some observers, it is the result of remorseless sellers' extracting unconscionable prices from desperate purchasers, where altruism and concern for one's fellow human beings should have been paramount considerations. To defenders of the market, however, there was nothing improper in charging the profit-maximising price, which if correct means that market-determined prices are morally sacrosanct.

Such events raise interesting questions concerning the ethics of market processes and the limits of voluntary arrangements. Of course, sellers can only demand prices that consumers are willing to pay. As a result, even ostensibly coercive or unconscionable contracts leave the contracting parties better off than they would be without any agreement. Yet, this conclusion overlooks the possibility that the parties could have apportioned the wealth surplus of their arrangement more equally.

Nevertheless, those who are quick to condemn perceived price gouging must not overlook that such sharp increases in price potentially carry benefits. They limit queues, spur increased production, and induce frugal consumption. The more urgent the situation, the greater the benefit occasioned by these price effects, for the great priority in responding to market shocks that significantly curtail supply or magnify demand is to increase the quantity of the scarce good as quickly as possible. The prospect of supracompetitive returns on sales would urge purveyors to manufacture and disseminate their produce to the afflicted area as promptly as they can.

These factors, however, are not an unassailable moral defence of vendors' charging whatever prices they can extract from consumers. In particular, the efficiency justification for such pricing is much diminished if the elasticity of supply for the relevant item is low. In the case of perfectly inelastic supply, even an infinite increase in price will not yield an increase in market output. Imagine that hotels in a discrete region devastated by a natural disaster increase their rental rate ten-fold for the duration of the emergency. It is unlikely that such high prices will spur the production of additional hotels, for the length of time and cost required to do this would render such production uneconomical. By the time construction was finished, market rates would likely have dropped to their pre-emergency levels. In such an event, the efficiency argument for the ten-fold increase in price would lie in eliminating queues, which would constitute at most a modest benefit, given that willingness to pay and subjective need for basic access to shelter may not be closely connected.

Nevertheless, one might distinguish moral judgments about the equity of individual price decisions in outlier cases from larger public policy. One can simultaneously criticise a vendor on moral grounds for choosing to demand an unusually high price without a cost justification, and yet recognise his legal right to set such a price.

Consider the problems of trying to do more. Legislating to outlaw unethical prices in extreme situations is complex. Some jurisdictions purport to forbid "price gouging" or "unconscionable" prices, but infusing those terms with economic meaning is difficult. Beyond constitutional problems with such ambiguous laws, one would have to inculpate in the law sufficient nuance to distinguish price hikes that carry sufficient efficiency gains to justify their imposition from the likely lesser number of price increases that carry net social costs. Price regulation at the micro level through *ex post* judicial enforcement would be imprecise, and likely counterproductive. It seems dubious that the government could effectively marshal resources as effectively as markets, even – and perhaps especially – in cases of exogenous shocks.

Ultimately, resolving abstract questions of justice is a subjective exercise, which resists objective falsification. The degree to which the efficiency of price-generating market processes coincides with morality in any particular instance is a relative question on which people can and will disagree.

4. Objection 3: markets and equality

Today's principal objection to capitalism is inequality. Many people take issue with the perceived excess that uncontrolled market processes lavish upon a lucky few. Hedge-fund managers, leading investment bankers, CEOs, sports stars, and other outlier but prominent earners earn annual pecuniary returns that dwarf average family incomes. More generally, the gulf in incomes between top and median earners has grown dramatically over the last three decades in the United States and elsewhere.[13] Discontent with such asymmetric wealth has fuelled protests, most visibly in the form of the "occupy movement" in 2011–2012 that sought to champion the cause of the "99 percent".

Wealth disparities result, in large part, from voluntary contracts. Interestingly, the top earners' rise in income has resulted not from taking money from those less well off, but in capturing a (much) greater share of new wealth created through economic growth. For instance, from 1993 to 2012, the top 1% of US earners saw their real income grow by 86%, while the real income of the remaining 99% grew by 6.6%.[14] Thus, income has grown sharply for some, but only slowly for others. Thus, the dispute is largely about more equal division of the spoils of economic growth.

Contemporary criticism may reflect peoples' claimed entitlement to a larger share of the wealth surplus that markets generate. This equitable claim may have teeth, especially if more equal income distribution is possible without negatively affecting long-term economic growth. Nevertheless, the objection would be more problematic if there were a tension between equity and efficiency. Economics suggests that directly intervening into markets to redistribute wealth can dilute incentives toward risky investment, entrepreneurship, and hard work, which are collectively indispensable for economic growth. If this insight is correct, it could be counter-productive to champion reforms that reduced the aggregate wealth of society to achieve greater horizontal equity when the discarded system promoted the well-being of all (albeit to asymmetric degrees). For that reason, economists typically reject an equitable function in constructing rules of decision in legal matters, preferring *ex post* taxation as more effective means by which to achieve horizontal equity.

A better explanation for the hostility to the growing wealth gap is the perceived disconnect between some people's outlier incomes and moral desert. It appears that, for many people, unusually great compensation is not in itself objectionable, but the belief that a person did not earn her reward most certainly is. For that reason, few quibble with the vast fortunes that such prominent innovators as Bill Gates and Steve Jobs amassed. People admire the radical technological leaps that such inventors oversaw and commercialised to the benefit of society. In contrast, the fact that bankers working for bailed out financial institutions received stratospheric bonuses struck a nerve when the reckless loans and investments that their banks had made crippled the world economy. Claims that such outlandish compensation was and remains necessary to attract "talent" ring hollow when the financial industries' best and brightest oversaw perilous behaviour that ultimately laid waste to global markets.

Are unequal incomes a symptom of market failure or are they the inevitable result of an economy founded on freedom of contract? The answer is predominantly the latter. This is an important point, which warrants additional discussion. In particular, a person's earning potential in a free market depends on such factors as one's genes, upbringing, and education.

---

13 *See* Congressional Budget Office, 'Trends in the Distribution of Household Income Between 1979 and 2007'. Available at: www.cbo.gov/publication/42729.
14 Emmanuel Saez, 'Striking it Richer: The Evolution of Top Incomes in the United States' (3 September 2013). Available at: http://elsa.berkeley.edu/~saez/saez-UStopincomes-2012.pdf.

The ethical quality of market processes depends on the distribution of opportunity. People born into extremes of circumstance experience vastly different realities in market economies, as the earliest capitalist systems demonstrated all too vividly. Dickensian reflections on unbridled capitalism hardly resonate with thinking people's conception of justice. The moral quality of market-generated outcomes ought to improve, however, as the *ex ante* distribution of income and opportunity becomes more just. Thus, markets work more ethically when society has in place an apparatus facilitative of social advancement. Such arrangements provide people with the opportunity to achieve their potential, which market forces will in turn reward.

Unfortunately, limits on parity are inherent in free-market economic systems. An infrastructure that promotes equality consistent with potential and ability will not satisfy those who yearn for a society in which everyone achieves pure equality (i.e. homogeneity). An ideal capitalist system would permit all those with ability and aptitude to succeed to a level commensurate with their natural (i.e. inherited) talents. While market mechanisms would bestow asymmetric awards upon people in such a community, the ensuing wealth distribution would reflect a number of factors. These would be, on the supply side, a person's innate talents and her predilection towards education and self-improvement and, on the demand side, the tastes that people in society happen to inherit and develop. Any injustice inherent in the ensuing distribution would be coterminous with that present in Darwinian nature. To the extent that such a system were to prevail, a form of public policy analysis that tied welfare to willingness to pay would possess a strong claim to legitimacy. The tax system, in turn, would redistribute wealth in a manner that society deems just.

Unfortunately, the modern world falls short of this aspirational ideal. Considerable disparities in opportunity exist, though education and other social advancement programmes improve matters by shrinking the gap between people born into circumstances of asymmetric privilege. The gulf, however, remains vast, and much remains to be done.

In short, markets do not move inexorably toward equality. This fact need not be objectionable if people own their talents, efforts, and labour, and hence the rewards that free contracts bestow upon them. Conversely, it may be arbitrary that some people have the skill set, education, and opportunity to offer services that consumers happen to value. From that perspective, the fact that "efficient" contracts promote the welfare of all parties privy to those agreements without violating anyone's else preferences does not necessarily mean that those contracts are morally sacrosanct, obviating any need for government intervention or *ex post* taxation. It is for the reader to decide the ethical limitations of efficiency within market processes.

Key Points

- The normative wing of law and economics promotes "efficient" laws. Efficiency refers to outcomes consistent with the Coase Theorem – specifically, allocations upon which stakeholders would agree in a zero-transaction-cost environment to maximise their collective welfare.
- Normative law and economics has roots in utilitarian moral philosophy, which holds that the right outcome maximises total "utility" or happiness. In its classical expression, it quantifies and aggregates the satisfaction and dissatisfaction of each stakeholder with an outcome to compute net utility. Each person whom a scrutinised policy, law, or action will affect matters, but only as a member of a larger collective.

  o Utilitarianism is influential, and its cost–benefit approach is a staple of much public-policy analysis.
  o Yet, classical utilitarianism has shortcomings:

- First, quantifying utility is rarely possible. Many experiences are incommensurate, subjective happiness is immeasurable, and there is no common scale on which to compare different people's utilities.

- Second, in its classical form, utilitarianism allows a majority to run roughshod over a minority's contrary interests. It can conflict with moral intuition by theoretically justifying horrific actions because of the subjective (e.g. sadistic) pleasure that those benefitting from them enjoy. It also makes the morality of an action contingent on people's perception, which can change over time.

    o John Stuart Mill sought to avoid some of these problems by disqualifying lower pleasures from inclusion in the social-welfare calculus.

- Neoclassical welfare economics has a different approach. Instead of using cardinal utility as classical utilitarianism does (i.e. rather than quantify and compare different people's utilities on a common scale) neoclassical economists use ordinal utility.

    o Neoclassical economists rely on individual preferences – as revealed by market transactions – and do no compare interpersonal utilities.

    o To measure the desirability of different outcomes, neoclassical economists look to whether resource reallocations satisfy stakeholders' preferences without doing violence to those of any other (i.e. whether they effect a Pareto improvement). The ultimate benchmark of efficiency is Pareto optimality where no further reallocations are possible without violating someone's preference.

    o Pareto optimisation, however, is unhelpful to many public-policy questions, the resolution of which creates winners and losers. In such situations, neoclassical economists rely on a more workable and less demanding criterion, Kaldor-Hicks efficiency.

    o Kaldor-Hicks efficiency results where a reallocation benefits certain entities more than it harms others, such that the former could fully compensate the latter and still be better off. There is no requirement under the Kaldor-Hicks criterion, however, that such compensation result.

- The Coase Theorem envisions free contract between stakeholders in zero-bargaining-cost settings. Economic analysis suggests using law in high-transaction cost settings to mimic the outcome of such market interactions.

- The weight that policymakers place on normative law and economics depends on the extent to which they find the efficiency benchmark, which focuses on individual autonomy and preference satisfaction, illuminative on the question of justice. That question itself depends on one's view as to the propriety of voluntary market transactions.

 ## References and Further Reading

Books

Hausman, Daniel M. and McPherson, Michael S., *Economic Analysis, Moral Philosophy, and Public Policy*, 2nd edn (2006).

Kaplow, L., and Shavell, Steven, *Fairness versus Welfare* (2006).

Mitchell Polinsky, A., *An Introduction to Law and Economics*, 4th edn (2011) Chs. 2, 20.

Piketty, Thomas, *Capital in the Twenty-First Century* (2014).

Posner, Richard A., *The Economics of Justice* (1983).

Posner, Richard A., *Economic Analysis of Law* (2011) § 1.2.

Sandel, Michael J., *Justice: What's the Right Thing to Do?* (2009) Chs. 2–4.

Sandel, Michael J., *What Money Can't Buy: The Moral Limits of Markets* (2013).

Shavell, Steven, *Foundations of Economic Analysis of Law* (2004) Ch. VII.
Zamir, Eyal and Medina, Barak, *Law, Economics, and Morality* (2010).

Articles
Dworkin, Ronald M., 'Is wealth a value?' (1980) 9 J Legal Stud 191.
Hardin, Russell, 'The morality of law and economics' (1992) 11 Law & Philosophy 331.
Johnsen, D. Bruce, 'Wealth is value' (1986) 15 J Legal Stud 263.
Kaldor, Nicholas, 'Welfare propositions in economics and interpersonal comparisons of utility'
    (1939) 69 Econ J 549.
Karni, Edi and Schmeidler, David, 'Fixed preferences and changing tastes (in the formation of
    economic values)' (1990) 80 Am Econ Rev 262.
Kronman, Anthony T., 'Wealth maximization as a normative principle' (1980) 9 J Legal Stud 227.
Posner, Richard A., 'The value of wealth: a comment on Dworkin and Kronman' (1980) 9 J Legal
    Stud 243.
Posner, Richard A., 'Utilitarianism, economics and legal theory' (1979) 8 J Legal Stud 103.
Shavell, Steven, 'Law versus morality as regulators of conduct' (2002) 4 Am L & Econ Rev 227.

Part 2

The Law of Tort

1   The Economics of Liability Rules and Accidents   65

2   An Economic Account of Tort Doctrine   88

Chapter 1

The Economics of Liability Rules and Accidents

Chapter Contents

A.	Introduction	66
B.	Which Liability Rule?	68
C.	Unilateral-Care Scenarios with Fixed Activity Levels	68
D.	Bilateral-Care Scenarios with Fixed Activity Levels	71
E.	Unilateral-Care Scenarios with Variable Activity Levels	76
F.	Bilateral-Care Scenarios with Variable Activity Levels	78
G.	Tort Law, Risk Aversion, Insurance, and Moral Hazard	82
H.	Is Law and Economics Theory Realistic about Optimal Remedies?	84
Key Points		86
References and Further Reading		87

A. Introduction

An ancient feature of the common law is that a person who unjustly injures another must make good the harm caused. This aspect of the law finds justification in a variety of sources, from the Aristotelian theory of corrective justice, which demands that a wrongdoer compensate his victim to re-establish the pre-harm equilibrium between the parties, to George Fletcher's influential account of the tort system as correcting a negligent person's creation and imposition of a non-reciprocal risk. Economics yields a distinct account of tort law. It views the tort system as a means for maximising social value by incentivising people to take cost-justified precautions and to regulate their activities. This perspective explains the subject's central doctrines, as well as the many liability regimes open to the courts.

Economists define efficiency by reference to satisfying individual preferences. An economic approach to tort law thus concerns itself with four economic factors that collectively inform the optimal distribution of care and activity levels:

- potential tortfeasors derive utility from behaviour that carries an incidental risk of harming others;
- such injurers suffer disutility in taking precautions to reduce the probability of an accident;
- would-be victims enjoy utility from engaging in activities that render them susceptible to harm; and
- potential victims experience disutility both in suffering injuries and in taking defensive precautions to reduce the likelihood of their being hurt.

The optimal number of accidents, amount of precautions, and time spent in potentially harmful activities thus depend on the interplay between these factors. Those principles yield many insights, not the least of which is that the efficient number of accidents generally exceeds zero.

This result might strike the reader as odd. Surely there is no such thing as a desirable accident that results in serious injury or worse? Of course, such an outcome is never in itself desirable, and those who might potentially experience such a fate would be willing to pay, or (equivalently) to sacrifice convenience, to avoid it. The important point, however, is that neither society nor individuals would agree to pay a sufficiently high price to eliminate risk entirely.

How much would people be willing to pay? Economists offer an answer: if all stakeholders could bargain *ex ante*, they would maximise their aggregate welfare pursuant to a social contract. That agreement would recognise the benefit of behaviour (e.g. playing sports, driving, or manufacturing products) that carries an incidental risk to others. Yet, it would require all actors to take the amount of care that reduces expected accident costs to the optimal level. Those ideal precautions are such that the cost of any further increment in care would exceed the associated reduction in accident costs. At the optimum point, the marginal benefit and marginal cost of taking care equal one another. Figure 2.1 illustrates the economic definition of due care. "B," the burden, represents the cost of precautions, while "PL" represents the probability of an accident multiplied by the loss associated with that event. The optimal level of precautions is P*, after which amount taking more care costs the tortfeasors more than it reduces the expected accident costs.

Some accidents, therefore, may inevitably follow from an efficient bargain. This is not to say, of course, that the contemporary number of fatal, serious, or mundane accidents is optimal – it is surely the case, for example, that the number of deaths on the roads (in 2012, 34,080 in the United States; 1,901 in the United Kingdom; and 161 in Ireland) is excessive from a public policy perspective. Indeed, if an optimal number existed, it would be comprised purely of economically unavoidable accidents that would occur in the event of all drivers on the road driving cautiously, taking all reasonable care, and driving only when the private benefits of doing so exceed the expected social cost of an accident associated with venturing out on the road. The number of driving accidents

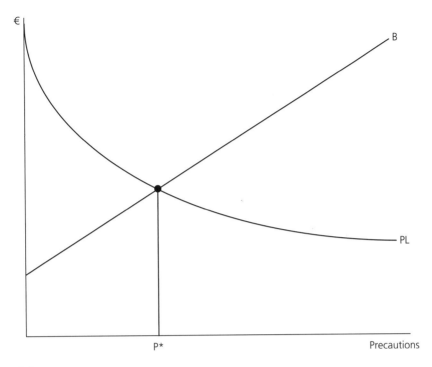

€

B

PL

P*

Precautions

Figure 2.1

today, however, is certain to exceed this "optimal" number, given the extent to which many drivers behave rashly and take unjustified risks behind the wheel.

This discussion invites an important question: Why is tort law necessary? The Coase Theorem would predict that, in a setting of no transaction costs and no income effects, the government's choice (i) to grant tortfeasors the right to behave negligently (i.e. to engage in risky conduct without taking cost-justified precautions to reduce the danger of harm to third parties) or (ii) to grant potential victims a right to be free of harm would not affect efficiency. The parties would allot rights efficiently between themselves to maximise their mutual welfare, consistent with the hypothetical bargain discussed above.

Would a potential victim ever allow a tortfeasor to behave negligently? It is one thing, after all, for a person to behave in a socially valuable manner, even if that conduct carries an incidental risk of third-party harm. For instance, the law should presumably allow people to drive and planes to take off and land over populated areas. It is another thing altogether, though, for would-be victims to agree to a person's driving far over the speed limit, drunk, while texting or in any other significantly impaired condition that all would deem negligent. This is especially so as neither the tort system nor budding tortfeasors ever compensate prospective victims *ex ante* for agreeing to undertake such a risk, and pecuniary damages make few victims of serious accidents whole.

The answer is somewhat nuanced. Potential accident victims would not agree to such egregious behaviour as drunk driving and extreme speeding. Save in outlier situations, such conduct is inefficient because the cost of precautions that would reduce accident costs are modest in comparison to the benefits. For instance, not driving drunk or overtaking on blind corners reduces expected accident costs more than it inconveniences drivers. Yet, there are more difficult cases because even careful behaviour can produce harm. For that reason, an optimal, non-zero amount of negligent behaviour generally exists. More specifically, taking care is "stochastic". It is probabilistic, such that one striving to be cautious cannot guarantee that he will not mistakenly injure a third party. Even the most skilled and assiduous surgeon's knife can slip.

Furthermore, there are circumstances in which the social benefits of ostensibly negligent and even reckless behaviour will outweigh the costs, and it is important that the law does not impose such a high penalty for tortious behaviour as to deter efficient instances of it. For example, it may be socially desirable that a person drives his grievously injured friend to the hospital at speed if time is of the essence. By imposing a price for such activity that would dissuade rational actors from undertaking inefficient, but not efficient, forms of dangerous conduct, the law would maximise social welfare.

Tort has a role beyond obviously dangerous conduct. Risk is ubiquitous in modern life. Even the most mundane behaviour entails some hazard, which translates, over time, into a guaranteed cost. Tort law's difficult task, then, is to induce people (1) to engage in the amount of risk-bearing activity that is optimal in light of its off-setting costs and benefits, and (2) to undertake those precautions that are cost justified with respect to their marginal tendency to reduce expected accident costs by more than the cost of the incremental precaution.

To determine the optimal legal standard, we can ask how stakeholders would have agreed to allot rights in a setting of low transaction costs à la Coase. The ensuing division of rights and obligations would lead to a Pareto-superior outcome if monetary damages fully compensate victims of accidents, and would otherwise produce a Kaldor Hicks-efficient result.

B. Which Liability Rule?

The law has multiple liability rules in its arsenal for inducing people to take care and to regulate their activity levels. These include negligence, strict liability, no liability, and combining negligence or strict liability with contributory or comparative negligence. Students often struggle to discern a coherent principle for choosing one over the other, but economics provides answers. Each of these liability rules imparts distinct incentives. One attuned to those effects can craft doctrine to the case at hand to identify the optimal rule.

The following sections explore four different accident models: unilateral care and bilateral care situations, both with and without activity-level changes.[1] The discussion assumes risk neutrality, but subsequently relaxes that assumption to consider how courts could employ the law of tort in cases where tortfeasors, victims, or both are risk averse. That analysis will implicate the interplay of the economics of insurance, moral hazard, and adverse selection.

C. Unilateral-Care Scenarios with Fixed Activity Levels

Two concepts are central to the law and economics of tort: precautions and activity levels. Where activity levels are fixed, so too are the benefits of potentially tortious conduct. Thus, in that setting, maximising social welfare is equivalent to minimising the expected cost of accidents. Depending on the context, achieving this goal can entail injurers' taking care, victims' taking precautions, or both. Where both the injurers and the victims can vary their activity levels, the law must not only induce the lowest cost avoider(s) to minimise the expected social cost of accidents, but also incentivise people to substitute their behaviour for more socially valuable activities. In such a context, tort law's economic goal is to maximise social welfare, recognising that the chosen activities of tortfeasors and victims are themselves sources of utility.

---

1 These examples draw on Professor Steven Shavell's influential work on the economics of tort. (Steven Shavell, *Foundations of Economic Analysis of Law* (2004) Chs. 8–12.)

In the most simple accident scenarios, activity-level changes do not affect efficiency and a single class of people, such as potential injurers, can minimise the expected cost of accidents on their own. In this context, the law should encourage would-be tortfeasors to undertake the amount of precautions that maximises efficiency. Which liability rule would create such incentives? The following model illustrates the incentive effects of various forms of liability.

This model makes simplifying assumptions. First, drivers are non-altruistic, and thus care only for their own welfare. Second, drivers alone can minimise the social cost of car accidents (we will relax this assumption later in this chapter when we consider the more realistic case where efficiency requires pedestrians, motorcyclists, cyclists, drivers, and other potential accident victims to take care). Third, drivers have insurance that covers their own medical expenses in the event of an accident, but this does not cover third-party liability. Finally, money can fully compensate for physical and emotional injuries, such that, in conjunction with the third assumption, drivers are indifferent to being injured themselves.

Drivers in this model can take four different levels of care. A representative explanation could be as follows:

1. *No care*: In this state, potential tortfeasors drive in a manner indifferent to the well-being of other people on the road – driving significantly above the speed limit, failing to signal, aggressively overtaking others on blind corners, declining to check their mirrors before changing lanes, not being attentive behind the wheel, not checking their lights before driving, and so on.
2. *Low care*: They now drive less aggressively and pay more attention to their surroundings, but still travel materially faster than the speed limit, overtake others who do not drive as quickly and do so despite visible oncoming traffic, only sporadically check their mirrors, and rarely signal.
3. *Moderate care*: Drivers exercising "moderate care" generally obey the speed limit, pay close attention to their environment and the actions of other drivers on the road, always check their mirrors and lights, only overtake on straight roads where there is no oncoming traffic, and so on.
4. *High care*: These most assiduous drivers maintain hyper-vigilance on the road, never play music or otherwise distract themselves whilst driving, never exceed the speed limit, driving only in the slow lane on the motorway, and drive defensively by maintaining a significant distance between their cars and those in front of them.

Each increment in care from none to high has two opposing effects. First, it reduces the probability of an accident. Second, it increases the cost to the driver. Each driver's insurance renders her indifferent to her own injuries, and every driver is non-altruistic. Thus, in the absence of legal intervention, each driver's preference is as follows: no care > low care > moderate care > high care. Potential victims prefer the opposite. The problem is therefore one of conflicting preferences, which raises the question of how the parties would resolve that conflict in a setting of no transaction costs. Figure 2.2 summarises the model.

The social-welfare optimum in this example is for drivers to take moderate care. As this outcome maximises the combined welfare of drivers and potential accident victims, the relevant stakeholders would have agreed that drivers drive with moderate care. Notice that the optimal amount of precautions does not minimise expected accident costs. This is true even though the cost of high precautions to drivers is less than the expected accident costs. The reason is because the *marginal benefit* of increasing care from moderate to high in reducing accident costs ($150 - 140 = 10$) is less than the *marginal cost* to drivers ($35 - 20 = 15$). That is why Judge Learned Hand's famous mathematical definition of negligence as B < PL is flawed.[2]

---

2 *United States v Carroll Towing Co*, 159 F2d 169 (2d Cir. 1947).

Precautions	Cost to Driver	Expected Accident Costs	Total Costs
None	0	200	200
Low	10	180	190
Moderate	20	150	170
High	35	140	175

Figure 2.2

With this example in hand, consider how various liability regimes may spur potential injurers to behave. We will discuss strict liability, negligence, and no liability.

1. No liability

First, if courts decline to impose liability, drivers will simply maximise their utility, which in this model, means minimising their costs. As the harm that victims suffer is not part of drivers' utility functions and because drivers are insured against their own injuries, they will ignore the cost of accidents and simply minimise their accident-avoidance costs. They will, therefore, take no precautions, which is inefficient. This is an externality problem – or bargaining failure – for the private costs of drivers' action do not align with the social costs.

2. Strict liability

Under strict liability, injurers must pay for any harm their actions cause others, regardless of whether the accident was avoidable. Such liability induces drivers to make their victims' costs their own – i.e. to include the welfare of potential accident victims in their utility functions. Drivers in our model can neither avoid paying, nor reduce the amount they have to pay, by changing activity levels (i.e. eschewing driving in favour of alternatives such as public transportation). Thus, all they can do is minimise their combined cost of taking precautions and paying for accidents that take place. That calculus is equivalent to the one that maximises efficiency, so drivers' private incentives align with the social optimum. Under a strict liability regime, therefore, rational drivers will exercise moderate care: this is the desirable outcome. Notice that strict liability in this example takes the form of a Pigouvian tax.

3. Negligence

What is the effect of implementing a negligence regime in lieu of strict liability? The answer, which surprises some law students, is that both negligence and strict liability create the same incentive to take precautions. In the setting of unilateral accidents that are not subject to activity-level changes, the incentive effects of both liability regimes are identical.

To understand why, consider the incentives associated with a negligence regime. The cost of an "unavoidable accident" (i.e. an accident that an injurer could avoid only by a marginal expenditure greater than the ensuing reduction in expected accident costs) is zero to an injurer who exercises due care under a negligence rule. One can define negligence as "the omission to do something which a reasonable man, guided upon those considerations which ordinarily regulate the conduct of human affairs, would do, or doing something which a prudent and reasonable man would not do".[3] If one

---

3 Blyth v Birmingham Waterworks Co (1856) 11 Ex Ch 781.

translates that standard into the language of economics, it means that negligence, in the case of fixed activity levels, is a failure to undertake the amount of precautions that minimises the expected social cost of accidents.

Applying this definition to our model, negligence is a failure to exercise at least a moderate amount of care. Thus, drivers can elect to take high care at a (private) cost of 35, moderate care at a cost of 20, low care at a cost of 190 (10 in precautions plus 180 in liability), and no care at a cost of 200 (0 in precautions plus 200 in liability). Confronted with these options, a rational driver would choose to drive with a moderate amount of care, which is the efficient outcome.

4. Negligence v strict liability

Should courts, therefore, be indifferent between strict liability and negligence in unilateral-care scenarios with fixed activity levels? The answer is: not necessarily. First, courts need distinct information to apply the different liability regimes. Under strict liability, courts need only determine the cost to victims of their injuries. In applying a negligence standard, however, the judiciary must not only determine that cost, but must also calculate the optimal amount of precautions, and then compare that ideal expenditure with the precautions that the defendant, in fact, exercised. These specific figures are, as a practical matter, often elusive. It is, therefore, easier for a court to apply strict liability. Furthermore, strict liability is preferable if victims are more risk averse than potential tortfeasors, because strict liability shifts risk away from accident victims and onto injurers.

Still, strict liability is not obviously better, even in this model. Strict liability results in more cases because victims of all accidents can successfully sue, whereas only those whom negligent conduct injured can successfully bring an action under a negligence regime. Thus, even though the average cost of a strict liability case is lower for the judiciary, the total cost of such cases may exceed that of cases under a negligence standard.

Finally, the reader should understand that the driving example discussed here is an abstract discussion meant to illustrate general principles. It does not imply that high care of the kind discussed above would not, in reality, enhance social welfare. It merely demonstrates that, due to the utility that those who undertake risk-bearing conduct experience, the optimum amount of care may not be what minimises the expected cost of accidents. The efficient level of precautions minimises expected social costs, which include the costs of both taking care and accidents.

D. Bilateral-Care Scenarios with Fixed Activity Levels

The preceding model may plausibly account for accidents in which potential injurers alone can minimise social costs through precautions and without changing activity levels. A good example may be airline crashes, as there is little that people on the ground can do to reduce the expected cost of such accidents. Furthermore, given the value inherent in flying, activity-level reductions among airlines that exercise all cost-justified precautions are unlikely to be efficient. In such cases, the economic goal of tort law should be to induce airline companies to undertake optimal precautions. In practice, society accomplishes this goal through a combination of *ex ante* regulation, *ex post* liability in tort, and potential criminal-law enforcement.

In most cases, however, minimising the social cost of accidents necessitates precautions on the part of both prospective injurers and victims. For instance, to reduce the cost of injuries on the road, not only must drivers take appropriate care – pedestrians and cyclists must do so, as well. Such cases are known as bilateral-care scenarios. The relevant question is how courts can employ liability rules to induce both tortfeasors and victims to undertake optimal precautions.

As before, prospective tortfeasors can engage in no, low, moderate, or high levels of care. Each successive increment in precautions by potential injurers reduces the expected cost of accidents by diminishing the likelihood of their occurrence. Each such increase in care, however, imposes a further cost on tortfeasors. In this model, however, the expected accident cost also depends on victims' precautions. We shall assume that they, too, can exercise four degrees of care, which likewise reduces the probability of accidents, though such precautions impose private costs that increase with the degree of care undertaken. Activity levels are fixed, and so we are unconcerned with spurring the injurers or the victims to substitute their current conduct for alternative forms of behaviour. This table demonstrates the relevant payoffs:

These possible outcomes depend on the respective care levels of the injurers and the victims. Consistent with its being a bilateral-care model, the social-welfare optimum is for both injurers and victims to undertake a moderate level of precautions. Notice once more that the efficient result (moderate–moderate) differs from the care combination that minimises the expected accident cost

Injurer Precautions	Cost of Care to Injurers	Victim Precautions	Cost of Care to Victims	Expected Accident Cost	Total Social Cost
None	0	None	0	500	500
Low	20	None	0	470	490
Moderate	50	None	0	430	480
High	80	None	0	415	495
None	0	Low	10	485	495
Low	20	Low	10	450	480
Moderate	50	Low	10	415	475
High	80	Low	10	400	490
None	0	Moderate	20	470	490
Low	20	Moderate	20	435	475
Moderate	50	Moderate	20	400	470
High	80	Moderate	20	380	480
None	0	High	40	455	495
Low	20	High	40	430	490
Moderate	50	High	40	390	480
High	80	High	40	375	495

Figure 2.3

(high–high). Minimising that cost is not necessarily the same as minimising the combined costs of accidents *and precautions*.

The question, then, is how to induce efficient behaviour through liability rules in tort. We shall consider the following liability regimes: no liability, strict liability, negligence, strict liability with contributory negligence, and strict liability with comparative negligence. To determine the rational choices of the injurers and victims in the strategic environment in which those actors find themselves, we shall use game theory. This branch of economic analysis is particularly useful when analysing strategic interrelationships and equilibrium. To determine whether a liability rule induces the right form of behaviour, one must ask of each party: given the other actors' anticipated decisions, what is her rational choice?

1. No liability

Given the absence of activity-level changes, actors' private interests are to minimise their expected costs. As each party is non-altruistic, third-party harm will not factor into any person's decision making. In a setting of no liability, the injurers' costs are limited to their precautions, if any. Victims' costs comprised both their own costs of taking care and the expected accident cost.

To determine rational behaviour in the presence of no liability, consider the normal form representation of the choices of injurers and victims. The left-hand figure in every cell is the injurers' payout; the right-hand one is the victims':

The efficient outcome is for both the injurers and the victims to take care, which minimises total social costs at 470. To determine what the players will rationally do, however, begin by identifying the injurers' dominant strategy. As the reader can readily affirm, regardless of whether victims take no, low, moderate, or high care, the best choice for the injurers is to take no care, which entails a cost of zero. This is the injurers' dominant strategy.

		Victims			
		No Care	Low Care	Moderate Care	High Care
Injurers	No Care	0, 500	0, 495	0, 490	0, 495
	Low Care	20, 470	20, 460	20, 455	20, 470
	Moderate Care	50, 430	50, 425	50, 420	50, 430
	High Care	80, 415	80, 410	80, 400	80, 415

Figure 2.4

What of the victims' strategy? Victims know that the injurers' dominant strategy is to take no care. Their best choice is, therefore, to take a moderate amount of care, which minimises their expected losses at 490.[4] The equilibrium is thus for injurers to take no precautions and for victims to act with moderate care. This is a Nash equilibrium because neither the victims nor the injurers can do better given the other parties' choices. This outcome, however, is inefficient because total social cost is 490 instead of the social optimum of 470 in which everyone takes moderate care.

2. Strict liability

Under a strict-liability regime, injurers must compensate victims for the full costs of their injuries. By assumption, such compensation perfectly restores victims to their pre-injury state, such that they are indifferent as to whether they were involved in an accident or not. To identify the outcome under strict liability, review the normal-form representation shown in Figure 2.5.

The victims' dominant strategy is obviously not to take care because doing so would entail a private cost without an offsetting private benefit.

Given victims' decision not to take care, drivers will minimise their expected costs. They could elect to take no care, in which case their expected cost will be 500. If they decide to take low care, drivers will experience a cost of 20 in precautions and expected liability of 470, for a total expected cost of 490. A rational, risk-neutral driver would thus prefer to take low care than no care. She could do even better, however, by exercising moderate care, as the increment in precautions costs of 30 (50 minus 20) would reduce the expected accident cost by 40 (470 minus 430), thus yielding an expected private cost of 480. It would be irrational for drivers to take a high amount of precautions,

---

4 Note, however, that regardless of what level of care injurers actually take, victims minimise their expected cost by taking moderate precautions. That level of care is therefore victims' dominant strategy.

	Victims			
Injurers		No Care	Low Care	Moderate Care	High Care
	No Care	500, 0	485, 10	470, 20	455, 40
	Low Care	490, 0	470, 10	455, 20	450, 40
	Moderate Care	480, 0	465, 10	450, 20	440, 40
	High Care	495, 0	480, 10	460, 20	455, 40

Figure 2.5

however, as the marginal cost of increasing care to that level would exceed the marginal reduction in expected accident costs. Given the victims' election not to take care, the drivers' rational choice is to undertake a moderate amount of care.

Thus, under strict liability, the equilibrium is for drivers to take a moderate amount of care, but for victims not to take any care. The result is a net social cost of 480, which in this model is superior to a setting of no liability, but still less desirable than the efficient outcome in which all parties exercise moderate care. That social optimum would entail a total cost of just 470.

3. Negligence

Negligence is the most common liability regime in tort law, and thus an important subject of economic analysis. As people perceive different connotations from the term "negligence", it is crucial to define the term in economic terms: a failure to undertake the amount of precautions that unilaterally minimises the expected social cost of an accident.

Under a negligence regime, if tortfeasors took care, the full social cost of any accidents that occur would fall on victims, save for those costs that tortfeasors incur in precautions. Conversely, if the injurers fail to take the efficient level of care, all accident costs would fall on them.

In the present model, optimal precautions for both injurers and victims constitute moderate care. If injurers took moderate or high care, the courts would not deem them negligent and the accident costs would lie with victims. Conversely, if injurers took low or no care, they would be negligent and would thus have to compensate victims for their injuries. With these concerns in mind, turn to the game-theory representation of a negligence regime, as applied to this bilateral-care scenario with fixed activity levels:

Regardless of victims' precautions, injurers' best choice is to take moderate precautions at a cost of 50. They would prefer this course to taking a high degree of care because their net costs under the latter approach would be 80. Conversely, if injurers took no care, the courts would find them negligent. Taking no care, tortfeasors' expected costs would be 500, 485, 470, or 455, depending on whether victims took no, low, moderate, or high care, respectively. Equivalently,

	Victims			
Injurers		No Care	Low Care	Moderate Care	High Care
	No Care	500, 0	485, 10	470, 20	455, 40
	Low Care	490, 0	470, 10	455, 20	450, 40
	Moderate Care	50, 430	50, 425	50, 420	50, 430
	High Care	80, 415	80, 410	80, 400	80, 415

Figure 2.6

tortfeasors' expected costs would be 490, 470, 455, or 450 if injurers took low care (which courts would deem negligent). Given these choices, it is rational for drivers to undertake a moderate amount of precautions and hence pay only 50.

What is the rational choice for victims? They know that injurers have an incentive to take a moderate amount of care. Given drivers' choice to do so, victims understand that they must pay the cost of unavoidable accidents. They will thus decide successively to increase precautions as long as each additional expenditure in care reduces the expected cost of accidents by more than that amount. Given drivers' election to take moderate precautions, if victims took no care, they would face an expected cost of 430. If they take low care, they will experience combined costs in precautions and accident costs of 425. If they take moderate or high precautions, victims will face a net expected cost of 420 and 430, respectively. Victims will minimise their expected costs, and will thus take moderate care, given drivers' decision also to take moderate care. Victims' taking moderate precautions does not affect drivers' incentive also to undertake moderate care, and so this is an equilibrium.

In the present model, a negligence standard is efficient, as it leads both injurers and victims to take optimal precautions.

4. Strict liability with contributory negligence

Strict liability alone is inefficient in the present model because it insures victims against all accident costs, thus inducing them not to take socially beneficial, but privately costly, precautions. Injecting contributory negligence changes this calculus because it insures victims only if they do not act negligently. As "negligence" means not taking the precautions that minimise the expected social cost of accidents, courts will deem victims negligent in this model if they take less than moderate care.

What level of care will potential victims take? The answer depends on the anticipated behaviour of drivers, and vice versa, as the following matrix demonstrates:

Take victims' strategy first. If injurers took no care, victims would minimise their expected costs by exercising moderate care, which would result in an expense of 20, as opposed to the costs of 500, 495, or 40 in taking no, low, or high care, respectively. The reader can readily verify that, regardless of which level of care injurers take, victims' rational choice is to take moderate care, which is thus their dominant strategy.

		Victims			
		No Care	Low Care	Moderate Care	High Care
Injurers	No Care	0, 500	0, 495	470, 20	455, 40
	Low Care	20, 470	20, 460	455, 20	450, 40
	Moderate Care	50, 430	50, 425	450, 20	440, 40
	High Care	80, 415	80, 410	460, 20	455, 40

Figure 2.7

Injurers do not have a dominant strategy. If victims take no care, injurers do best by also taking no care. If the victims take low care, the injurers again do best by not taking care. If the victims exercise moderate precautions, however, the injurers' best action is to take moderate care, which is also the rational choice if the victims undertake a high degree of care. Nevertheless, in this game, the injurers know that the victims' dominant strategy is to take moderate care, which means that the injurers will also take moderate care. This is the efficient result.

The victims, therefore, have an incentive to exercise a moderate amount of care when subjected to strict liability with contributory negligence. In light of the victims' decision to act in this way, the drivers also have an incentive to take moderate care if victims take care. Like negligence, strict liability with contributory negligence leads to the efficient outcome under the assumptions of this model. Notice, however, that strict liability with contributory negligence is more costly for a court to apply than a simple rule of strict liability.

5. Strict liability with comparative negligence

Strict liability with a defence of comparative negligence holds injurers responsible for harm to victims, though it discounts injured parties' recovery by the percentage to which they were negligent. This, too, leads to the efficient outcome in which both drivers and victims take moderate precautions.

To see why, first consider victims' incentives. They know that, under this liability regime, drivers must make good the harm caused, save to the extent that victims' negligent behaviour contributes to the relevant injury. So, if both injurers and victims take no care, the expected accident cost is 500, but the courts will limit victims' recovery to 470 on account of victims' failure to take moderate precautions at an expense of 20, which expenditure would have reduced the expected accident cost to 470. Victims would therefore be better off spending 20 on precautions. The reader can confirm that this result stays the same regardless of whether drivers take low, moderate, or high levels of care.

Given victims' incentive to take moderate care, it is rational for drivers also to exercise moderate care. The reason is that, absent negligence on victims' part, drivers must pay all accidents costs. To the extent that drivers can disproportionately reduce expected accident costs by undertaking precautions, they will do so. In this model, drivers' taking moderate care minimises their expected payout, which consists of the cost of their taking care plus their expected liability costs from the unavoidable accidents that occur.

E. Unilateral-Care Scenarios with Variable Activity Levels

In both of the preceding models, neither injurers nor victims could alter their activity levels. In reality, however, changing one's participation in a particular form of behaviour can be efficient. This is especially so for conduct that carries an unusually high risk of harm to others, such as transporting explosives or keeping dangerous animals, though it also applies to more prosaic conduct, including driving. In many such cases, maximising social welfare requires a person not only to take care, but also to reduce her engagement in an activity when the social costs of undertaking such behaviour exceed the benefits.

We now relax the assumption that injurers cannot alter their activity levels. So, for instance, we want drivers not only to take care while they drive, but to consider either not driving or driving less when the risk of going on the road (the expected cost both of taking care and of unavoidable accidents) exceeds the benefits. We want to impose the same incentives with respect to all manner of potentially tortious conduct.

Now consider the effects of various liability rules on care and activity levels in unilateral-care scenarios. For the sake of simplicity, assume that potential injurers either take care or they do not — gradations between low, moderate, and high precautions are not possible. In addition to deciding whether to take care, however, prospective tortfeasors must decide whether to engage in the risk-bearing behaviour and, if so, by how much. In this model, would-be injurers can eschew the risky conduct entirely or they can engage in that activity at a light, medium, or heavy rate. Assume that "medium" represents twice, and "heavy" three times, the amount of the activity that "light" participation represents.

Activity Level	Utility from Activity	Due Care	Cost of Care	Expected Accident Cost	Social Welfare
None	0	n/a	0	0	0
Light	50	No	0	70	–20
Medium	170	No	0	140	30
Heavy	200	No	0	210	–10
Light	50	Yes	20	30	0
Medium	170	Yes	40	60	70
Heavy	200	Yes	60	90	50

Figure 2.8

Consistent with this assumption, the cost of taking care while undertaking a medium amount of the activity is twice as great as the cost of precautions associated with spending only half the time (a light amount) engaging in the relevant conduct. The amount spent on precautions to take care while engaging in a heavy amount of the behaviour costs three times as much as it would under the light amount. Similarly, the expected accident cost increases proportionately with heightened levels of the risky activity.

Potential injurers derive greater utility by engaging in more of the risk-bearing behaviour. Nevertheless, because the marginal utility of the relevant activity eventually starts to decrease, potential tortfeasors experience a significant increase in utility from light to medium activity, but only a modest increase from medium to heavy (see Figure 2.8).

The social-welfare optimum is for potential injurers to engage in a medium amount of the relevant activity and to take due care while doing so. Now consider the degree to which different liability rules succeed and fail, respectively, to impart incentives for tortfeasors to engage in efficient behaviour.

1. No Liability

In a setting of no liability, injurers do not have to compensate accident victims, regardless of fault. By assumption, the well-being of potential victims does not feature in injurers' utility functions. In the absence of liability, then, injurers will maximise their utility, which in this model, involves engaging in a heavy amount of the pertinent activity (a private gain of 200) and taking no precautions (a private cost of 0). This is a classic externality – or bargaining failure under the Coase Theorem – because injurers do not internalise the expected accident cost of their behaviour (210). The tortfeasors' rational behaviour under a no-liability regime results in a social-welfare loss of 10.

2. Negligence

Under a negligence standard, tortfeasors pay only if they fail to take care. If the injurers engage in a light amount of the relevant conduct, they will have to pay 70 in expected accident costs if they do not take care. Alternatively, while undertaking a light activity level, they can pay 20 in precautions and pay nothing for the injuries that occur. Obviously, potential tortfeasors would rather take care. The reader can confirm that injurers will take due care regardless of whether they engage in a light, medium, or heavy amount of the pertinent behaviour.

How will tortfeasors determine how much conduct in which to engage? They would prefer a light amount over none – the former benefits them by 50 at a cost of only 20 in precautions, to yield a net private gain of 30. Likewise, injurers would rather engage in a medium conduct level than light because the former yields utility of 170, though precautions of only 40, at a total private gain over a light amount of 100. As noted, a medium degree of participation in the relevant activity, coupled with due care, is efficient.

Under a negligence regime, however, tortfeasors have an incentive excessively to partake in the risky behaviour. In the present model, injurers would benefit from increasing their activity levels from medium to heavy because doing so would yield a private utility gain of 30 (200 − 170), but would only increase expenditures on care by 20 (60 − 40). Although this outcome is privately attractive to the injurers, it is socially undesirable. The inefficiency arises because injurers do not have to pay for accidents that occur despite all cost-justified precautions. Here, the gain in utility to injurers from increasing their activity levels from moderate to high produces a private benefit to injurers of 10, which equals the utility increase of 30 minus the larger due-care costs of 20. The increase in expected accident costs of 30, however, outweighs the gain of 10.

A negligence standard is, therefore, inefficient in the present model. The reader will notice that this result only follows, however, if courts do not deem cost-justified engagement in activity levels to be an element of the negligence calculus. Courts do not consider whether a tort defendant engaged in too much of the relevant behaviour in determining whether he acted negligently. The information pertaining to the private benefit associated with undertaking different activity levels resides exclusively with the individual actor, such that the judiciary would have little basis to estimate it.

3. Strict liability

Under a strict-liability regime, injurers experience all the benefits and all the costs of engaging in the accident-producing activity. As the current model is a unilateral-care scenario in which only tortfeasors can affect efficiency, the fact that strict liability causes injurers fully to internalise the effects of their behaviour means that they will act efficiently.

Potential tortfeasors will choose to take care under any activity level. While undertaking the activity to a light degree, injurers could reduce their expected liability payout from 70 to 30 at a cost of only 20 by taking care. If they partook in the activity at a moderate rate, tortfeasors could reduce their expected liability costs by 80 through precautions that only cost 40, and so on.

Unlike in the negligence case, where the cost to injurers of unavoidable accidents was zero, tortfeasors subject to strict liability must pay the cost of all accidents. Thus, in contrast to their behaviour under a negligence standard, they will not engage in a heavy amount of the activity. Doing so would yield them extra utility of 30 over the medium activity level, which the expected accident cost of 30 would cancel out, but would also necessitate spending 20 more in precautions. Thus, the injurers maximise their welfare − and society's − by taking care and engaging in a moderate activity level.

F. Bilateral-Care Scenarios with Variable Activity Levels

The last model that we shall consider (see Figure 2.9) is simultaneously the most realistic and the most complicated account of tortious behaviour. The majority of accidents are most efficiently avoided by both potential injurers' and victims' taking care, and by all those parties undertaking optimal activity levels. Unlike the three models addressed above, no perfect liability rule exists for bilateral-care scenarios with variable activity levels.

In this model, the social-welfare optimum is for both injurers and victims to take care and to engage in a low activity level. Having identified the efficient outcome, consider the incentive effects of the relevant liability standards. We shall assume that the parties face a binary choice as to activity levels: low and high.

Injurer Activity Level	Injurer Utility	Victim Activity Level	Victim Utility	Injurer Care	Cost Injurer Care	Victim Care	Cost Victim Care	Ex. Accident Cost	S.W.
Low	100	Low	40	No	0	No	0	90	50
High	130	Low	40	No	0	No	0	130	40
Low	100	High	70	No	0	No	0	125	45
High	130	High	70	No	0	No	0	165	35
Low	100	Low	40	Yes	30	No	0	50	60
High	130	Low	40	Yes	30	No	0	90	50
Low	100	High	70	Yes	30	No	0	85	55
High	130	High	70	Yes	30	No	0	125	45
Low	100	Low	40	No	0	Yes	20	60	60
High	130	Low	40	No	0	Yes	20	100	50
Low	100	High	70	No	0	Yes	20	95	55
High	130	High	70	No	0	Yes	20	135	45
Low	100	Low	40	Yes	30	Yes	20	20	70
High	130	Low	40	Yes	30	Yes	20	60	60
Low	100	High	70	Yes	30	Yes	20	55	65
High	130	High	70	Yes	30	Yes	20	95	55

Figure 2.9

1. No liability

In a bilateral-care environment with variable activity levels, no liability is inefficient because it creates no incentive for tortfeasors to take care or to engage in the activity at the optimal rate. It does carry the benefit, however, of inducing victims both to take optimal precautions and to engage in the proper activity level. To explore these effects, consider the following payoff matrix:

Absent any liability in tort, neither injurers nor victims will consider the external costs of their various choices. As the injurers derive a benefit of 130 under high activity levels, rather than a mere 100 under a low activity level, they will choose the former course. Simultaneously, they will elect not to take care, which costs them zero, because taking precautions would cost them 30.

Given the injurers' decision to engage in a high activity level and not to take care, victims will choose between a cost of −90, −95, −80, or −85 corresponding to no care/low activity, no care/high activity, care/low activity, and care/high activity, respectively. As the third option minimises their expected costs, victims will rationally pursue this course.

		Victims			
		No Care/ Low Activity	No Care/ High Activity	Care/Low Activity	Care/High Activity
Injurers	No Care/Low Activity	100, −50	100, −55	100, −40	100, −45
	No Care/High Activity	130, −90	130, −95	130, −80	130, −85
	Care/Low Activity	70, −10	70, −15	70, 0	70, −5
	Care/High Activity	100, −50	100, −55	100, −40	100, −45

Figure 2.10

As the reader can readily confirm, a no-liability regime in this example leads to inefficient behaviour by injurers, though not by victims. The resulting social-welfare level of 50 is less than the optimum of 70. Let us see if an alternative liability standard would yield a superior result.

2. Strict liability

Under a strict-liability regime, injurers bear all accident costs. As a result, victims maximise their welfare by engaging in a high activity level (because it confers greater utility than pursuing a low activity level) and by declining to take care (because taking precautions would impose costs on the victims that would not translate into any private gain). Victims' decision not to take care, of course, is inefficient.

Given victims' choice, injurers' rational decision is to take care and to engage in a low activity level. Injurers' behaviour under a strict-liability rule is thus efficient. To understand the parties' decision making, consider this payoff matrix:

Regardless of injurers' choice, victims are best off by engaging in a high-activity level and by taking no care, which results in an expected value of 70. This choice is thus the victims' dominant strategy. Knowing this fact, injurers can choose between a cost of −25, −35, −15, and −25 by taking no care/low activity, no care/high activity, care/low activity, and care/high activity, respectively. Obviously, −15 is the least bad result for injurers.

The injurers' rational choice, therefore, is to minimise their losses by engaging in a low-activity level and by taking care. Net social welfare under strict liability is therefore 55. This is inefficient, as the social-welfare optimum would yield welfare of 70. The inefficiency results from the fact that strict liability, by insuring the victims against any loss, creates no incentive for them to take care or to reduce activity levels, even though it would be efficient for them to do so.

		Victims			
		No Care/ Low Activity	No Care/ High Activity	Care/Low Activity	Care/High Activity
Injurers	No Care/ Low Activity	10, 40	−25, 70	40, 20	5, 50
	No Care/ High Activity	0, 40	−35, 70	30, 20	−5, 50
	Care/Low Activity	20, 40	−15, 70	50, 20	15, 50
	Care/High Activity	10, 40	−25, 70	40, 20	5, 50

Figure 2.11

3. Negligence (with or without contributory or comparative negligence)

Under a negligence regime, injurers can avoid the entire cost of accidents by taking proper precautions. To see whether this liability standard induces optimal behaviour, we shall consider the model once more through the lens of game theory (see Figure 2.12).

Begin with injurers. If victims take no care and engage in low-activity levels, injurers can derive a return of 10, 0, 70, and 100 by taking no care/low activity, no care/high activity, care/low activity, and care/high activity, respectively. Injurers will, of course, choose the last option. In fact, the injurers will choose to take care and to engage in a high activity level regardless of victims' choice, thus making "care/high activity" injurers' dominant strategy. Knowing this fact, victims can only choose between −50, −55, −40, and −45. They will choose a combination of due care and low activity levels to minimise their expected costs at −40.

Thus, a negligence standard will lead accident victims to behave efficiently, but will not lead injurers to do so. Although injurers have an incentive to take care, they have no incentive to reduce their activity levels. This result holds true, regardless of whether the courts introduce contributory or comparative negligence to the legal standard.

4. Strict liability with contributory or comparative negligence

Strict liability induces potential tortfeasors to behave optimally, but imparts no incentive on victims to either take care or to efficiently reduce activity levels. We can improve on this result by introducing either contributory or comparative negligence to the strict liability standard. The injurers will behave as they do under pure strict liability, but now the victims will exercise due care because the cost of their doing so (30) is always less than the expected accident cost that their taking precautions enables them to avoid. Strict liability with contributory or comparative negligence, however, will not induce the victims to engage in a low- instead of a high-activity level. This is

		Victims			
		No Care/Low Activity	No Care/ High Activity	Care/Low Activity	Care/High Activity
Injurers	No Care/Low Activity	10, 40	−25, 70	40, 20	5, 50
	No Care/ High Activity	0, 40	−35, 70	30, 20	−5, 50
	Care/Low Activity	70, −10	70, −15	70, 0	70, −5
	Care/High Activity	100, −50	100, −55	100, −40	100, −45

Figure 2.12

because the reducing activity levels of the victim imposes a cost upon them of 30 (70 − 40), but no benefit, as the reduced accident cost of 35 inures solely to the benefit of tortfeasors.

5. No perfect rule

There is no liability standard that spurs both injurers and victims to act efficiently in bilateral-care scenarios with variable activity levels. As many accidents are avoided at lowest cost by both tort-feasors' and victims' taking care and by altering activity levels, this fact is significant. Courts, in implementing liability standards in tort, should therefore consider whether it is more important for injurers or victims to alter activity levels. If it is the former, the courts should impose strict liability with contributory or comparative negligence. If altered activity levels on the part of victims would have a greater impact on social welfare, the courts should use a negligence standard, with or without contributory or comparative negligence.

G. Tort Law, Risk Aversion, Insurance, and Moral Hazard

The preceding account assumed that both injurers and victims are risk neutral, which is unlikely to be realistic where the cost of an accident represents a sizeable portion of an affected party's total wealth or well being. With respect to catastrophic injuries, especially, potential victims are likely to be risk averse.

When such aversion is present, social welfare requires the law to do more than incubate incentives for potential tortfeasors and victims to take cost-justified precautions and to regulate activity levels. Risk-averse parties dislike fluctuations in their wealth, and would pay premiums to flatten their net income over time. Society can enhance welfare by shifting risk from risk-averse entities to risk-neutral, or even better to risk-preferring, parties. Both tort law and insurance can play important roles in this respect.

Putting the question of insurance aside momentarily, tort remedies can transfer risk. For instance, if potential victims are risk averse and tortfeasors, on account of their ability to diversify risk, are risk neutral, then a strict-liability regime would efficiently shift risk from victims to injurers. Such an arrangement would be unambiguously efficient overall if it is a unilateral-care scenario in which tortfeasors are the lowest cost avoiders of accidents. In bilateral-care cases, in which we care about tortfeasors' but not victims' activity levels, strict liability with a defence of contributory or comparative negligence will induce desirable behaviour on both sides and will also shift risk in a desirable manner. The transfer of risk, however, may be imperfect due to the probabilistic nature of taking care, such that potential victims, even if they take precautions, cannot ensure to a 100% certainty that the courts will not adjudge them to be either contributorily or comparatively negligent. Finally, if the injurers, but not the victims, are risk averse, then the law could shift risk to the victims by adopting a no-liability regime. Such a rule would be desirable, however, only if the victims were the lowest-cost avoiders or if their risk aversion were sufficiently pronounced as to outweigh the improper incentives weighing on their care and activity levels.

Notwithstanding this discussion, there is good reason to doubt whether the tort system can insure accident victims and effectively transfer risk. The problem arises primarily from the cost of accessing the legal system. For that reason, it is generally more efficient for prospective parties to accidents to self-insure.

Insurance works because insurance companies are risk neutral on account of their ability to diversify risk through a broad portfolio of investments the risk profiles of which are not positively correlated to a significant degree. Many individuals are not able to achieve such diversification, so there exists the possibility for mutually beneficial exchange.

Imagine a situation in which a person, A, faces a 1% risk of his sports car's being wrecked in an accident within the coming year at a cost of £100,000, thus creating an expected cost of £1,000. If A were risk neutral, he would be indifferent between paying £1,000 or facing a 1% risk of losing £100,000. If A were risk averse, however, he will see the 1% chance of such a loss as being worse than a fixed price of £1,000. Assume that he is risk averse to the point of being indifferent between a certain cost of £1,500 and the 1% probability of his car's being in a serious accident. An insurance company can grant policies to many drivers, thus pooling the risk and facing a high probability of making payments close to the expected cost of accidents. If such a company operated in a perfectly competitive industry – an unrealistic, but simplifying assumption – the price of its insurance policy would equal the expected cost of the accident. This is known as an "actuarially fair" policy. A would, therefore, pay a premium of £1,000, thus achieving a gain of £500.

There are problems, however, with the insurance process, so it is rarely possible to shift all of one's risk onto an insurance company. First, policies are never actuarially fair, thus inefficiently pricing some risk-averse prospective insureds out of the market. Second, there is a moral-hazard problem.

A recurring theme in law and economics is that people react to incentives. When completely insured, victims have no self-interested reason to take care or to change activity levels to reduce the probability, or severity, of accidents. For example, assume in the above example that the probability of A's car being destroyed in a crash is 1% only if A takes due care. If A took no precautions, however, the probability of such an accident rises to 5%, in which case the expected cost, and hence the insurance company's expected payout, rises from £1,000 to £5,000. If the insurance company agrees to compensate A for the £100,000 loss if it occurs, A would have no incentive to spend his own money (or time) on taking care because doing so would impose a cost upon him without any off-setting gain. This is the moral-hazard phenomenon.

Of course, insurance companies are not blind to this threat, and so they may make taking care a condition of the insurance contract. Unless such companies can accurately monitor their insureds to determine whether they are acting with due care, however, then a moral-hazard problem remains. In the above example, and assuming that the insurance company cannot monitor A's precautions, the company will demand a price of £5,000. Assuming that the cost of precautions is not preclusive, A will not pay the £5,000 premium and will instead take care and accept an expected cost of £1,000. This is inefficient because a risk-averse party experiences risk that could have been shifted to a risk-neutral entity.

H. Is Law and Economics Theory Realistic about Optimal Remedies?

The preceding models illustrate the positive effects of different liability rules in tort cases. To the extent these deductions are not only theoretically robust, but predict the manner in which potential tortfeasors and victims respond to distinct liability regimes, they are valuable. Legislators and judges should be mindful of the future consequences of the law. Economics provides a framework within which to understand how accident liability rules impact behaviour. In focusing on incentives, the theory provides a framework within which to produce a coherent and reproducible rule of decision. In a field as routinely subjective and contested as accident law, a theory's ability to yield objective conclusions is significant.

1. The realism of the economic account

Economic analysis generates insights that may surprise some students of tort law (e.g. in the absence of judicial error in calculating damages, strict liability does not create incentives to take more care than negligence). Other insights provide otherwise-elusive specificity. For example, one familiar with economic analysis can distinguish the distinct effects of strict liability, negligence, either of the previous two standards coupled with contributory or comparative negligence, or no liability at all.

The precision of these insights, however, depends on the relevant assumptions. These may include rationality, the ability of damages or insurance payments fully to compensate accident victims, due care is not being continuously variable, the propensity of courts accurately to quantify harm, and, in the case of negligence, the judiciary's ability to calculate both the optimal amount of precautions and the degree of care that the relevant party actually undertook. Certain of these assumptions are unrealistic at the individual level, which explains some commentators' scepticism as to the economic analysis of tort law.

The key to understanding the analysis and to appreciating its application to actual legal problems is to recognise the role played by the models explored in this chapter. Their aim is not to generate a realistic account of how individual tortfeasors and victims choose to engage in risky behaviour. People's real-life choices are beset by innumerable influences, the nature of which differs significantly from one individual to the next. No model could hope to encapsulate every variable that influences conduct. Law and economics is a theory of behaviour, which economists derive by abstracting from reality through assumptions. These enable one to focus on explanatory variables that the law can influence and that correlate in statistically significant fashion with behaviour. The fact that certain individuals' actions depart from the predictions of theory is of no concern if deviations are not systemically skewed in a particular direction.

For instance, no monetary judgment can render the victim of a serious accident indifferent between his pre- and post-injury state. As a result, potential tortfeasors prefer not to be in an accident, even in no-liability regimes. Conversely, strict liability will not lead potential victims to shrug their shoulders as to whether they are hurt in an accident or not. Similarly, the idea that third-party harm does not feature in tortfeasors' utility functions is often unrealistic: many, though sadly not all, people care about the harm that their actions may visit upon others.

Nevertheless, by assuming these complications away, the preceding models can identify rational behaviour. The fact that these assumptions do not hold perfectly true in practice need not deprive the models' theoretical predictions of their force. Specifically, the principal insight that externalities distort behaviour should hold true in practice. Even though a driver in a no-liability environment experiences a private risk to himself in behaving negligently, thus creating some deterrent, the fact that his expected cost does not include damages as to possible victims means that he will drive more dangerously than he would if the law forced him to internalise the full costs of his driving. The same is true of the potential victim whom strict liability partially insures – she is likely, as a practical matter, to be less careful in avoiding harm than if the law did not so insure her. These are specific examples of the moral-hazard problem.

The fact that people respond to incentives, however, does not in itself mean that potential liability in tort is itself a powerful explanatory variable as to people's decision to take care. In at least some settings, the incentive effect of tort law is probably modest vis-à-vis other factors. For instance, with respect to driving, anticipated liability is one of numerous incentives operating on potential tortfeasors. Others are self-interest in avoiding serious injury, adherence to social norms of acceptable behaviour, and, of course, the application of criminal law to extreme departures from reasonable care. In the commercial setting, market forces in the form of competition and the desire to maximise profit by maintaining high levels of demand cause companies to take steps to avoid injuring their customers. Ex ante regulation also plays an important role.

2. The empirical literature

Does evidence support law and economics theory? The answer is yes. Empirical studies show that, consistent with the insights explored above, both injurers and accident victims respond to incentives at the market level.[5] For instance, there is evidence that accident rates are higher in no-fault rather than tort-based jurisdictions, controlling for other explanatory factors.[6] No fault works by eliminating suits in tort for road injuries and instead requiring first-party insurance. The idea is to bypass the heavy administrative cost of the tort system. These findings suggest that the tort system materially affects the level of care that drivers take on the road. Consider a sampling of these studies.

In an early study, Elisabeth Landes ran a regression on all 50 US states, plus the District of Columbia, of which 16 states had passed no-fault laws between 1971 and 1976.[7] She found that introducing no-fault rules produced a statistically significant increase in fatal accidents. Jurisdictions adopting no-fault rules with relatively light restrictions on tort suits experienced a 2 to 5% increase in fatal accidents relative to those states that declined to adopt no-fault rules. Fatal accidents increased by 10 to 15% for no-fault states that more significantly restricted access to the tort system.[8]

A 2001 study of accident rates in the United States from 1982 to 1994 concluded that no fault significantly correlates with greater fatal accident rates.[9] In 2004, Alma Cohen and Rajeev Dehejia conducted an empirical study of all US states and Washington, DC over a 28-year period from 1970 to 1998. Controlling for the effects of compulsory insurance on behaviour (which prior studies had not done), they estimated that no-fault liability increased traffic fatalities by 6% due to its reducing accident liability.[10]

Why is this the case? Beyond the direct imposition of monetary damages as illustrated in the models above, the chosen liability rule may significantly affect insurance premiums and hence care. In addition, the categorical imposition or abolition of legal responsibility for accidents, such as

---

5   See, e.g., Ben C.J. van Velthoven, 'Empirics of Tort' in *Tort Law and Economics, Encyclopedia of Law and Economics* (2nd edn)(2009). See http://media.leidenuniv.nl/legacy/bvv-2009-04.pdf.

6   Rose Anne Devlin, 'Liability Versus No-Fault Automobile Insurance Regimes: An Analysis of the Experience in Quebec' in *Contributions to Insurance Economics* (1991) 499–520; J. David Cummins, Mary Weiss, and Richard Phillips, 'The Incentive Effects of No Fault Automobile Insurance', Wharton School, University of Pennsylvania, Working Paper 99–38 (1999); Frank Sloan, Bridget Reilly, and Christoph Schenzler, 'Tort liability versus other approaches for deterring careless driving' (1994)14 Int'l Rev L & Econ 53–71.

7   Elisabeth M. Landes, 'Insurance liability and accidents: A theoretical and empirical investigation and the effect of no-fault accidents' (1982) 25 JL & Econ 49.

8   But see S. Paul Kochanowski and Madelyn V. Young, 'Deterrent aspects of no-fault automobile insurance: Some empirical findings' (1985) 52 J Risk & Ins 269 (finding no statistically significant correlation between no fault and fatality rates).

9   J. David Cummins, Richard D. Phillips, and Mary A. Weiss, 'The incentive effects of no-fault automobile insurance' (2001) 44 JL & Econ 427.

10 Alma Cohen and Rajeev Dehejia, 'The effect of automobile insurance and accident liability laws on traffic fatalities' (2004) 67 JL Econ 357.

strict or no liability, is likely to affect activity levels where the relevant behaviour bears an unusual, and hence directly perceivable, propensity to impose costs on third parties. That is why strict liability is the standard tort regime applicable to ultra-hazardous activities.

Ultimately, the idea that tort law should not concern itself with creating desirable incentives is unconvincing. Public policy favours the injurers' and victims' taking care and altering activity levels when it is in their collective interest to do so. A variety of social policies and norms reflect this goal. If tort is but a component of a larger impetus toward efficient behaviour, then it does no disservice to the economic account of the law of accidents to say that liability rules are not the only driver of optimal conduct. Tort law can, and does, serve a complementary role with larger societal views of acceptable conduct – codified in communal norms of behaviour, criminal law, and fostering altruism – in achieving the right balance between the benefits of engaging in risk-bearing behaviour and the costs that such conduct imposes on potential victims.

Key Points

- If potential injurers and victims could bargain with one another at no cost (i.e. if the Coase Theorem applied) they would agree on the precautions and activity levels that maximise their combined welfare. This calculus would reflect the fact that people derive legitimate utility from pursuing conduct, such as driving, playing sports or selling a product, that may harm others.
- In the real world, transaction costs preclude such a bargain. Negative externalities accompany privately valuable, but socially costly, behaviour, thus causing tortfeasors to engage in risky activities too often and not to spend enough on precautions.
- The economic purpose of tort law is to induce both injurers and victims to take precautions and to regulate their activity levels to the point that maximises their combined welfare. The goal of the law should be to implement a liability regime that imparts those incentives.
- The optimal combination of care and activity levels is context specific. In unilateral-care scenarios, either injurers or victims alone can most efficiently minimise expected-accident costs. More commonly, however, efficiency depends on bilateral care, where all parties take precautions and/or adjust their activity levels.
- The following liability regimes are potentially available: (1) no liability, (2) strict liability, (3) strict liability with contributory or comparative negligence, (4) negligence, and (5) negligence with contributory or comparative negligence. Each one imparts distinct incentives.
- No liability causes victims to take due care and to alter their activity levels, and is thus the preferred rule when they are the lowest cost avoiders of accidents.
- Strict liability induces tortfeasors to undertake optimal precautions and efficiently to regulate their activity levels, and is thus the best regime when injurers are the lowest cost avoiders.
- Strict liability with contributory or comparative negligence causes both tortfeasors and victims to take due care, and for injurers to undertake an optimal amount of the risk-generating behaviour.
- Negligence leads injurers to take due care, but not to alter their activity levels.
- Negligence with contributory or comparative negligence causes both tortfeasors and victims to take optimal precautions, and provides an incentive for victims to regulate their activity levels.
- There is no rule of liability that incentivises both injurers and victims to take care and to regulate their activity levels.
- Empirical evidence supports the hypothesis that liability in tort deters negligent behaviour.

References and Further Reading

Books
Calabresi, Guido, *The Costs of Accidents: A Legal and Economic Analysis* (1970).

Kessler, Daniel P. and Rubinfeld, Daniel L., 'Empirical Study of the Civil Justice System' in *Handbook of Law and Economics* (2007) Vol. I, Ch. 5, § 3.

Landes, William H. and Posner, Richard A., *The Economic Structure of Tort Law* (1987).

Miceli, Thomas J., *The Economic Approach to Law*, 2nd edn (2008) Chs. 2–3.

Posner, Richard A., *Economic Analysis of Law* (2011) §§ 6.1–6.2, 6.5.

Shavell, Steven, *Foundations of Economic Analysis of Law* (2004) Chs. 8–12.

Shavell, Steven, 'Liability for Accidents', in *Handbook of Law and Economics* (2007) Vol. I, Ch. 2 (2007).

Articles
Calabresi, Guido, 'Some thoughts on risk distribution and the law of torts' (1961) 70 Yale LJ 499.

Calabresi, Guido, and Hirschoff, Jon, 'Toward a test for strict liability in torts' (1972) 81 Yale LJ 1055.

Kotz, Hein and Schafer, Hans-Bernd, 'Economic incentives to accident prevention: an empirical study of the German sugar industry' (1993) 13 Int'l Rev L & Econ 19.

Krueger, Alan B., 'Incentive effects of workers' compensation insurance' (1990) 41 J Public Econ 73.

Lee, Han-Duck, Browne, Mark J. and Schmitt, Joan T., 'How does joint and several tort reform affect the rate of tort filings? Evidence from the state courts' (1994) 61 J Risk & Ins 295.

Liang, Lan, Sloan, Frank A. and Stout, Emily M.,'Precaution, compensation, and threats of sanction: the case of alcohol servers' (2004) 24 Int'l Rev L & Econ 49.

Posner, Richard A., 'A theory of negligence' (1972) 1 J Legal Stud 29.

Schwartz, Gary T., 'Reality in the economic analysis of tort law: Does tort law really deter?' (1994) 42 UCLA L Rev 377.

Shavell, Steven, 'Strict liability versus negligence' (1980) 9 J Legal Stud 1.

Williams, Stephen F., 'Second best: The soft underbelly of deterrence theory in tort' (1993) 106 Harv L Rev 932.

Chapter 2

An Economic Account of Tort Doctrine

Chapter Contents

A.	Introduction	89
B.	The Injury Requirement	90
C.	Foreseeability, Proximity, and Causation	90
D.	Problems in the Determination of Liability	94
E.	Defective Products	96
F.	Intentional Torts	100
Key Points		101
References and Further Reading		102

A. Introduction

The law governing accidents implicates the problem of divided entitlements and inconsistent preferences. Externalities afflict the decision making of both injurers and victims and, due to transaction costs, no bargain toward an efficient allocation of rights occurs. Fortunately, the law can induce actors to internalise the consequences of their behaviour, and can thus remedy the externality problem that lies at the heart of tortious conduct. That possibility underlies the choice between various liability rules.

Tort law, however, is larger than the choice of liability rule. An economic account must explain such legal features as the reasonable person, causation, foreseeability, last clear chance, assumption of risk, products liability, and intentional torts. This chapter discusses the economics of these doctrines.

The first of these concepts – the reasonable person – finds straightforward meaning from an economic perspective. It refers to the behaviour that an individual would undertake were her interests aligned with those of society. That is why an individual acts "negligently" when he fails to take the precautions that would minimise the expected social cost of accidents (which cost comprises both expected accidents and taking care). Were judicial fact-finding sufficiently capable and cost-effective, the interwoven concepts of the reasonable person and negligence would even account for activity levels. They would judge a defendant unreasonable and, hence, negligent if she participated in the injury-producing conduct to a greater degree than social welfare justified.

The only complication surrounding the reasonable person concerns the degree to which the courts should juxtapose the characteristics of the particular defendant on that notional figure. In general, the reasonableness inquiry is indifferent to the idiosyncrasies of the relevant tortfeasor. In the famous case of *Vaughan v Menlove*, the Court of Common Pleas disagreed that the law should relieve the defendant of responsibility because he had the "misfortune of not possessing the highest order of intelligence".[1] Instead, the court demanded "caution such as a man of ordinary prudence would observe".

In a world in which the judicial apparatus were both flawless and free, the objective nature of the "reasonable person" inquiry would be questionable from an economic standpoint. In ignoring an individual's specific traits, the law fails to recognise that the cost of achieving a certain level of care varies across the population.

To adopt a simple example involving fixed activity levels, assume that certain behaviour, without precautions, entails an expected accident cost of 100. To simplify the analysis, assume that there are three potential injurers – A, B, and C. Being "a man of ordinary prudence", B can, at a cost of 20, reduce expected accident costs by 25 (to 75). His taking care is therefore efficient. A, being of above-average abilities, could achieve the same expected cost reduction of 25 by spending only 10. Yet, by spending 20, A could reduce expected accident costs by 40 (i.e. achieve an expected accident cost of 60). Efficiency therefore requires A to spend 20, rather than 10, in precautions, and thus to spend the same on precautions as B. Finally, C is a below-average person who can achieve a level of care that reduces expected accidents costs from 100 to 75 by spending 30. It is, therefore, inefficient for C to take such care.

An ideal tort system would compute the defendant-specific cost of taking care, compare that figure to the gains in reduced accident costs associated with such precautions, and thus determine whether or not the particular defendant acted negligently. The common-law tort system, however, does not operate in this manner. Does this feature depart from law-and-economics theory, or does

---

1 *Vaughan v Menlove* (1837) 132 ER 490 (CP).

a potential efficiency justification underlie this tenet of the law? It finds an economic explanation: the cost of the legal system. It is cheaper and less error-prone for courts to identify the average cost of taking a certain level of care and to compare it to the defendant's conduct than it is to examine each defendant's cost of taking care. Difficulties of proof and non-credible testimony would plague judicial assessment of individual precaution costs.

Yet, there is an exception. It applies when courts can easily determine that a defendant's cost of taking care greatly exceeds, or falls short of, that of the average person. Thus, the law does not hold a child to the standard of care required of an adult, nor will the courts deem it reasonable that one working in a higher profession, such as medicine, accountancy, or law, practice that profession at a level of competence comparable to that of an average layperson. This doctrine suggests that judicial analysis of "the reasonable person" bears an economic character. It recognises that assessing the cost of precautions to individual defendants is desirable when the courts can do so reliably and at low cost.

Thus, "the reasonable person" resting at the heart of tort law comports with an economic understanding of the legal system. Not all elements of the tort system, however, fit as comfortably within law-and-economics theory. This chapter next addresses a mysterious question concerning the nature of tort liability. Specifically, why is injury a requisite of liability? The chapter then tackles other vexing issues concerning the law and economics of tort.

B. The Injury Requirement

If the law-and-economics perspective on tortious behaviour is well founded, the tort system should presumably impose shadow prices on risky conduct. It should calibrate those prices to optimise output in the market — "output" being the number of accidents that occur, which in turn, depends on the amount of precautions undertaken and on activity levels. Thus, an economic approach to tort would create a price schedule for different kinds of potentially harmful conduct. Yet, if this is so, why must harm befall someone before the law recognises a tort? At first blush, this injury requirement might seem to reflect a non-economic function of the tort system – perhaps one founded on insurance, or simply the idea of "no harm, no foul".

The perceived tension, however, is superficial. In crafting optimal incentives, the law must foster "marginal deterrence". This concept refers to incentives that induce people who are already behaving inefficiently not to behave even more improperly. As Part 3 on criminal law explores, maintaining such incentives necessitates price steps, rather than uniform pricing. Applied to negligent conduct, a law that imposed a set penalty for identical behaviour regardless of whether injury ensued would not encourage those who are already acting dangerously to focus on not harming someone.

The risk created by driving at a certain speed beyond the limit, for instance, depends on many factors under the driver's control. In reality, care is continuously variable. A person's decision to behave negligently in one respect does not mean that there are no further gradations of care that she might simultaneously exercise. Conditioning liability in tort on an injury fosters marginal deterrence.

As an ancillary point, the injury requirement saves on costs by screening out cases of negligence that do not harm anyone. The legal system is expensive, so a doctrinal rule that excludes a class of cases without negatively affecting incentives is desirable.

C. Foreseeability, Proximity, and Causation

Economic analysis suggests that the law should impose a price schedule reflecting different accidents' harms, thus leading potential injurers and victims to internalise the social cost of their conduct. That effect, in turn, would induce those actors both to engage in optimal activity levels and to take optimal care. A challenge for the economic account, however, is that the law limits liability going beyond due care and causation. Specifically, the law conditions recovery on "foreseeability" in conjunction with proximity. Even if there were no dispute as to the negligence of an injurer's behaviour or as to causation, an accident victim cannot recover unless her injury was a foreseeable result of the challenged conduct. Indeed, a person owes no duty of care to those whose harm they could not reasonably foresee. As Lord Wilberforce remarked, in determining whether a duty of care exists:

> First one has to ask whether, as between the alleged wrongdoer and the person who has suffered damage, there is a sufficient relationship of proximity or neighbourhood such that, in the reasonable contemplation of the former, carelessness on his part may be likely to cause damage to the latter – in which case a prima facie duty of care arises. Secondly, if the first question is answered affirmatively, it is necessary to consider whether there are any considerations which ought to negative, or to reduce or limit the scope of the duty or the class of person to whom it is owed or the damages to which a breach of it may give rise.[2]

At first glance, this characteristic fits awkwardly with an economic account of accidents. If the courts relieve some tortfeasors of the injuries that they inflict, surely this facilitates negative externalities of the kind that justify liability in the first place? For some observers, the foreseeability and proximity conditions reflect a decidedly non-economic element of the tort system: fairness. If a person could not envisage his conduct's harming another, or if he possessed a sufficiently attenuated relationship with the ultimate victim, why should the law hold him to account for unfortunate consequences? This view is hardly ironclad, of course, as one can question the fairness of an innocent victim's being unable to recover when he is injured, albeit unforeseeably, by the negligent conduct of another. Regardless, the question from a law-and-economics perspective is whether foreseeability and proximity have an economic function. They do.

The law can only impart incentives to act efficiently if the actor can perceive the nature of any particular act to yield specific consequences. In this respect, foreseeability relates to causation. The tendency of an action to generate a particular outcome may depend on myriad factors, not all of which are predictable and all of which may interact in unexpected ways to yield atypical consequences. In this respect, a single "cause" for an outcome never exists. Instead, countless decisions and circumstances converge to produce a particular result, such that a vast number of "but for" causes invariably accompany any given conclusion.

This is not to say, of course, that every effect is unpredictable. Pushing someone in front of a train produces a foreseeable, even if not guaranteed, result. Conversely, prosaic actions can yield outcomes that one could not envision with any à priori confidence. An example might be the "butterfly effect", as to which some scientists postulate that the seemingly inconsequential act of a butterfly's flapping its wings in one part of the world can start a chain of events that culminates in a hurricane elsewhere. The larger point is that our universe is both overwhelmingly complex and interconnected, such that the ultimate result of a first action may not be discernible ex ante.

If a strict liability regime applied, then extricating the foreseeability requirement would create a de facto insurance regime for potential victims and tax activities that may be desirable. Even the most commonplace activities entail a non-eliminable risk of third-party harm. There are countless examples. One friend's phoning another for a chat may inadvertently lead to an injury by distracting the recipient of the call. If a worker takes a 15-minute mid-morning break to get a coffee at a

---

2 *Anns v Merton London Borough Council* [1978] AC 728, 751–52.

nearby café, it is possible that his walking along the sidewalk will lead another person to change his path and trip. Setting off for a long drive at one in the afternoon rather than at two could result in harm if, at a particular time and at a certain part of his journey, conditions are just right that his presence is a "but-for" cause of a crash.

In such circumstances, the action giving rise to an injury does not materially enhance the probability of the accident's occurrence. Harm may result from the act, such that cause and effect both exist, but that relationship is not such that one could discern a causative relationship *ex ante*. If we were to jettison the foreseeability condition for strict liability, the law would not spur additional cost-justified precautions. Nor would it change activity levels where compensable harms are sufficiently remote in light of the private gains of engaging in the behaviour.

Removing the foreseeability condition would affect efficiency. Employing strict liability without that condition would extend blanket insurance to victims through tort. The tort system, however, is an inefficient insurance mechanism. The social costs of employing judicial mechanisms are such that few, if any, accident victims achieve full recompense through the courts. Many are priced out of the judicial system altogether. Ultimately, inducing potential victims of unforeseeable accidents to self-insure is more desirable.

Strict liability applies at common law only to a subset of possible conduct, namely that which entails an unusually high risk of harm to others. This principle derives from *Rylands* v *Fletcher*, which held that the creator of an abnormally dangerous condition – in that case, the artificial accumulation of water on the defendant's land – "must keep it . . . at his peril, and if he does not do so, is *prima facie* answerable for all the damage which is the natural consequence of its escape".[3] Imposing strict liability in such circumstances comports with the economic account of tort, as activity-level changes are an especially important source of social welfare with respect to hazardous activities.

Outside the realm of such dangerous behaviour as keeping wild animals as pets or transporting explosives, some variant of the negligence standard typically applies. What is the economic function, if any, of the foreseeability requirement in these, more common scenarios?

The reader will recall that the economic goal of tort law is to maximise social welfare where activity levels are variable or (equivalently) to minimise the expected social costs of accidents where activity levels are fixed. In unilateral-care scenarios, victims or injurers, but not both, are best placed to minimise the sum of accident and care costs. In bilateral-care scenarios, both victims and injurers must take precautions to minimise expected social costs.

There are two situations in which efficiency requires potential injurers not to take care. First, unilateral-care scenarios where prospective victims are the lowest cost avoiders of accidents. Second, cases where no one is taking care minimises social costs. This last scenario is most likely to occur where the probability of an accident's occurring multiplied by the magnitude of associated injuries is low vis-à-vis the cost of precautions. That is likely the case with regard to those prospective plaintiffs whose vulnerability to harm is not the subject of a discernible causative relationship with potential injurers' behaviour.

When either of these two scenarios emerges, the courts should not hold the injurer liable. There are two ways in which the judiciary might achieve this result. First, if it applied a negligence regime, it could observe that the optimal amount of precautions spent by the injurer *with respect to the particular plaintiff* would be zero, in which event the court would not deem the relevant defendant, who declined to take care, negligent. Second, the courts could categorically absolve the defendant (and similarly placed potential defendants) of liability by holding that such prospective injurers do not have a duty of care toward certain classes of plaintiffs. In either event, the law would generate

---

3 *Rylands* v *Fletcher* [1868] UKHL 1.

desirable incentives with respect to victims. If victims are the lowest cost avoiders, a no-liability regime would spur them to take cost-justified precautions and to alter activity levels, if necessary. If the situation is one in which no parties should take care, a zero-liability rule will also lead to efficient behaviour.

The two approaches, however, are not equivalent. Consider a trial on: (1) the socially optimal level of care and (2) whether the precautions that the defendant took fall short of that ideal level. That approach has disadvantages. First, the social and private costs of employing the judicial process are considerable. If courts can exclude classes of cases in which the cost-justified level of care by certain kinds of plaintiffs toward a particular group of defendants is zero, then the law would save costs. The only caveat concerns possible Type I and II errors (incorrectly finding an injurer negligent when she was not, and falsely determining that an injurer was not negligent when she was, respectively) in both defining and applying the categorical exclusion, which necessitates caution with respect to both tasks.

Second, and consistent with the distinction between rules and standards (otherwise known as hard and soft law) a categorical rule of no liability creates legal certainty. A holding of no duty, therefore, may more effectively generate desirable behaviour. Judicial findings of negligence are apt to display a large standard deviation around the mean, such that, unless tortfeasors as a group are risk neutral, some potential injurers will be over-deterred or under-deterred, even if the courts succeed, on average, at setting liability equal to the socially optimal level.

The foreseeability condition may encapsulate situations in which it is better for a plaintiff not to take account of a particular defendant's vulnerability to harm. By holding that certain harms to certain individuals are unforeseeable – or (equivalently) by determining that plaintiff and defendant have an insufficiently proximate relationship – courts hold that no duty applies, and thus categorically relieve particular plaintiffs of liability. Efficiency justifies this approach if courts define non-foreseeability or inadequate proximity in a manner consistent with an injurer's maximising social welfare by not undertaking precautions with respect to the relevant victims.

Case law may illustrate this analysis. A leading UK decision on the scope of a person's duty, for example, is *Caparo Industries plc v Dickman*.[4] That case concerned an accountant's duty in preparing the financial statements of a company to the client's shareholders. There, the House of Lords determined that foreseeability was not in itself sufficient to warrant the imposition of a duty with respect to economic loss and, on account of inadequate proximity, held that "auditors of a public company's accounts owe no duty of care to members of the public at large who rely upon the accounts in deciding to buy shares in the company". The court quoted with approval Judge Cardozo's famous words that finding a duty in the absence of sufficient proximity would expose injurers to "liability in an indeterminate amount for an indeterminate time to an indeterminate class".[5] For a duty to exist, the court wrote, harm must be a reasonably foreseeable result of the defendant's conduct, there must be a proximate relationship between the parties, and it must be "fair, just and reasonable" to impose liability.

Economic analysis can give rigour to this standard, as well as to the court's holding. Such terms as "foreseeable", "proximate", "reasonable", "fair", and "just" pervade the law, but they are indeterminate. Although outlier cases residing at either end of the spectrum of applicable facts in tort cases will invite broad agreement as to the application of these terms, many cases lying in the middle will inevitably entail disagreement. Consistent with this observation, Lord Bridge in *Caparo* commented, with respect to "proximity" and "fairness", that the terms "are not susceptible of any such precise definition as would be necessary to give them utility as practical tests"[.] To say that an

---

4 *Caparo Industries plc v Dickman* [1990] 2 AC 605.
5 *Ultramares Corp v Touche* 174 N.E.2d 441 (1933).

economic approach to tort law can eliminate disagreement would be to go too far, but it can grant some specificity to legal standards.

As everything is, in a sense, foreseeable – because effects invariably have a vast number of "but for" causes – and since the concept of proximity is bewildering, there is significant benefit to the economic insight that courts should find that no duty attaches, whether on account of foreseeability or proximity, when the particular class of defendant is not the lowest cost avoider of the relevant risk. *Caparo* makes economic sense if the company's accountants were not the lowest cost avoiders of potential stock holders' mistaken investment decisions.

Rounding out this discussion requires one to specify what "unforeseeable" cannot mean. An intuitive, but incorrect, definition of the term is "of low probability". All manner of serious injuries are an unlikely result of a single act – for instance, the odds of dying in a commercial plane crash in the western world are several million to one. It does not follow, however, that low-probability injuries are unworthy of preventative precautions. The relevant criteria, rather, are the magnitude of the harm occasioned by an accident and the relative cost of precautions aimed at minimising that probability. It is for that reason that the duty of care may compel an airline to adopt a costly safety precaution, even if the percentage risk of harm that it negates is ostensibly small.

D. Problems in the Determination of Liability

1. The role of custom

A number of idiosyncratic features of the tort system warrant discussion. First, consider the relationship between the meaning of due care and the role of custom. We saw above that "due care" has a specific economic meaning: the private amount of precautions that minimises the expected social cost of accidents, where that cost includes the expense of taking care. With this in mind, what should we make of a defendant's argument that she was not negligent because her conduct comported with the customary level of precautions in the industry?

In the abstract, whether a defendant acted in a manner comparable to his peers in an industry would seem to be irrelevant to the question of whether he acted with appropriate care. As we have just seen, the definition of such care entails a comparison between the marginal benefit of an incremental increase in precautions and the marginal cost of that added care on the potential tortfeasor. In practice, however, courts have considerable difficulty in undertaking that analysis, so proxies may be helpful. Might industry custom be a suitable shorthand for due care?

From the perspective of economics, one can expect customary precautions to approximate the optimal level of care only if the custom arose in the absence of material externalities. When might this condition be satisfied? The economic purpose of the tort system, after all, is to correct a bargaining failure that arises between parties with inconsistent preferences due to high transaction costs. Thus, there are presumably few fields of tortious behaviour in which economists might expect the average tortfeasor to act with appropriate care in the absence of legal or regulatory intervention.

Nevertheless, bargaining failures concerning expected accident costs do not always occur. Modest transaction costs characterise these situations, such that regular contracting takes place between potential injurers and victims. The prime example involves professional services in which the expected cost of an expert's mishaps will affect the market price of her services. As a result, economists would expect the purveyors of such services, including doctors, lawyers, architects, and accountants, to experience incentives to take care independent of the tort system. The extent to which market forces induce those industries to adopt a customary level of care that approximates the optimal degree of precautions, however, depends on the level of competition in those markets.

Consistent with this analysis, the law of tort declines to draw an inference of due care when a defendant claims that he adhered to the level of precautions that are customary in high-transaction-cost environments. The courts would not alleviate a defendant of responsibility in a suit arising from a car crash should he argue that the speed with which he was driving was comparable to the average driver on the particular stretch of road on what the accident occurred. The courts reach a different conclusion, however, with respect to the relevance of custom in low transaction cost environments, where tortfeasors and victims routinely enter into contracts. This result, of course, is consistent with the preceding economic analysis.

Thus, under the classic *Bolam* test for the existence of negligence for professional negligence, the courts deferred to the relevant profession to determine the appropriate standard of care.[6] In *Bolam*, the High Court famously held that a person "is not guilty of negligence if he has acted in accordance with a practice accepted as proper by a responsible body of medical men skilled in that particular art". The House of Lords subsequently departed somewhat from that opinion in *Bolitho*, holding that "the court is not bound to hold that a defendant doctor escapes liability for negligent treatment or diagnosis just because he leads evidence from a number of medical experts who are genuinely of opinion that the defendant's treatment or diagnosis accorded with sound medical practice".[7] The court emphasised, however, that only in rare cases would the evidence justify a finding that a professional body of opinion is unreasonable.

2. Assumption of risk

If a plaintiff assumed the risk that led to his injury, the law will absolve the injurer of all responsibility. To assume risk in this fashion, a plaintiff must not merely have known a specific risk, but have affirmatively embraced it. For example, in *Ratcliff*, the court considered a plaintiff who had intentionally scaled barricades to be "the author of his misfortune".[8] In *Morris*, a person who, on the tail end of a pub crawl, got into a light airplane with his drunk friend in inclement weather assumed the risk of the inevitable.[9] The defence may also apply in less outlandish scenarios, most typically with respect to foreseeable injuries that people suffer while engaged in contact sports.[10] Assumption of risk will not apply, however, when the sports injury was intentional or otherwise outside the normal confines of the rules of the game.[11]

The doctrine of assumption of risk has a clear economic function. Specifically, assumption of risk applies in unilateral accident scenarios in which the victim is the lowest cost avoider. By declining to impose a duty on defendants in such circumstances, the law creates an incentive not only for potential victims to take care, but to reduce or eliminate activity levels. This makes eminent sense, as society should like to encourage people not to engage in such foolhardy escapades as getting into a plane with a drunk pilot or scaling protective enclosures.

3. Egg-shell-skull rule

An idiosyncratic feature of tort law is the egg-shell-skull rule. This doctrine, in its most simple expression, provides that an injurer must take her victim as she finds him. This does not mean that an injurer will be necessarily liable for any harm that befalls an unusually vulnerable person. For instance, an individual's coughing on a bus, thereby inducing a heart attack in a co-passenger, will not trigger liability in tort. This is, of course, because such harm is unforeseeable. Instead, liability

---

6 *Bolam v Friern Hospital Management Committee* [1957] 1 WLR 582, 587.
7 *Bolitho v City and Hackney Health Authority* [1997] 4 All ER 771.
8 *Ratcliff v McConnell* [1999] 1 WLR 670.
9 *Morris v Murray* [1990] 2 WLR 195.
10 *Wooldridge v Sumner* [1963] 2 QB 43.
11 *Smith v Emerson* [1986] ACTSC 36.

in tort only applies where it is reasonably foreseeable that a person of reasonable fortitude could suffer harm as a result of the injurer's actions. The egg-shell-skull rule applies when a tortfeasor breaches a duty, in which event the defendant will have to make good the harm experienced by the victim, even if that victim's injuries are greater than a person of typical fortitude would have suffered.

The egg-shell-skull rule plays an important economic function in ensuring that the law of tort properly aligns private incentives with the social optimum. If the courts declined to award damages sufficient to compensate for unusually severe injuries emanating from negligent accidents from which some injury was foreseeable, the result would be a windfall for some tortfeasors and a concomitant reduction in the price (expected liability) of engaging in risk-bearing activities. Specifically, if the law capped damages at the harm that an average person would suffer, negative externalities would continue to afflict potential injurers' decisions. Tortfeasors would reap the benefit of below-average damages for unusually strong victims, while escaping liability for the full amount of injuries to more vulnerable plaintiffs.

The law could avoid this result by awarding every successful tort plaintiff damages equal to the average harm experienced by victims of such accidents. Such a solution, however, would likely be unpalatable to the judiciary and, indeed, to the larger public because most accident victims would be variously under- and overcompensated.

E. Defective Products

Tort law forces people to internalise the consequences of their behaviour. It applies broadly, but defective products are among its most important objects. Countless goods are sold and consumed every day, making accidents ubiquitous. A 2010 US study estimated, for instance, that some 38,753,000 people sought medical help for injuries that they sustained related to a consumer product.[12] It also found that, in 2008, 35,900 deaths were related to such a product. The design, manufacture and use of goods are thus critical public-policy concerns.

1. Is tort necessary?

When should the law hold product manufacturers liable in tort for injuring their customers? One answer might be never. Recall that a premise underlying the economic account of tort is that transaction costs preclude injurers and victims from negotiating with one another. When bargaining is not feasible, the law steps in, imposing a price on a tortfeasor that approximates the one upon which the parties would have hypothetically agreed under the Coase Theorem. When it comes to products sold in the stream of commerce, however, transaction costs are not prohibitive. Manufacturers contract with distributors and retailers who, in turn, sell to consumers. Pervasive contracting is the defining trait here, which discounts the case for intervention by the tort system.

Yet, this analysis is incomplete. If perfect competition characterised real-world markets for consumable products, tort law would indeed be superfluous. Perfect information and choice would cause firms to implement all cost-justified precautions. Such conditions, however, are mythical. Information in most markets is asymmetric, and competition in some sectors is lacklustre. In the absence of the threat of *ex post* repercussions, profit maximisation may induce firms to avoid expensive precautions to which their customers will be oblivious. Thus, although widespread contracting

---

12 US Consumer Product Safety Commission, Consumer Product-Related Injuries and Deaths in the United States: Estimated Injuries Occurring in 2010 and Estimated Deaths Occurring in 2008 (2012). Available at: www.cpsc.gov/PageFiles/134720/2010injury.pdf.

indicates efficient behaviour, it does not guarantee it. Tort law can remedy information deficiencies, thus protecting consumers.

2. Strict liability for manufacturing defects

The defining trait of products liability – albeit a controversial one – is strict liability. The law holds companies liable for manufacturing defects that render a product dangerously defective, regardless of whether they took cost-justified precautions. This feature of the law derogates from the traditional legal principle, as expressed by Justice Holmes, that the "loss from accident must lie where it falls, and this principle is not affected by the fact that a human being is the instrument of misfortune".[13] Put differently, product liability reverses the principle of caveat emptor.

To contextualise this feature of the law, as well as the associated economics, we shall briefly discuss its development. Strict liability for defective products has long been a staple of US law, having emerged from the doctrine of *res ipsa loquitor*. Pursuant to that principle, a plaintiff could establish negligence by showing that a product would not ordinarily be defective absent negligence.[14] That rule emerged because injured consumers would often lack the information to establish neglect in the design or manufacturing process. In 1963, the California Supreme Court held that a "manufacturer is strictly liable in tort when an article he places on the market, knowing that it is to be used without inspection for defects, proves to have a defect that causes injury to a human being".[15] The court explained that this rule's point is to ensure "that the costs of injuries resulting from defective products are borne by the manufacturers that put such products on the market rather than by the injured persons who are powerless to protect themselves".

From there, strict liability quickly took hold in the United States. In 1965, the Second Restatement of Torts, § 402A, concluded that the seller of an unreasonably dangerous product that injures its user is liable, even if it "has exercised all possible care in the sale and preparation of [its] product[.]" Although the law varies from state to state, the predominant rule today is that manufacturers are strictly liable for manufacturing defects and for dangerously defective designs. As to the latter condition, establishing defectiveness entails a cost–benefit calculus reminiscent of assessing negligence or a consumer-expectation test.[16]

Strict liability took longer to take hold in Europe. A 1976 proposal by the European Commission, after much debate, gave rise to Council Directive 85/374/EEC.[17] At the time, most EU member states did not have strict liability for product defects. The 1985 Directive provided that a "producer shall be liable for damage caused by a defect in his product", which term encapsulates all movables, including electricity, excludes services and nuclear accidents, and was later amended to cover agricultural products. The injured consumer bears the burden of proving harm, a defect, and a causal relationship between the two, and faces a statute-of-limitations period of three years. Under the Directive, a "product is defective when it does not provide the safety which a person is entitled to expect[.]" It absolves producers in a number of instances, notably including when "the state of scientific and technical knowledge at the time when he put the product into circulation was not such as to enable the existence of the defect to be discovered" if the implementing Member State elects to include that provision in national law.

---

13 Wendell Oliver Holmes, *The Common Law* 94 (1881).
14 *Escola v Coca Cola Bottling Co of Fresno*, 24 Cal 2d 453 (1944).
15 *Greenman v Yuba Power Prods, Inc*, 59 Cal 2d 57, 62 (1963).
16 *See, e.g., Barker v Lull Eng'g Co*, 20 Cal 3d 413 (1978).
17 Council Directive 85/374/EEC of 25 July 1985.

3. Economic analysis of strict products liability

Having briefly surveyed the law, we can address the economics. Strict liability – in the absence of contributory or comparative negligence – induces cost-justified precautions and activity level changes on the part of the injurer. Such a liability regime is efficient in unilateral-care scenarios in which injurers are the lowest cost avoiders of accidents.

The economic purpose of no-fault liability for product defects thus seems axiomatic. Society wants manufacturers to produce merchandise that is safe for the consuming public. Strict liability in tort spurs companies carefully to manufacture their products. Yet, there is more to the economic account than just that. Recall that negligence imparts the same incentive to take care as strict liability. The latter regime, however, forces manufacturers to pay the full social costs of unavoidable defects in their products. This feature of the law has a number of economic effects.

First, by imposing all costs of product defects on producers, the law forces those companies to pool expected accident costs across their sales, thus increasing the price of the relevant product. The greater the non-eliminable risk of harm inherent in a product – that is, the greater the expected cost of accidents that cost-justified precautions cannot eliminate – the larger the increase in the price of the product will be. That price increase conveys otherwise-undiscernible information about product quality and safety to consumers. Without the price signal, they could not determine product defects at the time of purchase. This strict liability-induced price increase decreases output in the market for the relevant good, as marginal consumers shift their purchases toward safer (and hence, other things being equal, cheaper) substitute products.

Second, strict product liability shifts risk from consumers to manufacturers. Consumers are likely risk averse relative to companies that design, manufacture, and sell goods. A serious product accident may be catastrophic to an individual, and thus represent a large proportional loss of her utility. Diminishing marginal utility of income suggests that such consumers are likely to be risk averse. A manufacturer, however, can spread the risk of product accidents across its entire output, thus transforming into a near-certain expense what would be a probabilistic cost with respect to any one product sale. If strict liability shifts risk from risk-averse consumers to risk-neutral manufacturers, this effect is efficient.

These economic principles support strict- liability rules governing product defects. Nevertheless, for reasons explored in Part 6, the cost and associated inefficiency of the contemporary litigation process detract from these justifications. This is all the more true if, as theory predicts, strict liability increases the number of cases filed. Although strict liability reduces the average cost per case filed by eliminating the question of fault, the greater volume of lawsuits may magnify the total costs of litigation. Furthermore, if risk-shifting is the predominant goal of strict products liability, society and potential victims would be better off with insurance. Moreover, depending on competition and safety regulation in the relevant market, the tort system may have only a modest incremental effect on care. These concerns have led some economists to question the case for strict products liability.[18]

In light of these observations, what can we say about today's legal regime? Consider the EU's 1985 Directive on defective products. Its recitals justified the legislative act on several bases. These include: (1) divergent laws between the Member States may distort competition; (2) "liability without fault on the part of the producer is the sole means of adequately solving the problem . . . of a fair apportionment of the risks inherent in modern technological production"; and (3) "the contributory negligence of the injured person may be taken into account to reduce or disallow such liability[.]"

---

18 *See* A. Mitchell Polinsky and Steven Shavell (2010) 'The uneasy case for product liability', 123 Harv L Rev 1437. *But see* John C.P. Goldberg and Benjamin C. Zipursky, 'The easy case for product liability: A response to Professors Polinsky and Shavell' (2010) 123 Harv L Rev 1919.

A brief discussion of the economics frames these observations in an interesting light. First, as discussed above, strict liability forces producers to include in the price of their product a premium to cover the non-eliminable risk of harm. As goods manufacturers in a negligence setting pay a price of zero for non-economically avoidable accidents, their prices include no such increase. That being the case, asymmetric laws on liability governing producers may create unequal conditions of competition. Indeed, consumers would receive false price signals.

Second, the recital's reference to a "fair apportionment" of risk is intriguing. One might read the Council's language as suggesting that the only appropriate division is one in which all risk lies on manufacturers. Yet, many injuries are not fully compensable in pecuniary damages, for which reason even strict liability exposes consumers to economic risk. More generally, one can give this fairness concern economic expression through asymmetric appetite for risk. Large-scale producers can apportion small but non-eliminable risks across a large volume of output, such that they are close to risk neutral. Individual consumers vulnerable to injury accounting for a large share of their well-being, however, are more likely to be risk averse. Shifting risk from them to upstream producers thus enhances utility. Strict liability promotes this goal more than negligence, though it does not do so as well as insurance.

Third, the Council's view on contributory negligence comports with economics. Consumers are sometimes efficient avoiders of accidents, paradigmatically where they use products danger-ously or in a manner other than instructed. Strict liability without contributory or comparative negligence would impart no incentive to avoid taking those actions. Injecting that additional component, however, causes both producers and consumers to take care, and producers to raise prices. This produces a lower number of products bearing inherent dangers.

Other features of the Directive are consistent with economics. A producer will not be liable if he did not put the product into circulation or, if he did put it into the stream of commerce, the defect appeared afterward. Both features reflect straightforward principles of causation addressed above. An interesting element, however, is that no strict liability ensues if the producer did not sell the item for profit. Presumably, the provision reflects an aversion to "taxing" not-for-profit – and thus welfare-enhancing – activities. Nevertheless, it may not withstand economic scrutiny. An economic purpose of strict liability is to induce sellers to factor non-eliminable risks of harm into the sales price, thus signalling latent risks that cause consumers at the margin to substitute safer alternatives. That benefit holds true regardless of the profit status of the seller, and it is lost in this instance. Although strict liability suppresses activity levels by potential tortfeasors, the reduction is desirable when it reflects a trade-off between the pertinent social gains and losses.

Separately, in its 2000 (second) report, the Commission observed that the 1985 Directive "encourages producers to do their best to produce safe products . . . and[,] second, once these preventive measures have failed and accidents have happened, it allows the victims to obtain redress from the producers". An economist would observe that a negligence regime, properly enacted, would also encourage producers to do their best to produce safe products. The difference is that strict liability suppresses activity levels efficiently when placed on the lowest cost avoider. The second feature that the Commission identified is true vis-à-vis the negligence standard alternative. Strict liability does indeed serve an insurance function. The problem is that it serves that function inefficiently, due to the social and private costs of litigation. Actual insurance, be it public or private, is much better placed to promote this goal.

A final feature of the 1985 Directive concerns its impact on the prevalence of suit. By allowing suit by all of those whom a product defect injured, regardless of fault, strict liability opens up a larger number of positive value lawsuits. The result of moving from negligence to no-fault liability, holding other factors constant, ought to be an increase in the number of cases filed. Although each Member State has distinct legal systems and varying consumer-protection legislation that comple-ments defective-product liability, the evidence to date is consistent with the theory. In its fourth and latest report on the 1985 Directive, the Commission found that from 2006 to 2010, "some Member

States, including Austria, France, Germany, Italy, Poland and Spain, recorded an increase in the number of product liability cases brought under national laws transposing the Directive". Similarly, it found "an increase in the number of out-of-court settlements for compensation reached between the injured party and the person who caused the damage". Interestingly, it concluded that "the costs of the action discourage this type of proceedings in some Member States, for example the United Kingdom".

The final feature of the Directive suitable for fruitful discussion is the development-risks defence, which most countries have adopted. Specifically, most Member States do not recognise strict liability when the state of scientific or technological knowledge when the product was circulated was not such as to allow the defect to be discovered. This element of the law would be hard to explain if an insurance function were the predominant motivation. If EU legislators' larger aim, however, is to encourage due care and optimal activity levels, then this derogation of liability makes sense. As the section on foreseeability above explains, if tortfeasors cannot discern a causal relationship *ex ante* between an act or omission and an enhanced possibility of harm, then imposing liability will not alter behaviour.

F. Intentional Torts

Thus far, we have treated the preferences of tortfeasors as sacrosanct and worthy of equal inclusion in the social welfare calculus. By respecting both the desire of such individuals to engage in risky behaviour and the inconsistent preferences of potential victims to be free of danger, we invite application of the Coase Theorem. The application is, of course, hypothetical in light of the preclusive transaction costs that stymie any arrangement between potential injurers and victims. Nevertheless, this conceptual approach implies that a non-zero rate of accidents may be desirable in light of people's legitimate preference to engage in potentially harmful conduct.

Crediting potential tortfeasors' preferences makes intuitive sense, however, only when those preferences pertain to activities that enjoy some minimal level of social acceptance. The analysis becomes more problematic when we encounter instances of deliberate wrongdoing. In committing such intentional torts as battery, assault, false imprisonment, and intentional infliction of emotional distress, tortfeasors act with the purpose of bringing about a harmful result. As with the other kinds of torts considered above, the problem is one of inconsistent preferences, except that, here, the private benefit to the tortfeasor derives directly from the victim's suffering. This would be a distinction without a difference under a classic utilitarian approach that would incorporate all actors' utilities in the social-welfare function. Yet, there is something problematic about a person's deriving satisfaction from another's distress, and so many would argue that the law should decline to credit tortfeasors' preference in this setting.

If we give people's desire to commit intentional torts a zero weighting, it follows that, putting aside the costs of operating the legal system, the optimal output in the market for such torts is zero. In that event, the efficient sanction is one that, at the lowest possible cost to society, achieves the maximum deterrent to engaging in such behaviour. Consistent with that principle, the law permits victims of intentional torts to recover exemplary (or punitive) damages that go beyond the private harm that the relevant plaintiff suffered.

Yet, we do not need to reject tortfeasors' preferences to reach this result. Unlike many other torts, in which a defendant may engage in risk-bearing behaviour that bears dangers to a broad population of potential victims, in the intentional-tort cases, the defendant acts with specific intent as to a specific person or property. Transaction costs, therefore, are unlikely to be preclusive when the relevant parties are small in number and easily identified. Thus, if it were efficient for a positive amount of intentional torts to take place, we would expect parties to negotiate to that result.

Obviously, such arrangements rarely occur in reality. A person is unlikely to agree to be assaulted, battered, or falsely imprisoned at a price that the tortfeasor would be willing to pay. This fact reveals that those committing intentional torts bypass the implicit market process, and instead engage in a coerced transfer, the result of which is presumptively inefficient. As is always the case when people decline to avail of the market in low transaction cost settings, the law should impose on coercive transfers a price that is sufficiently high as to dissuade their occurrence. Mutual consent is the benchmark of efficiency.

This discussion marks an appropriate point at which to transition to a problem that closely relates to intentional torts – specifically, crime.

Key Points

- The "reasonable person" takes the precautions that an average member of society would have to undertake to minimise the expected social cost of an accident.
- Generally, the law declines to substitute a particular defendant's attributes for those of an average person because it is expensive and error-prone to estimate the cost of taking care for each individual before the court. Exceptions arise when it is easy to tell that a person's cost of achieving a certain reduction in expected accident costs is higher or lower than normal. Thus, for example, the law does not hold children to the same level of care as adults.
- The law will only hold a person liable in tort if he injures someone. This "harm requirement" helps to create marginal deterrence, encouraging a person acting negligently along a particular dimension of conduct to take what other steps are available to minimise the likelihood of injury. It also reduces the number of lawsuits filled, thus saving on litigation costs.
- The foreseeability requirement absolves an injurer of liability if no discernible causative relationship existed *ex ante* between the negligent conduct and the ensuing injury. Tort law creates valuable incentives only insofar as a rational actor could determine that altering her behaviour in a particular way would change the likelihood of an accident. Punishing utility-producing behaviour for a random result is unlikely to advance social welfare.
- Limiting the duty of care to reasonably foreseeable harm to a proximate victim may be an efficient proxy for unilateral-care scenarios in which victims are the lowest cost avoiders.
- Custom is a reliable shorthand for due care only where potential tortfeasors and accident victims regularly contract with one another, and where harms result from those contractual relations. In other settings, customs may incorporate negative externalities that the law should try to eliminate.
- Assumption of risk absolves a defendant of responsibility where the plaintiff embraced the danger inherent in the defendant's conduct. Its economic function is to eliminate liability in unilateral-care scenarios where victims are the lowest cost avoiders.
- Product defects are subject to strict liability, which economics justifies on account of forcing manufacturers to include in the price of their goods a premium reflecting the non-eliminable risk of a defect. That price increase signals valuable information to consumers about product risk, causing them to substitute toward safer goods. Nevertheless, as strict liability increases the number of lawsuits filed and may have only a modest effect on incentives to take care, some economists conclude that negligence would be the superior rule.
- Intentional torts implicate different concerns because it becomes difficult to credit the utility of engaging in injurious conduct when the purpose of the activity, as distinct from its unintended effect, is to hurt others. This feature raises the question whether the optimal number of intentional torts is zero. That issue serves as a suitable juncture to move to the economics of crime.

References and Further Reading

Books
Friedman, David D., *Law's Order: What Economics Has to Do with Law and Why It Matters* (2000) Ch. 14.

Miceli, Thomas J., *The Economic Approach to Law*, 2nd edn (2004) Ch. 2.

Polinsky, A. Mitchell, *An Introduction to Law and Economics*, 4th edn (2011) Chs. 4, 6, 9, and 14.

Posner, Richard A., *Tort Law: Cases and Economic Analysis* (1982).

Posner, Richard A., *Economic Analysis of Law*, 8th edn (2011) Ch. 6.

Shavell, Steven, *Foundations of Economic Analysis of Law* (2004) Ch. II.

Articles
Calabresi, Guido, 'Some thoughts on risk distributions and the Law of Torts' (1961) 70 Yale LJ 499.

Hylton, Keith N., 'Duty in Tort Law: An economic approach' (2006) 75 Fordham L Rev 1501.

Landes, William M. and Posner, Richard A., 'Causation in Tort Law: An economic approach' (1983) 12 J Legal Studies 109.

Part 3

Criminal Law

1   An Economic Account of Criminal Behaviour   105

2   Optimal Criminal Sanctions   112

3   Problems in Criminal Law   127

Chapter 1

An Economic Account of Criminal Behaviour

Chapter Contents

A.	Introduction	106
B.	Categorically Inefficient Crime	106
C.	Potentially Desirable Crime	108
Key Points		111
References and Further Reading		111

A. Introduction

From an economic perspective, a person commits a crime for the same reason that he undertakes any other action – it satisfies a preference. Jeremy Bentham famously opined that: "[T]he profit of the crime is the force which urges man to delinquency: the pain of the punishment is the force employed to restrain him from it. If the first of these forces be the greater, the crime will be committed; if the second, the crime will not be committed."

Law and economics assumes that people respond to incentives. If so, criminals' proclivity to offend is not fixed, but depends on the opportunity set and the relative price of goods (actions) within the consumption bundles. Thus, in deciding whether to commit an outlawed act, an individual would consider: (1) the private utility that she would gain from the prohibited behaviour, (2) the price – (i.e. the expected sanction that the state imposes, as well as other negative consequences) and (3) the utility associated with substitutable forms of behaviour, both lawful and unlawful. For any form of criminal conduct, then, one can theoretically chart a demand curve, which would allow society to set the desired level of output in the relevant shadow market (i.e. the amount of the relevant crime) by assigning an appropriate price for engaging in that prohibited behaviour.

This Part explains how economic theory can aid policymakers seeking to regulate criminal behaviour through an incentive mechanism. Much of this analysis is positive – focusing on the likely effect of proposed criminal laws on behaviour. This chapter, however, focuses on the normative question of what kind of conduct is appropriately condemned. Recall that the economic criterion is efficiency, which focuses on the satisfaction of revealed preferences. This perspective yields insights into the nature of criminal behaviour. The reader should be aware, however, that economics is by no means the only lens through which to analyse criminality. Part 1 above explored the nature of the efficiency criterion and its relationship to larger issues of justice.

We begin with the efficient amount of crime. If you thought the answer was zero, you may be incorrect. Determining the optimal amount of criminal behaviour depends on two questions. First, is there a basis beyond efficiency that justifies criminal prohibition? For instance, if obeying the law is an absolute ethical obligation, normative economics may be unconvincing. Second, should criminals' preferences inform the social-welfare calculus? Although this last query is weighty, its resolution may be unnecessary to crafting an economic theory of criminal law. It may be possible to identify the desirable amount of crime regardless of whether we credit criminals' preference to offend.

For the purpose of the ensuing discussion, this chapter employs the term "crime" broadly to encapsulate all acts that society affirmatively prohibits with threat of sanction. Such abolition distinguishes criminal prohibition from liability in tort, which is contingent on actual injury.

B. Categorically Inefficient Crime

There are at least two sorts of crimes that, in the absence of enforcement costs, society ought to eliminate on the basis of efficiency: (1) those motivated by a desire to harm third parties, such as murder and battery and (2) those that do not take hurting another as their principal goal, but that are coercive transfers that take place in low transaction cost environments.

1. Crimes that people commit to inflict suffering on others

Could there be an "efficient" murder? Beginning with the classic utilitarian view, it might be possible that the utility to a murderer (and to any third parties whom the victim's demise benefits) might exceed the disutility that the victim and those whom his passing negatively affects experience. Even if one embraced this possibility, despite its obvious moral problems, the difficulty of inter-personal comparisons of utility would preclude turning it into a workable rule of law.

Moving into the realm of neoclassical welfare economics, the act of murder represents a situation somewhat reminiscent of the problem of tort: inconsistent preferences. To resolve such incompatibility within the law and economics framework, we appeal to the Coase Theorem and ask how the parties would have resolved the conflict in a zero transaction cost environment. This inquiry yields three reasons why murder is necessarily inefficient.

First, we might ask whether the prospective murderer would agree to let the victim kill him in return for compensation. The parties would not reach such a deal, and so the act is inefficient. Second, murder – especially premeditated murder – takes place in low-transaction cost settings, as the stakeholders are few in number and identifiable. A person committing the crime therefore bypasses the bargaining process, running roughshod over another's autonomy. Finally, one might conclude that a person's preference to kill is entitled to zero weight. In that event, the act is obviously inefficient because victims and those close to them suffer, but no one (including, by assumption, the murderer) gains. Nevertheless, this last method by which to resolve the question of murder's efficiency – though straightforward in the case of this egregious crime – raises problems of its own.[1]

There is, however, a possible complication. What happens if our assumption that a victim would never agree to his murder fails to hold true? Part I referenced the gruesome 2001 case of Armin Meiwes, who killed and subsequently ate Bernd Jürgen Brandes with his permission. There is also the morbid tale of Sharon Lopatka, who, desiring to be tortured and killed, entered into such an arrangement in 1996 with Robert Frederick Glass. Both of these cases implicate the question whether consensual homicide is murder. From the perspective of law and economics, might one deem such arrangements "efficient"?

The short answer is that macabre agreements of this kind are theoretically "efficient" only if: (1) the contracting parties are both informed and competent, and (2) negative third-party effects do not negate the private "benefit" that the parties experience. Given the bizarre and horrific nature of Armin Meiwes's and Sharon Lopatka' agreements, the assumption that the parties were of sound mind and knowledgeable about the experiences to which they were agreeing is, to put it mildly, questionable. Furthermore, much of society experiences revulsion at the result of such arrangements. If one credits the preferences of third parties to live in a society in which such contracts do not take place, agreements of this sort are inefficient if the contracting parties could not compensate those negatively affected and still be better off themselves. It seems unlikely that this condition could be satisfied.

It follows that the prohibition on murder and other crimes the principal purpose of which is to harm victims are on sound economic footing. Zero output of such crimes would be efficient as an abstract matter, though, as we shall see, the cost of employing the legal system, and the fact that not all criminals respond rationally to incentives, mean that society has to accept a non-zero output in the "market" for such acts.

2. Property crimes that take place in low transaction cost settings

The second category of crimes that society should seek to eliminate, as a matter of efficiency, are coercive transfers that take place in low-transaction cost environments. Examples include robbery, burglary, and larceny in situations where the necessity defence would not apply. These acts are inefficient because those perpetrating them do so in circumstances where they could have bargained for the relevant resource, but chose not to do so.

---

1 *See* Part 1, Chapter 1, Section 2 *supra*.

Economists would not credit a larcener's argument that the stolen item is worth more in his hands than it was in his victim's. It would not even matter if the larcener happened to be correct. Had he, in fact, valued it more than the owner, the parties would have agreed on a mutually beneficial price. Such an arrangement would have effected a Pareto-superior outcome, assuming no third-party effects. If the larcener declined to bargain notwithstanding low transaction costs, then the law rightly condemns his act. Exceptions arise when the willingness and ability to pay metric upon which efficiency relies departs sharply from the subjective utility for which the proffered price is a proxy. For instance, few would disagree that stealing food to avoid starvation is justified. This point should remind the reader to be cognisant of the theoretical underpinnings of normative law and economics, so as to appreciate the limits of the theory.

Generally, though, the economic conclusion against coerced property transfers in low bargaining cost environments is sound. Zero output of such crimes is therefore economically desirable, free of such complications as the cost of the legal system and the difficulty of inducing some criminals to act rationally in response to punitive incentives. Nevertheless, this discussion does not suggest that property crimes could never be desirable, even within the framework of economics. Robbery, burglary, or larceny could conceivably enhance welfare in high-transaction-cost environments where the parties would have reached agreement, had they only had the opportunity to do so. Necessity applies to such cases.

C. Potentially Desirable Crime

Society should not eliminate all crime. Some readers may have difficulty accepting this assertion, but efficiency sometimes requires the reduction, rather than elimination, of certain criminal acts. The reasoning behind this view relates to the economics of tort law. There may be some desirable offences for the same reason that the efficient number of accidents is greater than zero.

Some readers may be sceptical that the law would outlaw an activity, and yet embrace greater than zero amounts of the behaviour. Holding that line, however, would require assuming that the fact of illegality is itself dispositive. If this were the case – in other words, if only the badge matters – the mere attachment of the "criminal" label would in itself deprive an action of all its social legitimacy. This cannot be correct. If it were, a despotic government, for example, could strip otherwise socially desirable behaviour of all substantive value simply by passing a statute outlawing it.

Let us explore crime that the law should not seek to reduce to vanishing point.

1. Necessity

Involuntary property transfers are presumptively inefficient. When parties freely reassign rights, the ensuing redistribution enhances social welfare in the absence of negative third-party effects. Coercive transfers, by contrast, need not satisfy the relevant parties' preferences, so there is no à priori basis to deem them desirable. That is the economic reason why society prohibits theft and other property crimes. Nevertheless, free bargaining is not always possible, even when the case for mutually beneficial exchange is compelling. Criminal law must take care, therefore, to avoid imposing so high a price as to preclude welfare-enhancing, albeit involuntary, property transfers in high transaction cost settings. It typically does so through the doctrine of necessity.

There are many examples of such conduct. Driving above the speed limit can be a crime in extreme cases. If the utility of the driver enjoys zero weight, then the optimal amount of such speeding is zero, so the law ought to calibrate its penalties to achieve that level of output. Yet, one must credit the preferences of drivers to drive above the speed limit in at least some circumstances. If one's friend is bleeding to death, one would properly drive unusually quickly, assuming that the benefit of getting to the hospital promptly exceeds the associated risk to others.

Second, suppose that a hiker were staggering through a remote part of the country during a blizzard and came across an unoccupied cabin that would provide refuge from the storm. Should he break into the lodge to save himself? The owner's absence creates preclusive transaction costs where it is surely efficient for the parties to agree to the hiker's taking refuge. The law would still be economically justified in punishing the unauthorised breaking and entering, as long as the price imposed were calibrated not to dissuade efficient instances of such conduct. In practice, the defence of necessity would apply, thus alleviating the hypothetical hiker of responsibility, save for an obligation to the lodge owner to make good any harm that the entry caused to the property.

2. Minor infractions

The second category of illegal, but sometimes desirable, conduct involves minor infractions that do not always require intent. As the social cost of such outlawed activities is modest, the private benefits can outweigh those costs. Representative "offences" include double parking, littering, and noise pollution. Zero output in the market for such infractions would be undesirable. For instance, few would argue that the law should impose such a high price on double parking that no rational driver would ever do it. There are situations in which even the most law-abiding citizen would temporarily double park to achieve a sufficiently important end. In setting a sanction − or "price" − for those who engage in such conduct, the government should take care only to dissuade improper incidences of such behaviour, where "improper" means where the social costs outweigh the benefits. Were the law to impose too great a penalty, it would deter some desirable behaviour.

3. Voluntary contracts with modest third-party costs

Voluntary contracts between informed adults are generally efficient under the Coase Theorem. Nevertheless, because negative externalities can harm third parties not privy to an agreement, some freely bargained arrangements reduce social welfare, and should thus be proscribed. The economic insight is that criminal law should impose a price equal to the negative externality. If all actors are risk neutral, such a sanction would deter the prohibited agreement in the average case, but not in outlier cases where its benefit is unusually great. This does not mean that the courts should decline to find a criminal violation in those unusual cases. Nor does it suggest that an actor should evade criminal sanctions in such an event. It merely implies that the optimal price is not one that would eliminate all such agreements.

Consider alcohol. Most western countries regulate the hours within which one may buy and sell such drinks. Suppose that a country bans alcohol transactions after 11 pm, as the United Kingdom did for many decades prior to 2005. If a customer both desires, and is willing to pay for, a beer at 11:30 pm and if the pub owner and staff are happy to work longer to make more money, then an opportunity for mutually beneficial exchange exists. As the arrangement would be efficient as between the contracting parties, the only law and economics case for prohibiting it would be if it carried sufficiently negative third-party effects. No doubt, such effects may exist and could justify the described law. If the prospective consumer of an additional beer is driving, for instance, the contract's negative repercussions are axiomatic. Other consequential effects of late-night drinking, such as public disorder or domestic abuse, would undermine the efficiency of the banned contract, though the capacity for such adverse consequences is context specific. Degraded work performance from late-night drinking during the work week is also an unwelcome result. Collectively, these negative effects may justify regulating the hours in which people may purchase alcohol. Yet, the consequences of some such contracts will be positive. To maximise social welfare, then, the law should impose a price that would deter all such agreements other than those carrying unusually great benefits or small costs. As pointed out above, however, this does not mean that the publican and customer should be let off the hook if caught.

The analysis is similar for gambling, against which the law has historically taken a dim view. Betting carries little capacity for third-party harm when the contracting parties act responsibly. Depending on the prevalence and magnitude of people's failure to make informed decisions as to their welfare and those for whom they are responsible, however, the law may justifiably prohibit gambling. Yet, there are many cases in which private actors' entering into such arrangements will be efficient, which suggests that the criminal sanction should not be prohibitively high. The law's prohibition of marijuana is less convincing still, as Chapter 3 of this Part explores in greater detail. Such soft drugs are to be distinguished from their powerfully addictive counterparts, of course.

Prostitution may be a more serious example. If two informed, competent, adults consensually agree that one will pay the other for sex, the arrangement would appear to be efficient in that it satisfies both parties' preferences. Of course, this assumes that the person providing the service is not herself a victim, whether of human trafficking or social circumstance. If she is, not only may her preference to enter into such contracts not be her own, but the typical link between satisfying a person's preference and advancing that individual's welfare becomes attenuated. Even where there is no victimhood or coercion – such that there is a voluntary contract between two knowledgeable adults – the arrangement still may not be efficient. It depends on off-setting third-party effects, for those whom the arrangement negatively impacts are not privy to the arrangement. There may be many victims: beyond significant others, there is the problem of the infrastructure that may grow up around prostitution services that make it more likely that more women in the future will wish to engage in the activity. In short, criminal prohibition of prostitution stands on solid economic footing. It is not obvious, however, that such contracts are inefficient in every case. Thus, attempting to eliminate every such arrangement through severe sanctions would be hard to square with normative economics.

In sum, many restrictions on contract are difficult to justify on efficiency grounds, especially when the law can separately regulate such contracts' undesirable third-party effects (such as by punishing drunk driving, human trafficking, domestic abuse, battery, and so on). The larger issue, though, is that punitive sanctions sufficiently severe to eliminate private contract with modest third-party effects would be undesirable. If arrangements of this sort, on the whole, reduce welfare, then the appropriate price equals the social cost of the crime (assuming unit demand elasticity). This is the familiar concept of a Pigouvian tax, which imposes a cost on an actor equal to the negative externality created by her behaviour. In the circumstances where the private gains of a disfavoured contract outweigh the concomitant social harm, the expected price should not be so high as to dissuade all instances of it.

Finally, contracts between consenting, informed adults become more difficult to condemn as third-party effects become increasingly attenuated. Consensual arrangements that are more obviously efficient within the law and economics paradigm are intimate acts between people behind closed doors. Despite the lack of material third-party effects, the law historically regulated such affairs with a heavy hand, prohibiting a range of sexual acts undertaken privately. It targeted homosexuality, in particular. The fact that the law has evolved toward a more permissive approach suggests that rules prohibiting efficient bargains (i.e. voluntary contracts between adults with modest third-party effects) are likely to erode over time.

4. Unilateral acts bearing private costs

The final category is minor crimes that do trivial violence to third parties. The prohibition of such unilateral acts is mysterious from the perspective of law and economics. Mysterious, that is, unless one rejects the preferences of those who are predisposed to commit the prohibited act. John Stuart Mill decried the prohibition of actions that do not violate the harm principle because such behaviour carries no material third-party effects. Consider, for examples, paternalistic rules against driving without a seat belt or riding a motorbike without a helmet. If individuals determine their own welfare better than the government can, then laws that deprive people of choice based on costs that are private to themselves are unjustifiable. Such a view can be either principled (i.e. invariant to the specific facts) or contingent on the question whether, in the particular circumstances, the government is a better judge of an individual's well-being that that person herself.

Key Points

- Economists view crime as a problem of inconsistent preferences.
- Some people prefer outlawed acts over their closest legal alternatives, and thus will offend unless the law imposes a price exceeding the private benefit of the crime.
- There are two categories of crime: those that are necessarily inefficient and those that efficiency may occasionally justify.
- The latter category bears similarities to tortious conduct, which the law wishes to restrict to a non-zero level reflecting the legitimate preferences of potential injurers and victims to engage in their desired behaviours. So, for example, necessity may justify otherwise-criminal, but life-saving, actions in dire circumstances. Society ought not to impose such a draconian price as to deter outlier, justified offences.
- Conclusively inefficient crimes include coercive transfers in low transaction cost settings and those driven by a desire to harm others. Examples include robbery where the defence of necessity would not apply and murder. The economic goal of criminal law is to achieve the lowest possible level of such crime at the least social cost.
- Assuming unit demand elasticity and risk neutrality, the right criminal sanction for potentially efficient offences equals the social cost of the crime. For instance, if double-parking costs society on average £100, the expected penalty should equal that amount. The price of the infraction in such cases should be fixed, and indifferent to the subjective value that an offender places on the act. For that reason, society can legitimately punish "efficient crimes".
- For categorically undesirable crimes, the optimal criminal sanction (assuming zero enforcement costs) is one that exceeds the private utility that the offender expected to derive in carrying out the act. The optimal price thus depends on the characteristics of each offender.

 ## References and Further Reading

Books:
Friedman, David D., *Law's Order: What Economics Has to Do with Law and Why It Matters* (2001) Ch. 15.
Miceli, Thomas J., *The Economic Approach to Law*, 2nd edn (2008) pp. 268–72.
Posner, Richard A., *Economic Analysis of Law* (2011) §§ 7.1, 7.8.

Articles:
Becker, Gary, 'Crime and punishment: An economic approach' (1968) 76 J Political Economy 169.
Ehrlich, Isaac, 'Crime, punishment, and the market for offenses' (1996) 10 J Econ Persp 43.
Ihlanfeldt, Keith, 'Neighborhood crime and young males' job opportunities' (2006) 49 JL & Econ 249.
Kelly, Morgan 'Inequality and crime' (2000) 82 Rev Econ & Stats 530.
Shavell, Steven, 'The optimal structure of law enforcement' (1993) 36 JL & Econ 255.

Chapter 2

Optimal Criminal Sanctions

Chapter Contents

A.   Introduction   113

B.   Regulating the Crime Level   113

C.   Driving Output to Zero: Minimising Inefficient
      Crime at the Lowest Cost   123

Key Points   125

References and Further Reading   126

A. Introduction

The previous chapter distinguished crimes that are always inefficient from those that may sometimes be meritorious. This chapter explores how the law should calibrate criminal sanctions to effect an efficient price schedule. The ideal price depends on whether one seeks to eliminate or merely to reduce the crime in question. Bear in mind, though, that one can use the following theory to effect a deterrence regime tailored to any policy goal, even if it means seeking to eliminate "efficient" crimes. The positive wing of law and economics, after all, is an analytic framework that one can use as a tool to advance a chosen policy.

With respect to necessarily inefficient crimes, the economic question is how to achieve the lowest level of output in the relevant market at the least social cost. As we shall see, the constituent elements of the term "cost" in this calculus are important. For those crimes that are typically, but not always, inefficient, the policy challenge is to set a price schedule that deters all inefficient criminal actions, but not efficient ones. With respect to both kinds of crime, the goals of reducing output and conserving resources are in tension, which complicates the definition of the optimal criminal sanction.

We shall begin with how to craft optimal prices for crimes that may sometimes enhance welfare. Section B undertakes this analysis, explaining the trade-off between the magnitude and probability of criminal punishment in imparting incentives at a given social cost and exploring the economic merits of such alternative sanctions as imprisonment, fines, shaming devices, and corporal punishment. All of these issues pertain to the question how best to calibrate criminal penalties to suppress output to the desired level.

Section C explores the distinct question how optimally to eliminate categorically undesirable offences. A principal insight is that, due to the social expense of operating the criminal-justice system, the economic challenge is to minimise the joint cost of unjustifiable crime and criminal law enforcement.

B. Regulating the Crime Level

For potentially efficient offences, one can think of the economic problem of crime as one of negative externalities. So construed, crime is another example of a recurring phenomenon explored in this book: a misalignment of private and social incentives drives inefficient behaviour. The law's challenge is to realign those incentives. In crime, as in tort, a lack of altruism leads some people to benefit themselves at others' cost.

How can society correct this problem? Where the person "causing" the harm happens to be the lowest cost avoider – typically, the offender rather than the victim is the lowest cost avoider in the criminal setting – a Pigouvian-tax solution is appropriate. Thus, to induce prospective criminals not to offend, the law should impose a sanction equal to the social harm of the crime. Such a tax would induce rational, risk-neutral people only to commit crimes where it is efficient for them to do so. Calibrating the criminal sanction to social harm is the right way to punish crimes that we generally, but do not always, want to deter. If the law were instead to impose a restitutionary remedy, imposing a price equal to or exceeding the criminal's gain, it would dissuade desirable instances of crime. Similarly, it may be a mistake to equate punishment with the principal victim's harm, which may understate the social cost. Thus, for potentially efficient crimes, the correct sanction equals the harm that the relevant act caused society.

This solution, however, masks complicating details. First, the "potentially efficient crimes" qualification is important. The optimal punishment outlined above makes sense only if the law credits the offender's preference to commit the crime. If society concludes that such preferences are under-serving components of social welfare, however, the optimal "price" does not equal the social harm of the act. That sanction would encourage a person to commit an act that bestows greater utility upon him than it imposes disutility upon society. Although this act may be desirable from a utilitarian perspective, it may be problematic from another. For such crimes, the desirable "price" exceeds the reservation price of any prospective criminal who might desire to commit the relevant act.[1]

In summary, some prohibited actions are potentially efficient. For such crimes, the optimal sanction introduced above – imposing a Pigouvian tax on the criminal – makes sense as a first approximation. A crucial question, however, concerns the constitution of that tax. Criminal punishment can take several forms, from traditional prison sentences and fines to shaming devices and draconian penalties like corporal punishment. Should society be indifferent between different forms of sanctions as long as the courts shape each individual punishment so that it equals the social cost of the prohibited act? May considerations of efficiency justify one form of punishment over another? We shall now address these questions.

1. The role of the probability of conviction

A punishment equal to the social harm of a criminal act will not deter if the probability of arrest and conviction is less than 100%. In reality, the odds of successfully prosecuting a criminal are far from a sure thing. The Crown Prosecution Service reported for 2010–2011, for example, that it successfully convicted 79.7% of defendants committed for trial in the Crown Court.[2] That statistic is impressive, but it does not reflect the probability that the state will not find, arrest, and charge offenders in the first place.

To understand the problem that less than certain punishment creates, consider this example: Assume that (1) the harm of a particular crime is equivalent to £100,000, (2) the criminal sanction equals that injury, (3) a criminal derives private satisfaction from committing the act of £80,000, and (4) the state has a 70% chance of apprehending and convicting him. In this event, the criminal will rationally commit the crime if he is risk neutral because the benefit of the act (£80,000) exceeds its expected cost (£70,000).

In reality, of course, few aspiring criminals compute numerical payoffs in deciding whether to offend. The law and economics model, though, abstracts from reality to generate testable predictions. The key insight from the preceding example is that, in imposing sentences that equal the social harm of the crime, courts under-deter outlawed behaviour if aspiring criminals perceive – as they surely do – that the odds of the government's catching and punishing them are less than 100%.

How might society remedy this problem? There are two possibilities. First, given a fixed punishment for a given crime, it could devote more funding to policing and prosecutorial services, thus increasing the probability of detection and, hence, the expected cost of committing the crime. The principal problem with this solution, however, is that the funds spent on financing the criminal-justice system are themselves a social cost, which the government must fund either through taxes that distort behaviour or by borrowing and thus further increasing long-term debt and reducing the future wealth of the country.

The second approach is to change the severity of the penalty. The idea is simple: to equate expected punishment with the social cost of the crime, the government must increase the sanction to offset the chance of getting off the hook. So, for example, if the probability that society will catch and convict a person who commits a certain crime is only 50%, the court will have to impose a

---

1 The reservation price in this context is the price at which a criminal is indifferent between committing the outlawed act and not doing committing it.
2 Crown Prosecution Service, Annual Report and Resource Accounts 2010–2011. Available at: www.cps.gov.uk/publications/reports/2010/annex_b.html.

penalty equal to twice the social harm of the offence to deter a risk-neutral prospective criminal. Only then will the expected cost of committing the relevant crime equal its social cost. In short, the optimal punishment varies in inverse proportion to the likelihood of successful prosecution.

One might employ this principle as a policy lever to minimise the combined social costs of crime and punishment. If the probability of conviction for a given crime is presently 20%, but the cost in terms of police, prosecutorial, judicial, and prison resources is great, society could maintain the same level of deterrence by sharply cutting back on funding for the criminal system and by enhancing the punishment. Assuming risk neutrality, this analysis implies that an ideal criminal system would involve: (1) a vanishingly small probability of detection and conviction; and (2) a penalty of near-infinite severity.

There are problems, however, with this approach. In the first place, penalties must become increasingly draconian as the probability of conviction becomes attenuated. This creates objections that are outside the law and economics framework, though they are of sufficient importance to warrant discussion.

Savage penalties for acts that, individually, carry only modest social harm create ethical issues concerning proportionality between crime and punishment. Few western countries would accept life sentences for such crimes as shoplifting, tax evasion, drug possession, unlawful consumption of alcohol, and less-serious instances of battery or assault. Not only would many people perceive an injustice based on such disproportionate punishment, but issues of horizontal equity also arise. If the law put in place a low-probability/high-sanction criminal justice system, would it be fair that a great many people would commit an act and get off scot-free, while one unlucky person would pay a terrible price for his misconduct? Judge Posner has written that such an outcome is unobjectionable because all parties face the same probability of punishment *ex ante*, so the few for whom the *ex-post* world proves unfortunate can no more be heard to complain than can the vast majority of people who play a lottery and lose. This point has teeth, but it remains true that asymmetric *ex post* punishment of similarly situated people conflicts with many people's moral intuition.

Furthermore, criminals have positive – often very high – discount rates. For that reason, attempts to magnify *ex ante* deterrence through longer jail times can flounder. This is because 20 years' imprisonment, for example, is less than twice as bad as 10 years in prison. To achieve an expected cost equal to the social harm of the relevant crime in a low-probability of detection environment, one might have to embrace increasingly long prison sentences or draconian corporal punishment. Few in the western world would consider flogging, let alone more severe instances of corporal punishment, to be an acceptable punishment, especially for acts other than the most serious imaginable crimes.

As the next section addresses in more detail, the high punishment/low probability approach to crime will be inefficacious to people who prefer risk or heavily discount the future. The group of individuals for whom this effect is most likely to be true is teenagers and young adults, whose not-yet-fully-matured faculties and judgment lead to heavy discounting of the future and embracing risk. For potential criminals drawn from these ranks, the opposite policy prescription may be true: society should implement a low punishment/high probability strategy. Empirical studies have shown that swift and certain punishment is more likely to change risk-preferring and high-discounting individuals' behaviour than attenuated risks of severe sanctions.[3]

---

3 *See, e.g.*, Raymond Paternoster, 'The deterrence effect of the perceived certainty and severity of punishment: a review of the evidence and issues' (1987) 4 Just Q 173; James Q. Wilson and Barbara Boland, 'The effect of the police on crime' (1978) 12 L & Soc'y Rev 367; Jack P. Gibbs (1968) 'Crime, punishment, and deterrence', 48 Sw Soc Sci Q 515. This is Beccaria's famous view. Cesare Beccaria, *On Crimes and Punishments* (Henry Paolucci trans., Macmillan, 1986) (1764) p. 58 ("The certainty of a punishment, even if it be moderate, will always make a stronger impression than the fear of another which is more terrible but combined with the hope of impunity; even the least evils, when they are certain, always terrify men's minds[.]").

Nevertheless, society can operate its criminal justice system more efficiently in some settings both by decreasing the probability of detection and conviction, and by increasing the magnitude of the sanction. It is, after all, no requisite of a legitimate criminal justice system that a punishment never exceeds the magnitude of the harm that the prohibited act inflicted upon society. Nor is it a requirement that society convicts everyone who has committed an offence before it can legitimately convict some who are guilty. For these reasons, the insight that society can lower the aggregate social cost of crime and punishment by lowering the likelihood of punishment and by increasing its magnitude is important. This holds true even though the criticism noted above may warrant rejection of the extreme implications of the low probability/high sanction approach to criminal law.

2. Price effects and risk preference

As we have seen, improbability of conviction and high discount rates are two factors that affect optimal criminal sanctions. Neither factor alters the theory that, for potentially desirable crimes, efficient punishments reflect the magnitude of the harm that the prohibited act visits upon society. Courts should craft punishments that, discounted to present value, create an expected cost *ex ante* equal to the negative externality inherent in the crime.

This conclusion assumes that criminals are risk neutral. Relaxing this assumption alters the optimal sanction. This section addresses the implications of risk aversion and risk preference, respectively, on the efficient price schedule for various crimes. The reader will recall that a risk-averse person would prefer (1) a 100% chance of losing £1,000 over (2) a 20% chance of losing £5,000 and an 80% probability of losing nothing. Conversely, a risk-preferring individual would prefer the 20% odds of losing £5,000 over the certain loss of £1,000. A risk-neutral person would be indifferent between the two.

Criminals' appetite for risk affects the incentives that sanctions impart. Suppose that the social cost of a crime is £10,000, that the probability of detection and prosecution is 100%, and that the sanction that the courts impose is also £10,000. Given the expense of maintaining the guaranteed conviction of offenders, however, society reasons that it can maintain optimal deterrence at lower cost by reducing the likelihood of arrest and conviction to 20% and by increasing the punishment to £50,000. Risk-neutral criminals would see the shadow price of an offence as identical under both regimes. For those potential offenders, the 20%/£50,000 is more efficient.

For risk-preferring criminals, however, the low probability/high punishment approach presents a lower price than the original regime. Thus, an expected cost equal to the harm of the crime may not adequately deter. Of course, the opposite holds true for risk-averse criminals: the 20%/£50,000 regime would encourage them not to commit crimes where it would be efficient for them to do so.

Thus, it may not always be efficient proportionally to increase the severity of the sanction and to reduce the probability of its imposition. If the potential criminals who are drawn to a particular crime prefer risk, the optimal policy is likely to increase the quality and number of policing, prosecutorial, and judicial resources, thus enhancing the likelihood that the state will catch and prosecute perpetrators. Although such a move would increase the cost of operating the criminal justice system, it would facilitate a more effective deterrence for risk-embracing prospective criminals.

Finally, the fact that substitutes for a particular crime may, in themselves, be illegal has potentially important policy implications. If the government seeks to crack down on unacceptably high levels of a particular crime, say burglary, by increasing the price to criminals of committing that act, the government may inadvertently increase demand for other substitute crimes, such as robbery. The result of the government's policy could be a reduction in burglaries and a proportional increase in robberies, which may not enhance social welfare. To avoid this result, the government would also have to increase the price of all illegal substitutes, though such a move may implicate marginal deterrence. Section 2 explores this in more depth.

3. Price elasticity and the cost of punishment

Venturing deeper into the efficient sanction compare: (1) the marginal benefit of increasing the expected punishment for a crime to (2) the marginal cost to society of imposing that greater sanction. The relationship between these marginal costs and benefits depends on the "price elasticity of demand" for the relevant crime – a concept that captures the extent to which an increase in price alters demand. If demand for a given crime is perfectly inelastic, even an infinite increase in expected punishment will not affect output in the market for the prohibited behaviour. The implication in such a case is that society should impose no criminal sanction; doing so would carry social costs without benefit. A representative example may be insane people, whose behaviour the law cannot influence through incentives. More generally, inelastic demand for a crime demonstrates that the marginal cost of increasing the sanction is positive (see Figure 3.1).

If demand for a crime is perfectly elastic ($\varepsilon = \infty$), any increase in price will drive output to zero. The more elastic demand is for crime, therefore, the more effectively the law can achieve its goal of spurring optimal activity levels. Indeed, where demand for a crime is elastic, incrementally raising the sanction enhances social welfare. Thus, the marginal "cost" of deterrence is positive. The implication is that the efficient criminal sanction *exceeds* the injury that the pertinent crime visits upon society. As a result, the government would efficiently deter some desirable crimes because doing so would occasion disproportionately large savings in policing, judicial, administrative, and penitentiary resources. This result may seem odd – why would we want to deter efficient offences? The answer is that, in the absence of necessity, it is not a defence that a crime was socially desirable, for which reason society punishes efficient and inefficient crimes alike. In the case just described, it is less expensive to deter a desirable crime than it is to facilitate it and punish it.

In reality, demand for most crimes is quite inelastic. For these crimes, the optimal sanction is *less than*, not equal to, the social harm of the offence. More specifically, the efficient penalty equals the social harm minus the marginal cost of achieving deterrence. The greater the demand inelasticity for a crime, the greater the marginal cost of effecting deterrence will be, hence the lower the optimal sanction. In the extreme case noted above of infinite inelasticity, the marginal cost is also infinite, so the efficient punishment is zero.

It is only for those crimes for which unit elasticity exists – such that an increase in price carries an exactly proportional decrease in demand – that society should equate the price of the prohibited

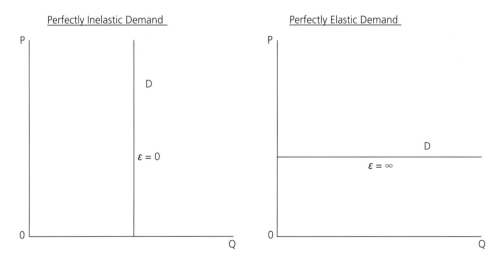

Figure 3.1

activity to its social harm. This, of course, is consistent with the first approximation of the optimal sanction for potentially efficient crimes introduced above. It holds true, however, only in rare cases where the price elasticity of demand for a given crime is neither elastic nor inelastic.

We now proceed to consider the nature of the criminal sanction. Governments can impose a given level of disutility on an offender in different ways. Some punitive mechanisms may deter at lower social cost than others. This fact yields a general conclusion that fines are apt to be superior to imprisonment in most settings.[4]

4. The relative superiority of fines over imprisonment

There are several reasons why fines are typically more efficient than incarceration. First, imprisoning a person is expensive. One report estimated that the cost per prisoner per year in England and Wales was £41,000.[5] The Irish Prison Service determined in its 2010 annual report that the average cost of a prison place was €70,513.[6] Economists have estimated US annual expenditure on corrections at approximately $75 billion.[7] Yet, the social costs of imprisonment exceed the pecuniary expense of funding the prison system. The opportunity cost of the punishment, in terms of prisoners' foregone productive contribution to economic activity, can be significant when those incarcerated had access to lawful employment. This lost benefit extends beyond the term of imprisonment as having been previously jailed detracts from a person's future employment prospects.

The human costs are also severe, not only in terms of families being torn apart, but also in incubating negative social traits, including violence, in those whom the law exposes to prolonged incarceration. Finally, positive discount rates and conditioning to the harshness of prison life mean that courts have to increase prison sentences disproportionately to affect a given increment in deterrence. Almost everyone has a positive discount rate, which means that, in the absence of deflation, a sum today is more valuable than the same amount in a year's time. If an individual has a discount rate of 5%, a prison sentence of 10 years is not 10 times more unpleasant than a one-year sentence. It is only 8.1 times worse.

This last point is important, for criminals, as a group, appear to have higher discount rates than the average member of society. This makes intuitive sense, for one would think that crimes would appeal to people who care about immediate satisfaction and less about future consequences. We would also expect people with such traits disproportionately to engage in pleasurable activities that inure to their long-term detriment, such as taking addictive drugs, which may increase the demand for crime over time, thus further enhancing the proportion of criminals with unusually high discount rates. It is no statistical anomaly, therefore, that young people commit a disproportionate share of crimes; the brashness associated with youth goes hand-in-hand with a tendency excessively to discount the future.

---

4 Although "fines" typically refer to the required provision of a certain pecuniary amount by a defendant, one can substitute "community service" for "fines" for the purposes of the ensuing discussion. Such service, of course, imposes a cost on offenders, which includes both physical effort and the opportunity cost of their time. Many of the advantages of fines discussed below apply equally to community service sanctions.

5 See, e.g., 'Prison Numbers in England and Wales Reach Record High'. Available at: http://news.bbc.co.uk/2/hi/uk_news/8640399. stm (23 April 2010); Kevin Marsh, 'The Real Cost of Prison: Moral, Social and Political Arguments for and against Prison Are All Very Well. But What About Value for Money?' Available at: www.guardian.co.uk/commentisfree/2008/jul/28/justice. prisonsandprobation (28 July 2008).

6 Irish Prison Service, *Annual Report* 2010 p. 36. Available at: www.irishprisons.ie/documents/Irish_Prison_Service_2010_Annual_ Report.pdf.

7 John Schmitt *et al.*, The High Budgetary Cost of Incarceration, Centre for Economic and Policy Research (2010) p. 2. Available at: www.cepr.net/documents/publications/incarceration-2010-06.pdf.

If it is true that criminals heavily discount the future, imprisonment may be an especially costly, and hence inefficient, means by which to achieve a desired level of deterrence. If the discount rate for a prospective criminal were, for example, 20%, a 10-year sentence would only be five times worse than a one-year sentence. In such circumstances, it may be more efficient to impose a penalty that imposes its full disutility in the instant time period.

Against the serious drawbacks associated with imprisonment, fines display a variety of attractive features. The first advantage is a lack of administrative expense. Suppose that a person is indifferent between a jail term of six months and a fine of £50,000. Implementing the latter sanction imposes the same level of disutility – thus achieving an equivalent level of deterrence – but entails none of the costly apparatus required to confine a person, such as the capital and labour costs of maintaining confinement facilities and hiring prison officers. Second, a monetary penalty does not remove a person convicted of a crime from the work force. Third, the pecuniary income which fines generate enables the government to fund welfare enhancing projects (e.g. those designed to reduce the demand for various crimes). Fourth, monetary penalties do not expose a convicted individual either to the violent culture common to many penitentiaries or to a network of criminals who may educate others on how best to carry out crimes and to evade police detection. For these reasons, properly enacted fines possess many advantages.

Furthermore, involuntary confinement harms actors other than those imprisoned. A person's loved ones and dependents suffer when society deprives them of the person whose support and company they need. This might not matter from the perspective of efficiency if the prospective criminal's utility function fully incorporated such third-party suffering, for the pain imposed on those close to the convicted person would, in itself, be a source of deterrence. Yet, a potential criminal's utility function will not often encapsulate the full injury that imprisonment imposes on her family and friends. Thus, prison sentences can carry welfare-reducing third-party effects that fines, as a substitute punishment, do not (at least to the same degree).

(a) Limitations on the use of fines

There are two major shortcomings to fines. The first is that there is a *de facto* ceiling to the disutility that they can impose. Some offenders would prefer any sum over a material stint in jail. For serious crimes, it may be impossible to craft a pecuniary sanction with sufficient bite to deter. Second, fines implicate problems of horizontal equity. The first such difficulty is that, for conclusively inefficient crimes, judges must calibrate fines to the circumstances of each defendant to impose appropriate disutility. Many would fault one person's having to pay £20,000 and another having to part only with £10,000 because the latter is a dedicated saver, for whom losing money produces severe anxiety, and the former is a spendthrift.

A further equitable problem is that some criminals are judgment proof. Thus, one cannot always craft monetary penalties to equal the harm that a crime creates. A criminal may be destitute and have neither the aptitude nor the inclination to obtain future work, and so the law can garnish no wages. As a result, a prison sentence may be necessary to achieve deterrence. Yet, the courts may be able to deter another person who has sufficient wealth through a pecuniary sanction. Efficiency would seem to justify fining the latter and imprisoning the former. The more serious the crime, and hence the greater the requisite fine to achieve optimal deterrence, the more pronounced this effect would likely be.

Would the courts' fining affluent criminals and imprisoning less well off offenders amount to unjust differential treatment? Many people would indeed see wealth- or class-based discrimination in such asymmetric punishment. Nevertheless, if courts moulded fines to impose a cost exactly equal to the equivalent jail sentence, punishing the offender with either sanction would not constitute differential treatment. Both punishments, by assumption, would impose precisely the same private cost on the offender. If society accepts this argument, it should expand the use of fines to more serious crimes. There would be much hostility to such a system, however, and this would probably reflect scepticism in the judiciary's ability to craft fines truly equivalent to corresponding jail terms. If a rich person would prefer a fine over what the court considers to be an equivalent jail sentence, then the judiciary's imposition of fines for well-off offenders and custodial sentences for those less well off would be both inefficient and unfair. It is presumably for such reasons that the law generally reserves monetary punishments for less serious offences, the social cost of which most convicts can pay for monetarily.

A further weakness in using fines is that they cannot incapacitate. There is a strong argument that society should lock up dangerous criminals who are predisposed toward violence and thus a menace to the populace. To be clear: this prescription does not justify the pre-offence internment of those whom the government deems threatening. For those whose actual crimes demonstrate an incurable propensity to savagery, however, imprisonment carries significant social benefits. Indeed, this may be one function that the prison system serves well; removing demonstrably unstable, vicious individuals from the streets makes society safer than it would otherwise be. Fines cannot achieve this.

In sum, there are strong efficiency reasons that favour society's making greater use of fines and less use of imprisonment, especially for non-violent crimes.

(b) Calibrating fines to the social cost of the offence

How should courts tailor monetary sanctions to the traits of the defendant before them? The answer depends, in part, on the nature of the crime. For offences that entail stealing money, the appropriate fine equals the amount of money stolen magnified to reflect the probability of evading detection and conviction. This holds true regardless of whether the relevant defendant is rich or poor because any given amount of money carries the same purchasing power in anyone's hands. A rational person contemplating stealing £1,000 will not do so if the expected cost of doing so equals or exceeds £1,000, regardless of whether that person is a billionaire or indigent.

The same does not hold true, however, of non-monetary crimes. Here, the optimal fine differs depending on whether the goal is to accept some efficient instances of the crime or to eliminate it entirely. If it is the latter, the judiciary must calibrate the fine such that it necessarily renders the crime unprofitable *ex ante*. The magnitude of that fine, however, depends on the marginal utility of income of the relevant defendant. If, as is commonly believed, each additional pound confers less utility on the recipient than the last, then the courts would have to impose larger fines on well-off defendants and more modest fines on those who are less affluent. Of course, if the goal of the pertinent criminal law is not to vanquish the prohibited act entirely, but to accept some efficient instances of the same, the optimal fine has nothing to do with the characteristics of the defendant before the court. Instead, assuming risk neutrality and unit elasticity of demand, the expected cost of the fine must equal the social harm of the pertinent crime.

More generally, how might the judiciary craft sanctions that reflect the social harm of different offences? The fact that the relevant variables are not always commensurate complicates the task. The easiest cases involve coerced transfers of wealth, in which the pertinent harm is coterminous with the amount of money stolen. More difficult cases arise when the relevant injury carries a significant emotional component. Violent crimes, in particular, cause emotional suffering and physical trauma that are difficult to quantify in pecuniary or custodial terms.

There is no simple answer. Nevertheless, resolving this dilemma is no more difficult than defining a sanction that either "fits" the crime from an equitable standpoint or that appropriately assuages victims' suffering. There is apt to be significant variation in courts' attempts to mould sanctions to equal social injury, but if the judiciary strives to satisfy this equality, it may be as likely to err on one side as the other, in which case the expected sanction will equal the harm of the crime. If offenders are risk neutral, this outcome would generate desirable incentives.

5. Alternative sanction mechanisms

(a) Shaming devices

An interesting sanction is the shaming device. Examples include a court's requiring an offender to display a prominent sign on his front garden, his front door, or on his car that states the crime that he committed. Some police departments use "name and shame" websites to display photographs and biographical information about those whom they arrest for sexual offences, such as soliciting prostitution. However, the fact that some such penalties apply to people who are not yet, and may never be, convicted is problematic.

Some perceive such punishments as crass and distasteful, while others consider it to be an appropriate sanction for those who commit acts of moral turpitude. From the perspective of law and economics, however, a striking feature of these punishments is the quite severe disutility they can impose. The impact of such penalties will vary considerably from person to person, but for some individuals, there is no question that social humiliation is a grave penalty. The greater a defendant's (self-perceived) stature in the community, the greater the disutility engendered in being shamed. For white-collar defendants in particular, these sanctions may be effective.

Also from the perspective of efficiency, shaming devices entail minimum expense for the state. They share many of the benefits of fines in achieving cost-effective deterrence and, unlike fines, they may be effective against judgment-proof individuals. Although shaming devices cannot create a price equal to the social harm of more serious crimes, they may be effective as applied to relatively minor offences. It will be interesting to see whether they become a more integral part of the judiciary's armoury.

(b) A case for corporal punishment?

To round out the present discussion, consider a controversial question: should the state employ corporal punishment, such as flogging, beating, or even killing, to deter criminal offences? Global beliefs on this subject vary tremendously. It is a central tenet of modern European political thought, for example, that physically punishing wrongdoers is unjust. By contrast, certain US states routinely execute people convicted of capital offences. Only four countries – China, Iran, Saudi Arabia, and Iraq – execute more people each year than the United States. Momentarily putting aside any moral views on the propriety of corporal punishment, consider this form of criminal sanction through the lens of deterrence alone.

First, like fines, corporal punishment imposes an immediate cost on the relevant criminal once the legal process has been exhausted. This could ameliorate the problem of high discount rates. Second, and unlike fines, physical punishment is not subject to wealth constraints. Third, corporal punishment potentially shares a common advantage with monetary penalties in that it does not necessarily require protracted expenditure by the state to maintain prison facilities and support infrastructure.[8]

There are, however, efficiency objections to the use of such punishment. The first concerns the expense of due process, which is necessary to reduce costly mistakes. Error costs rise in proportion to the seriousness of the crime and the severity of the relevant punishment. The greater the social harm of a prohibited act, the more exacting the penalty must be. The more draconian the criminal sanction, of course, the greater the cost of judicial error.

The death penalty is the most severe instance of corporal punishment that any western country presently imposes (though worse practices of torture and execution occurred under the sanction of law in historical times and certain non-western countries still use horrible means of execution). Before imposing the ultimate price, courts must be acutely sensitive to the danger of Type I errors (i.e. erroneously condemning an innocent person).[9] To minimise the cost of such "false positives",

---

8 This last point, however, is less strong and may, in fact, vanish if courts insist, as they should, on costly, heightened levels of due process to guard against mistakenly imposing serious corporal punishment.

9 William Blackstone famously commented that "[i]t is better that ten guilty persons escape than one innocent suffer".

the law demands more exacting levels of due process which, in turn, increases the social resources that the criminal justice system requires to implement capital punishment. Indeed, in the United States today, executing a person costs more than sentencing him to life imprisonment without the possibility of parole. This is due to the almost ceaseless appeals process and the associated cost of ongoing legal representation that takes place to satisfy due process requirements.

The due process cost of enforcing the more serious variants of capital punishment, in conjunction with the impossibility of compensating an innocent person whom the courts have accidentally sentenced to death, constitutes strong efficiency arguments against the use of the death penalty. The questionable economic case for such punishment is further exacerbated by the haphazard nature of its employment and the extended time that passes before the state carries out the sentence, both of which dilute any marginal deterrence that the death penalty creates.

Of course, the efficiency based discussion of corporal punishment may be little more than a detail for those who accept the moral premise that this form of criminal sanction is immoral, undignified, inhumane, and ultimately destructive of the legitimacy of the government that employs it. The law and economics treatment of such punishment, however, should remind the reader that the field does not purport to offer unqualified policy prescriptions on divisive, morally charged topics. It merely offers normative conclusions founded upon a particular set of values encapsulated within the efficiency paradigm. These values may or may not prove convincing to a legislature or court in any given case.

6. Conclusion

The preceding pages have explored optimal criminal sanctions. Lest the volume of information prove overwhelming, this section provides a summary of the key insights. First, many crimes have efficient output levels that exceed zero. Nevertheless, in the absence of legal intervention, markets for these proscribed activities will produce excessive criminal behaviour. Preclusive transaction costs prevent price systems' arising and coordinating behaviour. To remedy this market failure, the law should act in lieu of market mechanisms and impose a price on criminal conduct equal to the harm of the prohibited act. This conclusion assumes risk neutrality and unit demand elasticity.

Constructing this price, however, is not easy. First, not all ways of imparting a price are equally efficient. Where they are feasible, fines are generally superior to prison sentences. Second, as the probability of apprehending and successfully prosecuting a criminal will always be less than 100%, the court must increase the magnitude of the imposed penalty so that its *ex ante* expected value equals the social cost of the offence. Yet, even if the courts accomplish this task, the ensuing price that prospective criminals experience will be the efficient price only if they are risk neutral. Many criminals, however, are likely to embrace risk, which means that a price calibrated to risk-neutral offenders will under-deter them. The courts, therefore, have to increase the sanction further for risk-preferring offenders, though if the ensuing punishment is uniform this means that risk-neutral lawbreakers will be over-deterred, and risk averse criminals even more so.

A further difficulty with constructing an optimal price is that many prospective criminals discount the future at unusually high rates. The more that a person values today over tomorrow, the more likely he is to do something that most would consider foolish – specifically, to commit acts that inure to one's immediate benefit, but bring larger costs over time. There are a number of examples, but one is knowingly to start taking an addictive drug. Deterring people who engage in hyperbolic discounting with the threat of lengthy *ex-post* sanctions, such as long jail sentences, is ineffective. As a result, dramatic and potentially unjust hikes in the severity of punishment may be necessary to effect a given level of deterrence. Alternative punishments that society can impose in the short term, such as fines (or, more controversially, "name and shame"), are likely to provide equivalent deterrence at lower social cost.

A key factor in fashioning sanctions lies in the optimal trade-off between the magnitude of the sanction and the probability of its being enforced. Assuming risk neutrality, the optimal theoretical punishment is one that is almost infinitely severe and as to which a criminal has a vanishingly small probability of being subject. Such low probability/high punishment sanctions, however, are likely to be efficient when applied to risk preferring or future-discounting potential offenders. Here, it may be better to impose milder sanctions and to hire more police officers to increase the probability of detection and prosecution. For potential criminals who are more likely to be risk neutral or risk averse, however – such as older people and perhaps those in high-earning positions – the low-probability/high-punishment approach may be the correct one. So, for instance, one might efficiently tackle securities offences, such as fraud and insider dealing, in this manner.

C. Driving Output to Zero: Minimising Inefficient Crime at the Lowest Cost

Tailoring a price schedule that respectively suppresses and facilitates undesirable and efficient behaviour is, as we have just seen, complicated. Some crimes, however, never enhance social welfare. Such offences include murder, rape, kidnapping, and aggravated battery. How should society seek to eliminate crimes that are always undesirable? The answer is to impose a price greater than the expected benefit of committing the crime. Unlike the optimal punishment for potentially desirable crimes discussed above, this approach is restitutionary. Instead of looking to the magnitude of the harm done, it asks how much the criminal stood to gain from the act and imposes a penalty greater than this amount. Nevertheless, creating optimal deterrence remains devilishly tricky, even when the goal is to drive a particular crime to vanishing point.

1. Criminal penalties can harm social welfare

The first complication is that it is difficult to identify the subjective value that an offender places on a non-pecuniary crime. Without knowing that amount – the "reservation price" – a judge cannot ensure that the expected cost of the imposed sanction exceeds that value. Lacking means to estimate the utility that a crime conferred on a defendant, the judiciary might instead impose a sanction that greatly exceeds the social cost of the crime. Only by imposing a draconian penalty could the courts be confident that the price will necessarily exceed the criminal's gain, thus incentivising output to drop to zero.

Yet, this introduces a larger problem. Punishments that are sufficiently harsh to inculpate the desired incentive effect may be barbaric, such that their imposition would detract from social welfare. This is especially likely if the probability of detection and prosecution is not high, which requires an even greater punishment to deter. Thus, the first major difficulty in driving output to zero is that the cure may be worse than the disease. Punishment itself may detract from efficiency.

There are three ways in which criminal sanctions can undermine social welfare. First, if one credits offenders' welfare, punitive sanctions violate criminals' preferences and can therefore be efficient, if at all, only in the Kaldor-Hicks sense. Indeed, one could envision circumstances in which the cost of a sanction to the criminal would exceed the consequential incentive benefits occasioned by the fierce punishment.

Second, even if one disenfranchises criminals, such that their preferences are irrelevant to the social welfare calculus, law-abiding members of the community may abhor the infliction of punishments that they consider to be cruel. In such a society, draconian sentences may reduce welfare if they do not occasion gains that exceed those costs. The severity of those costs depends on the relevant community's tastes, which economists typically consider to be exogenous. For instance, citizens of western European countries generally oppose capital punishment, which is widely practised in the United States, China, Iran, Iraq, Saudi Arabia, Indonesia, and elsewhere.

Third, and again ignoring criminals' preferences, those who care about the offenders being sentenced surely represent a legitimate component of the social welfare calculus. Such people, who include defendants' families, friends, and other loved ones, suffer as a result of the imposed sanction.

There is a theoretical counter-argument, however, to the point that imposing severe sanctions can reduce welfare. This is that courts should never have occasion actually to impose the relevant sentence because, if the price were indeed sufficiently high, no-one would ever commit the forbidden act. All that is necessary is that the law credibly threaten to impose the relevant punishment.

Unsurprisingly, this point has little weight. It is true that, as the price elasticity of supply for all crimes is greater than zero, imposing a high price on inefficient crimes will cause the quantity of those offences to drop. Were it otherwise, supply would be perfectly inelastic, in which event the optimal criminal sanction would be no punishment at all. Imposing any sentence that reduced the welfare of an offender, that offended the sensibilities of the citizenry, or that simply entailed some administrative cost for the state would detract from social welfare without achieving an offsetting gain.

Nevertheless, output will never collapse entirely, regardless of the severity of the sentence imposed. As the next chapter explains, although prospective criminals react as a group to incentives in a manner consistent with the law of demand, individual actors' capacity for rational calculation varies considerably. This variance is not just from person to person, but within individuals themselves. Most people are prone to bouts of temper and other cognitive impairments that cause them temporarily to magnify the importance of the present over the future, thus leading them to make imprudent decisions. Regret, which is a universal emotion, evidences the fact that everyone is capable of making poor choices. This does not mean, of course, that anyone can commit appalling crimes or that, even in the blindest rage, the prospect of a probable, swift, and severe criminal sanction would not deter many people. It does mean, however, that even the cruellest penalty will not eliminate all crime.

Even if one dismisses criminals' preferences against punishment as irrelevant, and rejects the possibility that citizens may prefer not to live in a society that implements draconian criminal sanctions, other problems remain with creating a price schedule that exceeds a criminal's utility in offending. Foremost among these is the problem of marginal deterrence, which is the subject of the following discussion.

2. The marginal deterrence problem

If the optimal output of certain crimes is zero, one might impose a uniform, preclusively high price for all such offences. However, not all inefficient crimes are equally undesirable. An unprovoked battery is, among other things, inefficient, having no proper place in society. One can say the same of murder, of course, but few will argue that harm of these crimes is comparable. Thus, society ought to structure the price schedule to minimise the most harmful crimes vis-à-vis those that are less injurious.

To appreciate the risk, consider how best to enact statutory punishments for two kinds of crime: burglary and murder. If burglary is defined as at common law, such that there must be a breaking and entering of the dwelling of another at night with the intent to commit a crime inside, it is a crime that is never efficient. The offence amounts to a coercive transfer in a low transaction cost environment in which a private, contractual bargain was available through the market. Assume that the lawmakers in our hypothetical society believed that the harshest ethically permissible sentence was life without the possibility of parole. In that case, they may pass a law requiring life sentences for anyone convicted of burglary. Assume, for simplicity, that the probability that society will catch and convict a burglar for his crime is 100%.

The likely effect of such a law would be a precipitous drop in the amount of burglary. This isolated consequence would be desirable, but that benefit may mask two problems. First, a substitution effect may occur from burglary to a less costly alternative, such as robbery. There may be no net reduction in the amount of inefficient crime, and no efficiency gain.

There is a greater danger. Although the hypothetical law would decrease the number of burglaries that occur, it would be unlikely to eliminate all of them. As to those offences that still occur, life imprisonment would perversely alter burglars' incentives. Suppose that such criminals could reduce the chance of their being caught to 80% by killing any witnesses who happened to be in the house when it was burgled. As the maximum sentence for murder is also life imprisonment, burglars would, therefore, have an incentive to kill those residents.

Maintaining marginal deterrence is a recurring problem in criminal law. The key to solving it is always to have a harsher penalty available than the one that applied to the less-serious, preceding crime. This creates an upper limit on the optimal price for all but the most harmful imaginable crimes, such as mass murder or torture. The lower limit for all inefficient crimes, of course, is a price incrementally larger than the criminal's gain.

In short, marginal deterrence suggests that staggered, rather than uniform, prices are necessary, and that the severity of the relevant sanction should increase in proportion to the magnitude of the social harm of the crime.

D. Conclusion

Certain crimes are categorically unacceptable, and the overriding goal is minimisation. This might appear to be straightforward: to eliminate a particular form of conduct, one need only impose a harsh penalty with a sufficiently high probability. Some basic economic analysis, however, reveals that this is not so simple. Uniform draconian penalties across offences introduce perverse incentives to commit the worst kind of crimes subsumed within the blanket penalty. Other factors constrain the enactment of severe punishments. These include the preferences of criminals, their loved ones, and of interested third parties who dislike what they perceive to be disproportionate punishment. The result is that society must adopt an iterative approach, making a series of upward adjustments as the relevant offence become more grave, subject to not imposing sanctions that reduce social welfare by virtue of their draconian nature.

Notably, the law and economics of criminal punishment goes to incentives, but says little about the nature of criminals' preferences. It is surely the case, however, that social policy, re-education, and other reformative efforts are an important component of a criminological policy which seeks to eliminate categorically inefficient crime.

Key Points

- Calibrating an appropriate price for a crime depends on the *ex ante* perceived probability that the state will catch and punish the wrongdoer. For instance, if the social cost of a crime is £2,000 and the probability of being punished is 40%, a price less than £5,000 would not deter a rational, risk-neutral person inclined to commit the offence.
- Policing, prosecutorial, and judicial services are expensive, as is imprisonment. If potential criminals were risk neutral with low discount rates, the most efficient punishment would be a harsh one that bears a low probability of being enforced. In reality, however, criminals tend to have high discount rates and some prefer risk, which may make a low punishment/high probability sanction more effective. That approach may also be more just.

- The price elasticity of demand for a crime informs the optimal punishment. In the case of perfect inelasticity, the best sanction is none at all. That is why it makes economic sense not to punish insane people for committing otherwise criminal acts. Conversely, society efficiently imposes a penalty exceeding the social cost of the crime on those possessing elastic demand. That approach is efficient because, even though it deters some efficient offences, it achieves a disproportionate saving in policing, prison and related resources. Most criminals display relatively inelastic demand, however, thus making punishments less severe than the social injury of the crime appropriate.
- Economists typically prefer fines over imprisonment. Fines, unlike jail sentences, impose disutility in the short run, and may thus more effectively deter those with high discount rates. Similarly, fines achieve positive revenue for the state, while prison sentences are expensive and deprive the economy of the contribution those incarcerated would otherwise have made. In practice, however, fines are effective only for less severe crimes because prison sentences can typically impose greater levels of disutility, and can thus achieve more powerful deterrence.
- To affect marginal deterrence, the law must progressively impose ever-more-severe penalties against more serious crimes. If one applies the greatest possible sanction against a certain crime, say robbery, no greater punishment is available than to deter more serious offences, like murder. The law should thus implement price steps.

 ## References and Further Reading

Books

Garoupa, Nuno (ed.) *Criminal Law and Economics* (2009).
Harel, Alon and Hylton, Keith N. (eds) *Research Handbook on the Economics of Criminal Law* (2012).
Levitt, Stephen D. and Miles, Thomas J. (eds) *Economics of Criminal Law* (2008).
Miceli, Thomas J., *The Economic Approach to Law*, 2nd edn (2008), pp. 273–311.
Polinsky, A. Mitchell, *An Introduction to Law and Economics*, 4th edn (2011) Ch. 11.
Polinsky, A. Mitchell and Shavell, Steven, 'The Theory of Public Enforcement of Law' in *Handbook of Law and Economics* (2007) Vol. I, Ch. 6, §§ 1–11, 16–29.
Posner, Richard A., *Economic Analysis of Law*, 8th edn (2008) § 7.2.
Shavell, Steven, *Foundations of the Economic Analysis of Law* (2004) Chs. 20–22.

Articles

Alexander, Cindy, 'On the nature of the reputational penalty for corporate crime: evidence' (1999) 42 JL & Econ 489.
Ehrlich, Isaac, 'The deterrent effect of criminal law enforcement' (1972) 1 J Legal Stud 259.
Ehrlich, Isaac, 'Crime, punishment, and the market for offenses' (1996) 10 J Econ Persp 43.
Levitt, Stephen D. and Miles, Thomas J., 'Economic contributions to the understanding of crime' (2006) Ann Rev Law Soc Sci. Available at: http://pricetheory.uchicago.edu/levitt/Papers/annurev.lawsocsci.2.081805.pdf.
Posner, Richard A., 'An economic theory of the criminal law' (1985) 85 Colum L Rev 1193.

Chapter 3

Problems in Criminal Law

Chapter Contents

A.	Introduction	128
B.	Why Is Intent a Necessary Element of Most Crimes?	128
C.	Why Punish Unsuccessful Attempts?	130
D.	Price Discrimination	130
E.	Irrationality and the Realism of the Law and Economics Account of Crime	132
F.	Do Criminals Respond to Incentives?: The Empirical Literature	132
G.	Drug Policy	137
Key Points		143
References and Further Reading		143

A. Introduction

This chapter rounds out the economic account of crime, explaining how prominent features of criminal law reflect economic principles and examining challenges for the law and economics perspective. Most importantly, it reviews the empirical literature assessing whether the economics account of crime comports with real-life criminal behaviour. For example, does increasing the punishment for a particular offence, while holding constant the likelihood of prosecution, reduce the amount of that crime? Conversely, does increasing the probability of conviction whilst holding steady the relevant punishment lessen the number of relevant offences that occur?

We begin by asking why intent is a requisite of criminal liability for most offences.

B. Why Is Intent a Necessary Element of Most Crimes?

For those whose understanding of criminal law lies in retributivism, intent serves an axiomatic role. In their view of the criminal justice system, there is a world of difference between a person who commits a harmful act innocently or even negligently, and one who does so purposefully. An individual who knowingly contravenes his community's enacted laws violates the moral integrity of society and thus deserves to be penalised. Conversely, if somebody inadvertently carries out the same proscribed behaviour, the resolve underlying her actions comports with the social conscience. It follows that morality does not justify the latter person's punishment.

If the law and economics account is correct, however, the purpose of criminal law is to create a price schedule for various crimes which results in an efficient level of output in each relevant market. Hence, the economic account of crime (unlike the retributivist perspective) looks forward. The question of a person's guilty mind, therefore, would only be relevant to a consequentialist view of criminal law if it potentially alters behaviour in light of the price imposed on proscribed conduct. If creating an optimal price schedule is indeed the goal, however, why does the law generally require that a defendant act with intent to commit the crime?

The answer cannot relate to the magnitude of the injury occasioned by an act that, but for the absence of intent, would have been a crime. A person's good intentions do not diminish the injury that the victim suffers. Consider a traveller who accidentally takes another person's suitcase at the airport. The person deprived of his belongings suffers an identical deprivation regardless of whether the taking was an honest mistake (and thus not criminal) or intentional (and hence larceny).

From the perspective of efficiency, there is good ground to discourage accidental or negligent deprivations of property, as well as intentional ones. In punishing intentional or reckless behaviour, the law deters it. Failing comparably to sanction people who innocently commit otherwise identical acts, however, results in a zero market price for inadvertent harm. We might therefore expect too much innocent (i.e. non-deliberate) "crime".

Understanding this problem implicates an important fact: just because a person acts without intent does not mean that she could not envision the harmful event. If an individual can discern *ex ante* that his behaviour could produce an injurious result, and if he knows that the courts will impose a price equal to any such injury, he will have an incentive to take cost-justified precautions to prevent such harm's occurring. That criminal law generally absolves anyone who acts with less than criminal negligence – defined as a gross deviation from the standard duty of care – means that it fails to generate the full panoply of efficient incentives.

Simply because it does not punish as criminal those acts that lack the requisite *mens rea*, however, does not mean that the law fails to deter. In fact, when the law declines to condemn a harmful act as criminal due to the absence of intent, that act will nevertheless often be tortious. Part 2 explained how the tort system can induce potential injurers to adopt optimal precautions. The principal economic justification for the intent requirement is that it reduces the threat of over-deterrence.

From this perspective, not imposing criminal liability for negligent or innocent conduct, such as mistakenly taking another person's umbrella from a restaurant, is desirable because the threat of criminal sanctions would induce inefficient reductions in the amount of legitimate conduct.

For that reason, tort may be a superior vehicle to hold people to account for the non-purposeful costs that their behaviour imposes on others. The reality is that being deemed a criminal carries a negative impact independent of the sentence imposed. For example, even if a person only receives a fine of £1, the fact that he is convicted and thereafter has a criminal record means that the disutility that he experiences is considerably greater than the £1 fine imposed. Conceivably, then, it may not be possible to fashion sufficiently light punishments through the criminal justice system to instil appropriate incentives regarding unintended consequences.

The economic role of the intent requirement, then, may be to demarcate the boundaries within which tort and criminal law ought respectively to apply. What should we make, however, of strict liability crimes? These are offences for which the law requires no malicious intent. Some of them pertain to proscribed activities that society perceives to be less serious, such as regulatory infractions. The lack of any intent requirement for such acts fits with the explanation just provided, which posits that criminal convictions may over-deter because the stigma of criminality may result in a price that exceeds the social cost of the prohibited act. If the stigma associated with being convicted of a prosaic offence, such as double parking, is slight, imposing strict liability is efficient when the actor is the lowest cost avoider.

One cannot justify all strict liability crimes in this manner, however, as some of them entail serious repercussions. The most prominent example is statutory rape. To understand the economics of this offence, one must first discern the nature of the social harm that it creates.

At first blush, the crime may appear to be consistent with the Coase Theorem in that it entails a consensual arrangement that does not aim to harm any third party. The crucial distinction, however, is that one party lacks the capacity to determine her own welfare. If a person's revealed preferences conflict with her well being, facilitating the satisfaction of those preferences may undermine her welfare. This line of reasoning bears dangers, of course, as paternalism could potentially justify any governmental deprivation of liberty. Yet, regardless of one's general predilection for, or hostility toward, paternalistic intervention, it is hard to argue that minors have developed the requisite judgment to make potentially life-altering decisions in a manner that reflects their long-term interests.

Thus, if the age of consent is a legitimate proxy for informed decision making, the prohibition on statutory rape makes sense. In light of what we have said above about the economic role of intent, however, does the absence of an intent requirement make sense? The answer is yes. As this crime is one that society would likely seek to eliminate entirely, the goal is to impose a price on the conduct that exceeds the private gains to the offender. The only obvious economic cost to not requiring culpable intent, as we saw, is the risk of over-deterrence. If the optimal output of the activity that the law is seeking to regulate is zero, however, then over-deterrence is no longer a problem. Instead, the risk becomes one of maintaining marginal deterrence. Nevertheless, as long as more serious penalties than those imposed in statutory rape cases remain available to the courts, this risk is unlikely to be material. Furthermore, as Part 3 on tort law explained, strict liability creates an incentive to substitute toward alternative forms of behaviour. This is, of course, desirable in the setting of statutory rape.

This section concludes by referencing extreme cases in which a defendant cannot formulate intent. A child below a certain age cannot offend. In England and Wales, for example, this age is 10. In Scotland it is eight, and in Ireland it is 12. One must be at least 11 to commit a federal crime in the United States. Similarly, the law never deems an insane person guilty of a crime. These features of the law are consistent with law and economics because the price elasticity of demand for insane actors and those who are too young to understand the nature and consequences of their actions may be close to zero. As imposing a price on such people would not materially affect behaviour, but would nevertheless inflict social cost, the efficient result is no punishment at all. If an insane person is dangerous to the community, however, he may be locked up for the duration of his mental illness. If we are confident in the courts' ability not to commit Type I errors in this setting (i.e. not accidentally to find sane individuals incompetent) this, too, makes sense.

C. Why Punish Unsuccessful Attempts?

Harm is a requisite of tort, but not of crime. What explains this difference? Normative law and economics promotes behaviour to which affected parties would have agreed without transaction costs. The laws of crime and tort play closely related functions in fulfilling this role. They impose prices on wrongdoers that reflect the injury caused by the harmful behaviour. Applying this principle, however, would seem to suggest that the state should impose no penalty on a person who attempts, but fails, to commit a crime. This tentative conclusion might reflect the adage of "no harm, no foul".

Yet, it would be odd to absolve people who unsuccessfully try to commit certain offences. If someone planted a bomb under a car to kill an adversary, but by chance the explosives turn out to be dud, imposing a price of zero would hardly lead to efficient behaviour. This intuitive insight reveals why the law properly condemns attempt: tying the proper sanction to the harm of the proscribed act can be misleading. The problem lies in conceiving of punishment purely as a Pigouvian tax. While doing so can be illuminative, the Coase Theorem qualified the nature of Pigouvian taxes. As Part I discussed, inefficient market outcomes result from bargaining failures.

Applied to attempt, one employing law and economics would ask what the relevant stakeholders would have agreed to *ex ante* in a hypothetical setting of no bargaining costs. The outcome would reflect the nature of the crime. As the previous chapter discussed, two broad categories of crime exist. For those offences the benefits of which never exceed the social costs, the efficient level of output is zero. A potential victim would not agree to allow someone to try to commit such crimes.

Thus, the fact that an attempt failed to produce the actor's desired result does not mean that no harm occurred, as the actor's behaviour violated the target victim's preferences without consent (either expressly or theoretically implied). Furthermore, an unsuccessful attempt makes a repeat effort likely. Deterring attempts is efficient because such acts signal a danger that the harmful result will ultimately ensue. The only exception is where the sought outcome was not actually a crime, which explains the distinction between legal and factual impossibility. Only the former is a defence.

The final point is that the punishment imposed for attempt and other so-called "inchoate" crimes should be less than the sanction for successfully carrying out the target offence. This observation reflects marginal deterrence. As to those who offend, the law should always foster an incentive to refrain from proceeding further. By punishing a completed crime more than an attempt, society makes it rational for criminals at the margin to abandon their plans before they come to fruition.

D. Price Discrimination

For offences that may occasionally be efficient – assuming risk neutrality and unit demand elasticity – the law should impose an expected sanction that equals the social harm of the crime. In that way, a person will properly carry out the proscribed act only when the benefits to her of doing so exceed the social cost. As a result, for such crimes, we should expect to see punishments differ based not on the characteristics of the particular defendant, but on the extent to which the social injury arising from the act differs from one case to the next. In fashioning an appropriate penalty for one who double parks, for instance, the court should not ask what price would ensure that the offender never commits such an infraction again. Instead, the punishment – presumably a fine – should reflect the harm caused by double parking in the relevant neighbourhood and at the relevant time.

The matter is altogether different for those crimes that ought always to be deterred. For these offences, the price should depend on the defendant's characteristics, rather than on the harm occasioned by the proscribed act. If the optimal penalty depends on each defendant's unique characteristics, the range of sentences imposed for such crimes should vary. In short, an efficient criminal justice system would price discriminate, such that each imposed sanction marginally exceeds the offender's reservation price. To a significant degree, this is what we find.

Price discrimination pervades criminal law. For example, the courts punish repeat offenders more harshly than first-time defendants. The economic rationale is straightforward. If the price schedule previously put in place to minimise incidence of a categorically inefficient crime failed to deter a particular defendant, his offending shows that the price was too low. A person's proclivity to reoffend at a price that deters others suggests that his private benefit from engaging in the illegal behaviour is unusually high. If the law's goal is to promote zero output in the market for that proscribed activity, deterring that particular defendant in the future necessitates a greater price.

Much the same reasoning applies to considering post-arrest rehabilitation in determining an appropriate sanction. Proof of an offender's good-faith efforts to better himself, such as by enrolling in drug-treatment programmes, furthering his education, or by undertaking other activities that demonstrate a path of reform, generally leads to some sentence reduction. The economic reason is that such steps, if undertaken as part of a genuine, concerted effort toward self-improvement, indicate a diminished likelihood of committing the same crime again. The minimum price necessary to deter is, therefore, lower than it would be without such evidence. The same point holds true with respect to supportive factors that inform a judge's sentencing discretion and thus enable her to impose a lower than average penalty on an offender whose offence was out of character.

Other examples of price discrimination abound. It makes economic sense to punish premeditated crimes more severely than those committed on an *ad hoc* basis, which is of course what the law does. A person who plans a crime in advance is more likely to evade detection. Thus, to maintain a particular expected cost, one must magnify the penalty for a deliberate act beyond that imposed for an otherwise identical deed committed on the spur of the moment. Even putting the probability-of-detection question aside, though, an individual who takes the time and effort to think through his planned course of action is more likely to consider the law's imposed price and thus to reach a determination more consistent with rational-choice theory. If certain criminals are more likely to contemplate criminal penalties, their price elasticity of demand may also be higher, which would warrant a steeper punishment. One can "buy" a greater reduction in crime for a lower price by targeting criminals bearing elastic demand.

Related to this discussion, criminal law punishes people less who commit an offence pursuant to a sudden fit of passion that overwhelms their reason, thus rendering them less deterrable at any given price. Although this phenomenon might appear to justify a greater, rather than a lighter, penalty, this is not necessarily true. If a sudden bout of rage would lead even a reasonable person to commit the crime, the price elasticity of demand for the offence at the relevant point in time is apt to be low. In such situations, imposing a greater price may entail great administrative cost to the state but would yield little deterrence. Thus, criminal law recognises a partial defence of provocation if the incendiary act would have overwhelmed the self-control of even a normal person. The law properly declines to regard such an event as giving rise to a complete defence, however, because the price elasticity of demand in such conditions will rarely be zero, such that some deterrence is possible. The unsubtle point is that we want to encourage people to hold onto their reason even in inflammatory situations, even if we simultaneously recognise that not all individuals will do so and calibrate the optimal sanction accordingly.

More generally, the law often allows a partial defence of diminished capacity, such as when alcohol or drugs were involved when the offence was committed. At common law, a defendant could even evade criminal liability entirely for specific-intent crimes if his intoxication negated the required mental element for the crime. Recognising a diminished capacity defence, and imposing a lower price on people who did not have their usual control over their faculties, makes sense from the perspective of efficiency.

E. Irrationality and the Realism of the Law and Economics Account of Crime

The idea of the rational criminal – a calculating offender who makes cost–benefit-informed decisions – strikes many observers as unrealistic. Few would attribute superior reasoning prowess to drug addicts, gang members, hardened criminals, people with violent predispositions, and others drawn to serious crimes. The disconnect between the formal rationality of price theory and how people decide to offend might seem to undermine the law and economics account.

The validity of economic theory, however, does not rest on the degree to which it reflects the subjective reasoning that informs individual criminals' decision making. Instead, it depends on the ability of price theory to predict changes in criminal behaviour. The discipline identifies explanatory variables that materially affect crime. The last chapter explored a number of such variables. By tailoring the magnitude of punishment, the probability of detection and conviction, and the temporal period within which society imposes the relevant sanction, the law can instil an appropriate cost on outlawed behaviour. This price, in conjunction with supply and demand in the relevant market, will determine output (i.e. the quantity of the crime that occurs).

F. Do Criminals Respond to Incentives?: The Empirical Literature

1. Introduction

Do increases in the likelihood and magnitude of punishment result in less crime? The preceding economic account would predict that the answer is yes. Demand curves for crimes slope downward, and are not vertical. Thus, increasing the probability or severity of punishment makes an offence less palatable than it would otherwise be. For prospective, informed, criminals at the margin, such a price rise should induce them not to offend.

Of course, we would not expect output to drop to zero in light of a price increase. The demand curve for criminal behaviour is not horizontal – demand is not perfectly elastic. Some individuals' preferences to commit a crime will exceed the enhanced penalty which, if equal to the social cost of the proscribed act, means that carrying out the offence is (likely) efficient. A person's preference may outweigh the criminal sanction for one of two reasons. First, the individual may place an unusual premium on engaging in the prohibited activity. Second, he may consider the expected punishment to be less unpleasant than other people do. This latter result may be idiosyncratic – a given jail term, for instance, is more unpleasant for some individuals than it is for others.

Of course, changes in the magnitude or probability of punishment do not affect potential criminals who are ignorant of the law. For these reasons, we would expect some, but not all, potential criminals to respond to changes in the "price" that the law charges for committing an offence.

This is the theory, but what of the evidence? The short answer is that econometric studies generally support the preceding economic account. Overall crime rates react to changes in price, which demonstrates that criminals, as a group, respond to movements in the likelihood and extent of punishment.[1] A 1999 report concluded that "[a]s a whole, criminometric studies clearly indicate a negative association between crime and the probability and severity of punishment".[2] In 2007, a literature review concluded that "deterrence has a substantial but far from complete role in explaining patterns of criminal activity".[3]

2. Difficulties that hinder empirical research concerning the deterrent effect of crime

Before considering specific studies, it is worth stressing the complexity of the requisite econometric research. Econometricians face daunting obstacles, especially simultaneity bias. The crime rate, the number of police, the average prison sentence that the courts impose, and the probability of conviction are not independent. This causes a problem for statisticians. If high crime rates lead governments to hire more police, for instance, statistical studies may find a positive correlation between the number of police and the crime rate. Thus, if one does not control for simultaneity bias, it may mask the fact that increasing the number of police decreases crime. Indeed, ignorance of the problem could lead one to conclude that hiring more police increases crime! Of course, the causal chain operates in the opposite direction. It is the tendency of increases in crime to cause governments to hire greater numbers of police that produces biased results from straightforward – ordinary least squares – regressions. Early econometric studies fell prey to this problem,[4] which should remind readers that correlation does not imply causation.

A related bias results from incapacitation. A criminal cannot commit offences within larger society while in prison, so imprisonment may reduce the crime rate even if criminal sanctions do not deter. If the elasticity of supply for crime is high, incapacitation may dramatically reduce crime rates because few newcomers will replace criminals whom the government takes off the streets. Thus, in finding a statistically significant relationship between heightened imprisonment and a drop in crime rates, it is difficult to discern how much of the effect is variously due to deterrence and incapacitation. Put differently, in studying the effect of expected criminal sanctions on crime, statistical analysis that did not adjust for the crime-reducing effect of incapacitation would inflate the deterrent effect.

Notwithstanding these difficulties, econometricians have developed sophisticated techniques to minimise bias. For instance, measuring for so-called "Granger causality" in time-series data can demonstrate not only a correlation between two or more variables, but also a qualified form of causation. Although statistical determinations of such causality can be complicated, the basic idea is that one variable (X_1) "Granger causes" another variable (X_2) if incorporating prior values of both X_1 and X_2 collectively yield more accurate predictions of X_2 than previous values of X_2 alone.

As applied to whether increasing the number of police – the explanatory variable, which we will call "X_1" – leads to a decrease in the crime rate – the dependent variable, "X_2," – an ordinary regression would reveal a biased correlation between these variables. Furthermore, it would not indicate whether a causal relationship exists and, if it does, in which direction it operates. Instead, one could run a regression of the change in X_2 on lagged (prior) values of X_2. One could then run a separate regression adding lagged values of X_1. If the regression incorporating lagged values of both X_1 and X_2 correlates more closely with changes in X_2 than prior values of X_2 alone, one can conclude that movements in the number of police "Granger causes" changes in the level of crime.

---

1 To emphasise: the term "criminals" here refers not to individual offenders, but to large-scale groups.
2 Erling Eide, 'Economics of Criminal Behavior', in *Encyclopedia of Law and Economics*, Boudewijn Bouckaert and Gerrit De Geest (eds) (1999) p. 360.
3 *See* Steven D. Levitt and Thomas J. Miles, 'Empirical Study of Criminal Punishment', in *Handbook of Law & Economics* (A. Mitchell Polinsky and Steven Shavell (eds) 2007) p. 457.
4 Ibid. at 466–67.

Another technique designed to break the problem of simultaneity bias uses "instrumental variables". These allow an econometrician to estimate causation. The statistical challenge in measuring the effect, for example, of the number of police on crime is endogeneity bias (reverse causation). Specifically, police are endogenous with respect to crime rates. If researchers can identify a variable ("an instrument"), however, that correlates with the level of imprisonment but does not correlate with the crime rate, they can run a so-called two-stage, least-squares regression that avoids the bias that would otherwise skew the statistical results. A good example is Steven Levitt's use of election cycles as an instrumental variable which correlates with an increase in the number of police, but which is uncorrelated with crime rates.[5]

Unqualified conclusions as to the effect of subtle gradations in expected punishment on criminal behaviour remain elusive. Nevertheless, statistical evidence supports the conclusion that the law can affect criminal behaviour by adopting a price schedule of the sort discussed above. A discussion of some prominent empirical studies follows.

3. The empirical literature

(a) The scale of imprisonment

A threshold question is whether imprisonment diminishes the amount of crime. Economics suggests that the prospect of incarceration imposes a shadow price, increases in which will reduce the amount of the relevant criminal activity by inducing a potential offender to embrace other, less-costly forms of behaviour. It also suggests that incapacitation will diminish the level of crime if the supply of potential offenders is inelastic. If putting offenders behind bars does not reduce the offence rate, however, then this element of law and economics theory does not map to reality.

In fact, there is convincing empirical evidence that enhancing the prison population reduces the crime rate. Representatively, in 1994, Marvell and Moody concluded that a 10% increase in the prison population affected a 1.5% decrease in crime rates.[6] Two years later, Levitt determined that Marvel and Moody had understated the marginal reduction in crime that imprisoning one extra offender achieves by a factor of up to three.[7] Levitt's 1996 study suggested that releasing a prisoner produces an extra 15 crimes annually.[8] In 2000, Spelman concluded that "[m]ost studies show that doubling current U.S. prison capacity would reduce Index Crime rates by 20–40 percent".[9] The high-level implications of the law Fabsentand economics account of crime therefore seem secure.

Before the mid-1990s, however, a number of studies suggested that imprisonment had little effect on the level of crime.[10] Economists have subsequently debunked these reports, however, on the ground that they failed to account for simultaneity bias.[11] The number of people in prison in the United States grew significantly in the 1970s and even faster in the 1980s, as did the crime rate. The statistical error was failing to note that political hostility to enhanced levels of crime leads governments to magnify the incarceration rate. Increasing the number of people in prison does not lead to higher crime rates – higher crime rates lead to greater levels of imprisonment. More recent studies on the effect of imprisonment on crime used more sophisticated techniques, specifically

---

5 Steven D. Levitt, 'Using electoral cycles in police hiring to estimate the effect of police on crime' (1997) 87 Am Econ Rev 270.

6 Thomas Marvel and Carlisle Moody, 'Prison population growth and crime reduction' (1994) 10 J Quantitative Criminology 109.

7 Steven Levitt, 'The effect of prison population size on crime rates: evidence from prison overcrowding litigation' (1996) 111 QJ Econ 319.

8 Ibid.

9 William Spelman, 'What recent studies do (and don't) tell us about imprisonment and crime' (2000) 27 Crime & Justice 419.

10 See, e.g., Franklin Zimring and Gordon Hawkins, The Scale of Imprisonment (1991).

11 Levitt and Miles, supra note 3, at 470.

Granger causality and instrumental variables, to demonstrate that incarceration significantly depresses the crime rate.

Modern econometric studies find that increasing the scale of imprisonment significantly reduces the crime rate. One should not read this evidence, however, to conclude that governments should increase the number of people whom it incarcerates. Imprisoning a person is exceptionally expensive. The social benefits of incarceration are subject to diminishing returns in light of the fact that some convicts are more dangerous than others. Identifying the optimal level of imprisonment is complex, though there is evidence, for example, that the current level in the United States, which is less than that in western Europe, is excessive.[12]

The fact that the empirical literature supports the proposition that imprisonment deters crime, however, does not tell us whether that effect is the result of deterrence or incapacitation. Nor does it inform us whether the crime rate may be responsive to marginal adjustments in the expected cost of committing an offence. The following two sections discuss a number of studies that suggest that the deterrence effect is real.

(b) Magnifying the severity of punishment

Numerous studies have found that increasing criminal sanctions reduces the level of crime. In a particularly interesting 2009 study, three economists took advantage of a fruitful statistical opportunity when the Italian parliament passed the Collective Clemency Bill in July 2006.[13]

The legislation effected an immediate three-year sentence reduction for all criminals who had offended prior to 2 May 2006. Yet, the statute provided that, if a former inmate were to reoffend within five years following his early release, he would have to serve both the portion of his prior sentence that the act had suspended and the relevant sanction for his subsequent crime. Thus, the Clemency Bill effectively increased the cost of recidivism for those whom it had partially pardoned. Importantly, this enhanced price was not fixed, but varied randomly between released convicts depending on the amount of time that each one happened to have left on his sentence. This provided economists with a rare and illuminative natural experiment.

Studying a data set comprised of 25,814 individuals, Drago, Galbiati, and Vertova concluded that "prison sentences represent effective disincentives to individuals' criminal activity".[14] They found that reducing a sentence that a person was serving by one month, and adding that time to the expected sentence for a future crime, reduced the probability of recidivism by 1.3%. The authors opined that this effect amounted to a significant reduction in the propensity to recommit a crime. For a seven-month period, they estimated an elasticity of average recidivism with respect to expected punishment of −0.74. The authors explained that "[t]his means that increasing the expected sentence by 50 percent should reduce recidivism rates by about 35 percent in 7 months".[15]

A 2002 study concluded that violent crimes dropped in US states that adopted truth-in-sentencing laws that required violent offenders to serve at least 85% of their sentences.[16] Passage of those laws instantly affected a price increase for such crimes, which according to law and economics theory would result in a drop in output. The empirical findings were in accord. Similarly, a 1999 study examined the effect on crime of a California referendum that enhanced sentences for certain offences.[17] It

---

12 Ibid. at 471.
13 Francesco Drago, Roberto Galbiati, and Pietro Vertova, 'The deterrent effects of prison: evidence from a natural experiment' (2009) 117 J Political Economy 257.
14 Ibid. at 259.
15 Ibid. at 260.
16 Joanna Shepherd, 'Police, prosecutors, criminals, and determinate sentencing: The truth about truth-in-sentencing laws' (2002) 45 JL & Econ 505.
17 Steven Levitt and Daniel Kessler, 'Using sentence enhancements to distinguish between deterrence and incapacitation' (1999) 17 JL & Econ 343.

concluded that sentence enhancements reduced crimes by 4% in the year following adoption of the California law and by 8% within three years of the same.

A separate 1998 study by Levitt looked at how the transition from juvenile to adult criminal systems affected the level of crime for people reaching the age of maturity.[18] In some jurisdictions, punishment was significantly more severe for adults, while in other s the relevant sanctions are more comparable. This, too, provides a natural experiment suitable for fruitful research. In the jurisdictions that treat adults and juveniles relatively similarly, Steven Levitt found that violent crimes rose by more than 23%. In the jurisdictions subject to the harsher penalties for adults, however, these fell by almost 4% among people coming of age. The effect for property crimes was even starker. Where adults were punished much more harshly, such crimes dropped by 20% amongst those who transitioned from juvenile to adult status. Where sanctions were comparable, property crimes increased by 10%.

Not all empirical evidence, however, supports the hypothesis that increases in the magnitude of punishment correlates with statistically significant decreases in crime. Lee and McCrary in 2009 found that the tendency of individuals with criminal records to commit offences after reaching the age of majority decreased, but only in a statistically insignificant amount.[19]

(c) Increasing the number of police

There is strong empirical evidence that increasing the number of police correlates with a reduction in criminal offences. Most recently, and using data from US cities over half a century, Chalfin and McCrary estimated elasticities of crime with respect to police of approximately −0.35 for violent crime and −0.15 for property crime.[20] If correct, these results suggest that a 10% increase in the number of police officers results in a 3.5% and 1.5% drop in violent and property crime, respectively.

In 2007, Evans and Owens used law enforcement grants as an instrument that does not correlate with pre-grant trends in the crime rate.[21] The ensuing regressions estimated elasticities of robbery of −1.3, violent crime of −1.0, burglary of −0.6, assault of −1.0, murder of −0.8, car theft of −0.9, and rape of −0.4 with respect to police. In 2000, Corman and Mocan estimated that a 10% increase in the number of police led to a 10% drop in crime.[22]

In 2002, and using the number of firefighters as an instrumental variable, Levitt estimated elasticities of −0.435 and −0.501 for violent and property crimes, respectively.[23]

4. Concluding thoughts on the empirical literature

Econometric research on the deterrent and incapacitative effects of criminal law enforcement remains challenging in light of the statistical difficulties attendant upon the enterprise. Nevertheless, modern research has yielded insightful conclusions about the respective effects of imprisonment, changes in the severity of sanctions, and in the number of police. That modern studies report statistically significant relationships between these explanatory variables and the crime rate vindicates − or at least is consistent with − the key insights of the economic analysis of criminal law. Contrary to

---

18 Steven Levitt, 'Juvenile crime and punishment (1998) 106 J Political Economy 1156. But cf. Randi Hjalmarsson, 'Crime and expected punishment: Changes in perceptions at the age of criminal majority' (2009) 11 Am L & Econ Rev 209.
19 David Lee and Justin McCrary, *The Deterrent Effect of Prison: Dynamic Theory and Evidence* (2009) (unpublished manuscript, Department of Economics, Princeton University).
20 Aaron Chalfin and Justin McCrary, 'The Effect of Police on Crime: New Evidence from U.S. Cities, 1960–2010' (21 March 2012). Available at: http://emlab.berkeley.edu/~jmccrary/chalfin_and_mccrary2012.pdf.
21 William Evans and Emily Owens (2007) 'COPS and crime' 91 J Public Econ 181.
22 Hope Corman and H. Naci Mocan, (2000) 'A time-series analysis of crime and drug use in New York City' 90 Am Econ Rev 584.
23 Steven Levitt, 'Using electoral cycles in police hiring to estimate the effect of police on crime: reply' (2002) 92 Am Econ Rev 1244.

some people's expectations in light of the perceived irrationality of criminal actors, offenders do respond at the macro level to the incentives that criminal laws impart.

Nevertheless, it is important not to read the economic account of crime as the exclusive framework within which to analyse the dilemma of criminality within society. The fact that neoclassical analysis typically treats individual preferences as exogenous can be an attractive element of law and economics theory, in that it respects people's right to determine their own wants for themselves. It would be odd to insist, however, that public policy should never play a role in the inculpation, formation, and development of beliefs, attitudes, and tastes. A variety of sociological factors typically combine to instill a prediliction for criminality in certain people. To say that the law has no role in shaping preferences within the realm of criminal law, then, is to go too far.

Ultimately, to explain criminal behaviour and the preferences that underlie it, one must go beyond constructing optimal incentives through the criminal justice system – though that construction is itself an important component of criminal law and one upon which economics can cast much light. In crafting a comprehensive policy toward the problem of criminality, however, society must concern itself with influences on the crime rate beyond deterrence and incapacitation. A representative subset of such factors includes communal norms, the stability of familial structures within society, the quality of education, long-term unemployment rates, the wages available for lawful work, the availability of weapons, and illegal drug use. All are factors that governments can influence to varying degrees, with potentially important repercussions for attitudes toward and the prevalence of criminal offences in society.

It is on the last factor – illegal drugs – that the present chapter and Part conclude. The phenomenon of illicit drug usage, and the black markets that fuel the same, is perhaps the most divisive element of criminal law today.

G. Drug Policy

Few areas of criminal law ignite more passionate debate than the ongoing efforts to stamp out the sale and consumption of illicit drugs. Commentators fiercely contest the merits of such contrasting policies as ever-harsher enforcement, partial decriminalisation, and wholesale legalisation. The discussion, unfortunately, has not always been constructive. For some, prohibition is the manifestation of an unyielding moral stance against the impropriety of drug use which, as an ethical principle, should remain invariant to practical consequences. Others of a more pragmatic persuasion point to the failure and costs of the war on drugs. Hysteria and uncritical dogma too often crowd out rational analysis of this issue. As a tool by which to study policies' consequential costs and benefits, economics has important insights on this subject.

1. Should drugs be illegal?

A threshold question is whether one can justify the ban on drugs on law and economics grounds at all. First, in criminalising narcotics, the law forbids market transactions. This proscription is in apparent tension with the Coase Theorem, which suggests that contracts altering the pre-bargain allocation of entitlements are generally efficient. If one wishes to consume, and is willing to pay for, a particular drug, and if another person possesses and wishes to sell a suitable quantity of it, the ensuing "deal" renders both parties better off. What, then, is the ground for criminal prohibition?

One possible answer is that satisfying users' preferences to acquire and consume illegal drugs does not render them better off. Law and economics analysis typically defers to individual autonomy, recognising private choice as a superior determinant of one's well-being than third-party decisions based on paternalism. That deferential account, however, becomes more difficult to justify in the presence of intense physical cravings that overwhelm calculation and cause otherwise low discount rates to soar. There is at least some weight, then, to the argument that preferences and welfare may not closely align with respect to drug users.

Against this, however, lie two complications. First, a person's decision to consume a drug for the first time occurs before the onset of addiction. In that state of mind, why is an individual's informed decision to experiment with what he knows to be an addictive drug not entitled to deference? Second, not all illegal drugs possess such addictive qualities that they magnify discount rates in the manner described. If a person makes an ongoing decision to smoke marijuana without getting addicted, for instance, why is that person's preference not creditable?

A better economic answer to the question of why drugs should remain unlawful must lie in third-party effects. In analysing the economic nature of drug usage, it is important to understand that addicts do not internalise the full costs of their habit. Many addicts lack the cognitive capacity that participation in the work force requires. Many others do not possess the soundness of mind and stability required to parent children responsibly. Starved of an independent source of income, addicts must rely on state-provided welfare or rob others, instead of contributing to the economy (and hence to society) through work. Drug addiction has also played a terrible role in spreading disease among users, particularly among those who use substances intravenously. Unsurprisingly, then, the macro-level repercussions have been severe. The introduction of addictive hard drugs, such as heroin and crack cocaine, has devastated large segments of society, and working-class neighbourhoods in particular.

In light of these costs, contracts between consumers of addictive drugs and their suppliers are not obviously efficient. The relevant bargains affect many third parties who are not privy to those arrangements. Without their participation and consent, no *à priori* basis exists for deeming those agreements to be efficient.

Yet, it would be a gross oversimplification to group all prohibited drugs together, as such banned substances differ greatly in nature and effect. While consumption of heroin or crack cocaine can carry fiercely detrimental third-party effects, one cannot plausibly say the same about marijuana. There is some evidence that continuous use of the latter drug can negatively affect one's intellectual ability over time, though a number of critics have assailed the validity of those conclusions. The important point from the perspective of law and economics, however, is that whatever costs that marijuana consumption generates are largely unique to the user. Any third-party effects of the drug are modest, particularly vis-à-vis those generated by legal forms of drug ingestion such as drinking and smoking tobacco. As there is no basis within the law and economics framework to reject a person's preference to consume marijuana, an economic perspective provides little support for the ban on this particular drug.

The economic case for proscribing alcohol purchase contracts is probably stronger than for banning the sale of marijuana. The costs of alcohol consumption are extraordinary. Up to 40 percent of accident-and-emergency visits in UK hospitals are drink related.[24] Alcohol was a factor in almost one-third of all fatal road accidents in the United States in 2009.[25] In the UK, 17% of road fatalities were alcohol related in 2009.[26] The drug is a major factor in both public and domestic violence. One has to qualify these observations, of course, by the fact that the scale of alcohol consumption is an order of magnitude greater than cannabis.

---

24 Michalis P. Charalambous, 'Alcohol and the Accident and Emergency Department: A current review' (2002) 37 Alcohol & Alcoholism 307.

25 US Centers for Disease Control and Prevention. Available at: www.cdc.gov/MotorVehicleSafety/Impaired_Driving/impaired-drv_factsheet.html.

26 UK Department for Transport. Available at: http://dft.gov.uk/pgr/statistics/datatablespublications/accidents/casualtiesgbar/rrcgb2009.

This observation does not amount to an argument, however, that governments should ban the sale of alcohol. Many people have an evidently strong preference in favour of consuming the drug – a preference, indeed, that has become a material part of many western cultures. Deference to these preferences explains the legality of alcohol purchase contracts. Hostility to the preferences of those who like to smoke marijuana explains the different legal status given to that drug. From the perspective of neoclassical welfare economics, which treats individual preferences as exogenous, however, this is a distinction without a difference.

Nevertheless, the conclusion that the purchase of cannabis is likely to be efficient would seem to ignore potentially serious costs. In particular, money used to buy marijuana in most western countries goes to drug gangs, thus fuelling the often-brutal manner in which those entities compete with one another for sales. Is this not a cost of free exchange between sellers and consumers of marijuana? The answer is yes, but only insofar as society outlaws those contracts. If the law were to recognise such agreements as legitimate, both the government and lawful sellers would share the predominant portion of the producer surplus that the relevant contracts would generate.[27] One need only contrast the violence that organised crime visited upon the United States in supplying alcohol during Prohibition, which declined dramatically following passage of the Twenty-First Amendment.

Another objection is that marijuana is a "gateway drug", which leads users subsequently to try harder drugs. This argument, too, is dubious when one considers a lawful market for this particular drug. Consumers in such settings would not interact with unlawful dealers who offer more dangerous substances. Perhaps more importantly from the perspective of law and economics, however, the concern that legalisation would lead more people to choose an improvident course rests uncomfortably with the view that preferences are not an object of normative analysis.

In conclusion, it is difficult to justify as efficient most western governments' proscription of marijuana and comparable soft drugs, which lack significant, third-party negative effects.

2. Criminal sanctions and the price elasticity of demand for illicit drugs

Western governments have responded to the influx of drugs by enacting and enforcing harsh criminal sanctions. These vary between countries, but are almost uniformly severe when applied to those who engage in large-scale dealing. The western jurisdiction with the most draconian sentences is the United States. The US federal sentencing guidelines are complex and the penalties that they prescribe depend on myriad case-specific factors, but they are capable of producing extreme recommendations in drug cases. The US Controlled Substances Act imposes a minimum sentence of five years for manufacturing, distributing, or possessing with intent to distribute 500 grams of powder cocaine, 28 grams of crack cocaine, 100 grams of heroin, 1 gram of LSD, 10 grams of PCP, 5 grams of methamphetamines, and 100 kilos of marijuana.[28] Ten times those amounts trigger a mandatory minimum of 10 years.[29] The second such offence carries a mandatory minimum of 20 years and a third results in an obligatory life sentence without release.[30]

In England and Wales in 2010, those convicted of importing or exporting illegal drugs received average sentences of seven years. In 2006 in the same jurisdiction, the average custodial sentences that the courts imposed for trafficking were 38 months for powder cocaine, 37 months for heroin,

---

27 A black market would likely survive on a much smaller scale in the presence of legalisation and heavy taxation, offering cheaper access to drugs.

28 21 USC § 841(b)(1)(B).

29 21 USC § 841(b)(1)(A).

30 *Ibid.*

36 months for crack cocaine, 29 months for ecstasy, and 15 months for cannabis.[31] Ireland has a mandatory minimum of 10 years for certain trafficking offences.[32] The average sentence that Irish courts imposed on possessors and traffickers of drugs combined was 34 months.[33]

As the reader will recall, identical punishments do not impose the same cost on all prospective criminals. The price that a person experiences from a criminal sanction is subjective, depending on the individual's discount rate, aversion to jail time, appetite for risk, attitude to maintaining a law-abiding reputation, and opportunity cost (in terms of foregone time with family and friends and lost income from work). These characteristics vary tremendously from person to person. As a result, in order to reduce output in the markets for prohibited acts to desirable levels, it may be necessary to tailor penalties to the relevant individual.

It appears that, taken collectively, drug dealers and users tend to display common characteristics that dilute the potency of criminal sanctions. This is not to say, of course, that those involved in drugs constitute an homogenous group. Nor is it say that one cannot dissuade many such individuals. It is instead to point out that the ratio of profitability to opportunity costs on the supply side, and the physical compulsion that addiction creates on the demand side, mean that, for many people involved in these activities, preferences exceed the subjective price that the criminal laws impose. In short, the law cannot hope to eliminate drug consumption and sales.

Take the demand side first. This issue concerns those wishing to consume drugs. We have already discussed how addiction can magnify discount rates to extraordinarily high levels. This, in turn, dilutes the significance of future prison terms to a point where the threat of criminal prosecution provides scant disincentive. What of non-addictive, less-dangerous drugs? Society views consumption of these substances to be less serious, and thus (correctly) imposes more modest sanctions.

Ultimately, in cases of addiction, prison has modest deterrent value. To be sure, heavy sanctions for consumption of the most dangerous drugs should carry significant deterrent effect against initial use in the absence of any physical compulsion. Nevertheless, even one poor decision to experiment with certain drugs can lead to addiction, thus rendering users largely immune to subsequent deterrence. As for possession of small quantities of more innocuous drugs, the relatively light sanctions that the government imposes do not aim to eliminate all such consumption. The simple conclusion is that, for harmful drugs the consumption of which society should aim to eliminate completely, traditional criminal penalties are ineffective in light of the high discount rates that addiction instils.

Now consider the supply side, at which governments aim the most stringent criminal sanctions. The binding characteristic here is the pursuit of profit. The market for illegal drugs generates almost unimaginable returns for those who are willing and able to satisfy demand. Commentators have estimated, for instance, that Mexican drug cartels collectively reap profits between $18 billion and $39 billion annually, which grants them budgets comparable to those of small countries. It is not possible to craft criminal penalties that render the expected value of entering the market negative. This impossibility flows in part from the inability of police and prosecutors to increase the probability of successful prosecution beyond a low level. Drug gangs and cartels recruit heavily from communities characterised by poverty and chronic, often multi-generational, unemployment. The prospect of lucrative returns from dealing drugs will too often prove irresistible to down-on-their-luck young people whose second-best options are far from attractive.

Markets for illegal drugs thus possess qualities that hinder the ability of traditional criminal penalties to significantly reduce output. Specifically, the price elasticities of both supply and demand for drugs appears to be low. If increasing the price of purchasing and consuming a particular drug

---

31 See www.emcdda.europa.eu/attachements.cfm/att_92889_EN_onlineannex_SIsentencing.pdf.
32 Criminal Justice (Ireland) Act 2006 s. 84.
33 See, www.irishexaminer.com/ireland/kfaueysngbgb/rss2/.

has little effect, it may be inefficient to impose a significant price at all. This follows from the fact that criminal sanctions are themselves a source of (potentially great) social cost. If criminal law enforcement imposes such costs, but carries little gain in terms of reduced supply or demand for proscribed drugs, the case for continuing to apply draconian sanctions is weak. This conclusion follows the previous chapter's explanation that, in regulating criminal behaviour, society should increase the severity of the sanction until the marginal cost of a further, incremental increase in the magnitude of punishment exceeds the marginal benefit.

As the price elasticity of demand is low for many drugs, imposing a price equal to the negative externality that the purchase, sale, or possession of an illicit substance creates is inefficient. In other words, society can obtain superior results by imposing a price that is less than the traditional Pigouvian tax. The crucial question, then, concerns how elastic demand actually is. Empirical literature shows that changes in the price of drugs can affect the quantity of drugs that people purchase and consume, though the magnitude of the impact appears to change between drugs, and some observed effects are not statistically significant.[34] Demand thus appears to have an elasticity materially that is greater than zero, suggesting that criminal prohibition's price-increasing effect reduces drug usage, at least to some degree. Nevertheless, demand remains imperfectly inelastic, meaning that even high prices will not substantially eliminate consumption and severe criminal sanctions are unlikely to be efficient.[35]

3. A prescription for legalisation?

For some people, the goal of criminalisation has but one point: to eliminate the consumption of illicit drugs. For a variety of obvious reasons, this goal is not achievable. For those who hold strong anti-drug views, the real objective of criminal prohibition is to minimise consumption. From both perspectives, the function of prohibition is to increase the price of drugs, thus decreasing the quantity that people purchase and consume. This "price" encapsulates not only the pecuniary sum at which drugs sell on the street, but also the expected cost that criminal prohibition imposes on consumers.

There is no question that the cost of proscribed drugs today is far higher than would prevail in an unregulated and untaxed free market. As the price elasticity of demand is greater than zero, the law's forcing the price up reduces the number of people who choose to consume drugs. Viewed discretely, this element of the law is desirable. As noted above, however, criminal enforcement carries severe costs. Funding the requisite policing, prosecutorial, and imprisonment functions is vastly expensive. The lengthy prison sentences routinely imposed ruin the lives of individuals, families, and communities. Impure drugs that endanger those who consume them abound in an unregulated market. Perhaps worst of all, by creating and driving up the black market price, criminal prohibition feeds horrific violence among gangs who compete with one another for the extraordinary profits that are available. The fact that demand is not elastic exacerbates all of these costs by requiring ever-harsher punishments to affect a given decrease in demand.

Whether these costs outweigh the benefits in terms of reduced drug consumption is a matter of great debate. Those who live in communities that experience the full cost of the drug war are unlikely to think so. If all agree, however, that the point of the war on drugs is to reduce the quantity of consumption, a crucial question is whether alternative measures exist by which to achieve comparable price effects at a lower social cost.

---

34 National Criminal Justice Reference Service, 'Illicit Drugs: Price Elasticity of Demand and Supply' (2001). Available at: www.ncjrs. gov/pdffiles1/nij/grants/191856.pdf.
35 Gary S. Becker, Kevin M. Murphy, and Michael Grossman (2004) 'The economic theory of illegal goods: The case of drugs'. Available at: www.nber.org/papers/w10976.

Economics suggests a potential solution. Legalisation coupled with suitably heavy taxation could generate a price that limits output while dramatically reducing the terrible social cost that criminal prohibition entails. Tracing the economic effects of legalisation requires one to consider a number of conflicting effects on demand. In the first place, withdrawing the badge of criminality would increase the demand for drugs amongst law-abiding people. Conversely, taking away the thrill of committing a prohibited act would have a demand-decreasing effect among some others. The former effect would surely outweigh the latter, however, and probably by a large margin, such that legalisation would cause demand for previously illicit drugs to increase significantly. This probable effect is perhaps the main reason why many people support continuing prohibition.

Yet, increased demand would, in itself, augment consumption only if all other factors are held constant. By legalising drugs, the government would possess regulatory power over price. Through appropriate polices, such as the introduction of a sufficiently high tax (or, equivalently, limiting supply), society could theoretically increase price to a point at which the higher cost of purchasing a drug equals or exceeds the demand-increasing effect of legalisation.

The taxes that governments could charge to limit output would produce vast revenues, which society could then use for demand-reducing policies such as education, treatment for addiction, parental support, and so on. Economists have estimated that the US government could raise as much as \$46.7 billion in annual revenue through legalisation.[36] In light of these benefits, it is open to question whether the contemporary ban on drugs makes economic sense.

There is, however, at least one major complication. Depending on the magnitude of the increase in demand that legalisation would induce, governments may have to set exceptionally high taxes to suppress the demand-enhancing feature of legalisation. Dramatically high prices would carry disparate effects. Drug use in more-affluent areas may increase sharply beyond its current level. People from less-well-off backgrounds would be more likely to be priced out of the market (which would, in turn, feed an ongoing black market). Simultaneously, if the demand-increasing effect of legalisation were larger for middle-class neighbourhoods – it is possible, for instance, that those communities, on average, place a greater premium on complying with the law – one would expect to see a shift in relative consumption between the various socioeconomic groups even if overall output remains constant. If the middle class enjoys superior political clout, a possible increase in drug use among its ranks could act as a significant obstacle to legalisation.

Another factor may perpetuate criminal prohibition of drugs. This is an unjustified sense that legalisation would reflect a social affirmation of legitimacy. In light of the many terrible effects that hard drugs have on users, families, and neighbourhoods, casting a veil of approval over such products is anathema to many people. Their view is understandable, but ultimately uncritical. Morality and legality are not synonymous, and education can play an important role in remedying a perceived coincidence between the two.

The world would be a better place without drugs, but unfortunately they exist. Legalisation would implicitly recognise that governmental efforts to eliminate controlled substances have failed. Yet, failed it has. Drugs are here to stay. The question is how best to minimise the magnitude of the costs that use and addiction create. In light of the available evidence and economic theory, society could do better by legalising soft drugs, imposing sufficiently high taxes, and using the ensuing revenue both to mitigate the negative effects of drug use and to diminish long-term demand through education. The case is less clear with respect to hard drugs, but the cost of today's criminal enforcement provide a legitimate argument in favour of decriminalisation. No doubt, people will continue fiercely to debate questions concerning drug policy for a long time to come.

---

36 Jeffrey A. Miron and Katherine Waldock (2010) 'Making an Economic Case for Legalizing Drugs' (2010). Available at: www.cato. org/publications/commentary/making-economic-case-legalizing-drugs.

Key Points

- Intent is a requisite of most crimes. The economic justification for that aspect of the law is to demarcate civil liability in tort and criminal condemnation. If the latter applied to unintentional harmful acts, the law could over-deter certain socially beneficial conduct.
- The law punishes attempted, but inchoate, offences because they have the potential to create harm. To achieve marginal deterrence, the law properly imposes a sanction less than it would on those successfully carrying out the completed crime.
- The empirical literature supports the hypothesis that the probability and severity of punishment affect the crime rate. Although criminal law deters crime, and plays a substantial role in explaining the amount of crime, many other factors influence the crime rate.
- Economics sheds light on the drugs debate. On normative grounds, it questions the ban on voluntary transactions pertaining to soft drugs carrying modest third-party effects. With respect to harder drugs, the negative consequences of use do not inure solely or predominantly on informed users. For that reason, criminal prohibition may be justified. Nevertheless, cost–benefit analysis makes it difficult to justify the war on drugs as governments currently wage it.

 ## References and Further Reading

Books

Levitt, Stephen D. and Miles, Thomas J., 'Empirical Study of Criminal Punishment' in *Handbook of Law and Economics* (2007) Vol. I, Ch. 7.

Posner, Richard A., *Economic Analysis of Law*, 8th edn (2011) §§ 7.1, 7.5–7.7, 7.11.

Shavell, Steven, *Foundations of the Economic Analysis of Law* (2004) Ch. 24.

Articles

Avio, Kenneth L. and Scott, Clark C., 'The supply of property offences in Ontario: Evidence on the deterrent effect of punishment' (1978) 11 Canadian J Econ 1.

Becker, Gary S., Murphy, Kevin M. and Grossman, Michael, 'The economic theory of illegal goods: The case of drugs' (2004) Working Paper 10976. Available at: www.nber.org/papers/w10976.

Benson, Bruce L., Iljoong, Kim, Rasmussen, David W. and Zuehlke, Thomas W., 'Is property crime caused by drug use or drug enforcement policy?' (1992) 24 Applied Econ 679.

Block, Michael K. and Gerety, Vernon E., 'Some experimental evidence on differences between student and prisoner reactions to monetary penalties and risk' (1995) 24 JL Studies 123.

Boettke, Peter J., Coyne, Christopher J. and Hall, Abigail R., 'Keep off the grass: The economics of prohibition and U.S. drug policy' (2013) 91 Or L Rev 1069.

Buck, Andrew J., Hakim, Simon and Rengert, George F., 'Substitution between offence categories in the supply of property crimes: Some new evidence' (1987) 11 Int'l J Soc Econ 48.

Cloninger, Dale O., 'The deterrent effect of law enforcement: An evaluation of recent findings and some new evidence' (1975) 34 Am J Econ Sociology 323.

Ehrlich, Isaac 'Deterrence: Evidence and inference' (1975) 85 Yale LJ 209.

Part 4

Property

1   The Economic Role of Property Rights   147
2   Protecting Entitlements   160

Chapter 1

The Economic Role of Property Rights

Chapter Contents

A.	Introduction	148
B.	Ownership Rights and the Efficient Utilisation of Resources	149
C.	The Coase Theorem and Allocation of Scarce Resources	151
D.	Problems in the Creation of Property Rights	154
E.	Conclusion	158
Key Points		158
References and Further Reading		159

A. Introduction

Ownership rights lie at the heart of the common law tradition. Most philosophers agree that people either inherently enjoy, or can, through some course of conduct, acquire proprietary interests in themselves and in other things. The ubiquity of such rights is no historical accident, but reflects a storied tradition that justifies property as a foundational element of liberty and an indispensable component of a just society.

Despite its central role, "property" remains an abstruse concept. To say that a person "owns" a resource – be it real estate, personal property, his own body, or even an idea – is to invite a great many questions concerning the nature of the right that such ownership imparts. One might think of such incidental features of ownership as alienability, devisability, and descendability but the substantive qualities of property go far beyond these attributes. The most important characteristic of ownership is the scope of exclusivity that a property interest bestows. This quality implicates the question where one's rights begin and end. This is no abstract problem, as conflicts between separate ownership rights routinely emerge when the sphere of control that one right purports to cast invades another.

A simple example might entail a person's smoking in front of another. The right to smoke is presumably subsumed within the property right of self-ownership. Yet, a corresponding negative right to prevent a third-party invasion of one's own body also exists, which may permit a person to be free of another's second-hand smoke. The two rights cannot coexist in absolute form, so one or more of them must have limits. The difficult question is how to identify the optimal boundaries of those privileges. To approach the same problem differently, we might ask whether the law permits a landowner to grow tall trees on her grounds if they cast the bordering lot into sustained shadow. Is the right to grow foliage on one's land an incident of ownership or does a neighbour instead enjoy the right to be free of shade as a component of her property right?

Partially due to these difficulties, academics rarely think of ownership in absolute terms. Instead, scholars view property as imparting a "bundle of rights". From a consequentialist perspective, the rights included within this bundle should depend on the circumstances in which the property exists. Articulating a coherent theory by which to define the optimal constitution of any given bundle, however, is challenging.

To resolve such disputes, one must discern the policy that property rights serve. There are, to be sure, differing views on this question. Some commentators believe that property rights do not exist to forward any consequential goal, but instead reflect principles of independent moral significance. John Locke, for instance, famously conceived of property as a natural right that attaches to the fruit of one's labour.[1] Arguing from the premise that one owns oneself,[2] Locke contended that, by mixing her own work with otherwise un-owned natural resources, a person can obtain private property rights over the ensuing improved asset.

The law and economics account is distinct. In contrast to a rights-based explication of property, the economic view defends ownership on consequentialist terms. The idea is that exclusive rights cause scarce resources to gravitate to their highest value uses and to benefit from optimal investment. Furthermore, the optimal rights and duties subsumed within an ownership right properly depend on context.

---

1 John Locke, *The Second Treatise on Government* (1690).

2 Although the principle that a person should be the exclusive owner of himself is intuitively pleasing and no doubt resonates with many people, it is not axiomatic. John Rawls and many others have argued that the value of a person's attributes is "morally arbitrary" on account of its derivation from the genetic lottery, the social setting into which one is born, and so on.

This chapter explores the economic function of property rights. It begins by showing how ownership rights can spur private actors to coordinate the efficient use of resources, both statically and over time. The Coase Theorem finds its definitive expression in this setting, revealing the likely superiority of private arrangements over governmental decree in many, though not all, circumstances. The chapter also articulates an economic theory for defining the scope of property rights, which approach tackles the problem of incompatible uses.

B. Ownership Rights and the Efficient Utilisation of Resources

The property system's economic justification rests on a number of consequentialist rationales. In part, the absence of ownership rights would generate numerous inefficiencies, specifically short-term (static) costs in overconsumption and misallocation of scarce resources, and long-term (dynamic) losses in inadequate capital and human investment in resource development. Despite the overriding advantages of private ownership, however, circumstances do exist in which either public ownership or open use may be superior.

1. Static inefficiency

Collective action problems arise where conduct that may be in the aggregate interest of all is not in the private interest of any one person. If no one owns a lush resource, for instance, those who stand to benefit from its yield may purge the asset of its benefits in much the same way that locusts devour crops to the point of destruction. This is an instance of "static inefficiency".

Such inefficiency arises because people, in acting pursuant to their self-interest, fail to equate the well-being of others with their own. If non-altruistic, they will consume as much of a limited commodity as is necessary to render them fully satiated. If the resource in question is what economists refer to as a "private good", one person's consumption of the asset will deplete the quantity that remains available for others. This characteristic of "rivalry in consumption" is a trait common to all physical resources. As a negative externality afflicts each person's consumption decision, a systemic overuse of natural deposits ensures. The result is what economists refer to as "the tragedy of the commons".

This phenomenon is widespread, applying not only to overgrazing, but also to commercial overfishing in oceanic locations, deforestation in public areas, and traffic jams on public motorways. All such cases arise due to limited property rights.

How do ownership rights potentially solve static inefficiency problems? They do so because they align social and private costs by causing an owner to experience both. Consider a fertile piece of agricultural land. In the absence of exclusive rights, problems of the kind described above would arise. Suppose, however, that the government grants someone exclusive rights over the property. That owner may consume all of the land's resources himself or he may allow others to do so. In either event, he would have an incentive to coordinate efficient use of the property. As to third parties, he would charge an access fee no less than the loss in value of the extrication of minerals from the land associated with the licensed entry. He would do so because his interests are co-terminous with the aggregate value derived from the property. Of course, it is efficient to consume a resource where the marginal benefit of the unearthed deposit exceeds the marginal cost in reduced richness of the land. Ownership rights in valuable resources thus induce self-regulation in which owners act desirably because their incentives align with those of society. The ensuing pricing structure would foreclose inefficient gold rushes that lead to excessive depletion of the land.

Notwithstanding these benefits, it is worth highlighting an important qualification. Although property rights coordinate efficient uses of scarce resources, the introduction of such rights does not, in itself, guarantee efficiency. In particular, monopolists have an incentive artificially to enhance the scarcity of their owned resources, selling the same at above-marginal cost prices, thus creating allocative and static inefficiency. Part 8 explores the important roles of competition and, where necessary, government regulation in spurring desirable behaviour on the part of those who hold private ownership rights over valuable resources.

2. Dynamic inefficiency

The absence of property rights does more than spur over-consumption in the short term – it generates inefficiencies over time. Think of an entrepreneur who perceives of a way in which dramatically to increase the value of a natural resource. She would wisely decline to invest, however, if third parties would simply usurp the benefits for themselves. Free riding can reduce the private worth of socially desirable investment to the point that net present value is negative, thus deterring efficient behaviour. Property can prevent this dynamic-efficiency loss.

It is hard to understate the importance of property in generating incentives to invest in resources. A lack of ownership rights, for example, impedes economic development in the Third World. Not only does this lack of ownership spur over-consumption, it creates dynamic inefficiencies as occupiers of potentially arable plots decline to improve the land, such as by introducing superior crops, irrigation, and minerals. The decision not to pursue hard-won improvements that others can appropriate is privately rational, but the larger social costs are calamitous.

A simple game-theory model captures the problem (see Figure 4.1). Suppose that an un-owned forested area is within easy reach of two companies that compete in the logging industry. Most of the trees that lie within this expanse, however, are not yet mature. The timber is worth $15 million if one were to cut it today, but would be worth $25 million in five years' time discounted to present value. The social welfare optimum is to leave the forested tract untouched for the time being. In that event, the two competitors could receive $12.5 million each in five years' time rather than only $7.5 million each in the present.

There is, however, a collective-action problem. Each company knows that, if the other refrains from cutting down the trees, it can take them all for itself. If the first company holds back, its rival can clear the entire area itself and thus realise the full $15 million. Each competitor's dominant strategy is, therefore, to cut now, even though they would be collectively better off were they instead to cut later.

Granting either of the companies, or any other entity, a property right over the forested land would solve this dilemma. If a third party owned the land, for instance, it would not grant either company a licence to cut the timber today. This refusal would occur because the present value to the owner of allowing the trees to grow is $25 million, while neither logging company would rationally bid more than $15 million for a licence to cut today. If one of the rival companies owned the land and decided to cut the timber itself, it would cut five years from now rather than today because the former course of action yields a greater return. This example explains how property rights coordinate efficient resource consumption over time.

	Company Two	
	Cut Now	Cut Later
Company One	Cut Now	7.5M, 7.5M	15M, 0
	Cut Later	0, 15M	12.5M, 12.5M

Figure 4.1

As a general matter, whenever third parties can appropriate the value of a resource at will, individuals may have scant reason to devote their private time, effort, and other capital to improving it. Importantly, the value of most resources is variable, not fixed. By enabling private actors to capture at least some of the benefits of their enterprise for themselves, exclusive rights spur people to improve their property.

C. The Coase Theorem and Allocation of Scarce Resources

One of the central premises of economics is that some resource allocations are superior to others. Any consumable item invariably appeals to certain subsets of the population more than others – it is no secret that people possess a diverse array of idiosyncratic tastes. No resource commands an economic value that is independent of the uses to which one can put it. As different entities enjoy distinct opportunities to derive value from capital, efficiency requires an alienation mechanism by which resources can gravitate from lower- to higher-value uses. Society, therefore, needs an infrastructure that allows valuable assets in limited supply to end up in the hands of those who value them the most.

Such efficient allocations refer not only to resources that people seek for end consumption, but also to those principally valuable as inputs into larger manufacturing processes. Toil and technology, after all, can amplify and transform raw materials to yield superior resources for subsequent use. In this respect, individuals with superior skill, business acumen, technical knowledge, or access to necessary infrastructure can employ materials to create greater value than other people could achieve. In short, society must facilitate the transfer of rare resources to more productive ends. Ownership rights are the principal method by which to achieve such allocations, so they play an integral role in both maximising the intrinsic value of resources and in facilitating their efficient distribution.

How do property rights desirably allocate scarce resources? The answer lies in the most fundamental concept within the field of law and economics: the Coase Theorem. As Part I explained, this theorem provides that the initial assignment of a property right will have no effect on efficiency if transaction costs are zero. The reason is that private individuals will contract with one another to effect a superior assignment of rights when an initial resource allocation is inefficient. To the extent that stakeholders can bargain to desirable outcomes, the principal obligation of the government is to create and give legal force to ownership rights. Once in place, those property interests will give rise to market mechanisms that will allocate entitlements to their highest value uses.

To see how the Coase Theorem operates, envision the following simple scenario. Four companies, A, B, C, and D wish to excavate a mine in which all believe valuable mineral deposits reside (see Figure 4.2). Assume that the four companies, A to D, place values of £1 million, £1.2 million, £1.3 million, and £1.5 million, respectively, on procuring ownership rights over the mine. The differing values reflect each corporation's distinct ability to procure the deposited minerals at low cost. Imagine also that, due to the nature of the facility, a single company could extract the minerals at lower total cost than could several entities operating simultaneously. Granting someone an exclusive right over the mine, therefore, would create static efficiency benefits in foreclosing a gold rush in which multiple companies tried to excavate the deposits at the same time. Unfortunately, information concerning the value of acquiring prospect rights in the mine is private to all four companies, so no external body can reliably determine which company values the mine the most.

Upon which company should the government bestow the right? If the entities can bargain at no cost, it does not matter. Suppose that C acquires the right. That eventuality may appear to be inefficient, but in the absence of transaction costs, rights in the mine will end up in the hands

Firm	Private Value of Contract	Bargaining Surplus/Outcome Relative to Optimum
A	£1,000,000	£500,000/Suboptimal
B	£1,200,000	£300,000/Suboptimal
C	£1,300,000	£200,000/Suboptimal
D	£1,500,000	£0/Optimal

Figure 4.2

of D, who will pay an amount between £1.3 million and £1.5 million for the privilege. There is thus a bargaining surplus – that is, a potential value gain – of £200,000. Consistent with the Coase Theorem, the entitlement will end up in the same efficient place – in the possession of D – regardless of the initial allocation. Notice, though, that that allocation does affect the distribution of income between A, B, C, and D.

In the real world, of course, transaction costs are never zero, so the facile conclusion that government policy should limit itself to creating and enforcing property rights will not always or even generally hold true. This does not mean that the Coase Theorem, and by extension, the role of property rights in alienating scarce resources, have no application to public policy. First, the fact that transaction costs are positive does not mean that the Coase Theorem will fail. When the private benefits of reaching agreement exceed the negotiating costs, efficient bargaining should occur. It is, therefore, no surprise that contracts (both formal and informal) abound. Each one represents the Coase Theorem in action.

Private actors' ability to negotiate reallocations of resource assignments is indispensable to an efficient economy. To facilitate this process, the only absolute requirement is that government give legal force to property rights. The principal benefit of this phenomenon is that markets can ameliorate mistaken property allocations, which is apt to be a common occurrence given the government's inferior access to the information necessary to identify the highest-value allocations of entitlements. When private entities undo such mistakes, economists often refer to the ensuing arrangements as "private-ordering solutions".

Yet, impediments to voluntary exchange are ubiquitous. These transaction costs have a number of undesirable effects. In the first place, they foreclose some efficient reallocations of entitlements. This is apt to occur when the expense of negotiating an agreement exceeds the aggregate gain that the stakeholders would realise from reaching a bargain. Perhaps less obviously, transaction costs diminish the magnitude of the social value that even successful contracts generate.

Ultimately, where bargaining costs are so severe that no contracting can take place, initial property assignments are final. In these cases, unless the government allocates entitlements to their highest-value uses in the first instance, inefficiency will ensue.

Before considering how the law may reduce transaction costs to facilitate efficient exchange, however, contemplate the following question: is it possible for a market to develop that fosters inefficient, rather than mutually beneficial, exchange? Such a phenomenon may appear to be inconsistent with the Coase Theorem, as if large-scale contracting takes place, the cost of bargaining is, by definition, not preclusive, so ensuing market transactions ought to reallocate property rights from inferior to superior uses. The ensuing discussion addresses a famous piece of economic analysis, which explained how a "market for lemons" can emerge.

1. The "Market for Lemons"

In a 1970 article, George Akerlof explored the possibility that poor quality goods could predominate in markets in which sellers, but not consumers, are well informed as to the qualities of sold products.[3] Akerlof considered the used car market, in which industry terminology referred to high-quality vehicles as "cherries" and their defective counterparts as "lemons". The question that the article addressed was whether a market could develop which produced lemons, but not cherries.

At first glance, the idea that consumer demand would develop for dud products in a free market seems odd. If all parties were informed as to the nature of the relevant cars, the Coase Theorem provides that all ensuing sales would confer mutual benefits on the contracting parties, as vehicles moved from people who valued them less to people who valued them more. Those transactions would create a market for used cars in which prices would emerge that reflect the relative quality of the sold vehicles. One would therefore expect to see products of superior quality commanding a relatively high price and second-rate merchandise selling at low price points only.

Consider what happens, however, when we introduce information asymmetry to the market, such that owners of used cars know the attributes of their vehicles, but prospective purchasers do not. Potential customers' encountering difficulty in this regard is at least somewhat realistic, as many aspects of a used car's quality are not obvious upon superficial inspection. Vehicles are but one example of larger "credence goods" – products the material qualities of which are not apparent upon examination. Assume that all second-hand vehicles, bearing the full spectrum of potential quality from best cherry to worst lemon, are available for sale. Consumers immediately encounter a problem, as they cannot discern one from another. As indicia of quality, owners' representations are non-credible because each seller has an incentive to inform prospective buyers that the relevant car is a cherry, regardless of whether this is true.

When a rational, risk-neutral purchaser cannot distinguish between a number of products that are of heterogeneous quality, he will assume that any given product bears average attributes. The mean quality, of course, represents the expected value to a consumer of buying an item from within the relevant group of products. Applied to the example of indistinguishable used cars, this means that risk-neutral consumers will pay a price that reflects the value of the average used vehicle from within the group of cars that are available for purchase. This price, however, carries two, related, problematic effects. First, owners of lemons will rush to sell, as the market price will bestow a windfall upon them. Second, owners of cherries will refuse to part with their vehicles because the market price would under-compensate them.

The result is that the pool of used cars will dwindle, as owners of superior, used cars decline to sell them. Yet, the calculus does not end there, for as cherries leave the market, consumers will realise that the average value of sold cars has diminished. The new price, reflecting this updated mean value, will lead owners of better than average lemons to refuse to sell, so both the average value of cars, and hence the market price will drop further, and so on. This ongoing effect creates a death spiral in which market processes force high-quality products out, and leave only the worst goods available for sale.

Nevertheless, it is easy to exaggerate the prevalence of the "lemon effect" in the real world. Although serious information asymmetries can lead to transactions in which resources move to less-efficient uses in contravention of the Coase Theorem, the preceding account relies on consumers' being unusually passive. In fact, market processes are themselves likely to ameliorate, even if they do not eliminate, the lemon effect. Consumers will not be oblivious to the fact that cherries exist, and owners of such cars have an incentive to seek ways to sell them at a mutually attractive price. Both sets of potential parties have reason to search each other out and to solve their common problem. A prevalent solution has, indeed, emerged in conjunction with contract law: to make representations of quality credible, owners of high-quality goods can and regularly do issue binding warranties. Furthermore, markets may develop around the problems that create the lemon

---

3   George Akerlof, 'The market for lemons: Quality uncertainty and health insurance' (1970) 84 QJ Econ 488.

effect. A suitable example involves Carfax, which offers a private service detailing the full history of any vehicle of interest. Finally, and as we shall see, the law can play an important information-dispersing role in the marketplace.

This discussion illustrates an important principle in economics, which is that access to information is a prerequisite of efficient market processes. As information asymmetry is but a particular form of transaction cost, which collectively hinders a desirable bargain, the question is how the law should seek to ameliorate it. Section C below addresses this issue, explaining how law and economics offers insights into how society ought to formulate the legal characteristics of ownership. Foremost amongst these are policies that enrich the quantity and quality of information that pervade the marketplace and that bring clarity to individual property rights.

2. The market for mortgage-backed securities

It would be a major oversight in addressing the tendency of markets to increase social value by efficiently reallocating resources without addressing the economic calamity that was the 2008–2009 credit crisis. Believers in free markets were caught unawares, with Alan Greenspan famously testifying that "[t]hose of us who have looked to the self-interest of lending institutions to protect shareholders' equity, myself included, are in a state of shocked disbelief".[4]

D. Problems in the Creation of Property Rights

Ownership rights facilitate the transfer of entitlements and, hence, give rise to market transactions. They also coordinate desirable investment in, and consumption of, scarce resources. The preceding discussion, however, did not explain how the state should create and define property interests in the first instance. Law and economics offers much guidance on this subject.

The principal economic insight is that the design of ownership rights can itself affect transaction costs. As impediments to free exchange frustrate mutually advantageous bargain under the Coase Theorem, the government should craft proprietary interests to minimise the likelihood that a mistaken, initial allocation of an entitlement will be final. There are three major ways in which to mould property rights to minimise the transaction costs associated with their creation.

1. Clarifying property rights

First, society should design the property system so that one can both identify the relevant owner and demarcate the boundaries of ownership rights with ease and precision. Why does clarity affect transaction costs? The answer lies in the effect of uncertainty on the bargaining process. When the contours of a person's proprietary interest are obscure, stakeholders negotiating with respect to the pertinent resource must devote precious time and effort to determining the scope of the owner's entitlement and, sometimes, the identity of the owner himself. Competing claims to a resource of unclear breadth do not make for a smooth bargaining process. By contrast, it is relatively straightforward to hammer out a deal regarding an asset the ownership rights of which are clear.

The law knows the value of lucid property rights, and thus goes to some length to augment the clarity of ownership interests. Many jurisdictions require sellers to disclose latent defects of which they are aware, where "latent" refers to those defects that a purchaser cannot discern upon reasonable pre-sale inspection. The courts also protect consumers against misinformation by rendering

---

4 Greenspan Concedes 'Error on Regulation', *New York Times*, 24 October 2008, at B1.

those who make intentional misrepresentations liable in tort and in contract. Thus, the law improves market processes by facilitating greater levels of symmetric information.

The government undertakes other measures to clarify the boundaries of property rights. Land registries allow purchasers both to inspect the chain of title to property, thus verifying the seller's good title, and to verify the metes and bounds of relevant plots. Recording systems encourage those acquiring interests in land to record them promptly, by otherwise granting priority to subsequent good-faith purchasers for value. The law also encourages owners to make plain and to police the boundaries of their land by providing that those who fail to do so may lose their ownership rights. For instance, a person who encroaches upon the periphery of a neighbour's land will obtain ownership rights after the prescriptive period has run. In this way, the contours of ownership rights in land slowly move in tandem with appearances on the ground, thus enhancing clarity.

Other examples were prevalent in the law. For instance, common law courts favoured joint tenancies with a right of survivorship over tenancies in common. The former tenancy results in the surviving joint tenant's obtaining 100 per cent ownership of the property, while the latter tenancy provides that each owner's interest is fully descendible and devisable. By promoting the former, the law discouraged the complementarity problems that divided ownership can create. In particular, the common law's preference for joint tenancies promoted easy alienability. In contrast, one can imagine how numerous parties holding title to land as tenants in common may hinder the sale and transfer of the relevant property. For instance, if four people own land as tenants in common, and each dies leaving four heirs, 16 people may end up having ownership rights in the property. Should a third party later be able to achieve a higher-value use from the land, the sheer number of owners increases transaction costs and could potentially scupper the proposed, efficient deal.

Long a favourite of students of the common law, the rule against perpetuities ("RAP") prohibits future interests to property that are excessively speculative at the time of their creation. Specifically, the RAP renders void any future interest that may vest, if at all, outside the existence of a measuring life plus 21 years. The rule serves an economic function in ameliorating transaction costs. By reducing the possibility of shifting or springing executory interests vesting long after the initial disposition of property giving rise to the future interest, the RAP reduces the risk of unexpected conflicting claims to a resource. This rule simplifies the bargaining process by making it easier to establish the identity of the relevant owner.

Finally, the law has long been hostile to restraints on alienation, which represent the ultimate transaction cost. This feature of the law obviously comports with the Coase Theorem. By limiting restrictions on alienation to reasonable, time-limited purposes only, the law ensures that entitlements are free to move from lower- to higher-value uses.

2. Allocating entitlements to minimise *ex post* transactions

The law's first role in reducing transaction costs is to clarify ownership rights. The second is to minimise the need for *ex post* transactions. Specifically, in crafting property rights, the government should strive to anticipate the outcome of a free bargain in a zero-transaction cost environment.

This principle may appear to be straightforward, but in application it can run counter to intuition. Consider a case in which a factory emits pollutants that sully nearby occupants' houses, cars, and other outdoor property. In defining the parties' respective ownership rights, it is tempting to identify the "harmed" individuals, and conclude that their property rights have been infringed. This approach reflects the idea of requiring injurers to pay a Pigouvian tax equal to the magnitude of the externality.

Economic analysis, however, reveals that this line of inquiry can yield erroneous results. Delineation of the boundaries of a property right should focus not on who "invades" or "inflicts harm" on another's resource, but on who would acquire and exercise the entitlement in a zero-transaction cost setting. This inquiry, of course, results from the Coase Theorem. In the above example, it may appear that the polluting factory is the lowest cost avoider, but this need not always be true. It is possible, for instance, that the residents could move more cheaply than the factory or could take steps at lower cost to eliminate or to reduce the harm that they experience from the emissions. In the absence of transaction costs, and if it were cheaper for the residents to avoid the harm, the parties would agree that the residents, rather than the factory, take the requisite steps. Yet, if the law holds that the residents' property right protects against the factory's emissions even when residents are the lowest cost avoiders, the law risks perpetuating inefficiency if the cost of bargaining is high.

Note, however, that this discussion does not mean that the government would necessarily or even likely be wrong in granting the residents protection from pollutants as an incident of their ownership rights. The point is that the law would be correct in construing their property interests in this way only if that construction is consistent with what a hypothetical bargain between the affected parties in a setting of no transaction costs.

The relevant policy prescription, then, is that the government should attempt to identify the highest value uses of property, and allot ownership rights accordingly. Often, it will not be feasible to identify these uses at the individual level, and so the law must rely on heuristics. To the extent that one identifiable group of people is likely to value a resource more than other people, society should bestow proprietary interests over the same on the former group. This allocation reduces the number of *ex post* transactions required to reallocate resources to their efficient uses, and thus enhances social welfare.

3. Devising rights of appropriate scope

Third, the government must craft property rights so that they possess a sphere of exclusivity that is of appropriate scope for the circumstances. The manner in which one divvies up ownership rights can have profound consequences for the transaction costs involved in allocating the underlying resources to their highest value uses. This issue concerns the sphere of exclusivity. On the broad end of the spectrum, the government could acquire proprietary interest over all land within its borders. On the other end, society could create separate ownership rights in every square metre of land. Neither such allocation would be desirable.

Consider the problems of an all-encompassing property interest, which subsumes myriad distinct resources that would themselves be suitable for discrete uses. Although the owner would have an incentive to prevent over consumption of its property – such excessive use would degrade the value of her ownership interest – the benefit of property rights in allocating scarce assets efficiently would be either lost or greatly diminished. Such rights, as we have seen, play a fundamental role in assigning resources efficiently because they harness private information. A sweeping ownership right that relies on one entity to make value-adding decisions concerning assets about which it lacks intimate knowledge is unlikely to be efficient.

Yet, narrow ownership rights also create problems. These occur whenever a single property interest is insufficiently broad to effect the use or transfer of a relevant resource. In such instances, aggregating property rights is a prerequisite of consumption or alienation. Imagine, for instance, that a local authority wished to build a viaduct from a nearby spring to its town. Suppose, however, that a different person owns each metre of the five-kilometre stretch between the spring and the town. If each owner has the legal right to exclude third parties from trespassing on her property, the town would need to obtain permission from every one of the 5,000 owners to effect its plan. Even if the viaduct arrangement were independently efficient, the transaction costs implicated in achieving the same may be preclusive.

This phenomenon is known as the Cournot-complements problem, and is a direct result of divided ownership. If one must combine several property interests to achieve a larger goal, the owner of each interest possesses a veto, and hence a monopoly. This monopoly arises because each person's permission is indispensable. As a result, every owner has an incentive to "hold out" (i.e. to wait for other owners to grant permission before offering to license at a price only incrementally smaller than the social surplus that his granting a licence would generate). The successive waves of monopoly pricing and ensuing hold-out create the phenomenon of what economists deem "double marginalisation". People bargaining for an entitlement that is subject to multiple, discrete ownership rights must pay not one monopoly price, but several. This effect results in significant welfare losses, and may cause potentially efficient arrangements not to occur.

One solution lies in vertical integration, by which one entity assumes control over a series of complementary assets. In effect, this arrangement undoes the inefficiency that the government created in creating excessively narrow property rights. It does so by creating a single, larger property interest.

As the preceding explanations make clear, excessively broad and overly narrow property rights both create serious problems. How, then, should the government create ownership rights? As the reader may suspect, the answer displays a Goldilocks quality: property rights should be neither too expansive nor too narrow. Instead, one should bestow rights with the breadth of scope that is appropriate given the circumstances attendant upon the creation of the ownership interest. The relevant inquiry, then, is necessarily context specific. Part 8 explores these issues in more depth, while addressing the economics of the patent system.

An important concern is the use to which the owner will put the relevant resource. If the item around which the government creates an ownership right is primarily suitable for an independent purpose, complementarity issues are unlikely to ensue. So, for example, if the government believes that an off-shore location within coastal waters contains oil, creating a drilling permit allowing for a property interest in a single entity is likely to be efficient. The site at issue, and the oil it contained, have but a single, major use, so granting a single company a broad property right will not trigger complementarity problems. Conversely, if the resource on which society bestows a property right can only be consumed in conjunction with other resources, problems can emerge when there are a large number of narrow ownership interests held by different entities.

4. Allocations in the presence of preclusive transaction costs

The preceding discussion considered three significant ways in which the government can design property rights to ameliorate transaction costs. By moulding the contours of ownership to lubricate post-allotment contract, the government can facilitate the desirable qualities of exchange that the Coase Theorem envisions.

Yet, there are obvious limits to what the law can achieve in imparting property rights with characteristics designed to diminish bargaining costs. Conflicting claims to resources often emerge in circumstances where negotiations are not feasible, regardless of how one might construct the relevant ownership rights. In such settings, where transaction costs exceed the private benefit to the parties of reaching agreement, initial assignments are likely to be final. As Coasian trade is not possible, what should the law do? The first answer is that it should do its utmost to identify the highest-value use of the entitlement in question and allot the property right accordingly.

To the extent that efficient *ex ante* allocations are not feasible, however, the law can still play an important role. This concerns the nature of the protection that the courts give ownership rights. As the next chapter discusses, the judiciary may be able to undo the harm of inefficient *ex ante* allocations in high-transaction cost settings by protecting ownership rights through damage awards, rather than injunctions.

E. Conclusion

This Part has addressed a broad swathe of the economic issues surrounding property rights. An issue of momentous importance, however, remains to be addressed. How should the law protect property rights? Should an owner's rights be absolute or restricted? If the latter, how great should the limits on ownership be? Is property sacrosanct or simply an interest like any other that is subject to balancing and qualification?

William Blackstone made clear where he stood on these questions, famously characterising the right of property as "that sole and despotic dominion which one man claims and exercises over the external things of the world, in total exclusion of the right of any other individual in the universe".[5] This eloquent depiction likely comports with what many owners consider to be their rights vis-à-vis third parties. After all, if the hallmark trait of property is the power to exclude, it might seem that an owner's rights are indeed sacrosanct. Blackstone's account, however, is inconsistent with the modern law of property, which makes clear that absolute, inviolable ownership rights do not exist.

Today, property interests bestow qualified rather than absolute exclusivity. Ownership is not synonymous with freedom of action. As but one example, a person may not excavate on his property if the result of his doing so is to cause part of his neighbour's land to collapse in its natural state. Nor does ownership cast a pall of such inviolate exclusivity around a resource as to expel laws of general application: a person charged with growing illicit drugs on his land would not get far arguing that public rules cannot permeate the zone of exclusivity inherent in his property. Furthermore, the law routinely denies an individual power to prevent low-level, private invasions of her property. A person cannot enjoin, or obtain damages for, third-party conversations or music of mild volume during daylight hours that take place next door. Nor can a land owner generally enjoin commercial aircraft from flying overhead.

More generally, the law does not forbid all third-party appropriation of private property, especially where the use does not harm an owner. A person may own her house and the land upon which it rests, but the law does not entitle her either to restitutionary or other relief for the value that onlookers enjoy from appreciating the house's aesthetic qualities. Finally, and as the next chapter discusses in detail, the courts do not always grant owners the literal right to exclude, which would entail an automatic right to injunctive relief. In many cases, the law limits recovery to pecuniary damages, which contradicts the Blackstonian conception of property.

Key Points

- Economics justifies ownership rights on consequentialist terms. The Coase Theorem depends on alienable property interests that allow stakeholders to coordinate economic activity. Property is thus of great importance to law and economics.
- Property rights produce static-efficiency benefits by causing owners to internalise the costs and benefits of using their owned resources. As ownership allows one to reap the benefits of improving property, and to suffer losses from degradation of the resource, it encourages owners efficiently to regulate the use of their property. The "Tragedy of the Commons" illustrates problems that result from a lack of ownership. In particular, self-interested parties will act in their individual self-interest, but against their collective welfare, by excessively consuming a resource.

---

5 William Blackstone, *Commentaries on the Laws of England*.

- Property interests also induce dynamic efficiency gains by encouraging owners to invest capital in improving their land or other owned resources. Without exclusive rights, third parties could appropriate the hard-earned value flowing from prior capital investment.
- Governments can design property rights in the first instance to minimise the transaction costs needed to achieve efficient resource allocations.

  o First, they should assign rights to the entities that they consider most likely to value them the most. That process entails predicting the outcome of post-allocation Coasean bargain without transaction costs.

  o Second, they ought to fashion clearly demarcated property rights. Indeterminate ownership interests invite conflicting claims of right, which accentuate bargaining costs and stymie efficient resource allocations.

  o Third, they should devise property rights of appropriate scope. Narrow rights must be combined to achieve a particular use, such that high bargaining costs can frustrate efficient outcomes. This is the "Tragedy of the Anti-Commons". Conversely, broad property rights can also be problematic because the relevant owner may lack sufficient information to coordinate efficient use of the many assets underlying a single property grant.

References and Further Reading

Books

Barzel, Yoram, *Economic Analysis of Property Rights*, 2nd edn (1997).
Bouckaert, Boudewijn (ed.), *Property Law and Economics* (2010).
Ellickson, Robert C., *Order without Law: How Neighbors Settle Disputes* (1991).
Miceli, Thomas J., *The Economic Approach to Law*, 2nd edn (2008) pp. 140–55, 166–79, 189–222.
Posner, Richard A., *Economic Analysis of Law* (2011) §§ 3.1–3.2, 3.4–3.9.
Shavell, Steven, *Foundations of Economic Analysis of Law* (2004) Chs. 1–6.

Articles

Ayres, Ian and Talley, Ian, 'Solomonic bargaining: Dividing a legal entitlement to facilitate coasean trade' (1995) 104 Yale LJ 1027.
Bohn, Henning and Deacon, Robert T., 'Ownership risk, investment and the use of natural resources' (2000) 90 Am Econ Rev 526.
Demsetz, Harold, 'Toward a theory of property rights' (1967) 57 Am Econ Papers & Proc 347.
Epstein, Richard, 'Why restrain alienation?' (1985) 85 Colum L Rev 970.
Frischmann, Brett M., 'An economic theory of infrastructure and commons management' (2005) 89 Minn L Rev 917.
Hazlett, Thomas W., 'A law and economics approach to spectrum property rights: A response to Weiser and Hatfield' (2008) 15 Geo Mason L Rev 975.
Merrill, Thomas W. and Smith, Henry E., 'What happened to property in law and economics?' (2001) 111 Yale LJ 357.
Michelman, Frank I., 'Ethics, economics, and the law of property' (2004) 39 Tulsa L Rev 663.
Smith, Henry E., 'Semi-common property rights and scattering in the open fields' (2000) 29 J Legal Stud 131.
Smith, Henry E., 'Exclusion versus governance: Two strategies for delineating property rights' (2002) 31 J Legal Stud 453.

Chapter 2

Protecting Entitlements

Chapter Contents

A.   Introduction   161

B.   Protecting Ownership Rights in Zero-
      Transaction-Cost Environments   162

C.   Supporting Entitlements Where Transaction
      Costs are Positive but Not Preclusive   165

D.   Proprietary Interests in High-
      Transaction-Cost Settings   169

Key Points   170

References and Further Reading   170

Introduction

According to the once-prominent but now defunct Court of Common Pleas, the "law holds the property of every man so sacred, that no man can set his foot upon his neighbour's close without his leave[.]"[1] Interpreted to encapsulate not only realty (real estate), but also personalty (personal property), this view would ascribe a specific and powerful remedy to owners in the event of an unauthorised incursion. The relief in question would be a court-ordered injunction. Such an order, which grants an owner absolute control over the disposition of her property, would no doubt comport with what many people consider to be their ownership rights. So, for example, if a neighbour knowingly encroaches upon another's land in extending his house, the aggrieved owner could obtain a court order requiring the neighbour builder to tear it down. Similarly, if a person steals another's car, the owner has a right to compel the thief to return it. In the parlance of economics, invasions of such rights trigger a "property rule", pursuant to which courts award injunctive relief.

Yet, granting an injunction is not the only way to guard ownership rights. The other major remedy for a violation of another's entitlement is an award of damages. When courts give force to property by subjecting trespassers or other third-party appropriators to pecuniary fines, they employ a "liability rule".

At first glance, a monetary award that lacks an accompanying court order requiring the defendant to return the relevant asset and to refrain from future appropriation seems odd. If an employee discovers that his co-worker has taken his brand new mobile phone, for instance, he would probably be dismayed if the law permitted his colleague to keep the phone and merely to pay an amount equal to its replacement value (or perhaps original purchase price). It would be a strange world if people could take whatever they want without first asking permission from the owner, as long as they paid a fee set by a third party after the fact.

Nevertheless, liability rules play a central role in safeguarding entitlements. Injunctive relief is by no means ubiquitous in cases of property right invasions. For instance damages, rather than an injunction, is the traditional remedy for nuisance. The law regularly declines to grant specific performance against a promisor who, in reneging on his contractual obligations, does violence to the promisee's entitlement. The courts, however, will permit monetary recovery. A person whom a soon-to-go-to-print article will defame can rarely obtain a pre-publication injunction, but can sue for damages after the fact. In the realm of intellectual property, the typical recovery in a civil action for copyright infringement involves monetary damages. With respect to patent law, courts historically employed property rules, but now increasingly deny injunctive relief in favour of pecuniary remedies where the relevant patentee is a non-practising entity. As a general matter, an action for an injunction is equitable in nature, such that such relief will be unavailable if damages offer an adequate remedy (though comparable relief may be nevertheless available at common law through replevin or ejectment).

The choice between liability and property rules is one of the most important issues in the field of private law, and has been the subject of extensive research in law and economics literature. The issue goes beyond the field that most law students would consider to be "property law". Entitlements pervade the legal system, so the question of how the law should protect ownership interests implicates all manner of legal rights.

This chapter discusses the economic principles that govern how courts should protect ownership rights. There are simple rules of thumb as to when injunctions or damages are appropriate, but t they can be misleading in more complicated cases. Whether high or low transaction costs prevail is the primary consideration. Yet, such issues as information asymmetries between the parties, the

---

1 Entick v Carrington 95 Eng Rep 807 (CP 1765).

cost of accessing the legal system, judicial error, and assessment costs that parties experience in seeking and processing information complicate analysis.

We begin our discussion of this complex, but important, topic by examining the simplest possible example, which concerns how best to protect entitlements when the cost of bargaining is zero.

B. Protecting Ownership Rights in Zero-Transaction-Cost Environments

The Coase Theorem provides that all property assignments are efficient in zero-transaction-cost settings. Does this conclusion depend on how the law protects the relevant property right? The answer is no, but only in the absence of judicial error. In this setting, property rules are efficient if courts correctly identify and enforce ownership rights. Liability rules are likewise efficient in zero-transaction-cost environments only if courts do not err in calculating damages.

Relaxing certain assumptions demonstrates that the choice between injunctions and damages is complex, even in the simplest (i.e. transaction cost free) case. To illustrate why, and to appreciate the interplay between (1) the legal rights that ownership bestows and (2) the manner in which parties allocate assets through bargain, consider the following basic hypothetical:

1. Property and liability rules are both efficient: no transaction costs; no judicial error; no litigation costs; and damages lie within the spectrum of prices upon which the parties would hypothetically agree

A owns a chattel that B would like to obtain. A would sell the good for £230 or more, while B would pay £250 or less for it. For the purposes of this example, each party's willingness to sell equals her willingness to purchase.[2] Figure 4.3 summarises the bargaining situation, highlighting the efficient bargaining zone and cooperative surplus available to the parties. P_A and P_B reflect A's minimum sell and B's maximum sell prices, respectively.

In lieu of bargaining for the item, B could consider simply take it. Should B do so, A, being the owner, could appeal to the courts. If the law protects A's interest in the chattel through a property rule, the judiciary would compel B to return the chattel. Were the courts to enforce A's entitlement

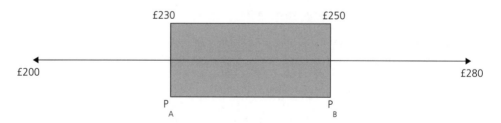

Figure 4.3

---

2 This common, simplifying assumption is a neoclassical economic analysis, though the cognitive psychology literature and accompanying empirical data reveal that real-life conduct is often at odds with this supposition. Part 9 discusses the burgeoning field of behavioural law and economics.

to the chattel through a liability rule, however, they would award monetary damages only. Assume that the courts would award A his minimum selling price − £230. Note, though, that the same result would hold true if damages equalled any amount between £230 and £250. A liability rule tailored to any damages amount within the spectrum of mutually advantageous prices will facilitate an efficient assignment of the property right.

Assuming that (1) damages equal the price at which the owner would have been indifferent between selling and not selling the resource ("the reservation price"); (2) courts do not err, (3) litigating a case costs nothing, and (4) no transaction costs exist, B will acquire the chattel regardless of the initial allocation of the property right. Should the courts employ a property rule, the only way that B could obtain ownership of the resource − which is the efficient outcome − is for him to bargain with A for permission. Given the absence of transaction costs and the parties' respective preferences, B will purchase it from A at a price between £250 and £230.

Should the judiciary apply a liability rule, however, B could either negotiate the same deal as above or it could reject negotiations with A, take the chattel, and pay damages of £230 *ex post*. In these circumstances, B would be rationally indifferent between bargaining for the item through a contract and taking the resource without permission at the cost of £230. Observe, however, that the availability of damages at £230 sets a cap on the price that B would agree to pay. This reflects the fact that parties bargain in "the shadow of law". Thus, under the assumptions of this hypothetical, the access price will be £230 under a liability rule regardless of whether the parties bargain or B takes the good subject to the court's damages determination. Notice that the outcome under both the property and liability rule regimes is efficient because B, the party who valued the chattel more than A, acquires it.

2. Only property rules are efficient: damages are less than the subjective value that the owner places on the relevant asset; no transaction costs; and no litigation costs

Remedies can affect efficiency, even in zero-transaction-cost settings, by setting the strategic context in which bargaining takes place. If the parties anticipate that the courts would grant damages less than the owner's subjective value, inefficient outcomes may ensue.

Suppose, now, that A, an owner, and B, a prospective buyer, value a chattel at £250 and £230, respectively. Efficiency therefore requires that A remain the owner. Under a property rule, A and B may attempt to bargain, but B would never offer a price that A would be willing to accept. The threat of injunctive relief would thus lead to the efficient outcome. If courts underestimate A's minimum sell price at £220, however, a liability rule regime would lead B to dispossess A and simply pay under-compensatory damages. This outcome is inefficient, even though no transaction costs exist. The problem flows from the judiciary's mistaken valuation of the asset, which skews *ex ante* contract negotiations. Such under-compensatory damages generate further inefficiencies by spurring owners to adopt costly precautionary measures that they would not have to undertake under an optimal legal regime.

A recurring problem is that when courts award damages rather than injunctions − as the law does with respect to compulsory purchase orders or other governmental exercises of eminent domain − they award an amount equal to the estimated "market price" of the pertinent resource. Importantly, the market price and the minimum price at which a plaintiff would have been willing to sell are rarely the same. Awarding owners the market price of their expropriated assets thus often under-compensates them. Had an owner valued her property at or less than the prevailing market price, she would likely have already sold it. The fact that she did not suggests that her reservation price exceeds market value.

In light of these economic problems, why do courts use market prices? They do so as a proxy because measuring the property owner's reservation price requires the court to identify the plaintiff's subjective value. This worth is infamously – often preclusively – difficult to estimate accurately. An owner's assertions concerning her reservation price are non-credible, for she has an incentive to exaggerate the relevant amount and thus garner greater damages. She faces little-to-no downside in lying because her claims are not easily falsifiable. Meanwhile, a court has limited ability to look to external sources by which to estimate the pertinent amount. It might fruitfully look to price offers that the owner previously turned down, thus implying that her subjective value exceeds those prices, but this, too, is potentially misleading because of hold-out concerns. The owner may have steadfastly refused to part with her property in the strategic hope of convincing a court to award her an even larger amount later.

In short, courts' underestimating plaintiffs' minimum sell prices may lead to inefficient resource allocations in the presence of a liability rule. This danger is particularly acute when courts use market prices as proxies for plaintiffs' subjective value.

3. Damages awards greater than the appropriator's maximum purchase price are efficient in the absence of transaction and litigation costs

Courts are fallible institutions. This observation entails no criticism, for the judiciary faces formidable challenges. In particular, much of the information necessary to render informed judgments is private to the parties, such that, even with the benefit of admitted evidence, information asymmetries often afflict judicial determinations of fact. The inevitable deficiencies inherent in the litigation process have important implications for the choice whether to protect entitlements through property or liability rules.

Consistent with these concerns, determining the economic value of an expropriated resource is an error-ripe process. Thus, even if the judiciary strives to calculate the economically appropriate figure – the dispossessed owner's minimum willingness-to-sell price – there is no guarantee that it will, on average, reach an amount that approximates the correct value.

As we have just seen, courts' underestimating the worth of an asset to its owner can lead to inefficient resource allocation, even in the absence of transaction costs. If a liability rule undercompensates the initial owner, it will cause at least some inefficient property transfers to take place. Thus, if mean damage awards in appropriation cases involving no transaction costs are likely to be too low, the courts should employ a property rule.

Suppose, however, that courts systemically award *inflated* damages awards, such that the mean pecuniary judgment exceeds the willingness-to-sell figure. This analysis shows that liability and property rules are potentially equivalent. Return to the example in which an owner A, and an interested third party, B, possess minimum willingness to sell and maximum willingness to buy values of £230 and £250, respectively. Assume, however, that the courts erroneously calculate damages at £260. Anticipating this *ex ante*, both A and B know that, in the event that B appropriates the resource without A's permission, the court will impose damages of £260. As that figure exceeds his maximum purchasing price, B will not appropriate the chattel.

This liability regime – in which courts award inflated damages awards – creates a legal backdrop that imparts the same incentive as a property rule. Both remedies render it unprofitable for B to take the asset without permission. If B wishes to obtain the resource, he would have to enter into a contract *ex ante*. As transaction costs are absent, A and B will reach a mutually beneficial agreement à la Coase, in which the parties agree to transfer the property right from A to B for a price between £230 and £250.

This leads to a surprising conclusion: where no bargaining costs exist, we ought to be indifferent between (1) property rules and (2) liability rules that impose financial penalties equal to or exceeding the owner's subjective value. The economic effect of both such remedies is identical: both impart efficient incentives to bargain *ex ante*. This equivalence reveals that property rules are simply a particular kind of liability rule: they impose a price on a taking that is sufficiently high to deter appropriation *ex ante*.

Consistent with this analysis, the judiciary takes a hard line with a defendant who appropriates another's chattel in low transaction cost settings without bargaining for permission. Specifically, the courts use a property rather than a liability rule, unless restitution is impossible due to destruction of the asset. This is efficient for the economic reasons just outlined.

Of course, restitutionary remedies are not always practical after a gratuitous dispossession of one person's property by a non-governmental actor: after all, the wrongdoer may have compromised the economic value of the asset. Where injunctive relief is not available in zero-transaction-cost environments, then, the law implicitly heeds the deficiencies involved in tying damage awards to market value. Instead, the judiciary will generally impose damages that are punitive in the sense that they will exceed both the rightful owner's reservation price and the defendant's maximum willingness to purchase price. This remedy is, of course, efficient because it imparts the same incentives as a property rule.

As explained below, however, this analysis does not suggest that courts should always err on the side of injunctions or inflated damages awards. This is because, in the presence of transaction costs, efficiency may require *ex post* use of the judicial process in lieu of an *ex ante* bargain. An optimal remedy would encourage parties to use the courts instead of contracting when it is efficient from them to do so. In such settings, excessive damages and property rules may stymie efficiency.

C. Supporting Entitlements Where Transaction Costs are Positive but not Preclusive

A key assumption underlying the analysis undertaken thus far is that the parties interested in a resource can negotiate with one another at no expense. When this is true, property rules are efficient. The threat of an injunction – or, equivalently, damages that equal or exceed the owner's subjective value – induces parties who are interested in a resource to bargain for permission *ex ante* with the owner. This is because, in the presence of such a remedy, the cost of a non-consensual transfer to a defendant exceeds the private benefits of appropriating another's entitlement. Assuming no bargaining costs, either a property rule or a high-damages award will desirably allocate resources at no social cost. Property rules and high-damages awards distribute income in favour of the initial entitlement holder. A damages award equal to the owner's subjective value confers the full social value of the property reallocation on the taker.

An assumption of no judicial error, however, is critical to the conclusion that liability rules are efficient. If courts err, awarding damages *less* than the property owner's reservation price, undesirable outcomes may ensue because a liability rule regime in which monetary compensation systemically under-compensates an entitlement holder will spur undesirable transfers from higher- to lower-value uses in at least some circumstances. It thus follows that, for zero-transaction-cost environments in which courts are prone to render excessively low pecuniary damages, property rules are superior.

In reality, however, there are few, if any, situations where no bargaining costs exist. This section explores more plausible cases in which positive, but non-preclusive, transaction costs prevail.

As we know, the Coase Theorem's thesis that efficiency is invariant to the situs of an initial property right applies only where contracting is free. Yet, the essential tenets of the theorem should hold true where the mutual benefits that the parties stand to gain from agreeing exceed the necessary transaction costs. This section addresses the relative superiority of property and liability rules in cases characterised by such conditions. It begins by exploring how transaction costs arise, then addresses the relative merits of property and liability rules where bargaining costs are positive, but not prohibitive.

1. How transaction costs arise: numerous parties, strategic bargaining, information asymmetries, and bilateral monopoly

Bargaining is never free. Even the most amicable and straightforward exchanges entail some expense in identifying the person with whom one must deal, conveying and processing information, weighing one's options, and transferring value. Such impediments to agreement, of course, are often trivial, and will not materially affect the predictions of the Coase Theorem. As a general matter, however, the difficulty and expense of contracting increase in proportion to the number of parties who are privy to an arrangement. If a sufficiently large number of entities are indispensable to alienate a particular entitlement, market-based transactions may not be feasible. In such cases, absent legal intervention, an initial property grant is likely to be final. This phenomenon implicates the relative virtue of property and liability rules.

It does not follow, however, that arrangements involving only a small number of parties are subject to such low transaction costs that a bargain is inevitable. Many deals, even those to which only two parties are privy, entail costly negotiation. This phenomenon is especially pronounced when a large spectrum of mutually acceptable terms exists between the extremes at which prospective promisors and promisees would respectively refuse to contract. The greater the disparity between these terms, the broader the array of terms upon which the parties may reach an accord. Of course, a wide spectrum of mutually acceptable terms may make ultimate consensus more likely. Such a broad range, however, may also render negotiations more protracted because each side will strive for a deal that lies at its most favourable end of the spectrum. The opportunity for such wrangling can both enhance the social cost of successful contracting and may even lead to a bargaining failure in situations where agreement would have been efficient. Information asymmetries, which often exist, may further exacerbate bargaining costs in strategic negotiations because neither party knows the terms that are minimally acceptable to the other.

To illustrate problems with strategic behaviour, return to the prior hypothetical in which A will accept any price greater than or equal to £230 to part with his entitlement and B will pay an amount up to and including £250 to acquire it. Suppose that neither A nor B knows the value that the other places on the resource and assume further that the law protects A's ownership right through a property rule.

B knows that she cannot take the resource without permission: the court would simply require her to return it. To get negotiations moving, either A or B will first suggest a price. What price might each one suggest? Strategic considerations pervade the choice. Each party will push not only to achieve a deal that falls within her range of acceptable prices, but to negotiate the best possible price.

Should A float a figure far above his reservation price, such as £300? In suggesting such an amount, A might hope that the offer would lead B to conclude that A's reservation price is considerably higher than it is. In other words, A is aware that his opening selling price serves as a signalling mechanism to B, such that an initial high offer may result in a greater price than he otherwise would receive. Conversely, though, such an inflated offer could lead B to think that A's willingness to sell price exceeds B's willingness to buy price, thus inducing her to cease negotiations – an inefficient and mutually disadvantageous result.

B's opening price bid would be no less simple. The lowest price at which A will voluntarily part with his entitlement is his reservation price. Yet, B cannot observe this value and A has limited ability credibly to disclose the same. B's bidding low, for instance at £200, might spur A's outright rejection without further interest. Should B convey a generous offer close to her maximum purchase price, say £249, she would likely garner an acceptance, if one is to result at all, but that acceptance would result in B's receiving less-favourable a deal than she may have otherwise achieved. Ultimately, one or both parties may stubbornly hold out, even in the face of a mutually beneficial offer, to extract even-better deals in the future.

How great a danger of scuppering negotiations does such strategic bargaining pose? The answer is case specific, but the principal factor that tempers haggling-induced bargaining costs is competition. When potential parties to a contract can turn to substitutes for comparable performance, the spectrum of terms upon which the parties will agree will narrow. This is because a third party is likely to better a skewed offer that would bestow a disproportionate benefit on the offeror at the offeree's expense.

It follows that transaction costs are more likely to be significant in cases involving a small number of negotiating parties when competition is absent. Economists use the term "bilateral monopoly" to encapsulate a special class of such cases, which involve high bargaining costs between two parties. These monopoly conditions arise where neither party to a would-be contract has access to a viable substitute from whom to obtain the desired performance. Unlike competition, which fosters agreement, bilateral monopoly can frustrate efficient bargain. The strategic bargaining between A and B above is a good example because, by assumption, there is no third party to whom either A or B can look for equivalent performance. A less abstract example involves two opposing parties in a criminal prosecution. The defendant can bargain with no one other than the state; the state with no one other than the defendant. A large spectrum of terms upon which both parties would agree may therefore exist, but, due to the absence of competition that would narrow that spectrum, the parties may engage in protracted negotiations that either delay or even frustrate agreement.

Having thus explored the circumstances in which transaction costs are likely to arise, we can now consider the relative virtue of property and liability rules as applied to cases of positive, but non-preclusive, bargaining costs.

2. A simple case in which liability rules are superior: positive transaction costs; no judicial error; and no litigation costs

We return to the example of the parties, A and B, who value A's property at £230 and £250, respectively. Once more, no third party has an interest in the chattel. Positive transaction costs of £15, however, now exist. As they are less than the combined benefit to the parties of reaching an agreement to transfer A's ownership interest to B, these bargaining costs are not preclusive. The Coase Theorem would predict, therefore, that the market will ensure that the chattel's final allocation will be efficient. Consider the relative effects of the law's protecting A's entitlement through injunctive relief and pecuniary damages, respectively.

Under a property rule, B's choice is to bargain with A for permission to obtain the relevant chattel or to abandon his interest in it. Since a range of mutually acceptable prices in the amount of £20 exists, and because the transaction costs that the parties must overcome in finalising a deal are only £15, the parties will enter into a contract the price of which depends, in part, on the distribution of the bargaining costs.[3] The ensuing allocation of the chattel to B is efficient. The arrangement is a Pareto improvement because it satisfies the preferences of both A and B without negatively impacting those of any third party. Despite the favourable outcome, however, the parties jointly would have been even better off if the circumstances had not required them to suffer an expense of £15 to achieve the benefit of the bargain.

Under a liability rule regime, in which litigation costs are zero, the outcome will be efficient if the parties know that the judiciary will award damages within the spectrum of £230 to £250. In

---

3 If A assumes the full expense of transacting, the parties will settle on a price between £245 and £250. If B assumes all the transaction costs, the price will be between £230 and £235. If the parties split the bargaining costs equally, they will agree on a price between £237.50 and £242.50.

such an environment, B will not bargain with A, but will instead take the chattel and pay the court-ordered price.[4] B's ensuing acquisition of the property is efficient, but in this case, society facilitates the desirable property reassignment at zero cost because litigation is free and bargaining is expensive (£15). A liability rule in this setting thus avoids a societal wealth reduction of £15, and is superior to a property rule for that reason.

3. A simple case in which property rules are superior: positive transaction costs and judicial error

Lest the reader think that liability rules are categorically preferable to property rules when positive, but non-preclusive, transaction costs exist, consider the following case. Suppose that now the courts would erroneously grant A damages of £200 should B appropriate the chattel without A's permission.

As parties bargain in the shadow of the operative legal rule, B knows that he can acquire the good for a mere £200. Even though A values the good at £230, his refusal to sell at less than that price is irrelevant because judicial damages establish a *de facto* price ceiling of £200. In this example, B would inefficiently take the chattel.

What happens if the courts instead protect A's ownership with a property rule? An efficient bargain would ensue. A and B both stand to gain from an arrangement. The threat of an *ex post* injunction would force B to negotiate, such that A and B will agree on a price between £230 and £250. They would have to suffer the transaction costs of £15, but because their aggregate gain from contracting exceeds that expense, an efficient bargain would transpire. Observe that property rules unlock the benefits of private information that may not be available to the courts in setting a damages award.

It therefore follows that, if courts are prone to err downward in damages calculations, property rules are likely superior to damages awards where transaction costs are positive, but not preclusive. If the judiciary correctly determines the magnitude of a deprived property owner's loss, however, liability rules are preferable because they permit the efficient alienation of entitlements without the parties' having to experience the relevant bargaining costs. Recall, of course, that this result holds true only if one assumes away the cost of accessing the legal system. As Part 6 explores, the expense of availing of the judicial process is significant. When litigation costs exceed transaction costs in this setting, property rules are to be preferred.

4. Conclusion

Conventional wisdom holds that courts should use property rules rather than liability rules where bargaining costs are slight. It is important to understand, however, precisely why property rules are often superior in this situation. A person who commits larceny may claim to value the stolen chattel more than the owner does. He may even be right. Yet, the court should award the owner relief that ensures that the asset rests with the person who is willing to pay the most to obtain it. One manner in which to achieve this is to grant the owner an injunction, compelling return of the chattel. This forces the larcener, if he wants to retain or reacquire possession, to bargain for permission.

---

4 It does not matter what amount the court awards within the spectrum of mutually satisfactory prices. Suppose, for instance, that the court awarded A the damages amount within this range that are most favourable to him and least favourable to B: in this case, £250. B would still pay this amount rather than bargain for what would be to her a superior price because, were B to offer any price less than £250, A would not accept it. The parties do not need to know each other's reservation price for this to hold true. They need only know the amount that the court would award in damages. As the cost of bringing suit to A is zero, the damages that the judiciary would award him represent a floor. Yet, that damages figure is also a ceiling, for B will not agree to pay A more than A would get in damages. To emphasise, these conclusions hold true only because the cost of litigation is zero. We shall relax this unrealistic assumption momentarily.

The other avenue by which to ensure efficiency is to award the original owner damages equal to or exceeding her minimum-sell price. To fashion an effective monetary remedy, the court need not know the subjective value that the larcener places upon the appropriated chattel. It need only identify the owner's reservation price. Knowing *ex ante* that he would have to pay that amount *ex post*, a prospective larcener would take the asset without permission only if he valued it more than the amount at which the owner would be willing to part with the same.

Yet, there is a critical shortcoming in the use of a liability rule in this setting, which is a deficiency that a property rule does not implicate: if courts cannot accurately determine the owner's subjective value, or if the larcener is judgment proof, there is no guarantee that a liability regime will impart incentives on third parties to invade another's entitlement only when it is efficient for them to do so. In situations where bargaining costs are low, a strong efficiency case exists for employing a property rule.

D. Proprietary Interests in High-Transaction-Cost Settings

The general rule is that injunctive relief is appropriate where transaction costs are low and that damages are preferable when those costs are large. The reasoning is straightforward: the threat of injunctive relief imposes a prohibitively high price on one who invades an entitlement without permission, thus inducing him to bargain for it through the market. That justification largely evaporates, however, when the market is unavailable, as when the expense of bargaining is preclusive. The law can solve this problem by establishing a price *ex post* that reflects what the parties would have agreed upon *ex ante*, had low transaction costs prevailed. In such settings, a damages regime facilitates the efficient consumption of resources. In contrast, a property rule regime would cause the relevant entitlement to lie with the one who happened first to acquire it. This would be an inefficient result if the initial owner's subjective value is less than the prospective buyer's maximum purchase price.

Although there is good reason generally to favour damages in high-bargaining-cost settings, situations do exist in which injunctive relief may be appropriate. First, employing the litigation process to determine the hypothetical price at which the parties would have reached agreement is itself costly. Thus, property rules may be superior, notwithstanding high transaction costs, if overcoming those expenses through private contract is less costly than the price of discovery. Of course, if one construes "high transaction costs" to refer to bargaining expenses that exceed the benefit to the parties of reaching agreement, then neither property nor liability rules will be preferable where litigation costs are even higher. This point reveals an unfortunate fact, which is that there may never be a better rule.

The second possibility concerns the recurring issue of judicial error. Imagine that courts either systemically under- or overestimate an entitlement's value. The result would be inefficient invasion or non-invasion, respectively, of a resource. The false price signals that erroneous judicial damage awards create may therefore fuel inefficiencies that could be even worse than a property rule's rendering a resource inalienable.

Third, where it is unclear which of transaction or litigation costs are the greater, implementing a property rule may be preferable if affected parties can reach private ordering solutions. For instance, in an influential article, Professor Robert Merges observed that, where it is efficient for them to do so, patentees have voluntarily agreed to convert their property rights to liability rights.[5]

---

5 Robert P. Merges, 'Contracting into liability rules: intellectual property rights and collective rights organizations' (1996) 84 Calif L Rev 1293.

This insight potentially favours protecting valuable rights through injunctions. If courts err in calculating damages in a liability regime, the result may be welfare diminishing reallocations. Conversely, if the initial assignment of an ownership right is inefficient, then even in high transaction cost settings, owners may voluntarily and efficiently transform their rights into a liability rule. Whether the evidence that Professor Merges marshalled in favour of this argument is controlling, however, depends on whether owners protected by an inefficient liability rule regime can also privately contract to convert their ownership rights into a property rule. There are some grounds to believe that they can do so.[6]

Key Points

- The fact of property ownership is distinct from the manner in which the law protects it. The law can safeguard entitlements pursuant to a property, liability, or inalienability rule.
- A property rule triggers injunctive relief, permitting an owner to compel a third-party appropriator to return an item or to end any ongoing incursion.
- A liability rule entitles a property owner to monetary damages in the event of a taking. An appropriator must pay the ordered amount, but can continue to invade the relevant property right without the owner's permission.
- The law protects certain fundamental interests with an inalienability rule. Owners of property rights subject to that protection cannot assign their interests. So, for example, the law will not recognise or enforce an agreement to one's organs.
- A voluminous literature exists clarifying the circumstances in which a property or liability rule is appropriate. Generally, economists do not favour inalienability rules because, if the law misallocates a property interest subject to such protection, parties cannot reassign it to a higher value use à la Coase.
- As a rule of thumb subject to many exceptions, property rules are superior to liability rules in low transaction cost environments. The underlying rationale is that parties can more effectively determine their interests than third parties, including courts. When a property owner is armed with the right to an injunction, one wishing to acquire the resource must bargain for permission.
- The choice of rule influences the manner in which parties negotiate. That is, "parties bargain in the shadow of the law". So, for example, when courts systemically err upward or downward in calculating damages, parties bargaining *ex ante* will inform their positions in light of what they expect the judiciary will do *ex post*.
- Identifying the optimal rule in a particular setting requires comparing transaction to litigation costs (which informs whether bargaining or litigation is relatively efficient) and whether courts systemically overinflate, underestimate, or correctly identify damages. Liability and property rules can be more desirable than the other regardless of whether transaction costs are modest or heavy.

 ## References and Further Reading

Books
Cooter, Robert and Ulen, Thomas, *Law and Economics*, 6th edn (2011) Ch. 5 (IV).
Friedman, David D., *Law's Order: What Economics Has to Do with Law and Why It Matters* (2000) Ch. 5.

---

6 Mark A. Lemley, 'Contracting around liability rules' (2012) 90 Calif L Rev 463.

Miceli, Thomas J., *The Economic Approach to Law*, 2nd edn (2008) pp. 155–61.
Posner, Richard A., *Economic Analysis of Law* (2011) §§ 3.10.

Articles

Calabresi, G., and Melamed, A. Douglas, 'Property rules, liability rules and inalienability: One view of the cathedral' (1972) 85 Harv L Rev 1089.

Epstein, Richard A., 'Why restrain alienation?' (1985) 85 Colum L Rev 970.

Frech, H. Edward III, 'The extended Coase Theorem and long-run equilibrium: The non-equivalence of liability rules and property rights' (1927) 27 Econ Inquiry 254.

Kaplow, Louis and Shavell, Steven, 'Property rules versus liability rules: An economic analysis' (1996) 109 Harv L Rev 713.

Krier, James E. and Schwab, Stewart J., 'Property rules and liability rules: The cathedral in another light' (1995) 70 NYU L Rev 440.

Lewinsohn-Zamir, Daphna, 'The choice between property rules and liability rules revisited: Critical observations from behavioral studies' (2001) 80 Tex L Rev 219.

Mnookin, Robert N. and Kornhauser, Lewis, 'Bargaining in the shadow of the law: The case of divorce' (1979) 88 Yale LJ 950.

Polinsky, A. Mitchell, 'On the choice between property rules and liability rules' (1980) 18 Econ Inquiry 233.

Schwartz, Alan, 'The case for specific performance' (1979) 89 Yale LJ 271.

Part 5

The Law of Contract

1   An Economic Theory of Contract Law   175
2   The Economics of Contractual Remedies   197

Chapter 1

An Economic Theory of Contract Law

Chapter Contents

A.	Contracts and the Coase Theorem	176
B.	Frustration, Impracticability, and Impossibility	179
C.	Mistake, Duress, Undue Influence, and Misrepresentation	184
D.	Problems in Interpretation	188
E.	Limits on Autonomy: Unconscionable Agreements	190
F.	Third-Party Effects and Inefficient Accords: Contracts Against Public Policy	194
Key Points		194
References and Further Reading		196

A. Contracts and the Coase Theorem

Contracts lie at the heart of law and economics, as the exchange inherent in every such bargain represents the Coase Theorem in action. By entering into mutually advantageous agreements, contracting parties create value, correct inefficient assignments of rights, and remedy externalities. In the absence of third-party effects, agreements into which informed, competent adults enter constitute Pareto improvements because they render contracting parties better off without violating the preferences of anyone else.

These economic benefits explain the rules with which law students first become familiar when learning contracts. These rules, of course, concern the fact of offer, acceptance, and consideration: three prerequisites to the formation of a legally enforceable agreement. The first two conditions require the unambiguous articulation, communication, and affirmation of the material terms upon which the parties are willing to contract. By holding that equivocal offers or acceptances do not give rise to contracts, the law makes it less likely that parties will inadvertently bind each other at cross-purposes, entering into arrangements that may not be mutually beneficial. Similarly, the common law rule that, in order to be effective, an acceptance must be the mirror image of the offer played a role in ensuring that the binding terms are, in fact, those to which the parties agreed.

Consideration, in turn, reflects the central economic role of exchange. Contracts can only be mutually beneficial if the relevant promises confer value on all of the parties. So, for instance, if a person gratuitously offers to pay his co-worker £100 the following week, but subsequently reneges on his promise, absent any reliance, the co-worker will have no recourse under the law. If the promisor had premised his offer to pay on the co-worker's ceasing an irritating practice that the co-worker had a lawful right to do, for example, consideration would exist and the contract would be enforceable. The difference in the latter case is that an exchange has taken place. Were the law to jettison this requirement, the courts would encounter many more contracts into which promisors inadvertently entered. Many of these agreements would involve prosaic, family-orientated promises.

Thus, in promoting exchange, contracts serve a critical economic function. A prefatory question, however, asks what independent role the law promotes with respect to these arrangements. At first blush, there seems to be little need for the state to foster agreements under the Coase Theorem. Consistent with the previous Part, if people bargain independently through the market to allocate entitlements, the law's sole function would seem to be to create and to recognise property rights. If contracts are mutually beneficial, why would the state ever need to enforce them?

1. Enforcing contractual promises to remedy monopoly

As the posed question suggests, if all voluntary agreements are reciprocally beneficial, it is not obvious why contract law is necessary at all. Mutually advantageous arrangements ought to be self-enforcing, regardless of whether they have binding force under the law.

In fact, though, the law has a central part to play in fostering efficient agreements because contracts are self-enforcing only in certain circumstances. For instance, there is little need for the law to involve itself in bargains that entail simultaneous performance on all sides. An example would be barter of items the qualities of which are immediately verifiable upon cursory examination. The same is true of deals that arise in competitive markets among parties for whom repeat business is indispensable to long-term survival. Yet, where parties do not exchange bargained-for promises at the same time and where competition imperfectly constrains opportunistic behaviour, sequential performance invites strategic breach in order to take advantage of another's post-performance vulnerability.

The problem is monopoly, which arises to some degree in almost all contracts. To understand why this is the case, envision a straightforward agreement that seems to involve near-simultaneous performance, such as buying dinner at a street food stand. In theory, such a contract should be a Pareto improvement because it simultaneously satisfies the preferences of both the customer and the restaurateur without harming those of any other. Will the parties fulfil their arrangement independent of legal intervention? It depends.

If the diner never expects to return to the vendor again, if there are no legal repercussions, and if he is not altruistic, then he has an incentive to take the food and then skimp on the bill. The risks, however, are not unique to the owner. In the hours and days after he has eaten, the customer hopes that the vendor's food will not make him ill. Yet, if the vendor serves a transient customer base – for instance, he may operate in a tourist-heavy location or he may be able to move his stand to different parts of the city with little difficulty – he can make more money by purchasing sub-standard ingredients at low cost. Prospective customers have little independent ability to protect themselves from poor cooking and bad ingredients because they can only tell so much from a visual inspection and a sample taste. By taking advantage of customers' vulnerability to maximise short-term profit, vendors would reduce the expected value for consumers of buying from food stands. Simultaneously, customers' incentive to eat food without paying for it reduces the expected value to vendors of setting up shop. Violated agreements will, therefore, result in both diminished demand and supply, and reduced levels of welfare for both customers and vendors.

Contract law thus protects against the monopoly that promisors enjoy once promisees have tendered performance under the agreement. In the absence of the legal enforcement of bargained-for promises, property owners who had paid part or all of the contract price would be at the mercy of builders who had yet to finish constructing a house. Having moved into the house and paid the remaining balance, the new homeowners would be vulnerable to shoddy workmanship, as to which they would have no recourse. To render agreements secure, contracting parties would have to engage in protective measures that would be expensive and only partially efficacious. The law thus facilitates the entitlement-shifting function of private arrangements. Contracts and the Coase Theorem go hand in hand.

2. Contracts as risk-shifting devices

The law plays an economic role beyond preventing promisors from reaping windfalls by reneging on their agreed obligations. In a simpler world, that might be the law's sole substantive role. Governments would foster harmonious relations between contracting parties simply by foreclosing strategic behaviour associated with sequential performance. By policing agreements to hold promisors to their word, the law would enable people to perform pursuant to what are, by definition, mutually beneficial agreements. Since every contract would benefit each party privy to the same, few disputes would arise.

The real world, however, is not so simple. Ours is a turbulent reality where certainty as to the future is elusive. A challenging question for the law of contract is what to do when the circumstances surrounding an agreement change in a manner that one or both of the parties did not anticipate. Many students of contract law struggle to formulate coherent principles with which to resolve contested questions of contractual obligation. For some people, the best approach entails a case-by-case, post hoc fairness determination. This backward-looking approach, however, does not consider the rule of decision's effects on future behaviour. Furthermore, as fairness is subjective, inconsistent rules may emerge if reasonable judges reach differing conclusions. Economics, in contrast, offers a forward-looking, consequentialist framework within which to resolve contractual disputes.

Consider some representative examples. If a band obtains a three-day licence for a music venue, but the chief performer loses her voice shortly before the gig, should the courts enforce the agreement and hold the band liable for the licence fee? Imagine an entrepreneur who opens a new electronics store and purchases the relevant stock from a manufacturer. If a freak accident destroys the goods while they are in transit, upon whom should the law impose the loss? Assume that an investor sells a put option that compels her to sell the relevant asset at a particular price in the future. She agreed to the contract because she was confident that the market price of the asset would drop precipitously. If the price instead rises sharply, thus rendering her insolvent if the law were to enforce the contract, how should the court rule? If a person books a flight for a conference that she did not realise is actually the following week, should she be able to rescind her agreement with the airline?

Analysing such problems requires one to appreciate a truth behind the economics of contract law: people can enhance their welfare by binding themselves to positions that may ultimately inure to their detriment. This insight is counter-intuitive, as it is within everyone's common experience to lament prior decisions: "If only I hadn't agreed to that." Ex post regret, however, no more proves that an *ex ante* agreement was undesirable than a happy outcome establishes the wisdom of the underlying, predicate choice. The crucial question is whether a contract, given the information then available, produced a positive expected return for each party who was privy to it.

To clarify this point with concrete examples, contrast two outlandish scenarios. In the first, one person offers to pay another £1,000 if the latter throws a dice and gets a 1. If the offeree throws any other number, however, he must pay the offeror his lifelong savings of £1 million. If the offeree agrees, subsequently throws a 1, and ends up better off by £1,000, does that mean his decision was an intelligent one? Conversely, investors agreeing to fund a start-up company that all agreed to be promising in light of then-available evidence, but that ultimately realises a net loss, may well not have been the correct decision.

The point underlying these examples is that the fact of Pareto improvement is consistent with contracts' rendering some parties worse off *ex post*. Only the fact of *ex ante* expected benefit is relevant. The fact that an arrangement turned out to be against the promisor's expectations, then, is no ground for rescission. In allowing disappointed promisors to renege on their commitments, the law would promote their well being only on a myopic, short-term basis. A rule of law that viewed *ex post* regret as a permissible basis upon which to withdraw a contractual promise would ultimately hurt all entities potentially privy to contracts. As it is the risk-shifting function of contracts that create value for many promisors, allowing the person for whom the negative event materialises to rescind the arrangement would mean many efficient contracts would never come into existence.

3. Contractual liability as an incentive mechanism

As the following pages explain, the law serves two economic functions in regulating parties' contractual obligations. These functions, however, are at least partially in tension. The first is to ensure that contracts are welfare enhancing (e.g. imagine a person who was mistaken about the pertinent facts that existed at the time of an agreement). There is some economic basis to rescind the contract if the accord effected a net welfare reduction. Had the parties known the facts that existed at the time of the contract, they would not have entered into the arrangement. In such circumstances, the assumption that agreements are welfare-enhancing is not valid.

The second economic function is to instil incentives that lead contracting parties to behave efficiently. From this perspective, the law should bind the individual who was ignorant of the operative facts to the contract if she could have learned the relevant truths through cost-justified inquiries. In such a case, liability is less a matter of contract than it is a penalty system designed to inculpate desirable behaviour.

Other contract law problems exist as to which economics similarly offers useful prescriptions. Prominent amongst these are questions of substantive interpretation. How should the courts interpret ambiguous terms or resolve disputes that the terms of the contract did not envision? Questions of capacity also arise. To what degree should the courts defer to autonomy or adopt a paternalistic perspective, thus relieving promisors of ill-advised contractual duties that inure to their detriment?

Should the courts honour one-sided deals? Ought a person's drunkenness be a defence to enforcement? Finally, contracts exist that are inefficient on account of the negative third-party effects that they create. Where negative externalities outweigh the private gains that arrangements impart on contracting parties, the courts should generally refuse to enforce the relevant agreements. We encountered a related example in Part 3 on criminal law, which discussed the economics of illegal drugs.

This chapter addresses all of these questions, explaining how price theory provides clear answers to what may otherwise be intractable problems.

B. Frustration, Impracticability, and Impossibility

1. Introduction

A primary economic function of contracts is to manage risk. This role is often explicit. For instance, investors routinely enter into futures contracts, in which one party goes long and the other goes short as to the expected price of the underlying asset. The division of risk in such arrangements is plain, and constitutes an integral component of many hedging strategies. Another obvious example includes insurance contracts. Pursuant to such agreements, risk-averse individuals transfer the chance of a negative event's occurrence to an insurer. The insurer can achieve risk neutrality by virtue of its ability to pool a large number of risks that are not positively correlated, thus achieving superior diversification than an insured could achieve himself. Such arrangements are mutually beneficial because a risk-neutral insurer can accept a risk at an actuarially fair rate (i.e. at a price equal to the expected cost of the insured-against outcome) while a risk-averse insured will happily pay a price greater than the expected cost of the event to be rid of that chance. The level of the insured's risk aversion and the degree of competition that drives insurance prices toward actuarially fair levels create the spectrum of mutually advantageous prices within which agreement can occur.

Yet, many contracts serve a more subtle insurance purpose. Consider employment agreements in which a company pays its workers a set salary. Such contracts shift part of the risk of fluctuations in the company's profitability away from employees and toward the company's owners. Think also of supply agreements. If an airline is concerned about the volatility of the cost of aviation fuel – a justifiable concern in light of the narrow margins in the airline industry and the ensuing tendency of spikes in key input prices to induce bankruptcy – it can enter into a medium-term supply agreement at a set price. The airline (the promisee) assumes the risk that the cost of fuel will decrease below the agreed-upon price over the relevant time frame, while the supplier (the promisor) accepts the danger that the price will rise. Consider the real-life example of Southwest Airlines, which in 2008 reaped the benefit of a supply agreement that allowed it to obtain more than 70% of its fuel at $51 per barrel, when the market price had risen to over $125 per barrel.

These examples illustrate an economic element of contracts: allocation of risk. The previous section introduced the seeming paradox that mutually advantageous agreements can yield outcomes in which the afflicted parties rue the day they entered into the relevant contracts. The paradox dissolves when one distinguishes the *ex post* and *ex ante* states of the world. Given the lack of certainty that exists at the time of contract formation, the principal question of interest to the economist is whether, in light of then-available information, the agreement produced a positive expected return for each of the parties at the moment it came into being. For these reasons, the fact that a risk materialised to the detriment of one of the contracting parties provides no economic basis upon which to rescind the agreement. Even if one rescinding such an agreement had to pay restitution, contracts could no longer serve a meaningful risk-shifting function. Much investment and economic activity occur on the basis of underlying, risk-regulating agreements. Take away the latter, and one loses much of the former. The law is, therefore, correct to hold that a party cannot rescind a contract on the basis of an event as to which he assumed the risk.[1]

We will now consider three complicating questions, which should be familiar to all students of the common law: the doctrines of frustration, impracticability, and impossibility. The relevant economic principles are common to all three situations, which differ only with respect to the aspect of the contract that the unanticipated event impacts. Specifically, when an *ex post* occurrence reduces or eliminates the value of performance to the promisee, it is a possible case of frustration. When the event severely magnifies the cost to the promisor of delivering the relevant performance, it may be a case of impracticability. If the unexpected incident makes it not only expensive, but physically impossible, for the promisor to deliver what the contract requires, it is potentially an incidence of impossibility.

2. Frustration of purpose

Envision a contract that bestows mutual advantage upon the parties *ex ante* for the typical reason: (1) the bargained-for performance is worth more than the contract price to the promise; and (2) that price exceeds the promisor's costs in delivering that performance. This is a trait common to all efficient contracts, and should reflect every agreement into which informed, competent, adults enter. What happens, however, if events transpire in such a way as to deprive the promisee of the benefit that he would have reaped from the relevant bargain?

In such a situation, enforcing the contract *ex post* may effect a welfare reduction because performance may now be worthless to the promisee, and the contract price may be more valuable in his hands than in those of the promisor. Yet, one cannot simply conclude that efficiency justifies absolving the parties of their obligations in all such circumstances. In particular, one must distinguish events that strip contractual performance of its value, thus justifying rescission on economic grounds, from the materialisation of a risk subsumed within the contract. We have just explored why the realisation of a risk to one party's misfortune generally provides no basis for rescission. Why should a post-formation event that eviscerates the value of the subject matter of a contract produce a different result?

This challenging question lies at the heart of many students' struggles with the related doctrines of impossibility and of frustration of purpose. The economic distinction between (1) the occurrence of a risk that renders performance unprofitable for a party, but that does not justify rescission, and (2) an event that obviates the value of performance to the promisee and that warrants undoing the contract comes down to one thing: whether one party implicitly or explicitly embraced the danger of the relevant event's occurring. If a party did so, then the issue is one of assumed risk and rescission is inappropriate. This distinction would beg the question, however, in the absence of an articulable rule by which to determine whether a party assumed the pertinent risk. Economics provides such a rule.

Where a seller agrees to bear the cost of a potential peril, the contract price will rise to offset the diminished expected value of the arrangement to the seller and to reflect the increased value of the agreement to the purchaser. If a buyer accepts the risk, the effect would be in the opposite direction. The magnitude of the price effect, of course, will depend on the probability of – and magnitude of the harm occasioned by – the pertinent risk's arising. Assumption of risk need not be explicit, as long as the legal environment is such that the entity to be charged with having accepted the danger could determine that implied term.

How should courts determine whether a party assumed the relevant risk? One way is to identify the party best placed to minimise the chance of the harmful event's occurrence. If the parties

---

1 *Great Peace Shipping v Tsavliris Salvage (International)* [2002] 4 All ER 689.

had been able to negotiate in a setting of no transaction costs, thus agreeing to provisions that would settle every conceivable contingency, they would likely have put the risk of loss on the party best able to stop that loss from occurring. Finding the contract enforceable against the lowest cost avoider of a harmful event, which diminishes or eliminates the value of the contract to one party, is essentially a form of strict liability that can induce efficient behaviour.

In short, rescission is economically appropriate on the ground of frustration only where neither party explicitly assumed the risk of the value-eliminating event's occurrence – which assumption would affect the contract price – and where neither party is better placed to minimise the probability of the outcome's actually transpiring. To place these economic principles in context, consider a representative, landmark opinion.

A famous common law opinion concerning frustration is *Krell v Henry*, in which the defendant rented a flat to observe King Edward VII's coronation procession.[2] The defendant's offer made plain that he should "have the entire use of these rooms during the days (not the nights)" of the relevant dates. When the king's illness necessitated the rescheduling of the procession, the flat owner sued for the rent on which the parties had agreed. Nothing in the parties' correspondence referenced the coronation or the repercussions for their agreement if the government were to postpone the event. How should the court have solved this quagmire?

Approach this problem from the perspective of law and economics. Had the procession proceeded as scheduled, the contract would likely have been socially efficient. As the defendant preferred viewing the coronation to holding onto the contract price, and because the plaintiff preferred to receive that sum over maintaining exclusive use of his property for the relevant time period, the agreement would have been mutually beneficial. Did the contract anticipate the disruptive event? If it did, then enforcing the accord correctly promotes the parties' *ex ante* well-being, even if it harms one of them *ex post*. As noted above, an agreement can do so implicitly, as where one party is better placed than the other to prevent the risk from occurring. In *Krell v Henry*, both parties knew that the defendant's sole purpose in renting the room was to view the procession. Neither party, however, had any more control over the timing and details of the coronation than the other. Nor did the court reference evidence that the parties had agreed to adjust the price in a way that would suggest one party's assuming the risk of a delay.

In these circumstances, the court was therefore correct to discharge the defendant's duty to pay the agreed price, for the agreement, viewed *ex ante*, did not anticipate the event and enforcing the agreement *ex post* would have been as likely to reduce aggregate welfare as it would have been to improve it.

It is important, however, that courts apply the doctrine of frustration sparingly. In most circumstances, a sustained examination of the circumstances of the parties' arrangement will reveal that the parties implicitly chose to subject one party to the risk of an event's occurrence or non-occurrence. Often, one party will be better placed than the other to minimise the probability of the undesirable event.

3. Impracticability

Frustration arises when a post-formation incident reduces, by a sufficiently severe margin, the value that the promisee experiences from the promisor's performance. US law refers to the corresponding effect that a promisor experiences as "impracticability", though some courts in the United Kingdom encapsulate both phenomena with the penumbra of frustration.

---

2 [1903] 2 KB 740.

English and Welsh law excuses a promisor from performing only if there is "such a change in the significance of the obligation that the thing undertaken would, if performed, be a different thing from that contracted for".[3] In more recent times, the House of Lords has explained that "frustration . . . takes place when there supervenes an event (without default of either party and for which the contract makes no sufficient provision) which so significantly changes the nature (not merely the expense or onerousness) of the outstanding contractual . . . obligations from what the parties could reasonably have contemplated at the time of its execution[.]"[4] In the United States, the law excuses a person from performing on the ground of impracticability if the event was unexpected, neither the contract nor custom assigned the risk, and the occurrence renders performance commercially impracticable.[5]

The economics of impracticability are indistinguishable from those applicable to frustration. Should an unforeseen disruption in the promisor's operations occur, such as if a natural disaster severely compromises a party's ability to perform, enforcing the contract as written may impose costs on the promisor that swamp its gains under the agreement. An order of specific performance could potentially lead, therefore, to a net welfare reduction as between the parties. Notwithstanding this possibility, courts should find contracts enforceable if they expressly or impliedly imposed the risk on one of the parties.

As with frustration, the risk should lie with the party best able to avoid the danger. So, for instance, consider an agreement between a manufacturer and retailer of household items, such as batteries. The written contract assiduously lays out details and conditions regarding price, quality, time of performance, the means of delivery, termination date, and so on. It makes no reference, however, to the following event: Shortly after signing the agreement, but before the first delivery, the manufacturer's workers go on strike, such that the factory can operate only on a skeleton crew. Assume that the producer could still meet the retailer's order without being rendered bankrupt, but would suffer a disproportionate loss. Should a court grant rescission in such a case?

The economic answer is no. The manufacturer is better placed than the retailer to anticipate a labour-relations dispute, to minimise the cost of such an event if it does happen, and to reduce the likelihood of its occurring. If the law were to relieve the producer of contractual liability, it would temper the manufacturer's incentive to take optimal steps to maintain smooth labour operations. Denying the manufacturer rescission, and thus subjecting it to expectation damages in the event that the strike leads it not to perform, means that the producer will take all cost-justified steps to prevent the labour dispute.

It bears emphasising what categorically falls outside the realm of impracticability: events that increase the cost of performance, but not to the point that approaches the promisor's solvency constraint. It is an incident of every contract that the promisor assumes the risk that the cost of performing will rise. This is part of the risk-shifting function inherent in almost every contract. The only increase in cost that may amount to impracticability is one that threatens to render the promisor insolvent and incapable of further performance should the law enforce the contract as written.

4. Impossibility

Impossibility is a more extreme case of impracticability, differing in degree rather than in kind. The condition arises when a post-formation occurrence not only makes the promisor's obligation more expensive to fulfil, but forecloses any possibility of his carrying it out. The economic issues at play

---

3 *Davis Contractors v Fareham UDC* [1956] AC 696.
4 *National Carriers Ltd v Panalpina (Northern) Ltd* [1981] AC 675.
5 See, e.g. *Transatlantic Financing Corp v United States*, 363 F2d 312, 315–16 (DC Cir 1966).

are identical to those applicable to impracticability, so the courts should not allow a party to rescind an agreement simply because it can no longer complete the required task.

The reader might object that it invites an absurdity to compel a promisor to do what cannot be done. In finding a contract enforceable, however, the law does not necessarily require performance. Instead, it permits a promisor to deliver either the bargained-for performance or its monetary equivalent (expectation damages). Imposing such an obligation, even in the event of impossibility, can instil desirable incentives on behaviour. In particular, if the operative contract is silent and if one party is better able to anticipate, mitigate, or prevent the impossibility generating condition, making that party liable for the expectation value of the contract in the event of such an occurrence imposes incentives to devote an efficient amount of resources to reducing the expected cost of that condition.

Consider a representative example of impossibility, which demonstrates how courts can miss the pertinent economic issues. There is no better illustration than the celebrated case of *Taylor v Caldwell*, in which a music hall burned to the ground shortly before the people who had rented it were to hold a series of concerts.[6] The owners of the property brought a suit to recover what they claimed was rent due under the contract, which had no provision pertaining to the risk of loss of the rented facilities. As the unanticipated event – the destruction of the property – foreclosed the promisor's ability to provide the amenities, but did not reduce the value to the promisees of receiving their bargained-for performance, the case was one of impossibility rather than of frustration. The promisor could no longer carry out his contractual obligation to provide the specific premises, which no longer existed.

In a famous passage, Blackburn, J., opined:

> There seems no doubt that where there is a positive contract to do a thing, not in itself unlawful, the contractor must perform it or pay damages for not doing it, although in consequence of unforeseen accidents, the performance of his contract has become unexpectedly burthensome or even impossible . . . But this rule is only applicable when the contract is positive and abso-lute, and not subject to any condition either express or implied: . . . where . . . it appears that the parties must from the beginning have known that it could not be fulfilled unless when the time for the fulfilment of the contract arrived some particular specified thing continued to exist . . . there, in the absence of any express or implied warranty that the thing shall exist, the contract is not to be construed as a positive contract, but as subject to an implied condition that the parties shall be excused in case, before breach, performance becomes impossible from the perishing of the thing without default of the contractor. There seems little doubt that this impli-cation tends to further the great object of making the legal construction such as to fulfil the intention of those who entered into the contract.

From an economic perspective, there is much that is correct in this piece. Judge Blackburn rightly focused on what the parties would hypothetically have agreed to, had the issue been brought to their attention. For reasons discussed in Section D below, this inquiry lies at the heart of the law and economics assessment of implied terms. The thought process is as follows: in a conjectural, zero-transaction cost environment, contracting parties would include an express provision for every conceivable contingency, no matter how improbable its occurrence. In divvying up their respective obligations, including the assumption of risk, the parties would maximise the total value of the contract. Achieving this goal would entail imposing risk on the party best able to avoid it. Moving from this hypothetical bargain to the real world, positive transaction costs make it

---

6 [1863] 122 ER 309.

inefficient expressly to contract for outlandish outcomes. Instead, the law efficiently imputes terms to which the parties would likely have agreed *ex ante* in the absence of bargaining costs.

The quoted passage in *Taylor* is consistent with this fundamental principle. Judge Blackburn's analysis departs from the mainstream economic view, however, in concluding that the parties would have made the leased premises' continuing existence a condition precedent to the parties' obligations under the contract. This supposition ignores the fact that the probability of the premises' burning down is not fixed. If the promisor can affect the likelihood of that outcome, which surely he can, then the parties may not have made the bargain rescindable by the promisor should the premises have been destroyed. By requiring the promisor to pay expectation damages, the law would instead spur the owner to take all cost-justified measures to prevent the building's destruction.

Given the facts of the case, it seems quite clear that the promisor had superior ability to protect against pre-performance fire than the renters. If that were indeed true, the outcome in *Taylor* may have been wrong from the perspective of economics, even though the larger principles that Judge Blackburn espoused were and remain correct.

We now move from contracts that are mutually beneficial *ex ante* but not *ex post* to consider agreements that fail that potential Pareto-improvement standard from the moment of their inception.

C. Mistake, Duress, Undue Influence, and Misrepresentation

1. Introduction

The key assumption underlying the Coase Theorem, and hence the desirability of contract, is that voluntary arrangements efficiently reallocate entitlements between the contracting parties. This assumption is generally well founded, as people make binding commitments only if they prefer doing so over their alternatives. As explained above, it is often desirable to restrict one's future freedom. Given the risk-shifting function of contracts, *ex post* regret in itself gives a disappointed party no ground on which to back out of an agreement.

Yet, the postulate that voluntary exchange efficiently alienates property interests rests on a series of critical assumptions. The first is competence. If a person is an incapable arbiter of her own well being, her decision to contract does not necessarily satisfy any stable, coherent, or otherwise creditable preference. For that reason, the law allows a minor, at his discretion, to rescind or enforce an agreement into which he entered with an adult. Insane people cannot enter into legally enforceable contracts. Nor can an intoxicated person. Each of these prohibitions lies on a secure economic foundation, as tying an incompetent person's action to advancements in his welfare is a dubious proposition.

These limitations are straightforward. What should we make, however, of an arrangement between two competent adults based on a misunderstanding of fact? What if a promisee influences or pressures a promisor to agree to disadvantageous terms? Should the law require a person to disclose facts of which a prospective contracting party is ignorant? This section explores these questions from an economic perspective.

2. Mistake

A contract should mutually benefit the parties if each knows the relevant facts. In some cases, however, one or both parties may be mistaken as to the relevant circumstances. From an economic perspective, whether rescission is available should depend on the nature of the mistake. If it undermines the assumption of mutual advantage, the arrangement did not presumptively reallocate entitlements in a desirable way. There may still be an economic basis for enforcing the arrangement, but only if one party failed to avail of the cost-justified means by which to learn the truth. If both parties are equally culpable or innocent, however, then no à priori basis exists to believe the arrangement efficient or for assuming that imposing liability on one party will impart desirable incentives for future behaviour. In such a case, the courts should rescind the agreement.

A classic example of mutual mistake lies in the 1864 case of *Raffles v Wichelhaus*.[7] There, the parties entered into a sales contract for cotton, which the promisor would deliver via the ship "Peerless", which was leaving from Bombay. Unbeknownst to the parties, two ships bearing that name existed; one sailed in September and the other in December. The promisor and promisee did not have the same ship in mind, and so they were at cross purposes. The court therefore determined that no contract existed. This is the correct economic result because no there is no reason to suppose that the arrangement promoted the net welfare of the parties. Neither party was more culpable than the other for the misunderstanding.

The common law approach to mistake is broadly consistent with the insights of economics. The seminal 1932 House of Lords' decision in *Bell v Lever Brothers* established that not all instances of mutual (or common) misapprehension render a contract void.[8] Instead, the court espoused the economically sound principle that: "[A] mutual mistake as to some fact which, by the common intention of the parties to a contract, whether expressed or implied, constitutes the underlying assumption without which the parties would not have made the contract they did, and which, therefore, affects the substance of the whole consideration, is sufficient to render the contract void." By framing the legal issue in these terms, the court unwittingly embraced the Coase Theorem. If the parties would still have agreed had they been aware of the relevant facts, the contract still effects, absent third-party effects, a Pareto improvement.

Lord Denning in *Solle v Butcher* later expanded the role of common mistake by finding that equity could render a contract voidable, as opposed to void *ab initio*, on the lesser ground that "a common misapprehension either as to facts or as to their relative and respective rights, provided that the misapprehension was fundamental and that the party seeking to set it aside was not himself at fault".[9] The efficiency of this formulated standard depends on the construction given the quali-fier "fundamental". The economic question is whether knowledge of the mistake as to a then-existing fact would have scuppered the deal, inducing one or more of the parties not to enter into the contract *ex ante*. The issue is not whether the mistake concerned an issue that only proves funda-mental to one or more of the parties *ex post*.

In 2002, the Court of Appeal disapproved of the decision in *Solle v Butcher*, focusing instead on whether the mutual mistake rendered the agreed-upon performance impossible.[10] This modern approach to the problem of mutual misapprehension in entering into a contract is too narrow. Of course, if the parties did not know that the relevant performance was impossible at the time of contract formation, the purported agreement lacks the exchange that is a requisite of an efficient reallocation of entitlements. The performance that an agreement requires, however, may be simultaneously feasible and welfare reducing. In such situations, enforcing the contract as written may effect a reduction in efficiency if neither party was more at fault than the other for the mistake.

The Court of Appeal was therefore right in *Great Peace Shipping v Tsavliris Salvage (International)* to emphasise:

---

7 [1864] 2 H&C 906.
8 [1932] AC 161.
9 [1950] 1 KB 671.
10 *Great Peace Shipping v Tsavliris Salvage (International)* [2002] 4 All ER 689.

> Supervening events which defeat the contractual adventure will frequently not be the responsibility of either party. Where, however, the parties agree that something shall be done which is impossible at the time of making the agreement, it is much more likely that, on true construction of the agreement, one or other will have undertaken responsibility for the mistaken state of affairs.

Now consider a misconception that is limited to one party. Against so-called unilateral mistake, the law takes a harder line than against mutual error. Generally, the law refuses to absolve the mistaken party of liability under the contract, even if enforcing the agreement imposes great hardship on the misguided party. Why does a different rule apply?

Economics provides a ready answer. Where only a single party is mistaken, it suggests that the relevant information was accessible in a cost-justified way. Even though the law speaks of "enforcing" the contract, that terminology is somewhat misleading. In the case of unilateral mistake as to a foundational element of the contract, there is no meeting of the minds and hence no actual agreement for the law to implement. Instead, the law imposes liability on the mistaken party, requiring that it either perform as understood by the promisee or pay expectation damages. The effect is comparable to the economic role of liability in tort law. By imposing such a price on unilateral mistake, the law spurs prospective parties to a contract to devote an efficient amount of resources to educating themselves about the material facts attendant upon their potential agreement. In cases of mutual mistake, by contrast, the fact of both parties' ignorance suggests that learning the relevant fact may not have been feasible at the time of entering into the contract. Where all parties are mistaken about an essential term of the contract, and there is no reason to deem one more at fault than the other, then no presumption of efficiency can exist, and so rescission is appropriate.

3. Undue influence and duress

(a) Undue influence

Unless an exchange is "voluntary", there is no reason to suppose it efficient. Free consent is, therefore, a predicate condition of presuming mutually valuable exchange. Yet, such terms as "coercion" and "voluntary" are not always clear. The question of whether a promise was freely made does not necessarily invite a binary answer. At one end of the spectrum lie informed decisions into which promisors enter after thoughtful deliberation, with full knowledge of the facts, and without pressure from third parties. The other extreme involves "your money or your life" scenarios. Few decisions lie at these limits. It cannot be the case, however, that any degree of external pressure, stress, coaxing, or immediacy deprives a contractual promise of its legitimacy. Few of the routine choices that people make in life arise in a neutral vacuum, untouched by emotion, stress, urgency, or third-party cajoling.

Thus, mere pressure by one prospective party to a contract rarely results in a void or voidable agreement. People bargain with each other all the time, and negotiations invariably entail efforts to persuade another of the virtues of a position. In this respect, the negotiation process carries a preference-shaping function. How, then, can a court distinguish pressure of the kind that precedes a valid, efficient contract from that which amounts to duress?

The first question is whether the circumstances surrounding a promise were such that the promisor's binding himself to a contractual obligation does not reflect his preference. For example, if a promisee secures the commitment he seeks by subjecting a person who is easily manipulated to protracted pressure, the promisor may agree to a course contrary to self-interest. In such a case, instead of being stable over time, the preference upon which the promisor acted may be fleeting. Contracts based upon the satisfaction of transitory and soon-to-be-contradicted preferences do not obviously effect a Pareto improvement. In such cases of undue influence, a person in a dominant position can manipulate a promisor's thinking, such that he transplants his own preferences onto the promisor.

(b) Duress

Cases of duress are different than undue influence. In particular, a coerced person's choice may represent a clear and stable preference that will not change over time. How should the courts approach these problems? The case law often asks whether a promisor's entering into the impugned contract was "a voluntary act".[11] Resting alone, this language is unhelpful because, as the next paragraph explains, even a coerced choice is, in some respects, voluntary. Economics can inject meaning into such terms as "duress" and "involuntary", thus giving rise to workable definitions.

The problem with cases of duress is that a third party manufactures a false choice for an offeree. The coerced offeree may have a decided preference for one presented outcome over another yet, but for the duress, would have been able to satisfy that overriding preference without bearing the cost that the coercing party has created.

For instance, imagine a situation in which a criminal broke into a banker's house, tied up his family, and told him that, if he did not get a certain amount of money from his employer, the criminal would kill them. From a narrow (and misleading) perspective, the potential for a mutually beneficial exchange does exist. The banker would prefer to keep his family safe than to take money from the institution for which he works. At the same time, the criminal would rather get the money than kill the banker's family. Does it follow that the ensuing arrangement effects a welfare improvement between the parties? The answer is yes only if one assumes that the choice with which the unfortunate promisor was presented was inevitable. One should not conduct the relevant efficiency analysis in a manner divorced from the consequential effects of rendering such agreements enforceable under the law.

Economic analysis explains the intuition: the bank-robbery arrangement is inefficient. The criminal artificially manufactured conditions to facilitate the relevant agreement, which works a reduction in the long-term welfare of the banker and that bestows a windfall on the criminal. The relevant contract, though "voluntary" in the sense that the promisor was free to choose between unpalatable options, was involuntary because the choice was itself a contrived construct. Bankers are better off in a world in which the courts do not recognise such coerced agreements as legally enforceable. By declining to bestow legal status upon such arrangements, the law reduces the expected gain to criminals of bringing them about. The ensuing drop in activity levels, of course, is desirable.

This is the economic reason why the law refuses to recognise contracts into which one party forced another to enter. Where duress is a "but for" cause of a person's accepting an offer, the preference that the arrangement satisfies relates only to a choice that the coercing party generated. If the law were to enforce agreements into which parties entered while under duress, it would spur inefficient expenditures in manufacturing and in defending against coerced agreements.

4. Misrepresentation and omission

This section concludes with the related issues of misrepresentation and omission. The first point is that problems of prospective parties' manufacturing lies or failing to disclose material truths would not arise in zero-transaction cost environments. These are characterised by perfect, symmetric access to information. In the real world, of course, many contractual negotiations take place in information-deprived settings.

---

11 *See, e.g. The Sibeon and The Sibotre* [1976] 1 Lloyd's Rep 293; *The Universe Sentinel* [1982] 2 All ER 67.

It makes little sense to suppose contracts are mutually beneficial if a party has a fundamental misapprehension as to a material fact. For that reason, mutual mistake permits rescission if both parties were equally culpable in their ignorance. Yet, the law may efficiently impose liability, notwithstanding a party's error to induce people to apprise themselves of the relevant facts. As in tort law, the efficient rule is to impose liability on the lowest cost avoider of the relevant mistake.

In cases of intentional misrepresentation, there is no ambiguity concerning the identity of the lowest cost avoider. When a offeror manufactures a mistruth to convince an offeree to contract, the courts should and do enforce the agreement as understood by the lied-to party. This holds true even if the recipient of the lie could have learned the truth at low cost – the reason is that the misrepresenting party had even less difficulty undoing the lie. The law was therefore correct to hold that: "[i]f a man is induced to enter into a contract by a false representation it is not a sufficient answer to him to say, 'If you had used due diligence you would have found out that the statement was untrue. You had a means afforded to you of discovering its falsity, and did not choose to avail yourself of them'."[12]

A key element of this rule, however, is that the recipient of a misrepresentation should reasonably understand that the communication amounts to a statement of fact. Thus, sales puff and assertions of broad opinion generally do not render an ensuing contract voidable at the instance of the misinformed party.[13] This element of the law makes sense, as it incentivises people subject to implausible claims of largesse free from specific facts to receive those claims with warranted scepticism.

An interesting asymmetry exists between how the treatment that the common law treats misrepresentations and omissions. The general rule is that a vendor need not disclose a material fact to a prospective purchaser, which reflects the age old adage of *caveat emptor*. Representatively, Judge Blackburn famously declared in 1871: "A mere abstinence from disabusing the purchaser of that impression is not fraud or deceit, for, whatever may be the case in a court of morals, there is no legal obligation on the vendor to inform the purchaser that he is under a mistake which has not been induced by the act of the vendor."[14]

Is there an economic basis for this distinction? The rule creates an incentive for a prospective purchaser to investigate the qualities of the relevant item and to put pertinent questions to the seller, who by virtue of the rules discussed above cannot lie his way into an enforceable contract. Given that the would-be purchaser has the most information about the characteristics that are important to her in the subject matter of the proposed contract, it may be efficient to place the duty of discerning the relevant traits on her.

This efficiency justification would not hold true, however, as so-called "latent defects" – those deficiencies that one could not identify upon a reasonable inspection. The majority rule today holds that, if a seller knows of a latent defect in the property that he seeks to sell, he must disclose it to aspiring purchasers. This approach makes economic sense.

D. Problems in Interpretation

Contractual disputes routinely arise when a post-formation event, for which the underlying agreement does not provide, materially affects the nature, cost, or effect of the relevant performance. This creates a quandary for the law. If the courts' task is to hold promisors to their obligations, thus

---

12 *Redgrave v Hurd* (1881) 20 ChD 1.
13 *See, e.g. McKeown v Boudard-Peveril Gear Co* [1896] 65 LJ Ch 735.
14 *Smith v Hughes* [1871] LR 6 QB 597.

protecting promisees against opportunistic breach, what can the judiciary do when the operative contract simply fails to address an issue? Is it appropriate for the law to inject a term to which the parties did not actually agree? Most people would say that it is, at least if the introduced term is a reliable proxy for what would have transpired under the relevant counterfactual. Yet, how can the judiciary delve into the mysteries of a "but for" world and arrive at an accurate prediction? Economics provides a methodology by which to approach this problem.

The first step is to understand why gaps and ambiguities arise. Positive transaction costs accompany all contractual negotiations. There are an almost infinite number of eventualities that may arise post-contract formation, even though the probability of many of their occurring is remote. To provide specifically for every possible contingency would entail vast expense. The law, however, can alleviate this defect by implying provisions upon which the parties would have agreed had bargaining costs been lower.

Second, the economic approach to implying terms and to extrapolating meaning from ambiguous provisions assumes that the parties meant to maximise the aggregate value that their arrangement created. Is this assumption justified? At first blush, one might think not. After all, each individual privy to an agreement cares only about his own return (i.e. in extracting the greatest value possible) rather than in ensuring a just or equal distribution of wealth to other contracting parties. How can one, therefore, extrapolate from an individual objective to a potentially inconsistent collective goal?

The answer is that, to achieve the largest private gain from a contract, the first step is to maximise the net value of the arrangement. All things being equal, the more profitable the agreement, the greater the amount of wealth available for individual distribution. If slices increase in proportion with the size of the pie, those entering into a contract would agree on terms that maximise their collective wealth. Law and economics seeks to give effect to that supposition by implying and interpreting terms to maximise value.

Some examples illustrate the point. One of the most well-known implicit terms in contract law is the implied covenant of good faith and fair dealing. Another is that the goods that a vendor sells are fit for their ordinary purpose. Another still is that a retailer will use its best efforts in marketing a manufacturer's goods that it has agreed to sell. There are many such examples, but the trait common to each one is that, if parties decided not to agree on such terms, it would probably effect a net welfare reduction. For instance, if promisors and promisees declined to deal in good faith with each other, there would be potential for opportunistic behaviour in light of the sequential nature of performance. Similarly, a manufacturer would be unlikely to pay a retailer to distribute its goods if it had no contractual basis for ensuring that the retailer would actively attempt to market them. In all of these instances, the law predicts that the parties would have agreed on the implied terms, had they only thought to include them.

One can thus see that the *ex ante* bargaining process, *ex post* litigation, and the underlying legal framework enjoy a symbiotic relationship. Prospective parties to a contract bargain in the shadow of law. If the law implies terms to which most parties would agree, those provisions become the default components of any contract. Such implication may be efficient because it spares the parties any need to brave the transaction costs required to make the implied term an explicit part of their contract.

This constitutes an important, efficiency enhancing function of the legal system, but it does not follow that the law should always imply terms. The complication is that the legal process is itself costly, not just in terms of lawyers' fees and consuming the courts' limited resources, but in terms of potential error. When a promisor and a promisee agree to make a term an explicit part of their arrangement, they suffer the transaction costs necessary to reach consensus on the point, but gain a guarantee of mutual benefit. By contrast, in implying terms, courts engage in a hypothetical exercise by appealing to a non-existent counterfactual. The cost of employing the judicial apparatus in this matter may be less than the transaction costs involved in private agreements because one ruling that creates a precedent can substitute for countless drafting sessions. Nevertheless, when courts venture beyond terms that would obviously have enhanced the aggregate value of the relevant contract, they engage in an increasingly speculative exercise which threatens to inject an incorrect default term. In that event, negotiating parties either have to spend their limited resources on overcoming the incorrect default rule or suffer the repercussions of that implied term should the pertinent event come to pass.

For that reason, courts refuse to imply a term where the parties are clearly the lower-cost determinants of the relevant provision. The quintessential common law example is the judiciary's refusal to impute a price where the parties failed to agree upon a figure themselves. The capacity for error here is severe, as a mistaken judicial estimate of the appropriate price may create a welfare-reducing contract. The parties themselves have private information which is crucial for determining the relevant price. Only where the bargain is such that courts can determine price by reliably appealing to an objective metric will they impute a price term. A good example concerns the introduction of a default "reasonable price" between merchants who regularly deal in certain goods under the US Uniform Commercial Code. In such cases, regular market prices provide a reliable benchmark, mainly because the value of the sold goods to merchants lies in their commercial value, rather than their idiosyncratic, subjective, worth.

In light of these concerns, the constrained approach to judicial implication of terms adopted by the common law has much to commend it. In *Southern Foundries* (1926) *Ltd* v *Shirlaw*, the House of Lords provided what is perhaps the most famous exposition of the rule: "Prima facie that which in any contract is left to be implied and need not be expressed is something so obvious that it goes without saying; so that, if, while the parties were making their bargain, an officious bystander were to suggest some express provision for it in their agreement, they would testily suppress him with a common 'Oh, of course!'"[15]

This approach correctly encapsulates the law and economics goal of implying terms, which is to minimise the combined resource and error costs of drafting and litigation. The courts promote this goal only by implying terms where they are confident that the implied provisions would have been a constituent part of a value-maximising contract *ex ante*. To go full circle, one can understand the doctrines of frustration, impracticability, and impossibility as default terms around which parties are free to bargain. Where any of those doctrines applies to render a contract voidable, the law recognises that a term excusing further performance in light of the operative event would have been a value-enhancing provision. The economic insight that no such excuse should apply where one party is better able to avoid the event also reflects the ex ante hypothetical bargain that would generate the greatest possible ex ante wealth from the contract.

E. Limits on Autonomy: Unconscionable Agreements

How should the law treat "unfair" or "one-sided" contracts? One possibility is to dismiss perceived inequity as an irrelevant detail. A person should stand by her promises, even improvident ones, or those that fail to seize a proportionate share of the wealth surplus that the contract generated. This cold line, however, would be anathema to those who believe that courts should free parties from imprudent assurances that they uttered from disadvantaged positions. The law adopts a middle course, generally holding people to their ill-considered promises but, in extreme cases, refusing to enforce "unconscionable" bargains. This section explores the questions of whether unconscionability makes economic sense and whether rendering contracts with oppressive terms voidable fulfils an economic role distinct from the excuses for performance explored above.

---

15 [1940] AC 701.

1. Procedural unconscionability

First consider procedural unconscionability. This arises where a person innocently signs an agreement while oblivious to a draconian provision that the promisee later seeks to enforce against him. As explored throughout this chapter, contracts presumptively yield mutual gains only if the parties were aware of the material terms. If a promisor were justifiably ignorant of a punitive term (e.g. the drafter may have buried it within the fine print of an adhesion contract) enforcing the contract would carry two negative economic effects. First, it could reduce the parties' combined welfare, as the harm to the ambushed promisor may exceed the gain to the promisee. Second, enforcing such terms would encourage drafters to devise novel ways of injecting harsh terms to catch unwary promisors. That, in turn, would induce promisors to take costly self-protection measures. Both such effects, of course, would be inefficient because they would require spending scarce resources on a non-welfare-enhancing goal.

Yet, the prohibition on unfair surprise engendered in the previous rule should not benefit a person whose ignorance of a term is not justifiable. It is generally incumbent on the party who is signing to familiarise himself with the terms of the contract. If the terms ultimately inure to his disadvantage, the courts will not entertain claims of unconscionability. This rule makes good economic sense, even if the agreed-upon terms reduce welfare *ex post*. The reason lies in forward-acting incentives: in most circumstances, the signing party can determine the terms of a contract at low cost. Holding a promisor to the terms of the papers that she signs, inculpates a powerful incentive to learn those terms *ex ante*. Only in rare circumstances (e.g. where a drafter hides a term that contradicts reasonable expectations within a voluminous contract) will the court discharge a promisor from his duties.

2. Substantive unconscionability

Now, consider substantive unconscionability – otherwise known as "oppressive terms". This encompasses a variety of scenarios, of which the usury laws are a specific example. The law characterises outcomes producing oppressive provisions by reference to "inequality of bargaining power".[16] That asymmetry produces outcomes skewed in favour of the party in a superior position. One can impart economic meaning on the term "bargaining power" by equating the term to "monopoly" or "monopsony". In either such event, competition exists on one side, but not both sides, of a market. One party to a potential bargain may be able to walk away, while another cannot. While vast differences in bargaining power implicate questions of fairness, it is more difficult to discern an efficiency objection.

Take the following example: a person's car breaks down as he is driving through desolate terrain in severe weather conditions, far from the nearest town, without mobile phone reception. Desperate to escape his plight, he is elated to spot another car driving in his direction. The would-be saviour, however, is a cold-hearted person who spies a way to profit from the man's misfortune. The driver announces that the price of her helping the stranded man by driving him to the town is £30,000. Knowing that the alternative would be a dangerous night stranded in his car in inclement weather, he agrees. What should the courts do if, after the woman had driven him to the nearest town and to safety, the man refuses to pay on the ground that the agreement was substantively unfair?

Pause here to consider the difficulty of finding an economic objection corresponding to the substantive unconscionability that many readers would read into this contract. The parties knew the terms and embraced them willingly. Few would doubt the urgency that underlay the man's preference

---

16 *See Lloyds Bank Ltd v Bundy* [1975] QB 326.

to get to the nearby town, but, unlike the case of duress considered above, the promisor driver did not create that urgency. The voluntary contract satisfied both parties' preferences – the man preferred to part with £30,000 than to spend a dangerous night in the wilderness and the woman preferred the money over the convenience of not having to drive to the town. If we assume that the agreement carries no third-party effects, it effects a Pareto improvement. What, then, is the problem?

The answer, from the perspective of efficiency, is not obvious. If "unconscionability" refers only to an unequal divide of benefits, the concept rests awkwardly with an economic account of contract. Is a win–win arrangement necessarily enough to trigger legal enforceability, or must the gains be symmetrical? Those who adhere to norms of distributive justice may answer yes to the latter question, but their point of view would not resonate with many economists. From an economic perspective, it would be perverse to undo an arrangement that enhances the wealth of all based on concerns of equal distribution. Is it a better state of affairs if everyone is simultaneously worse off and more equally deprived? Most economists working in the neoclassical tradition would conclude that the answer is no.

Thus, the tension between distributive justice and aggregate wealth maximisation comes down to a conflict between two partially conflicting norms. The manner in which different individuals weigh these norms gives rise to distinct preferences, on which of course the law and economics framework generally takes no position. Thus, one can see that law and economics is a powerful analytic tool, the reach of which is not universal. It treats preferences as exogenous, leaving it for other disciplines to explain the same and to make the case for influencing them in a particular direction, if at all.

Economists generally resolve the tension between fairness and aggregate wealth in the following manner: They acknowledge that many people prefer to live in a world in which at least some horizontal equity exists between individuals, such that sharp differences in affluence can be a social ill. Economists predominantly argue, however, that law is an inappropriate mechanism by which to achieve such equity. Court decisions only affect the well being of the parties privy to the case; they represent an arbitrary minority of a larger pool of similarly situated people. More importantly, using the law to this effect may reduce aggregate wealth in society, not least because adjusting doctrine to achieve wealth redistribution creates an unpredictable legal environment. Instead, economists advocate using the tax system to redistribute wealth more efficiently. Properly designed taxes will distort behaviour less severely than wealth-shifting legal rules.

Returning to the hypothetical with the stranded driver. One objection is that the parties could have reached a mutually advantageous agreement on more equal terms. This is not an efficiency objection. It simply states that an equally efficient, but fairer, arrangement could have ensued. The reason why the woman could demand such a high price was monopoly. If another driver had simultaneously happened by, the man could have bargained with both drivers, each of whom would have sought to undercut the other. If the law prohibited a monopoly price – principally in the form of refusing to enforce substantively unconscionable contracts generating oppressive terms – it would create a price constraint, thus capping the parties' bargaining range. The driver, then, would not demand £30,000 in such a legal environment because the expected return in court would either be £0 or, more likely, restitution in the form of petrol costs and the inconvenience of driving the man to the town. Instead, the driver would likely float a more reasonable price – say £1,000 – which the courts would presumably enforce. The result would be a contract that would simultaneously fulfil the bargaining parties' preferences and promote fairness.

Yet, using unconscionability as a price cap may itself be problematic. The issue is that the rule prohibiting monopoly terms may inadvertently scuttle some efficient potential contracts. For instance, if for idiosyncratic reasons £10,000 were the driver's reservation price, the law's imposing a cap of, say, £5,000 would result in no contract. The driver would pass by the stranded man, leaving both parties worse off. The economic danger here relates to error costs. The courts must tailor price constraints so as not to foreclose economically desirable transactions. Unfortunately, the judiciary is poorly placed to perform such a function. This point relates to Part I, which addressed the problem of free market pricing in the event of supply shocks, such as those associated with natural disasters. We saw that allowing markets to produce unusual prices in response to major external events involves a trade-off between inducing incentives towards speedy market self-correction and what many people would regard as decent behaviour.

The short conclusion is that, if substantive unconscionability corresponds to an unequal division of profit under a fully informed agreement between mentally sound parties with different bargaining power, the common law prohibitory rule is hard to justify from the perspective of economics.

3. An illustration: Council Directive 93/13/EEC on Unfair Terms

To illustrate the preceding analysis, consider the EU's Directive on Unfair Terms in Consumer Contracts. Passed in 1993 and subsequently incorporated into domestic law by the Member States, it renders certain unfair contractual terms unenforceable against consumers. The quality of "fairness" is, of course, subjective. The Directive imparts some meaning, however, by explaining that a term that the parties did not individually negotiate is unfair if "it causes a significant imbalance in the parties' rights and obligations arising under the contract, to the detriment of the consumer". Through an annex, it provides a non-exclusive list of unfair terms. The law applies only to contracts into which consumers – meaning: "Any natural person . . . acting for purposes which are outside his trade, business or profession" – enter with sellers or suppliers "acting for purposes relating to [their] trade, business or profession[.]"

These provisions reveal that European lawmakers were concerned about asymmetric bargaining positions, whether they arise from a seller's superior sophistication or economic power relative to the consumer. What might an economist make of the Directive? There is an important distinction between procedural and substantive unfairness. The former is generally of greater economic concern. So economists would generally embrace striking a contractual provision that "irrevocably bind[s] the consumer to terms with which he had no real opportunity of becoming acquainted before the conclusion of the contract" if its known inclusion may have induced the consumer not to sign the contract. Generally, the law incentivises consumers to familiarise themselves with the terms of agreements that they sign by holding them to disadvantageous terms. This is one example of *caveat emptor*. Yet, when there is no meaningful ability to discern a contractual provision that runs counter to expectation, enforcing that term may detract from welfare. This aspect of the Directive makes sense.

As for terms to which consumers knowingly agree, the fact of "detriment" is more elusive. Most contracts contain individual provisions that promote the buyer's interest over the seller's, and vice versa. That is the nature of compromise. Striking individual terms from contracts that promote the interest of the supplier to the detriment of the customer would undo some welfare-enhancing contracts. It is possible, then, that the Directive could scuttle desirable agreements. Fortunately, it limits its scope in several important ways. First, it applies only to disadvantageous terms that create "a significant imbalance" in the parties' rights and that are "contrary to . . . good faith". Thus, it construes terms collectively to determine whether they weigh heavily in favour of the supplier. Second, it assesses unfairness "at the time of conclusion of the contract". That *ex ante* approach is correct because many risk-shifting contracts appear unfair after the fact for the party who embraced a risk that later materialises.

Most significantly, though, individual negotiation over a term brings it outside the scope of the Directive. This holds true regardless of whether it would otherwise be considered "unfair". This feature makes economic sense. If the parties bargained over whether to include a term, its incorporation into a duly executed contract suggests that the agreement effects a Pareto improvement between the contracting parties.

Thus, the Directive focuses on contracts of adhesion. There is no general economic reason to invalidate provisions in adhesion contracts, which economise on transaction costs. Yet, because of the Hobson's choice presented in many such settings, terms will reflect a fair apportionment of the surplus that the contract realises only if adequate competition exists on the seller's side. Under monopoly, adhesion contracts may include terms allowing sellers to appropriate the lion's share of the value of the agreement. As noted above, rules against substantive unconscionability can induce parties to divide the benefit of their bargain more equally. The risk is that, in limiting the degree of asymmetric profit, the law may reduce the private value of some contracts to sellers below their reservation level, thus preventing some efficient agreements from taking place. However, as the Directive aims at narrow terms that are apt to act against consumers' interests and are unlikely to be a "but for" cause of reaching agreement, it is improbable that this risk will materialise.

F. Third-Party Effects and Inefficient Accords: Contracts Against Public Policy

This chapter concludes with a brief word on agreements that, though privately beneficial to the parties, are nevertheless inefficient because of third-party effects. We have seen that informed people voluntarily bargain with one other when that arrangement is to their mutual advantage. For that reason, economists assume that contracts are welfare-enhancing when negative externalities are absent.

Yet, many contracts carry negative consequences for third parties. Unless those affected individuals were privy to contractual negotiations and had an ability to veto any agreement, one cannot presume that externality producing contracts are invariably efficient. This is a significant problem, of course, because many of those whom contracts affect will not be parties. The law generally assumes that the private benefits of agreements outweigh third-party effects. However, it tempers the potential for inefficient contracting through liability in tort for certain damages caused by externality producing agreements. In certain cases, the law abandons the presumption of contractual efficiency altogether (e.g. it will not permit contracts that seek to harm third parties). The presumption of efficiency in such causes obviously does not hold true. Thus, agreements to kill, injure, or defame third parties are not enforceable. Such arrangements fall within the larger rubric of contracts against public policy, which the courts will not recognise.

The externality issue is most vexing when the trade-off between negative third-party effects and the private gains occasioned by the relevant agreement does not lead to a clear-cut conclusion. This observation allows us to circle back to Part III, which discussed challenging questions concerning the efficiency of gambling, prostitution, and the purchase and sale of drugs. In such cases, the desirability of the underlying contract depends on a case-specific weighing up of the private benefits and social costs that the impugned arrangement generates.

As many agreements carry third-party effects, and because transaction costs preclude many stakeholders from negotiating in the underlying arrangement, one cannot rely on the fact that a free market will always produce contracts that maximise social welfare. The externality problem remains central to efficiency. Part 8 addresses an important example, which is that the law forbids horizontal competitors from entering into cartel agreements. Such arrangements yield significant gains to the contracting parties, but inflict disproportionate losses on society. In that example, as in many others, economics provides a useful tool with which to determine whether the net welfare effect of an agreement is positive or negative.

Key Points

- The Coase Theorem predicts that, in zero-transaction cost settings, parties will bargain to reallocate property interests to ensure optimal assignments. The theorem finds expression in the real world through contracts, which are thus an important field of study within law and economics.

- Informed, competent parties voluntarily negotiate with one another only if it is in their mutual interest *ex ante*. That is why contracts typically create a Pareto improvement in the absence of negative externalities. The law may still be necessary, however, where agreements call for sequential performance. By enforcing contractual promises, the law solves the monopoly problem that arises when a performing entity is at the mercy of one that has yet to perform.

- Parties often contract to shift risk. When contracts serve an insurance function, they typically benefit one party and harm the other *ex post* depending on whether the insured condition arises. To determine whether an agreement was and is efficient, one must analyse it *ex ante*. Thus, the fact that a contract hurts a promisor is no basis for rescission.

- Nevertheless, the law permits rescission in the event of frustration, impracticability, or impossibility.

- Frustration entails an occurrence the risk of which neither party assumed which eliminates the value of performance to the promisee. To tell whether a party embraced that risk, in the absence of an express provision, one should ask whether either party was better placed than the other to stop its occurrence. If neither is so situated, rescission is appropriate.

- Impracticability and impossibility are equivalent to frustration, except that they concern an event that renders prohibitive the cost of performance to the promisor.

- Contracts are presumptively efficient because the parties understand the terms of their arrangement. If one or both parties misapprehend a material term, however, that presumption is no longer justified. There is no "meeting of the minds". One might imagine, therefore, that all significant errors justify rescission. That is not the law, however, and for good reason. Enforcing a contract against a mistaken party imposes a cost that spurs future promisors to make themselves aware of the conditions to which they agree. Thus, in the absence of wrongdoing by the other party, unilateral mistake should not allow the misguided party to annul the contract. In contrast, mutual mistake suggests that neither party could reasonably have known about the error, so more readily gives rise to rescission.

- Duress, undue influence, and misrepresentation allow the victim to rescind the contract because they deprive the "agreement" of its voluntary character, thus upsetting the assumption that the arrangement effects a Pareto improvement. In the case of duress, even though a promisor may eagerly accept a proposed offer (e.g. "your money or your life") that is a false choice that the wrongdoer inefficiently created.

- Ambiguity arises in contract because parties do not expressly account for an outcome. That failure typically occurs due to transaction costs. The law can efficiently impute terms that the parties could not cost-effectively have provided for in their agreement. The principal economic insight is to construe the agreement to maximise the joint surplus of the contract *ex ante*. That hypothetical construction attempts to recreate the outcome had the Coase Theorem applied.

- Courts will set aside an unconscionable contract, relieve the burdened party of its obligations under the agreement, or strike an offensive term in one of two settings. First, procedural unconscionability may lead a disadvantaged party unknowingly to embrace a term, such as when a sophisticated vendor buries an oppressive condition in the fine print of an adhesion contract. Economics justifies rescission in such settings if the promisor could not reasonably have known about the term. Second, substantive unconscionability arises where the terms – though knowingly adopted by the parties – are sufficiently unfair. This provision of the law is more difficult to understand from an economic perspective because it goes not to whether a contract mutually benefits the parties, but to an unequal division of the surplus. While fairness considerations may justify rescission, the economic danger is that the ceiling thus created may deter some sellers from contracting.

References and Further Reading

Books

Cooter, Robert and Ulen, Thomas *Law and Economics*, 6th edn, 2011, Chs 8 (I, II, IV, & V) & 9 (II).
Miceli, Thomas J., *The Economic Approach to Law*, 2nd edn (2008) Ch. 4.
Posner, Richard A., *Economic Analysis of Law* (2011) §§ 4.1–4.9, 4.15.
Shavell, Steven, *Foundations of Economic Analysis of Law* (2004) pp. 291–303, 325–85.

Articles

Aghion, Philippe and Hermalin, Benjamin, 'Legal restrictions on private contracts can enhance efficiency' (1990) 6 JL Econ & Org 381.
Ayres, Ian and Gerner, Robert, 'Filling gaps in incomplete contracts: an economic theory of default rules' (1989) 99 Yale LJ 87.
Bayern, Shawn J., 'Rational ignorance, rational close-mindedness, and modern economic formalism in contract law' (2009) 97 Cal L Rev 943.
Ben-Shahar, Omri, 'An ex-ante view of the battle of the forms: inducing parties to draft reasonable terms' (2005) 25 Int'l Rev L & Econ 350.
Bruce, Christopher J., 'An economic analysis of the impossibility doctrine' (1982) 11 J Legal Stud 311.
Craswell, Richard, 'Property rules and liability rules in unconscionability and related doctrines' (1993) 60 U Chi L Rev 1.
Craswell, Richard, 'Offer, acceptance, and efficient reliance' (1996) 48 Stan L Rev 481.
Davis, Kevin E., 'The demand for immutable contracts: another look at the law and economics of contract modifications' (2006) 81 NYU L Rev 487.
Epstein, Richard A., 'Unconscionability: A critical reappraisal' (1975) 18 JL & Econ 293.
Epstein, Richard A., 'The neoclassical economics of consumer contracts' (2008) 92 Minn L Rev 803.
Hart, Oliver and Moore, John, 'Incomplete contracts and renegotiation' (1988) 56 Econometrica 755.
Hermalin, Benjamin E. and Katz, Michael L., 'Judicial modification of contracts between sophisticated parties: A more complete view of incomplete contracts and their breach' (1993) 9 JL Econ & Org 230.
Johnston, Jason Scott, 'Strategic bargaining and the economic theory of contract default rules' (1991) 100 Yale LJ 615.
Katz, Avery, 'The strategic structure of offer and acceptance: Game theory and the law of contract formation' (1990) 89 Mich L Rev 215.
Kornhauser, Lewis A., 'Unconscionability in standard forms' (1976) 64 Cal L Rev 1151.
Posner, Eric A., 'Economic analysis of contract law after three decades: Success or failure?' (2003) 112 Yale LJ 829.
Posner, Richard A., 'The law and economics of contract interpretation' (2005) 83 Tex L Rev 1581.
Posner, Richard A., and Rosenfield, Andrew M., 'Impossibility and related doctrines in contract law: An economic analysis' (1977) 6 J Legal Stud 88.
Rasmusen, Eric and Ayres, Ian, 'Mutual and unilateral mistake in contract law' (1993) 22 J Legal Stud 309.
Schwartz, Alan and Scott, Robert E, 'Market damages, efficient contracting, and the economic waste fallacy' (2008) 108 Colum L Rev 1610.
Schwartz, Alan and Scott, Robert E. 'Contract interpretation redux' (2010) 119 Yale LJ 926.

Chapter 2

The Economics of Contractual Remedies

Chapter Contents

A.	Introduction: Efficient Breach and Optimal Reliance	198
B.	The Effect of Damages on Breach and Reliance Decisions	199
C.	Consequential Damages	204
Key Points		205
References and Further Reading		205

A. Introduction: Efficient Breach and Optimal Reliance

"Efficient breach" is an essential concept in the law and economics of contract. It provides that a promisor should renege on his contractual obligations where a third party would benefit from his performance more than the original promisee. The view that a contractual duty is a contingent promise rather than an absolute guarantee found its most famous expression in the words of Oliver Wendell Holmes, who wrote that: "the duty to keep a contract at common law means a prediction that you must pay damages if you do not keep it, – and nothing else."[1]

Suppose that A is a manufacturer, the capacity limitations of which enable it to produce no more than 1,000 widgets per year. Consider a widget retailer, B, who commands a moderate business reputation in his neighbourhood and who wishes to purchase 1,000 widgets from A. The minimum selling price of A for its full output is £10,000 (£10 per widget). In light of its expected sales opportunities, B would pay no more than £20,000. Consistent with the Coase Theorem, A and B enter into a contract at a price between £10,000 and £20,000 (say £15,000). This arrangement, of course, renders both A and B better off.

Now imagine that a rival widget seller, C, arrives on the scene. Due to its sterling reputation, access to a larger market, and superior efficiency, C could sell each unit at a greater profit than B. C would therefore offer up to £25,000 for A's 1,000 widgets. Suppose that, after A & B had entered into the contract described above, C offers A £21,000 to break its contract with B and to supply C instead. Efficiency requires that A accept C's offer and abandon its contract with B. As the widgets are scarce, they should end up in the possession of the party that values them the most – in this case, C.

The observant reader may protest that A need not breach its contract with B at all, as, if C values the widgets the most, it could simply buy them from B. This view would be correct in a low transaction cost environment. Suppose, however, that circumstances foreclose agreement between B and C. Perhaps they are hated rivals, which steadfastly refuse to deal with each other. In that event, A's giving the 1,000 widgets to B creates less value than selling the widgets to C. The A–C contract is Kaldor Hicks efficient, but not a Pareto improvement because, although the arrangement enhances net welfare, it nevertheless injures B. However, as the A–C agreement is Kaldor-Hicks efficient, those parties could fully compensate B and yet still remain better off. If they were to do so, the breach would give rise to a Pareto improvement. Damages for breach of contract can play this role.

Efficient breach is controversial in some quarters. Charles Fried famously argued that "[p]arties enter into contractual relations with certain expectations; for the state to disappoint those expectations is on its part a form of tyranny and deception".[2] He espoused the view that "[t]he moral force behind contract as promise is autonomy: the parties are bound to their contract because they have chosen to be". Ultimately, Fried believed that "[t]o renege [on a contract] is to abuse a confidence he was free to invite or not, and which he intentionally did invite".

Fried's view of the sanctity of one's word is superficially attractive. Yet, as a commercial matter, it is not at all clear that a person's signature on a contract should constitute an unbreakable bond, which obligates the signer to fulfil his obligation no matter what the circumstances. Sacred promises like wedding vows have few parallels with most contracts that appear throughout the economy. In the realm of business, contracts often reflect ongoing commercial arrangements, pursuant to which companies strive to satisfy orders given limited inventories, uncertain business environments, and unforeseeable future opportunities. Infusing agreements with a moral inviolability seems incongruous in such circumstances.

---

1 Oliver Wendell Holmes, *The Path of the Law* (1897) 10 Harv L Rev 457, 462.
2 Charles Fried, *Contract as Promise: A Theory of Contractual Obligation* (1981) p. 91.

More generally, it is hard to take seriously the idea that any contract is unbreakable. Every agreement is at least somewhat contingent. Furthermore, in many settings, common sense recoils at the idea of ordering a promisor to perform, paradigmatically in the employment setting, where requiring one to work for another smacks of involuntary servitude. Ultimately, to say as Fried did that parties are bound to their contract because they have chosen to be is to beg the question: the manner in which parties bind themselves depends on the legal interpretation that the courts give the operative contractual language. One may promise to paint another's house, but if the law reads that assurance as being either to paint or to pay, the painter has not in fact bound himself to perform.

To argue that a contractual promise is qualified, however, is not to say that a promisor is free to renege on his word without consequence. To applaud a particular breach as efficient is not to relieve the promisor of responsibility under the contract – she still must pay damages for failing to make good her promise. This chapter is concerned with the nature of those damages.

Efficient breach accounts for half the story of the law and economics treatment of remedies. The other significant issue is reliance. The benefit that a promisee experiences under a contract is rarely fixed, but instead depends on the various preparations that he makes in anticipation of the promisor's performance. For instance, a business owner may order the necessary volume of inputs for her business, but the arrival of those inputs means little if she has not already put the requisite infrastructure in place to transform those inputs into outputs. As a general matter, the more that a promisee spends in reliance on a promisor's anticipated performance, the greater the value that he will experience if that performance materialises.

The conditional term "if", however, is important. There are no guarantees in life and a promisor's performance is no different. The money that a promisee expends in anticipation of the contract's being fulfilled is likely to be sunk, and therefore wasted, if the performance does not occur. Efficiency, therefore, requires that a promisee only expend as much capital on reliance as is cost justified in light of the probability that the promisor will fail to fulfil his end of the bargain.

Inducing promisors to breach only when it is optimal, and spurring promisees to spend no more or less than the correct amount of reliance damages, are the twin economic goals of contractual damages. The following pages explore three major forms of remedies: expectation, reliance, and restitution damages. We will see that each one has distinct effects on the decisions when to breach and how much to spend in reliance of promised performance. Unfortunately, no rule induces efficient decisions as to both factors. The following discussion assumes risk neutrality, such that all parties make the choice that maximises expected value.

B. The Effect of Damages on Breach and Reliance Decisions

1. Expectation, reliance, and restitution damages

To determine the effect of various damages regimes on promisors' breach decisions, one must first specify the nature of those remedies. Expectation damages seek fully to compensate a promisee by rendering him indifferent to whether or not the promisor performed. Thus, if a teacher stood to gain £20,000 from a year-long contract at a local school, which figure included not only pecuniary gain but also subjective reward, the expectation remedy in the event of the school's reneging on its agreement is £20,000.

Reliance damages attempt to put the disappointed promisee in the same position as if she had never entered into the contract, by returning to her any expenditure that she incurred in its anticipation. Thus, in the teaching hypothetical, if the prospective teacher had obtained a year-long lease with a non-returnable, upfront deposit of £1,000 in the vicinity of the school and had parted with no other sunk expenses, the reliance damage figure would be £1,000.

Finally, restitution damages return to the promisee any benefits that he had conferred on the promisor prior to the latter's breach. In the example of the waylaid teacher, if, in furtherance of her position, she had provided the district with a series of free lectures concerning modern teaching techniques, the restitution award would be a monetary figure equal to the value of those lectures.

As the reader can see, each of these damages differs significantly from the others. It should not be surprising, therefore, that each one imparts distinct incentives as to the breach and reliance decisions. To illustrate the effects of these different remedies, consider the following variants of a single hypothetical.

2. Exploring the incentive effects of different damages regimes

Imagine a two-person information technology practice, "Tech Solutions", which specialises both in installing interconnected computer systems and in providing technological solutions for small- to medium-sized businesses. Given its small scale, the partnership can service only one significant client at a time.

A technology start-up ("Alpha") approaches Tech Solutions, expressing an interest in the installation of an intranet and supporting computer network. Alpha would agree to pay up to £40,000 for the job, which Tech Solutions would be willing to carry out for no less than £20,000. Suppose that the parties have equal bargaining power, such that they ultimately agree on a price of £30,000, of which Alpha must pay £5,000 up front. Alpha promptly makes that payment, and, in anticipation of the contract's performance, hires an engineer, to whom it pays a market-level, non-refundable hiring bonus of £3,000. Spending the £3,000 to hire that employee would permit Alpha to hit the ground running when its IT systems come online. Having the engineer in place to begin immediately would create an extra £4,000 in revenue.

After these events, but before Tech Solutions begins performing, a third party, Beta, approaches the partnership about a time-critical project. Numerous bugs that severely handicap its ability to make and deliver on sales have plagued its computer systems. With its peak sales season rapidly approaching, Beta is eager to fix the problems and to realise the profit that properly functioning IT systems would allow it reap. Beta, which would pay up to £37,000 for Tech Solutions' timely services, offers to pay £36,000.

Offeree	Offeree's Max. Price	Tech Solutions' Min. Price	Cooperative Surplus
Alpha	£40,000	£20,000	£20,000
Beta	£37,000	£20,000	£17,000

Figure 5.1

(a) The optimal outcome

Begin by identifying the social welfare optimum. Tech Solutions should not breach its contract. Alpha would pay up to £40,000, while Beta would pay no more than £37,000. This is not an example of efficient breach.

Should Alpha hire the engineer? It might appear to be efficient that Alpha do so because it would yield additional revenue of £4,000 at a cost of just £3,000, but, in fact, it may be inefficient. Whether this is the case depends on the probability that the promisor will provide the bargained-for service. Assume that the likelihood that Tech Solutions will perform under its contract with Alpha is 70% (e.g. business may be poor, such that there is a 30% probability of Tech Solutions' becoming insolvent prior to performing). In that event, Alpha's hiring the engineer entails a sunk cost of

£3,000, but provides an expected return of only £4,000*0.7, or £2,800. The social expected value of hiring the engineer on reliance of the contract is, therefore, negative. It would, therefore, be inefficient for Alpha to hire the engineer in reliance on its contract.

(b) Expectation damages

Suppose that an expectation damages regime is in place. In this environment, Tech Solutions must either deliver the services that it promised to Alpha or pay damages equal in value to Alpha of the bargained-for performance. This damages regime is tantamount to a legal guarantee that the promisee, Alpha, will receive the benefit of its bargain.

Take the breach decision first. Having agreed to install an intranet and supporting computer systems for Alpha for a price of £30,000, Tech Solutions may be galled to learn that, in so agreeing, it foreclosed an even-more-lucrative deal with Beta at £36,000. Will the IT partnership rationally abandon Alpha in favour of a better deal with Beta? If expectation damages apply, the answer is no.

If it performs under its contract with Alpha, Tech Solutions would obtain £30,000. Breaching its agreement would yield Tech Solutions an additional £6,000, making that option the preferred one in the absence of contract law. Due to expectation damages, however, the cost to Tech Solutions of breaching its contract would be the value that Alpha would derive from Tech Solutions' performance of £40,000 (for reasons explained below, Alpha will hire the engineer under this damages rule) minus the contract price of £30,000, for net damages of £10,000. Tech Solutions will not breach because doing so would entail paying damages of £9,000 or £10,000 for a mere benefit of £6,000. Expectation damages thus efficiently induce Tech Solutions not to breach the contract.

This result is not an accident of the model, but is a general result. Expectation damages are equivalent to a Pigouvian tax, which corrects the negative externality inherent in a promisor's decision to breach. In making the breach decision in the absence of legal consequences, a promisor would compare the private costs and benefits of deciding whether to abandon a contract, and would not consider the deleterious effects of its decision on the abandoned promisee. As with all negative externalities, the result is an excessive amount of the externality producing activity – in this case, breach. Expectation damages make the promisee's losses the promisor's own. This causes the promisor's private incentives to mirror the social optimum, such that she will breach only if the gains that she realises outweigh the costs to the promisee. This leads to a specific conclusion: expectation damages ensure that rational promisors will breach only when it is efficient for them to do so.

Now consider the question of reliance. We already saw that Alpha's hiring the engineer before Tech Solutions performs is inefficient because the cost of doing so is a certain £3,000, while the off-setting, expected benefit is merely £2,800. Yet, expectation damages will lead Alpha inefficiently to hire the engineer before its IT systems go online. Why? The answer lies in the effect of expectation damages on Alpha's incentives. Such damages guarantee Alpha the performance for which it bargained or its pecuniary equivalent. Alpha will thus reason as follows: "If Tech Solutions performs, I will realise £1,000 more in profit by hiring the engineer in advance. If Tech Solutions does not perform, it will nevertheless owe me the same profit that I would have made in hiring the engineer and in receiving full performance under the contract." Expectation damages thus transform the actual probability of Tech Solutions' non-performance from 70% to a private probability of 100% for Alpha.

As with the promisor's breach decision, this result is not random. By guaranteeing performance or its monetary equivalent under the contract, expectation damages introduce a negative externality into the promisee's reliance decision. Promisees will spend money on reliance, even if there is a high probability of non-performance, because they will experience the full upside of that investment, but not the downside. Expectation damages therefore induce excessive reliance expenditures.

(c) Reliance damages

Now suppose that reliance damages apply. If Tech Solutions breaches its contract with Alpha, the relevant damages figure would again depend on whether Alpha hired the engineer in anticipation of performance. As explained momentarily, however, Alpha will hire the engineer under this damages regime. For that reason, reliance damages would be £8,000, comprised of £3,000 for the engineer's signing bonus plus the £5,000 down payment. In either event, reliance damages would put Alpha in the same position in which it would have been had it never entered into the contract.

How would these damages weigh against the gains to Tech Solutions of breaching its contract? The value to Tech Solutions of finishing the Alpha contract would be £25,000, which equals the contract price minus the £5,000 deposit that it had already received. What about the value to Tech Solutions of abandoning Alpha in favour of Beta? This would be £36,000 minus reliance damages, which would be £8,000. The benefit of breach to Tech Solutions (£28,000) exceeds the benefit of performing under the Alpha contract (£25,000). Thus, Tech Solutions will inefficiently breach its contract.

Once more, this result is not random. The problem is that reliance damages do not cause promisors to experience the full social costs of their decisions to breach. They must merely return promisees to their pre-contract states of well being. A negative externality thus accompanies the promisors' breach decisions in the presence of reliance damages, and so one can expect excessive levels of breach in agreements subject to such contractual remedies.

Might there be a silver lining with respect to Alpha's reliance decision? Unfortunately, the answer is no. Reliance damages insulate promisees against the possibility that their investment in anticipation of performance will be wasted. Applied to the present hypothetical, if Tech Solutions installs the IT systems, Alpha's having spent £3,000 on hiring an engineer will boost its revenue by £4,000. If Tech Solutions fails to perform, however, there is no downside to Alpha's having hired the engineer because it will get the full £3,000 back in reliance damages.

This leads to a straightforward conclusion about reliance damages: they fail to induce promisors to breach only when it is efficient for them to do so, and they fail to spur promisees to spend an efficient amount in reliance on anticipated performance. They are, therefore, an imperfect remedy for breach of contract.

(d) Restitution damages

The last damages regime is restitution, which requires a breaching promisor to return any value that the promisee bestowed upon the promisor. Applied to our hypothetical, the restitution measure would simply be the £5,000 deposit that Alpha paid under the contract.

Begin with the promisor's incentive to breach. By embracing a £36,000 contract with Beta in lieu of the £25,000 still remaining under its agreement with Alpha, Tech Solutions stands to gain £11,000 minus any relevant damages. In the present case, those damages are the £5,000 restitution measure. As Tech Solutions stands to reap a private gain of £6,000 by breaching its contract, it will do so. This result, of course, is inefficient.

Yet, restitution damages bear a significant advantage: they spur efficient reliance expenditures. The reason is that a restitution award will not return any investment made in anticipation of the promisor's performance. As a result, the costs and benefits that a promisee experiences in deciding whether to spend money in reliance on a promised benefit align with the social optimum – a promisee will engage in such expenditures only if the expected return is positive.

Applied to the Tech Solutions example, Alpha will not hire the engineer in advance of its IT systems' coming online. Although hiring that employee would enhance revenue by £4,000 at a cost of only £3,000 if Tech Solutions' fulfils its end of the bargain, there is only a 70% chance that that performance will be forthcoming. As a result, the expected value to Alpha of hiring the engineer is −£400. Unlike expectation and reliance damages, restitution does not shield Alpha against the 30%

chance that its up-front bonus payment to the engineer will be wasted. Restitution damages thus induce efficient reliance expenditures.

3. General insights

The preceding analysis yields a disappointing conclusion: there is no perfect remedy for breach of contract. Expectation damages prevent inefficient breach, but invite excessive reliance expenditures, while restitution carries the opposite effect. Reliance damages instil optimal incentives with respect to neither breach nor reliance.

To appreciate why this result arises, consider an analogy to the law and economics of tort involving bilateral care scenarios. Where care on the part of both tortfeasors and victims is a predicate of efficiency, a rule that imposes full liability on only party – specifically, strict liability or no liability – will not minimise social cost. So, too, a remedy that imposes contractual liability on only one party is imperfect when efficiency requires constrained behaviour by multiple parties with respect to both breach and reliance. Maximising the welfare that contracts generate requires two outcomes: (1) promisors must only breach when it is socially efficient for them to do so; and (2) promisees must engage in only the socially cost-justified level of reliance expenditures. An absolute rule that forces one party to experience all costs cannot be efficient in such a case because it would induce only one party, but not both, to behave desirably.

This is why none of the explored damages regimes is perfect. Optimal damages, of course, are theoretically identifiable. One would award expectation damages to a promisee in the event of breach, but would reduce those damages so that they reflect the subjective value that the promisee would have experienced had it spent only the socially optimal amount in anticipation of the promisor's performance. As such information is rarely available to the court, however, moulding contractual remedies in this manner is not feasible.

As a practical matter, then, courts are left with three imperfect choices. Nevertheless, in choosing which damages regime to apply, the judiciary can fruitfully determine whether, given the facts surrounding the contract at hand, inefficient breach or excessive reliance is apt to be the graver problem from the perspective of efficiency. For example, if there is simultaneously a high probability of non-performance and a tendency for promisees to engage in large-scale reliance expenditures, there may be a strong case for employing a restitution remedy. Conversely, where there is considerable danger of inefficient breach, but limited prospect of excessive reliance, expectation damages are apt to be superior.

Other times, information constraints will stymie the judiciary's ability to apply what would in the abstract be its preferred remedy. The expectation measure can be difficult to compute when idiosyncratic, subjective, factors account for much of the value that a promisee would experience from the promisor's performance. It may also be impractical if great uncertainty surrounds the benefit that the promisee would have derived from performance. For instance, if a promisor fails to deliver a necessary input to the promisee's new business, which subsequently fails, computing the expectation measure requires the court to delve into an imponderable counterfactual. Would the business have succeeded but for the breach? If so, how lucrative would it have been? It is not always feasible to answer such questions. If expectation damages are too speculative reliably to apply, but if the court is concerned about the danger of inefficient breach, reliance damages may be superior than restitution. The reason is that, although both reliance and restitution damages permit promisors rationally but inefficiently to breach, reliance damages are greater and thus permit a narrower range of inefficient breach than restitution awards.

A related point concerns the economic role of mitigation. A promisee must take reasonable steps to minimise the extent of the losses it experiences from a promisor's breach. The reason is that, given the promisor's decision to breach, abating the social cost of that action falls on the promisee, who is then the lowest cost avoider. The mitigation principle thus serves a clear economic function.

Having considered the effect of different damages regimes on breach and reliance, this chapter concludes with a discussion of the limits of expectation damages. In particular, at what point, if any, are the costs that a promisee experiences from a promisor's breach too remote for the law to include them in a damages award? This is the question of consequential damages.

C. Consequential Damages

The preceding account implicitly assumed that the various damages regimes incorporated all relevant monetary effects. For instance, expectation damages encapsulate all the foregone benefit of the contract to the disappointed promisee. Similarly, reliance damages capture all pecuniary sums that a promisee expended in anticipation of performance. These assumptions are not always justified, however, as it is a staple of remedies law that only foreseeable damages are recoverable.

The foreseeability limitation engrained in the common law finds its definitive expression in *Hadley v Baxendale*.[3] A Gloucester miller, having suffered a broken crank shaft, contracted with a carrier to bring the crank shaft to Greenwich for repairs. As a result of a delay in the shipment, the mill remained closed and suffered a considerable loss in profits. In the mill's ensuing action for breach of contract, the court denied the miller damages for those particular losses, holding that only foreseeable consequential damages are recoverable for breach of contract.

One might construe foreseeability as a fairness-based limitation on recovery. After all, why should a promisor have to pay for harms that he could not reasonably envision? This construction would mask the central economic function of the *Hadley* rule. Limiting consequential damages to those that a promisor could foresee is best understood as a default rule – an implied term – around which the parties are free to bargain. In this respect, the analysis relevant to foreseeability limitations on contractual damages dovetail with the previous chapter's discussion of why and how the law reads unwritten terms into agreements.

The *Hadley* rule is all about information. Where perfect, symmetric access to information surrounds a bargain, the parties will understand the consequences of non-performance and, if transaction costs are sufficiently low, will agree on terms accordingly. Yet, asymmetric information characterises most contracts, as many promisees have private knowledge that they do not share with promisors. The foreseeability limitation incentivises high-damage promisees to inform promisors of that characteristic, thus allowing the parties to decide who should bear the risk of non-performance. If the promisor agrees to accept the danger of his failing to perform, one would expect an increase in the contract price. Alternatively, if the promisee embraces that risk, the agreed-upon price would be lower.

The term upon which the parties are likely to agree will reflect the identity of the lowest cost avoider. This will often be the promisor, who can typically control the probability of her non-performance better than the promisee, but this will not always be the case. Sometimes a promisee, who stands to suffer unusually severe losses from a breach, can more effectively insure against those losses.

Consider a person who books a taxi to the airport so that he can make a flight for a critical business meeting. If he misses his flight, he would lose a lucrative contract. The taxi driver has little upon which to distinguish this particular client from any other. If the driver failed to show or was sufficiently late that the businessman missed his flight, holding the driver liable for the full costs of his breach may not be efficient. The *Hadley* rule makes it incumbent upon the businessman to communicate the dire urgency of the taxi ride, thus permitting the driver expressly to reject liability

---

3 [1854] EWHC 70.

for breaching or to embrace that danger, likely for a higher price. In the circumstances, the parties might agree that the businessman accept the risk. He can control the consequential business costs of non-performance by booking an earlier flight, making alternative travel arrangements in advance to cover the danger that the taxi might be late, organising an emergency back-up video conference, and so on.

Key Points

- The opportunity cost of contractual performance is the highest value that another promisee would have placed on that performance. Although a contract may effect a Pareto improvement, the welfare surplus it creates may be less than a foregone contract opportunity that arose after the promisor signed the agreement and before he performed. To maximise efficiency, law and economics encourages "efficient breach".
- Efficient breach requires that the promisee valuing a promisor's performance the most, obtains its benefit. It does not imply that the original promisee should receive nothing. Damages should compensate parties who do not receive the performance for which they bargained under the contract.
- Expectation damages bestow upon promisees a monetary reward equivalent to the performance for which they contracted. Such damages thus make a promisee indifferent between receiving damages or performance. As expectation damages force promisors to internalise the cost of their decision to breach, they will do so only when the value of contracting elsewhere is greater. Thus, expectation damages create incentives only to breach when it is efficient to do so.
- Reliance damages put promisees in the same position in which they would have been if they never contracted. They thus deprive promisees of the benefit of their bargain. With such a damages regime in place, it may be rational for promisors inefficiently to breach their contracts because they do not have to pay the full social costs flowing from their breach.
- Restitution damages require promisors to return all value that promisees conferred pursuant to the contract. As these damages do not provide promisees with the full value that they would have enjoyed had the promisor performed, they facilitate inefficient breach.
- Promisees often invest resources in anticipation of the performance due to them under a contract. If that investment is sunk, however, promisees should reduce it to account for the probability that a breach of contract may occur. Expectation and reliance damages, however, guarantee that promisees will not lose their reliance expenditures. Thus, they encourage excessive reliance. Only restitution damages spur efficient reliance expenditures because they force promisees to factor in the probability of non-performance.
- Should a promisor breach his contract, the law only allows a promisee to recover ensuing damages that were reasonably within the promisor's contemplation. This limitation on consequential damages is a default term around which parties can bargain. It induces promisees who place unusually great value on the sought-after performance to disclose that information to the promisor. The parties can then allocate the risk and adjust the contract price accordingly.

 ## References and Further Reading

Books
Cooter, Robert and Ulen, Thomas, *Law and Economics*, 6th edn (2011) Chs. 8 (III) and 9(I).
Hermalin, Benjamin E., Katz, Avery W., and Craswell, Richard, 'Contract Law' in *Handbook of Law and Economics* (2007) Vol. I, Ch. 1.

Miceli, Thomas J., *The Economic Approach to Law*, 2nd edn (2008) Ch. 5.
Polinsky, A. Mitchell, *An Introduction to Law and Economics* (2011) Chs 5 and 8.
Porat, Ariel (ed.), *The Economics of Remedies* (2012).
Posner, Richard A., *Economic Analysis of Law* (2011) §§ 4.10–4.14.
Shavell, Steven, *Foundations of Economic Analysis of Law* (2004) pp. 304–24.

Articles
Barton, John H., 'The economic basis of damages for breach of contract' (1972) 1 J Legal Stud 277.
Cooter, Robert, 'Unity in tort, contract, and property: The model of precaution' (1985) 73 Cal L Rev 1.
Craswell, Richard, 'Contract remedies, renegotiation, and the theory of efficient breach' (1988) 61 S Cal L Rev 629.
Kornhauser, Lewis A., 'An introduction to the economic analysis of contract remedies' (1986) 57 U Colo L Rev 683.
Kull, Andrew, 'Restitution as a remedy for breach of contract' (1994) 67 S Cal L Rev 1465.
Rogerson, William P., 'Efficient reliance and damage measures for breach of contract' (1984) 15 Rand J Econ 39.
Schwartz, Alan, 'The case for specific performance' (1979) 89 Yale LJ 271.
Shavell, Steven, 'The design of contracts and remedies for breach' (1984) 99 QJ Econ 121.
Shavell, Steven, 'Damage measures for breach of contract' (1990) 11 Bell J Econ 466.

Part 6

Litigation

1   An Economic Theory of Litigation   209

Chapter 1

An Economic Theory of Litigation

Chapter Contents

A.	Introduction	210
B.	Explaining the Litigation Process	211
C.	Negative-Value Lawsuits	217
D.	English and American Rules Compared	222
E.	The Optimal Level of Litigation	226
F.	Conclusion	229
Key Points		230
References and Further Reading		231

A. Introduction

A hallmark of western society is that people embroiled in disagreements can appeal to neutral arbiters to resolve their conflicts. By channelling disputes away from violent resolution – thus fostering stability and economic development – the courts serve an imperative function. The modern litigation system, however, does more than hand down Solomonesque judgments on private disputes to keep the peace. In enunciating rules that demarcate the contours of acceptable behaviour and by creating rights, legislatures and courts induce people to bargain in the shadow of law.

That the law can guide behaviour, however, does not tell us in what direction one ought to employ it as a policy lever. Much of this book has used economic principles to elucidate laws that impart efficient incentives. Positive analysis enables courts and legislators to make conclusions informed as to the economic costs and benefits of alternative policies. To the extent lawmakers embrace efficiency as the guiding lodestar, normative economic analysis identifies optimal rules. If economics can help to inform the substantive law, however, what is the economic purpose of the litigation process itself?

Litigation is the vehicle by which abstract norms become substantive law, and thus it serves a crucial economic function. As important as identifying specific laws, however, is enforcing them, and in this respect the judicial process is indispensable. Unless governments force people to recognise rights, any legal privilege would be edentulous. The point of the litigation process, therefore, is both to identify and to give force to the rule of law. By viewing the courts' role in this way, one can appreciate how the judiciary and the Coase Theorem go hand-in-hand. By recognising and implementing laws, the courts bestow rights upon people and thus allow them to bargain among themselves. The point of courts, therefore, is not directly to resolve every justiciable disagreement, but to give force to rights, which make assertions of legal privileges credible and which facilitate efficient bargaining. The availability of non-cooperative solutions through trial drives cooperative solutions in the form of settlement.

It is for that reason that, "in most matters[,] it is more important that the applicable rule of law be settled than that it be settled right".[1] Once a law is in place, society has granted entitlements that, in the absence of inalienability rules, stakeholders are free to reallocate between one another. Obviously, this is not to say that any entitlement – and hence any law – is valid, as positive transactions costs that hinder alienability abound. It is to point out, however, that by creating and enforcing clear rules, the law facilitates private agreements that achieve Pareto improvements vis-à-vis the initial allocation.[2]

Courts' institutional purpose within society is therefore clear. A more interesting and less easily answered question, however, is why do parties litigate cases at all? If the prospect of a binding judgment consistent with well-established rules of law accompanies every dispute, why would parties ever eschew settlement in favour of trial? If theory suggests that people should privately resolve conflicting claims to entitlements, the fact that we observe pervasive litigation, encompassing a vast spectrum of controversies from low-stakes feuds to multi-billion dollar commercial disputes and beyond, reveals that bargaining failure precludes agreement in many cases.

This Part articulates an economic theory of litigation, explaining the circumstances in which rational litigants choose to become embroiled in, and to settle, judicial proceedings. This theory reveals, as indicated, that the litigation process's primary economic purpose is to induce a Coasian bargain. By identifying the factors that frustrate settlement, one can begin to contemplate ways in which to improve the efficiency of the litigation process.

1 Burnet v Coronado Oil & Gas Co (1932) 285 US 393, 406.
2 Of course, to the extent that legislatures can adopt rules that mirror those to which stakeholders would agree in a hypothetical, zero transaction cost environment, it is desirable that they do so.

The fundamental insight is that legal uncertainty fosters litigation in lieu of agreement. Asymmetric expectations concerning a plaintiff's success at trial can foreclose mutually advantageous bargain. The litigation process therefore not only renders threats to sue credible, it distributes information more evenly among the parties, thus causing their respective estimates of the complainant's odds of victory to merge. Such alignment in expectations will precipitate settlement, which is the outcome for the vast majority of legal disputes. The fact that professional lawyers typically represent parties is also an important contributor to settlement, as the former's ability more objectively to assess the merits of a case enhances the probability of reaching an accord.

In analysing litigation using neoclassical economics theory, this Part considers two different rules governing the outcome of legal disputes. The first is what many refer to as "the American rule", which provides that each side to a controversy must bear its own legal costs, regardless of who wins. The "English rule", by contrast, provides that the loser pays. As one might expect, the operative rule has a significant effect on litigants' incentives throughout the litigation process. The following chapter proceeds under the American rule, which is analytically more straightforward. The last section, however, explores the different results that ensue under the English rule, and addresses the possible bases for preferring one rule over the other.

B. Explaining the Litigation Process

Many choices underlie the litigation process. This section explains the circumstances in which a rational litigant will file suit, settle, proceed to trial, and appeal an unfavourable judgment. To facilitate analysis and to identify the key incentives weighing on litigation, we shall assume that all litigants are risk neutral and thus maximise expected value. A potential plaintiff will sue if the sum of all possible outcomes multiplied by each outcome's corresponding probability exceeds zero. From that perspective, a person would not file a complaint if doing so would entail litigation costs of £15,000 coupled with a 10% chance of winning £50,000, a 20% chance of winning £40,000, and a 70% chance of winning nothing. This is because the expected value would be −£2,000.

Assuming that relevant actors are risk neutral, and thus follow the dictates of expected value theory, why might people endure the cost of litigation when they could simply settle their underlying dispute?

1. Settlement depends on how closely the parties' expectations align

(a) Parties should settle when they agree on the expected outcome

Since most disputes giving rise to lawsuits entail a discrete number of readily identifiable parties, and because going to trial is expensive, the Coase Theorem would seem to predict that litigating parties should agree on terms rather proceed to judgment. Although the perceived prevalence of trials may obscure this fact in some people's eyes, the vast majority of cases do settle. In fact, less than five percent of lawsuits result in an adjudication on the merits.

To understand when parties will settle, consider the following example, which illustrates that symmetric beliefs as to the likely outcome at trial will drive settlement. Suppose that two parties – a potential plaintiff "P" and a defendant "D" – were involved in an accident. If P sues, he has a 70% chance of convincing the jury that D was negligent and liable for causing him harm in the amount of £100,000, and a 30% chance of recovering nothing. Both P and D agree that these are the respective probabilities of P's prevailing and losing at trial. They both agree that a verdict for P would result in a £100,000 judgment. Litigation, of course, is not free. It would cost P and D £15,000 and £20,000 respectively, in layers' fees and expenses to bring the case to trial. The following table summarises the relevant facts:

	P	D
Odds of prevailing	0.7	0.3
Payoff if P succeeds at trial	£100,000	−£100,000
Litigation costs	£15,000	£20,000
Expected value of suit	£55,000	−£90,000
Bargaining range	£55,000–£90,000	£55,000–£90,000
Available cooperative surplus	£35,000	£35,000

Figure 6.1

The first question is whether P will be inclined to enforce his claim. The answer is yes because the expected value of his filing suit is £55,000, which equals the jury verdict if he wins (£100,000) multiplied by the chance of his winning (0.7) minus his litigation costs (£15,000). Meanwhile, D is an unfortunate situation. Having been sued or threatened with suit by P, he faces an expected cost of going to trial of £90,000 equal to the possible jury verdict (£100,000) multiplied by the odds of his losing (0.7) plus his litigation expenses (£20,000).

The parties have a strong incentive to settle. P stands to gain £55,000 from going to trial, while D stands to lose £90,000 from doing so. Both can do better. At any price between these two points, both parties will experience mutual gains, so we should expect a settlement under the Coase Theorem.

In the graph below, A–B represents the parties' expected outcome from proceeding to trial. X–Y signifies the hypothetical expected outcome from litigating a case to judgment when doing so entailed no costs, which would simply be the expected jury award of £70,000. It is the expense of accessing the litigation system that shifts the parties' expected returns from X–Y to A–B, thus rendering both parties worse off. Nevertheless, the parties can bargain to avoid the inefficiency of trial. Summing the differences between A and X and Y and B produces the cooperative surplus from reaching settlement, which is £35,000.

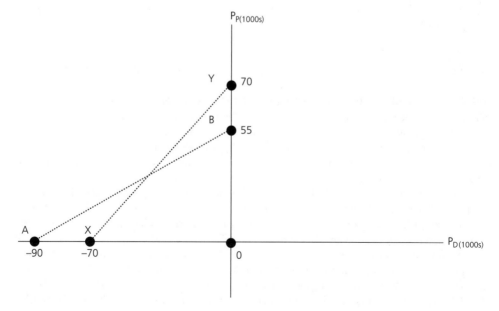

Figure 6.2

The £35,000 "bargaining range" equals the sum of P's and D's litigation costs. Those expenses determine the zone of mutually beneficial settlement terms. What matters to the settlement question, therefore, is not necessarily the magnitude of litigation expenses – though the mutual benefit and hence the likelihood of reaching an accord increases in proportion to the cost of going to trial – but how closely the parties' respective calculations of the plaintiff's expected jury verdict align. Observe that the £35,000 bargaining range is the aggregate cost that the parties save in not going to trial, and thus the "cooperative surplus" that they realise through agreement.

Although a bargaining range exists, however, settlement is not assured. The problem is bilateral monopoly, which introduces transaction costs even though there are only two parties to the negotiations. Observe that each party must deal with the other, as to whom there is no substitute. While both parties would be better off agreeing on a settlement amount from £55,000.01 to £89,999.99, it should be clear that P would much prefer the latter figure, while D would equally prefer the former amount. The parties will therefore devote great energy to achieving the most favourable possible division of the aggregate profit represented by the bargaining range.

Furthermore, depending on whether the lawsuit between P and D is a one-off or one of many lawsuits in which the parties are involved, reputational effects may justify either party's rationally rejecting ultimatum offers at its least favourable end of the bargaining spectrum. Doing so may signal to future adverse litigants that it will only accept generous offers, thus potentially granting it future boons that outweigh the foregone cost in rejecting an offer this time within the bargaining range. Game theory illustrates why this may be a rational strategy. In a one-shot game, rejecting a mutually beneficial settlement offer is contrary to self-interest and hence irrational. In a repeat-play game, however, it may be possible to send a credible signal to future potential litigants. If this signal successfully deters potential plaintiffs from bringing suit, it will have been a rational strategy if the value of the deterred future lawsuits discounted to present value exceeds the lost gain in the present period of rejecting the beneficial settlement offer.

The larger the bargaining range, the greater the impediment that bilateral monopoly will create to settlement. This is because a large spectrum between each party's minimally acceptable terms translates into a lucrative award should one party's threat of stubbornly holding out induce the other side to relent. Might this mean that a vanishingly small, but-still positive, negotiating range is more likely to result in settlement? It seems improbable, not least because parties cannot always identify the borders of the relevant bargaining range. In practice, although expansive bargaining spectra induce bilateral-monopoly conditions, they also increase the mutual cost of failing to reach an agreement. For that reason, agreement probably becomes more likely as the negotiating range grows larger.

(b) Divergent expectations can stymie settlement

The discussion thus far explains why the vast majority of cases results in settlement. Under what circumstances, however, might litigants press ahead to trial instead of settling? There is no mystery. Incentives to proceed to trial are simply the converse of settlement conditions: when the parties' perceptions as to the plaintiff's likelihood of success at trial differ sufficiently, no agreement will take place.

To see why this is true, revisit the example of P and D. Suppose that P again estimates that he has a 70% chance of prevailing at trial and earning damages of £100,000 at a cost of £15,000. Once more, then, P calculates an expected value of going to trial of £55,000. This time, however, D is more confident in his prospects at trial. He believes that P merely enjoys a 50% chance of winning, and further believes that, in such an event, the jury would only award P £40,000. D calculates his expected cost in going to the jury, therefore, as being £40,000 minus the £40,000 calculated jury award multiplied by its 0.5 estimated probability plus £20,000 in litigation costs (see Figure 6.3).

Now the parties will not settle. In pressing ahead to trial, P stands to reap £55,000, so he will not agree to give up his claim for less than that amount. D, meanwhile, expects to lose only £40,000 in

	P	D
Odds that P will prevail	0.7	0.5
Payoff if P succeeds at trial	£100,000	−£40,000
Litigation costs	£15,000	£20,000
Expected value of suit	£55,000	−£40,000
Bargaining range	None	None
Available cooperative surplus	−£15,000	−£15,000

Figure 6.3

going to the jury, so he will not pay more than that amount to end the lawsuit. As the reader can see, it is the parties' divergent calculation of P's prospects in proceeding to trial that forecloses settlement.

The fact that parties may reach different conclusions regarding the plaintiff's expected verdict, however, does not mean that settlement will always be impossible. If litigation costs are sufficiently large vis-à-vis the asymmetric valuation of the plaintiff's odds of success, a mutually beneficial bargaining range will exist. For example, in the above case, if the parties' litigation costs doubled – such that it costs P and D £30,000 and £40,000 respectively to litigate to judgment – settlement should occur. Under those conditions, P would expect a gain of £40,000 and D would expect a loss of £60,000, so they will agree on a settlement figure between those two sums.

(c) Appetite for risk affects the likelihood of settlement

The discussion thus far has assumed risk neutrality. In many cases, however, parties will be somewhat risk averse. This is especially likely where the amount in dispute constitutes a significant portion of the litigants' total wealth. The reader will recall that a person is risk averse if he would accept a guaranteed sum of lesser amount than the expected value of a gamble. For instance, an individual who is indifferent between a 100% chance of £9 and a 10% chance of £100 would be mildly risk averse.

How does a person's appetite for risk affect the potential for settlement? The answer, unsurprisingly, is that risk aversion makes settlement more appealing, while risk preference increases the allure of trials. Recall that a risk-averse person places a premium on a sure thing, while a risk-preferring individual prefers to take a chance rather than to obtain a guaranteed payoff. Trials are, of course, probabilistic (i.e. risk-filled) affairs. Settlement converts an uncertain outcome into a guaranteed one, and is thus relatively attractive to risk-averse litigants and off-putting to risk-preferring parties.

Consider the following example. A defendant, D, accidentally injures a plaintiff, P, in the amount of £50,000. The parties agree that P has even odds – 50% – of prevailing at trial. It would cost each party £5,000 in lawyers' fees and litigation costs to proceed to trial. Will they settle? They certainly would if they were risk-neutral actors. P's expected value of going to trial is £20,000, while D's expected cost is £30,000, so any price between those limits would translate into mutual gains.

Suppose, however, that P prefers risk to the point that he would favour a 50% chance of £45,000 (damages minus his lawyer's fees) over a 100% chance of £30,000 (D's maximum settlement offer). In that event, the parties will not settle if D is risk neutral or risk preferring. If D is risk averse, however, she would be willing to pay a price greater than £30,000 to secure a guaranteed expense in lieu of a 50% chance of a £55,000 loss. Depending on the severity of D's risk aversion and P's risk preference, the parties may settle for more than £30,000.

The parties' appetite for risk can permit settlement even when no bargaining range would exist for risk-neutral parties. Change the above example so that P thinks he has an 80% chance of prevailing at trial, while D thinks P only has a 40% chance of winning. If the parties both agree that a verdict for P would result in damages of £50,000, P's expected value of going to trial is £35,000, while D's expected cost is £25,000. No settlement would occur if the parties were risk neutral because D wouldn't pay more than £25,000, while P would not give up his claim for less than £35,000. If either or both parties are sufficiently risk averse, however, the bargaining range may expand to the point where settlement is mutually attractive.

People are generally risk averse, which increases the likelihood and hence prevalence of settlement by expanding the relevant bargaining range. Are there circumstances in which litigants are more likely to depart from slight-to-moderate risk aversion? The behavioural economics literature, which Part IX addresses, provides an important insight. Specifically, people are likely to prefer risk when facing the prospect of large losses and to be risk averse when encountering a large potential gain. This psychological phenomenon results from reference points. When faced with an unpleasant choice between bad odds at trial and an unattractive settlement, many people tend to cling to the hope of prevailing at trial. This phenomenon explains risk preference, which leads some litigants to reject settlement offers greater than the expected value of trial. Conversely, when people face a potential large return, the fear of losing that award induces them to accept offers less than the expected value of trial.

When this phenomenon arises, it tends to frustrate settlement when the effect of the defendant's risk preference exceeds that of the plaintiff's risk aversion.

(d) The larger the amount in controversy, the less likely the parties are to settle

We have seen that parties' beliefs concerning the expected outcome of trial is the primary determinant of whether a settlement will be possible. We also saw, however, that the magnitude of the parties' litigation expenses can affect the feasibility of agreement by setting the range of the potential bargaining zone. Other things being equal, the greater the cost to the parties of litigating the case to judgment, the larger the mutual benefit of reaching agreement, hence, the greater the likelihood of settlement. Litigants' appetite for risk can further affect the boundaries of a settlement range, sometimes foreclosing agreement when the expected value of a deal is larger than going to trial for both parties and other times permitting settlement when the expected value of proceeding to judgment is greater for both parties than reaching an accord.

The last factor relevant to the settlement question concerns the magnitude of the amount in controversy. Specifically, and holding other factors constant, does settlement become more likely as the plaintiff's potential recovery becomes larger?

The answer is a qualified no. First comes the qualification: if the parties' expectations perfectly align, the desirability of settlement will be invariant to the stakes involved. Contrast two otherwise identical scenarios in which P and D agree that (1) P has a 50% chance of prevailing and (2) the cost of litigating to judgment for each party is £20,000. In one scenario, the amount in controversy is £100,000. In the other, it is £1 million. The parties should settle in both cases. In the former, P's expected value from trial is £30,000 and D's expected cost is £70,000. In the latter case, the expected values are £480,000 and -£520,000, respectively. In both cases, the width of the bargaining range is precisely the same, reflecting a cooperative surplus of £40,000.

When the parties' expectations diverge, however, increasing the stakes may reduce the feasibility of settlements. This will necessarily be so when the parties are risk neutral and when their efforts at trial are fixed. In such circumstances, the fact of mutual optimism means that the probability of settlement drops with increases in the amount in controversy. The reason is that enhancing the financial stakes magnifies the disparity caused by asymmetric expectations.

To illustrate this effect, revisit the preceding example except that now P calculates his probability of success at trial at 60% and D estimates P's likelihood of prevailing at 40%. Once more, the parties are risk neutral and their costs are £20,000 each. In the first case, the amount in controversy is £100,000 and in the second it is £1 million. The parties should settle the first case. P's expected value is £40,000, while D's expected cost is £60,000. A bargaining range exists between these figures, with a cooperative surplus of £20,000.

Although the parties' relative optimism remains the same, the parties will not settle the second case. P's expected value is £580,000 and D's expected cost is £420,000. A gulf of £160,000 separates the parties, thus precluding any agreement. The difference between the two cases comes down only to the amount in controversy. As the stakes grow larger, the gap between the parties' calculated expected values will expand if any divergence in expectations exists.

Despite this effect, it is not possible categorically to conclude that greater amounts in controversy translate into lower probabilities of settlement. In particular, if the parties are risk averse, larger stakes enhance the risk of trial, thus making settlement more attractive.[3] Furthermore, if the parties can affect the likelihood of their prevailing at trial by changing the amount of resources that they devote to litigation (e.g. by hiring better lawyers), increasing the amount in controversy will lead the parties to expend greater resources at trial. This latter effect will increase the likelihood of settlement by enhancing the combined expense – the opportunity cost – of proceeding to trial.

2. The role of lawyers and discovery in spurring settlement

We have just seen that parties' expectations concerning the outcome of trial is the principal factor determining the likelihood of settlement. Optimism thus leads some litigants to reject settlement offers that more objective analysis would identify as being mutually beneficial.

What could account for such asymmetric predictions, which hinder settlement? Two factors plausibly explain it. The first is overconfidence bias, which may lead litigants systemically to inflate what they consider to be their chances at trial. Where one or both parties to a lawsuit fall prey to this bias, a wedge may result between their respective expectations, thus foreclosing settlement. The second reason why parties may attach different likelihoods to the outcome of trial is asymmetric access to information. If one party has private knowledge that is indicative of either magnified or reduced prospects for the plaintiff at trial, the more informed party may correctly identify the expected outcome at trial, but the other may not. Both such effects may foreclose settlement. Fortunately, the judicial system is cognisant of such impediments to efficient bargain.

Consider what is likely the definitive feature of a just legal system: people mired in legal difficulties need not face the state or their private opponents alone, but can engage a lawyer whose sworn duty compels her to make her client's interests coterminous with her own. To be sure, lawyers' exalted role in many constitutional systems has axiomatic virtues going beyond settlement. In rendering expert advice concerning how best to resolve the disputes at hand and in mounting a vigorous presentation of their clients' cases, attorneys ensure that governments respect clients' legal rights. This role safeguards people against abuse of power and, in holding opponents to their proof, reduces the prevalence of error and hence of miscarriages of justice. Yet, the fact that lawyers act on behalf of parties in dispute also carries an important benefit to the efficiency of the litigation process: it injects otherwise-absent objectivity to the proceedings.

Knowledgeable, experienced, lawyers can subject cases to a level of dispassionate and informed scrutiny that lay people embroiled in passionate conflict could not match. Being experts in both law and procedure, having seen how comparable proceedings were resolved, and being one step removed from the controversy, attorneys should reach more-accurate predictions concerning the expected outcome of trial. If this prediction holds true, legal representation fosters settlement by more closely aligning parties' expectations.

---

3 Recall that risk-averse people will pay a premium to smooth their income stream over time, thus avoiding fluctuations in their wealth.

A second feature of the litigation system also fosters settlement: the compulsory dissemination of relevant information among the parties. In the United States, for instance, a case which survives the initial pleading stage proceeds to formal discovery, in which the parties can demand a generous range of information from the opposing side. By serving document requests, subpoenas, interrogatories, and requests for admissions, and by taking depositions, lawyers unearth the relevant facts surrounding a case. Other common law jurisdictions have less expansive (and less expensive) procedures for bringing the truth to light in advance of trial, but have information-sharing mechanisms in place nonetheless. In England and Wales, for example, during the "disclosure" stage of commercial litigation parties must produce documents (broadly defined) upon which they rely or which affect their or another party's case.

Discovery causes relevant information formerly known only to one party to come to light. As the litigation process unveils such private knowledge, the parties' information about the relevant facts become more symmetrical. This will induce litigants to make more-informed determinations of their chances at trial, thus causing expectations more closely to align. As mutual optimism diminishes, of course, settlement becomes more probable.

A further feature of formal, fact-disclosing procedures – and especially in the United States where discovery costs are notoriously high – is that the expense of proceeding from the initiation of a lawsuit to trial fosters settlement. Given any set divergence in expectations concerning the outcome of a proceeding, the larger litigation costs become, the more likely settlement will be. This does not necessarily mean that high discovery costs are socially efficient – indeed, as the discussion below on negative value lawsuits explains, the opposite may be true, as discovery costs are wasteful and may increase the number of filed cases. Nevertheless, regarding the discrete question as to the probability of settlement over proceeding to trial, greater litigation costs enhance the likelihood of cooperative solutions.

C. Negative-Value Lawsuits

If plaintiffs are risk neutral, rational, and wealth maximising, they file suit because the expected value of doing so is positive. Yet, people regularly initiate lawsuits that bear negative expected value if litigated to judgment. This section explores the economics of such "nuisance" lawsuits, asking whether cases of this sort are an artefact of irrational behaviour or consistent with expected value theory.

In fact, unravelling the mystery of negative-value lawsuits is straightforward. First, litigation is not a binary process, but is rather an amalgam of many sequential choices. There are, after all, many steps between an act giving rise to a grievance and an ensuing judicial remedy. Second, especially under the US rule in which each side bears its own expenses, even a defendant who successfully refutes a claim suffers an uncompensated loss. Combined, these conditions make it possible for mutually advantageous bargaining zones that are (1) less than defendants' expected cost in litigating to judgment and (2) more than plaintiffs' costs in filing suit.

Negative value lawsuits may appear to be synonymous with frivolous ones, which bear a low probability of success. In fact, the concepts are distinct. Not all negative-value lawsuits are frivolous. Suppose that a footballer committed a technical battery by deliberately kicking a ball at, and striking, an onlooker, who was not hurt as a result. If the onlooker sued for battery, he would surely prevail, but his damages would only be nominal. As the cost of bringing suit exceeds that amount, the battery claim possesses a negative expected value, even though it is not frivolous.

To illustrate in more detail how negative-value lawsuits arise, consider a hypothetical claim involving two risk-neutral parties, P and D. The possible path of litigation comprises several sequential choices, beginning with P's decision whether to file suit. Figure 6.4 reveals each step and the corresponding cost to the parties.

Decision Number	Decision or Event	Decision maker or actor	Marginal cost to plaintiff £	Marginal cost to defendant £	Plaintiff's probability of success
1	File suit, or	P	1,000	0	n/a
	don't file suit		0	0	n/a
2	File motion to dismiss, or	D	1,000	2,000	0.8
	don't file motion to dismiss		0	0	n/a
	Settlement Offer	P	n/a	n/a	n/a
3	Accept settlement offer, or	D	(P_0), if accepted	P_0, if accepted	n/a
	proceed to discovery		48,500	80,000	n/a
4	File motion for SJ, or	D	2,000	4,000	0.5
	don't file SJ motion				n/a
	Settlement Offer	P			
5	Accept settlement offer, or	D	(P_0), if accepted	P_0, if accepted	n/a
	proceed to trial		15,000	20,000	n/a
	Trial		[1,000,000] if won	1,000,000 if lost	0.2
6	Appeal verdict, or	D	5,000	10,000	0.5
	don't appeal		0	0	n/a

Figure 6.4

The following diagram illustrates the possible outcomes of this hypothetical litigation.

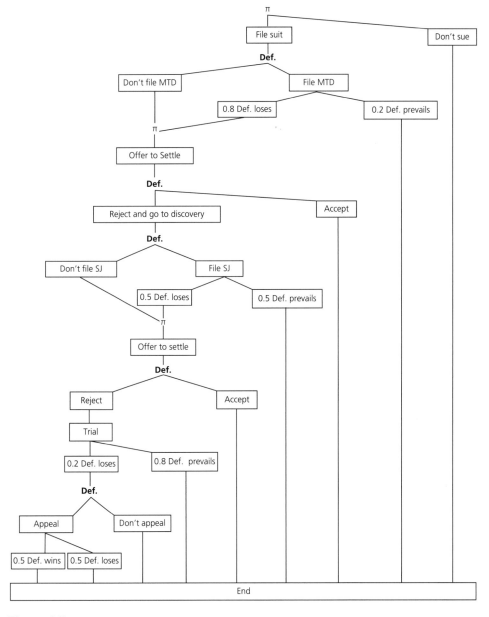

Figure 6.5

The parties' litigation costs depend on the choices they make throughout the proceedings, such as whether they settle, and when, and whether D files dispositive briefs, such as to dismiss (MTD) and for summary judgment (SJ).[4] Assuming that the parties eschew settlement and the defendant files dispositive motions whenever it can and would appeal a negative verdict at trial, the expected value of litigation to P is −£50,000. The expected verdict amount is £40,000 (£1 million multiplied by the probability of its being realised of 4% (0.8*0.5*0.2*0.5)). Yet, P's expected litigation costs are £90,000.[5] This is an example of a negative value lawsuit.

Yet, P may nevertheless sue. If P brings the action, D might agree to pay a settlement amount sufficiently large to make filing the complaint profitable. After all, D also suffers litigation costs, which may exceed the settlement sum that would make filing the lawsuit profitable for P.

As litigation takes place in a strategic environment in which one party's rational choice depends on opponents' likely choices, game theory can determine whether P should file suit. We shall begin by computing the expected value to the parties of each decision, beginning with the last choice and moving backwards. We will identify the attractiveness of settlement to the parties in light of the payoffs of their litigation decisions. The settlement amount at any given stage depends on the expected value to the parties of proceeding further into the litigation from that point.

1. The appeal decision

Employing backward induction, begin with the last move in the game, which arises after the jury verdict. Of the two possible outcomes from trial, the first is that P prevails, obtaining a £1 million verdict. In that event, what is D's rational move? Bear in mind that all prior expenses undertaken by the both parties during the trial are now sunk and hence irrelevant to the decision. It is obvious that D would appeal because it would enjoy a 50% chance of overturning the verdict, obtaining a benefit of £1 million at the expense of appellate litigation costs of merely £10,000. The expected value to D of appealing would thus be £490,000.

What if D wins at trial, leaving P with zero recovery? By assumption, the court will not reverse a finding for D. Therefore, P would not appeal because doing so would grant it a 0% likelihood of obtaining a reversal, but would entail costs of £5,000. In other words, the expected value to P of appealing would be −£5,000.

It thus follows that, that if P prevails at trial, an appeal will take place, but not otherwise.

2. The post-discovery settlement decision

Having completed the discovery process, and if D has filed but not prevailed on a motion for summary judgment, the parties are ready for trial. Before they engage in that process, they have an opportunity to confer regarding the possibility of settlement. Whether such an accord is possible depends on the parties' respective expected values of proceeding to trial. P faces a 20% chance of securing a £1 million judgment, at a cost of £15,000. P also knows that, if he wins, D will appeal with a 50% likelihood of overturning the judgment, but that, if P loses, P will not appeal. The appellate process would cost P £5,000, though there is only a 20% chance that it will incur that cost. P's expected value in proceeding to trial is therefore £84,000.

D would experience £20,000 in litigation costs at trial and would face a 20% chance of the jury finding her liable for £1 million at trial. She knows that, in such an event, she would appeal

---

4 Note that, if P prevails, he will obtain £1 million in damages, but will receive nothing if he loses. In the event that he loses at trial, assume that P cannot appeal because the appellate court will not disturb a jury's factual finding of no liability. Yet, given the novel legal issue on which P's case rests, D has a significant chance of overturning a jury verdict in favour of P (50%).

5 Without settlement, and assuming that D files every dispositive motion and appeals a negative trial verdict, expected litigation expenses are £90,000. This equals 1.0*£1,000 (the expected cost of filing suit); 1.0*£1,000 (the expected cost of opposing a motion to dismiss); .8*£100,000 (the expected discovery expenses); .8*£2,000 (the expected cost of opposing summary judgment); .8*0.5*£15,000 (the expected trial costs); and 0.8*0.5*0.2*£5,000 (the expected appeal costs).

and would enjoy a 50% likelihood of securing a reversal at a cost of £10,000. D's expected cost in foregoing settlement is therefore £122,000.

A mutually beneficial settlement range therefore exists between £84,000 and £122,000. Assume that the parties have equal bargaining power and thus meet half way at £103,000. Theory thus predicts that no trial and hence no appeal will take place.

This is not the end of our inquiry however, as we must determine whether the lawsuit would even proceed to the post-discovery stage.

3. The summary judgment decision

After the close of discovery, but before P makes a post-discovery settlement offer, D can move for summary judgment. Doing so would provide D with a 50% chance of success at a cost of £4,000. The alternative is not to file the motion, and instead to proceed to settlement talks, which as we have just seen would cost D £103,000. D will, therefore, file the motion for summary judgment because the expected value of doing so is £47,500, which equals $0.5(£103,000) - £4,000$. None of the costs previously incurred in the litigation bear on D's decision to file the motion because those expenses are sunk.

4. Whether to settle in advance of discovery

If the case makes it to the point where D has filed an answer, the parties are ready to proceed to discovery. Before doing so, however, they will have an opportunity to settle. To determine whether a settlement is feasible, compare P's and D's respective expected values in proceeding forward.

If the parties do not settle, they will proceed to discovery, costing P £48,500. Based on the preceding analysis, P knows that D would then file a motion for summary judgment, against which it would cost P £2,000 to defend. Should D not prevail on that motion – there is a 50% chance that she would not – the parties would settle at £103,000. The expected value to P of proceeding to discovery is therefore £1,000.

Consider D's situation. If P chooses to press on in the litigation, D would have to pay discovery costs of £80,000, then £4,000 to file a motion for summary judgment, and then a 50% chance of paying £103,000 in settlement. The expected cost to D of proceeding to discovery is £135,500. Thus, proceeding to discovery would cost D more than P, and therein lies the opportunity for a lucrative settlement in P's favour.

A bargaining range exists between £1,000 and £135,500. Assuming once more that the parties have equal negotiating power, they will settle at £68,250.

5. Whether to file a motion to dismiss

Having been served with the complaint, D can file a motion to dismiss. As courts treat all well-pleaded facts in the complaint as true in reviewing such a motion – granting it only if those facts do not support a plausible right to relief – it is difficult to win such a motion. D's odds of success are 20%. Filing the motion would cost D £2,000. Will she move to dismiss or go straight into discovery? The answer lies in the expected value to D of moving to dismiss, which equals the foregone cost if she prevails (£68,250) multiplied by the probability of succeeding on the motion (0.2), minus the expense of bringing the motion (£2,000). As the expected value is positive (£11,650), she will file the motion.

6. Whether to file the complaint

Having worked backward from the last decision in this sequential game, we now arrive at the first, which represents the ultimate question of interest: will P file this negative value lawsuit?

P knows that his suing will cause D to move to dismiss and, in the eventuality that the motion fails, the parties will settle for £68,250 before discovery. The expected value to P of filing the lawsuit, therefore, is £52,600, which equals 0.8*£68,250 (the settlement amount multiplied by the likelihood of its realisation) minus £1,000 (the filing fee) minus £1,000 (the cost of opposing D's motion to dismiss).

This is a negative value lawsuit. Given the assumptions outlined above, P would expect to lose £50,000 in litigating to final judgment. Yet, the sequential actions underlying the litigation, which all generate discrete costs, and the prevailing defendant's inability to recoup its litigation expenses, combine to make this a profitable action for P.

7. Conclusion

The preceding model demonstrates that negative value lawsuits can be profitable because plaintiffs can sometimes impose sufficient litigation costs on defendants to make it cheaper for those defendants to settle than to proceed to a trial.

Taken on its own, this model would suggest that negative value lawsuits abound because defendants will settle in lieu of proceeding to more expensive trials. There are at least two reasons why they do not. First, and as the next section explores, the incentives are different for common law jurisdictions following the English rule, where the losing party bears all the costs. Second, dynamic analysis suggests that it may be rational for defendants repeatedly hit with negative value lawsuits steadfastly to refuse to settle. If such defendants can establish a hard reputation for "irrationally" proceeding to trial against nuisance suits, prospective plaintiffs may eschew those potential defendants for softer targets. The ensuing savings in lawsuits that do not arise, discounted to present value, may exceed the cost savings that settlement would have achieved. In such an event, it may be rational for a defendant to forego settlement in favour of more expensive trials!

Nevertheless, working to foster a "never settle" reputation will not always, or even generally, promote the financial interests of defendants that are subject to lawsuits. Furthermore, asymmetric information may make it difficult for defendants to ascertain whether particular plaintiffs are bringing negative value suits or are actually litigating positive expected-value actions. Limited ability to distinguish the two may lead defendants mistakenly to settle negative value suits even where those defendants wish to generate a reputation for litigating negative value actions to judgment.

D. English and American Rules Compared

In the United States, each side bears its own costs. There are limited exceptions, such as in civil rights cases or where a defendant establishes that the operative claim was frivolous, but this is the predominant rule. Other common law jurisdictions, however, typically follow the "English rule", which requires the loser to pay both sides' costs.

Commentators have long debated which system is preferable. Champions of the English rule contend that the "loser pays" requirement deters frivolous claims, discourages nuisance lawsuits, and suppresses the aggregate amount of litigation, which many people believe to be excessive. Supporters further claim that the English rule spurs people to file meritorious lawsuits. United States' lawmakers would seem to accept at least some of these purported benefits, as Congress has enacted fee shifting in settings such as civil rights and antitrust with the purported goal of encouraging private enforcement.

Proponents of the American rule, however, argue that a "loser pays" system closes the courthouse doors to plaintiffs of lesser means. If everyone is entitled to her day in court, such commentators argue, the American rule is superior. A recurring concern is that individuals would not sue companies who could afford to hire an army of defence lawyers as this would translate into cataclysmic costs if they were to lose.

This section subjects the American and English rules to economic scrutiny, tracing the incentive effects of each. The ensuing conclusions refute some conventional wisdom regarding the effects of these rules, but vindicate others. No one rule is superior in all circumstances but, depending on the legislature's policy preferences, there may be valid grounds for preferring one over the other.

1. The English rule discourages lawsuits with a low probability of prevailing and encourages high probability lawsuits

To compare the incentives that the English and American rules generate regarding whether to file suit, consider how a plaintiff's expected value differs under each. Although this book generally avoids equations, it is useful in this context to generate inequalities representing complainants' sue/do not sue decision. In the ensuing discussion, "P_P" represents the plaintiff's probability of success, "$1-P_P$" equals the defendant's likelihood of prevailing (as estimated by the plaintiff), "D" is the damages if the plaintiff wins, "C_P" reflects the plaintiff's litigation costs, and "C_D" constitutes the defendant's litigation expenses.

Under the simpler American rule, the expected value from filing a complaint and litigating to judgment is $P_P*D - C_P$. Under the expected-value criterion, therefore, a plaintiff will sue under the US rule if:

$P_P*D - C_P > 0$ ["condition 1"].

This makes sense of course, as a risk-neutral person will sue if each side pays its own costs and the damages it expects to garner from trial exceed the costs entailed in securing that judgment.

The file suit condition is somewhat more complicated under the English rule. In that context, the expected value to a plaintiff of filing suit and proceeding to final verdict is:

$P_P*D - (1-P_P)(C_P + C_D)$.

In other words, under a "loser pays" system and in the absence of settlement, a plaintiff's expected value in suing is the probability of his prevailing multiplied by the judgment he would obtain minus the likelihood of his losing multiplied by the sum of his and the defendant's litigation costs. A plaintiff will sue under the English rule if:

$P_P*D - (1-P_P)(C_P + C_D) > 0$ ["condition 2"].

What can we learn about the US and English rules when comparing these inequalities? By rearranging condition 1, it follows that a plaintiff will sue under the US rule if:

$P_P*D > C_P$.

This is intuitive — a risk-neutral complainant will bring an action only if the expected judgment surpasses his expected costs. By similarly rearranging condition 2, a plaintiff under the English rule will sue if:

$P_P*D > (1-P_P)(C_P + C_D)$.

This also makes sense: a risk-neutral person will sue if the damages multiplied by the likelihood of her obtaining them are more than the costs she would have to pay were she to lose.

To determine the circumstances in which a lawsuit will be more attractive under one rule than under the other, look at the relationship between P_P*D and the right-hand sides of the rearranged conditions above. For any given value of P_P, D, C_P, and C_D, a lawsuit will be more likely under the American rule if:

$$C_P < (1-P_P)(C_P + C_D).$$

This yields the conclusion that a plaintiff will more likely sue under the American rule when:

$$P_P < C_D/[C_P + C_D].$$

Holding costs constant, this inequality tells us two important things about the English and American rules. First, as P_P shrinks, it becomes more likely that the inequality will be satisfied; thus it becomes more probable that a plaintiff would sue under the American rule rather than the English. Conversely, as P_P grows larger, it becomes more likely that the inequality will not be satisfied, so a prospective plaintiff would probably bring an action under the English rule.

These two insights make sense. Where a plaintiff has a slim chance of prevailing, it would rather bring suit under a regime where each side bears its own costs. There is a large probability that, if he sues, he will ultimately have to pay both his own expenses and those of his opponent. Conversely, for a complainant whose odds of success are great, a "loser pays" system is attractive because not only is the plaintiff likely to obtain her sought judgment, she would do so free of any litigation costs.

Therefore, economic theory supports the view that a "loser pays" system discourages frivolous lawsuits. Such a system, however, is likely to increase the number of lawsuits filed which have a high probability of prevailing.

This latter effect will not always be desirable. When the ratio of litigation costs to the judgment amount is high, it is likely that lawsuits will be inefficient because the social cost of employing the litigation system may well exceed the worth of the verdict's deterrent value.

2. The English rule may discourage settlement

A "loser pays" regime deters frivolous actions, but encourages suits that plaintiffs are likely to win. For those opposed to nuisance claims, the English rule has much to commend it. Under which rule, however, will litigants be more likely to settle than to go to trial?

Recall that the parties' expectations for trial and litigation costs determine the fact and spectrum of a settlement range. If risk-neutral parties agree on the expected verdict at trial, settlement will always be possible. If the parties' expectations differ, the feasibility of agreement depends on whether the factors fostering settlement – the magnitude of the parties' litigation costs, for instance, or risk aversion – outweigh those frustrating it. In particular, given asymmetric expectations the probability of settlement decreases with any increase in the amount in controversy: the larger the stakes, the greater the pecuniary impact of a marginal change in the percentage likelihood of the plaintiff's recovery.

This recap is useful because it permits one to focus on the settlement incentives that the English and American rules create. Neither rule necessarily changes the probability that the parties ascribe to the possible outcomes at trial. Nevertheless, the choice of rule affects the remaining factors, changing both the magnitude of the verdict and the amount that the parties rationally spend on litigation. Furthermore, in the event that either or both of the litigants are not risk neutral, the likelihood of settlement depends on whether the loser pays or each side bears its own costs. Consider each effect in turn.

(a) The English rule increases the amount in controversy, thus diminishing the likelihood of settlement

First, for any given amount of damages, the English rule will yield a greater net award than the American rule because the victor will also get her litigation costs. The American rule, of course, bestows a comparatively meagre award, essentially under-rewarding the prevailing party by denying him any recovery of the costs he has expended in successfully vindicating his rights. As the English rule increases the amount in controversy vis-à-vis the American rule, the former will encourage a trial when the parties have different expectations concerning the ultimate verdict.

(b) The greater stakes under the English rule spur parties to spend more on litigation; this makes settlement more likely

Yet, the greater amount in controversy under a "loser-pays" system does not necessarily make a trial more likely. At least one incidental feature of the English rule has an opposing effect – encouraging settlement. As it bestows a richer bounty on the prevailing party, the English rule will spur the parties to spend more on a trial. Specifically, the possibility that the other side will bear all the costs decreases the private marginal costs of greater expenditure to both parties, thus spurring further financial investment in the trial. Second, greater stakes propel further spending at trial because, for any given positive change in the probability of the desired outcome, an increased amount of controversy translates into a larger marginal benefit.

As the parties' litigation costs establish the extent of a bargaining zone, if any, increasing those costs makes settlement more likely. Holding all other factors constant, then, this aspect of the English rule makes it more probable that the parties will reach an accord.

(c) Risk-averse litigants are more likely to settle under the English rule, while risk-preferring parties are more likely to go to trial

For any given case, the possible payoffs under a "loser pays" system vary more than under the American rule. For that reason, a trial is even less attractive to a risk-averse litigant under the English rule than it is under a regime in which each side bears its own costs. It follows that settlement is more appealing to such litigants in the presence of the English rule. The opposite, of course, is true for risk-preferring parties.

Thus, there is no definite answer to which of the English and American rules makes settlement more likely. The ultimate tendency of one rule more heavily to promote settlement will depend on which factors, given the circumstances of the case, control.

3. Both rules can exacerbate the problem of excessive litigation

There is widespread belief that certain western societies have become overly litigious. This view is not bereft of support. In the US in 2011, plaintiffs filed 294,336 civil lawsuits in the federal system alone.[6] The Court Statistics Project reported that, in 2009, there were no less than 106 million pending cases in US state courts.[7] Courts in England and Wales saw more than 1.2 million claims for financial damages in 2011.[8] In 2007, in the same jurisdiction, claimants brought approximately 2.1 million civil cases.[9] In Ireland in 2010, there were over 150,000 new civil cases.[10] There is a sense in these and other common law jurisdictions that people have become too quick to summon

---

6 *See*, www.uscourts.gov/Statistics.aspx.
7 *See*, www.courtstatistics.org/.
8 *See*, www.justice.gov.uk/statistics/courts-and-sentencing/judicial-quarterly.
9 *See*, www.unece.org/fileadmin/DAM/env/pp/compliance/C200823/Amicus%20brief/AnnexOJacksonvolume1.pdf.
10 *See*, www.courts.ie/.

their lawyers at the first sight of trouble and too hesitant to resolve differences in a less formal, and doubtless more civilised, manner.

Of course, high-stakes disputes concerning complex issues routinely emerge. A formal litigation system is, therefore, essential. For prosaic matters, however, a "sue first and talk later" culture creates problems going beyond the unattractive quality of litigiousness. Accessing the courts is expensive, and contemporary rates of litigation are excessive with respect to certain causes of action. For this reason, one might ask whether the English or American rule is more likely to curb the problem of excessive litigation.

Yet, this question does not yield a clear answer. As the next section explains, contemporary litigation levels are apt to be excessive in certain situations and inadequate in others. The choice of rule predictably affects the incidence of different kinds of law suits. A "loser pays" regime increases the number of cases in which plaintiffs have an above-average chance of prevailing. Importantly, though, not all such actions are socially desirable. Contrary to intuition, the English rule may exacerbate the problem of excessive litigiousness. What of the American rule? Many lawsuits with a low probability of success are, of course, inefficient. A system that causes each side to bear its own costs magnifies the number of such actions, aggravating the problem.

Both rules, therefore, invite too many lawsuits. Yet, each carries a distinct benefit in suppressing particular forms of inefficient litigation. The English rule makes negative value and frivolous claims unprofitable for plaintiffs, while the American rule limits plaintiffs' incentives to file lawsuits that plaintiffs are more likely than not to win.

E. The Optimal Level of Litigation

Thus far, much of the analysis has implicitly assumed that injured parties can appeal at zero cost to the courts to make whole their losses. With that assumption, it follows that the law can induce efficient behaviour by imposing prices on risk-neutral actors equal to the negative externalities attendant upon their conduct. Thus, expectation damages impart incentives only to commit efficient breach of contract; strict liability induces tortfeasors to regulate their activity levels and to take all cost-justified precautions; and sanctions equal to the probability adjusted harm of an offence can regulate the amount of criminality. In all of these examples, the law causes actors to internalise the effects of their behaviour, which is efficient when they are the lowest cost avoiders of the relevant harm.

This account, though yielding rich insight into the theoretical underpinnings of law, overlooks the expense of vindicating one's rights in court. Private costs – predominantly in the form of attorneys' and filing fees – prevent some prospective litigants from accessing the legal system. The fees are but a subset of larger litigation costs, which the state provides at significant cost to the taxpayer. The amalgam of private and social costs yields a variety of problematic effects. First, litigation costs do not simply transfer wealth: they distort behaviour and cause wealth losses. If the law concerns itself with curtailing social costs – such as accidents, crime, opportunistic breach of contract, invasions of property rights that undercut investment and beyond – the costs that it minimises must also include litigation expenses.

This insight has an important implication: in light of positive litigation costs, some negative-externality-producing conduct will go uncorrected. For example, suppose that a tortfeasor could reduce the expected cost of his causing an accident by £200,000 by taking precautions of £150,000. His failure to take such care would, of course, be negligent so, all things being equal, it would be efficient to find him liable for £200,000. All things are not equal, however, as litigation is not free. Suppose that the social cost of litigating the case is £60,000. In that event, the victim's litigating to judgment and obtaining damages would reduce welfare by £10,000, even though it would spur more efficient behaviour on the part of future tortfeasors.

One might object that this inefficient result would not ensue if, under the Coase Theorem, stakeholders could contract to avoid social welfare losses. Yet, the fact that the social cost of bringing a lawsuit is £60,000 does not mean that the plaintiff's private cost is the same amount. If the plaintiff pays just £20,000 in litigation expenses and is assured of victory, he will rationally bring the suit. Although his doing so would indeed reduce social welfare, those taxpayers whom the lawsuit negatively affects are far too diffuse to have an individual incentive to become involved. Nor, indeed, does any taxpayer have a veto over (i.e. a property rule interest in) how the government spends her taxes. Obviously, then, transaction costs are too high to prevent inefficient litigation.

This phenomenon represents a broader problem: litigation choices reflect private, not social, welfare. This issue should be familiar to the reader by now, for departures between private and social cost are pervasive. The litigation sphere is no different, so plaintiffs will sometimes sue when they should not and other times inefficiently decline to bring suit. This section looks at these questions.

1. The social and private costs of litigation

Judicial proceedings entail two distinct forms of expense. The first are private costs that litigants alone experience in bringing and defending lawsuits. The second are social costs that the government, but not the parties, bear in making the judicial arm of the state available for public use. Both sums are significant.

Begin with the public price of litigation. This includes the salaries of judges and supporting staff, the acquisition and upkeep of the necessary infrastructure, administrative expenses, and so on. Government funding for the judiciary comes either directly from taxpayers or from sovereign debt markets, but in neither case do the litigating parties provide all of the capitalisation themselves. In the United States, the public largely funds the judiciary, at a cost of $6.97 and $6.91 billion in 2012 and 2011, respectively.[11] The Court Statistics Project reported expenditure in 2004 of approximately $8.5 billion. Even this figure significantly understated the total cost because the report lacked figures from several prominent states.[12] In England and Wales, taxpayers pay approximately £130 million per annum to fund the civil and family courts; this amounts to roughly 20% of the overall cost.[13] Litigants in England and Wales pay the remainder through fees.[14]

What of litigation costs that are private to the parties? These pertain chiefly to lawyers' fees, which eat up a sizeable portion of the amount in controversy. Of course, in enhancing the accuracy of fact finding and legal analysis, lawyers play a potentially important role in an efficacious litigation process. Yet, the enhanced process associated with their involvement comes at a heavy administrative and pecuniary cost. The fact that contracting parties increasingly agree to forego formal litigation in the event of a dispute in lieu of less formal, less expensive, resolution procedures proves the point. Lawyers are themselves an impediment to the achievement of the theoretically ideal goals explored throughout this book.

Combined, litigation costs are immense. They are greatest in America, where the expense of tort litigation alone peaked in 2003 at a staggering 2.2% of GDP, but are significant in all common law jurisdictions.[15] A 2013 study found that liability costs as a percentage of GDP were 1.66% in the

---

11 *See* www.uscourts.gov/FederalCourts/UnderstandingtheFederalCourts/AdministrativeOffice/DirectorAnnualReport/annual-report-2012/fiscal-year-funding-cost-containment-initiatives.aspx#funding; and www.uscourts.gov/annualreport_2011/Budget.aspx.
12 Court Statistics Project. Available at: www.courtstatistics.org/Overview.aspx.
13 *See* www.unece.org/fileadmin/DAM/env/pp/compliance/C200823/Amicus%20brief/AnnexOJacksonvolume1.pdf (p. 63).
14 *Ibid.*
15 Suing Companies: On Top of a Wave, *The Economist* (20 May 2010).

United States, 1.05% in the United Kingdom, and 0.78% in Ireland.[16] The authors found that a common law tradition and a high number of lawyers per capita strongly indicate high litigation costs.[17]

The following sections explore the ramifications of these costs for the efficiency of the legal system. The discussion concludes that the litigation system, as presently constituted, fails to foster optimal incentives of the kind explored in previous chapters. This suggests that complementary government policies are desirable.

2. When is litigation efficient?

When is a lawsuit desirable? This is a loaded question, which implicates conflicting views about the meaning of justice, the role of the courts, and the relationship between aggregate welfare and individual rights. Depending on one's jurisprudential view, the question of whether a lawsuit is efficient may be distinct from whether the same legal proceeding is right or otherwise justified. From the consequentialist perspective of law and economics, however, lawsuits serve a single function: to induce efficient behaviour by generating optimal incentives. A civil proceeding is, therefore, economically desirable only if the incentives that it produces generate gains that exceed the underlying litigation costs.

This perspective warrants rejecting some intuitively attractive propositions (e.g. actions that plaintiffs are sure to win are desirable). Many people discern the normative quality of a lawsuit based on whether the underlying claims are well-founded in law and fact. If a plaintiff initiates an action bearing a high probability of success, it follows that she is legitimately vindicating her legal rights in court. If a problem exists, it is with the substantive law, which the legislature or judiciary can revisit. This view rests, at least implicitly, on the perspective that justice is invariant to, and independent of, the expense required to achieve it.

In terms of economics, however, litigation is merely a conduit by which the law imparts incentives and guides behaviour. The judicial process carries no intrinsic value apart from that function. Viewed from this perspective, one can readily demarcate the boundaries of desirable lawsuits, and thus identify those actions that are inefficient. Consider a pedestrian hit by an assiduously careful driver following a freak combination of events beyond the parties' control. There is no dispute that the driver hit and injured the plaintiff. Nor is there any question that the defendant was on the road for justifiable reasons, such that an efficient activity level change would not have altered the likelihood of the accident. Based on these facts, under a strict liability regime, the pedestrian would surely prevail. His odds of success may even approach 100%. Yet, if the social cost of bringing the action is anywhere above zero, this lawsuit is categorically inefficient. Why? It is because the driver's behaviour was efficient and the accident was unavoidable in the economic sense explored in Part II. The litigation between the parties results in a wealth transfer from defendant to plaintiff, a social cost incurred in employing scarce judicial resources, and no concomitant benefit in the form of incentive generation.

One might protest by invoking the pedestrian's right to compensation. Is a victim's recovery not a defensible goal independent of economic concerns? Perhaps, though many economists believe that matters of distributive justice are ill-suited goals of the legal system. It is better, from the perspective of efficiency, that potential accident victims obtain insurance, which compensates people at lower social cost than litigation. These benefits are not just economic, as if the goal of the

---

16 David L. McKnight and Paul J. Hinton, 'International Comparisons of Litigation Costs: Europe, the United States and Canada' (May 2013). Available at: www.instituteforlegalreform.com/sites/default/files/NERA%20Study%20of%20International%20 Liability%20Costs%20FINAL.pdf.

17 Ibid., p. 2.

litigation system is to compensate injured parties, it performs that function poorly. Even omitting the public expense of suit, private costs in lawyers' fees and expenses swallow much of the available recovery.

Inefficient lawsuits are more likely to arise under a strict liability, rather than a negligence, regime. In fact, if courts defined negligence as the failure to take the precautions that minimise the expected social cost of accidents – where that cost includes the public expense of litigation – and if courts operated free of error, there would be no inefficient tort litigation under a negligence standard. As it is, of course, courts operate imperfectly, thus undesirable actions do arise under negligence regimes.

3. Should parties have to pay the full cost of litigation?

As the private and social costs of litigation diverge, economists would not expect litigants' collective behaviour to match the social welfare optimum. When parties do not bear the full cost of an activity from which they derive benefit, a rudimentary insight of economics – rooted in the negative-externality literature – is that they will engage in an excessive amount of that conduct. Translated to the setting of a court, the fact that plaintiffs need not pay the marginal cost that their lawsuit adds to the judiciary's operations suggests that they will bring too many actions. Standard theory might suggest that the government should correct the externality (or bargaining failure in the parlance of the Coase Theorem) by rendering private and social costs co-terminous. Does this suggest that litigants should shoulder the full burden of running the litigation system, freeing the taxpayer of any expense?

The answer is no. A litigant's decision to sue carries not one, but two, offsetting externalities – one being negative, and the other being positive. The negative externality is as just described – suing entails the expenditure of scarce judicial and administrative resources that would otherwise be available for other purposes. Furthermore, much litigation amounts to rent-seeking, as each party's efforts simply counteract those of the other. The quintessential example involves the expensive production of conflicting reports by equally credentialed and persuasive experts. To the extent such efforts do not aid the court in correctly resolving a complex issue, they are socially wasteful. Yet, an important positive externality accompanies many decisions to file suit; this is the precedential value of the ensuing disposition on future behaviour. A prevailing litigant does not internalise the full benefit of her victory, which may impart valuable incentives.

This yields an interesting conclusion. Although there is presently too much litigation, in light of the great expense of employing the judicial process, there are not enough socially valuable lawsuits. This is a public goods problem, which the government is well placed to solve by subsidising the legal system. Thus, the state should encourage certain kinds of unusually valuable litigation, the consequential benefits of which exceed the private value available to a prevailing plaintiff. For example, the US Congress has encouraged civil rights action by granting successful complainants their lawyers' fees, but not permitting defendants to recover their lawyers' costs should they win. The government also fosters such lawsuits through the provision of free legal aid. In other settings, for example with respect to private antitrust litigation, the law automatically trebles a prevailing plaintiff's recovery. To the extent the state targets private lawsuits that enhance social welfare, rather than those that are simply politically favoured, the provision of such incentive mechanisms is proper.

F. Conclusion

Litigation is profoundly important to the economic analysis of law. Viewed from the perspective of economics, the legal system should induce actors to behave as if the full consequences of their behaviour, both good and bad, fall upon them alone. To fulfil this function, the law imposes prices that correct negative externalities, and subsidises behaviour that yields positive spill over effects.

Litigation is the mechanism by which the law accomplishes this end. Unfortunately, the cost and inefficiency of legal proceedings obstruct the law's ability to realise its economic purpose.

First, to access the court system, a plaintiff must consume costly administrative resources provided by the state. The fact that legal proceedings are socially costly means that one must include litigation within the sum of aggregate costs that the law should minimise. As a result, the efficient amount of torts, crimes, and other negative externality producing behaviour is higher than it would be in a hypothetical world in which litigation is free.

Second, litigants' incentives rarely align with those of society. As the private and social costs accompanying parties' decisions diverge, the amount and type of proceedings may be imperfect. Some parties may inefficiently decline to sue. For instance, lawyers' compensation, filing fees, and other costs impede some meritorious lawsuits. This allows injurers to evade liability where the expected cost of their challenged behaviour exceeds the social cost of bringing the relevant action. Unless the courts impose disproportionately greater damages in cases that come before them, negative externalities will remain. In other circumstances, entities may bring suit when they should not. Frivolous lawsuits are a prominent example, but there are others. Even cases that plaintiffs are almost sure to win may be inefficient, such as when the complained of action was efficient or could not be deterred or when the gain in deterrence is less than the social cost. Strict liability regimes are the most likely to drive such lawsuits.

The overarching policy prescription that flows from this account is straightforward: governments should lower the social cost of the litigation process, and should subsidise private actions where the social value exceeds the private value. Restrictions on competition between lawyers facilitate supracompetitive prices. These limit citizens' access to the courts, thus diluting the law's deterrent effect. Procedural inefficiencies cause actions to stagnate, delaying final judgments and reducing the expected cost of violating a legal rule due to positive discount rates. The principal constraint on minimising the cost of litigation is due process. There is thus a trade-off between ensuring accurate determinations of law and fact, on the one hand, and reducing cost, on the other. Nevertheless, reform is both possible and warranted, and should target aspects of the contemporary litigation system that delay proceedings or drive up cost by more than they enhance accuracy.

Finally, as we have seen, economics provides a rich theoretical account for why parties litigate at all, and what conditions foster settlement. The principal function of trials is not to resolve disputes, but to give parties credible threats with which to substantiate their legal position, thus facilitating settlement. Furthermore, where the parties' sole concern in litigation is financial, the lone factor that leads to settlement or trial is the parties' relative expectations at trial. For that reason, legal certainty and objective legal representation are key elements driving cases toward settlement.

Key Points

- Courts enforce rights. Access to the judiciary permits a rights holder credibly to threaten to sue when facing an invasion of a legal entitlement. That threat should induce private bargain between stakeholders, thus making resort to the courts unnecessary.
- Lawsuits arise when the parties have divergent views on the plaintiff's expected verdict. Thus, legal certainty inversely correlates with the rate of litigation. When parties' expectations align, settlement will occur. When the parties agree on the expected damages, their combined litigation costs create cooperative surplus from settling.
- Appetite for risk affects the likelihood of settlement. Risk aversion makes settlement more attractive, while risk preference has the opposite effect.
- The greater the amount in controversy, the less probable it is that the parties will settle. If the parties attach different probabilities to the plaintiff's winning, a growing sum at issue magnifies the disparity between the parties' estimates of the likely verdict.

- Legal representation and discovery both precipitate settlement by making it more likely that the parties' expectations from trial will align.
- Plaintiffs may rationally file negative-value lawsuits – those for which the expected value of litigating to trial is less than zero – if they credibly threaten to impose sufficiently large discovery costs on defendants to make it mutually attractive for the parties to settle.
- As compared to the American rule under which each side bears its own costs, the English rule spurs a higher number of lawsuits in which plaintiffs have greater than even odds of prevailing, and discourages lawsuits with a low probability of success.

 ## References and Further Reading

Books

Baird, Douglas G., Gernter, Robert H. and Picker, Randal C., *Game Theory and the Law* (1998) Ch. 8.
Bone, Robert G., *Civil Procedure: The Economics of Civil Procedure* (2003).
Cabrillo, Francisco and Fitzpatrick, Sean, *The Economics of Courts and Litigation* (2008).
Cooter, Robert and Ulen, Thomas, *Law and Economics*, 6th edn (2011) Chs. 10 & 11.
Miceli, Thomas J., *The Economic Approach to Law*, 2nd edn (2008) Ch. 8.
Polinsky, A. Mitchell, *An Introduction to Law and Economics* (2011) Ch. 16.
Posner, Richard A., *Economic Analysis of Law* (2011) Ch. 21.
Shavell, Steven, *Foundations of Economic Analysis of Law* (2004) Chs. 17–19.
Spier, Kathryn E., 'Litigation', *Handbook of Law and Economics* (2007) Vol. I, Ch. 4.

Articles

Bebchuk, Lucian Arye, 'Litigation and settlement under imperfect information' (1984) 15 RAND J Econ 404.
Braeutigam, Ronald Ray Owen, Bruce, M. and Panzar, John C., 'An economic analysis of alternative fee shifting systems' (1984) 47 L & Contemp Probs 173.
Cooter, Robert D. and Rubinfeld, Daniel, 'Economic analysis of legal disputes and their resolution' (1989) 27 J Econ Lit 1067.
Friedman, Ezra and Wickelgren, Abraham L., 'No free lunch: How settlement can reduce the legal system's ability to induce efficient behavior' (2008) 61 SMU L Rev 1355.
Gould, John P., 'The economics of legal conflicts' (1973) 2 J Legal Stud 279.
Katz, Avery, 'Measuring the demand for litigation: Is the English rule really cheaper?' (1987) 3 JL Econ & Org 43.
Landes, William M., 'An economic analysis of the courts' (1971) 14 JL & Econ 61.
Polinsky, A. Mitchell and Rubinfeld, Daniel L., 'The deterrent effect of settlements and trials' (1988) 8 Int'l Rev L & Econ 109.
Posner, Richard A., 'An economic approach to legal procedure and judicial administration' (1973) 2 J Legal Stud 399.
Priest, George L., 'Regulating the content and volume of litigation: An economic analysis' (1982) 1 Sup Ct Econ Rev 163.
Reinganum, Jennifer F. and Wilde, Louis L., 'Settlement, litigation, and the allocation of litigation costs' (1986) 17 RAND J Econ 557.
Rosenberg, David and Shavell, Steven, 'A model in which lawsuits are brought for their nuisance value' (1985) 5 Int'l Rev L & Econ 3.
Shavell, Steven, 'Suit, settlement, and trial: A theoretical analysis under alternative methods for the allocation of legal costs' (1982) 11 J Legal Stud 55.
Shavell, Steven, 'The fundamental divergence between the private and the social motive to use the legal system' (1997) 26 J Legal Stud 575.

Part 7

Innovation Policy

1	Innovation Policy	235
2	The Patent System	251
3	Copyright Law	283

Chapter 1

Innovation Policy

Chapter Contents

A.   Introduction   236

B.   Building a Platform for Technological Progress   236

C.   Conclusion   249

Key Points   249

References and Further Reading   250

A. Introduction

Innovation is a crucial determinant of long-term welfare, and thus a priority for public policy. Its value is twofold. First, scientific progress lifts constraints that had previously restricted a community's wealth potential. A society's technological ability to transform scarce inputs into valuable consumables and services limits the potential value of the economy. Second, technological advancement may make entirely new products and services possible, thus creating value for consumers where none existed before. The same is true of novel forms of artistic expression, from music to literature to art, which enriches people's lives.

Both such effects – greater productive efficiency and new sources of utility – enhance the magnitude, and not just the distribution, of wealth in society. In 2010, for instance, the US Chamber of Commerce tied three-quarters of post-World War II, US economic growth to innovation.[1] Similarly, a recent study concluded that innovation was responsible for two-thirds of UK private-sector productivity growth between 2000 and 2007.[2]

Of course, innovation is not always desirable, as it depends on the ends to which society uses the resulting invention. Some people have devoted their visionary and technical talents to nefarious goals: creative techniques of torture and ever-more-lethal weapons are obvious examples. Nevertheless, innovation is on the whole an overwhelmingly positive generator of social welfare, which is why governments strive to create environments conducive of progress in the arts and technology. Yet, identifying and building an infrastructure in which innovation will flourish is a complex endeavour. As social scientists devoted to understanding the nature and effect of incentives, economists have a lot to say about how best to inculpate innovation.

Fortunately, the aggregate quality and amount of innovation are contingent on many factors within the government's control. Understanding the stimuli that drive innovators' efforts is therefore indispensable to effective policy. Having studied the various catalysts underlying artistic and industrial progress, economists can recommend policies to maximise output of pertinent creativity and science.

Economics can thus help, but so, too, can law. If economics provides the policy recommendations upon which to build an innovation platform, law is the mechanism by which governments can enact rules that inculpate incentives to invent. This fact creates the potential for positive achievement, but also for harm. Indeed, current laws drive many instances of innovation, but impede others. Economic analysis can identify ways in which to achieve superior results.

This chapter identifies the distinct roles that private enterprise, universities, the public sector, and individuals play in modern innovation policy, and explores the background conditions conducive of innovation that the government can foster independent of patent and copyright law. Chapter 2 focuses on technological, engineering, and scientific progress, with which the patent laws have traditionally concerned themselves. Chapter 3 explores the economics surrounding the development of creative content, which relates primarily to music, film, computer software, books, and art more generally. Copyright is the traditional legal mechanism enacted to foster innovation in those fields.

B. Building a Platform for Technological Progress

Why do people innovate, and what can governments do to spur the process? The answers are not obvious. Inventors toil in their proverbial basements on all manner of potential inventions, and

---

1 US Dep't of Commerce, 'Patent Reform: Unleashing Innovation, Promoting Economic Growth, & Producing High-Paying Jobs' (13 April 2010). Available at: www.commerce.gov.
2 NESTA, 'The Innovation Index: Measuring the UK's Investment in Innovation and its Effects' (2009). Available at: www.nesta.org.uk/library/documents/innovation-index.pdf.

their motivations are as diverse as their ideas. Some strive for pecuniary gain, while others crave social recognition and the esteem of their peers. Others still derive such innate joy from the process that they would do it regardless of reward. Crafting a comprehensive innovation policy is thus complex, as it appears that, in order to be effective, such a strategy must promote diverse and potentially conflicting inducements to invent.

Although the circumstances surrounding different innovators' productive efforts are heterogeneous, two broad conclusions are possible. First, some sources of invention are more important to modern innovation policy than others, such that one can fruitfully inquire what conditions are most conducive to R&D in the former context. A government would responsibly direct a disproportionate share of its efforts to foster such conditions. Second, certain inducements are likely to spur innovation in many contexts and are unlikely to impede it in others. Fostering those catalysts is likely to enhance the aggregate value of innovation in the economy.

This section begins with a high-level overview of the roles that private industry, the government, universities, and individual inventors play in fuelling innovation in industrial technology. That synopsis informs the *ex ante* – or background – conditions that infuse economic incentives to invent.

1. Exploring the source of modern innovation

(a) The central role of private companies

Private enterprise is the principal driver of technological progress today. In the last 20 years alone, it has generated a bewildering array of revolutionary innovations. The information technology industry has produced Google's Internet search algorithm; Facebook; Apple's array of game-changing products beginning with the iPod and iTunes; the BlackBerry and ensuing smart phone revolution; YouTube; small-scale GPS devices for cars; high-definition Blu-Ray and DVD systems; and much more. Computer-hardware and software companies, such as Intel, Microsoft, and Apple continue to advance computing power and applications by leaps and bounds. Car manufacturers have designed safer and ever-more-efficient vehicles, including electric cars. Biopharmaceutical companies continue to research and to manufacture life-saving drugs and biologics, though the recent ratio of new blockbuster drugs and biologics to mere reformulations and follow-on biologics has been disappointing.[3] Nevertheless, notable pharmaceutical products of the last 20 years include Lipitor, a cholesterol-reducing statin which is the best-selling drug in history; Plavix, an anti-blood-clot agent; Nexium, a drug that inhibits gastric acid production; and Seretide, an anti-asthma formulation.

The trait common to all such commercial innovators is pursuit of profit, which has important public policy ramifications. If private enterprise is the powerhouse creator of modern technology, it is imperative to foster conditions conductive to innovation in that setting. Companies must, therefore, be able to extract at least some of the value of their commercialised inventions. Appropriation mechanisms are therefore indispensable to high rates of private sector research and development (R&D). Of course, the individual employees and owners of innovating enterprises derive non-pecuniary benefits from their technological contributions. The point, however, is that, within the context of industry, these benefits are ancillary to positive expected returns on investing in innovation.

What accounts for the private sector's disproportionate success in producing novel technologies? The answer lies in the uniquely powerful incentives that a confluence of factors creates: (i) the prospect

---

3 "Me-too" variants of pre-existing drugs yield lower prices, but little long-term value relative to such historical blockbuster drugs as penicillin, morphine, aspirin, ether, thorazine, and insulin.

of great financial awards for companies that successfully introduce technologically superior products, (ii) fierce competition among companies to achieve that goal, and (iii) a broad pool of talent combine to drive creativity. The public sector is not subject to comparable incentives. This is not to deny, of course, that the government cannot and will not achieve revolutionary innovations. It is merely to point out that superior incentives for ground-breaking invention generally lie with private industry.

Notwithstanding private industry's leading role in modern innovation, it would be a mistake to construe private enterprise independent of other important actors. In fact, much high-value R&D undertaken today entails sophisticated and coordinated efforts between the private sector, universities, and the public sector. Illustratively, the National Institute for Health ("NIH") contributes more than a quarter of all US funding for biomedical research, while the Medical Research Council in the United Kingdom spent almost £800 million on such research in 2010–2011. Another prominent example is the US National Science Foundation, which, with a budget of roughly $6.9 billion, funds research in mathematics, computer science, and social science.

(b) Universities

Much funding of this kind goes to universities, which play an especially important role in conducting basic research. A high risk of failure characterises initial-stage research, which often makes such work unattractive for private companies who possess higher discount rates than society and focus on projects possessing profit-generating potential. Instead, universities do much of the early legwork, identifying subsets of promising technologies, developing them to a stage where they have credible potential for commercial application, and then selling them to private companies. These companies, in turn, undertake the remaining research with the ultimate aim of marketing the underlying technologies.

Universities, therefore, are key incubators of modern-day industrial innovation. The factors driving R&D there, however, are somewhat distinct from private industry. For full-time academics, much of the reward from successful research lies in tenure, promotion, and reputation among peers. For these inventors, pecuniary awards of the kind necessary to induce commercial research are probably less important.

Nevertheless, monetisation still matters, not only at the level of the individual academic, but also for the larger university that provides its faculty and students with the requisite funding and infrastructure. To induce university-level innovation, then, not only is capitalisation sufficient to cover research costs indispensable, but financial rewards representing a portion of the social value of successful research endeavours are likely to spur ever-greater efforts. As universities are not themselves profit-maximising entities – which is, of course, a desirable trait given third-level institutions' unique and important role in undertaking valuable, but not readily monetised, research – adequate external funding is crucial. Depending on the jurisdiction and particular institution, of course, significant capitalisation may come in the form of tuition and alumni donations. All universities rely on external grants for much of their research, however, which is why the government must support innovation in the university sector.

(c) The government

As noted, governments are important sources of innovation. In identifying scientific goals of interest to the larger community, the government can devote public funding to worthy projects free of the risk that may hinder private investment and with more concern for potential long-term payoffs. Beyond facilitating the research of others, however, the government can conduct its own innovation, which has historically been significant and has had many desirable spillovers into public life. Government research in military and space technologies is especially on point. Indeed, such modern-day technologies as the internet, jet engines, radar, and GPS resulted from military research. Of course, the public sector can play an important role in pursuing worthy research projects that profit-maximising enterprises would spurn.

The reader might object that, if a research endeavour does not bear a positive expected value – such that no risk-neutral, profit-maximising company would pursue it – the government should also eschew the project. If a research project bears negative expected value, surely it is inefficient and best jettisoned? The answer, however, is that unprofitable research endeavours are sometimes in the public interest.

Whether the government should conduct research that the private sector eschews depends on the reason why the project does not possess positive expected value at the private level. If the answer is that the research would bear an expected profit but for companies' inability to capture a sufficient share of the social value of an ensuing invention, then the research endeavour is a worthy one. In such an event, the government should enact policies permitting more effective appropriation by private enterprise or undertake the research itself.

Yet, there are research opportunities that both the private and public sectors should rightly shun. The efficient amount of innovation is not the maximum possible level. The R&D process requires spending scarce resources. The optimal rate of industrial invention arises at the point where a marginal increase in inputs to the innovation process yields an expected gain in social welfare equal to the cost of that incremental input. Boosting innovation beyond this level is bad public policy. There is a danger here, as the state experiences imperfectly aligned incentives to invest because, unlike private enterprise, it has the luxury of spending other people's money.

(d) Individual inventors

Rounding out the population of innovators are researchers who invent independent of any larger entity. Such inventors enjoy a romantic image in the public eye, as many people still conceive of innovation in the style of Thomas Edison. Although many people, working alone, strive to accomplish some modicum of technological advance, the reality is that the lion's share of innovation today results from institutional R&D. This observation does not denigrate individual innovation. The fact of the matter, however, is that the capital funding needed for effective research in many technologies precludes garage-based efforts at the individual level. This observation does not apply, of course, to computer programming and software. In such settings, the contributions of individual innovators remain significant.

2. Background conditions conducive to private-sector innovation

Modern industrial innovation entails a complex interplay between private enterprise, the public sector, and institutions of higher learning. As we have noted, the private sector has demonstrably superior vision and incentives with respect to such innovation. This suggests that industry should be the foremost focus of a responsible innovation policy. Governments should, therefore, foster an environment that spurs businesses to realise their potential to conceptualise, invent, and commercialise novel technologies. Public sector, university-based, and other research plays an important role, but one most fruitfully construed as complementary, focusing on research that companies pursue at sub-optimal rates.

This raises a crucial question: how can the government unleash the innovative potential of private enterprise? From the economic perspective of incentives, the necessary impetuses lie at both the front and back end. Most obviously, the quality and rate of innovation depend on the inputs that are available to feed the R&D process. Even the most ingenious and visionary management can accomplish little without adequate capitalisation, sufficiently talented engineers and other employees, and a larger business environment facilitative of its work. This chapter focuses on inputs that underlie private-sector innovation. The next focuses on the patent system's discrete role in spurring industrial R&D. That system operates as a post-innovation appropriation mechanism, which can infuse desirable *ex ante* incentives to invent, as well as *ex post* incentives to commercialise.

Economics identifies at least eight background conditions that governments can foster to nurture private-sector innovation. These are political stability; education; a functioning legal system;

efficient capital markets; suitably targeted government funding that does not crowd out private investment; bankruptcy laws that spur a desirable level of entrepreneurial risk-taking; immigration rules that enable technology companies to hire the best minds; and employment laws that foster fluid labour markets. Notwithstanding the heterogeneous forces driving innovation, addressing these factors is likely to drive high rates of scientific advance. We shall address each factor in turn.

(a) Political stability

Political stability is a requisite of sustained industrial innovation. Unstable governmental systems frequently undermine both the rule of law and macroeconomic conditions – two effects that do much violence to innovation. Such instability also harms incentives to invent in its own right. Uncertainty freezes industrial capital investment in the R&D process. A capricious form of government, subject to frequent coups or unpredictable fluctuations in policy, poisons the business environment on account of its unpredictability.

The reader will recall the distinction between risk and Knightian uncertainty. The former involves payoffs to which decision-makers can apply known or calculable probabilities, while the latter entails conditions in which no meaningful calculation of odds is possible. To be sure, the borders between risk and uncertainty are porous rather than precise, but one can meaningfully distinguish circumstances lying at respective ends of the certainty spectrum.

Businesses can rationally invest in risky environments because, by diversifying their portfolios, they can achieve risk neutrality and devote capital to projects bearing positive expected values. Where uncertainty prevails, however, businesses lack means by which to reach informed decisions. In politically unstable countries, investors encounter grave difficulty in ascribing even approximate numeric probabilities to political events that could ruin their investments.

The rewards from successful innovation generally inure over time, while inventors experience the cost of investment in the present. Faced with political instability, private entities will typically turn to safer investment opportunities – even those bearing lesser potential returns – because those prospects are more susceptible to net-present-value analysis. It follows that, to foster an environment conducive of private investment in R&D, a country must work to ensure stable mechanisms of government. Unsurprisingly, the empirical literature is in accord.[4]

(b) Education

Human capital is an obvious input into the knowledge economy. Innovation advances the state of the art beyond its pre-existing level, which obviously requires a threshold level of training in the applicable field on the part of the relevant innovator. At the level of a national economy, private enterprise cannot engage in fruitful R&D without having access to a pool of knowledgeable workers. An educated workforce is therefore a critical prerequisite of technological innovation.

In a broad sense, this conclusion must be true – for without a threshold level of knowledge, workers cannot contribute meaningfully to the R&D process – but it may also be misleadingly simple. While eradicating a country's education system would have catastrophic effects on technological innovation, it does not necessarily follow that reduced funding for education would suppress a country's long-term economic growth founded on R&D. Nor does it necessarily suggest that enhancing public funding would magnify long-term technological and artistic progress.

This may surprise the reader. After all, if the knowledge base in an economy is a principal input in the R&D process, one would expect expanded education to yield greater innovation and economic growth. Indeed, a strong correlation exists between an individual's education and her income, which may be a proxy for productivity. Yet, the empirical literature only weakly supports the hypothesis that education enhances productivity at the macro level. "Productivity" and

---

4 *See, e.g.*, Gayle Allard, Candace A. Martinez, and Christopher Williams, 'Political instability, pro-business market reforms, and their impacts on national systems of innovation' (2011) 41 Research Policy 638.

"innovation" are, of course, distinct concepts, though the latter feeds the former. If promoting education correlates only weakly with productivity-led economic growth, this relationship has profound implications for innovation policy.

The empirical disconnect between education and productivity at the micro and macro levels requires explanation. One answer – though not necessarily the most probable one – is that education and productivity may not be strongly correlated at either level. This possibility rejects human capital theory, which holds that education is a productivity-enhancing investment that magnifies a people's value in the economy. From this view, education boosts productivity by instilling otherwise-absent skills in prospective workers.

Another view, however, is the screening hypothesis, which holds that education is a sorting mechanism that sends credible signals to prospective employers concerning the traits of the relevant students. More productive people will rationally invest in education to demonstrate their superior aptitude and skills to employers, which signal will enable them to obtain higher paying jobs and thus enhance the productivity of the economy (as compared to the alternative state of the world in which, absent a signal-generating education system, less-productive individuals may have obtained the relevant positions). From this perspective, education may impart little, if any, substantive knowledge to students that translates into otherwise-absent, work-applicable skills.

Education serves a valuable function under both theories, though the policy implications for how best to structure educational policy differs under each. In particular, if the screening hypothesis holds true, society may realise modest or even negative returns from further investing in education. Conversely, if education bestows on students otherwise-absent skills and knowledge that have productivity-magnifying applications, increasing the quality and length of schooling through additional funding is more likely to yield positive social value.

Yet, there may be another explanation for the strong statistical relationship between education and income at the micro level and the weak correlation between education and productivity at the macro level. Education and productivity may, consistent with intuition, be correlated at all levels, but statistical problems may frustrate econometricians' efforts to identify that relationship. As it turns out, many such problems exist. In the first place, reverse causality poses a significant difficulty because jurisdictions that experience increasing productivity and macroeconomic growth are more likely to increase educational funding and vice versa. In addition, an inability to measure educational investment directly forces econometricians to rely on the number of years' schooling, which is a poor proxy.[5]

Education likely carries both effects, enhancing industry-relevant skills and serving as a valuable signalling device to employers that candidates possess abilities that predispose them to the particular jobs for which they are applying. The relative weight of those effects, however, is surely contingent on a variety of circumstances, including the specific discipline studied, the reputation of the relevant educational institution, and the rigour of the prescribed curriculum. As an illustrative example, a person admitted to a prestigious institution on the basis of her intellect, who skips classes, crams for exams, and acquires little long-term knowledge, but subsequently obtains a job on the basis of the signalling value of her high-calibre education would fit the screening hypothesis to a tee. Conversely, an individual who studies a technical discipline at a rigorous, though less-prominent university, and who devotes his time to mastering the substantive material underlying the curriculum is more likely to graduate with a skill set that would enable him to be a more productive employee.

There is some reason to believe that university-level education in sciences and in engineering is more likely than most disciplines to instil productivity enhancing abilities. This does not necessarily mean that training in the hard sciences always or usually yields a skill set of immediate

---

5 *See* P. Aghion, L. Boustan, C. Hoxby, and J. Vandenbussche, 'The Causal Impact of Education on Economic Growth: Evidence from U.S.' (2009). Available at: www.economics.harvard.edu/faculty/aghion/files/Causal%20Impact%20of%20Education.pdf.

relevance to employers. It does suggest, however, that advanced study in such fields enhances human capital, predisposing graduates for quicker and more-effective training at the hands of employers.

Thus, at the university level, the so-called "STEM" subjects – science, technology, engineering, and mathematics – are likely to be more conducive of high rates of technological innovation in an economy than studies focused on the humanities and social sciences.[6] This is not to deny the rich benefits associated with the latter fields of study, but governments put a premium on technology-based economic growth and should do what they can to promote STEM fields of study among those bearing a suitable aptitude.

(c) The legal system

Private-sector innovation depends on the rule of law. The absence of demarcated and consistently applied laws results in a tumultuous business environment, antithetical to R&D investment. Such phenomena as the selective enforcement of rules, a non-independent judiciary, and a systemically corrupt police force impede technological advancement. In such environments, bribery may be a *sine qua non* of doing business, and legal recourse may be unavailable in the event of opportunistic breach of contract. Even contracts with the state may be subject to the latter's whim. Corruption distorts market processes, which would otherwise direct resources to higher-value uses. Extortion may be a problem, as will unchecked expropriation of proprietary interests in technology. The latter effect may be particularly harmful, as the next chapter on the economics of the patent system explains. Collectively, a compromised legal system is a serious barrier to entrepreneurship, foreign direct investment, and private enterprise's devotion of capital to the research and commercialisation of promising technologies.

Consistent with these factors, economists have consistently found a positive relationship between the strength of the rule of law and economic growth.[7] States with flawed legal systems that wish to achieve enhanced long-term economic growth through innovation would reap significant gains by tackling deep-rooted corruption, promoting judicial independence, and strengthening the rule of law.

(d) Capital-market efficiency

Much industrial innovation is investment heavy, and thus depends on inventors' access to capital. Of course, the funding required to innovate is heavily context dependent. The most capital-intensive research industry is biopharmaceuticals. PhRMA, the US biopharmaceutical industry representative, has estimated that the average cost of developing a marketable drug is $1.3 billion (though this figure is probably overstated). The semiconductor industry, another high-cost field of innovation, spent $53 billion on R&D in 2012.[8] It is a requisite of ongoing innovation in resource-hungry research sectors that aspiring inventors possess access to capital sufficient to finance promising projects.

Debt or equity funding is indispensable to capital intensive projects due to the protracted temporal gap between incurring research expenses and reaping the ensuing reward. In the pharmaceutical industry, for example, the average time to develop a promising chemical compound into a marketable drug is 12 years.

The availability of capital funding – be it in the form of equity, credit, or grants – serves a critical function in bridging the gap between expense and return. The government should therefore enact policies that promote macroeconomic growth and capital availability. It is difficult to overstate

---

6 *See, e.g.*, U.S. Congress Joint Economic Committee, 'STEM Education: Preparing for the jobs of the future' (2012).
7 *See, e.g.*, D. Kaufman and A. Kraay, 'Growth without governance' (2002) 3 Economica 169; R. Hall & C. Jones, Why do some countries produce so much more output per worker than others?' (1999) 114 QJ Econ 83.
8 The McClean Report 'A Complete Analysis and Forecast of the Integrated Circuit Industry' (2013).

this point. Jurisdictions in which venture capital seeks investment opportunities facilitate innovation, driving bold research projects and entrepreneurship. Thriving venture capital activity, for instance, played a key role in the rise of Silicon Valley as the world's innovation centre. Without such funding, many successful technology start-ups would have floundered in their incipiency.

Consistent with this discussion, numerous studies find a close connection between efficient financial systems, innovation, and economic growth.[9] Unfortunately, ongoing problems in the wake of the international banking crisis have exposed just how difficult it is to identify macroeconomic policies aimed at securing efficient and stable financial markets. There is at least some tension between the two, as banking systems are inherently unstable. Unfortunately, economists do not yet sufficiently understand financial economics and macroeconomics to identify long-term policies around which consensus can emerge.

(e) Competition policy

A long-disputed question is whether competitive or concentrated industries are superior incubators of innovation. Making the latter case, Joseph Schumpeter famously argued that monopoly is the best driver of invention because the large profits associated with supracompetitive pricing produce surplus funds for research and development. Furthermore, he maintained, dominant companies have incentives to invest private capital because their installed client base and scale efficiencies lessen the chance that fringe rivals can appropriate the value of any successful inventions. According to Schumpeter, competitive markets with low profit margins will not drive innovation. Thus, monopoly may provide a "more stable platform" for R&D investment.

The Schumpeterian view counsels a *laissez faire* approach to antitrust policy with respect to dominant-firm behaviour. If competition law were to restructure monopolised markets, the long-term result may be lower prices and higher output, but reduced innovation. Assuming that policy-makers wish to promote dynamic over static efficiency, interventionist antitrust policy aimed at fostering competition may have unintended results.

Kenneth Arrow rejected Schumpeter's view, arguing that competition best spurs innovation. He explained that dominant firms have relatively weak incentives to research ground-breaking technologies because they face a high opportunity cost in doing so. Specifically, because monopolists earn monopoly profits on the basis of then-existing technology, their spending those profits to realise a new marketable technology may simply displace one profit base for another. This phenomenon, known as "the replacement effect", reduces the value of an invention.

By contrast, a company subject to competition has more to gain by achieving a breakthrough discovery because it will experience a significant increase in demand, thus taking profitable sales opportunities from its rivals. Arrow showed that for a drastic process or method innovation – one for which the monopoly price is lower than the previous technology's marginal cost – the reward from developing a novel process is the same for both a monopolist and a previously competitive firm, but the monopolist faces a larger replacement effect. Thus, the firm subject to competition faces a stronger incentive to invent.

The Schumpeter-Arrow debate has generated a considerable body of empirical and theoretic work, but few hard answers. Arrow's model concerned innovation in technological methods, which can diminish a company's marginal costs. The model did not address product innovations, which arguably represent a sphere of invention that is more important to the economy. As an improvement product is less likely to render an old product defunct, a monopolist's invention of the former may allow it to price discriminate and hence to achieve greater profitability. Thus, although a competitive firm's replacement effect is likely to be less, a monopolist may have a greater incentive

---

9 *See, e.g.*, European Central Bank, 'The Role of Financial Markets in Productivity and Growth in Europe' (2007). Available at: www. ecb.int/pub/pdf/scpops/ecbocp72.pdf.

to invent a novel product. Even if a product invention is sufficiently revolutionary as to constitute a drastic invention, as per Arrow's definition, a competitive firm will not necessarily have the greater incentive to invent unless the discovery is so significant that the monopolist cannot use it for price-discrimination purposes.

An authoritative 2006 synopsis of the economic literature concluded that the evidence "does not support a conclusion that large firms promote innovation because they provide large and stable cash flows, economics of scale (above some threshold), or risk diversification. At the same time, neither theory nor empirical evidence supports a strong conclusion that competition is uniformly a stimulus to innovation".[10] Economic models, therefore, do not lend themselves to an unqualified policy prescription.

Complicating matters further is the question how best to interpret Arrow's and Schumpeter's views from an antitrust perspective. In the first place, it may be a mistake to over-emphasise the replacement effect. This phenomenon may be serious only where a dominant company actually enjoys a market position that fringe rivals or other potential competitors do not threaten. In fact, monopoly positions in technology markets are less secure than one might suppose, even in the presence of network effects. Even dominant technology companies must continue innovating to maintain their positions.

Second, the fact of monopoly is consistent with Arrow's model, which relied on exclusive rights over one's innovation. Enforcing open standards, thus eschewing legal recognition of propri-etary rights in information, would lead to suboptimal innovation on account of insufficient incentives to invent. In this respect, a policy that sought to maximise competition – literally defined – would run counter to Arrow's view. It would myopically substitute technological compe-tition in R&D for price-based competition.

The relevant prescription is, therefore, more subtle. One advancing Arrow's view would respect intellectual property rights, even if they produced monopoly conditions, but would presumably adopt a variety of policies aimed at ensuring that the inventor obtaining such dominance would not use its position to quash actual or potential competition. In this respect, an inventor would not have the right to control follow-on paths of technological research, use its dominant position to fetter rivals' attempts to research and to commercialise new generations of products, or otherwise appropriate value for itself that goes beyond the nature of the claimed invention itself. In contrast, a Schumpeterian approach might be more willing to allow a dominant company to enjoy the fruits of that position because an absence of immediate competition over future avenues of R&D would not harm long-term innovation. Empirical and theoretical investigations of these alternative approaches, however, have failed to yield a robust policy prescription.

As the dynamics of innovation are both complex and context specific, and because general principles are elusive, it is difficult to determine whether a particular form of dominant-firm behaviour enhances or depresses efficiency. We shall revisit this question in Part VIII, which addresses the economics of competition.

(f) Regulation and bureaucratic red tape

There are many ways that governments can enrich the inputs that feed private sector R&D. As we have just seen, they can adopt policies promotive of education, political and macroeconomic stability, and law. Yet, the state can inadvertently stymie the process. A classic example is the bureaucracy that emerges as an incident of regulatory systems that governments enact to "protect" consumers. Compliance costs, regulatory delays, and red tape suffocate much entrepreneurship in its incipiency. The bureaucracy inherent in the administrative state is a negative input into the innovation process.

---

10 Richard Gilbert, 'Looking for Mr Schumpeter: Where are we in the competition-innovation debate?' in Adam B. Jaffe, Josh Lerner and Scott Stern (eds) *Innovation Policy and the Economy* (2006) p. 159.

This problem does not lend itself to a simple solution, as regulatory measures serve an important economic function – dispersing information. Symmetric and complete access to information is a requisite of economic models that predict Pareto efficiency. Information is vital to the efficacy of market processes, and its absence is a major reason why real-world markets depart significantly from the hypothesised predictions of neoclassical models premised on perfect competition. By requiring disclosure of pertinent data concerning one's product or service, the government can allow consumers to make more-informed choices. This effect will lead, in turn, to market prices that better reflect the value of the commodity in question, thus sending superior signals to the market. There is thus a tension between the compliance costs of regulation and the benefits of consumer protection.

When *ex post* regulation in the form of legal liability is inadequate, *ex ante* oversight by the state steps to the fore.[11] Such before-the-fact regulation is pervasive in the modern economy. Well-known examples include the regulatory processes accompanying the aviation and drugs industries. Further prominent examples include the US Securities and Exchange Commission and the Bank of England, which has recently taken over many obligations of the recently abolished UK Financial Services Authority. The principal justification for agencies of this kind is to ensure that publicly owned and traded companies disclose all material information concerning their businesses. In the absence of securities laws, much knowledge important to the accurate valuation of companies would remain private.

Regulatory laws and the agencies that enforce them, however, also impose heavy compliance costs on business. A prominent example is the much-maligned Section 404 of the Sarbanes-Oxley Act, which requires management and an external auditor to report on the adequacy of the company's internal control on financial reporting. Enacted in the wake of public company scandals of WorldCom, Enron, and Tyco International, Congress passed the act to restore confidence in the accuracy of securities filings and hence in securities markets. Commentators widely see Section 404, however, as an overreaction that imposes costs in excess of associated benefits.[12]

The compliance costs associated with regulatory oversight are staggering. Illustratively, for 2008, economists estimated that the cost of US federal regulations in exceeded $1.75 trillion, which roughly equalled 14% of US national income.[13] Worse still for innovation policy, the impact of regulations falls disproportionately on small businesses. Compliance costs for such businesses amounted to $8,086 per employee in 2008.[14] As a further example, a 2003 report for the UK Financial Services Authority (FSA) determined that the median incremental cost of complying with FSA regulations was 1.6% of non-regulatory operating costs.[15]

A 2011 *Economist* article illustrated how consumer protection regulations can hinder entrepreneurship, and thus innovation.[16] The piece recounted the trials of an Iranian immigrant in trying to launch a yogurt business in California. Having spent a year obtaining the required permit from Orange County and delving at last into business, the entrepreneur received a shutdown notice from California's Department of Food and Agriculture (CDFA). The regulator required her to establish a "Grade A" dairy plant, into which she had to install "'a pasteuriser with a recorder" 'culture tanks,' and a 'filler', which apparently also required a 'mechanical capper' to screw lids on jars."[17] Her

---

11 It is for this reason that, from the perspective of public policy, the 2008–2009 banking crisis was primarily a regulatory failure.
12 For the SEC's 2009 review of the costs of complying with Section 404, see US Secs & Exch Comm'n, Study of the Sarbanes-Oxley Act of 2002 'Section 404: Internal Control over Financial Reporting Requirements' (2009). Available at: www.sec.gov/news/studies/2009/sox-404_study.pdf.
13 Nicole V. Crain and W. Mark Crain, 'The impact of regulatory costs on small firms' (2010). Available at: www.sba.gov/sites/default/files/rs371tot.pdf.
14 *Ibid.*
15 Europe Economics, 'Costs of compliance' (2003). Available at: www.fsa.gov.uk/pubs/other/cost_compliance.pdf.
16 'Red Tape in California: Beware of the Yogurt', *The Economist* (19 May 2011).
17 *Ibid.*

ordeal not yet over, the regulator informed her that the operative regulations forbade milk to be pasteurised twice, requiring her to appeal for an exemption from the head of the CDFA.

That there are good reasons to adopt *ex ante* administrative rules over business in some circumstances does not justify ubiquitous regulation. As regulatory rules become more pervasive, they do more damage to the market and the innovation process.

(g) Bankruptcy laws

Debtor protection might not be the first thing that jumps to mind when one thinks of innovation policy. Yet, laws governing the relationship between borrowers and creditors can significantly affect R&D investment.[18] To understand why, one must first discern bankruptcy laws' basic economic effects.

In the absence of a bankruptcy code, borrowers would remain liable for the full amount of any debt that they incur. This may be a draconian, environment for imprudent or unfortunate debtors, but it would not be bereft of any economic benefit. Holding a borrower liable for the full amount of her debt would be an instance of strict liability because the legal obligation to repay would be invariant to fault. Such liability, as we saw in Part II, causes actors to internalise the negative externalities that would otherwise accompany their conduct. Applied to borrowers, the absence of bankruptcy protection would incentivise debtors to borrow responsibly and to take every cost-justified step to ensure solvency. The benefit would be lower interest rates, and lower costs of capital for entrepreneurs and other innovators. Notice that lenders' unqualified right to demand repayment would benefit not just creditors, but would also confer a collective benefit on debtors, who would enjoy cheaper access to financing.

Yet, grave problems would afflict any legal system that refused ever to discharge a person's debt. The most obvious are grounded in unfairness. Even the most responsible borrower's ability to repay is contingent on factors over which he lacks absolute control. Life can spring a plethora of misfortunes that might compromise even an able debtor's ability to repay. It is not obvious that the law would properly compel a person to devote her life to servicing an outstanding loan that she could never afford to repay, where that inability arose only from the vicissitudes of circumstance.

Economics provides equally strong reasons for discharging a person's debt in appropriate circumstances. Likely the most powerful justification is risk aversion. To unleash the full value of entrepreneurship and innovation, the law must endeavour to make socially valuable prospects attractive to investors. The psychological literature makes clear that people and institutions alike are highly risk averse when faced with the possibility of a loss accounting for most or all of their wealth. Many of the most valuable R&D prospects face a high rate of failure. The vast majority of technological start-ups fail, for instance, yet a small subset of those that succeed (including Google, Apple, Amazon, and Hewlett-Packard) bestow overwhelming benefits on society.

Budding inventors face odds stacked against them in creating a new business. At the individual level, most people would decline to launch a start-up in the absence of bankruptcy protection. The prospect of a cataclysmic failure and ruinous debt would deter technological development that has great potential value, but a low probability of success. If they are risk averse, potential innovators will shun some prospects that bear positive expected value. Similar principles would apply to the R&D investments of larger companies. Although such corporations are generally less risk averse than private individuals (because of companies' superior ability to diversify their investments) it will rarely be possible for corporate entities to invest their R&D funds on research projects the risk profiles of which are not correlated at all. It follows that, in the absence of bankruptcy protection, companies would discard bold, risky, but potentially lucrative forms of innovation in favour of safer

---

18 This section focuses on bankruptcy codes, though it bears noting that much of the ensuing discussion also applies to corporate organisations that possess legal status distinct from their owners.

R&D projects that build incrementally on the status quo and that bear less chance of imperilling the company's solvency over time.

By limiting the downside potential of a failed investment, bankruptcy law plays an important economic role in limiting risk aversion's suppressive effect on innovation. The reality is that we live in an era in which technological advance often requires perseverance in the fact of repeated failure. One could appeal to any number of specific sectors to make the point. For instance, less than one out of 5,000 chemical compounds investigated for pharmaceutical suitability will become a marketed drug. More generally, even successful entrepreneurs typically prevail only after several botched start-ups. Multiple attempts of that kind would not be possible in the absence of limited liability. For governments wishing to promote innovation, there are compelling economic reasons to enact a bankruptcy code.

Bankruptcy protection, however, is no panacea, as it introduces moral hazard problems of a kind that should now be familiar to the reader. By shielding borrowers from creditors' demands to repay voluntarily incurred debt, insolvency laws have two related, negative effects. First, by reducing the cost of default to the borrower, they introduce an asymmetry between the potential upside and downside of investment opportunities. As we have just seen, this constitutes an important benefit in inducing risk-averse inventors to embrace entrepreneurial opportunities bearing positive expected value. Yet, an improperly calibrated bankruptcy code that is too generous to borrowers who encounter difficulty in repaying their debts will introduce unwelcome distortions. As debtors enjoy the full benefit of successful, loan-financed investments, but experience only a fraction of the total cost of failure, they have an incentive to borrow excessively and to devote too much capital to high-risk, high-reward projects. As a necessary incident of this phenomenon, creditors will demand higher payment to compensate them for the risk of not being repaid. The higher interest rates that ensue slow economic activity and may stifle entrepreneurship.

Overall, though, this discussion creates a strong case for a bankruptcy system. Given that such codes are now ubiquitous in the western world, however, the more interesting and difficult question concerns the optimal contours of bankruptcy protection. Demarcating the proper boundaries between a creditor's right to demand repayment, even in the face of a borrower's financial distress, and a debtor's right to discharge an impractical burden is possible as a matter of abstract theory. Identifying an optimal bankruptcy code for a specific economy, however, is quite another matter.

Interestingly, it is not just law, but culture, that drives the relationship between bankruptcy and innovation. Studies detailing the manner in which aspiring entrepreneurs and the larger community in which they operate perceive bankruptcy reveal a remarkable transatlantic disparity. In Silicon Valley, which many see to have been the global hub of technological innovation for the past 20 years, budding innovators and the larger community see bankruptcy as a badge of honour. The sense is that if a person did not experience failure at some point throughout a career, she was not trying hard enough. Many spectacularly successful entrepreneurs in Silicon Valley fell flat, before winning big. By contrast, attitudes are notably different in Europe. There, a person whose business becomes insolvent is more likely to perceive himself, and to be perceived, as a failure. An environment conducive of innovation will see bankruptcy resulting from calculated investments in technology as a step on the way to greatness. Indeed, the fact that the law permits a person to wipe the slate clean and to press forward with a new idea itself recognises this principle. Governments should do what they can to promote a culture that sees innovation-based bankruptcy in such a light.

A tension thus exists between limiting debtors' repayment obligations when investments fail and promoting lower interest rates by protecting creditors' right to demand repayment. The crucial question, of course, concerns the optimal balance. The empirical literature generally supports the view that debtor-friendly bankruptcy codes are superior drivers of innovation.[19]

---

19 *See, e.g.,* Viral V. Acharya, 'Bankruptcy codes and innovation' (2008) 22 Rev of Fin Stud 4949.

(h) Immigration rules and employment law

Human capital is the *sine qua non* of industrial innovation. This is an unremarkable observation, as even prodigiously inventive entrepreneurs and managers could not transform abstract ideas into marketable products without engineers, scientists, and other professionals. As human ingenuity, skill, and dedication comprise the engine of innovation-based economic growth, they should be the foremost concern of those who seek to promote technological advancement. The question from a policy perspective is how to craft a labour pool teeming with skill.

Education is an important component of human-capital development, as we have seen, but this section explores two distinct policies that can dramatically enhance the number of employees available to R&D-focused institutions and companies. The first is immigration law. If one wishes to promote industrial innovation, the policy conclusion is straightforward: countries should embrace liberal immigration policies directed at skilled workers. By making visas easily and cheaply available for foreigners with advanced training, governments can provide technology companies with access to the employees whom they need to engage in cutting-edge research. As the best minds are never going to be unique to a single country, fluid cross-border movement of skilled human capital is conducive to innovation and efficiency.

As clear as this normative conclusion may be, political impediments routinely frustrate optimal immigration rules. Domestic workers have strong incentives to lobby against foreign competition, which suppresses prices in labour markets and ejects some domestic employees from their previously held jobs. Such lobbying is a classic form of rent-seeking, as incumbents strive to capture public policy and to set it on a course against the interests of larger society. The benefits of free movement of skilled labour are vast in the aggregate, but are also diffuse and hence relatively modest at the level of the individual voter. Conversely, the costs to incumbent employees who stand to suffer reduced compensation and greater competition for jobs are localised and thus command a greater impact in the public mind. Given many people's predilection in favour of those from home rather than abroad, the political apparatus often adopts inefficient immigration policies.

Amongst the most vocal critics of such protectionism are the technology companies that find themselves starved of the talent that they need to achieve their potential. Microsoft, Google, Apple, Intel, and similar companies are prominent advocates of more-liberal immigration laws for foreigners with advanced training in science, engineering, and mathematics. In 2013, the United States hit its annual cap for H-1B skilled foreign workers in less than a week.

Employment law plays a related role in enriching, or limiting, human capital as an input to the innovation process. Unfortunately, few issues are more politically contested than the degree to which governments should promote economic efficiency in labour markets. Economic theory suggests that fluid labour markets are conducive to innovation because they permit employers readily to hire the most skilled employees and to part company with those who fail to perform at expected levels. An illustrative feature of Silicon Valley that some believe to have been facilitative of its success is that non-compete agreements between employers and employees are unenforceable. As an incidence of this California law, a technological start-up or company with a good idea can acquire the necessary talent simply by luring them away from a rival enterprise. Were such agreements enforceable, a new company faces a restricted pool of potential employees.

Few, if any, labour markets work efficiently, as almost all are best with restrictions on competition. Particularly prevalent are laws that promote the interests of current job holders over job applicants. The nature of these laws depends on the jurisdiction and industry, though it is rarely permissible in Europe for an employer to fire an employee on the basis that a superior applicant has applied for the relevant position. Such rules stymie efficiency, but promote the welfare of those enjoying protected positions.

Although an extended discussion of labour market economics is outside the confines of this book, the basic policy prescription from the perspective of innovation policy is clear: governments can generally unleash greater innovative potential by liberalising employment laws. By making it easier for companies to hire talent, and to let those underperforming go, governments can enhance private industry's ability to secure the strongest possible work force. Whether this goal is politically achievable is a distinct question, of course, as it implicates profoundly divisive political questions.

(i) Public investment

Finally, the state can spur innovation through public subsidies. As the opening of this chapter explained, government funding can stimulate valuable research on projects that are not sufficiently conducive to monetisation to entice private investors. By funding shortfalls that stymie worthy research efforts, the state can spur a more comprehensive and socially valuable innovation platform.

There is a real danger, however, which arises when governments try to identify and pick victors in the market. Misdirected government subsidies may also crowd out private investment. If that were indeed to occur, it would be problematic because the private sector, which is subject to keener incentives, is better than the bureaucratic state at identifying promising technological research. If one were to look for a topical example, one might point to Solyndra, a solar-energy company that received more than half-a-billion dollars in loan guarantees from the US Government. It promptly went bankrupt.

C. Conclusion

Industrial innovation is a function of inputs that governments can manipulate to create an ideal innovation platform. By investing in macroeconomic and political stability, education, and the rule of law, by minimising unnecessary administrate red tape, by passing immigration and employment laws conducive to the free movement of skilled labour, by adopting suitable bankruptcy laws, and by subsidising research in valuable projects that are unattractive to the private sector, governments can craft an effective, over-arching innovation policy.

The next chapter explores an important limitation in the ability of markets to produce optimal rates of industrial innovation, even in the presence of rich inputs to the R&D process. The public goods nature of inventions, as we shall see, gives rise to positive externalities, which may induce prospective inventors and their financiers to under-invest in innovation. The degree to which this risk holds true, and in what settings, is a critical question for innovation policy. The major government effort built on solving this perceived market failure – the patent system – is currently under fire for hurting innovation more than it spurs it. In determining whether these and other criticisms are well founded, the following chapter addresses the economics of the patent regime and its relationship to R&D.

Key Points

- Innovation policy is a critical factor in long-term economic growth.
- Private enterprise, universities, and the public sector are all important sources of innovation. Distinct incentives accompany R&D investment in each of these settings. The private sector may generally be a superior outlet for innovation, so public spending should not crowd out private investment. Nevertheless, given its focus on profit, industry will not engage in some socially valuable R&D projects. Government research and funding should target such projects.
- Government can materially influence the rate of innovation by fostering background conditions conducive to it.
- Those conditions include: political stability; education; the rule of law; efficient capital markets; competitive industries; limiting regulations that stifle innovation and entrepreneurship through red tape; bankruptcy laws that facilitate justified risk taking; immigration and employment laws

that induce free movement of labour toward its highest value uses; and an appropriate rate of public investment.

- The law can incentivise R&D that would otherwise be vulnerable to third-party appropriation by enacting a suitably crafted intellectual property regime. That is the subject of the next two chapters.

 ## References and Further Reading

Books
Atkinson, Robert D. and Ezell, Stephen J., *Innovation Economics: The Race for Global Advantage* (2012).
Jeffe, Adam B., *Innovation and its Miscontents: How Our Broken Patent System is Endangering Innovation and Progress, and What To Do About It* (2006).
Lerner, Joshua, *The Architecture of Innovation: The Economics of Creative Organizations* (2012).
Scotchmer, Suzanne, *Innovation and Incentives* (2006).

Articles
Agarwl, Rajshree and Gort, Michael, 'First-mover advantage and the speed of competitive entry, 1887–1986' (2001) 44 JL & Econ 161.
Borjas, George J. and Doran, Kirk B., 'The collapse of the Soviet Union and the productivity of American mathematicians' (2012) 127 QJ Econ 1143.
Furman, Jeffrey L. and Stern, Scott, 'Climbing atop the shoulder of giants: The impact of institutions on cumulative research' (2011) 101 Am Econ Rev 1933.
Marx, Matt, Strumsky, Deborah and Fleming, Lee, 'Mobility, skills, and the Michigan non-compete experiment' (2009) 55 Mgmt Sci 875.
Moser, Petra, 'Innovation without patents' (2012) 55 JL & Econ 43.

Chapter 2

The Patent System

Chapter Contents

A.	Public-Goods Theory and the Economics of Innovation	252
B.	A Primer on Patent Law and Economics	258
C.	Incentives to Invent Independent of the Patent System	266
D.	Industry-Specific Innovation Profiles	269
E.	Alternatives to Patents: Prizes, Buy-Outs, and Regulatory Exclusivity	276
F.	Conclusion	280
Key Points		280
References and Further Reading		282

A. Public-Goods Theory and the Economics of Innovation

The first step of innovation policy is to create an environment conducive to effective research and development (R&D). The last chapter explored how this might be done. The Coase Theorem ought to take over from there. Consumers generally prefer products entailing superior technologies, and will pay to get them. Those endowed with creative and technological prowess stand to gain from this fact, and should innovate to avail of consumer demand. Even monopolists have incentives to invent, for attractive technologies shift demand curves outward, thus increasing profit. Incentives may be even more pronounced in competitive markets, where Darwinian survival requires innovating enterprises not to fall behind their rivals. More generally, the race to be the first to unearth a valuable technology, and thus to reap the benefit of first-mover advantage, will spur further heightened efforts.

Consumable products, however, are not the exclusive abode of useful inventions. Many valuable discoveries are applicable only to manufacturing and distribution processes. The Coase Theorem, however, should be no less conducive of such process inventions. Fed by inputs of the kind explored in the previous chapter, companies should innovate due to market forces alone. Pursuit of profit should spur firms, even dominant ones, to develop novel, cost-reducing production and delivery methods. Such innovations diminish companies' marginal cost of production, thus boosting productive efficiency, saving scarce resources, increasing demand and thus profit for the innovating companies. In the presence of competition, such process-based innovations may be indispensable to long-term survival, as enterprises that fail to keep pace with the technological advances of their rivals will find themselves asphyxiated by decreasing margins. Ultimately, when exposed to competition, companies that lack productive efficiency will become insolvent and will be forced to exit the market.

For these reasons, one might expect innovation to flourish with state involvement limited to that explored in the preceding chapter. But will it?

1. The economic foundation of the patent system

Economics suggests that market failure may suppress innovation. The problem (though we shall see that it can also be a benefit) is copying. Reverse engineering another's technology denies the inventor the ability to extract the full social value of her innovation. Knowing the vulnerability of their hard-earned discoveries to free riding, innovators may no longer be prepared to devote the time, effort, and money necessary to advance the art.

Every inventor requires a different minimum return to engage in R&D. To incentivise every potential innovator society could allow each one to appropriate the full social value of his discovery. In that event, social and private interests are fully aligned, such that an innovator will engage in R&D only if the expected social value of her doing so is positive. Ex post appropriation of others' technology reduces the expected value of invention at the private level, thus leading at least some inventors not to innovate when they should. In short, innovation generates positive externalities, and so it is subject to underproduction in a free market.

This economic account of innovation has been extraordinarily influential. Indeed, it constitutes the principal justification for patent regimes the world over. Yet, is technology vulnerable to copying? The answer lies in the long-held, though as we shall see increasingly criticised, assumption that technology is a "public good". To invent or to discover is simply to attain information. Knowledge, however, is difficult to keep private, as reflected in the mantra that "information wants to be free". If third parties can discern the nature of an invention through inspection or reverse engineering, the technology is "non-excludable". This trait is common with respect to technical know-how, as keeping an idea secret is more difficult than cordoning off one's physical property.

Exacerbating this problem is the fact that information is "non-rivalrous in consumption", which means that, once discovered, knowledge yields an infinite supply. That is why content industries' frequent analogy between stealing a car and digitally copying a movie is inapt. Taking a person's vehicle deprives him of its use, but bootlegging a film does not reduce the amount of that film available for others to consume. Of course, this does not necessarily justify unauthorised downloading or other forms of copying. The absence of supply constraints in information increases the difficulty of excluding others. If new discoveries can be consumed by all, it may be preclusively difficult for the inventor to control the dissemination of information, and thus to reap compensation sufficient to have made the expected value of his *ex ante* research greater than his opportunity cost of capital.

These details would be without significance if the innovation process was costless, but it is not. Inventors have to devote money and effort to unearthing new knowledge. They will do so less, or not at all, if they cannot recoup risk-adjusted R&D costs *ex post*. As innovation drives long-term economic growth, correcting market failures in the production of technology should be a priority.

Enter the patent system, which is governments' traditional solution to the positive-externality problem in invention. A patent confers an exclusive right to practice the claimed invention. Its economic function is to bestow private-good traits upon inventions that would otherwise lack them. Once an owner has an enforceable proprietary interest in her invention, she can more securely sell or licence the technology, thus capturing more of its social value. Knowing this *ex ante*, prospective inventors may rationally devote private capital to the R&D process when, without patent protection, the expected value of doing so would be less than the opportunity cost of capital.

In short, the patent regime creates a lawful monopoly within the scope of the relevant invention. Its economic function is to correct the market failure that would emerge in the presence of copying and competition. In particular, as R&D costs are sunk and because competition drives price toward marginal cost, a free market would deny some inventors the ability to recoup their investment. The following graphs illustrate the classic justification for a patent system:

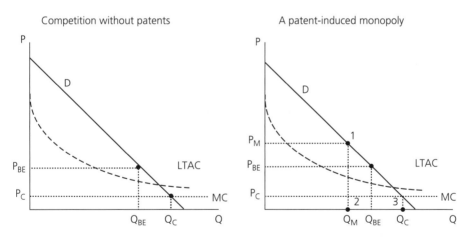

Figure 7.1

The graph on the left depicts the problem that emerges for an inventor of a hard-earned technology that bears a low and constant marginal cost to sell to consumers. The combination of high sunk costs and constant, low marginal cost results in a downward-sloping, long-term average cost ("LTAC") curve. Of course, to maintain solvency over time, a seller must sell at or above long-term average cost.

If third parties can copy the inventor's technology at no cost, an asymmetry emerges between the inventor, who made a large sunk R&D investment, and his competitors, who have no sunk costs.

Under conditions of perfect competition, the price will drop to marginal cost. In that event, the inventor in the left graph will be unable to command a price beyond P_C. As that price is below the LTAC curve, the inventor will be unable to recoup her sunk investment costs and will have to exit the market. Knowing this outcome *ex ante*, the inventor would rationally decline to devote the scarce capital required to innovate, knowing that third parties would appropriate the benefits of that innovation *ex post*.

The graph on the right portrays the patent solution. By granting the inventor an exclusive right, in this case over a valuable product or process for which no comparable substitutes exist, the patent regime may grant an economic monopoly. In that case, the innovator can sell at the monopoly price, P_M. This lies above the LTAC curve and hence the breakeven price, P_{BE}, thus ensuring profitability. The inventor would rationally engage in the requisite R&D *ex ante* knowing that patent protection will enable him to recoup his innovation costs.

Patents do more than instil incentives to invent: they spur the commercialisation of inventions. Much work can separate an initial invention from a sold product. Indeed, conceptualising a promising insight is often not the end of the process, but just the beginning. The patent system can operate as a bridge, encouraging an initial inventor either to devote the necessary toil required to market the technology or to licence someone else to do it for him. In the absence of exclusive rights enforceable by law, anticipated free riding may delay, or even foreclose, the marketing of technology.

2. The economic cost of the patent regime

Notwithstanding its benefits, the patent system carries a hefty price. The first problem is allocative inefficiency. Consider, again, the right-hand graph above. As a result of the monopoly pricing, the quantity of the technology sold in the market drops sharply from the competitive level, Q_C, to the monopoly level, Q_M. The result is a loss of economic value represented by the 1–2–3 triangle. Economists refer to this elimination of wealth as "deadweight loss", which arises when supracompetitive pricing deprives consumers of a product or service that they value more than the cost to society of making one more unit. By generating this deadweight loss, the patent regime eliminates wealth.

Patents create inefficiencies beyond the monopoly pricing just discussed. Exclusive rights fetter other inventors' access to technical know-how that they need to fuel their innovative efforts. In certain industries, the lion's share of innovation entails continuous, incremental improvements over what was recently new technology. Such settings involve a high ratio of follow-on to breakthrough inventions. When these conditions exist, patents that hinder inventors' access to state-of-the-art technology can interfere with, rather than promote, innovation. Patents are most likely to cause this problem when their scope is expansive.

A third problem arises when patents' boundaries are vague, thus creating overlapping claims to the same technology. When this occurs, a "patent thicket" can emerge, which forces companies wishing to sell patented technologies to hack their way through a dense web of coinciding patent rights that lay claim to the same product or process. Related to this problem is the anti-commons effect that can emerge in situations of fragmented ownership of numerous patented technologies, which one must combine to market a product. This situation can create high-transaction costs which frustrate commercialisation. We discuss patent-thicket and anti-commons effects in greater detail below, when considering the innovation profiles of certain industries.

The fourth economic cost lies in patent races, which are a specific example of the larger gold-rush problem. The fact that intellectual-property rights bestow exclusive rights on the first to file a successful patent application diverts competition to the *ex ante* research process. As a general matter, this is desirable because it spurs the invention of new technologies, thus promoting dynamic efficiency at the cost of less-important static efficiency. Furthermore, to the extent R&D efforts are not duplicative, this effect can generate desirable positive spill-over effects, adding new insights to the storehouse of human knowledge. Nevertheless, duplication is wasteful. Patents induce too many prospective inventors to compete to be the first to invent a technology. Patent races thus lead potential patentees to dissipate the expected rents that they would acquire from a patent.

Consider a hypothetical in which ten identical companies must determine in which of two research projects they should invest their R&D capital. The first investment is a safe choice, as it involves effecting a modest improvement in a well-known technology. Each of the ten companies knows that its engineers can accomplish that incremental advance in technology. Patent protection is unavailable for this research project because it is obvious to one skilled in the art. Nevertheless, consumer preference for the improved technology would boost demand, thus increasing profits. A company pursuing this opportunity would have a 100% chance of securing a return of £20,000, discounted to present value. Neither the probability nor the amount of the return depends on how many other companies pursue that opportunity. As the R&D costs of pursuing that project are £10,000, the expected private value (and also, by assumption, social value) of investing in it for each company is £10,000.

The second research project is a risky and expensive investment opportunity, which involves working on a ground-breaking technology. Consistent with the nature of that advance, a company achieving the requisite breakthrough would obtain a patent and realise large profits as a result. The investment carries a risk both because the research project has only a 50% chance of success and because the likelihood of getting a patent also depends on how many others invest in the same R&D project. A company's probability of successfully inventing and being the first to get a patent is 50% if no other competitor also pursues this second research opportunity, 25% if one other company competes for the patent, 12.5% if three other companies compete, and so on down to 5% if all ten companies compete.

The second research project is a winner-takes-all proposition because the first inventor to file a patent application over the technology will secure its full value. R&D costs are £500,000, but the present value of successfully inventing and being the first to acquire a patent is £1 milion. The following table summarises the relevant facts underlying the model.

	R&D Project 1	R&D Project 2
Return if successful	£20,000	£1,000,000
Social R&D costs	£10,000*n	£100,000*n
Prob. technology will be invented	1	0.5*n, lim. 1.
Prob. success for each company	1	0.5/n
Expected return for each company	£10,000	$[0.5/n](£1,000,000) - £100,000$

Figure 7.2

What is the social welfare optimum? The answer is that two companies should pursue the second R&D project and the remaining eight should invest in the first R&D opportunity. Society gains £10,000 when any given company pursues project 1. The social value of a company's investing in project 2, however, depends on how many companies have already invested in it.

Society expects to gain £400,000 from each of the first two companies that decide to invest in project 2. Each company's entry increases the probability that the technology worth £1 million to society will be invented, for a social benefit of £500,000, and at a social cost of only £100,000. The result is different for the third and subsequent companies, however, because none of their investment decisions affects the probability that the breakthrough technology will be invented. Should the third or any successive company pursue project 2, there would be a social R&D cost of

£100,000, but no off-setting benefit to society. As project 1 carries a £10,000 expected social value for each of the third to the tenth companies, they should all invest in that R&D endeavour.

The desirable outcome is thus clear, but what will actually happen? Assuming that the companies move sequentially, each will pursue the project that then bears the greatest private expected value. The expected values of projects 1 and 2 for the respective movers are as follows:

	Private expected value for R&D Project 1	Private expected value for R&D Project 2
First mover	£10,000	£400,000
Second mover	£10,000	£150,000
Third mover	£10,000	£66,666
Fourth mover	£10,000	£25,000
Fifth mover	£10,000	£0
Sixth mover	£10,000	(£16,666)
Seventh mover	£10,000	(£28,571)
Eighth mover	£10,000	(£37,500)
Ninth mover	£10,000	(£44,444)
Tenth mover	£10,000	(£50,000)

Figure 7.3

The opportunity cost of pursuing the second R&D project is always the £10,000 that the company could have earned by investing in the first project, therefore a company will engage in the second project if the expected value of doing so exceeds £10,000. The first four companies will decide to invest in the second research endeavour, which is inefficient. There is a £220,000 loss of social value, which equals the wasted R&D capital expended on the second research project and the benefit that consumers would have derived from the third and fourth movers' pursuing the first R&D project.

This illustrates the patent race that attracts an excessive amount of capital to the R&D process, causing inefficient duplication of research. The problem is rent seeking, as prospective patentees attempt to capture the monopoly profits that patent protection makes available. It is yet another example of private and social interests diverging, which leads individuals to act in a manner contrary to public welfare.

3. A parsimonious approach to patent law

The fact that calibrating the patent system entails a trade-off between costs and benefits leads to an important concept: parsimony, which is qualified by the propensity for error. We have seen that law's economic role is to internalise the consequences of people's actions. The law of tort, crime, contract, and beyond seeks to align the private and social costs of behaviour yielding third-party effects.

In the realm of intellectual property, however, the problem is positive, rather than negative, externalities. Nevertheless, a full Pigouvian subsidy may be undesirable. The law should not give inventors such comprehensive property protection that they fully internalise the benefits of their discoveries. Instead, it should strive to identify inventors' reservation returns – the minimum reward that would have been sufficient *ex ante* to spur the relevant act of innovation – and to award that amount. The reason lies in the public-goods nature of technology. Given the low marginal cost of disseminating knowledge, and the non-rivalrous nature of information, society can maximise welfare by providing a sufficient reward to spur initial acts of invention, and then by making that invention freely available to the public for consumption and to inform cumulative innovation. Relying on contract to ensure the optimal dissemination of patented technology is imperfect because of the post-patent grant transaction costs involved in licensing. Making that technology part of the public domain, by contrast, will allow efficient allocation. Numerous features of the patent system reflect this trade off, including the 20-year time limit.

Unfortunately, imperfect access to information makes it difficult to identify inventors' reservation rewards. Given this uncertainty, a critical public policy question is whether society should err on the side of dynamic efficiency – thus granting generous awards in unclear cases – or on the side of static (allocative) efficiency, providing frugal awards and thus fostering price competition. Economists have concluded that dynamic efficiency is a greater source of long-term welfare than static efficiency. This translates into a general policy prescription in favour of generous compensation for successful innovators.

The distinction between breakthrough and incremental innovation, however, complicates this insight. In industries where cumulative, follow-on improvements over the status quo are the principal source of innovation, patent policy that errs on the side of promoting dynamic efficiency would actually grant narrow patents rights, thus reducing patentees' ability to restrict improvements on their technology. Where bargaining is difficult, broad property protection for baseline inventions would frustrate sequential improvements. Crafting the optimal contours of a patent right is therefore complicated and context specific.

4. A closing observation

Notwithstanding the classic economic case for the patent regime, a cautionary note is necessary. Modern patent systems have strayed from their economic foundation, embracing public goods theory in an uncritical fashion. Copying can produce economic benefits, so the law should not correct all positive externalities. The "positive spill over effect" accompanying innovation is important, as it fuels follow-on innovation, improvements, competition, and consumer welfare. That is why competitors are generally free to use one another's consumer-pleasing ideas and innovations. Patents are a limited exception to the general policy in favour of unbridled competition. The default position should embrace copying and competition, rather than monopoly.

From the perspective of economics, patents are appropriate only if they are a but-for cause of valuable innovation (including commercialisation). The reason is that patents come at a hefty price. One can justify that cost only if it comes with a larger benefit. Although patents are important in certain industries, such as biopharmaceuticals, they may impose costs that exceed their benefits in others, such as information technology. A radical overhaul of the system is unlikely, however, because of the industry that has built up around it. As an industry-specific abolition of the patent system would be disruptive in the short term, near-term reform is likely to be incremental.

This chapter now explores patent doctrine from an economic perspective, and identifies factors that may drive industrial innovation independent of any intellectual property protection. Understanding the dynamics that may instil incentives to invent absent intellectual property is important, for if one can promote innovation without suffering the costs of the patent system, it is prudent to do so. Having identified the various factors that influence inventors' decisions whether to engage in R&D, the chapter explores how innovation profiles in various industries map onto public good theory. An alignment failure goes a long way to explaining today's patent crisis, which has fuelled calls for an overhaul, or even abolition, of the patent regime.

B. A Primer on Patent Law and Economics

It is difficult to understand the economics of the patent system without appreciating the essential features of than system. Most people are familiar with the principal characteristic of a patent, which is that a deserving inventor obtains enforceable rights over her innovation. Nevertheless, the patent laws display idiosyncratic features with which uninitiated readers may not be familiar. This section traces the contours of patentable subject matter, identifies the technical requirements of patentability, explores the rights associated with patent ownership, and analyses some of the more nuanced elements of patent doctrine. In doing so, it explores these principles through the lens of economics.

1. Patentable subject matter

Not all fields of innovation are entitled to patent protection. The law in the United States allows inventors of qualifying processes, machines, manufactures, and compositions of matter to apply for patent protection, while the European Patent Convention (EPC) authorises the patenting of inventions that are capable of industrial application. Most people in the patent industry distinguish two kinds of patent-eligible inventions: products and processes. The former are objects, while the latter are methods of accomplishing a given end. Both are generally entitled to protection under the patent laws, if the invention satisfies the other conditions of patentability addressed below.

While the field of patentable subject matter is broad, there are certain innovations for which patent protection is unavailable. Note, in particular, that the products and processes susceptible to industrial application do not include abstract information or knowledge. The most important exclusion thus relates to laws of nature, intangible ideas, mental processes, and physical phenomena. A classic example is that Einstein could not have patented the famous equation: $E = mc^2$. Nor can a person who discovers a new mineral or naturally occurring product obtain a patent over it. As the US Supreme Court commented, such "manifestations of nature . . . [are] part of the storehouse of knowledge . . . free to all men and reserved exclusively to none".[1]

These categorical exclusions form the bedrock of the patent system, and serve a valuable economic purpose. At first blush, the principle that laws of nature and pre-existing natural phenomena are patent ineligible might fit awkwardly with economics. Many discoveries in physics and science of this sort are ground breaking and are a source of immense social value; for that reason, they are worth incentivising. It seems odd, then, to deny patent protection to some of the most valuable forms of innovation. The mystery unravels when one recognises that abstract rules of nature bear ubiquitous application, such that granting one person even a temporary monopoly over those rules would hold up downstream research and applications due to transaction costs. Simultaneously, the intellectual property system does not deprive those discovering abstract principles of any reward. *Applications* of universal rules and naturally occurring phenomena are patent eligible; these exclusive rights may be lucrative in light of the myriad uses of the underlying processes.

Tensions have arisen, however, when new technologies run into these categorical exclusions. This phenomenon is not surprising, of course, as courts articulated those prohibitionary rules in a time when inventions were predominantly mechanical in nature. Two important fields of innovation, in particular, have encountered difficulty with respect to patent eligibility: computer software and biotechnology.

Computer software has obviously been a field of unprecedented innovation, so it is an important concern of public policy. Software is simply a programme, however, that instructs computers what operations to perform and when. In that respect, algorithms are simply mental steps that have long been deemed to be unpatentable. Consistent with that view, US law holds that software is

---

1 Funk Bros. *Seed Co* v *Kalo Inoculant Co*, 333 US 127, 130 (1948).

unpatentable in isolation as a mathematical algorithm.[2] The European Patent Convention (EPC) similarly disqualifies computer software from patent protection.[3] Nevertheless, algorithms may form part of a patentable method or product, which is an exception that can swallow the rule. Computer software does not render an invention unpatentable, even if it constitutes a significant part of the innovation. The key to patentability lies in practical application, rather than in abstraction; however the precise delineation of the border between patent-eligible and ineligible uses of computer software remains elusive.[4]

Biotechnology also has a tortured history with patent eligibility, in particular because naturally occurring organisms do not qualify for protection. Innovation in biotechnology bears a stunning array of uses, such as medical diagnostic tests, the large-scale production of useful biological substances like insulin and antibiotics, gene therapy, personalised medicine, genetic modification in agriculture, and pharmacogenomics. Much of this work involves manipulating biological processes, purifying naturally occurring material, and isolating DNA.

The US Supreme Court famously announced that "anything under the sun made by man" is patentable.[5] As long as extracted genetic and other biological material is "distinctly different in character" from that within the body, it can be patented. Nevertheless, biotech patents are controversial, not least because of hostility to the idea of private ownership over living matter. In Europe, biotech patents can generally be patented, save for methods of surgery or therapy and medical diagnostic techniques.[6] The law in the United States on this matter is still in flux. In 2012, the US Supreme Court invalidated two patents on medical diagnostic tests for monitoring drug dosages.[7] In 2013, the Court found isolated DNA segments to be unpatentable, but held that cDNA is patent eligible.[8] The patentability of gene patents more generally remains in question.

Two fields of innovation that many believe to be unworthy of patent protection are methods of doing business and tax planning. Tax patents have been controversial in the United States for some time, but the 2011 America Invents Act effectively prohibited them. Methods of conducting business were long deemed to be unpatentable in America, but that changed with the (in)famous *State Street Bank* decision in 1998.[9] A veritable flood of business method patents followed, driven in part by the growth of the internet and e-commerce, and comprising a large number of data-processing technologies. The US Supreme Court subsequently circumscribed the scope of such patents in its 2010 decision, *Bilski*, finding that a method of hedging losses was an unpatentable, abstract, idea.[10] Nevertheless, such patents remain broadly patentable in the United States. In Europe, "[s]chemes, rules and methods for ... doing business" are generally not patentable under the EPC, though methods that solve technical problems may be.

The final field of innovative activity that may fall outside the confines of patentable subject matter entails immoral inventions. The EPC explicitly forbids patenting inventions "the commercial exploitation of which would be contrary to ... morality"[.][11] That convention also provides, however, that the mere fact that use of the invention would be illegal is not, in itself, enough to bar patentability. Immorality used to be an impediment to obtaining certain US patents, though recent case law means that morality is unlikely to bar any patent application.[12]

---

2 *Bilski v Kappos*, 130 S Ct 3218, 3230 (2010).
3 European Patent Convention (EPC), Art. 52.
4 *See CLS Bank Int'l v Alice Corp.*, 2011–1301 (Fed Cir. 9 July 2012).
5 *Diamond v Chakrabarty*, 447 US 303 (1980).
6 EPC, Arts. 52 and 53(b). The EPC also bars patents over plant and animal varieties and essential biological processes for the production of plants and animals. Ibid.
7 *Mayo Collaborative Servs v Prometheus Labs., Inc.*, 132 S Ct 1289 (2012).
8 *Ass'n for Molecular Pathology v Myriad Genetics, Inc.*, 133 S Ct 2107 (2013).
9 *State Street Bank v Signature Fin. Grp*, 149 F3d 1368 (Fed Cir 1998).
10 *Bilski v Kappos*, 130 S Ct 3218 (2010).
11 EPC, Art. 53(a).
12 *See, e.g., Juicy Whip, Inc v Orange Bang, Inc*, 185 F3d 1364 (Fed Cir 1999).

In sum, the key to understanding patentable subject matter from the perspective of economics is to see it as a policy lever. Commentators broadly accept the utilitarian view that the patent system's purpose is to spur innovation. The bar on patenting abstract ideas and natural phenomena is generally consistent with that economic rationale, for reasons just discussed, but could be problematic if given an absolute quality in all cases.

2. The requirements of patentability

(a) Novelty

The patent system exists to spur innovation, an act that, by definition, requires the discovery of unprecedented knowledge. The law thus refuses to give exclusive rights to those who learn what others already knew. Inventions anticipated by a single, prior-art reference are ineligible for protection, as they are not inventions at all.

This feature of the patent regime might seem to be so intuitive as to be unworthy of any further examination. In fact, though, the novelty requirement bears some idiosyncratic traits that are relevant to economic analysis. In particular, the law gives the "prior art" an expansive definition in assessing whether a claimed invention is indeed new. An anticipatory reference need not reside in the field as the invention, nor must it be widely known, circulated, or used in any way. For example, a prior-art reference that rendered claimed technologies ineligible for US patent protection included an unpublished PhD dissertation in a German university library.[13]

This feature of the novelty inquiry means that the law will deny protection to some innovators who independently uncover and plan to commercialise technologies that would not otherwise be available in the market. An obscure reference may anticipate a claimed invention, but it will seldom have been marketed. Furthermore, even if the scientific community is aware of the prior art, commercialisation may not occur if it would be vulnerable to free riding. The point is that, with respect to a certain subset of inventions, novelty may sometimes be a technicality.

Economics thus suggests that, in some instances, non-novel discoveries should be either patentable or subject to an alternative incentive system. The best example comes from the field of pharmaceuticals. In that industry, ideas alone are of modest value due to the cost of bringing a promising compound through clinical trials. If a prior publication discloses a promising chemical compound, pharmaceutical companies will be loath to spend the sums required to obtain regulatory approval to market it. This is especially so because generic drug producers can reverse engineer drugs, and can rely on pioneer drug manufacturer's safety and efficacy studies to obtain regulatory approval on an expedited and far-cheaper basis. In such cases, dogmatically applying the novelty requirement would deprive society of valuable drugs.

The fact that a rule leads to undesirable outcomes in some cases, however, is in itself insufficient ground for jettisoning the rule. There is a great deal of scholarship on the economic effects of rules and standards, otherwise known as hard and soft law, and rules may be preferable even though they produce imperfect results in some cases. Were the patent system to embrace a more comprehensive examination as to novelty, asking not only whether an anticipatory reference existed but whether invalidation would serve the utilitarian goals of the patent system, it would upset predictability and burden the courts and regulatory agencies charged with running the patent system. The better solution may be to rely on alternative incentive mechanisms. In the case of pharmaceuticals, bestowing regulatory exclusivity on the company developing anticipated drugs may sometimes be appropriate.

---

13 *In re Hall*, 781 F2d 897 (Fed Cir 1986).

(b) Non-obviousness or inventive step

Even never-before-seen technologies cannot be patented if they were obvious in light of the prior art. Described as "the ultimate condition of patentability", the non-obviousness or inventive-step requirement is the principal impediment to the success of most patent applications. Although this requirement, like novelty, depends on the prior art, obviousness considers the analogous prior art only. Whether an innovation satisfies this condition depends on the view of a hypothetical person having ordinary skill in the art ("PHOSITA"). Thus, the degree of inventiveness needed to achieve patent eligibility depends on the characteristics with which the law bestows that person.

The non-obviousness condition performs a valuable economic function, primarily in siphoning off discoveries that were inevitable in the short term. Patents impose costs in the form of allocative inefficiency, inducing a gold rush, and foreclosing downstream uses of technology in high transaction-cost environments. These weighty costs are justifiable only if society gets something larger in return. That something is new technologies that would otherwise not arise or would do so only after a sufficiently protracted delay.

If the law permitted the patenting of trivial improvements over the status quo, the result would be a tsunami of 20-year exclusive rights over trifling products and processes. The costs associated with such an outcome would outweigh any concomitant benefit, for obvious inventions are predominantly inevitable. The optimal quantum of inventiveness is what maximises the incentives to invent that the patent system generates.

An important concern, however, involves research that is not only obvious, but also expensive and risky. Early innovation in biotechnology was in some respects obvious in light of the prior art, but it was also capital intensive and haphazard. Literal or dogmatic application of the non-obviousness bar would have limited the scale of innovation in this field, delaying research in fields such as medical-diagnostic techniques founded on monoclonal antibodies. Instead, courts infused the PHOSITA with limited foresight, thus lowering the obviousness bar for patentability in the field of biotechnology. This reveals that the non-obviousness or inventive-step condition is a policy lever that courts and patent agencies can and should use to maintain optimal incentives.

(c) Utility or susceptibility of industrial application

One might imagine that inventors of worthless technologies would have no claim to patent protection. Ths is reflected in the rule that innovations must be "useful" in the United States or bear "industrial applicability" under the EPC. In practice, however, this requirement is edentulous. To show utility, one must merely identify a "concrete, specific, and real-world use".[14] Contrary to some people's expectations, there is no requirement that a prospective patentee convince the patent office that her invention is superior to a pre-existing state of the art. She need merely demonstrate that it bears an actual application. So, for example, if one were to discover a new method of making tea that resulted in a foul-tasting cup every time, the innovation would nevertheless pass the utility bar. In most fields, only outlandish inventions, such as perpetual motion machines, fall at this hurdle.

Does the minimally low utility bar make economic sense? At first blush, the answer might appear to be no because it facilitates many useless patented inventions. In most circumstances, however, such patents will have little or no economic value in the marketplace. Non-asserted patents with no valuable uses will typically be of little social cost. Conversely, there may be an economic case for spurring the invention of novel, non-obvious products and processes that do not yet bear lucrative application. It is often difficult to discern at the time of invention whether the unveiled technology will have valuable uses in the future. If the patent system can incentivise the

---

14 *See* Craig A. Nard and R. Polk Wagner, *Patent Law (Concepts and Insights)* (2007).

dissemination of potentially valuable inventions at modest social cost, the potential for positive spill-over effects may justify patentability. From that perspective, the current low bar on industrial application and on utility makes economic sense.

There is one field of innovation, however, in which the utility requirement poses a material impediment to obtaining patent protection. This is upstream research in biotechnology, in which field-identified products and processes do not immediately lend themselves to an identifiable downstream use. Given the difficulty of ascertaining an immediate use, but also the potential value of such uses once discovered, it is not clear that a stringent utility requirement in biotechnology is desirable.

(d) Disclosure

To obtain patent protection, an inventor must disclose her claimed technology. Often portrayed as a quid pro quo, disclosure disseminates knowledge that society can use to promote further innovation. Under US law, a patent application must meet the enablement, which requires disclosure sufficient to enable one skilled in the art to practice the invention without undue experimentation. There is also a best-mode requirement, which demands than an inventor reveals the best way known to her of practicing the claimed invention.[15] Under the EPC, disclosure must be sufficiently clear and complete for one skilled in the art to be able to carry out the invention.

The widespread diffusion of technology is of great value to cumulative inventions that incrementally build and improve upon the prior art, which in most industries, accounts for the lion's share of innovation. There are two problems. First, the contemporary patent regime does a poor job in fulfilling its disclosure function. Second, to the extent that the patent system succeeds in making vivid disclosure a requisite of patentability, this feature may bear hidden costs. By requiring inventors to give up all the intricacies of their claimed technologies, the patent system benefits those innovators' competitors by making it easier for them to design around the intellectual property. These effects will often be socially desirable, as this precipitates competitive pricing that inures to the benefit of consumers, at least in the short term. Nevertheless, a rigorous disclosure requirement may paradoxically do violence to the goal of promoting the dissemination of technological know-how through the patent system. For inventors of technologies that are potentially, though not readily, susceptible to reverse engineering, demanding disclosure conditions may induce some of them to choose trade secrets in lieu of patent protection. Trade-secret protection, of course, involves inventors' positively investing to keep their technologies secret.

3. Essential characteristics of patent rights

The preceding discussion explored what kinds of invention are patentable. We saw that this form of intellectual property is potentially available for a vast array of discoveries, save those entailing abstract principles of ubiquitous application and for naturally occurring phenomena. If an innovation falls within the broad spectrum of patentable subject matter, it need only be new, non-obvious, useful, and sufficiently disclosed to be patent eligible. These characteristics of the patent system generally make economic sense.

A different question concerns the nature of the legal rights that patents impart on their owners. Most people are broadly aware that a patent gives a deserving innovator a monopoly over his invention. Some aspects of patent ownership, however, surprises those studying intellectual property law for the first time. The following discussion reviews patent rights' fundamental traits, and briefly identifies their economic significance:

---

15 Under the America Invents Act of 2011, however, failure to disclose the best mode is no longer a defence to a patent infringement lawsuit.

(a) A patent does not grant a right to practice

A patent provides no affirmative right to practice; it merely bestows the legal ability to exclude others. Newcomers to patent law often confuse these rights, but the differences between the abilities to practice and to exclude can be dramatic. The distinction comes into focus when one realises that patents routinely cast overlapping spheres of exclusivity.

For instance, imagine that someone invents and patents a new kind of fridge. A different inventor subsequently designs a modified and superior variant, over which she secures an improvement patent. Despite her intellectual property rights, the latter inventor will not be able to build or to sell her fridge because it likely falls within the first inventor's patent rights. Yet, the first inventor will not be able to sell the improved version of his fridge without the subsequent improver's blessing. Given this defining characteristic, which often creates mutual blocking positions, the modern patent system envisions private contract in a manner consistent with the Coase Theorem.

If improvers cannot practice their new technologies, and if original inventors cannot practice superior versions of their initial breakthroughs, the potential for mutually beneficial arrangements exists. The law thus induces such inventors to bargain with one another in lieu of practising without permission. The right to exclude, but not to practice, spurs bargain if accompanied by a stick to deter infringement. The result should be an *ex ante* market for the licensing of technology, in which patentees cross-licence one another and grant licences to third-party manufacturers to commercialise technologies. Unfortunately, efficient markets for *ex ante* technology transfer have not emerged.

(b) There is no clean room defence in patent law

Unlike copyright, patent law has no independent invention defence. It is no answer to a claim of infringement that the defendant developed the accused product or process in a "clean room" or was otherwise oblivious to the asserted patent. This feature of the patent system surprises some newcomers who envision intellectual property as a solution to third-party appropriation of others' hard-won innovation. There is a world of difference, after all, between deliberately copying another's invention and independently discovering the same technology. Intellectual property's economic purpose is to regulate the former.

For better or for worse, however, strict liability for infringement lies at the heart of the contemporary patent system. Indeed, recent empirical literature reveals that less than 10% of US patent-infringement complaints even allege copying.[16] These findings evidence the failure of *ex ante* technology-licensing markets to emerge.

(c) A patent protects what one claimed, not what one invented

Patentees do not obtain exclusive rights over what they invented, but what they *claimed*. This distinction is also important. Suppose that you were a wine connoisseur and an expert in winemaking and that you discovered a new method of making high-quality wines. To obtain a patent, you would have to do more than disclose your invention and how it works. These elements of a patent document do not themselves define the contours of your exclusive right. Instead, you must describe the parameters of your innovation in words.[17]

---

16 Christopher A. Cotropia and Mark A. Lemley, 'Copying in patent law' (2009) 87 NCL Rev 1421.

17 This might, for example, entail: "A wine-making process of the type in which clear grape must is obtained as an intermediate product, which comprises the steps of (a) introducing the grapes to a pressing-stalk stripping operation wherein the grapes are stripped from the stalks and the grape skins are broken; (b) feeding the resulting product thus obtained under a pressure which increases to a value of between 7 and 13 bars and for a time of between 4 and 8 minutes, into a variable volume chamber with soft walls permeable to the liquid phase; and (c) pressing and filtering the grapes under a pulsating pressure which increases to a value of between 13 and 18 bars, for between 12 and 16 minutes and recovering a substantially clear liquid fraction." US Patent No. 4,568,549 (wine-making process).

The claims define the scope of the patented invention. In reading a patent, however, one is most unlikely to encounter just a single claim. Instead, patents ascribe many claims of varying scope even to only one invention. The reason for this is strategic. There is a tension between the law's requirement that a claimed invention be non-obvious and a patentee's desire to cast as wide a net as possible. The wider that net, the greater the value of the intellectual property right, but the more likely it is that a court or patent office on re-examination will invalidate the patent.

(d) Patents are time limited

A patent endures for up to 20 years from its filing date. This feature of the patent system distinguishes patents from traditional forms of property ownership, which has no temporal limit. This distinction is no accident, but serves a valuable economic purpose.

The reason for treating traditional and intellectual property differently in terms of duration lies in the distinction between private and public goods. As a private good is rivalrous in consumption, only one person can generally consume the item at a time. Perpetual property rights are therefore desirable because the right to exclude induces people to bargain under the Coase Theorem, thus causing ownership rights to gravitate toward their highest value uses. Public goods are different, however, because they are non-rivalrous in consumption, thus not subject to the conditions of scarcity that necessitate market prices to allocate goods and services.

Public goods are different. Anyone can consume them without reducing the quantity or quality that remains for others. Efficiency thus ensures that those goods be sold at marginal cost. Patent rights artificially limit the supply of public goods, causing prices to rise and creating allocative inefficiency. This effect is justifiable only if it sufficiently rewards inventors to justify their innovation. Rewards beyond that minimally sufficient return bestow windfalls on inventors, at the expense of allocative efficiency. The 20-year time limit recognises that innovators require only a threshold level of compensation, and that once the patent system has bestowed the necessary incentives to invent, it should withdraw and allow competitive pricing to take place.

(e) Patents are a form of property

There are, as we have just seen, differences between patents and traditional property, but there are also many parallels. The quintessential characteristic of property – a right to exclude – is common to ownership of patented technology, realty, and chattels. As with traditional property, patentees can licence, assign, or abandon their rights. The alienability of intellectual property, of course, reflects the Coase Theorem, which envisions the transfer of property rights from lower- to higher-value uses.

An important debate concerns the nature of the right to exclude. Some law and economics scholars, who are broadly characterised as belonging to the "property rights movement", advocate the view that a property rule should apply in most cases of patent infringement, as they do in cases of trespass.[18] Property rules, of course, grant owners injunctive relief. Other commentators argue that liability rules are superior in patent cases. Although patents are a form of property, and bear many characteristics common to traditional ownership, they also bear unique characteristics that make uncritical parallels between traditional and intellectual property misleading.

(f) Maintenance fees

One must periodically pay maintenance fees to the government to maintain one's patents rights. In the United States, fees are due 3.5, 7.5, and 11.5 years from the date of the original patent grant. The requisite sums are $1,130, $2,850, and $4,730, respectively. The European Patent Office

---

18 Compare Peter S. Menell, *Intellectual Property and the Property Rights Movement* (2007) 30 Regulation 36 with Richard Epstein, *The Property Rights Movement and Intellectual Property: A Response to Peter Menell* (2008) 30 Regulation 58.

requires renewal fees every year from the third year after the relevant patent issued, from £445 in the third year to £1,495 in the twentieth year. If patentees fail to make these payments, their claimed inventions fall into the public domain. This characteristic of the patent regime contrasts with the copyright system, which lacks any such requirement.

Maintenance fees make economic sense. All things being equal, public policy should maximise the scale and richness of the public domain, which feeds cumulative innovation and permits competition based on technology free of proprietary restrictions. Patents are an exception to principles of free competition, and are justifiable only to the extent that they cure market failures in the production of new technology. We noted above that the commercial worth of an innovation will not always be apparent at the time of a patent grant, which is why the law is generally correct to set the utility or "industrial application" condition low. In the years following a patent grant, however, if the intellectual property lacks sufficient value to the owner to be worth paying renewal charges, the claimed technologies should be removed from the patent system and dedicated to the public domain.

(g) Patents do not necessarily grant an economic monopoly

It is a common mistake to assume that the monopoly conferred by a patent is an economic monopoly. Indeed, the US Supreme Court fell prey to that fallacy for several decades, until it reversed itself in 2006.[19] Patents do bestow a monopoly of sorts on their owners – an exclusive right to practice the claimed technology. When economists use the term "monopoly", however, they refer to a significant level of market power, which is the ability profitably to raise price above marginal cost for a sustained period of time. This power comes from a combination of consumer demand for the product and a lack of effective substitutes for the same.

Most patents do not bear these traits. For example, if one invents and patents a novel toothbrush, the patentee would have to compete with the purveyors of different toothbrushes falling outside the scope of the patent. If those products are sufficiently interchangeable in the eyes of the consumer, the patentee would be unable profitably to charge supracompetitive prices.

4. Patent scope

A patent's "scope" reflects the spectrum of technology that falls within the associated zone of exclusivity. A patentee's right to exclude extends no further than the periphery of his intellectual property, such that products or processes residing outside the scope of patent protection lie in the public domain. As scope dictates the contours of a patent's monopoly, it lies at the core of any question of infringement.

Unfortunately, the language that patentees use to claim their inventions is rarely clear. There are exceptions. For instance, chemists use commonly defined terminology that generally allows one skilled in the art to discern what a pharmaceutical patent does, and does not, capture. Other industries, however, lack an accepted vocabulary with which to identify the contours of claimed technologies. Patents in the information technology sector, for example, are notoriously indeterminate, not allowing people skilled in the art to identify the limits of the claimed technology.

Identifying a patent's scope is, of course, a prerequisite of finding liability. For that reason, "claim construction" – the process by which courts determine the reach of the asserted patent as a matter of law – is the single most important component of the patent litigation process. Unfortunately, it is often difficult to predict the outcome of this interpretative process. "Fuzzy" ownership rights cause high transaction costs, which obstruct efficient markets for *ex ante* technology transfer.

---

19 *Illinois Tool Works, Inc v Independent Ink, Inc*, 547 US 28 (2006).

An idiosyncratic element of patent law complicates matters further. Under the US doctrine of equivalents, the fact that an accused product or process falls outside the scope of the claims, as literally interpreted, will not always bar a finding of infringement. If the accused product or process performs substantially the same function, in substantially the same way, to yield substantially the same result as the patented technology, a finding of infringement will follow. A comparable principle exists under the EPC. The Protocol on the Interpretation of Article 69 of the EPC requires a balanced approach between strict literalism in interpreting the claims and delegating patent claims to mere guidelines. Another doctrine operates in the opposite direction. When an improvement over a prior technology is sufficiently revolutionary, the reverse doctrine of equivalence frees that improvement from the original patentee's sphere of exclusivity, even if the terms, literally defined, encapsulate the new technology.

There is an economic justification for not limiting patent scope to the claims as literally interpreted. The reason is to prevent potential infringers from evading patent claims through trivial alterations that do not change the nature of the technology. The doctrine of equivalents and related law in Europe thus expand patent scope, but do so at the cost of predictability. This has aggravated problems in industries in which patent claims are inherently vague.

Patent clarity depends on the law's disclosure conditions. Lax requirements, which oblige patentees to reveal few details concerning the nature of their inventions, lead to broad scope. Conversely, stringent disclosure requirements make it harder for patentees to claim technologies by pointing to claim language when the detailed invention disclosed by the patent specification does not appear in the accused device. High disclosure obligations thus lead to narrow patent scope. As we shall see below, the law may have failed properly to calibrate disclosure obligations in certain industries.

These are the elements of patent law bearing on patent scope, but what about the normative question of optimal scope? The economic answer is that the law should craft the ownership right to induce invention and to minimise transaction costs. The correct scope therefore depends on the ratio of initial to follow-on innovation, the degree of capital investment underlying the claimed technology, the expense of commercialisation, and the rate of technological advance, which factors the next section explores in greater detail.

Suffice it to say for now that, where an invention yields a breakthrough and stand-alone technology as to which there is limited room for immediate improvement and which is expensive to turn into a marketable product, optimal patent scope is broad. This reflects Edmund Kitch's "prospect theory" of patent law, in which the law bestows a generous property right in a technology, thus leading the owner to invest in the invention, commercialisation, and improvement of the product or process. This approach obviously goes hand-in-hand with the Coase Theorem, and works well when transaction costs are low. Where such costs are high, the economically desirable patent scope is more narrow.

C. Incentives to Invent Independent of the Patent System

The tendency of markets to generate inventions at a suboptimal rate will be more acute in some circumstances than in others. Certain market conditions may spur optimal rates of innovation without any patent or equivalent protection at all. Others would suffer catastrophic shortfalls in innovation output in the absence of government intervention. This section explores the factors that affect incentives to innovate independent of the patent regime. The following section explains how those factors apply to distinct industries.

1. Susceptibility to reverse engineering

Markets may under-produce technologies that are vulnerable to appropriation. Yet, few technologies are equally susceptible to reverse engineering. This has important implications for the optimal design of the patent system.

At one end of the spectrum lie inventions that are immediately self-disclosing. A person skilled in the art can discern the workings of such technologies upon cursory inspection. These innovations epitomise public goods. Third parties can disassemble such products into their constituent components, and can determine how the good operates with minimal difficulty. Holding other factors constant, the need for patent protection over such technologies may be compelling. Lacking legally enforceable exclusive rights, prospective inventors of easily reverse-engineered products may decline to invent. The threat of prompt free-riding may reduce the expected value of innovating below the reservation level. Appropriation may, therefore, deny consumers valuable technologies.

At the other end of the continuum are inventions the workings of which are preclusively difficult to discern *ex post*. Inimitable technologies are not public goods, so there is no economics-based justification for patent protection. Even if this were available, however, inventors of such technologies would rarely avail of it. To obtain a patent, a person must disclose her invention so that one skilled in the art can recreate it without undue experimentation. Coupled with an exclusive right limited to 20 years, this disclosure condition will render patents unattractive to inventors of excludable technologies. They will instead embrace perpetual trade-secret protection. The classic example is Coca-Cola, which has maintained its invaluable formula for more than 125 years.

Most inventions lie between these extremes, and the vulnerability of these technologies to *ex post* appropriation involves varying degrees of time, effort, and capital. In general, the less excludable an innovation is, the more pronounced both the positive externalities and hence the danger of under-production will be. Whether the degree of non-excludability associated with a particular innovation endangers *ex ante* incentives to invent, however, depends on other factors, which we shall now address.

2. Capital investment

The incentive-to-invent rationale of the patent system holds that competition will render inventors insolvent by denying them the ability to recoup their sunk investment in R&D. If competitors can copy an inventor's technology, the price of that novel product or process will drop toward marginal cost in an open market. Knowing this *ex ante*, prospective innovators will not invest capital in a research endeavour that bears negative expected value in light of the probability of third-party expropriation.

That rationale does not apply in blanket fashion, however, to all technological discoveries. If imitability informs the need for a patent system, so too does a particular invention's requisite capital investment. R&D costs, which vary dramatically, implicate the design of an optimal patent regime. Some inventions require vast expenditure over a protracted period of time. Unless resistant to reverse engineering, such innovations are vulnerable to under-production. Other insights may be spontaneous. Such spur-of-the-moment, "eureka" moments may be tremendously valuable, but they occupy an interesting niche in the economic theory of innovation. If a person happens upon an idea by chance and without purpose, his efforts lacked direction and so the prospect of a financial reward would seem to have been meaningless.

Does this mean that spontaneous innovations are unworthy of patent protection? The answer is: not necessarily. In the first place, it may not be the prospect of solving a specific problem that drives an inventor, but instead the possibility of happening upon a useful, but as-yet-unidentified, insight. By rewarding those who unintentionally discover useful technologies, the patent system spurs inventors to pursue promising lines of inquiry, even if the end result of that research process is unclear.

Second, although a particular invention may come to a person without effort or investment, it does not mean that commercialising that technology and making it available to consumers will be cost free. On the contrary, marketing technology is often laborious and is itself vulnerable to free-riding. Patents can promote the emergence of such products. These considerations counsel against an outright prohibition of patent protection over such innovations. It is the case, however, that inventions happened upon by chance and without sunk capital investment in R&D depend less on intellectual property than costly research endeavours. The optimal breadth of patent scope, other things being equal, increases in proportion with the expense of the underlying innovation process.

3. The risk of failure

Closely related to the capital investment required to achieve a given technological breakthrough is the risk of failure attendant upon that R&D process. The more likely it is that sums devoted to innovation will fail to yield a marketable technology, the greater the level of profitability that will be necessary to spur an inventor's *ex ante* research efforts.

Consider two research projects. The first requires the expenditure of £1 million, bears an 80% chance of yielding a return of £5 million, and yields a 20% chance of providing a return of zero. The expected value of that research project is £3 million. The second investment opportunity would cost only £500,000 and would generate a return of £10 million, but bears a mere 30% chance of doing so. There is a 70% chance that this research investment would produce a return of zero. Its expected value is £2.5 million. A risk-neutral investor would thus pursue the first R&D investment, even though it requires a greater sunk investment and would yield half the return, if successful. In short, the risk of failure matters.

The greater the probability of failure, the stronger the case for patent protection (holding other factors constant). Where the likelihood of successfully innovating is low, but the social value of a successful invention is high, society will have to accept seemingly excessive profits on the part of those who prevail in their R&D efforts. The return on a single investment may be great, but when viewed in the correct *ex ante* state (i.e. discounted by the probability of failure) the profit may be far more modest. In such settings, some inventors may cross-subsidise ultimately fruitless, but *ex ante* justified, R&D projects with the returns from successful ones.

4. First-mover advantage

Another major factor that affects the rate of innovation is "first-mover advantage". Even if a research project is laborious and expensive, and the ensuing technology is vulnerable to appropriation, innovating may nevertheless be attractive if the market rewards the first entrant. Consumer familiarity with a leading brand may reap dividends long after comparable goods become available at lower prices. The greater the lag time between an initial innovator's marketing a new technology and rivals' copying and selling equivalent goods, the more likely it is that the initial inventor will have cemented its place as an incumbent. The ensuing brand-name advantage may far outlast the onset of any competition.

First-mover advantage is particularly strong when "network effects" or "positive externalities in consumption" exist. These occur when the value of a good increases with the number of people who already consume it. The classic example is a telephone grid. When only a single person has a phone, the network has no value. Yet, as more people connect to the grid, the value of joining the network climbs exponentially.[20]

Network industries tend to produce "path dependence" or "tipping effects", causing monopolisation. It may be difficult to displace an incumbent monopolist, even if a new entrant offers a

---

20 Network effects may also be indirect, as occurs when the number of consumers using a product affects the amount and quality of supportive products and services applicable to that product. Computer operating systems are a good example. The more popular an operating platform, the greater the market for programmers who write applications for it becomes. Yet, the more and better software that exists for an operating system, the more attractive that system will be to the marginal consumer.

lower price or a better technology. From the perspective of patent policy, the presence of powerful network effects suggests that initial inventors are likely to reap significant gains, even if third parties can copy their technologies.

5. Speed of obsolescence

The speed with which technologies become obsolete affects the case for patent protection. Where technological progress is incremental and rapid, inventions are likely to become quickly defunct. As patents often take up to three years to issue, such innovations are not optimal candidates for this protection. Indeed, here, patents likely suppress innovation by encouraging rent-seeking by those holding patents over outdated technologies, who try to extract value from those marketing profitable goods. Conversely, if invention in a particular industry tends to entail irregular, but revolutionary, innovations, the patent system is likely to be far-more effective.

D. Industry-Specific Innovation Profiles

Many factors affect the case for, and optimal breadth of, patent protection. These features include susceptibility to reverse engineering, the capital investment required to innovate, the risk of failure, first-mover advantage, and the pace of technological progress. To demonstrate how these characteristics affect patent policy, this section explores the innovation process in industries where patents are significant. The public goods justification for patent protection does not map neatly onto many of these sectors.

1. The pharmaceutical industry

The pharmaceutical industry is the poster child for the patent system because the research and development of drugs falls squarely within the public goods paradigm. In the first place, developing pharmaceutical products is staggeringly expensive. PhRMA, the representative body for the US biopharmaceutical industry, has estimated the average cost of developing a single successful drug to be approximately $1.3 billion. Although the study underlying this figure has been subject to some criticism – in particular for employing a cost of capital that inflates the average-cost figure and for omitting R&D expenditures' favourable tax treatment – the average cost of bringing a drug successfully to market is at least in the nine figures.

What accounts for this? A major contributor is failure. Industry experts often report than merely one in 10,000 initially screened chemical compounds results in a marketable drug, and candidate molecules fail at all stages of the innovation process. The principal cost of developing new chemical entities, however, lies in time- and capital-intensive clinical trials. An overview of this process, which takes an average of 12 years, shows why R&D in new drugs is so expensive. The need for a scrutinising regulatory review, of course, lies in the potential toxicity of insufficiently screened chemical compounds.

The first stage involves pre-clinical (animal- and laboratory-based) research in which scientists screen and validate isolated or synthesised chemicals to determine their potential viability through in vitro studies. Even this pre-clinical stage is costly, as a great majority of scrutinised compounds prove unworthy of further study. The small fraction of chemicals that emerge from this process proceed to Phase I clinical trials, in which researchers administer the drug to human volunteers. The focus on Phase I trials is not on efficacy, but on safety. Scientists investigate the pharmacological and pharmacokinetic qualities of the candidate drug, determining how the human body absorbs, metabolises, and breaks down the compound. These studies, which typically involve 20 to 80 subjects, identify safe dosage ranges and side effects.

Phase II trials are larger, focusing on 100 to 300 volunteers suffering from the targeted condition. These trials focus on both safety and efficacy. Researchers often randomise these studies. By far the most costly stage are Phase III trials, in which researchers administer the experimental drug to large groups of people, typically in excess of 1,000. To ensure the greatest possible accuracy, Phase III trials are usually randomised and double blind. The nature of the outcome being scrutinised dictates the scale of the trials. Where companies test a drug's effect on mortality, for instance, the population of volunteers may be enormous, potentially in excess of 10,000.

Following a successful completion of Phase III trials, a drug company can seek and obtain regulatory approval from the FDA. The agency may nevertheless require additional, post-approval information concerning the drug, which involves Phase IV trials. These are post-marketing studies that yield further information about the side effects, efficacy, and optimal dosage of the drug.

Many drugs flounder even in the late stages of clinical testing, after the relevant innovator has sunk vast amounts of capital into the process. Even in the tiny subset that go on to become marketable drugs, however, the majority fail to achieve sufficient profitability in the market to recoup the relevant R&D costs. Instead, the pharmaceutical industry depends on a modest number of "blockbuster" drugs to cross-subsidise the losses that it suffers in the many fruitless research processes.

It is conceivable that average research costs in the hundreds of millions of dollars per drug would not be fatal to sustained innovation if the active pharmaceutical ingredients in drugs resisted reverse engineering. In fact, though, generic drug producers can identify the chemical compound underlying a drug of interest. Thus, pharmaceutical innovation epitomises the economic concept of public goods. Even among those who take a dim view of the contemporary patent system, most acknowledge that the patent system is a key but-for cause of pharmaceutical R&D.

Ultimately, if one abolished the patent regime and failed to replace it with a substitute incentive mechanism, the output of pharmaceutical innovation would decline catastrophically. To appreciate the industry's vulnerability to changes in patent protection, one need merely witness the "patent cliff" that occurred in 2011 when the patents on a small number of high-profile drugs, including Lipitor, Plavix, and Nexium, expired. This event caused Pfizer, Inc.'s and Eli Lilly's profit to drop by 50% and 27% in the fourth quarter of 2011, as generic competition emerged. For an industry that in the United States alone devoted $65.3 billion in R&D expenditures in 2009, the industry's dependence on the patent system suggests that policymakers should maintain strong intellectual property rights in that setting. This is particularly so because the time lag between identifying a patent-eligible chemical compound and acquiring marketing authorisation from the FDA means that average drug-substance patents typically enjoy little more than ten years of sales under patent protection.

Despite the benefits of patent protection in the pharmaceutical industry, the patent system's costs are also most painfully apparent in that setting. By granting pharmaceutical companies exclusive rights in the form of drug-substance, drug-product, and method-of-use patents, the law causes drugs to sell at prices far in excess of their marginal costs of production. Although such monopoly pricing is the fuel for feeding the breakthrough medical treatments of tomorrow, and thus justifiable, it exacts a terrible cost on those who cannot afford to buy life-saving and other important drugs at those rates. The final section of this chapter considers alternative incentive mechanisms that may produce comparable rates of innovation by solving the public-goods problem, whilst avoiding the draconian nature of monopoly pricing.

2. Biotechnology

Biotechnology is an exciting field of innovation in which engineers manipulate cellular and bio-molecular processes to a variety of remarkable ends. In agriculture, scientists have altered the genetic make-up of crops to render them resistant to diseases and insects, and to boost productive output. Researchers have mapped the human genome, locating genes and sequencing the nucleotides that comprise human DNA. In medicine, biotechnology has ushered forth exceptionally accurate medical diagnostic tests and has produced a variety of drugs, known as biologics. These include allergenics, vaccines, gene therapy, and genomics. Biotechnology also permits industry, using recombinant-DNA technology, to develop large-scale amounts of biologic material that naturally occurs in small amounts, such as insulin, human growth hormone, and human-blood-coagulation factors. Although innovation in biotechnology has already bestowed an abundance of novel products and processes, many exciting research possibilities lie in the future, particularly with respect to personalised medicine. This allows doctors to mould treatments and drugs specific to each patient's condition, instead of prescribing a course aimed at treating the median patient in the population of those suffering from the relevant ailment.

There seems to be little question that cutting-edge biotech research has extraordinary potential. The conditions underlying biotech innovation are broadly comparable to those in the pharmaceutical industry. In particular, the public goods rationale behind innovation in traditional chemical-based drugs applies in similar fashion to biologics and related biotech research, much of which is capital intensive. Biologics are large, complex molecules that scientists manufacture with recombinant DNA technology. Researching and developing biologics are expensive in light of their structural complexity, which supports the need for strong patent protection. Innovators in this field must also incur vast costs in securing regulatory approval to sell biologics and related technologies to the public. Furthermore, such innovations are often susceptible to reverse engineering. With respect to gene sequencing, the expense of biotech innovation lies not so much in the act of initial invention, which is increasingly automated, but in commercialisation. These features of the industry suggest that free markets may lead to inadequate capital investment in R&D, thus triggering a need for governmental intervention.

Notwithstanding these industry characteristics, which fall within the public goods rationale, the patent system is less warmly embraced in the biotech sphere than in the pharmaceutical industry. Gene patenting, in particular, is controversial. Commentators typically view patents as a form of ownership, but many people believe that living organisms are not properly subject to propertisation. Is molecular biology thus properly within the purview of the patent system, or should living processes fall outside the sphere of intellectual property protection? From the perspective of economics, the questions are whether a higher level of biotech innovation is preferable than less, and if so, whether patents are an effective mechanism by which to spur greater levels of R&D in this field.

Given the nature of gene patenting, however, there is a danger that property rights may impede, rather than promote, R&D investment in the biotechnology industry. This potential obstacle relates to the economic reason why patents are inappropriate over abstract ideas or scientific principles. Rules of nature lie upstream and bear countless downstream uses. By granting patents at the top of the vertical chain, society could impede efficient diffusion of the technology due to the transaction costs involved in countless prospective licensees' securing permission to use a foundational technology. In the field of biotechnology, researchers have patented specific genes. Those individual genes, however, bear myriad downstream uses in further research, medical diagnostic techniques, and so on. In acquiring exclusive rights over individual genes, patentees may impede efficient use of those genes given the sheer number of their applications. If every person or organisation wishing to use those genes must bargain for permission, the transaction costs involved may hinder efficient advancement and commercialisation of technology.

Economists refer to this problem as the "tragedy of the anticommons". This condition lies in contradistinction to the "tragedy of the commons", which is an economic phenomenon that justifies property rights due to the tendency of users to over-consume unowned resources and to decline to invest in the betterment of those resources. As Part 4 explained, granting exclusive rights over such property internalises owners' incentives, spurring them to coordinate investment in, and consumption of, the resources, and to sell them to those who value them more.

The tragedy of the anticommons is the opposite problem, emerging from too many property rights rather than too few. When ownership interests are narrow, many, and held by different people, coordination costs can frustrate efficient use of the owned resources. The term arose in an article of the same name that explained that full kiosks on the street stood right next to empty storefronts in post-Communist economies due to an excessive fragmentation of property rights. This fragmentation created transaction costs that prevented mutually beneficial exchange from taking place.[21]

Some scholars fear that patents threaten to create an anticommons in biotechnology because, if people hold exclusive rights over narrow upstream technologies, biotech companies that endeavour to research and develop new downstream therapies may be unable to acquire licences to the necessary, patented knowledge.[22] Despite this academic concern, however, empirical studies to date reveal little evidence of an anticommons effects in the biotech field.[23]

These issues have recently come to a head in the United States. In 2012, the US Supreme Court ruled in *Prometheus Laboratories*, which involved patents claiming a medical-diagnostic method that permitted doctors to determine whether the doses of thiopurine drugs that they were administering to patients with autoimmune diseases were too high or too low.[24] The process worked by monitoring the blood level of certain metabolites, which levels correlated with the probability that a particular dosage of a thiopurine drug would be ineffective or harmful. Prometheus, which was the exclusive licencee of the patented process, sold diagnostic tests encompassing the method. The defendant, Mayo, was initially a purchaser of the diagnostic method, but subsequently decided to use its own tests, which precipitated a suit for infringement. The Supreme Court held that the patents were invalid because the patented three steps merely informed doctors about laws of nature and further actions that were known in the scientific community. To be patent-eligible, an inventor must claim steps that "provide practical assurance that the process is more than a drafting effort designed to monopolize the law of nature itself".

Prometheus is a decision of vast significance to the biotech industry, which has developed a wide variety of targeted medical treatments and diagnostic tests. Such innovation lies at the heart of personalised medicine, and private biotech companies have sought to protect their investments in this novel branch of medicine through patents. The US Supreme Court stripped much of that protection away in 2012, and went further still in 2013 in *Myriad Genetics*, holding that isolated DNA is unpatentable.[25]

The discussion thus far supports a strong intellectual property system. Patents and innovation are inseparable in the pharmaceutical industry. Patents are also an important driver of private R&D in biotechnology. Although these settings are not free from controversy, IP protection is unquestionably a "but-for" cause of much innovation in those fields. The patent system operates well here because patents permit efficient markets for the alienation of technology to develop. As language claiming the chemical composition of a patented drug bears a distinct and clear meaning to one skilled in the art, there is little uncertainty concerning the scope of pharmaceutical patents. Furthermore, drugs are typically subject to a small number of patents. Due to the limited number of patents in the pharmaceutical field, coupled with the clear periphery of patentees' exclusive rights, manufacturers can search the prior art to identify blocking patents and to negotiate licences. In addition, the lengthy life-cycle of biopharmaceuticals fits well with the three-year, patent-acquisition process, and the ensuing 20 years of protection.

21 Michael Heller, 'The tragedy of the anticommons: Property in transition from Marx to markets' (1998) 111 Harv L Rev 621.
22 Michael Heller and Rebecca Eisenberg, 'Can patents deter innovations? The anticommons in biomedical research' (1998) 280 Science 1.
23 See, e.g., Richard A. Epstein and Bruce N. Kuhlik, 'Is there a biomedical anticommons, regulation' (2004); David E. Adelman, 'A fallacy of the commons in biotech patent policy' (2005) 20 Berkeley Tech LJ 985.
24 *Mayo Collaborative Services v Prometheus Labs*, 132 S Ct 1289 (2012).
25 *Association for Molecular Pathology v Myriad Genetics, Inc*, 133 S Ct 2107 (2013).

3. The semiconductor industry

The semiconductor industry, which designs and manufactures the silicon chips at the heart of computers, is one of the world's most innovative and important industries. The pace of technological advance in the sector has been extraordinarily fast, producing chips that roughly double in performance every two years, consistent with Moore's law. The industry also occupies a unique position in that the technology it produces is not self-contained, but feeds the larger electronics industry. The industry had worldwide sales of almost $299.5 billion in 2011, and $291.6 billion in 2012. Given the overriding importance of semiconductors to all manner of electronic devices from personal computers and smart phones to televisions and cars, it is obviously a crucial hub of innovation.

Certain aspects of semiconductor design and manufacture suggest a need for patent protection. The reverse-engineering of semiconductor products, though technically challenging, is feasible. Furthermore, the industry pours billions of dollars' worth of private capital into the research process.[26] Nevertheless, R&D in the semiconductor industry fits awkwardly with the patent system. Getting a patent is a laborious, time-consuming process, and the exclusive protection that results lasts for an extended period of time. Given the pace of innovation in this industry, however, semiconductor devices bear unusually short life cycles. New technologies rapidly become defunct, which means that patents are an imperfect way of protecting chip-related inventions that enjoy a brief stint at the cutting edge. By the time an inventor secures a patent over an invention, which will often be between two and three years after filing the application, the inventor will possess exclusive rights over an outdated technology. Compounding the problem is the fact that each semiconductor combines a vast number of discrete, patent-eligible technologies. Indeed, modern chips integrate billions of individual devices. A single new microprocessor potentially implicates thousands of patents.

The problem with so-many patent-eligible technologies underlying a single silicon chip is that semiconductor manufacturers must obtain permission to produce new products. When the ownership of necessary technologies is fragmented, manufacturers must secure licences from many different patentees. Even if chip producers can identify the relevant patent rights and corresponding owners, another economic problem emerges. The discrete components that one must combine to create an end product are complements: a decrease in the price of one will increase demand for the others, and vice versa. The so-called "Cournot complements" problem arises when those components lie in the hands of different owners. Each such owner will try to extract a monopoly price for its licence because it knows that the manufacturer cannot achieve its purpose without its permission. As no owner takes into account the fact that lowering its price will increase demand for complements owned by others, each owner's price will be too high. The result is a hold-out problem.

The traditional economic solution to the Cournot-complements problem is vertical integration. If one entity acquires ownership rights over all the complements, the problem dissolves. In the semiconductor field, another partial solution is to restrict the inventions that are patent eligible. By reducing the number of separate ownership rights, one can alleviate the burden. Nevertheless, the reality of the modern semiconductor industry is that companies have acquired as many patents as possible and stockpiling an arsenal of intellectual property rights. Illustratively, IBM, Intel, Broadcom, Micron Technology, and Qualcomm acquired 6,148, 1244, 1164, and 947 US patents, respectively, in 2011.

---

26 The European Commission measured worldwide R&D investment in larger technology hardware and equipment in 2011 as being the second largest in the world at over £70 billion. Directorate General Research & Innovation, Monitoring Industrial Research: The 2011 EU Industrial R&D Investment Scoreboard (2011).

An anticommons therefore exists in the semiconductor industry. This phenomenon could drastically inhibit innovation, but it has not done so. The reason lies in what economists refer to as a "private-ordering solution". This corresponds to voluntary private agreements designed to minimise the inefficiency of background conditions. As applied to the semiconductor industry, companies negotiate clearing positions with each other through voluntary cross-licensing arrangements. Innovation in the industry continues to advance at a staggering rate, so it is difficult to conclude that the system in place is problematic and in need of revision.

Notwithstanding this fact, it does not follow that the patent system drives innovation in the semiconductor industry. In fact, although semiconductor patents are valuable, that value is predominantly defensive. Other than semiconductor-design houses that license newly developed technologies to larger chip manufacturers, there is little market for the *ex ante* transfer of patented knowledge in the sector. Instead, companies amass patents for strategic purposes; this enables them to negotiate cross-licensing agreements with comparable competitors, thus avoiding patent-infringement claims. A company's ability to avail of this mechanism thus depends on the extent of its patent portfolio. For entities that lack access to such portfolios, entering the semiconductor industry is difficult. Indeed, to do so, a new entrant would likely have to pay up to $200 million in patent-licensing royalties alone.

From an economic perspective, it is difficult to conclude that patents serve a compelling role in spurring R&D in the semiconductor industry; there is at least some reason to conclude that the patent system inhibits competition in a number of ways. Nevertheless, in light of the high level of technological output in the industry, a compelling need substantially to reform patents in this sector does not yet exist. It is worth emphasising, though, that, were the prevailing equilibrium and associated détente between chip manufacturers to be disturbed, the patent system could descend into wide-scale litigation. Such an eventuality could create serious problems for innovation in the industry.

4. The information technology industry

If pharmaceuticals are the poster child for the patent system, the information technology ("IT") industry epitomises the case for reform. There is widespread agreement that the patent regime is broken in the IT field.

The problems are multitudinous. First, there are simply a vast number of IT patents. Individual products in the IT industry, including smart phones, BlackBerries, computer software, internet technologies, and telecommunications products routinely implicate hundreds and even thousands of them. The volume of intellectual property rights potentially reading on IT devices means that manufacturers must overcome vast identification and bargaining costs to negotiate clearing positions. Compounding that difficulty is the fact that the claims in IT patents are notoriously vague. Due to the lack of any accepted terminology in the IT field to which one skilled in the art can ascribe a specific meaning, it is often impossible to demarcate the boundaries of an IT patent.

Furthermore, the law has imposed remarkably light disclosure requirements on IT inventors. Illustratively, a patent application claiming a novel process that uses an algorithm need not disclose the source code underlying the software. The combination of imprecise language and patent specifications that do not disclose what patentees have claimed has generated a chronic lack of certainty. The worst example is functional claiming, which, if insufficiently tethered to a particular means of accomplishing the claimed result, results in an immensely broad right to exclude. The ensuing exclusive right far exceeds the technology actually invented. The result is an impenetrable patent thicket in which numerous patents arguably claim the same technology, further increasing transaction costs for companies that wish to manufacture products and to sell them to consumers.

These problems have become increasingly severe as patent trolls have proliferated. More formally known as "patent-assertion entities" ("PAEs"), such businesses acquire otherwise unenforced patents, sometimes at a discount from bankrupt technology companies and other times from small firms using shell companies. PAEs neither commercialise their claimed technologies nor licence them *ex ante* to manufacturers. Instead, PAEs wait for manufacturers independently to invent technologies and to market products that arguably infringe on their intellectual property rights. To avoid claims of wilful infringement, and potential exposure to treble damages, IT manufacturers routinely instruct their engineers to ignore patents and to solve technical problems that they encounter on their own volition. Few patents in the IT field are useful to engineers, so the patent system performs little, if any, disclosure function in that setting.

A case might nevertheless be made for patent protection in the IT industry on public goods grounds if intellectual property were necessary to avoid market failure on account of *ex post* appropriation. In fact, though, the fear that unchecked third-party copying will undermine private investment is probably misplaced in this environment. The capital required to innovate in the IT field is relatively modest. Although not impervious to reverse engineering, the technology underlying most IT products is not immediately self-disclosing. It is no simple task, for instance, to translate object code underlying software into instructions that can be read by humans. Combined with the fact that cutting-edge technology in the IT industry is rapidly rendered obsolete and that the ratio of original-to-follow-on innovation in that setting is low, the economic case for patent protection is weak.

Caught in this maelstrom, service providers and manufacturers in the IT sector are engaged in an ongoing patent war, as each tries to amass as many patents as possible for defensive purposes. Highlights in 2012 include Google's $12.5 billion acquisition of Motorola Mobility for its more than 16,000 patents relating to the Android device; Microsoft's $1.1 billion purchase of patents from AOL, and Apple's $4.5 billion purchase of more than 6,000 patents from bankrupt Nortel, beating out Google. An equilibrium of the kind that exists in the semiconductor industry has not persisted in the IT industry. Judge Posner, sitting by designation on the federal district court, threw out a 2012, high-profile infringement case between Apple and Motorola involving IT patents on the ground that the sought relief was not in the public interest. Later the same year, Apple secured a $1 billion judgment against Samsung on account of the latter's copying certain patented features of the iPhone. Samsung has controversially retaliated by asserting standard-essential patents subject to fair-and-non-discriminatory licensing obligations. It successfully obtained an exclusion order from the International Trade Commission in June 2013, barring Apple from importing certain of its iPhone and iPad products. President Obama, however, vetoed the order in August 2013.

In short, innovation occurs in the IT industry despite, rather than because of, the patent system. If abolition in the IT sector, however, is not feasible – and politically that seems to be the case for the foreseeable future – the question is what kind of less-radical reforms are appropriate going forward. Law and economics provides some important insights in answering this question. In the first place, high transaction costs foreclose an efficient market for the *ex ante* licensing of technology in the IT industry. For that reason, liability rules are superior to property rules. Courts should, therefore, deny injunctive relief in most settings involving IT patents, and strive to avoid excessive damages awards, which – as we have seen – carry an economic effect equivalent to a property rule. Second, patent agencies, courts, and legislatures should do more to promote disclosure. Potentially helpful examples include enhanced disclosure requirements, which would narrow patent rights; use of IT-industry dictionaries to infuse IT patents with greater clarity; further use of prosecution history, holding applicants to disclaimers made during that process; and liberal use of the reverse doctrine of equivalents in the United States to find that IT patents do not read on products entailing significantly improved technologies compared to those claimed in the asserted patents.

E. Alternatives to Patents: Prizes, Buy-Outs, and Regulatory Exclusivity

The patent system has no lack of shortcomings. It fosters monopoly pricing, invites undesirable patent races, starves some second-generation researchers of much-needed technical know-how, frustrates downstream uses of proprietary technology in high transaction-cost settings, and fetters commercialisation when anticommons or thicket conditions emerge. Although the patent regime generates net benefits in many situations, as epitomised by the biopharmaceutical sector discussed above, the severity of its costs warrants consideration of other options. This section discusses three major alternatives to patents: prizes, buy-outs, and regulatory exclusivity. For reasons explained below, these may best be construed as complements to the patent system.

1. Prizes

Markets under-produce knowledge goods because of positive externalities. When the social value of innovation exceeds the private returns, economists predict that suboptimal investment in R&D will follow. The patent system solves this problem somewhat circuitously, by introducing monopoly. An alternative solution would be directly to impose a Pigouvian tax, which in the case of positive externalities, takes the form of a subsidy. By granting deserving inventors a reward equal to the difference between the social and private values of their discoveries, the government can eliminate the market failure that would otherwise cause a dearth of invention.

Prizes have a storied history in spurring innovation. A famous example was the British government's 1714 announced reward of £20,000 for the first person who devised a method of calculating longitude within five-tenths of one degree. The government had deemed the reward necessary in light of a series of terrible nautical disasters that had befallen sailors who had misapprehended their positions. The prize spurred a tremendous amount of activity in R&D, which finally resulted in John Harrison's conceiving a solution. His invention used chronometers that enabled mariners to compare their local time to Greenwich time, and thus to calculate the longitudinal position of their ships. Another celebrated example was the 1795 reward that Napoleon offered to the person who discovered an effective way of preserving food, which the French military needed for sustained operations. The prize, which Nicolas Appert received in 1810, spurred the invention of canned food. There is no lack of contemporary examples. A prominent one is the $10-million Ansari X Prize for privatised space flight, which went to Burt Rutan and Paul Allen in 2004 for their SpaceShipOne design. A recent McKinsey study concluded that the total prize sector, as of 2009, could be as great as $2 billion, involving rewards in aviation and space, science and engineering, climate and environment, and the arts.[27]

From the perspective of economics, prizes display many attractive features. First, they avoid the problem of monopoly. By declining to impart exclusive rights on inventors and by requiring complete disclosure in return for the reward, prize systems spur *ex post* competition. This process promotes conditions of allocative efficiency, as prices gravitate toward marginal cost. Such static efficiency carries more than academic benefits. Monopoly pricing may not be excessively problematic for patented luxury goods, but when applied, for instance, to life-saving drugs, the exclusive rights engendered in intellectual property rights can produce cruel results. Marginal-cost pricing for such goods means saved lives.

This fact does not in itself justify the abolition of patent protection for, as noted above, the absence of such ownership rights in pharmaceutical innovation would deny the world many of the

---

27 See, www.mckinseyonsociety.com/downloads/reports/Social-Innovation/And_the_winner_is.pdf.

life-saving drugs of tomorrow. Nevertheless, if society can spur competitive pricing without under-mining R&D investment, it should do so. Prizes may be an important means by which to accomplish this end. Furthermore, there is increasing concern that too much modern pharmaceutical innovation consists of prosaic reformulations and "me too" drugs, which add little in terms of efficacy. Monopoly prices in return for close variants of pre-existing drugs entail a different value proposition than such prices for brand new medicines. Governments can target precisely the kind of pharmaceutical research that they desire through suitably crafted rewards.

Second, the private sector is not adequately incentivised to solve problems that are not readily monetised through patents. States and charitable organisations can use prizes to correct this failure of the patent system. For instance, the biopharmaceutical industry experiences greater incentives to develop drugs and biologics that treat ailments prevalent in the western world, such as obesity-related conditions, than it does to devise cures to conditions that primarily afflict those in the third world, such as malaria. As the return on patent-protected drugs depends on consumers' ability to pay, the medical industry may not focus its efforts on solving conditions that cause the greatest level of human suffering. Similarly, small-population conditions may not constitute a sufficiently large pool of consumers to warrant R&D in drugs that companies would finance in reliance on patent protection. In both such cases, domestically or internationally funded prize pools can create incentives for private industry to devote the appropriate level of capital to the innovation process.

These benefits are weighty, but does it follow that prizes are categorically superior than patents? The answer is no, for several reasons. First, although rewards result in competitive markets for the production and sale of technology, prizes do not eliminate the monopoly problem. Prizes must be funded, and the requisite capital generally comes from taxation or sovereign-debt markets. Elevated taxes distort behaviour, and increased levels of sovereign debt suppress long-term economic growth. In either event, public funding of prizes entails inefficiencies, which are simply less localised than the deadweight loss that patents can create.

Second, when prizes are socially funded – as they typically are – a great deal of cross-subsidisation takes place. With taxpayer-funded prize systems, many people pay for technologies that they have little interest in consuming. Conversely, in a patent regime, only the people who wish to use a new technology will pay for it. Third, prizes depend on the government's identifying problems *ex ante*. Many valuable innovations, however, involve feats of ingenuity that few governments would have foreseen. It follows that rewards are suitable only for solving known problems. Patents are vastly superior at harnessing creative efforts toward accomplishing technological feats that give consumers something that they had never previously envisioned.

Fourth, patents have the distinct advantage of harnessing private information. In computing optimal rewards, governments must try to predict the demand curve for the hypothetical technology or, even better, the sum that is minimally sufficient to induce inventors to try to solve the problem *ex ante*. Both such sources of information are difficult for governments to discern. Fifth, prizes do not eliminate the gold-rush problem, for the prospect of a reward will often induce multiple candidates to vie to solve the technical challenge. These multifarious efforts will often entail duplication of effort and capital, which carries inefficient results. Notwithstanding this fact, though, governments can control the severity of the gold-rush phenomenon by calibrating the scale of the reward and by altering the stage of development at which an inventor can claim the prize. For example, depending on the nature of the innovation process, it may be more efficient to award prizes upon attaining specific milestones, rather than requiring that an innovator complete the full R&D process. This may translate into an advantage in favour of prizes.

Finally, for products the marketing of which requires high levels of post-invention investment, prizes alone may lead to suboptimal commercialisation of technology. In appropriate settings, patents can serve a valuable purpose in spurring owners to guide the marketing and improvement of new products and processes. This is the prospect function of patenting that Edmund Kitch famously identified, and it is one that prizes alone are ill-equipped to serve.

These limitations render prizes an unsuitable replacement for the patent system, at least on a categorical basis. Nevertheless, rewards are a potent complement to the patent regime, particularly in those settings where monopoly pricing produces unjust outcomes. Prizes are also particularly useful for solving keenly felt problems that are subject to accurate valuation.

2. Patent buy-outs

Patents create monopoly, and prizes can only solve problems that can be identified *ex ante*. A promising third way involves so-called "patent buy-outs", in which governments rely on a patent system, but use public funds to purchase intellectual property rights and then place the acquired technologies in the public domain. This approach eliminates the waste of reverse engineering and design around, by-passes the allocative inefficiency of monopoly pricing, and frees valuable technical knowledge for use in cumulative innovation. Unlike prizes, however, patent buy-outs do not require governments to discern the technical challenge to be resolved. By purchasing patent rights from those who discover valuable new technologies, governments can achieve the benefits of prizes free of at least some of their costs.

The problem lies in valuation. How much should the government offer an inventor for her patented technology? Asymmetric information limits the state's ability to calculate the optimal sum. To prevent patentee under-compensation in conditions of uncertainty, there is a strong argument that all patent buy-outs should be voluntary. If the state were to offer an inadequate price, the relevant inventor would decline the offer and would recoup his investment through monopoly prices. Using a property rule to protect inventors' intellectual property is desirable in that it capitalises on patentees' private information. Note the interesting point, however, that the optimal buy-out price may exceed the monopoly value of the patent to the inventor since the deadweight loss associated with supracompetitive pricing ensures that, absent perfect price discrimination, the monopoly worth of a technology is less than its social value.

The property rule approach is no cure all, however, as it introduces the possibility of over-compensation, which may also be harmful. Specifically, if the government offers too generous a price, a patentee will eagerly accept and reap a windfall. Were the government systemically to inflate the value of the patents that it purchases, the result would be too much innovation.[28] Furthermore, insisting that any buy-out be voluntary invites strategic behaviour on the part of patentees. Inventors may resist government overtures that entail optimal prices in the hope that the state's inadequate knowledge may lead it to inflate its offers. Furthermore, where a patentee has an exclusive right over one of many complementary technologies that one must combine to create a marketable product, it may have an incentive to hold out. In such cases, inventors may be able to extract a price from the government that exceeds the *ex ante* value of their proprietary technology by threatening to enjoin the larger use that the state seeks to accomplish. The social value of that larger use, rather than the *ex ante* licensing value of the patented technology, sets the ceiling on a patentee's hold-up price.

Thus, what should the government do if patentees refuse "reasonable" prices? Should the state force a sale pursuant to its eminent domain or compulsory purchase power? One's attitude to the government's use of this power depends on the capacity for its abuse, and that capacity is considerable. Given the *ex post* nature of the world in which states negotiate to acquire patents, hindsight bias distracts from the reality that the invention at issue was not inevitable. The temptation is always great, given the existence of a particular technology, to expropriate the value of that invention in

---

28 This may sound oxymoronic, but because the R&D process involves the expenditure of scarce resources, efficiency requires that those inventors devote those inputs to R&D only if doing so reaps a social value greater than the next best alternative use. For that reason, there is such a thing as "too much" innovation.

the name of the public interest. Combined with the insight of decision theory that is better to err on the side of too much innovation than too little, this observation suggests that voluntary patent acquisitions are superior.

Economists have not been blind to the danger, however, that this approach may over-reward patentees. A prominent, proposed solution is to make use of an auction process in which the government would solicit sealed bids, which it would use as a measure of private value and to which it would add a mark up to reflect the larger social value.[29] The state would then make an offer at the ensuing price, which the relevant patentee could either accept or decline. To deter inflated bids, however, the government would sell a subset of the acquired patents to the highest bidder. This approach might be expected to be a viable solution to the problem of monopoly pricing associated with intellectual property. Indeed, economists consider buy-outs to be particularly desirable with respect to pharmaceutical patents, where optimal rewards are indispensable to ongoing R&D, but the allocative-inefficiency costs of exclusivity are most acute.

Notwithstanding the benefits of a patent buyout system, there are some related difficulties. In the first place, it is often difficult to value technology at the time of a patent grant. In many cases, a patent's worth may become clear only many years after it was issued. Furthermore, given the high rate of patent invalidity, there may be a significant cost to purchasing patents many of which would ultimately have been found invalid upon re-examination or in litigation. Indeed, studies reveal that courts invalidate almost 50% of patents that parties litigate to judgment, which is not a reassuring statistic.[30] Still, these problems are surmountable. As long as the government strives to make accurate valuations and to discount the value of a patent for the possibility of invalidity, the mean price that the state pays should approximate the correct value, as fluctuations around the mean should cancel each other out. Furthermore, it is easy to overstate the invalidity problem. If the government limits itself to buying out only the most socially valuable patents, most defects compromising the validity of acquired patents would lie on technicalities that should not obviously, on economic grounds, warrant depriving inventors of a reward.

3. Regulatory exclusivity

The last incentive mechanism that we shall explore, regulatory exclusivity, occupies a strong complementary position alongside the patent system. Patents provide unsuitable means for promoting innovation in every setting. This is particularly likely when the law deprives worthy inventors of protection based on economically suspect grounds. A good example would be denying patents to inventors of expensive and risky innovations that were technically obvious to try in light of the prior art.

In circumstances like these, policymakers can step in to correct the patent system's failure to create efficient incentives. A principal tool is regulatory exclusivity. Such an exclusive licence from the state results in a certain business environment, in contradistinction to the probabilistic nature of patent ownership. The most well-known examples of regulatory exclusivity lie in the biopharmaceutical sphere. For instance, Article 39 of the Trade-Related Aspects of Intellectual Property Rights ("TRIPS") requires members to protect the data underlying the development of new chemical entities against unfair commercial use. In the United States, chemical drugs enjoy five years' data exclusivity, while pioneer biologics obtain 12 years, which inventors can extend by six months if they conducted paediatric studies. In contrast to such data exclusivity, the US Orphan Drugs Act provides seven years' marketing exclusivity for companies that develop small-population drugs

---

29 Michael Kremer, 'Patent Buy-Outs: A Mechanism for Encouraging Innovation', NBER Working Paper (1997). Available at: www. nber.org/papers/w6304.pdf.

30 *See*, e.g., John R. Allison and Mark A. Lemley, 'Empirical analysis of the validity of litigated patents' (1998) 26 Am Intell Prop L Ass'n QJ 185.

treating fewer than 200,000 people in the United States. EU law provides ten years' marketing exclusivity for orphan drugs.

There is an economic argument that regulators should use marketing and data exclusivity to safeguard R&D investment in industries characterised by capital-intensive, high-risk innovation. Targeted application of generous regulatory exclusivity could help to spur greater efforts in the biopharmaceutical field, for instance, to develop brand new treatments in lieu of increasingly prevalent "me too" reformulations of existing drugs.

F. Conclusion

As the principal legal mechanism for promoting industrial innovation, the patent regime serves an economic role of extraordinary importance. The basic insight is that free markets will under-produce technology, which is a form of public good. If accurate, that theory provides a strong justification for legal intervention given R&D's powerful effect on long-term economic growth.

A more in-depth exploration of the economic characteristics of industries in which patents feature prominently, however, reveals that the public goods theory of innovation does not map neatly onto many sectors. Biopharmaceutical R&D does display the classic traits that justify patent protection, namely high capital-investment requirements, a great risk of failure, large commer-cialisation costs, a high ratio of pioneer-to-follow-on innovation, and vulnerability to reverse engi-neering. For that reason, drug patents rest on a sturdy economic foundation. The same cannot be said, however, for many other sectors, and the information technology industry in particular. It is difficult to square the economic rationale for the patent system with the nature of innovation in the IT sector, where inventions are rapid, modest, cheap, and quickly displaced. Given the low ratio of breakthrough-to-cumulative innovation in that setting, granting original inventors broad exclusive rights puts the brakes on follow-on R&D. Indeed, a scrutinising review of the IT industry suggests that the contemporary patent system is broken.

As policymakers struggle to resolve the many difficulties that afflict the patent regime, law and economics can provide useful guidance. By focusing attention on the question of optimal incen-tives rather than on interest groups, and in explaining how optimal patent scope depends on the nature of innovation in the relevant industry, the discipline can help lawmakers, regulators, and courts to mould a more effective innovation policy. Policymakers can accomplish this end, in part, by availing of alternative incentive-to-invent mechanisms suggested by economics, including prizes, patent buy-outs, and regulatory exclusivity.

Key Points

- Economics justifies patent protection on two principal grounds.

  - First, for technologies that bear public-good characteristics, novel insights may be vulner-able to third-party appropriation. Without enforceable proprietary rights, a firm may not devote scarce capital to R&D projects upon which its competitors can free ride. Patents thus encourage investment in technology.

  - Second, patents spur firms to commercialise existing technologies. It can be expensive to develop an idea from conception to a marketable product. Thus, free-riding can discourage companies from devoting the necessary capital to translate cutting-edge know-how into consumable goods.

  - Thus, the economic problem is that innovation spawns positive externalities, meaning that free markets will engage in too little R&D. One can thus think of the law's role as being to create a Pigouvian subsidy.

- The patent system imposes costs, as well as benefits.

  - First, it confers economic monopoly power on inventors of valuable technologies for which no substitutes exist. Monopoly pricing distorts market outcomes by generating lower output than would exist under competition. Economists refer to the ensuing welfare costs as "deadweight loss".

  - Second, because transaction costs are pervasive, proprietary interests in technology fetter the universe of cutting-edge knowledge available for follow-on innovation.

  - Third, in industries that must combine discrete technologies to create a single product, patenting can create anticommons and thicket problems. The former arises when many different entities own the patents needed to create an end product, such that a firm must secure licensing permission from numerous licensors. Cournot-complement effects cause those patentees to charge more than they would in the presence of vertical integration. Thicket effects arise when patents' claims are vague, allowing multiple patentees to claim the same technology. Both of these problems magnify transaction costs, and suppress commercialisation of technology.

  - Fourth, patents create a race by firms that result in inefficient duplication of R&D efforts. In some cases, however, positive spill over effects from this process can facilitate new insights, making the net welfare effects of patent races to be ambiguous.

- The law holds that rules of nature, abstract discoveries, and stand alone computer software are not patentable. That prohibition makes economic sense because each such discovery, if patentable, would lie upstream and bear myriad applications. Due to real-world transaction costs, upstream monopolies would stymie the downstream application of technology. The law, however, permits patenting of useful downstream applications of such principles.

- To be patentable, an invention must be novel, useful, and non-obvious. The economic explanation for those requirements are as follows:

  - *Novelty*: anticipated inventions are not inventions at all. Generally, allowing one to claim a monopoly over what others already knew would impose a tax without a corresponding gain. Nevertheless, economics suggests that the law should provide patents or alternative incentive awards when bringing a known technology to market is expensive and vulnerable to free-riding. An example is certain unpatentable drugs.

  - *Utility*: patenting useless inventions would add to an already large universe of IPRs, increasing transaction costs for firms wishing to secure clearing positions.

  - *Non-obviousness*: if an invention is obvious, it was likely inevitable. In that case, granting a patent imposes a social cost but this is not a "but for" cause of innovation. Simultaneous invention on a wide scale may suggest inevitability, and thus evidence obviousness.

- Several factors affect the need for patent protection over an invention. These are: susceptibility to reverse engineering; the quantum of necessary capital investment; the risk of failure and the sunk nature of the associated R&D; first-mover advantage, including network effects; and speed of obsolescence. As different industries bear dissimilar characteristics along these lines, the need for the patent system varies markedly between them.

- Patents are not the only means by which to solve under investment in easily appropriated technology. Prizes calibrated to exceed inventors' reservation returns can accomplish the same goal. As compared to patents:

  - *Prizes offer advantages*: In particular, they do not confer economic market power on inventors, and thus facilitate competitive markets for the acquisition and use of technology; and

  - *Prizes are subject to disadvantages*: Two are especially noteworthy: First, government funding of prizes created distortions elsewhere in the economy and require those not using the ensuing technology to cross-subsidise those who do. Second, prizes can only spur the discovery of solutions to known problems.

● Patent buy-outs and regulatory exclusivity are also available to governments as alternatives or complements to traditional patent systems.

 ## References and Further Reading

Books

Boldrin, Michele, and Levine, David, *Against Intellectual Monopoly* (2008).
Kieff, F. Scott, 'On the Economics of Patent Law and Policy' in *Patent Law and Theory* (Toshiko Takenaka (ed.)) (2008).
Landes, William M. and Posner, Richard A., *The Economic Structure of Intellectual Property Law* (2003) Chs. 11–12.
Lemley, Mark A. and Burk, Dan L., *The Patent Crisis and How the Courts Can Solve It* (2011).
Miceli, Thomas J., *The Economic Approach to Law*, 2nd edn (2008) pp. 180–83.
Shavell, Steven, *Foundations of Economic Analysis of Law* (2004) Ch. 7.

Articles

Dam, Kenneth W., 'The economic underpinnings of patent law' (1994) 23 J Legal Stud 247.
Gilbert, R. and Shapiro, Carl, 'Optimal patent length and breadth' (1990) 21 RAND J Econ 106.
Harhoff, Dietmar, Narin, F., Scherer, F.M. and Vopel, K., 'Citation frequency and the value of patented inventions' (1999) 81 Rev Econ & Stats 511.
Heller, Michael A. and Eisenberg, Rebecca S., 'Can patents deter innovation? The anticommons in biomedical research' (1998) 280 Science 698.
Jaffe, Adam B. and Lerner, Josh, 'Reinventing public R&D: Patent policy and the commercialization of national laboratory technologies' (2001) 32 RAND J Econ 167.
Judd, Kenneth L., 'On the performance of patents' (1985) 53 Econometrica 567.
Kieff, F. Scott, 'Property rights and property rules for commercializing inventions' (2001) 85 Minn L Rev 697.
Lanjouw, Jean O. and Schankerman, Mark, 'Patent quality and research productivity: Measuring innovation with multiple indicators' (2004) 114 Econ J 441.
Lemley, Mark A. and Burk, Dan L., 'Policy levers in patent law' (2003) 89 Va L Rev 1575.
Lerner, Josh, 'Patenting in the shadow of competitors' (1995) 38 JL & Econ 463.
Merges, Robert P. and Nelson, Richard R., 'On the complex economics of patent scope' (1990) 90 Colum L Rev 839.
Moser, Petra, 'How do patents law influence innovation? Evidence from nineteenth-century world fairs' (2005) 95 Am Econ Rev 1214.
Posner, Richard A., 'Intellectual property: The law and economics approach' (2005) 19 J Econ Persp 57.
Sakakibara, Mariko and Branstetter, Lee, 'Do stronger patents induce more innovation? Evidence from the 1988 Japanese patent law reforms' (2001) 32 RAND J Econ 77.
Scotchmer, Suzanne, (1991) 'Standing on the shoulders of giants' (1991) 5 J Econ Persp 29.
Wright, Brian D., 'The economics of invention incentives: Patents, prizes, and research contracts' (1983) 73 Am Econ Rev 691.

Chapter 3

Copyright Law

Chapter Contents

A.	Introduction	284
B.	Copyright Law and the Incentive to Create Expressive Works	285
C.	The Optimal Scope of Copyright Protection	290
D.	The Efficient Copyright Term	294
E.	Piracy Wars: File-Sharing, DRM, and ISP Injunctions	295
F.	Conclusion	297
Key Points		298
References and Further Reading		298

A. Introduction

The literary and performing arts enrich people's lives and contribute greatly to consumer welfare. Fostering artistic talent and spurring the outlay of creative works is thus a key priority for society. Music, literature, film, theatre, painting, and other artistic phenomena, however, possess fundamentally different characters than industrial research and development (R&D) of the kind explored in the previous chapter. Expressive creations thus warrant a distinct form of public policy treatment than technological innovation. From the perspective of law and economics, the threshold question is whether artists and content creators would produce optimal amounts of expressive works without state intervention. This chapter addresses this question and explores the economic role of the copyright system as an "incentive to create" mechanism.

We would be amiss, however, to begin without a prefatory observation: even more so than the patent regime, copyright is controversial. The debate is about more than innovation policy; it concerns the relationship between consumers, creators, and government, and entails conflicting claims to the use and ownership of artistic creations. A sizeable community believes that "information wants to be free", concluding that the state should abolish or radically curtail the institution of copyright. Adherents to that position contrast a copyright-free world with the permission culture that accompanies widespread proprietary rights in creative content. On the other side of the spectrum lie content industries, which have been waging a war to maximise the value of their artistic output. Their principal target is piracy, though we shall see that the scope of what certain industries consider as piracy has expanded over time. Nevertheless, unauthorised copying has indeed accelerated, principally in tandem with the proliferation of access to digital technology and to the internet. Alarmed by this threat, the film, publishing, and recording industries have equated downloading with theft, and have lobbied courts and legislatures to magnify their exclusive rights. They have been successful, profitably securing anti-circumvention laws that criminalise attempts to crack digital rights management ("DRM"), which companies use to protect the copying and distribution of digitised works, and securing a seemingly endless array of copyright extensions.

Most recently, and frustrated by their inability effectively to target individual downloaders, content industries have sought legislation aimed at Internet Service Providers ("ISPs"), through which pirates access the internet to download and share copyrighted material. In 2011, these efforts brought about controversial proposed US legislation in the form of the Stop Online Piracy Act ("SOPA") and Protect IP Act ("PIPA"). The acts failed to pass following unprecedented protest, led by internet companies including Wikipedia, Google, and Flickr. This legislation would have permitted copyright holders to enjoin websites that enabled or facilitated infringement. The severity of the reaction illustrates the importance of the copyright debate, as well as its implications both for the democracy-enabling virtues of unfettered internet access and for freedom of speech.

This chapter explores the law and economics of the copyright system, and its effect in spurring expressive content. Although economic analysis supports the case for a copyright system, certain aspects of contemporary doctrine are difficult to justify from an economic perspective. In particular, governments should reduce copyright terms, which are presently excessive; they should introduce registration requirements and renewal fees; they should create databases identifying all copyright holders; and they should amend anti-circumvention laws to permit bypass efforts aimed at achieving fair use of underlying content.

The key economic condition underlying these prescriptions is the fact that progress in literary and performing arts is cumulative. As a result, a larger and richer public domain is apt to be conducive of more rapid and superior artistic output. The state should thus maximise the public domain, subject to not reducing pecuniary rewards from expressive works below the level at which artists would decline to create. Copyright systems, as presently constituted, do not seem to reflect this approach. Of course, none of these points does violence to the essential truth that proprietary interests in creative content are appropriate and potentially important to the promotion of artistic works.

B. Copyright Law and the Incentive to Create Expressive Works

1. The copyright system

It is helpful to begin with a basic description of copyright law, which is the primary incentive mechanism that governments have employed to spur artistic creativity. As we shall see, however, it is a matter of some controversy whether copyright promotes an economic, incentive-to-create function or serves a different role founded on moral rights. From the perspective of economics, however, the premise underlying the copyright system is akin to that justifying the patent regime: deserving innovators should enjoy proprietary rights enforceable by law. As with patents, the idea is to remedy positive externalities. Proprietary interests permit content creators to capture a greater share of the social value of their artistic expression.

Copyright is available in the United States for all original works of authorship that are fixed in a tangible medium of expression. In the United Kingdom, original works involving independent creative effort are copyright eligible once reduced to physical form. Subsumed within the field of matter than can be copyright protected are literary and performing arts of the kind mentioned above, as well as architectural works, photographs, and computer software. A copyright holder enjoys certain rights. In the United States, this is the exclusive rights to reproduce the copyrighted work; to make derivative works; to distribute copies of the work; and publicly to display and perform the work. In the United Kingdom, it is the exclusive right to copy the work; to issue copies to the public; to rent or to lend it to the public; to perform, show, or play the work in public; to communicate the work to the public; and to make an adaptation of the work or to do the preceding acts in relation to an adaptation.

Although copyright is a form of intellectual property, it differs from the patent system. First, there is no registration or application process to obtain a copyright. A qualifying author receives immediate protection under the law once she fixes a copyrightable expression in a tangible form. Unlike patents, no maintenance fees are required to maintain a valid copyright. In the United States, however, an author must register his copyright with the US Copyright Office before bringing a suit for infringement. Second, copyright provides no ownership rights in an idea; it merely gives an author a proprietary interest in the form of her original expression. Thus, you can quite properly lift all the novel ideas underlying an author's work and use them in your own as long as you do not employ the same manner of expression. This marks a major departure from the law of patents, which grant exclusive rights in substantive technologies.

Third, copyright merely protects a content creator against actual copying. A clean-room defence therefore exists in copyright law, but not in patent law. Fourth, other than in circumscribed instances, the patent system prohibits copying and restricts experimental use. United States copyright law, however, authorises a broad array of direct copying of protected work in circumstances falling within the rubric of "fair use". UK law has a narrower, but still material, provision that allows copying in cases of "fair dealing".

These principal characteristics render copyright protection far narrower than patent ownership. A further distinction, however, strengthens copyright by providing protection of much-longer duration. At present, copyright protection lasts for the life of the relevant author, plus 70 years. Patented inventions, in comparison, fall into the public domain after only 20 years from the date of application.

Having identified some of the key attributes of the copyright system, we can delve into the economics of expressive works, the vulnerability of art and expression to free riding, and the law's economic role in instilling optimal incentives with respect to the literary and performing arts.

2. Artistic creation and the public domain

Artistic expression is a uniquely cumulative endeavour. No piece of expressive writing is the entirely independent creation of the author, free of influence from pre-existing works. This does not mean, of course, that artists simply regurgitate the work of others. Rather, they assimilate prior literature and infuse it with their own personal creativity, thus creating transformative works. That background literature inspires acts of creative expression is well understood. To draw just three examples, Homer's *Odyssey* was a major influence on Joyce's *Ulysses*; *Romeo and Juliet* on *West Side Story*; and *King Lear* on *A Thousand Acres*.

This aspect of artistic creativity has significant public policy implications, particularly for the optimal scope and duration of copyright protection. As pre-existing literature is an essential input into the creation of original expressive works, society must not fetter authors and artists' creativity by hindering their ability to use background literature. The public domain refers to the universe of works that are free for all to use. The larger and richer the body of works upon which creators can freely draw, the more likely it is that such creators will produce a greater number of superior works. The constraint that limits the free availability of those inputs, however, is ensuring a return to producers of expressive works sufficient to spur them to create.

A possible economic goal, then, is to maximise the size of the public domain subject to not undercutting the incentive of artists and authors to create the material that subsequently become inputs into later expressive works. This objective is far removed from eliminating positive externalities by enabling creators to extract the full social value of their works. A property right that permitted producers of expressive works to extract such value would align creators' and society's interests to create a given work. This approach could only work, however, in the absence of transaction costs.

In the real world, the transaction costs that accompany the licensing of copyrighted works are high, as evidenced by the emergence of centralised purchasing and selling organisations like ASCAP, BMI, and SESAC, which pool copyrights from similarly situated artists and sell blanket licenses to consumers. To craft a copyright that would enable its holder to extract the full social value of the creative expression, the government would have to create perpetual intellectual property of such all-encompassing scope that any use of the work, no matter how tangential, would be subsumed within the artist's exclusive right. This copyright would also have to be coupled with an effective enforcement mechanism. This would obviously be impractical.

In the first place, tracing costs would quickly become overwhelming. If copyrights were ever-lasting, one would have to locate the rights holder to every work that influenced one's contemporary expression. Yet, the literary and other artistic influences that collectively form our background knowledge are innumerable. Tracing the current holders of centuries- and millennia-old copyright interests would be impossible. Similarly, fully aligning the private and social benefits of creative expression would entail scope so broad as to capture all derivative works and adaptations. Prospective creators of such follow-on works would decline to create if the costs of securing permission were excessive. Conversely, open access to previously created works provides free inputs to new forms of expression upon which artists and authors can draw to craft original forms of expression.

For these reasons, some positive externalities are desirable in the sphere of copyrighted works. Economists refer to the benefits that creators do not internalise as "positive spillover effects", which profit society. Governments should not eliminate such effects, but should rather strive to narrow the gap between private and social value to the point where the pecuniary return of original expression is sufficiently lucrative to supply the necessary incentive to create.

3. Expressive works as public goods

The principal economic concept bearing on expressive works is the familiar theory of public goods. If creative content is expensive, arduous, or risky to generate – but easily copied if successful – third-party appropriation of the value of artistic creation would undermine *ex ante* investment. The result would be an impoverished society deprived of the inestimable benefits of an artistically rich culture. As in the case of the patent system, though, whether this risk translates from abstract theory to reality depends on the nature of the expressive material, the traits of the relevant artist, and the larger market setting in which the creator sells or otherwise distributes his art. In fact, it is not clear as a universal matter that copyright enhances the output of artistic works.

Factors unrelated to the copyright system are often paramount in inducing the creation of artistic works. The innate compulsion toward creative expression is particularly important, which observation holds true for all manner of artistic expression. Poets are driven to capture life's poignant moments in words. People writing books typically do so for the sense of accomplishment associated with sharing one's thoughts with others. For all but the most famous authors, the expected pecuniary return is modest. People edit Wikipedia for free. Innovation in the early years of the internet was explosive, notwithstanding the absence of property rights in the underlying TCP/IP protocols and the presence of open-source licences to relevant code. Countless people contribute to open-source software, such as Linux, Mozilla Firefox, and the Apache HTTP Server Project, which have proven to be of high quality. Musicians the world over play for the joy of the experience itself. Precious few make lucrative returns.

The fact that an innate urge to self-expression drives much creation output has important ramifications for the law. If artists have independent preferences to create, then the law has no role to play in inducing creation through the provision of monetary rewards – at least when the capital requirements of creation are modest. Within the law and economics framework, such preferences are exogenous and unrelated to the incentive structure that the law creates. In this respect, incentives to create expressive material exist independent of intellectual property.

To understand the economic importance of the motivations that drive people to create, contrast two extreme circumstances. In the first, pecuniary concerns alone motivate the creation of original expressive works. The economic theory of copyright is at its zenith in this case, as *ex ante* expectations of capturing the social value of artistic expression drive artists and authors to create. In the second situation, artists will create expressive material regardless of pecuniary reward, though they would prefer to receive a monetary return for their creations than not. Assume that the marginal cost of distributing the relevant expression is zero. There are no fixed costs. The following graph contrasts the different economic situations see Figure 7.4.

In the absence of copyright protection, artists and authors have sufficient incentive to create. Free copying of the expressive material results in infinite supply, represented here by S_C ("$_C$" represents "under competition"), which equals the marginal cost curve bearing a constant value of zero. Under these conditions, the amount of material consumed satisfies all demand, represented by point Q_C. The creator and copiers of the pertinent work enjoy zero economic profit, while consumers reap welfare equal to the triangle 6–5–3.

If one were to introduce copyright protection, however, the creator of the relevant work could prevent third-party duplication and thus effect an artificial restriction in supply. By unilaterally restricting the supply of the artistic work, the monopolist would capture consumer surplus to realise profit. In this example, a profit-maximising monopolist creator would produce quantity Q_M at price P_M.

Introducing copyright protection in this case is inefficient. As the reader can readily verify, the provision of exclusive rights results in an output restriction from Q_C to Q_M. Although the creator receiving copyright protection gains in the amount of 1–4–5–2, that benefit is less than consumers' loss – it is not a zero-sum game. There is a deadweight loss equal to the triangle 1–2–3. That efficiency loss would be justifiable if it were a "but for" cause of a larger gain, but in this case there is no off-setting benefit because a monopoly return was not needed to spur creation.

Other reasons beyond inherent reward drive creative efforts. Reputational effects, for instance, drive much creation, as when faculty publish to promote their standing within the academic

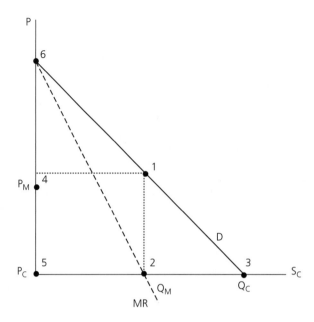

Figure 7.4

community. In other cases, a person will create as a means to achieve a larger purpose. For example, proprietary rights in their dissertations do not drive PhD students to write; the prospect of earning a doctorate does. In other cases, pecuniary rewards may indeed be pertinent in driving the production of expressive content, but the monetary return does not come from copyright protection. A prominent example involves the music industry. iTunes and CD sales contribute little financially to artists, as the great majority of proceeds goes to the relevant recording companies. Musicians make most of their money from live performances; this means that they have a reason to distribute their music freely to increase demand for their gigs. This does not mean, of course, that copyright is unimportant to the recording industry. However, it would be correct to say that copyright incentives are dominant only in certain portions of that sector.

Even where money matters, copyright protection is not always a prerequisite of creation. Copying will never deprive creators of all private value. First, artists can protect their work through contract. By insisting on terms that limit or forbid the copying of their work, and by policing their agreements, content creators can restrict the availability of their art, thus increasing its price and private value. To the extent this ability is present, of course, it means that artists can privately transform public into private goods. Second, lag time permits artists to sell their work in the absence of competing sales for a period before a sufficient volume of copying takes place to neutralise the creator's market power.

Third, original content often carries a higher status than duplicates, and thus commands a price premium that benefits the artist. One need merely compare, for example, the respective values of a Rembrandt and its carbon copy. Fourth, first-mover advantage infuses familiarity with the artist in the public's mind, which may carry pecuniary benefits then and for future works, too. Finally, the fact that a work is susceptible to duplication may sometimes enhance demand for that work, thus increasing the original price, as might be the case when a person buys a CD if he can burn a copy of it for his wife. In light of these factors, the private value of content creation is invariably positive. Even without copyright protection, an artist's expected gain in both pecuniary and non-monetary terms may be sufficiently high to drive her efforts.

The foregoing account does not make a compelling economic case for the copyright system, but nor are there convincing economic grounds for abolishing it. The preceding factors merely show that a certain amount of expressive content will take place in the absence of copyright protection. They do not show that all or even most socially desirable art produced in the presence of copyright would take place in its absence. The previous chapter explained that the ease of *ex post* appropriation and the amount of capital investment underlying the R&D process influence the vulnerability of innovation to free riding. The same is true in the copyright setting.

In times past, the expense of copying literary works, such as books, limited the vulnerability of such innovation to expropriation. Historically, making handwritten copies or using ink printing presses was a time-consuming and resource-heavy means of copying another's work. More recently, photocopying expressive material, though faster, is not instantaneous, and results in successively inferior copies at each element of the vertical chain. Such means of replication do undermine the private value of original writers' and artists' creations by denying them the opportunity to licence or sell their works to consumers who would otherwise have bought them. Nevertheless, the technical limitations on these forms of copying constrain third-party appropriation.

The digital revolution has changed all that. Coupled with ubiquitous internet access, digital technology has reduced the cost of copying and distributing electronic goods almost to zero. Music, film, television programmes, video games, newspaper articles, and comparable products are widely produced in electronic form. Unlike traditional means of copying, such as photocopying, digital duplication results in no qualitative degradation, thus enabling an endless vertical stream of copying. Users can distribute digital copies on an almost cost free basis through e-mail, online file-sharing services, burning content onto DVDs, and beyond. This technology, though extraordinarily valuable for society, threatens to undermine *ex ante* incentives to create if left unchecked.

Of course, even imputing a pecuniary motive to content creators, easy duplication and sharing would not fatally corrupt *ex ante* incentives if the cost of creation was itself minimal. Although this is indeed the case for some forms of art, a tremendous amount of capital investment underlies modern content industries. The average development budget underlying a contemporary video game is in excess of $10 million. A recent report by the International Federation of the Phonographic Industry ("IFPI") stated that industry invests $5 billion a year in artists. The movie industry operates on no less modest a scale. The US component realised over $10 billion in revenue in 2010. The book publishing industry is subject to significant upfront costs in terms of editing, printing, and marketing. Collectively, these content industries rely on copyright protection to monetise their heavy upfront investments. Abolishing copyright would lead to a disorderly collapse of the contemporary business model in those industries. Abolition would not eliminate creative content in those sectors, but it would transform the nature of the expressive content produced, likely reducing its short- and perhaps its long-term quality.

Furthermore, even if copyright is of ancillary importance to many authors and artists, it does not follow that the prospect of a monetary return holds no allure at all to such creators. Most people understandably prefer a greater financial return on their efforts than less, holding everything else is constant. Thus, even if other factors are paramount in spurring certain forms of creativity, intellectual property may still act as a modest spur to create and thus be desirable for that reason. If the institution of copyright affects even a modest increment in the volume and quality of expressive materials in society, it is worth having. Even at the individual level, it seems likely that copyright provides at least some marginal contribution to artistic expression. Take the classic example of books. Authors toil over their work for countless hours as they struggle through various drafts. The material and opportunity costs subsumed within those efforts can be significant, as is the work involved in the editing process. Although writing books is rarely lucrative, the prospect of achieving a pecuniary return is a material component of at least some authors' incentive to write. As we have just seen, the recording, film, and television industries operate on enormous, copyright-dependent budgets.

In sum, a great deal of capital investment and individual effort goes into the creation of art, and non-copyright factors are, in themselves, probably insufficient to drive optimal levels of artistic output. In light of the prominent role that copyright plays in spurring creative expression in many settings, it would be an economic mistake to abandon copyright. A more promising and responsible approach is to calibrate the existing system so that it tracks more closely its underlying economic rationale. Copyright scope and duration, the subject of the next two sections, are particularly fruitful objects of examination.

C. The Optimal Scope of Copyright Protection

"Copyright scope" bears two components. The first concerns the kind of creative expression that qualifies for copyright protection. The second encapsulates the legal rights subsumed within copyright ownership. Both elements have radically expanded over time. Before recounting these changes, however, we should make the economic issue plain.

Scope reflects a trade-off between providing sufficiently generous protection to spur original acts of creativity and freeing up artistic work to feed the cumulative process of creating new expressive material. If the law expands the sphere of copyright-eligible expression, it enhances the incentive to create the newly subsumed material, but it also increases the cost of third-party use of it. Similarly, if the law magnifies the exclusive rights that copyright holders enjoy, it narrows the divide between private and social value of expression, thus enhancing the incentive to create, but fettering third-party use of the proprietary material. This section explains how copyright scope has expanded over time and addresses the economic analysis pertaining to that expansion.

1. Copyright's ever-expanding scope

In its earliest days, copyright law, as encapsulated in the 1710 Statute of Anne, had a narrow scope. It encompassed only book publication. The US copyright statute of 1790 had a slightly larger reach in that it also applied to maps and charts. Early UK and US copyright law thus did not apply to music, theatre, architecture, or painting. Even with respect to publications, authors' rights were meagre. Third parties could freely copy protected books, as long as they did not republish them. Moreover, copyright holders could not prevent the publication of so-called "derivative works", which are forms of expression based on underlying works, such as translations and sequels.

Today, copyright scope is unrecognisably broader than it has been historically. Presently, in the United States, an author instantly acquires copyright protection when he fixes his original expression in a fixed medium of expression. As a result, even e-mails and hastily scrawled post-it notes qualify for copyright protection. Third parties are no longer free to copy protected expression, even if they refrain from republishing it. Copyright holders now have exclusive rights over derivative or adaptive works that are "substantially similar" to the protected expression. The right to translate works, to adapt them into different forms (e.g. from a novel into a play), to remix music, to create sequels, and the like now reside exclusively with the copyright holder.

An especially notable enlargement of copyright scope arose with the advent of computing. Before then, people who had purchased rights to copyrighted content enjoyed considerable freedoms to consume that material as they saw fit. By definition, copyright only applies to acts of copying, and so consumers of copyrighted material could do whatever they wanted with it as long as they did not copy the work. They could, for example, read a book as many times as they wish or sell it to a third party. The internet and the digital age has changed that. Any time a person uses an electronic file – be it a book, song, movie, or computer algorithm – her computer creates a copy of that file in its memory, thus triggering copyright law. This feature of the computer age radically expands the scope of copyright, potentially allowing copyright holders to restrict uses in all manner of ways that are not possible for physical copyrighted material.

This dramatic expansion in the ambit of copyright protection changes the economic role of copyright. Authors and artists today enjoy far-richer proprietary interests in their work, and stand to reap greater benefits by creating popular works. In this respect, expanded scope is economically desirable because it imparts greater incentives to create original works. Yet, the enlarged ambit of copyright protection also magnifies the cost of building on prior literature and imposes allocative inefficiency losses on society. The unprecedented enlargement of scope that the online world and digital technology entails has disrupted the prior balance built into copyright. The result is potentially excessive power in the hands of copyright holders, which impedes creators' use of others' expressive works. The remaining guardian of balance in this setting is fair use, to which concept we now turn.

2. Restrictions on copyright: fair use and fair dealing

The fact that copyright casts a broad net does not mean that an author or artist enjoys unqualified exclusive rights over expressive material falling within the purported sphere of ownership. Limitations serve a crucial economic function, particularly in spurring positive spillover effects.

The principal tool that US law uses to limit copyright holders' exclusive rights is "fair use". When applicable, the doctrine relieves a person of infringement for copying protected work without permission. Section 107 of the Copyright Act 1976 articulates a four-part test for when the defence applies, though the elements are non-exhaustive, and in any event, courts enjoy discretion in distinguishing fair use from infringement. The test is as follows: (1) the purpose and character of the use, including whether such use is of a commercial nature or is for nonprofit educational purposes; (2) the nature of the copyrighted work; (3) the amount and substantiality of the portion used in relation to the copyrighted work as a whole; and (4) the effect of the use upon the potential market for or value of the copyrighted work.

Fair use plays a critical role in facilitating third-party use of copyrighted material in high transaction cost settings. The Coase Theorem explains the circumstances in which copying should be fair use. Specifically, the defence ought to apply where, in a hypothetical costless bargain, prospective creators and consumers of expressive content would have agreed to free copying because such use would maximise their collective welfare. Legal intervention is necessary, notwithstanding the efficiency of licensing in such circumstances, because of bargaining costs. For instance, authors and filmmakers *ex post* might refuse to allow a critic to write a negative review, even though all stakeholders would have agreed to allow such uses *ex ante* in the absence of bargaining costs. Content creators may decline to permit other artists to create parodies of their work. The law can cure such market failures by introducing a compulsory licence at no cost in the form of fair use.

Copying is efficient where the proposed third-party use would result in expression that complements rather than substitutes for the underlying work. In the economic literature, two goods are complements if decreasing the price of one increases demand for the other. A classic example would be ice cream and cones. Goods are substitutes if increasing one product's price increases demand for the other good. If the price of Coca-Cola were to rise by 50%, the demand for Pepsi would presumably rise, thus indicating some substitutive relationship between the two.

This distinction is important to the fair-use inquiry because, viewed *ex ante*, using a copyrighted work to generate a complementary work benefits all. So, for example, critical reviews efficiently increase the demand for films and books by distributing credible information to the consuming public. It is only *ex post*, when an artist has created a sub-par product that a published critique of his work may prove harmful. Granting content creators an *ex post* right to veto third-party complementary use of their expressive works would undo the economic value of reviews. In the presence of a veto power, reviews would lose their information-signalling value because consumers would know that copyright holders would only agree to positive discussions of their work. Enforcing the *ex ante* hypothetical bargain through fair use thus maximises welfare, and is economically equivalent to enforcing a contract that was mutually wealth-enhancing, even if it turns out to disadvantage one of the parties *ex post*. In short, fair use should apply when copying would be efficient, but transaction costs foreclose licensing.

United Kingdom law does not recognise fair use, but instead employs the concept of "fair dealing". Sections 29 and 30 of the UK's Copyright, Designs and Patents Act 1988 provide that no liability for copyright infringement arises for copying for the purposes of non-commercial research or private study, for criticism, or for reporting current events. Fair dealing does not apply to copying undertaken for other reasons, regardless of whether one might reasonably deem those purposes to be "fair". As a result, fair dealing is narrower than fair use.

Fair use stands on sturdier economic footing than fair dealing. The broad distinction between these doctrines is that the former embodies a standard or "soft law", while the latter uses rules or "hard law". The economic differences between rules and standards are well known. The former provide legal certainty by specifying the boundaries of the relevant law (e.g. a law providing that "the speed limit is 70 mph" is clear). Standards employ loose language, providing little certainty, but reaping the benefits of flexibility. To continue with the preceding example, a standard might provide that "the speed limit is what is reasonable under the circumstances".

Standards are generally preferable when legislators lack sufficient information *ex ante* to craft specific laws that will prove efficient. In such circumstances, courts enjoy superior access to information because they encounter cases *ex post*. Over time, precedent that the judiciary lays down will clarify the boundaries of the law, thus creating more legal certainty, but maintaining flexibility should novel or otherwise unforeseen circumstances arise. Fair use enjoys a considerable advantage because it is impossible to envision, *ex ante*, all scenarios in which copying may occur. Notwithstanding the economic benefits of fair use, however, Article 9(2) of the Berne Convention and Article 5 of EU Directive 2001/29/EC constrain European countries' ability to embrace the doctrine in lieu of fair dealing.

In sum, scope is a crucial determinant of the copyright system's efficiency. It is clear, as a question of economics, that scope should not be all encompassing. There are many industries in which copying is both rampant and lawful, yet innovation flourishes. As Kal Raustiala and Christopher Sprigman recount in The Knockoff Economy, competitors in football, comedy, fashion, and food routinely adopt their rivals' innovations, be they dress designs, jokes, recipes, or strategies. Copyright law does not prohibit such copying, which would appear to be the correct result because market forces, and especially competition, provide adequate incentives to create in those settings. Whether the current scope of creativity subject to copyright protection is itself excessive, however, is a more difficult question. As we have seen, there are important limitations built into the right to exclude underlying copyright; limitations which include the permissibility of trivial copying, non-substantially similar use of expressive material, and fair use/fair dealing.

Nevertheless, there is reason to worry that copyright scope has expanded excessively in the digital arena, as computerised consumption of literary and performing arts radically expands "copying" and hence the reach of copyright. It is an open question whether the fair-use doctrine is sufficiently potent to maintain optimal balance in light of this expansion, particularly in light of the high cost of litigation, and the large damages available to a prevailing copyright holder. United States law, for instance, provides for up to $30,000 in statutory damages for non-wilful, and up to $150,000 statutory damages for wilful, copyright infringement.[1] These sums can apply regardless

---

1 17 USC § 504(c)(1)–(2).

of the harm that the copyright holders actually suffered, thus permitting them to threaten copiers relying on fair use with crushing damages, should the latter not prevail in court. This dynamic impedes fair use as a safeguard against excessive copyright scope.

3. Registration requirements and the conflicting economic and moral rights views of the copyright system

Closely related to copyright scope are the requisites of copyright eligibility. Policymakers can change the proportion of original expressive works that fall into the public domain by adjusting the preconditions of copyright protection. Whether the government should employ these policy levers, however, is a matter of some controversy. The utilitarian case for funnelling original expression into the public domain by requiring creators to satisfy minimal formalities is compelling. Nevertheless, such requirements are anathema to those who conceive of copyright as a legal embodiment of artists' natural rights in their creative works. From their perspective, an author or artist inherently owns her expressive material, such that the government cannot legitimately make ownership contingent on formalities. The economic approach rejects this view, particularly when a moral rights conception of ownership operates against the interests of larger society. We shall discuss two factors on which the law could precondition an enforceable copyright interest in expression: notice and registration.

Of these two potential conditions, notice is the most prosaic. Requiring an author or artist to adorn her work with the famous copyright symbol, ©, the date, and her name in order to acquire the right to sue another who copies the work would be a trivial requirement. Yet, this modest condition would separate at low cost those for whom copyright is a material consideration from those for whom it is irrelevant. Third parties would be free to copy works falling in the latter category, thus promoting the creation of derivative and other original acts of expression. The Berne Convention, however, made notice optional for all works published during or after March 1989, so copyright notice is no longer required. This is an economic mistake.

There is an even stronger case for introducing a registration requirement. This obligation would require creators of expressive works to provide information to a government agency concerning their work, the date of creation, the identity of the copyright holder, and relevant contact information. This modest requirement would have little effect on those for whom the pecuniary value of copyright protection is an important spur to creative expression. For the many people who create for non-copyright-based purposes, however, registration would be a mild burden without a benefit. Registration requirements would thus expand the public domain, without diminishing incentives to create. It would also reduce transaction costs by providing third-party users of copyrighted material with contact information for securing licences.

Unfortunately, contemporary copyright systems the world over have jettisoned a registration requirement. The problem lies in the Berne Convention, which provides that "the enjoyment and the exercise of [copyright] shall not be subject to any formality". This provision led countries to abolish registration and notice requirements. As a result, copyright now attaches to every original piece of writing fixed in a tangible medium of expression. As of 1976, US law no longer requires that an author or artist register her work with a government agency to receive copyright protection. This move harmonised US law with copyright systems elsewhere. Loosening formalities in this way inefficiently expanded the scope of copyright protection and restricted the public domain.

Whether one approves of this state of affairs depends upon how one perceives intellectual property. Economists view it as an instrumental mechanism that promotes social welfare by creating incentives to create more and better creative expression. Some others, however, view copyright as a social recognition of an artist's ownership over himself, of which his creative expression is a component. The moral rights view, popular in Europe, underlies many aspects of the Berne

Convention, including the right to claim authorship of one's work and to object to its distortion, mutilation, or modification.

As explored throughout this chapter, certain elements of the copyright system are in tension with economics. Moral rights may offer a superior descriptive account of contemporary copyright laws. That does not mean, however, that a moral rights-based perspective yields a superior normative account of how governments *ought* to craft their copyright laws. From an economic perspective, introducing modest notice and registration requirements on authors and artists would do minimal disservice to those creators' interests, but would reap disproportionate gains for future creativity by enlarging the public domain.

D. The Efficient Copyright Term

Copyright law's principal economic function is to promote incentives to create. Duration is, of course, relevant to this function. Longer copyright terms enable artists to appropriate a greater amount of the social value of their expressive material, thus boosting initial incentives to create. This effect would warrant lengthy duration were it not for offsetting considerations, namely that copyright facilitates supracompetitive pricing, and fetters artists' ability to build on prior literature. Enhancing the duration of copyright thus increases original incentives to create, but at the expense of both static efficiency and follow-on creation.

How to resolve this tension? The answer lies in positive discount rates, which means that increasing copyright terms yields decreasing marginal benefits to prospective creators. Beyond a certain amount of time, further enhancements in the length of copyright yield vanishingly small enhancements in *ex ante* incentives to create. Suppose that a book of unusual lasting power would command sales under copyright of £10,000 every year for the duration of the copyright term, and £0 otherwise. If the author possessed a 10% discount rate, her expected value in creating the work would be £85,135 under a 20-year term, £90,770 under a 25-year term, £99,148 under a 50-year term, and £99,992.74 under a century-long term. As a general matter, extending copyright terms beyond 25 years will have a modest effect on *ex ante* incentives to create.

A complication, however, is that positive discount rates also reduce the present cost of term extensions. It might thus appear that we should be indifferent about lengthening the duration of copyright because the present cost of doing so is as tenuous as the present benefits thus created. These difficulties pertain only to prospective changes in the copyright term, such that any adjustment in duration will impact artists' *ex ante* incentives to create. Where a change in the term is *retroactive*, however, the calculus is different. In such cases, legislatures increase the term of already-existing works. Ex *post* term extensions do not affect incentives to create material that artists have already produced. If the copyright system exists to spur the creation of expressive material, retroactive extensions are improper.

An interesting wrinkle in the typical economic story of copyright, however, is the possibility that proprietary control in some artistic expression may actually increase its social value by limiting its duplication. It may be that introducing such material into the public domain results in a loss of social welfare. The economic phenomena responsible for this effect are congestion externalities which William Landes and Richard Posner have used to support their proposal of indefinitely renewable copyright protection. Such externalities theoretically arise where widespread derivative uses of copyrightable expression degrade the quality of the expression in consumers' minds. Some have floated the example of Walt Disney's Mickey Mouse, hypothesising that the ubiquitous use of that character in all manner of settings and for all manner of purposes would cause the public quickly to tire of it.

Nevertheless, there is reason to be sceptical that congestion externalities justify copyright term extensions without generating incentives to create. First, such externalities have no effect on the majority of modern copyrighted material, particularly those created in digital form. Movies, television shows, music, video games and computer software are not susceptible to overexposure of a kind that would lead to a loss in value, and certainly not to a loss in value exceeding the static- and dynamic efficiency benefits of introducing them into the public domain. Indeed, certain of these products entail the opposite phenomenon: network effects that cause the marginal value of a good to increase with larger numbers of users of that good. For example, the demand for multiplayer video games rises with an increase in the number of online players. Second, there is, as yet, no empirical evidence that making easily copied expressive material, for which there is consumer demand, freely available reduces welfare.

All told, these factors coalesce into a weak economic case in favour of copyright terms in excess of 25 years. Further extensions yield immaterial effects on *ex ante* incentives to create, but fetter future expressive content by restricting the public domain. Moreover, retroactive extensions are categorically inefficient, unless congestion externalities exist. For these reasons, it is dubious that such externalities justify lengthy or perpetual copyright protection.

The economic case against this is strong. One might be forgiven, then, for supposing that the state would not extend terms in the absence of theoretical or empirical evidence that the prevailing incentive to create is inadequate. Although term extensions are contrary to the public interest when incentives to create are sufficient, copyright holders have an incentive to lobby the government to pass laws in their favour. Such inefficient rent seeking is a key prediction of public choice theory, which suggests that interest groups will strive to capture the political process, subverting it to serve their ends rather than those of society.

Unfortunately, copyright law is a lesson in subversion of the political process. There has been a never-ending succession of term extensions, as legislatures on both sides of the Atlantic have continually extended copyright protection at the behest of those holding soon-to-expire copyrights over valuable works. A brief history of copyright reveals the dramatic nature of these extensions.

The world's first copyright act, the 1710 Statute of Anne, vested in authors a copyright term of 14 years, which would expand by an additional 14 years for authors who were alive at the expiration of the initial term. All books falling within the remit of the act would thus fall into the public domain after at most 28 years. This legislation profoundly influenced future copyright law. Indeed, the first US statute, the Copyright Act of 1790, adopted precisely the same copyright terms.

The United States expanded its initial copyright term from 14 to 28 years in 1831, such that an author could obtain a maximum of 42 years' protection. Congress then lengthened the renewal term to 28 years, thus permitting a maximum copyright duration of 56 years. The US copyright term accelerated exponentially from 1962 to 1998, as Congress extended the term eleven times in 36 years. The US Copyright Term Extension Act of 1998, grants copyright for a term of the author's life plus 70 years. The 1998 legislation was particularly controversial, given the campaign led prominently by Walt Disney because a number of the company's key characters are coming out of copyright. For that reason, critics derisively dubbed the 1998 act as the "Mickey Mouse Protection Act".

This lengthy copyright term is not unique to the United States. European Union law similarly provides authors with copyright of a duration equal to the life of the author plus 70 years. Following an extended campaign by the music industry, the EU extended copyright protection for sound recordings from 50 to 70 years in 2011. Had they not so voted, famous 1960s recordings by the Beatles, the Rolling Stones, and the Who would have fallen into the public domain. Copyright extensions of this sort, economically construed, harm the public interest.

E. Piracy Wars: File-Sharing, DRM, and ISP Injunctions

The digital technology revolution has forever changed copyright law. It has simultaneously expanded copyright scope – because every electronic use of a digital good entails making a copy – and yet has rendered content creators more vulnerable to third-party appropriation. The calibration underlying copyright law in the physical realm seems ill-suited to the distinct circumstances of the digital world. Copyright infringement is pervasive on the internet, which threatens to deprive artists and authors – for whom pecuniary returns are important – of sufficient profitability. Yet, ongoing efforts to control online use of copyrighted content threaten cumulative innovation, potentially yielding windfall returns on some copyright holders.

The ease of duplicating and disseminating digital files has given rise to a copyright war as the content sector – most prominently, the recording, film, video-game, and publishing industries – has engaged in ever-more-desperate efforts to stem the flood of online piracy. Those industries' early efforts focused on individual users who uploaded and distributed copyrighted materials, suing them for vast sums, often millions of dollars, in an effort to make an example out of them and thus to deter infringement by others. These enforcement actions were not well received by the public. In many instances, the industries did themselves no favours by suing sympathetic defendants, including children and grandparents, as well as non-infringers whom the industries had misidentified.

Notwithstanding the scale and prominence of these lawsuits, and the lofty damages sought by copyright holders, the industries strategy of suing individual consumers was doomed to failure. The odds of even a large-scale distributor of copyrighted material being sued were remote. The fact that most cases settled out of court in four-figure amounts meant that the expected cost to a risk-neutral internet user of sharing copyrighted content was too small to create an adequate deterrent.

Content industries switched their efforts to peer-to-peer (P2P) networks that allowed online users to swap digital files en masse. Although these technologies were and remain equally conducive to the sharing of non-copyrighted material, the reality was that millions of users were using the P2P services to engage in wholesale infringement. The most famous P2P was Napster, which the American recording industry successfully sued for contributory infringement in 1999. After being enjoined in 2001, the company was liquidated under the US Bankruptcy Code. Alternative P2P services soon emerged, including Kazaa, Gnutella, and more recently LimeWire. The content industries have secured court orders against these services, but internet piracy remains widespread today, not least from Pirate Bay, a Swedish-based file-sharing website.

Notwithstanding the widespread opportunities for illegal downloading of copyrighted goods, private industry has been able to create a lucrative commercial market for the lawful, online sale of copyrighted content. iTunes, for instance, generated more than $10 billion in revenue in 2013 alone. Moreover, industry claims concerning the extent of the financial losses from piracy are probably inflated. As a matter of economics, illegally downloading protected content harms the copyright holder only if it deprives them of a sale that would otherwise have occurred. If the downloader's reservation price for the good exceeds the good's marginal cost of production, which is close to zero, but is less than the market price for the good, downloading does not harm the copyright holder.

The piracy war has recently focused on Internet Service Providers ("ISPs"), as content industries attempt to secure their assistance in preventing infringement by ISP customers. Those industries have sought a "three-strikes" approach in which ISPs monitor their customers' activities, and impose a series of sanctions for successive instances of uncorrected infringement. Such sanctions might include bandwidth limitation and account suspension. These efforts have been controversial, particularly due to their invasion of web users' privacy and what many consider to be a fundamental right to online access. In the US, ISPs have agreed to implement a copyright alert system, pursuant to which serial offenders will find their internet connection speed reduced. In Ireland, the country's biggest ISP, Eircom, agreed in 2009 to implement a "three strikes" policy that would ultimately result in disconnection after it was sued by a number of prominent content creators, including Warner Music Group, Universal Music Group, and Sony. In 2011, the European Court of Justice ruled that monitoring web users for copyright infringement constituted an impermissible invasion of privacy.

Later the same year, the Data Protection Commissioner ordered Eircom to cease this policy, which order the High Court overruled in 2012. Such legal wrangling will no doubt be representative of the difficulties that lie ahead as copyright holders vie to limit unauthorised downloading and opponents fight to maintain an open internet. As noted above, the debate reached its crescendo in the US in 2011 with the failed attempt to pass two pieces of legislation, SOPA and PIPA, which would have authorised copyright holders to secure injunctions against ISPs in certain circumstances.

The last means of protection available to content creators is known as digital rights management ("DRM"), which is a technology that prevents users of digital files from using, copying, or distributing them without authorisation. To the extent DRM technology works, it transforms public goods into quasi-private goods, by rendering them excludable. This is not necessarily desirable. The reader will recall that a benefit of digital goods is their capacity for flawless and costless re-creation, which permits the satisfaction of all consumer demand. The economic goal is to provide content creators with just enough to warrant their investing in *ex ante* creation, and then to place the relevant expression in the public domain. If DRM is effective, it potentially allows authors and artists to capture a great deal more social value than that. This deprives consumers of low-cost or free access to valuable works and limits the positive spill-over effects that feed creative expression. The fact that legislators have passed statutes criminalising attempts to hack DRM compounds the problem if there is no accompanying exception for circumvention for the purpose of fair-use copying. The US Digital Millennium Copyright Act contains no such exception, which facilitates a worrying extension of copyright scope.

In any event, DRM is unlikely to solve the problem of widespread, online dissemination of copyrighted content. The technology irritates consumers – a recent, unpopular example involves video-game DRM that required gamers to maintain a constant internet connection to keep playing – thus reducing demand for the protected work in the first place. Furthermore, hackers devise new methods of circumventing DRM technologies almost as quickly as content industries invent them, which limits their ability to prevent piracy.

F. Conclusion

As this three-chapter discussion of innovation policy draws to a close, it is fitting to revisit the economics of inventions and expressive works. The principal economic justification for intellectual property laws is public goods. If technology and artistic expression are costly to create but easy to appropriate, there will be an inadequate amount of innovation. The problem is familiar fare to the economic analysis of law. Like the cases of tort, contract, property, crime, litigation, and competition addressed in this book, the issue lies in externalities or, in the terminology of the Coase Theorem, bargain failure. Unlike those other cases, however, the externalities accompanying technology and expression are positive, leading to too little innovation. As with the other subjects addressed in this book, the solution lies in narrowing the gap between private and social utility. The intellectual property laws accomplish this by granting property rights to inventors, authors, and artists, thus permitting them to extract a greater proportion of the social value of their discoveries and creations.

The devil, of course, is in the detail, and the problem for policymakers is to identify each innovator's *ex ante* reservation return. There is no workable mechanism by which to accomplish this goal, as the necessary information is private to each artist, author, and inventor. Nevertheless, there are basic steps that governments should take to limit windfall profits inuring to innovators. With respect to copyright, policymakers should circumscribe today's excessive terms. Jurisdictions that have yet to embrace the fair-use doctrine should do so. Finally, the law should introduce registration requirements, which would expand the public domain while preserving the incentive-generating function of the copyright system.

Key Points

- Copyright's economic role is to spur artistic expression by limiting third-party appropriation. Exclusive rights allow artists to capture more of their works' social value, thus inducing them to create in circumstances where otherwise they would not.
- Proprietary control of expression, however, carries costs.

  o Artistic endeavours are cumulative, improving prior work and drawing on it for inspiration. Since the universe of literature, music, and art is the principal input in future expression, granting authors vetoes over the use of their work stymies future creation. In short, in a static setting, copyright shrinks the public domain.

  o Copyright can also bestow authors and artists with economic market power, enabling them to charge supracompetitive prices, which create deadweight loss. The static inefficiency may be severe for digital goods susceptible of flawless and costless recreation.

- Many incentives other than copyright drive artistic expression. The innate urge to self-expression, competition, social norms, pursuit of status, altruism, and many other factors can spur the creation of expressive works. Where copyright is unnecessary to create incentives to create, its enforcement can reduce social welfare.

  o Open systems free of proprietary rights may be the best incubators of creation in certain settings. For instance, innovation flourished in the early days of the Internet based on TCP/IP protocols that no one owned.

- The public-goods theory justifying copyright is greatest with respect to investment-heavy creation that third parties can easily appropriate, such as the commercial film and video-game industries.
- Copyright scope has expanded over time, simultaneously enhancing incentives to create, the social costs of monopoly, and the portion of existing works that do not lie in the public domain.

  o The economic goal is to adjust copyright scope to achieve the optimal balance between these factors.

  o Particularly valuable adjustments expand the public domain without materially reducing incentives to create. For instance, registration and notice requirements induce the portion of artists/authors for whom copyright is important to self-select into protection. Creators who express themselves for non-pecuniary reasons may not go to the trouble, thus making their expressive material free for the world to enjoy.

- Fair use and fair dealing are doctrines that limit copyright scope. Their economic function is to facilitate socially valuable third-party use of expression in high transaction-cost settings.

  o Fair use is likely superior to fair dealing as a public-policy tool because its flexibility allows courts to permit copying expression in new circumstances that the legislature could not have envisioned.

- Present copyright terms of the life of the author plus seventy years are economically excessive, absent congestion externalities. Discount rates mean that the increment in protection from, say, 50 to 70 years is negligible to a present-day author contemplating an expressive work.

 ## References and Further Reading

Books
Landes, William M. and Posner, Richard A., *The Economic Structure of Intellectual Property Law* (2003) Ch. 6.

Lessig, Larry, *Free Culture: How Big Media Uses Technology and the Law to Lock Down Culture and Control Creativity* (2004).
Miceli, Thomas J., *The Economic Approach to Law*, 2nd edn (2008) p. 183.
Posner, Richard A., *Economic Analysis of Law* (2011) pp. 52–59.
Shavell, Steven, *Foundations of Economic Analysis of Law* (2004) pp. 138–50, 155–59.

Articles
Adelstein, R.P. and Peretz, S.I., 'The competition of technologies in the market for ideas: Copyright and fair use in evolutionary perspective' (1985) 5 Int'l Rev Law & Econ 209.
Besen, Stanley M., and Kirby, Sheila Nataraj, 'Private copying, appropriability, and optimal copyright royalties' (1989) 32 JL & Econ 225.
Boyle, James, 'Cruel, mean, or lavish? Economic analysis, price discrimination and digital intellectual property' (2007) 53 Vand L Rev 53.
Breyer, Stephen, 'Copyright: A rejoinder' (1972) 20 UCLA L Rev 75.
Breyer, Stephen, 'The uneasy case for copyright: A study of copyright in books, photocopies and computer programs' (1970) 84 Harv L Rev 281.
Cooter, Robert, 'Expressive law and economics' (1998) 27 J Legal Stud 585.
Dam, Kenneth W., 'Some economic considerations in the intellectual property protection of software' (1995) 24 J Legal Stud 321.
Easterbrook, Frank H., 'Intellectual property is still property' (1990) 13 Harv JL & Pub. Pol'y 108.
Ginsburg, Jane C., 'Creation and commercial value: Copyright protection of works of information' (1990) 90 Colum L Rev 1865.
Gordon, Wendy J., 'Fair use as market failure: A structural and economic analysis of the betamax case and its predecessors' (1982) 82 Colum L Rev 1600.
Hurt, Robert H. and Schuchman, Robert M., 'The economic rationale of copyright' (1966) 56 Am Econ Rev 421.
Johnson, William R., 'The economics of copying' (1985) 93 J Political Econ 158.
Landes, William M. and Posner, Richard A., 'An economic analysis of copyright law' (1989) 18 J Legal Stud 325.
Leval, Pierre, 'Toward a fair use standard' (1990) 103 Harv L Rev 1105.
Liebowitz, Stan J., 'File-sharing: Creative destruction or just plain destruction?' (2006) 49 JL & Econ 1.
Merges, Robert, 'Of property rules, Coase, and intellectual property' (1994) 94 Colum L Rev 2655.
Oberholzer, Felix and Strumpf, Koleman, 'The effect of file sharing on record sales: An empirical analysis' (2004) 115 J Political Econ 1.
Stanley M. Besen, Kirby, Sheila N. and Steven, C., 'An economic analysis of copyright collectives' (1992) 78 Va L Rev 383.
Varian, Hal, 'Copying and copyright' (2005) 19 J Econ Persp 121.
Zentner, Alejandro, 'Measuring the effect of music downloads on music purchases' (2006) 49 JL & Econ 63.

Part 8

Competition Law and Natural Monopoly Regulation

1	Antitrust and The Regulation of Business Strategy	303
2	Antitrust Limits on Contract	334
3	Monopolisation	348
4	The Regulation of Natural Monopoly	370

Chapter 1

Antitrust and The Regulation of Business Strategy

Chapter Contents

A.	Introduction: The Economic Role of Competition Policy	304
B.	The Evolving Schools of Antitrust Economics	305
C.	The Economics of Competition and Monopoly	309
D.	Industrial Organisation: Imperfectly Competitive Markets	314
E.	The Role of the Market: Definition, Power, and Self-Correction	323
Key Points		330
References and Further Reading		332

A. Introduction: The Economic Role of Competition Policy

Left to their own devices, firms would eliminate competition to earn monopoly profits at consumers' expense. Antitrust law protects the economy by prohibiting contracts and unilateral behaviour designed to suppress rivalry. More than 100 countries now have competition laws that proscribe price-fixing cartels, monopolisation, and other harmful restraints of trade.

Prohibiting anticompetitive practices may seem straightforward, but regulating business strategy both to encourage competition and to deter harmful practices is difficult. Commercial behaviour is almost limitless in its variety and is always evolving. Due to that complexity, it is easy to confuse efficient conduct and harmful behaviour. The principal tool that antitrust policymakers use to scrutinise business strategies is economics. They look to price- and game-theoretic models to understand the likely effects of impugned conduct, and use empirical methods to determine the consequences of behaviour already undertaken. As a result, antitrust has grown in economic sophistication over the last several decades, so much so indeed that – to a significant degree – antitrust has become a field of applied economics. This Part explores economic principles relevant to competition policy, explaining antitrust law's economic purpose and analysing a variety of business phenomena.

Before addressing the economics of competition law and exploring the schools of thought that have influenced this field, it is first necessary to address antitrust's purpose. At a broad level, the role is axiomatic: to promote competition. The conviction that competition is desirable lies at the heart of antitrust policy. When companies strive to outdo each other by developing new and better products, lowering prices, increasing operational efficiency, and reducing costs, tremendous gains ensue for consumers and the economy alike.

Commentators widely accept, though not universally, that economic efficiency is the principal goal of US antitrust law. On this view, liberalising markets to enable firms to innovate and compete – but modestly limiting firms' freedom of operation under the antitrust laws – increases wealth, economic growth, and international competitiveness, while reducing inflation. Competition causes price to drop toward marginal cost, allowing consumers to purchase products or services that they value more than they cost society to provide. This effect not only promotes consumer welfare, it enhances the amount of wealth in society. Similarly, Darwinian competition forces companies to make the most efficient possible use of scarce inputs, getting more from less, thus freeing up resources that society can use elsewhere. Construed in this way, antitrust serves a function that goes arm in arm with economic theory. A competition policy founded on maximising efficiency finds its direction in microeconomic theory.

Yet, in some quarters, policymakers understand competition to serve an end other than efficiency. Some view dispersion of economic power as a valuable goal. The concentration of wealth in the hands of a few may negatively affect democracy, equity, and equality of opportunity. By ensuring that companies do not grow to the point that they inhibit access to markets and consumers, competition law can serve a goal independent of efficiency. This perspective has been particularly influential in the development of EU competition law. Ordoliberal thought, which emphasises individual freedom, underlies antitrust jurisprudence of the European courts and Commission, especially under Article 102 of the Treaty on the Functioning of the European Union (TFEU). Much more so than US antitrust, EU competition law places a "special responsibility" on dominant firms not to abuse their positions, such as by restricting competitors' or consumers' freedom of action. In Europe, claims of efficiency may sometimes be inadequate to justify restraints seen as inhibiting access to markets and consumers.

Problems emerge, however, when efficiency and goals such as the diffusion of economic power come into tension. Especially in the new economy, which innovation and information goods characterise, efficiency may be associated not with an atomised market structure, but with a series of ephemeral monopolies in the manner envisioned by Joseph Schumpeter.[1] If policymakers dismantle dominant firms in technology industries, or impose broad duties to deal, the result will be higher price competition in the short term, but potentially reduced innovation and investment in the long term. The appropriate policy turns, in part, on how one understands the purpose of antitrust law.

The next section explores how competition rules have developed over time, and explains why policymakers sometimes disagree on the appropriate response to certain forms of business conduct.

B. The Evolving Schools of Antitrust Economics

1. The limits of economics

Competition law is a form of passive regulation that limits freedom of contract to ensure that firms do not usurp market processes for their private advantage. It is a daunting challenge. Business conduct takes myriad forms, and it is not easy to ascertain whether a given restraint promotes or harms competition. Even if a restraint is anticompetitive, one must determine whether intervention is cost justified given the expense and duration of judicial or regulatory proceedings. Empirical data may be the best way to determine the propensity of commercial behaviour to injure competitive processes, but they are not always available. In their absence, the law must rely on theory to predict the effects of challenged restraints.

That is a fraught exercise because no single theory can hope to model the countless incentives that buffet firm and consumer decision making at the individual level. Nor can theory yield empirically falsifiable answers where the necessary counterfactual is unobservable, as is often the case. For instance, if one asks whether the law should require a network owner to share its infrastructure with its rivals at a price set by a third party, the answer turns on whether the short-term boost to competition made possible by mandatory sharing exceeds the potential – though uncertain – long-term costs to incentives to invest if the access price is too low. Theory can outline the nature of the possible benefits and costs, but it cannot identify the optimal rule. Due to uncertainty about the constitution of ideal competition laws, regulators often rely – if only implicitly – on politically and historically shaped assumptions concerning markets' ability to self-correct and the tendency of private enterprise, unrestrained, to promote or injure social welfare.

It is on account of economics' limits – and jurisdictions' differing experiences with markets, state oversight, and competition – that distinct schools of antitrust economics have evolved, and notable divergences between the world's various antitrust regimes have emerged. Nevertheless, it is hard to underestimate the impact of economics on competition policy and easy to overstate the differences between the antitrust "schools" that have developed over the last several decades. There is now broad consensus among policymakers that economics yields important answers to many antitrust problems. Most experts agree that an evidence-based approach to competition law is ideal, and that microeconomic and game-theoretic models usefully illuminate the optimal rule of decision where empirics are unavailable. The modern schools of antitrust – namely, the Chicago, post-Chicago, and neo-Chicago schools – bear modest differences, and indeed one can readily construe the neo-Chicago school as being a contemporary version of Chicago. The exception lies in the behavioural antitrust movement, which, though lying in the periphery of competition policy, is quite distinct.

This section now discusses the relevant schools of antitrust that have influenced competition policymaking in the last half century.

---

1 Joseph Schumpeter, *Capitalism, Socialism, and Democracy* (1942) p. 83.

2. The Harvard School

The "Harvard School" is a structuralist approach to competition policy that held sway in the United States from the 1930s to the 1960s, which has influenced the development of EU competition law. The structuralist view derives from the Cournot theory of oligopoly, explored below, which links the number of firms in an industry to the efficiency of market outcomes.[2] Its essential insight was that concentrated industries – those in which few firms compete – cause market power, low output, high prices, and inefficiency. The ensuing paradigm came to be known as the Structure–Conduct–Performance ("SCP") model because it linked market structure (e.g. a concentrated market subject to entry barriers) to firm conduct (e.g. tacit collusion – otherwise known as "conscious parallelism" – between strategically interdependent firms in an oligopolistic market) to economic performance (supracompetitive prices and inefficiency).

The SCP approach lent itself to a straightforward policy prescription: governments could improve market efficiency by reducing concentration. This view informed an aggressive antitrust policy, aimed at remedying not just conduct (which is but a function of industry) but the structure of the market itself. The Harvard School thus looked unfavourably on mergers that increased concentration, emphasised defendants' market share, and required no more than modest showings of exclusionary behaviour in monopolisation cases because market structure itself suggested anti-competitive conduct.

The SCP approach was influential in America, particularly during the Warren Court's inhospitable approach to antitrust in the 1950s and 1960s, and was evident in the US Department of Justice's 1968 Merger Guidelines. It also influenced the formation of EU competition law, which took a structural approach to antitrust problems in the first several decades of its existence – a trait that continues to characterise parts of EU competition policy, especially dominant-firm conduct. European law focuses, for example, on market share rather than entry barriers, views increasing concentration with suspicion, and (as evidenced in the then Court of First Instance's 2007 decision in *Microsoft*) is more willing to impose mandatory sharing obligations in an effort to improve industry structure. These features distinguish today's EU competition rules from those of the US.

The SCP literature bore a notable empirical component, which Section D below briefly summarises. In short, Harvard scholars tried to validate their theory by showing that firms in concentrated industries earned greater rates of return than those in competitive markets. Their studies revealed that profits and concentration positively correlate with one another. This showing, in conjunction with the intuitive nature of the Harvard School's policy conclusions, convinced policymakers for several decades that anticompetitive outcomes were principally a structural problem, and that an interventionist competition policy aimed at reducing market concentration was appropriate. It was not until the emergence of the Chicago School that a more permissive approach to antitrust law, founded on microeconomic theory, took hold.

3. The Chicago School

The price-theoretic approach to antitrust law is today the dominant methodology for analysing competition problems in the United States and is influential in Europe. It took centre stage in the 1970s when economists, particularly those affiliated with the University of Chicago and UCLA, discredited the SCP paradigm and scrutinised antitrust doctrine using neoclassical economics. In Chicagoans' view, the SCP approach was descriptive, rather than analytic, and thus of limited use in predicting the future effects of restraints of trade.

---

2 "Oligopoly" refers to an industry in which there are a small number of firms, each of which can materially affect market price and output, such that each firm's profit-maximisation choice depends on the anticipated actions of rivals.

The Chicago School assaulted the SCP view that high profits in concentrated industries evidence anticompetitive market power. On the contrary, it pointed out, industries subject to scale economies will naturally result in high levels of concentration. Antitrust intervention aimed at reducing concentration would thus harm productive efficiency. Moreover, equating accounting and economic profits is a mistake, not least because the former does not account for risk. Furthermore, even in concentrated markets, supply-side constraints can limit market power if entry barriers are low. This critique seriously undermined the unadulterated structuralist view. Although market structure remains a material part of modern competition law, many economists today view the classic SCP paradigm as discredited.

The measure of a school of thought, of course, lies not in tearing down what came before, but in providing a superior theory with which to guide enforcement. The principal tool of the Chicago School is neoclassical price theory. Armed with that analytic tool, Chicago scholars inherited an antitrust jurisprudence suspicious of market concentration and distrustful of novel business practices that did not lend themselves to obvious explanations. The Warren Court had fashioned prohibitory rules against a wide variety of vertical restraints, including product tying, bundling, minimum and maximum resale price maintenance, and even territorial restrictions that a manufacturer might impose on its retailers. Certain joint ventures were deemed *per se* illegal, and the law took a hard line against perceived acts of predatory pricing by large firms. The US Supreme Court had even construed section 7 of the Clayton Act to forbid mergers between firms possessing no market power in industries experiencing increased concentration.

Subjecting these rules to microeconomic analysis, Chicago economists found judicial understanding of economic phenomena to be facile and lacking in rigour. Chicago School empiricists – George Stigler, in particular – analysed the effects of vertical restraints, block-booking practices, scale economies, the effects of the antitrust laws, and more. As the movement grew, it ushered in an era of liberalisation, as economists revealed that business conduct presumed to be anticompetitive lent itself to benign explanations often founded in efficiency. Neoclassical economists analysed a host of impugned restraints within the framework of rational utility maximisation, deriving results suggesting that ostensibly anticompetitive business practices were actually efficient.

Neoclassical economics has yielded far too many nuanced insights into industrial organisation to recount in detail, but some notable contributions stand out. For instance, a profit-maximising manufacturer would impose vertical restraints on its distributors only if doing so would either lower the cost, or improve the quality, of distribution. A dealer-imposed price or territorial restriction, far from being infected with anticompetitive effect, is presumptively efficient. Firms can form joint ventures to achieve together what none could achieve alone, suggesting that ancillary restraints on competition should be lawful if required to effect the arrangement and no more restrictive than necessary. Vertical integration, and hence product tying and bundling, eliminate negative externalities occasioned by disaggregated ownership of complements. Bundling complementary goods in a single sale reduces search and negotiation costs, but in fixed proportions cannot create additional monopoly power because consumer rationality would make any attempt to earn a second monopoly mark-up profit-reducing.

Mergers effecting modest changes in market concentration are unlikely to yield unilateral or co-ordinated effects in light of models indicating profit-maximising responses to attempted exercises of market power by firms with limited market share. For the same reason, exclusionary conduct by dominant firms is unlikely to succeed. Predatory pricing, for instance, would attract entry *ex post* because the entrant would know that the incumbent's profit-maximising reaction would be to share the market.

Although the Chicago School is sceptical that unilateral conduct generally harms consumers, the movement is not opposed to antitrust enforcement. It takes a hard line against price-fixing cartels and mergers to monopoly, for instance, and has laid the economic groundwork for demonstrating how dominant firms could raise their rivals' costs. Critics sometimes wrongly conflate the school's scepticism with denial.

The Chicago School's impact was transformative. As a result of rational-choice theory's insights, a consensus has emerged in the United States that microeconomics lies at the heart of antitrust analysis. In analysing the propriety of a challenged restraint, predictive models and empirical investigation invariably focus on whether the business practice at issue is apt to yield durable price increases over the "but for" world. Indeed, "beginning in the 1980s . . . [e]fficiency became the only generally accepted goal of antitrust".[3] Importantly, the impact of the Chicago School is by no means limited to the United States: EU competition law relies heavily on economics and has done more so over time: an evolution for which the Chicago School is largely responsible.

4. The Post-Chicago school

The Chicago School's contribution to competition policy is hard to understate, and its enduring legacy lies in antitrust's deep-rooted commitment to the economic method. Nevertheless, some of those espousing the neoclassical view were too sanguine about their pro-market beliefs, resulting in an excessive swing away from the uncritical hostility to business practices that had defined the preceding era. Further research after the 1970s led to refined economic models – many of them founded on game theory – demonstrating that some business practices, previously thought innocuous by Chicagoans, could actually harm competition. For instance, information asymmetries may allow dominant firms strategically to exclude competition, in particular by raising rivals' costs, or to exercise monopoly power in aftermarkets populated by locked-in consumers. Sufficient scale economies may allow an incumbent to exclude equally efficient competitors, even by pricing above cost, a phenomenon known as limit pricing. Models of imperfect competition proliferated, suggesting that a rule of *per se* legality was improper in most settings.

Nevertheless, the post-Chicago literature did not suggest that most business conduct, even by large firms, was suspect. On the contrary, game-theoretic models showing that certain practices were capable of excluding equally or more-efficient competitors depended on restrictive assumptions unlikely to be met in the real world. Post-Chicago scholarship thus painted a more complicated picture than the neoclassical models that preceded it – one recognising that anticompetitive effects were the exception rather than the rule and that many traditionally suspect unilateral actions were efficient, but granting that harmful consequences were sometimes possible. The post-Chicago School thus supports the US rule of reason, which subjects challenged restraints to exhaustive scrutiny to determine their overall effect.

Despite the enhanced theoretical vision that the post-Chicago movement made possible, it suffered from a flaw that similarly afflicts the contemporary behavioural movement. Unlike the deductive methodology that the Chicago School employed, post-Chicago models did not yield predictions susceptible to empirical testing. The value of the post-Chicago movement, then, stands in tempering claims that theory necessarily predicts market self-correction, and in elucidating the theoretical circumstances in which dominant firms can raise rivals' costs. The game theory emblematic of this account is now a staple of modern antitrust analysis, resting comfortably alongside the price-theoretic models residing at the heart of the Chicago School. In short, the post-Chicago contribution was one of incremental adjustment, reaffirming the economic insight that much business conduct that the Warren Court condemned had pro-competitive rationales.

Finally, it bears noting that the post-Chicago School has been especially influential in Europe, which has often justified taking a hard line on abusive behaviour by dominant firms by referring

---

3 Richard A. Posner, *The Problematics of Moral and Legal Theory* (1999) p. 229.

to economic models showing that exclusionary practices may be both rational and effective in at least some circumstances.

5. Neo-Chicago

Some academics have recently come to speak of a "Neo-Chicago School" of antitrust. Its prominent characteristics include combining neoclassical price theory with game theory and error analysis built on weighing the relative harm of Type I errors (accidentally condemning efficient conduct) and Type II errors (mistakenly permitting anticompetitive behaviour). It is unclear whether this is in fact a distinct school of competition economics, as opposed to a modest evolution of the Chicago and post-Chicago literature outlined above.

6. Behavioural antitrust

A final note on the Chicago method is important. Neoclassical economics is deductive, which means that it reasons from theoretical norms to conclusions that one then tests empirically. It operates from the premise that economic actors maximise their preferences subject only to their budgetary or other constraints, such as imperfect information. By assuming rationality, economists can extrapolate conclusions about the likely behaviour of those actors. This process of drawing conclusions from background premises is the defining characteristic of a predictive theory. Deductive analysis thus involves hypothesising (i.e. predicting) future conduct from a theoretical framework. It reasons from assumptions and axioms to anticipated truth. Importantly, empiricism plays a critical role here. Evidence-based inquiry serves not as the foundation of the theory, but as the means by which to evaluate it. Ultimately, theory proves itself through a single barometer of quality: the degree to which its predictions track real-world outcomes.

In this way, neoclassical economics contrasts with inductive analysis, the starting point of which is empirical. Through statistical analysis, surveys, and experiments, economists engaging in inductive analysis aggregate data from which they draw general conclusions. The Harvard School's SCP paradigm is a good example. The inductive process begins with empiricism, which is where the deductive method ends. There is nothing wrong with inductive analysis; its efficacy depends, however, on the ability to craft a theory from empirical observations.

A new school of antitrust thought, known as behavioural antitrust, adopts an inductive approach to problems in competition law. As Chapter 9 below explores in more depth, behaviouralists look to cognitive psychology to understand how people and firms actually make choices. Behavioural scholars reject what they consider to be the unrealistic assumptions of neoclassical theory, observing that companies and especially consumers often behave irrationally. Instead, behavioural antitrust scholars look to cognitive biases that lead economic actors to make decisions contrary to those that expected-value theory predicts. For instance, the endowment effect causes people to value what they own more than equivalent items they do not, thus cementing consumer lock-in for post-sales service.

Behavioural antitrust is in its incipiency, and the scholarly literature addressing is, as yet, undeveloped. Its principal contribution thus far has been to focus attention on empirics rather than theory, reminding competition policymakers not to tie themselves slavishly to mathematically attractive theories in the neoclassical tradition when the evidence runs counter to model projections.

C. The Economics of Competition and Monopoly

Antitrust fosters competition by eliminating firm-created restraints on trade. It does so because economic theory shows that competition promotes social welfare, while monopoly detracts from it. As with other areas of law explored in this book, antitrust cures a market failure stemming from stakeholders' inability to contract with one another at no cost.

Purveyors and purchasers of goods have conflicting interests. Sellers wish to maximise profit, while buyers seek the lowest possible prices. Transaction costs typically preclude each participant in a market from contracting with every other to ensure optimal outcomes. The economic problem is thus one of incompatible preferences. To solve such conflicting claims within the sphere of law and economics, one would ask how stakeholders would have resolved their conflicting interests in a hypothetical, *ex ante*, zero-bargaining cost environment. The reader will recall that, in such a situation, the Coase Theorem suggests that the parties would bargain to an efficient outcome.

Economics explains that competition between sellers does more than transfer wealth to consumers; it increases the amount of value in society. The choice between monopoly and competition is not a zero-sum game. Consistent with the Coase Theorem, then, prospective stakeholders negotiating freely would embrace competition. Consumers would compensate sellers for their foregone monopoly profits, but would still be better off themselves. The ensuing outcome of perfect competition would be Pareto optimal. Armed with that economic insight, policymakers can enact laws in the form of antitrust rules that foster competition. Although competitive markets will not compensate manufacturers and distributors deprived of the opportunity to charge monopoly prices, the outcome will nevertheless be Kaldor-Hicks efficient.

1. Perfect competition

The economic model of perfect competition is a useful analytic baseline, though real-life markets never attain that state. Perfectly competitive industries involve atomised competition on both the selling and purchasing sides of the market. Thus, there are many vendors and buyers, none of whom wields any individual power over the market price. The goods being bought and sold are homogeneous (i.e. identical) and there are no fixed costs or barriers to entry or exit. Each market participant enjoys perfect, symmetrical access to information.

In such a situation, any person who tries to sell a good at a price higher than what another vendor offers will encounter no demand for the product, and will thus be unable to make any sales. Demand is therefore perfectly elastic. The minimum price at which any seller would rationally sell is the marginal cost of producing one more unit. At any lower price, the vendor would be better off not making the extra product and would thus cease further production.

It follows that an industry bearing the above attributes can bear just one price: one that equals firms' marginal cost of production. Thus, any company failing to achieve an incremental cost of manufacturing and distribution equal to that of its competitors will be priced out of the market, and will have to exit. That is why "antitrust and bankruptcy go hand-in-hand".[4] Perfect competition thus fosters "productive efficiency," which means that sellers use the socially optimal number and quality of inputs in the production and distribution processes. Every company in equilibrium produces at "minimum efficient scale" – the lowest point of its long-term average-cost curve. As such inputs are scarce, anything saved through productive efficiency gains becomes available for use elsewhere in the economy.

The concept of marginal cost bears an important attribute from the perspective of social welfare. Consumers prefer a greater number of products and services than fewer, but it is efficient for consumers to acquire them only if their willingness-to-buy price exceeds the marginal cost to society of making those goods and services. If it costs £10 to manufacture and deliver an additional widget, but the marginal consumer will not pay more than £8 for it, then it is wasteful for society

---

4 Frank H. Easterbrook, 'When is it worthwhile to use courts to search for exclusionary conduct?' (2003) Colum Bus L Rev 345, 345–346.

to produce it. Perfect competition is desirable from this perspective because it results in allocative efficiency. This means that every consumer who values the competitively priced good at or beyond its incremental cost of production will acquire it. The following graphs illustrate the long-term equilibrium in a perfectly competitive market:

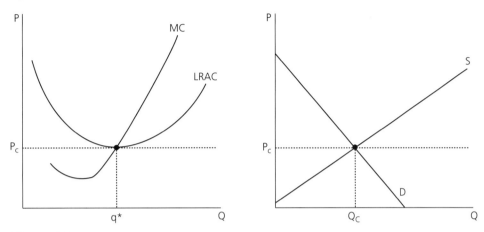

Figure 8.1

The graph on the left shows the situation facing each individual firm, while that on the right demonstrates the market outcome. Under perfect competition, each surviving firm must produce the quantity, $q*$, which minimises its long-term average cost, and can sell its products for no more than its marginal cost of production, P_C (the competitive price). As the graph on the right illustrates, the long-term output equilibrium lies at Q_c with price equal to P_C.

2. Monopoly

In a monopoly, just one company sells a product or service for which no adequate substitute exists at the competitive price level. An important prerequisite of monopoly are entry barriers, which prevent third parties from entering the market to compete with the incumbent and to avail of supracompetitive pricing. The best example of such barriers is government-controlled entry – when the state limits the number of competitors in a market. When there is but a single purveyor of a desirable good, and no actual or potential competition, the monopolist's demand curve is the same as the industry demand curve. As the monopolist wishes to maximise profit, it will create an artificial scarcity in the market to increase the marginal revenue it derives from each sale and hence its margin. The seller will restrict output to the point that producing one less unit would reduce its profit because the resulting drop in demand would outweigh the greater revenue per sale. Economists identify this profit-maximising point as the price–output combination: marginal cost equals marginal revenue.

Output restriction is the primary economic evil of monopoly. Increasing price beyond marginal cost inefficiently prices some consumers out of the market. The result is deadweight loss, which represents a foregone value that society could have realised, but did not. Deadweight loss means that monopoly is allocatively inefficient.

To illustrate the costs of monopoly, consider the following example. The market demand curve is $P = 100 - Q$, such that consumers will buy 40 units at a price of 60; 70 units at a price of 30; and so on. For simplicity, assume that there are no fixed costs, and that the marginal cost of production is constant at 10. Thus, a firm must spend £10 to manufacture and sell one more good.

The following graph demonstrates this market, showing the outcome under perfect competition. As the reader will recall, such competition causes price to equal marginal cost. Thus, the

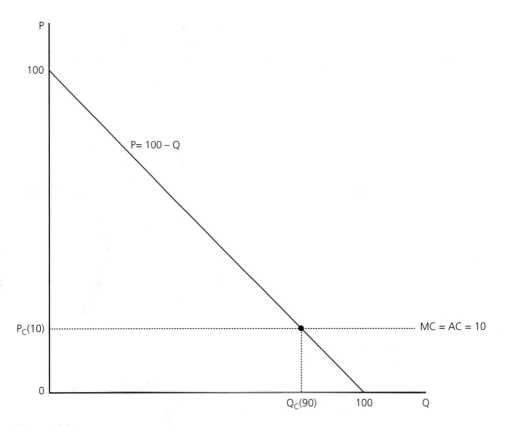

Figure 8.2

market will produce 90 units at a price of £10. Producer surplus (the economic profit that manufacturers in the industry earn) is zero, while consumer surplus is £4,050 (the area under the demand curve and above the marginal-cost curve).

The outcome is different under monopoly. The demand curve facing a monopolist is the industry demand curve, P = 100 − Q. By assumption, firms maximise profits. A monopolist would do so as follows: First, its profit (Π) equals its total revenue minus total costs. Total revenue equals the price charged for each good (P) multiplied by the quantity of goods sold (Q). Total cost equals the number of products built (Q) multiplied by the average marginal cost of making those goods (MC), plus any fixed costs. Thus, Π = P.Q − (Q.MC + FC). Plugging in the numbers, Π = (100 − Q).Q − (10Q + 0) = 90Q − Q².

To maximise profits, one would differentiate this profit function with respect to Q and set the first derivative equal to zero. Thus, dΠ/dQ = 90 − 2Q = 0. The profit-maximising quantity, Q_M, equals 45, and the monopoly price, P_M, equals 55 (see Figure 8.3).

The reader can immediately appreciate the differences between monopoly and competition. The most serious economic problem is deadweight loss. By reducing supply, thus creating an artificial scarcity, the monopolist can charge a price (55), which exceeds marginal cost (10), and thus earn positive economic profits. Consumers are worse off, and the monopolist is better off, by £2,025. There is not simply a wealth transfer, however, from consumers to the dominant firm. The 1–2–3 triangle represents a loss of value, here equal to £1,012.50, which represents the foregone gains that society would have reaped "but for" the exercise of monopoly power. There is a net loss to society.

There is a further cost that the preceding graph does not illustrate. Supracompetitive profits

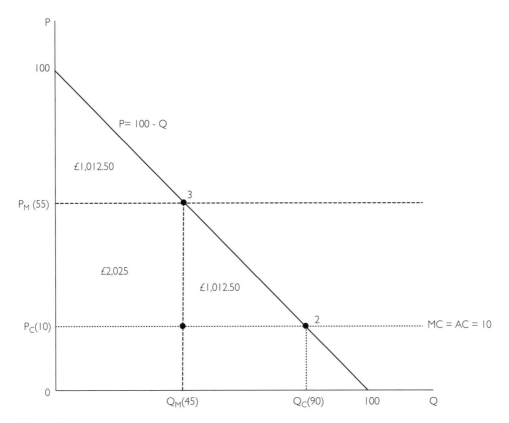

Figure 8.3

induce would-be monopolists to compete for the prize of the dominant position. If such competition duplicates capital with no positive spill over effects, it is socially wasteful. The race to obtain a monopoly is thus another example of rent-seeking.[5] In the limit, prospective monopolists would rationally convert the entire expected monopoly surplus into money spent trying to attain a dominant position. This is, of course, productively inefficient.

In sum, the differences between competition and monopoly create a strong prescription in favour of the former. The next two chapters explore the antitrust rules that governments have enacted to promote competition. Before engaging in this analysis, however, a prefatory issue remains: why not simply regulate prices?

The answer informs the role and limits of competition policy. Antitrust rules are passive, rather than affirmative. They prohibit behaviour destructive of competition, but do not compel conduct that maximises it. For example, a company can lawfully acquire or maintain a monopoly, and charge monopoly prices.[6] One might ask why this is the case if monopoly is, as just presented, undesirable. In fact, there are important reasons why competition law might not always require efficient market pricing. In particular, assailing the monopoly prize may suppress competition.

Ultimately, antitrust is a complementary tool that assists the market. The underlying rationale is that competition will produce desirable outcomes, and there is no greater spur to competition

---

5 The first person to make this observation was Gordon Tullock in 'The welfare costs of tariffs, monopolies, and theft' (1967) 5 W Econ J 224.
6 EU competition law has an economically odd provision in TEU Art. 102 that prohibits unfairly high prices. No EU case, however, has ever applied this provision, which has no analogue in US antitrust law.

than the prospect of the monopoly reward that awaits the most successful companies. In general, this prospect will be a self-defeating prize, for the efforts of many to achieve it will result in none of them doing so. Consumers and larger society reap the benefits. It is only in circumstances where our *à priori* belief in the efficient functioning of markets no longer holds true that competition law's passive role may no longer suffice. The last chapter in this Part explores situations in which competition may be an inadequate guarantor of acceptable market outcomes. In that setting, however, policy makers may lack attractive options, for industrial regulation is itself a devilishly tricky undertaking, the historical efficacy of which inspires little confidence in governmental efforts to mimic market incentives.

D. Industrial Organisation: Imperfectly Competitive Markets

Neoclassical models of perfect competition and monopoly do not approximate real-life markets, even though they serve as an important baseline in price-theoretic analysis. Most markets are imperfectly competitive, typically being "oligopolistic". That term refers to industries in which there are sufficiently few sellers that each affects the market price and output level, and so must factor its competitors' anticipated actions into its profit-maximising decision. The economics literature devoted to studying imperfectly competitive markets is industrial organisation. This section introduces the three most famous models addressing "oligopoly", and briefly addresses empirical work in industrial organisation.

1. Cournot competition

The classic model of oligopoly is "Cournot competition". In that setting, non-colluding firms in a concentrated industry that sell homogenous goods make profit-maximising output decisions assuming that their competitors' production levels are fixed. The essential insight is that oligopolistic rivals will continue changing their output in response to one another's production levels until they reach an equilibrium. At that point, each oligopolist's expectation as to every other firm's output will be satisfied, and no further changes will take place. The model produces the intuitively pleasing result that industry output increases toward the competitive level as the number of firms competing in the market grows larger.

At one time, the Cournot model purported to be static, even though each firm moved sequentially. Today, game theory has changed the analysis to a more illuminative dynamic model, which operates as follows. Assume the simplest case, in which two companies compete. The industry demand curve is again $P = 100 - Q$, such that at a price of zero, consumers purchase 100 units, and at a price of 100, they buy none. The marginal cost of production is 10, and so it costs every firm £10 to make one extra good. The reader will recall that, under perfect competition, output would be 90, price would equal marginal cost at 10, and the outcome would be allocatively efficient with a deadweight loss of 0. The result under monopoly would be an output of 45, a price of 55, and a deadweight loss of 1012.5. These are the polar-opposite baselines.

Now suppose that there are two firms in the market. Unlike monopoly, each firm's profit-maximising output depends not on the industry demand curve, but on how much demand remains after the other company has satisfied part of it. The greater one company's production, the less demand there is for the other competitor's goods. Thus, each company uses the idea of a *residual* demand curve to determine its optimal output. Firm A's residual demand curve is $P_A = 100 - Q_A - Q_B$. Firm B's is $P_B = 100 - Q_A - Q_B$.

Suppose that Firm A believes that Firm B will produce 50 units. In that event, A's residual demand curve would be $P_A = 50 - Q_A$. Thus, A would sell 20 units at a price of 30. But B would realise that it would not make sense to make 50 units, because it would face a residual demand curve of $P_B = 80 - Q_B$. So, B would produce 35 units at a price of 45. This would, in turn, upset A's profit-maximisation calculation, leading it to identify a revised residual demand curve of $P_A = 65 - Q_A$. Thus, it would produce 27.5 units at a price of 37.5.

This process would continue until their best response functions intersect. To derive Firm A's best response function, identify A's profit, which equals total revenue minus total cost:

$$Q.P - Q.MC \text{ or } Q_A(100 - Q_A - Q_B) - 10Q_A \text{ or } 90Q_A - Q_A^2 - Q_A.Q_B.$$

To maximise profit, A would differentiate this function with respect to Q_A and equate the derivative with zero. The result would be:

$$90 - 2Q_A - Q_B = 0.$$

Thus, Firm A's optimal output is:

$$Q_A = (90 - Q_B)/2$$

and Firm B's profit-maximising output is:

$$Q_B = (90 - Q_A)/2.$$

The intersection of those best response functions is the equilibrium point:

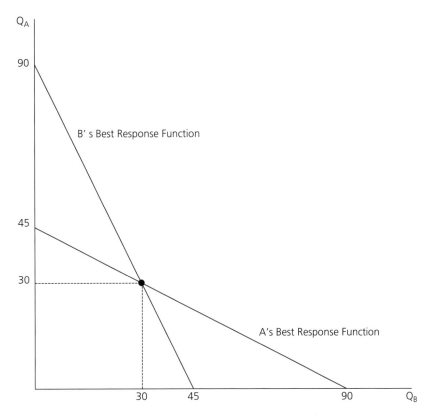

Figure 8.4

ANTITRUST AND THE REGULATION OF BUSINESS STRATEGY

In this model, the only equilibrium is for each duopolist to produce 30 units at a price of 40. Only at that point will each firm's expectation as to the other's output decision be satisfied. As each company is maximising its profit given the choice of the other firm, this result is a Nash equilibrium. Industry output of 60 is better than the monopoly output of 45, but less than the perfectly competitive outcome of 90. As the number of firms engaging in Cournot competition increases, the predicted market outcome grows progressively closer to the competitive level. Some experimental evidence supports the predictions of the Cournot model.

2. Bertrand competition

Under the Cournot model, firms set their output levels rather than the prices they charge, which seems unrealistic. The Bertrand model of oligopolistic competition yields a surprising result: assuming homogeneous products, constant marginal costs, and perfect access to information, the equilibrium is the same as under perfect competition. Oligopolists that compete on price while selling identical goods will ultimately charge an amount equal to their marginal costs of production.

What accounts for this odd result? The answer lies in the combined assumptions of homogeneity and symmetric information. If Firms A and B both sell identical goods, the only basis for consumer choice is price. If Firm A charges even a small amount less than Firm B, and has sufficient production capacity to satisfy market demand without experiencing increased marginal cost, every consumer will abandon Firm B. No matter what above marginal cost price that one oligopolist charges, its rivals can profitably steal all its sales by charging just a little bit less. The downward process continues until one arrives at the floor of marginal cost. That is why Bertrand competition rests in equilibrium at that point.

Figure 8.5 illustrates the residual demand curve facing Firm B.[7] Notice that the demand for its product turns entirely on whether Firm A's price is greater than, equal to, or less than its own. When P_B exceeds P_A, the quantity of P_B demanded is zero. When P_B equals P_A, Firms A and B share the market. When Firm B charges less than Firm A, it captures the entire market, though the lower it cuts its price the more it sells (because the demand curve slopes downward).

Although the Bertrand model's predictions are extreme, they depend on strict assumptions. When products are heterogeneous, such that consumers perceive competitors' goods differently, the model does not predict marginal-cost pricing. Nor will that result follow if oligopolists face capacity constraints that prevent them from increasing output to the point sufficient to satisfy all consumer demand. Indeed, switching or transaction costs can have the same effect. Most firms' long-term average-cost curves slope upward beyond a certain range of output, meaning that a rival charging a higher price will experience positive residual demand.

Nevertheless, the Bertrand model approximates competition in some real-life markets, particularly those involving homogeneous goods. For example, competition on certain routes in the aviation industry displays this quality, as consumers abandon airlines charging even a little more than their competitors. Some price wars in that industry have seen prices being driven down close to cost on busy routes.

3. The Stackelberg leadership model

The final traditional account of oligopolistic competition is the Stackelberg leadership model, in which one firm enjoys a first-mover advantage and sets a profit-maximising quantity à la Cournot in anticipation of what it knows the second-mover's quantity decision will be. Suppose that two firms compete in selling identical goods, they move sequentially, and the leader's output decision

---

7 Dennis W. Carlton and Jeffrey M. Perloff, *Modern Industrial Organization*, 4th edn (2005) p. 172.

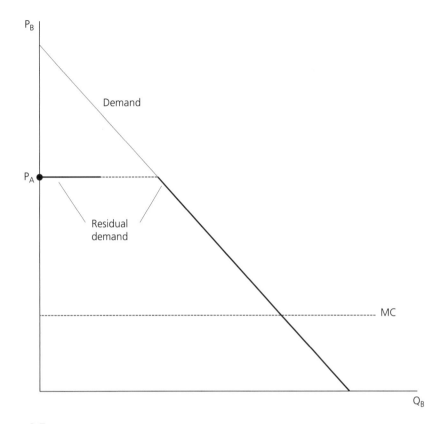

Figure 8.5

is irreversible. Again, the industry demand curve is P = 100 − Q, and each firm's marginal cost is constant at 10. Because it is a sequential game, we can solve it through backward induction, and so begin with the follower's output decision.

Firm B, the second mover, acts as under Cournot. It maximises its profit based on what it observes to be A's output, Q_A. Thus, it faces residual demand of P = 100 − Q_A − Q_B. As before, Firm B's reaction function is Q_B = (90 − Q_A)/2.

The first mover, Firm A, knows that this function will drive Firm B's output decision. Profit, of course, is the difference between total revenue ("TR") and costs ("TC"). Total revenue for Firm A is:

$$TR_A = P.Q_A = (100 - Q_A - Q_B).Q_A = 100Q_A - Q_A{}^2 - Q_A.Q_B.$$

Total cost for Firm A is: $TC_A = 10Q_A$. Therefore, Firm A's profit is:

$$\Pi_A = 90Q_A - Q_A{}^2 - Q_A.Q_B.$$

But Q_B is not fixed, because it is a function of Q_A. Substituting Firm B's reaction function in for Q_B, we get:

$$\Pi_A = 90Q_A - Q_A{}^2 - Q_A[(90 - Q_A)/2].$$

To maximise profit, we get:

$$d\Pi_A/dQ_A = 90 - 2Q_A - 45 + Q_A = 0.$$

Thus, Firm A's profit-maximizing quantity is 45, and Firm B will produce 22.5 units.

Total industry output of 67.5 is greater than the two-firm Cournot equilibrium of 60, but short of the efficient outcome under perfect competition and Bertrand of 90. The following graph illustrates how a leader in an oligopolistic market determines quantity under Stackelberg competition:

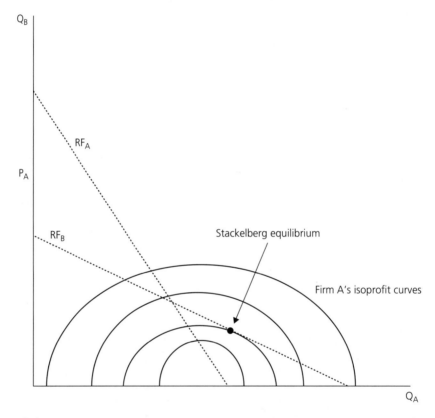

Figure 8.6

This graph shows the duopolists' reaction functions, RF_A and RF_B. Firm A experiences the same profit on any point of the same isoprofit curve. The lower the curve, the greater its profit. Firm A's profit-maximising decision is to produce the quantity corresponding to the point where Firm B's reaction curve is tangential to Firm A's lowest isoprofit curve.

4. Game theory

The three preceding models of oligopolistic competition are classics. The emergence of non-cooperative game theory significantly expanded economists' modelling of how firms behave in settings of strategic interdependence. The principal insight is that, although cartels are inherently unstable in static settings, companies may be able to achieve a collusive equilibrium in infinitely repeated dynamic games.

(a) Static game

Envision a situation in which duopolists compete in a single period, and must move simultaneously. They set their output levels and choose between Cournot and monopoly production levels. We shall again assume that the industry demand curve is: $P = 100 - Q$, and marginal cost is 10. Thus, each company's Cournot and monopoly outputs are 30 and 22.5 units (the monopoly output split both ways), respectively. What outcome does game theory predict?

The Nash equilibrium is for both firms to set output at 30. This is another example of the prisoners' dilemma. Firms A and B would be collectively better off if both colluded jointly to produce the monopoly output of 45. Antitrust laws prohibit such agreements, however, and game theory predicts that the companies will not reach a monopoly outcome through non-cooperative behaviour as each firm has an incentive to cheat. Firm A reasons: "Regardless of whether Firm B produces the Cournot or collusive (i.e. monopoly) output, I will make more money by setting output at the Cournot level." Firm B thinks the same thing, so they will not set output at the monopoly level.

		Firm B	
		Monopoly	Cournot
Firm A	Monopoly	1,012.5, 1,012.5	984.38, 1,476.56
	Cournot	1,476.56, 984.38	900, 900

Figure 8.7

This demonstrates the payoffs to the parties under the four possible outcomes. The duopolists maximise their combined wealth at 2025 (1,012.5 each) by both producing the collusive/monopoly output, but individually each firm would do better still (1,476.56) if it produces the Cournot output while its competitor sets output at the monopoly level. Because both firms' dominant strategy is to produce the Cournot output, the Nash equilibrium is Cournot–Cournot.

(b) Infinitely repeated game

Despite the single-period incentive to increase output, game theory reveals a troubling insight when players repeat a game through infinity. There, a Nash equilibrium can exist at the monopoly outcome even without express collusion. This possibility suggests that markets with more than one competitor could nevertheless produce the full allocative and productive inefficiencies of monopoly.

This result can ensue when a firm signals both a willingness to set output at the monopoly level contrary to short-term self-interest and a threat to punish other oligopolists that fail to match its output restriction. The firm's threat is to increase output and thus to make all competitors worse off. Competition law prohibits express communications of this sort, but firms can legally do so implicitly. For example, an oligopolist may sharply reduce output, thus signalling to its rivals that it is willing to limit its production to the new level indefinitely if the others follow suit. If those competitors similarly restrict output, the law does not object, as no formal agreement has arisen. Deviations from the ensuing tacit collusion may be punished through future increases in production.

To consider how this process may create a Nash equilibrium at the monopoly outcome, continue the hypothetical from the previous section, except that now the firms repeat the game indefinitely. Suppose that Firm A sets output at the monopoly level, such that Firm B can earn 1,476.56 in that period producing the Cournot output or 1,012.5 also producing the monopoly amount. In one period, it is rational for Firm B to go with Cournot. Suppose, however, that Firm A rationally signals that it will set output at the Cournot level forever if Firm B does not match its monopoly output (a so-called "grim trigger strategy"). In that case, Firm B would benefit by 464.06 (1,476.56 − 1,012.5) by "cheating" in the first period, but would give up 464.06 in every single future period in fore-going joint-monopoly profits of 1,012.5 for Cournot profits of 900. Absent a bizarrely high discount rate, Firms A and B will therefore produce the monopoly output in this example.

Although this is an important insight, one should not overstate it. It is difficult for an oligopolist to threaten credibly that it will increase output indefinitely in the future. The reason is that, once its rival has "cheated" in a period, that loss is sunk, and the punisher's choice to increase output forever is then irrational. Nevertheless, economists generally believe that prices are likely to be higher, and output lower, in concentrated oligopolies in which firms compete indefinitely over time than they are in one-period settings.

5. The empirical literature

Many of the economic models explored above relate industry structure to economic performance. The perfect competition model predicts that markets with many competitors, free entry, symmetric information, and homogeneous products tend towards allocative and productive efficiency over time, with competitors earning zero long-term economic profits. Conversely, monopoly results in deadweight loss and sustained economic profits. Between these extremes, models of oligopolistic competition suggest that efficiency inversely correlates with concentration. The Cournot model shows that the greater the number of firms in an industry, the more closely the ensuing Nash equilibrium approaches the competitive outcome. So, too, does the Stackelberg model. The Bertrand model, by contrast, produces the odd result that the only equilibrium in an oligopolistic market for homogeneous goods is the perfectly competitive outcome. This prediction does not hold, however, in the presence of product differentiation or asymmetric information. More recently, game theory shows that oligopolistic competition of indefinite or perpetual duration is likely to produce less-competitive outcomes than single-period competition. In general, the fewer firms in a market and the more homogeneous the sold goods, the more likely it is that oligopolists can tacitly collude.

The relationship between industry concentration and efficiency matters enormously to competition policy. If concentration enhances market power, thus enabling firms to earn long-term economic profits by restricting output, then mergers reducing the number of competitors in a market should be viewed with suspicion. Antitrust agencies should have little patience for dominant-firm behaviour that may inhibit entry or incumbent expansion if the dominant position does not reflect scale economies. More generally, evidence that firms earn long-term economic profits in concentrated industries due to sustained output restrictions would warrant aggressive antitrust policies aimed at restoring competition that market forces cannot.

Countless empirical studies have explored the relationship between industry structure, firm conduct, and market performance ("SCP"). The takeaway point is that, although early studies suggested a strong causal link between concentration and sustained market power, more recent insights have discredited that conclusion. Much of the SCP literature suffered from serious deficiencies. Today, although there is some evidence that concentration correlates with market power (i.e. the ability sustainably to charge prices in excess of marginal cost) it is unclear whether inadequate competition, efficiency, a combination of these, or some other factor explains this statistical relationship.

(a) SCP studies

The SCP movement began in the late 1930s at Harvard under Edward Mason, accelerating under Mason's students, especially Joe Bain. Since then, empirical studies have attempted to measure the relationship between structure and performance. The overarching thesis is that concentration and/ or entry barriers allow firms to earn supracompetitive profits in the long term. To investigate that hypothesised relationship, SCP researchers historically used cross-sectional studies to compare multiple industries at a fixed moment in time. In a given study, they measured each industry's profits over a certain period of time, typically using accounting data, and calculated each market's structure using four-firm or eight-firm concentration ratios. For instance, an industry in which the four largest companies make up 75% of sales has a four-firm concentration ratio of 0.75. SCP economists then regressed observed profitability against concentration across the relevant markets to see if industry structure explains variations in performance.

The empirical work in the SCP tradition is far too voluminous to recount here in any detail.[8] Nevertheless, we will address some of the most influential studies. In 1951, Joe Bain published an influential study comparing the respective rates of return of 42 industries based on two measures of industry structure: markets in which the eight largest firms accounted for more than 70% of sales, and those in which they accounted for less.[9] He found that profits were 4.3% higher in the relatively concentrated markets (11.8%) than in the others (7.5%). Five years later, he found that concentrated markets subject to conditions he defined as entry barriers (such as scale economies, high capital requirements, and advertising) enjoyed higher profits than less-concentrated industries not subject to such barriers.[10]

Subsequent studies found similar results. In 1966, for example, Mann used data from 1950 to 1960, and largely reproduced Bain's 1951 findings.[11] He found that more-concentrated industries experienced an average rate of return of 13.3% vis-à-vis 9% for the others.[12] In 1974, a literature review concluded that there was a statistically significant relationship between structure, conduct, and performance.[13]

(b) Debunking the SCP literature

Literature of the kind outlined above held sway for several decades, giving rise to aggressive anti-trust enforcement. Much of that empirical research, however, has now been discredited. As a result, little work regressing accounting profits against concentration or other endogenous industry conditions now takes place. This section identifies the statistical problems that plague many SCP studies.

First, the explanatory variables that the classic SCP literature seeks to measure are endogenous, potentially generating biased results. To regress profitability against concentration (or entry barriers or advertising) to see if the latter causes the former, profitability must not – but sadly does – affect concentration. This is the same simultaneity bias we saw in the empirical literature addressing crime – one derives skewed results in comparing the number of police to crime because not only does greater police volume reduce crime, but higher crime increases the number of police. Similarly, profitability affects concentration. Supracompetitive returns attract entry, and hence a greater number of firms and lower concentration, even if higher concentration also causes supra-normal profits. In formal terms, market structure is endogenous (i.e. explanatory variables within the model affect it) not exogenous. So, for example, regressions using firm-concentration ratios may produce spurious results. An authoritative literature review concluded that "essentially all variables that have been employed in such studies are logically endogenous".[14]

Tests meant to control for simultaneity bias suggest that concentration and supra-normal profits still correlate with one another.[15] Nevertheless, correlation does not imply causation. In a

---

8 The references section at the end of the chapter include authoritative literature reviews of the empirical industrial organisation literature.

9 Joe S. Bain, 'Relation of profit rate to industry concentration: American manufacturing, 1936–1940' (1951) 65 QJ Econ 293.

10 Joe S. Bain, *Barriers to New Competition: Their Character and Consequences in Manufacturing Industries* (1956).

11 Michael Mann, 'Seller concentration, barriers to entry, and rates of return in thirty industries 1950–60' (1966) 48 Rev Econ & Stats 296.

12 *See also*, W.S. Comanor and T.A. Wilson, 'Advertising, market structure and performance' (1967) 49 Rev Econ & Statistics 423; N. Collins and L. Preston, 'Price-cost margin and industry structure' (1969) 51 Rev Econ & Statistics 271.

13 Leonard W. Weiss, 'The Concentration-Profits Relationship and Antitrust' in Harvey J. Godschmid, Michael Mann, and J. Fred Western (eds.) *Industrial Concentration: The New Learning* (1974) pp. 201–220.

14 Richard Schmalensee, 'Inter-Industry Studies of Structure and Performance' in *Handbook of Industrial Organization* (1989) p. 954.

15 Leonard W. Weiss, 'The Concentration–Profits Relationship and Antitrust', in Harvey J. Godschmid *et al.* (eds.) *Industrial Concentration: The New Learning* (1974) pp. 201–220.

devastating critique of the SCP literature, Harold Demsetz showed that efficiency may cause high concentration and greater-than-normal profits.[16] Even if the empirical literature correctly finds a correlation between structure and performance, that result is meaningless insofar as a causative relationship is concerned. Such studies do not allow the researcher to ascribe causative effect to the explanatory variables being measured. Profits may be partially a function of structure, and yet structure a function of profits.

Second, most SCP studies mistakenly rely on accounting, rather than economic, profits to measure performance. The various models of oligopolistic competition speak only to economic profits, which can be most unlike the accounting equivalent. In particular, accountants measure capital costs using book value (i.e. purchase price reduced over time, such as by straight-line depreciation). Economically understood, however, capital costs should be defined by replacement value, which may be different. For instance, an expensive investment in infrastructure in year 1 may become a stranded cost by year 4 if the relevant technology becomes defunct. In that case, the capital's economic value would be low – showing that no further investment would efficiently take place, even if its yet-to-be-fully-depreciated worth is high on the books. Furthermore, accounting profits do not properly measure investments in advertising, research, and development. The cost of such devoted capital appears in a single period, even though the benefits ensure over many. The potential result is bias. Other complications include the improper use of before-tax rates of return, and a failure to discount profits by the ex ante probability of failure.[17]

Third, researchers derive concentration ratios from industry statistics, not from formal economic analysis. This is problematic because the government defines industries differently than economists define relevant economic markets.[18] Similarly, published statistics group distinct products together, generating potentially misleading averages. Biased results ensue.

Fourth, an interpretive difficulty with SCP cross-sectional studies is whether observed data concerning performance and structure are in disequilibrium.[19] In the long term, supracompetitive profits should attract entry, thus reducing concentration, while capital will leave industries experiencing modest returns, hence increasing concentration. If this occurs, performance across industries will converge over time.

Such problems, and particularly the fact that industry structure is endogenous, have resulted in a "barrage of criticism", which "has caused most research in this area to cease".[20] Furthermore, more-recent empirical work has found that a correlation between structure and performance is tenuous. Carlton and Perloff have concluded that "there is at best weak evidence of a link between concentration and the various proxies for barriers to entry and measures of market performance".[21] Instead, today's work in industrial organisation – sometimes referred to as the "New Empirical Industrial Organization" – focuses on one industry at a time, estimating market power and hypothesising the effect of events relevant to antitrust, such as proposed mergers.[22] This approach avoids many of the simultaneity problems that plagued inter-industry comparisons in the earlier literature, and produces more-focused insights that significantly benefit antitrust law.

---

16 Harold Demsetz, 'Industry structure, market rivalry and public policy' (1973) 16 JL & Econ 1; Sam Peltzman, 'The gains and losses from industrial concentration' (1977) 20 JL & Econ 229.
17 Dennis W. Carlton and Jeffrey M. Perloff, *Modern Industrial Organization* 4th edn (2005) pp. 249–52.
18 The next section discusses the economics of market definition.
19 For a famous criticism of Bain's work on this ground, see Yale Brozen, 'Bain's concentration and rates of return revisited' (1971) 14 JL & Econ 351.
20 Dennis W. Carlton and Jeffrey M. Perloff, *Modern Industrial Organization*, 4th edn (2005) p. 268.
21 *Ibid.* at p. 265.
22 *See generally* Liran Einav and Jonathan Levin, 'Empirical industrial organization: A progress report' (2010) 24 J Econ Persp. 145.

E. The Role of the Market: Definition, Power, and Self-Correction

1. Why study the market?

This chapter provides the reader with the background economics and context with which to understand antitrust analysis of specific restraints, which the following two chapters explore. It concludes with what is almost always the most critical part of an antitrust case: market definition.

With the exception of hardcore cartels, the law requires plaintiffs to prove a relevant market in which the alleged anticompetitive effects occurred. The market inquiry seeks to identify the economic environment in which the alleged restraint or exclusionary practice took place. It should include every material constraint on the defendant's ability to exercise market power (i.e. independently to curtail industry output and thus cause the market price to rise). Thus, companies that sell interchangeable goods belong in the relevant market, as they can increase production in response to the defendant's attempted exercise of market power, thereby neutralising it. Firms that would enter the industry to compete should prices rise to supracompetitive levels might also belong in the market, though courts and agencies typically account for such supply-side constraints in analysing market power rather than market definition. Typically, reputational and other non-market-imposed price constraints do not form part of the relevant market.

Every non-cartel antitrust case follows the same path in market definition. Plaintiffs argue that the relevant market is narrow and that the defendant occupies a significant share of it, while defendants argue the opposite. A firm's share of the market matters because the law draws a variety of conclusions from that statistic. In America, for example, no firm with less than 40% market share can commit monopolisation as a matter of law. These inferences follow from the economic theory that competitors will increase output in response to attempted exercises of market power.

In short, the law focuses on the relevant market not as an end in itself, but in its value as a proxy for whether the scrutinised firm or firms can affect market outcomes. The technical proxy is to the company's price elasticity of demand at marginal cost.

2. Measuring market power: The Lerner index and price elasticity of demand

Market power reflects the price elasticity of demand ("PED") that the scrutinised firm encounters at the competitive price level. The PED measures the percentage change in demand that results from a 1% increase in price. A PED of 1 means that a 1% rise in price reduces demand for the good by 1%. That is unit elasticity. A score greater than 1 means that demand is elastic, and the firm lacks market power. A PED of 2 means that an incremental rise in price reduces demand by twice as much. A PED between 1 and 0 demonstrates that demand is inelastic, and the firm can exercise market power. Perfect inelasticity occurs when PED is 0, at which point price changes do not affect demand.

Where demand is elastic at a price equal to the company's marginal cost, the company will have little, if any, ability to exercise market power. Should it attempt to do so, its customers will abandon it in favour of its competitors' products. Conversely, if demand is inelastic, the firm will be able lucratively to raise prices beyond the competitive level without suffering an off-setting decline in sales. Inelastic demand arises when there are no good substitutes to the relevant product or service at competitive price levels. A defendant's market power thus informs the economic question of whether an alleged restraint of trade is harmful. Without market power, any effort by a company to corrupt the competitive process will fail, as the relevant firm will be unable to raise prices above its marginal cost of production.

The "Lerner index" measures a company's market power, defined by the formula:

$$L = (P - MC)/P$$

where L is the Lerner index, P is the firm's price at the firm's profit-maximising output, and MC is the firm's marginal cost at its profit-maximising output.

It is equivalent to the inverse of the firm's price elasticity of demand *at the profit-maximising output*, such that $L = 1/E_d$. The Lerner index ranges from 0, which indicates no market power, to 1, which reflects the greatest possible level of market power.

As the demand facing a firm becomes less elastic, the Lerner index increases, indicating greater levels of market power. At a PED of 5, the Lerner Index is 0.2. As the PED drops to 2, the index increases to 0.5. The index reaches its maximum possible value, reflecting the greatest level of market power, at 1, which occurs when the PED is 1. A PED of 1 reflects "unit elasticity", at which point a marginal increase in price will cause demand to decline by an exactly proportional amount.

Why can the Lerner index not exceed 1? Such a result would require a firm to be selling at a PED of more than 1, which would involve selling in the inelastic portion of its demand curve. No profit-maximising firm would ever do this. When demand is inelastic, a company can profitably increase its price. Suppose, for example, that the price elasticity of demand were 0.4, such that a 1% increase in price would reduce demand by only 0.4%. It increases profit to raise price in that environment. The firm would continue to increase price further until demand became elastic – less than 1 – at which point a 1% increase in price would reduce demand by more than 1%.

The Lerner index is a theoretically powerful concept for defining a firm's market power, but unfortunately it has limited practical efficacy because it is notoriously difficult to estimate a company's marginal cost of production. Nor is it easy to measure the elasticity of demand facing a firm at the level of output that maximises profit. Should the firm being investigated not then be producing the profit-maximising output, one would have to speculate about what the hypothetical elasticity of demand would be. As it is often prohibitively difficult to measure the inputs necessary to calculate the Lerner index, economists typically appeal to a proxy: market share. It is important to remember, though, that the point of measuring a firm's share of the market is to gain insight into the price elasticity of demand facing the company at the competitive price level.

3. Market share as a proxy for market power: Demand-side substitution

As is too commonly the case, theory yields sharper answers in abstract models than in practice. The market power question lying at the heart of antitrust is a case in point. Economics tells us that a company's ability profitably to increase price to supracompetitive levels is a key consideration in analysing the propriety of a restraint imposed by that firm. Should it lack such power, the firm will be unable to injure the competitive process. Unfortunately, the key economic variable at issue – demand elasticity at marginal-cost pricing – is elusive, and thus unsuitable as a practical component of antitrust analysis.

Lacking first-best information with which to inform their analysis, economists instead look to proxies for price elasticity of demand. The most prominent of these is market share. The underlying concept is straightforward: the greater the proportion of sales that a firm enjoys in an industry, the more likely it is that it can sustainably set supracompetitive prices. Should they have limited production capacity, rivals cannot significantly increase output in the short term to neutralise their competitor's attempted price increase. Expanding capacity in such a way is expensive, which means that firms' short-term, average-cost curves rise sharply as their output increases beyond their prior capacity limitations.

Imagine two firms that are targets of separate antitrust investigations. The first has a market share of just 5%, while the other has a share of 90%. One can reasonably infer that the latter enjoys greater market power. Take the company with the 5% share. Even if it restricts output severely, the impact of that supply reduction on the market price would be slight. Furthermore, to the extent that the output restriction successfully raised price, the firms comprising the remaining 95% of the market would only have to increase their output by a trivial percentage to satisfy unmet consumer demand. Conversely, the firm with 95% of the market will likely be able to induce a sharp decline in market supply by reducing its own output. The companies accounting for the remaining 5% of the market would have to increase their production dramatically to re-establish the competitive level of output.

The nature of the rival firms accounting for the remainder of sales in a market also matters. The smaller the scale of a rival's operations, the less probable it is that that competitor can dramatically ramp up operations to undo a competitor's output restriction.

Such is the theory why firms with significant market share typically enjoy market power. To calculate that share, however, one must first define the relevant market. How should competition law determine which products and services fall within a single market? The answer is crucial, as the result of the inquiry typically determines the outcome of an antitrust lawsuit. The economic answer is that only those products or services that constrain the target firm's pricing power should fall in the relevant antitrust market. Consistent with that theory, competition law considers that rival products fall within the same market as the scrutinised company if they are "reasonably interchangeable" with the goods sold by the target company.

The quality of "interchangeability" or "substitutability" implies a positive cross-price elasticity of demand ("CPED"). CPED measures how a 1% change in the price of one good affects demand for the other product. A positive CPED means that an increase in price for one good enhances demand for the other product, thus suggesting substitution. The higher the CPED, the more sensitive the relationship between the target goods' respective price and demand and the more likely it is that those products reside in the same market. Conversely, goods with zero or low CPED are not substitutes, and thus do not belong in the same market. The two charts immediately below contrast goods that belong in the same market and those that do not:

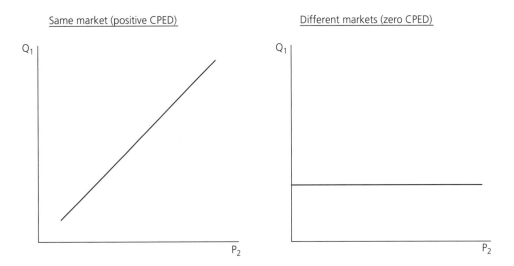

Figure 8.8

The concept of CPED informs the most influential technique for defining a market. This is the "small but significant non-transitory increase in price" ("SSNIP") test. This first focuses on the accused firm's product and the nearest substitute product. The SSNIP test asks whether a hypothetical monopolist owning both of those goods could profitably increase price from the competitive level by 5 to 10%. If the answer is yes, the relevant market is comprised exclusively of those two products. If the answer is no, it means that a sufficient number of consumers would abandon the two higher-priced products in favour of substitutes. Those substitutes thus form part of the relevant market because they limit the hypothetical monopolist's pricing power. One applying the SSNIP test would then introduce the next closest substitute, and ask whether a hypothetical monopolist owning all three goods could profitably increase their price by 5 to 10%. That iterative process continues by adding further substitutes until a hypothetical monopolist would be able profitably to increase price by 5 to 10%.

The SSNIP test yields a more rigorous form of market-definition analysis than subjective or survey-based assessments of substitutability. By framing inter-changeability in terms of how price increases affect purchases, the test illuminates the economic relationship between particular goods or services.

Application of the SSNIP test, however, can provide surprisingly narrow, counter-intuitive market definitions, suggesting that certain products belong in separate markets even though they appear to bear similar functional attributes. For instance, although one instinctively thinks that Coke and Pepsi belong in the same market, many people's deep-rooted preferences for one over another mean that the relative demand for each may be invariant to modest price movements. If the cross-price elasticity of demand between Coke and Pepsi is indeed low, it suggests that neither product significantly constrains the other.

Nevertheless, it may be a mistake to read too much into static market definition. For example, many consumers irrationally adhere to brand-name drugs when chemically identical, but far cheaper, generic versions first come to market. The lack of immediate wholesale substitution from the much-more-expensive pioneer drug to the generic may suggest, under a snapshot application of the SSNIP test that the goods belong in different markets, even though the products are substantively identical. More dynamic analysis, however, would reveal large-scale erosion of the pioneer drug's sales over time by generics. Furthermore, brand-name pharmaceutical companies go to great lengths to delay generic entry, thus indicating that differently branded versions of the same drug do belong in the same market. Recognising the importance of such dynamic effects, the US antitrust authorities' new horizontal merger guidelines rely somewhat less heavily on the SSNIP test, and more closely embrace empirical evidence of real-life competitive effects over time.

Market definition is binary. Courts or enforcement agencies will either find that a certain good belongs in the market or they will not. This "in-or-out" approach is somewhat misleading. The fact that a good does not fall within the same market as a defendant's product does not mean that the goods do not influence each other. Substitutes constrain one another to varying degrees, and the quality of "substitutability" itself occupies a spectrum. Nevertheless, the binary quality of market definition may be justifiable for practical reasons – employing a more expansive analysis involving minute gradations in pricing constraints would excessively complicate antitrust analysis.

4. Entry as a constraint on market power: Supply-side substitution

Demand-side substitution, as we have seen, is a critical element of market definition. Two products belong in the same market if consumers consider them to be good alternatives at competitive prices. Market power, however, also depends on supply-side substitution. Third parties may enter a market on the selling side to capitalise on profit opportunities. Consider a firm that increases its prices by 10%. One constraint is that some consumers will shift their purchases elsewhere. Another is that rival companies will enter the market, undercut its higher prices, and take sales away from it.

In free-market economies, capital tends to flow to where it can earn the highest return. In the absence of significant entry barriers, monopoly prices should be ephemeral because they will attract new competitors. The question for market-power analysis is whether such entry is likely to be sufficiently prompt and effective to make the attempted monopoly price unprofitable. Whether this is likely depends, in turn, on the barriers to entry that hinder the rapid emergence of viable competition on the selling side.

Entry barriers are hugely important to market power. For example, in 1990, the US Court of Appeals for the Ninth Circuit found that a chain of cinemas lacked monopoly power, even though it had 100% of the market share in Las Vegas, because entry barriers were light.[23]

Barriers to entry are subject to competing definitions. The classic account is that of Joseph Bain, who argued that they are anything that benefit established sellers over their potential competitors. On his view, scale economies (a "percentage effect") and high capital requirements hinder entry because they permit incumbent firms to earn supracompetitive profits without the threat of supply-side substitution. Bain's account has an intuitive quality. High capital requirements, after all, seem obviously to impede entry. Furthermore, if incumbent companies achieve the production volume necessary to operate at minimum efficient scale, they enjoy a cost advantage over any competitor entering the market on a modest scale.

Neither such intuition, however, is robust. First, as to high capital requirements, the question is not whether many or even most people could afford to enter a market. The correct inquiry is whether, in the event of supracompetitive profits in the industry, private companies have sufficient access to capital to take advantage of the attractive pricing opportunity. Depending on the availability of debt and equity (which depend on capital-market efficiency), companies may be able to secure the requisite funding to enter a capital-intensive industry and compete.

Second, on the question of percentage effects, assume that incumbents would not reduce output in response to entry. This assumption is not generally warranted. Maximising profit in the short-term often requires an incumbent to reduce output in the event of a new competitor's arrival. Bain thought that pre-existing competitors would adopt a limit-pricing strategy, at which they set prices at a level that would be loss-making for an entrant, given its smaller scale, but still profitable for incumbents, given their larger output and hence lower marginal cost. Although this may occasionally be a rational strategy, modern game theory suggests that, in the absence of creating excess capacity (a costly endeavour), the threat of limit pricing is non-credible.

The more economically rigorous definition is that of George Stigler, who characterised entry barriers as costs that an entrant must bear, but that firms already in the industry need not. From that perspective, high capital requirements and scale economies are not barriers to supply-side substitution because they are impediments that incumbents have already overcome. Although there have been many more definitions of entry barriers articulated since those espoused by Bain and Stigler, their conflicting views remain the two most important.

It would be a mistake to exaggerate the divide, however, for there are important conditions that constitute entry barriers under either view. The most potent, and hence anticompetitive, barriers to entry are those that the government imposes. Regulatory restrictions on entry – the paradigmatic example are caps on the number of competitors in an industry – are a case in point. Patents and other lawful monopolies can also foreclose entry, removing supply-side substitution as a restraint on incumbents' pricing power. More generally, competing definitions of entry barriers can obscure

---

23 *United States v Syufy Enters*, 903 F2d 659 (9th Cir 1990).

the fundamental point of interest in an antitrust case, which is whether entry is likely to be timely and sufficient in a particular industry to remedy an output restriction. The answer to that question is likely to be context-specific and often empirical.

5. Market-power assessments without economics: Judicial error

The market-power discussion undertaken thus far is of profound importance to antitrust analysis, but it is also complex. To appreciate the importance of economics to judicial decision making, and to illustrate how even eminent jurists can lose their way in this complex arena, we pause momentarily to explore two notable instances of judicial error, one from each side of the Atlantic.

The US Supreme Court famously erred in 1956, when it had to determine whether EI du Pont, a cellophane manufacturer, had monopoly power.[24] The question was whether cellophane, a plastic wrapping material, constituted its own market, or whether it competed with other flexible packaging materials. The answer was important, for the defendant sold 75% of the cellophane in the United States, but only 20% of all wrapping materials. As the government had charged the company with monopolisation, the market-power question was determinative.

In demarcating the relevant market, the Court inquired into the cross-price elasticity of demand between the various products. In doing so, however, it committed a critical error. The reader will recall that one must apply the SSNIP test at the target firm's competitive price level. In alleged monopolisation cases, this will often require one to abstract away from the price that the scrutinised firm actually charges. The reason is that a profit-maximising firm will always charge a price at which the demand for its product is elastic. Were demand inelastic, the company could profitably increase price further. Absent reputational constraints, a rational firm will necessarily keep increasing its prices until demand becomes elastic.

If a target company has indeed achieved a monopoly as alleged, and if the firm is, in fact, exercising its monopoly power, its demand will necessarily be elastic. That means that other goods constrain any further increases in the monopolist's price, but it does not follow that those other goods are economic substitutes. Two goods may not be interchangeable at competitive price levels, but may become substitutes when one is sold at monopoly prices. For example, cars and bicycles are not functionally interchangeable over anything other than trivial distances, so bike manufacturers will not constrain the pricing decisions of car producers. Yet, if all cars were owned by one company who raised prices to near-prohibitive levels, one would see more and more consumers eschewing such vehicles in favour of cheaper bikes. If one were to use a sufficiently high car price as the baseline for the SSNIP test, one might find that a 5 to 10% further increase in price would not be profitable because so many consumers would defect toward bicycles. The test would thus produce the erroneous result that a high cross-price elasticity of demand exists between cars and bikes, incorrectly suggesting that those products belong in the same market.

The Supreme Court committed just this mistake when it asked whether a price increase over the current market price for cellophane would be profitable, incorrectly concluding that, because consumers would substitute their purchases toward alternative wrapping materials, cellophane did not occupy its own market. This result came to be known as the "Cellophane Fallacy". The correct approach would have been to estimate EI du Pont's marginal cost of production and hence competitive price, and to apply the SSNIP test to that amount.

Errors in market power analysis are by no means unique to the United States. In 1978, the European Court of Justice had to determine whether United Brands, a producer and seller of the Chiquita brand of bananas, occupied a dominant position in the retail market for bananas in

---

24 *United States v EI du Pont de Nemours*, 351 US 377 (1956).

continental Europe.[25] In an important opinion articulating the definition of monopoly power under EU law, the ECJ characterised a "dominant position" as "a position of economic strength . . . which enables [its holder] to prevent effective competition . . . by giving it the power to behave to an appreciable extent independently of its competitors, customers and ultimately of its consumers".[26] This definition lacks specificity and hence descriptive power, but in focusing on a monopoly's ability to act independently, the ECJ's definition is broadly consistent with the economic meaning of monopoly.

It is not clear that the ECJ meant to ascribe economic meaning to its account of dominance and to the factors that contribute to it. Nevertheless, from an economic perspective, important components of the *United Brands* opinion going to dominance are erroneous, for the ECJ improperly equated size with market power. The court construed vertical integration as contributing to a dominant position, concluding that United Brands' integration, which included owning plantations and a shipping fleet, granted the company "commercial stability and well being". Such factors are economically irrelevant, however, if they do not illuminate the price elasticity of demand facing the firm at its competitive price level. The ECJ provided no basis for supposing that United Brands' vertical integration affected the company's ability profitably to raise the price of bananas in the European retail market, which ability depends not so much on the firm itself, but on the ability of its rivals to increase output in the short term.

A similar mistake occurred in the European Commission's controversial veto of a merger between GE and Honeywell, which combination US authorities had already cleared. The Commission viewed GE's financial arm and ensuing access to capital, as well as its commercial success, as indicating dominance. Such analysis does not align with neo-classical economics, for alone it sheds no light on an ability to restrict industry-wide output.

Notwithstanding such errors, the economic analysis that agencies and courts employ on both sides of the Atlantic has become increasingly sophisticated. The US Department of Justice and Federal Trade Commission routinely employ complex econometric evidence of direct competitive effects to analyse market power more accurately than ever before. Furthermore, in late 2005, the European Commission articulated a new position in which it would equate dominance with "substantial market power", an approach that would align closely with the economic approach outlined above.[27] Even if competition policy has yet to reach its economic zenith, price theory is in the ascendancy.

6. Two-sided markets

This section concludes with a special case. The previous discussion has focused on "one-sided markets" in which one or more vendors compete with one another to sell directly to consumers. More complicated cases involve two-sided networks, in which platforms serve as intermediaries between sellers and purchasers.

There are many examples of such two-sided markets. Manufacturers of video game consoles act as intermediaries between gamers and title developers. Credit-card companies like MasterCard and Visa connect sellers and buyers of all manner of goods. Performing rights organisations such as ASCAP, BMI, SESAC and PRS for Music in the United States and PPL in the United Kingdom act as a link between consumers and copyright holders of musical compositions and recordings. Internet Service Providers are platforms that connect consumers to internet content and application providers.

25 *United Brands v Commission of the European Communities*, Case 27/76 [1978] ECR 207.
26 Ibid. at para. 65.
27 European Commission, DG Competition Discussion Paper on the Application of Article 82 EC of the Treaty to Exclusionary Abuses, (2005). Available at: http://ec.europa.eu/comm/competition/antitrust/art82/discpaper2005.pdf.

One might ask why platforms arise in these settings, when prospective sellers and purchasers could simply bargain with one another directly. The answer lies in reducing transaction costs and in availing of network effects. Consider copyright licensing. Given the number of musical compositions and recordings, it would often be prohibitively expensive for a consumer to search out and negotiate a licence. An intermediary that aggregates rights and licences them on a blanket basis reduces such transaction costs, albeit at the cost of restricting competition between copyright holders (which is why certain performing rights organisations are subject to competition-ensuring consent decrees).

Network effects similarly drive the emergence of platforms. Such effects exist when the value of joining an interconnected network to the marginal consumer increases with the number of people already subscribed to the platform. The classic example is a telephone network. With only one linked phone, the network is valueless. As additional users join the grid, however, its value rises exponentially. Two-sided markets typically display strong network effects. For example, developers and consumers of video games would like to find each other, but unless developers can agree upon a common platform, each title developed by a different publisher would work only for that publisher's console. Deprived of the benefits of an interoperable platform on which many, if not all, developers' titles run, consumers would place less value on video games. As a result, a smaller market would exist for commercial developers, which would produce a smaller number of titles, thus further reducing consumer demand, and so on in a vicious cycle. Platforms in the form of video game console manufacturers solve this coordination problem, thus creating value on both sides of the market.

These are the essential characteristics of two-sided networks, but what does this discussion have to do with market definition and market power? The answer lies in the fact that the standard methodologies for defining markets such as the SSNIP test (or the related concept of critical-loss analysis) generally yield erroneous results if applied to one side of a two sided network. Consider a two-sided market for online dating, in which a website serving heterosexual consumers connects men and women to one another. In analysing whether the business has market power over men, one might be tempted to ask whether the website could raise price to men by 5 to 10% above marginal cost without suffering a critical loss of men. Suppose that the answer happens to be yes because other websites and more traditional fora for dating are not adequate substitutes in the eyes of most men who avail of the company's services. Thus, an increased price for men would reduce the number availing of the service, but only modestly. A regulator or court might incorrectly conclude that the website enjoys monopoly power. This determination could overlook the feedback effect that reduced numbers of men would have on women's demand for the service. As fewer men are available through the website, the value of that site to the marginal female customer will decline, reducing the number of women availing of the service. This effect, in turn, would reduce the number of men using the website, and so on.

Due to these indirect network effects, one wishing to define a relevant market over a two-sided network must be concerned not only with the price elasticity of demand facing the platform on the side of the network in which one is interested, but also on the price elasticity of demand on the other side of the network, as well as on the potency of the network effects at issue. For these reasons, the market-definition process is considerably more complicated in two-sided networks than it is with respect to more traditional one-sided markets.

Key Points

- Antitrust law prohibits monopolisation and anticompetitive agreements. Its economic function is to prevent inefficient conduct that would otherwise take place due to high transaction costs.

- Economics, including price theory and game theory, is indispensable to competition law because it allows judges and regulators to determine whether a restraint on trade is likely to enhance market output (and thus be approved) or to reduce it (and thus be condemned).
- Nevertheless, economics cannot answer all antitrust questions, in particular those that require balancing long- and short-term effects. For instance, to answer whether competition law should require a dominant firm to "open" its platform to render it interoperable with its rivals' products, one must weigh the static benefits of increased competition in the short term with the potential dynamic costs to incentives to invest in future technologies and platforms. The information necessary to answer such questions definitively is unavailable.
- Multiple schools of antitrust thought have emerged over time.

    o   The Harvard School
    o   The Chicago School
    o   The Post-Chicago School
    o   The Neo-Chicago School
    o   Behavioural Antitrust.

- The two models underlying price theory are those of perfect competition and monopoly.

    o   Perfectly competitive markets are allocatively and productively efficient. To arise, there must be many sellers and buyers of homogeneous goods, with perfect access to information, and zero cost of entry and exit.
    o   Monopolies create deadweight loss, and are thus allocatively inefficient. Furthermore, profit-maximising monopolists do not produce at the minimum point on their long-run, average-cost curves. For monopolies to exist, there must only be one seller, many buyers who lack purchasing power, and entry barriers.

- Industrial organisation is the field of economics that studies imperfectly competitive markets. It has produced several classic models that relate the efficiency of outcomes to market structure.

    o   *The Cournot model*
        –   Assuming that its competitors will not change their output, a firm in an oligopoly will set its profit-maximising output based on residual demand. Firms will continue to adjust their output until their expectations as to their rivals' output levels are satisfied. That occurs at an equilibrium point. In a duopoly, the equilibrium price is lower than under monopoly, but higher than under perfect competition. The equilibrium price falls as the number of oligopolists in the market increases.
    o   *Bertrand competition*
        –   In an oligopolistic market comprised of homogeneous goods in which firms compete on price, the only equilibrium price equals the marginal cost of production. The perfectly competitive outcome ensues.
    o   *The Stackelberg model*
        –   In an oligopolistic market again comprised of identical products, firms compete using sequential output decisions. In a duopoly (a two-firm oligopoly), one firm leads, picking an output level, after which the second firm picks its profit-maximising output based on residual demand. Knowing what the follower's output decision will be given any output choice that the leader makes, the leader uses backward induction to pick its profit-maximising output. The equilibrium is inefficient, though the welfare loss is less pronounced than under a Cournot duopoly.

- Prior to the 1970s, industrial-organisation economists produced a large volume of empirical work, finding that industry concentration positively correlated with rates of return. This research supported the SCP approach, which suggests aggressive antitrust enforcement to reduce industry concentration.

- Subsequent advances in economics have discredited the SCP empirical literature.

  ○ SCP empirical studies used market structure as an explanatory variable as to profits. Structure, however, is not exogenous to the model – structure may affect profit, but profit may also affect structure. Thus, its use creates a biased model.

  ○ Even if structure correlates with profit, that observation does not imply a causative relationship between the two variables. The economist Harold Demsetz showed that efficiency may cause high concentration and supra-normal profits.[28] Furthermore, cross-sectional observations may capture a freeze-frame picture of markets that are in disequilibrium.

  ○ SCP studies used accounting profits, which are different than economic profits.

  ○ Today, the predominant view among industrial-organisation economists is that evidence of a connection between structure, conduct, and performance is weak, at best. Current research, known as "New Empirical Industrial Organization", focuses on one industry at a time, estimating market power and hypothesising the effect of events relevant to antitrust.

- Market definition is probably the most critical aspect of all antitrust cases, other than those involving hardcore cartels. The relevant market includes all products that are reasonably interchangeable with each other at competitive price levels. Its economic function is to gain insight into the price elasticity of demand that the scrutinised firm would experience at the competitive price level. If demand is elastic at that point, the firm lacks market power and the restraint of trade being scrutinised is unlikely to harm competition. If demand is inelastic, however, the company may have significant market power and be able to effect anticompetitive outcomes.

- Assessing market power is more complicated in two-sided markets, where a platform or network links two groups to one another. Examples include dating websites and video game platforms. Feedback effects can explain below-cost pricing on one side of the network, and above-cost pricing on the other. Any conclusion drawn by studying only one side of a two-sided market will be reliable.

 ## References and Further Reading

Books

Bork, Robert H., *The Antitrust Paradox: A Policy at War with Itself* (1978).

Cabral, Luis, *Introduction to Industrial Organization* (2000).

Carlton, Dennis W. and. Perloff, Jeffrey M., *Modern Industrial Organization*, 4th edn (2005).

Elhauge, Einer (ed.), *Research Handbook on the Economics of Antitrust Law* (2013) Ch. 3.

Mankiw, N. Gregory, *Principles of Economics*, 6th edn (2011) Chs. 13–17.

Martin, Stephen, *Advanced Industrial Economics*, 2nd edn (2002).

Miceli, Thomas J., *The Economic Approach to Law*, 2nd edn (2008) pp. 315–29.

Pitofsky, Robert (ed.), *How the Chicago School Overshot the Mark: The Effect of Conservative Economic Analysis on U.S. Antitrust* (2008).

Posner, Richard A., *Antitrust Law Part I*, 2nd edn (2001).

Posner, Richard A., *Economic Analysis of Law* (2011) §§ 10.5–10.6.

Schmalensee, Richard, 'Inter-Industry Studies of Structure and Performance' in *Handbook of Industrial Organization* (1989).

---

28 Harold Demsetz, 'Industry structure, market rivalry and public policy' (1973) 16 JL & Econ 1; see also Sam Peltzman, 'The gains and losses from industrial concentration' (1977) 20 JL & Econ 229.

Articles

Crane, Daniel A., 'Chicago, post-Chicago, and neo-Chicago' (2009) 76 U Chi L Rev 1911.

Hovenkamp, Herbert, 'Antitrust policy after Chicago' (1985) 84 Mich L Rev 213, 225.

Hovenkamp, Herbert, 'Post-Chicago antitrust: A review and critique' (2001) Colum Bus L Rev 257.

Kovacic, William, 'The intellectual DNA of modern US competition law for dominant firm conduct: The Chicago/Harvard double helix' (2007) Colum Bus L Rev 1.

Kovacic, William E. and Shapiro, Carl, 'Antitrust policy: A century of economic and legal thinking' (2000) 14 J Econ Persp 43.

Posner, Richard A., 'The Chicago school of antitrust analysis' (1979) 127 U Pa L Rev 925.

Robert Pitofsky, 'The political content of antitrust' (1979) 127 U Pa L Rev 1051.

Wright, Joshua D., 'Abandoning antitrust's Chicago obsession: The case for evidence-based antitrust' (2012) 78 Antitrust LJ 241.

Chapter 2

Antitrust Limits on Contract

Chapter Contents

A.	Introduction	335
B.	Horizontal Restraints on Competition	336
C.	Vertical Restraints on Competition	342
D.	Conclusion	344
Key Points		345
References and Further Reading		346

A. Introduction

Contracts play a celebrated role within law and economics, which generally deems voluntary transactions to be efficient. As the reader now knows, private agreements can enhance social welfare by transferring scarce resources to higher-value uses and by coordinating economic activity. Nevertheless, the law restricts private contract in a number of important ways. As Parts 3 and 5 explore, the law respectively criminalises and declines to enforce certain agreements that have as their object or effect the infliction of harm on third parties. This chapter addresses a particular form of inefficient contract: namely, one into which companies enter to suppress competition. Why are such arrangements inefficient when the Coase Theorem would seem to predict the efficiency of private agreements?

The answer, of course, lies in transaction costs and third-party effects. As Part 5 explained, a contract is presumptively efficient only if all stakeholders are privy to the arrangement. When a victim is not a signatory to the arrangement that injures him, the fact of the contracting parties' voluntary consent is of no moment. One cannot presume the contract to be efficient. When two or more rivals agree to restrict competition, negatively affected consumers lack a seat at the bargaining table. Even though the law recognises a *de facto* right to pay only those prices that emerge from a competitive process uncorrupted by private accord, the sheer number of purchasers and the clandestine nature of most anticompetitive contracts mean that transaction costs are high. Competition law plays an important role in suppressing such inefficient behaviour.

The law's underlying premise is that markets generally work as long as private actors do not corrupt that process. As a result, competition law simultaneously operates as an exception and complement to the free market. This is consistent with the Coase Theorem, which suggests that markets are efficient in low transaction-cost environments.

The most basic rule in antitrust law is that horizontal rivals may not agree to eliminate competition, unless doing so is necessary to achieve a larger pro-competitive goal, such as in a joint venture. "Horizontal" means that the companies sell substitutable products or services, and thus actually or potentially compete with one another for sales. Although horizontal restraints are the principal concern of competition law, the gamut of antitrust is broader, regulating vertical agreements within the supply chain, mergers and acquisitions, and unilateral conduct by dominant firms.

Competition law concerns itself almost exclusively with economic phenomena, which is why price theory and the larger economic field of industrial organisation are particularly illuminative here. Indeed, there is no field of law that economic analysis has more fundamentally transformed. Modern US antitrust doctrine, for instance, bears little resemblance to the rules that existed in the 1960s. Although EU competition law has yet to evolve to the same level of economic sophistication as the United States, the European Commission in particular has recently progressed in leaps and bounds. There is no longer any question that law and economics are inseparable in the field of competition policy.

This chapter focuses on concerted behaviour (i.e. conduct taking place pursuant to agreement between two or more companies). Explicit cartel agreements that entail naked price fixing, market-sharing or boycott provisions are the most odious from the perspective of efficiency, and are easily condemned on economic grounds. Yet, economic analysis of other horizontal deals is more complicated. To be sure, horizontal agreements always raise competitive dangers, but many can produce offsetting efficiencies. Quantifying the pro- and anticompetitive features of such arrangements requires assessing market definition, market power, price effects, and dynamic consequences.

The next chapter addresses monopolistic behaviour. The last chapter in this Part tackles problems that emerge when the essential premise underlying antitrust policy – namely that free markets produce efficient results when private conduct does not corrupt them – fails. In such circumstances, regulation may be economically justified if such state intervention is less problematic than free-market processes.

B. Horizontal Restraints on Competition

1. Cartels as artificial monopolies

Four antitrust rules apply without regard to market power. Specifically, horizontal rivals may never agree nakedly: (1) to limit price competition; (2) to limit output; (3) to divvy up their sales territories; or (4) not to deal with third-party competitors. Each of these arrangements falls within the rubric of illegal, cartel behaviour. In the United States, the prohibition takes the form of a *per se* proscription. Once a plaintiff establishes such an agreement, an antitrust violation follows without regard to market definition, entry barriers, or actual anticompetitive effect. In the European Union, such arrangements have as their object the restriction of competition, and are thus summarily condemned.

The justification for these rules is straightforward. The last chapter explained that monopoly is generally undesirable. When horizontal competitors enter into a cartel, they become a single economic unit. Where such competitors account for a sufficient proportion of the market, the economic effect is equivalent to creating a monopoly. The only difference is that, rather than a single entity reaping the windfall profits associated with supracompetitive pricing, several companies divide the bounty among themselves. Consumers suffer equally under both scenarios.

There is no economic distinction between agreements to raise price and those to reduce output. Price and output are two sides of the same coin. When an entity with market power raises its prices, it causes the quantity sold in the market to drop (save in the rare cases where the relevant portion of the demand curve is vertical), and vice versa.

One might wonder why market-sharing agreements lie in the same category as price and output agreements. In fact, divvying up the geographic locations in which cartel members can sell is worse because it eliminates both price and quality competition. When rivals agree not to increase their prices, each has an incentive to capture a greater share of the profits of the arrangement by competing in a manner not prohibited by the cartel. As it is rarely possible for a cartel to monitor compliance with the quality of goods and services, price agreements limit price, but not quality, competition. Conversely, assigning each cartel member a separate geographic market can foreclose both forms of competition.

There might nevertheless be a case for relaxing the automatic prohibition of such hard-core restrictions on competition if they were prone to yield off-setting efficiencies in at least some settings. Economists and courts agree, however, that cartels are so unlikely to produce economic benefits in excess of their costs that the efficient rule is simply to forbid them all. Nevertheless, we shall consider the possibility that price-fixing agreements and related "naked" restraints on competition might sometimes produce benefits.

2. Should the law ever permit cartels?

Two factors temper the harms that cartels visit upon society. First, cartels are inherently unstable and generally break down. Second, markets tend to self-correct because supracompetitive profits entice new competitors, whose emergence will eventually re-establish a competitive equilibrium.

As to instability, game theory explains why every cartel member has an incentive to cheat, which can lead to a breakdown in collusion. The principal insight is that the profit-maximising price for the entire cartel is greater than the short-term, profit-maximising, price for each cartel member. If cartel members raise price to the monopoly level, any one conspirator can increase their profit by undercutting that monopoly price. Depending on the price elasticity of demand, even a slight reduction in price can significantly increase demand for the cheating firm's product. Every other member reasons the same way, however, which will cause the cartel to collapse. The situation is another example of the prisoner's dilemma:

		Company 2	
		Collude	Cheat
Company 1	Collude	8, 8	0, 14
	Cheat	14, 0	2, 2

Figure 8.9

The preceding static game is an example of what economists call "Bertrand price competition"; consumers care only about price, such that undercutting will result in an immediate collapse in demand for that product. Although real markets do not display such extreme sensitivity to pricing (though some sectors, such as the airline industry, occasionally come close), it provides a useful illustration.

Suppose that Companies 1 and 2 are embroiled in competition. Determined to do better, they agree to charge the monopoly price. As soon as the agreement is in place, however, consider each company's incentives. If Company 2 colludes as promised, Company 1 can earn 8 by also colluding or can cheat for a return of 14. Obviously, it would prefer to cheat. What if Company 2 cheats? In that event, Company 1 should again cheat because doing so would yield it a return of 2 as opposed to 0. Each company's dominant strategy is to cheat, and so cheat–cheat is the Nash equilibrium. Game theory would predict that this cartel will fail.

Should we decline to condemn price fixing for this reason? The answer is no, for several reasons. First, even if a cartel rapidly decays, the period of supracompetitive pricing inflicts efficiency losses that the threat of criminal sanctions and fines may have dissuaded. Furthermore, if collusion is lawful, failed agreements can be reinitiated. Antitrust enforcement can arrest this harmful phenomenon in its incipiency. Second, real-life cartels do not occur statically, but operate over time. Dynamic game theory suggests that cartel members may be able to overcome the dilemma outlined above. In that event, parties to a price-fixing agreement may be able to manufacture a new Nash equilibrium at cheat–cheat. The economic case for prohibition is iron clad.

Suppose that Companies 1 and 2 must decide whether to collude or to cheat in successive periods. Cheating yields a greater profit in any given period, but now each company must factor in the consequences. Suppose that Company 2 credibly threatens that, in the event that Company 1 cheats, Company 2 will price at the competitive level forever. This is a so-called "grim strategy". If that threat is credible, then, in deciding whether to cheat or to collude in any given period, Company 1 will have to weigh the financial benefit of cheating in the instant period against the present value of the foregone benefits of future collusion-level profits. Depending on the trade-off, the dominant strategy may be for both companies to collude.

Might exceptional circumstances justify hardcore restrictions on competition? There are two possibilities, but neither holds water.

The first involves a cartel comprising such a miniscule market share that it cannot affect market price or output. Consider, for example, two neighbourhood grocery stores that lie on different sides of the same city and that many supermarkets separate. Should the owners of those two stores agree to increase price by 5%, for instance, there will be no effect whatsoever on the market-clearing price. Nevertheless, antitrust condemnation is sound, principally because the price-fixing agreement is unlikely to generate any cognisable efficiency benefits. If a certain form of behaviour almost-always harms efficiency and almost-never yields offsetting benefits, outright condemnation is desirable. Any other rule would require unjustifiable administrative expense in distinguishing exceedingly rare innocuous price-fixing from the inefficient kind. Moreover, even if the grocery-store example does not involve efficiency losses, it does implicate equitable concerns. Specifically, to the extent information-deprived consumers pay inflated prices there is a wealth transfer unconnected to any legitimate conduct.

The second possibility is that relaxing antitrust rules against price-fixing might be beneficial in times of economic distress. This view became real policy during the Great Depression in the 1930s, when the United States suspended certain antitrust rules in the hope that, by boosting firms' economic profits, it would induce those companies to hire more workers, thus reducing the unemployment rate. In fact, cartelisation had precisely the opposite effect. Monopolies restrict output. Recessions, of which depressions are a more extreme variant, are defined by sustained economic contractions in the form of lower output. Cartelisation therefore aggravates economic distress by compounding the output restrictions responsible for wealth losses, unemployment, and reduced economic activity. Today, there is a broad consensus that competition enforcement should be especially vigorous during times of economic contraction. This is all the more so because companies' incentive to enter into cartel agreements may be more pronounced during times of falling demand and profitability.

3. Tacit collusion

The principal goal of competition policy is to eliminate cartels. One new to antitrust, however, may be surprised to learn of a major loophole in the law. Although the law condemns both price-fixing and market-sharing agreements, competitors may silently to reach precisely the same arrangements through parallel conduct. "Tacit collusion" or "conscious parallelism" occurs when rivals collectively embrace monopoly pricing and output through independent action. It is perfectly lawful.

Imagine an "oligopoly", which is an industry in which a sufficiently small number of firms compete that each one must consider its competitors' actions. Suppose that four firms strive to outdo each other, which competition results in the market price approaching each company's marginal cost. Frustrated by its meagre profits, one firm decides to charge the monopoly price. If the other three companies decide to follow that price lead, the market price will rise through a process known as "barometric price leadership". As a matter of law, those competitors would be free to maintain their prices at those levels indefinitely, as long as they do not agree with one another to do so or embrace such facilitative practices as sharing pricing, sales, or sensitive cost information. This aspect of the law is no small detail. It is a gaping hole in the antitrust mandate against price fixing.

One might argue that, in the absence of a formal agreement, there can be no contract sufficient to trigger the "concerted action" requirement of Section 1 of the Sherman Act or Article 101 TEU. Such an argument would be incorrect. Note the close analogy between tacit collusion and unilateral contract at common law. In the latter case, an offeror announces that it will contract on particular terms should an offeree accept. Acceptance takes the form of affirmative action, rather than an expression of assent. In much the same way, an oligopolist that increases its price to the monopoly level sends a message to the market that it will maintain its price, should its competitors follow suit. Those rivals need not sign a contract or shake the first mover's hand to embrace the offer. They need merely raise their prices to the monopoly level. The law could regard barometric price leadership as a form of agreement.

Ultimately, competition law grudgingly accepts tacit collusion. The first problem lies in enforcement. Strategic interrelationship between competitors defines oligopolistic markets, such that rational choice depends on the actions of one's rivals. How, then, would one enjoin tacit collusion? The injunction would arguably have to order a company to ignore important market information and act irrationally.[1] This may be a decree with which an enjoined party could not comply.

Two economic phenomena dilute the problem of tacit collusion. First, cartels are inherently unstable because each "conspirator" has an incentive to cheat to secure larger profits in the short term. Second, entry, rather than antitrust intervention, may be the proper solution to tacit collusion. In the absence of significant entry barriers, conscious parallelism will attract new competition into the market.

4. Lawful restrictions on horizontal competition

Adam Smith famously commented that "[p]eople of the same trade seldom meet together, even for merriment and diversion, but the conversation ends in a conspiracy against the public, or in some contrivance to raise prices". Hardcore restrictions of the kind discussed above epitomise those dangers. Nevertheless, the view that inter-competitor collaboration always degrades efficiency is misplaced. Rivals efficiently interact with one another in all manner of fora. Competitors enter into joint ventures, seeking to accomplish together what neither could achieve alone. Rivals enter into standard-setting organisations and patent pools, which respectively agree upon interoperable technological platforms and clear blocking positions by dispensing essential patents. Industry trade groups meet periodically to discuss matters of common concern to the industry, though antitrust lawyers who are present ensure that participants do not discuss any sensitive issue of importance to competition. In short, some restrictions on competition between horizontal rivals are efficient.

So, how are antitrust enforcers to distinguish good combinations from bad? First, scrutinise the agreement to determine whether its principal aim or consequence is to eliminate price, output, or quality competition at the horizontal level. If it is, the arrangement is a "naked" restriction and, hence, illegal. The fact that an arrangement eliminates competition, however, does not in itself establish its inefficiency. The question is whether restricted competition is a necessary feature of an agreement that carries a larger benefit.

Envision a joint venture between pharmaceutical companies to develop a high-risk, capital-intensive drug. Both firms have complementary scientific expertise that would help to realise the pharmacological breakthrough. A legitimate corollary of such an arrangement may be the joint administration and pricing of the ensuing drug, insofar as the accord does not extend beyond the confines of the venture to affect separate aspects of each firm's business.

The fact that a horizontal non-price restriction serves a function beyond eliminating competition, however, does not guarantee its legality. Consider a famous 1984 opinion of the US Supreme Court, which scrutinised the National Collegiate Athletic Association's deal with television networks. The arrangement restricted the number of American football games that the networks could broadcast in a season and prohibited member colleges from individually negotiating additional broadcasts.[2] The Court declined to condemn the contract on its face, despite its "horizontal" and "output restrictive" effects, but instead observed that "what is critical is that this case involves an industry in which horizontal restraints on competition are essential if the product is to be available at all".[3] Given the NCAA's failure to articulate a pro-competitive justification for the restriction, however, the contract was found to violate antitrust laws.

---

1 This argument is not iron clad. The author has argued elsewhere that the law could benefit by outlawing tacit collusion in certain, narrow circumstances. *See* Alan Devlin, 'A proposed solution to the problem of tacit collusion in oligopolistic markets' (2007) 59 Stan L Rev 1111.

2 *Nat'l Collegiate Athletic Ass'n v Bd. of Regents of Univ. of Oklahoma*, 468 US 85 (1984).

3 Ibid. at 101.

More generally, to determine the efficiency and hence legality of most concerted practices, one must determine their net effect. This approach finds its clearest application under the US rule of reason, under which a plaintiff must first establish that a challenged restraint eliminates competition, after which showing the defendant must demonstrate that the restraint carries off-setting benefits. Should the defendant make that showing, the ultimate burden of persuasion falls on the plaintiff to prove that the net effect of the arrangement is negative.

5. Monopsony

Interesting issues arise when monopoly arises not on the selling side of the market, but on the buying side. This occurs when a single buyer faces competing sellers that have no viable substitute outlays for their goods. Economists use the term "monopsony" to characterise this market condition. While monopoly drives market prices above marginal cost, monopsony results in prices falling below the point at which the marginal social benefit of an input equals its marginal expense of provision. Neither result is efficient.

Monopsony most often occurs in an intermediate portion of a vertical supply chain, when a sole manufacturer forces the purveyors of its inputs to reduce their prices below competitive levels. The unilateral acquisition or exercise of monopsony power is lawful in the absence of predatory or exclusionary practices. The result is different, however, when competing buyers fix the price at which they purchase inputs, thus coercing upstream sellers to accept a lower price. Antitrust condemns buyer-side cartels in the same way that it prohibits seller-side price fixing and market sharing. This holds true even though one might think of buyers as "consumers" whom the competition laws protect.

Imagine that all the hospitals in a city agreed to reduce nurses' wages. This agreement would obviously make nurses worse off and hospitals better off. In that labour market, nurses are sellers of health-care services and hospitals are purchasers, so one might thus think the conspiracy desirable if one focuses on consumers alone. Yet, hospitals are part of a vertical chain of distribution, and are not the ultimate consumers of health-care services: patients are. What happens to those patients as a result of the wage-suppressing agreement? Intuition might suggest that health-care prices will decline because of hospitals' lower operating costs. From that perspective, the monopsonistic agreement would appear to be desirable, at least for the ultimate consumer.

Economic analysis, however, reveals that monopsonistic accords are every bit as destructive of efficiency as cartels on the selling side of the market, though the reasons why are more complicated. The relevant analysis looks at two distinct market segments. Using the hospital wage-setting conspiracy as an example, consider the agreement's effect on output and price in the nursing-services market.

In an input market, the quantity supplied increases as price rises (in the employment setting, "price" comes in the form of a wage or salary). To continue with our example, if hospitals increase nurses' salaries, the supply of nurses in the market will increase. By the same token, reduced salaries cause fewer nurses to apply for jobs. As direct purchasers of nursing services, hospitals would like to pay less for each person they hire. If they acquire monopsony power, the hospitals could force down the market price. Doing so would increase their profits, but it would also reduce the number of inputs supplied. Hospitals would attempt to compensate for the shortfall by substituting alternative inputs for nurses, but the substitution would be imperfect. We can be confident in this conclusion because, if substitute inputs were more efficient, the hospitals would already have been using them.

The net result is twofold. First, the buyer-side conspiracy reduces output in the input market (here, nursing services). Second, unless demand is perfectly inelastic in the downstream market, output will decrease there, too, because of higher marginal costs, thus harming ultimate consumers. This is counter intuitive, as manufacturers' forcing the price of their inputs to sub-competitive levels actually *increases* the prices that consumers pay downstream. The following graph illustrates the exercise of monopsony power:

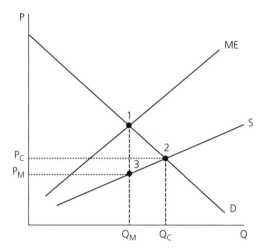

Figure 8.10

The graph demonstrates how monopsony power reduces price from the competitive level, P_C, to the monopsony level, P_M. A deadweight loss in the form of the 1–2–3 triangle results from a drop in the input sold in the market from Q_C to Q_M. Why will price and output fall to P_M and Q_M, respectively? The answer lies in the monopsonist's profit-maximising decision. While a monopolist maximises profit by producing the output at which marginal cost equals marginal revenue, a monopsonist produces at the point where the marginal expense of purchasing one more unit of the relevant input equals its marginal product (i.e. the incremental, private benefit to the monopsonist of acquiring that input). In the preceding graph, the demand curve represents the marginal product of the relevant input. Thus, the profit-maximising point occurs where the marginal-expense curve, ME, intersects with the demand curve, D.

A final note concerns the goal of antitrust law. Competition enforcers often frame the antitrust mandate in terms of consumer welfare. The Coase Theorem can clarify analysis by making clear that the pertinent economic issue encompasses not just consumers, but society as a whole. For that reason, it makes more sense to speak of aggregate welfare, rather than consumer welfare. Consistent with that fact, there is no need to appeal to the downstream economic effect of a cartel on the buying side. Monopsony suppresses the quantity of inputs produced and sold in the segment of the vertical chain in which buyers exercise their power over price. This is not a zero-sum transfer, but entails a deadweight loss that reduces aggregate welfare. Buyer-side price-fixing agreements are, therefore, inefficient.

The one conceivable exception involves purchasers' agreeing on price in response to monopoly on the selling side of the market. When monopoly and monopsony meet, the result is bilateral monopoly. In the absence of superior bargaining power or skill on one side, one might expect the competitive level. Note, however, that this academic possibility does not justify buyer-side cartels, which economics predicts to be inefficient in virtually all circumstances.

6. Conclusion

Antitrust enforcement is a complex endeavour, and the case for intervention against perceived anti-competitive practices is often unclear. Competition enforcers must weigh industry dynamics, the possibility of error, the likelihood and speed of market self-correction, and off-setting short- and long-term effects in deciding whether to bring an enforcement action. The problems are especially weighty in the field of single firm behaviour, as the next chapter makes clear.

Against this backdrop, the prohibition on naked restrictions on horizontal competition stands out as a clear policy dictate. The primary goal of a competition-enforcement agency should be to eradicate cartel agreements, which produce the full costs of monopoly or monopsony without offsetting benefits. The prospect of attaining a dominant position drives companies to be more innovative, to achieve greater efficiency, to manufacture superior products, and to provide superior customer service. Accepting periods of monopoly achieved on such a basis is a price worth paying. Appropriation of consumer welfare through private contract between horizontal competitors, however, generates no such boon, and ought to be flatly condemned.

Governments routinely sanction cartels and monopolies – even though they are as destructive of efficiency as any other hardcore restriction – and impede entry into various occupations and professions. Trade unions, for example, would be unlawful were they not exempt from competition law. A rationale for legalising union activity is to correct an imbalance of power between purchasers and sellers of labour. Should employers enjoy monopoly power, allowing prospective and current employees to achieve monopsonistic power through private agreement results in bilateral monopoly? The same justification can support the introduction of a higher minimum wage, which can increase employment where employers enjoyed monopsony power over the market wage. This justification falls away, however, where competition exists among prospective employers or where workers are skilled and hence command market power on the selling side.

C. Vertical Restraints on Competition

Restrictions on horizontal competition endanger efficiency because they tend to restrict output and to raise price. Vertical competition, however, is different. Verticality refers to the chain of distribution through which a manufactured good makes it way via distributors and retailers to consumers. An important question in competition law concerns restrictions that manufacturers residing at the top of the vertical chain impose on those operating below. We shall consider three specific cases, which entail a producer's: (1) assigning exclusive sales territories to its dealers; (2) fixing a maximum price on the resale of its goods; and (3) insisting on a minimum price for its products.

To analyse vertical restraints, one must distinguish inter- and intra-brand competition. Envision a manufacturer of high-end cars. Once it has produced those vehicles, the company will need to get them from its factory to consumers. The firm could vertically integrate, creating a private distribution and retail network. Alternatively, the manufacturer could contract with third parties to accomplish that process on its behalf. Producers want to minimise the cost of distribution because consumer demand for their goods will decline with an increased price, which will rise in tandem with higher delivery costs. Manufacturers thus have an interest in spurring competition among their dealers. The greater this competition, however, the lower the incremental cost that the distribution process adds, and the producers will realise greater profits. Price and quality competition between distributors and retailers of the *same* product is "intra-brand competition".

"Inter-brand competition", by contrast, exists between different manufacturers' substitutable products. In the luxury car example, our manufacturer must strive to outdo sellers of other high-end vehicles. If inter-brand competition is sufficiently forceful, an absence of intra-brand rivalry is irrelevant because even a monopolist distributor and retailer cannot increase price in the downstream market if consumers enjoy access to competitively priced interchangeable goods.

Armed with this knowledge of inter- and intra-brand competition, as well as of manufacturers' incentives to minimise the cost of distribution, consider three forms of vertical restraints that have triggered antitrust concern. These agreements are generally efficient, though their potential to cause harm justifies scrutiny under competition law.

1. Exclusive dealerships and territories

Horizontal market-sharing agreements are the most destructive of efficiency because they eliminate both price and quality competition. For that reason, rivals agreeing to divvy up geographical zones between themselves is a hardcore offence, which many jurisdictions punish with a criminal sanction. Vertical non-price restraints, in which manufacturers bestow separate sales territories on their respective dealers, however, are entirely different.

First, ask why a producer would ever grant only one distributor/retailer the right to carry its merchandise? As manufacturers wish to minimise the cost of getting their produce to consumers, is competition between dealers carrying the same good desirable? Generally, the answer is yes, but it does not follow that restrictions on dealer-level competition are inefficient. In fact, there are important pro-competitive justifications for vertical non-price limitations on competition.

First, a manufacturer of new goods for which a market has yet to emerge may have difficulty finding retailers that will carry and aggressively promote its product line. To compensate for the risk in selling an unknown product, a manufacturer may need to offer the retailer an exclusive sales opportunity to justify the requisite investment. Second, even for well-known brands, the low profit margins associated with high levels of intra-brand competition may lead dealers not to advertise or to provide superior customer service. In return for contractual guarantees of lofty marketing efforts by a particular retailer, a supplier can offer exclusive marketing opportunities.

United States' law recognises the potentially potent efficiency benefits of vertical non-price restraints, but EU law has taken a harder line. The reason lies not in economic principles, but in distinct goals. The defining objective of the EU has been to promote the common market. Construing country-specific exclusive dealerships as being incompatible with this fundamental goal, the ECJ has struck down such restrictions without considering the relevant economics.[4] Once can question the ECJ's reasoning, however, as if vertical non-price restraints promote inter-brand competition, the net result would likely be greater levels of cross-member-state commerce.

Economic analysis suggests that manufacturer-imposed vertical restraints are presumptively efficient and hence should be lawful, precisely because suppliers have an incentive to minimise the cost of distributing and marketing their inventory. To analyse the propriety of a vertical restraint, therefore, one should identify its source. If the insistence on geographic market separation comes from competing downstream dealers, which conditions they force upon the relevant manufacturer, the restriction is probably inefficient.

2. Maximum resale prices

Many manufacturers prohibit their dealers from charging more than a certain price. One might question the danger of a maximum price, or price cap, even in the horizontal setting. After all, if competition law concerns itself with fostering lower prices and higher output, isn't a restriction that sets a ceiling on price to be applauded? The answer is no. In the first place, if such a limitation emanates from private agreement between rivals, it is likely to be in those competitors' interests rather than in those of the public. Second, a price ceiling is a facilitative device that allows oligopolists to collude by providing them with a benchmark. In the simplest case, if rivals set a "maximum price" equal to the monopoly price, the arrangement is simply a cartel. Finally, in times of deflation, setting a price at an agreed-upon, fixed ceiling constitutes a *de facto* price increase over time.

---

4   *Consten SA and Grundig Verkaufs-GmbH v Commission* [1966] ECR 299.

Thus, the prohibition on horizontal maximum-price agreements stands on a solid footing, but what of price ceilings that manufacturers impose in a vertical setting? Vertical resale price maintenance can be efficient for several reasons, most obviously in limiting the exercise of monopoly power that a manufacturer's dealers may possess or acquire in the downstream retail market. As noted above, producers wish to minimise the incremental cost incurred in moving their goods through the chain of distribution. Suppressing the price that their dealers can charge downstream directly promotes that interest. It is only if the downstream retailers are themselves the source of the maximum price that the vertical restriction may reflect a horizontal price-fixing conspiracy at the retail level.

3. Minimum resale prices

Resale price maintenance can also take the form of a minimum retail price. At first blush, it is not obvious why a manufacturer would wish to maintain a price floor for its product downstream. After all, producers generally benefit when dealers compete on price because such competition increases consumer demand for the relevant manufacturers' products.

Nevertheless, a producer might want to prevent prices from dipping below a certain level in the downstream market. Vertical, minimum-price restraints can prevent free riding. Suppose that two dealerships both carry a manufacturer's car. One dealer puts together a lavish showroom and offers a luxurious range of pre-sale services to prospective customers. Such efforts, of course, inure to the benefit of the car producer, as it boosts demand. Yet, if one retailer undertakes such efforts, another may take advantage by offering none of those services, and using the ensuing cost saving to undercut the marketing dealer's price. Knowing its vulnerability to such free riding *ex ante*, no dealer may actively promote the manufacturer's products. A suitably tailored minimum resale price can cure by this problem by giving each dealer a sufficient mark up.

A minimum resale price can also protect a risk-taking dealer as an exclusive sales territory can, as a retailer benefitting from a generous minimum resale price will know that no other dealer carrying the same product line will be allowed to undercut its price. By enhancing the *ex ante* expected value of carrying a producer's goods, minimum resale prices can induce retailer investment.

Nevertheless, minimum resale prices bear capacity for anticompetitive effects. This is especially true if downstream dealers insist on their introduction. Depending on the nature of inter-brand competition, moreover, horizontally competing manufacturers could use resale price maintenance to coordinate a cartel. Given the off-setting potential for pro- and anticompetitive effects, the US Supreme Court was correct in 2007 to rule that minimum resale prices are not illegal *per se*, but should be construed under the rule of reason.[5] EU law, however, has yet to evolve to that point. In that jurisdiction, an uncritical hostility to vertical restrictions remains.

D. Conclusion

The Coase Theorem suggests that market transactions reallocate scarce resources desirably. That assumption underlies modern competition policy. Instead of intervening in markets to engineer superior outcomes, antitrust serves a passive, prophylactic role that prevents companies from corrupting market forces. Although it can be difficult to determine whether antitrust intervention produces net gains or losses in particular cases, economics yields at least one unequivocal prescription: the law should condemn naked restraints of trade between horizontal rivals. Cartel agreements

---

5 *Leegin Creative Leather Prods, Inc v PSKS, Inc*, 127 S Ct 2705 (2007).

are economically comparable to those inefficient contracts explored in Part V because they seek to benefit the contracting parties at the expense of third parties. As those third parties are not privy to the agreements, there is no *à priori* basis for assuming them efficient. In fact, economic analysis makes clear that both price-fixing and market-sharing arrangements affirmatively reduce welfare.

In light of the dangers of inter-rival contracts, the law properly views collaboration between competitors with suspicion. Still, horizontal restraints can enhance efficiency when they make larger benefits possible. Joint ventures, trade associations, patent pools, and standard-setting organisations are thus properly subject to antitrust oversight, but not to outright condemnation. Careful economic analysis of horizontal restraints, including market-power analysis, is indispensable to ensuring proper competition enforcement.

When one moves away from horizontal agreements to consider vertical restraints on competition, the relevant analysis changes. Resale price maintenance, exclusive dealerships, and market division among retailers are likely to be efficient when manufacturers impose them. As profit-maximising producers wish to minimise the cost of distribution and retail, vertical restraints upon which manufacturers insist are likely to be socially desirable. Nevertheless, competition oversight is warranted to ensure that such restraints are neither the means of implementing a horizontal conspiracy between manufacturers nor the result of a downstream cartel among retailers. Economics indicates that US antitrust law is generally correct within the field of vertical restraints, though EU competition law has yet to adopt an equally sophisticated body of jurisprudence. One explanation for this disparity, however, may lie in EU objectives going beyond economic efficiency, which goals include market integration.

Key Points

- The cardinal rule of antitrust is that horizontal competitors may not fix prices or allocate markets, save where those restraints are ancillary to a larger, pro-competitive arrangement.
- Agreements eliminating competition are a species of contract contrary to public policy. They are inefficient because they create costs in excess of private gains to the conspirators. In a world without transaction costs, firms and consumers would contract to the point that perfect competition prevailed. That outcome would be Pareto optimal. Price-fixing and market-sharing conspirators violate that social contract, destroying value in the process.
- Nevertheless, firms may tacitly collude without breaking the law. Although it may not explicitly agree to terms, an oligopolist is free to raise its price to the monopoly level – a move that is contrary to short-term self-interest because it is loss-making if other firms do not follow. If the other firms in the market follow the price lead, the result will be monopoly price and output.

  o Competition law declines to condemn tacit collusion because it would be difficult to enjoin. In oligopolistic markets, firms must factor their rivals' anticipated reactions into their price-setting decisions. An injunction ordering a company not to take account of its competitors' prices would thus require irrational conduct. Entry may be the best remedy for tacit collusion.

  o Static models in game theory suggest that tacit collusion is difficult to maintain. Implicit cartels should erode because every firm has an incentive to "cheat" by undercutting its rivals. Dynamic models in which conspirators can "punish" defectors through price wars, however, suggest that collusion may become a Nash equilibrium.

- Monopsonistic agreements – those between purchasers that create buying power – are equally destructive of efficiency as seller-side cartels. They cause output reductions upstream that also distort outcomes in downstream markets.

- Vertical restraints occur between firms at different levels of the distribution chain. They are less likely to create anticompetitive effects than horizontal restraints. As a general rule, manufacturers wish to minimise the cost of the distribution and retail process, for which reason restraints upon which they insist are likely to be efficient.

  o A producer may award its dealers exclusive sales territories. Although doing so limits intra-brand competition, it may enhance inter-brand competition by compensating dealers for embracing risk in marketing the producer's goods. US law analyses such restraints under the rule of reason, while EU law takes a strong line against any vertical contracts that divide markets by member state. The EU rule reflects the non-economic goal of market integration.

  o Vertically imposed, minimum resale prices can protect a dealer against free-riding, while maximum resale prices can limit mark ups, thus stimulating demand for the manufacturer's product. Where such restraints emanate from an agreement between downstream retailers, however, they are likely to be anticompetitive. The same is true if the impetus for them lies in concerted action between upstream manufacturers of competing products.

 ## References and Further Reading

Books
Posner, Richard A., *Antitrust Law Part II*, 2nd edn (2001).
Posner, Richard A., *Economic Analysis of Law* (2011) §§ 10.1–10.3, 10.12–10.13 (2011).
Miceli, Thomas J., *The Economic Approach to Law*, 2nd edn (2008) pp. 320–24.
Elhauge, Einer (ed.), *Research Handbook on the Economics of Antitrust Law* (2013) Chs. 4, 7–8.
Williamson, Oliver E., *Markets and Hierarchies: Analysis and Antitrust Implications* (1975).
Blair, Roger D. and Harrison, Jeffrey L., *Monopsony in Law and Economics*, 2nd edn (2010).
Viscusi, W. Kip, Vernon, John, Harrington, Joseph, *Economics of Regulation and Antitrust*, 4th edn (2005).
Baird, Douglas G., Gertner, Robert and Picker, Randal, *Game Theory and the Law* (1994) pp. 165–78.
Stigler, George J., 'A Theory of Oligopoly', in *The Organization of Industry* (1968) p. 39.

Articles
Baker, Jonathan B., 'Identifying cartel policing under uncertainty: The U.S. steel industry, 1933–1939' (1989) 32 JL & Econ 47.
Blair, Roger D. and Harrison, Jeffrey L., 'Antitrust policy and monopsony' (1991) 76 Cornell L Rev 297.
Dick, Andrew R., 'When are cartels stable contracts?' (1996) 39 JL & Econ 241.
Green, Edward J. and Porter, Robert H., 'Noncooperative collusion under imperfect price information' (1984) 52 Econometrica 87.
Hay, George A. and Kelley, Daniel, 'An empirical survey of price-fixing conspiracies' (1974) 17 JL & Econ 13.
Hovenkamp, Herbet, 'The law of vertical integration and the business firm: 1880–1960' (2010) 95 Iowa L Rev 863, 911.
Meese, Alan J., 'Intrabrand restraints and the theory of the firm' (2004) 83 NCL Rev 5.
Philipson, Thomas J. and Posner, Richard A., 'Antitrust in the not-for-profit sector' (2009) 52 JL & Econ 1.
Posner, Richard A., 'Oligopoly and the antitrust laws: A suggested approach' (1969) 21 Stan L Rev 1562.
Posner, Richard A., 'The next step in the antitrust treatment of restricted distribution: per se legality' (1981) 48 U Chi L Rev 6.

Posner, Richard A., 'Vertical restraints and antitrust policy' (2005) 72 U Chi L Rev 229.

Spengler, Joseph, 'Vertical integration and antitrust policy' (1950) 58 J Pol Econ 347.

Turner, Donald F., 'The definition of agreement under the Sherman Act: Conscious parallelism and refusals to deal' (1962) 75 Harv L Rev 655.

Williamson, Oliver E., 'Assessing vertical market restrictions: antitrust ramifications of the transaction cost approach' (1979) 127 U Pa L Rev 953.

Chapter 3

Monopolisation

Chapter Contents

A.	Monopoly as an Elusive Prize: The Dilemma for Competition Regulators	349
B.	Product Tying	352
C.	Anticompetitive Pricing	355
D.	Refusals to Deal	359
E.	Loyalty Rebates	361
F.	Vertical Integration	362
G.	Anticompetitive Mergers: Unilateral and Coordinated Effects	364
Key Points		367
References and Further Reading		368

A. Monopoly as an Elusive Prize: The Dilemma for Competition Regulators

Given the evil of monopoly, one might expect antitrust to attack the condition in all its forms. After all, if competitive markets tend toward efficiency, why would antitrust enforcers not break up dominant undertakings? Chapter 1 explored the industrial organisation literature, a portion of which suggests that firms in concentrated markets earn supracompetitive economic profits. Should structural remedies be the order of the day, restoring competition and lower prices for consumers? The answer is no.

Dominance is itself perfectly lawful, as long as the monopolist neither achieves that position by predatory means nor artificially maintains it by exclusionary practices. This aspect of the law reflects a considered position. Although a structuralist view continues to hold sway in Europe, the Chicago and post-Chicago literature have diminished its influence. Instead, competition law polices dominate firm behaviour to ensure that it does not erect barriers to incumbent expansion and rival entry. This section explains these aspects of modern antitrust policy.

1. Antitrust should rarely assail market structure

The reason not to condemn dominance is that monopoly is itself a powerful spur to competition. In capitalist systems, firms compete to maximise profit, and the prospect of supracompetitive returns drives companies to ever-greater efforts. To the extent those endeavours result in lower operating costs, superior products, and lower prices, they are desirable. The typical result is not necessarily dominance on the part of a single company, but a competitive equilibrium in which efficient firms survive and others fail.

When monopoly results from superior performance, competition enforcers should not assail the dominant position – at least not in the short term – because doing so would dilute the expected reward of successfully outcompeting one's rivals. It is only if companies seek monopoly through improper means – defined as practices capable of excluding equally or more efficient competitors – that antitrust condemnation is sound. As the US Supreme Court has explained:

> The mere possession of monopoly power, and the concomitant charging of monopoly prices, is not only not unlawful; it is an important element of the free-market system. The opportunity to charge monopoly prices – at least for a short period – is what attracts 'business acumen' in the first place; it induces risk taking that produces innovation and economic growth. To safeguard the incentive to innovate, the possession of monopoly power will not be found unlawful unless it is accompanied by an element of anticompetitive conduct.[1]

A second reason not to condemn monopoly is that it may be a desirable condition in some industries. In the "new economy", which is founded on technology rather than on conventional manufacturing, the most valuable competition occurs in the laboratory. Firms compete using scientists, engineers, and physical capital to be the first to unearth valuable technologies. Such industries may display Schumpeterian "gales of creative destruction", which result in a sequence of ephemeral monopolies. At any one time, a single company may be dominant in an industry, yet its monopoly may be vulnerable. In the technological world, even a dominant undertaking cannot survive if it does not stay abreast of others' scientific advances. In such settings, monopoly is, in fact, the necessary reward that drives innovation. Efforts to maintain competitive market structures may therefore advance static efficiency at a disproportionate cost to dynamic efficiency.

---

1 *Verizon Communications Inc v Law Offices of Curtis V Trinko, LLP*, 540 US 398, 407 (2004).

The third justification for not attacking monopoly is the presumption that uncompromised market processes work reasonably well. Antitrust's mandate, therefore, is simply to arrest private efforts to corrupt market processes. As a result, competition enforcers should only target monopolists that seek to perpetuate, or achieve, their dominance by suppressing competition from equally or more efficient rivals.

Finally, monopolisation cases are notoriously protracted and expensive. It takes many years for them to progress to final appeal. By then, industry developments may have rendered the challenged exclusion defunct. That makes any behavioural or structural remedy irrelevant, and a sanction laudatory only in sending a message to future firms tempted to exclude rivals. To be sure, deterrence matters, but depending on the circumstances, it may not be worth the cost of litigation, especially where the relevant market is likely to self-correct promptly.

All told, these factors suggest that agencies should not challenge dominance for its own sake. US law has long recognised this principle, as Judge Learned Hand observed in 1945 that "[t]he successful competitor, having been urged to compete, must not be turned on when he wins".[2] Consistent with that guiding metric, US antitrust law does not hold a company guilty of the offence of monopolisation if it grew or developed "as a consequence of a superior product, business acumen, or historic accident".[3] Similarly, EU competition law only forbids the *abuse* of a dominant position. It does not condemn the fact of monopoly itself.

Nevertheless, a hands-off approach to monopoly makes sense only if competition is likely to erode the company's market power over time. Should a monopoly endure for reasons other than efficiency, the dominant firm is likely to achieve a windfall that exceeds the prize necessary to spur fierce competition *ex ante*. The degree to which monopoly endures over time is contested, and would seem to depend on the industry in question. Even if one could identify monopolised markets resistant to competition, competition law may not be an appropriate mechanism to solve the problem. There is some precedent for successful use of antitrust laws to restructure monopolised industries. The best example is the 1984 divestiture of the long-time telecommunications monopolist, AT&T, into seven regional holding companies subject to equal-access duties. This remedy dramatically increased competition in the US long-distance telecommunications market. More generally, though, empirical evidence suggests that structural remedies are often ineffective in reinvigorating lost competition.[4]

2. Antitrust should challenge exclusionary behaviour

Intervening in markets to engineer more desirable industry structures is to be distinguished from condemning exclusionary practices by dominant firms. Society best applies antitrust to facilitate competition, constraining monopolists' ability to hinder rivals from developing viable market positions. This chapter explores five forms of potentially exclusionary conduct: product tying, predatory and limit pricing, refusal to deal, loyalty rebates, and vertical integration. Each of these practices can sometimes exclude competition, even though they do not generally do so. The analytic difficulty lies in the fact that such practices can create off-setting benefits, simultaneously enhancing a dominant undertaking's efficiency and encumbering rivals' ability to expand market share and to acquire a competitively significant position in the market.

Three factors affect the severity with which antitrust enforcers should assail single-firm conduct. First, how a dominant firm acquired its monopoly power affects the case for intervention. Where a company achieves success because of efficiency, the case for aggressively limiting the firm's

2 *United States v Aluminum Corp of America* 148 F2d 416, 430 (1945).
3 *United States v Grinnell Corporation*, 384 US 563, 570–71 (1966).
4 *See, e.g.*, Robert W. Crandall, 'The failure of structural remedies in Sherman Act monopolization cases' (2001) 80 Or L Rev 109.

freedom of action is less compelling. Of course, that does not mean that a firm may monopolise by competing on the merits, and thereafter occupy an antitrust-free zone. Conversely, if an undertaking inherits a dominant position from the government through the privatisation of a previously state-owned enterprise, for instance, the case for acquiescence is diminished.

Second, in jurisdictions that allow aggrieved consumers and competitors to sue under the antitrust laws, more permissive rules concerning dominant-firm conduct would be wise. Given the number of lawsuits and the incentive of competitor-plaintiffs to launch actions contrary to the public interest, holding plaintiffs to a demanding burden of proof is sensible.

Third, whether competition enforcement should be stringent or lax turns in part on one's faith in market processes. Determining whether an alleged abuse of a dominant position enhances or detracts from welfare is challenging. One must often weigh short-term restrictions on competition that detract from static efficiency against possible long-term incentives that enhance dynamic efficiency. Long-term effects, however, are inherently speculative, so the relevant calculus requires a comparison between terms that are almost impossible to quantify and that are thus incommensurate.

One solution is to appeal to error analysis. Type I errors – or false positives – occur when a court erroneously condemns a monopolist for an efficient practice. Type II errors – or false negatives – arise when a court mistakenly blesses anticompetitive behaviour. An influential view is that Type I errors are worse than Type II because the former will be ephemeral.[5] As the market will erode monopoly profits and eventually re-establish competition, the cost of a false negative is temporary. Conversely, market forces do not affect judicial decisions that forbid desirable practices, so a Type I error in the monopolisation context will endure, at least until it is overruled. Some use this line of thought to justify a permissive approach to single-firm conduct, most notably the US Department of Justice in its 2008 report.[6] In an unprecedented move, the Federal Trade Commission refused to join, and in fact denounced, the report stating that it was a blueprint for weakened antitrust enforcement against monopoly. The Justice Department withdrew the report the following year under the Obama administration.

Beyond the asymmetric influence of the SCP paradigm, the preceding factors – the manner in which monopoly arose; whether the jurisdiction authorises private actions; and one's faith in the market – accounts for a transatlantic divide between US and EU competition policy. The European approach is more aggressive than that of the US. In Europe, many dominant undertakings are former state-owned enterprises; antitrust enforcement has been predominantly public rather than private; and faith in the market is less pronounced than in the United States. By contrast, in America, most successful companies largely acquired their positions by being superior competitors and innovators; private enforcement is widespread; and a belief in the capitalist process, though shaken by the Great Recession of 2008–2009, remains more firmly engrained than in Europe.

Still, there has been criticism – some of it justified – that EU competition law has occasionally protected competitors, rather than promoted efficiency. Furthermore, EU jurisprudence over single-firm conduct is, as a general matter, less economically sophisticated than US precedent. The Court of First Instance's 2009 opinion in *Microsoft* was emblematic of this shortcoming.[7]

Having explored some of the broad issues underlying the law of monopolisation, we now turn to the so-called "exclusionary" business practices that competition law has often condemned – sometimes uncritically – when dominant firms carry them out. Assume for the purposes of the following discussion that the company employing a challenged practice has monopoly power. In the absence of the existence or prospective attainment of such power, a firm is free unilaterally to

---

5 Frank H. Easterbrook, 'The limits of antitrust' (1984) 63 Tex L Rev 1.
6 US Department of Justice, Competition and Monopoly: Single-Firm Conduct Under Section 2 of the Sherman Act (2008) [withdrawn 2009].
7 Case T-201/04, *Microsoft v Commission* [2007] ECR-II-3601.

undertake any of the conduct explored below. This chapter limits its analysis to unilateral, dominant-firm behaviour.

B. Product Tying

Competition law has long condemned dominant-firm product tying, which occurs when a company insists that consumers wishing to purchase one good also buy another. Tying generally takes one of two forms. Bundling, or fixed-proportions tying, occurs when a vendor sells the tying and tied goods as a single package. For example, a smart phone (the tying product) comes with pre-loaded software (the tied product). Requirements contracts, or variable-proportion tie-ins, arise when a seller compels a consumer to purchase inputs (the tied products) needed to run the tying product only from the seller. For instance, a printer manufacturer may require its customers to buy all the ink that they need in the future from it and not from its competitors.

1. The (largely) misplaced case against product tying

Product tying raises a number of long-standing concerns. Foremost amongst them is coercion – namely that tying forces consumers to buy products that they do not want, thus stripping them of choice. Second, bundling and requirements contracts allow a dominant firm to "leverage" its monopoly power in the tying market to an otherwise-competitive tied market. Having obtained two monopolies via its tying strategy, the tying firm can extract supracompetitive prices from two markets instead of just one. Third, tying creates barriers to entry into the tied market by making it essential to enter both the tying and tied markets instead of just the tied market itself. These objections are intuitively attractive, but lie on dubious economic footing.

Why are these objections misplaced? The "coercion" objection is, as a general matter, facile because tying complementary goods typically serves consumer convenience. Consider the annoyance of getting home with a new remote to learn that batteries are not included. Furthermore, to the extent that capital markets provide sufficient funding to enable companies to enter markets to avail of supracompetitive profits, the necessity of entering two markets rather than just one need not foreclose entry. For that reason, even product tying that bestows monopoly market share on a tying firm in the tied market does not necessarily foreclose entry.

The larger issue is whether a dominant firm can use tying arrangements to leverage monopoly power into the otherwise-competitive tied market. An important economic insight is that such leverage is not always possible. According to the single monopoly profit theorem, a monopolist cannot extract a second supracompetitive return by employing a fixed proportions tie-in between goods the demand for which are positively correlated. Suppose that a single fast-food restaurant enjoys monopoly power because consumers do not see the restaurant's food as being interchangeable at the competitive price with other foods available nearby. The restaurant also sells soft drinks. However, suppose that a series of next-door establishments sell exactly the same beverages, so that the market for those drinks is competitive. Can the restaurant leverage its monopoly over fast food into the market for soft drinks by bundling its food with soft drinks, and thus enjoy two monopoly profits?

The answer is no. Suppose that the monopoly price of the food alone is £10 and the competitive price of the soft drinks is £2. If the restaurant bundles the two together, it cannot profitably charge a price greater than £12. Should it attempt to do so by charging, say, £13 for the bundle, it will actually reduce its profits. The reason is that charging £13 is indistinguishable from separately vending the food at £11 and soft drinks at £2. Since £10, rather than £11, is the profit-maximising price for food any *de facto* price increase beyond £10 will be less lucrative because lost sales will swamp the greater margin per sale thus achieved.

The same result holds for variable proportions tying arrangements if consumers enjoy perfect access to information at the time of purchase, such that they factor in any supracompetitive cost of the later-purchased tied product into the *de facto* price that they pay for the tying good. For example, if a dominant camera manufacturer requires its customers to purchase all their film from it, it will be unable to earn two monopoly profits as long as its customers factor the *ex post* cost of film into their upfront purchase decision.

The single-monopoly-profit theorem has clarified the counter-intuitive economic effects of product tying, and has demonstrated that ostensibly nefarious business practices need not carry malign effects. Price discrimination and/or producer- and consumer-side efficiencies are more likely to cause sellers to use tying arrangements. As we shall see below, however, the single-monopoly-profit theorem does not always hold.

Nevertheless, there is widespread hostility to product tying. EU law condemns it in strong terms. Indeed, Article 102 TEU provides that an abuse of a dominant position "may . . . consist in . . . making the conclusion of contracts subject to acceptance by the other parties of supplementary obligations which, by their nature or according to commercial usage, have no connection with the subject of such contracts". European courts have repeatedly condemned tying arrangements imposed by dominant undertakings.[8] US law adopts a qualified *per se* rule against the practice, though the prohibition is less severe than in Europe. Recent US decisions have retreated from the *per se* rule, which in any event, requires both a showing of monopoly power and that the tie have "a substantial potential for impact on competition".[9] In the DC Circuit's 2001 decision in *Microsoft*, the court rejected a *per se* rule, but instead used the rule of reason because of the potential efficiencies of bundling in high-technology markets.[10]

Competition law's continuing hostility law to product tying is disappointing. The probable explanation is two fold. First, economic analysis is counter-intuitive in this setting, perhaps leading policymakers to discount its conclusions. Second, tying is often efficient, but harms competitors. Competition enforcers generally agree that consumer welfare is the principal goal of competition enforcement. To the extent enforcers silently embrace protectionist objectives, particularly in favour of politically favoured companies (such as national champions), hostility to product tying is unsurprising.

2. Tying arrangements are generally efficient

What are the potential economic benefits of product tying? There must be some because tying is ubiquitous, including in competitive markets. Shoes are sold with laces; cars typically come with built-in radio and sometimes with navigation systems; cable and satellite television packages incorporate a bundle of programmes; restaurants often insist that consumers purchase wine only from the relevant establishment's cellar; schools routinely provide a mandatory curriculum of classes that students must take; and so on. This fact alone puts a blanket prohibition on weak footing. Sure enough, economists have identified several efficiencies that tie-ins can generate.

First, where tying and tied goods are complements[11] (as is typically the case), bundling eliminates search and negotiation costs for consumers. Most purchasers want their remote controls to come with batteries, and are aggravated when they do not. Most consumers prefer computers that

---

8 Case T-201/04, *Microsoft v Commission* [2007] ECR-II-3601; Case C-53/92P, *Hilti AG v Commission* [1994] ECR 1-667; *Napier Brown v British Sugar*, Commission Decision 88/519/EEC, 1988 OJ (L 284) 41; Tetra Pak II, Commission Decision 92/163/EEC, 1992 OJ (L 072) 1.

9 *Jefferson Parish Hospital Dist (No 2) v Hyde*, 466 US 2, 16 (1984).

10 *United States v Microsoft Corp*, 253 F3d 34 (DC Cir. 2001).

11 Two products are complementary if reducing the price of one increases the demand for the other, and vice versa.

have sufficient software pre-installed to allow them to begin using their new systems. Few buyers of ice-cream from a mobile vendor want the product without an accompanying cone or container. By bundling an array of goods that consumers generally wish to possess, a seller provides convenience, thus enhancing demand for its product and reducing the transaction costs that its customers endure. These benefits are equally real whether the relevant merchant is a monopolist or subject to competition.

Indeed, the efficiencies of combining complementary goods can be so strong that it makes more sense to think of the tying and tied products as a single unit. For instance, cars come with wheels and shoes are sold with laces. Both are examples of product ties, but each is more fruitfully understood as an example of technical integration. A dispositive dispute at the outset of many monopoly-tying cases is whether the tie combines two separate products at all. For instance, when sued for bundling its Windows operating system with its Internet Explorer browsing software, Microsoft argued (unsuccessfully) that no tie existed because the two products formed a unitary whole.

Second, tying solves the double-marginalisation problem that arises when two different vendors with market power sell complementary goods. Where different firms sell complements, none considers the fact that decreasing its price would increase demand for the other product. Each firm thus sets a higher price than it would if it experienced the benefit of greater demand thus created. When a single company ties such products, thus vertically integrating, it internalises the positive externality. The result is an overall lower price and higher output over the tying and tied products, which benefits both consumers and the tying company.

Third, variable-proportions tie-ins facilitates price discrimination. Such conduct is not always, or even generally, inefficient. Indeed, perfect price discrimination where a monopolist charges every customer his reservation (or "walk away") results in allocative efficiency – the same result as under perfect competition. There is no deadweight loss. First-degree price discrimination, however, is impractical. Second- and third-degree price discrimination can enhance or detract from efficiency depending on market conditions.[12] There is no general rule, then, that imperfect price discrimination reduces market output. Such discrimination, however, does enhance sellers' profits, and thus the return from innovating, which suggests that it may enhance dynamic efficiency.

A company can use tying arrangements to price discriminate by charging a competitive price for the tying product and charging a supracompetitive price for the complementary tied product. High-volume users will consume a greater amount of the latter good, thus paying a higher average price. Some prominent economists who have studied product tying as a price-discrimination mechanism have concluded that the great majority of tie-ins enhance social welfare.[13]

Fourth, product tying can produce savings for manufacturers. Offering consumers à la carte options can increase producers' expenses by denying them the scale and scope economies conducive of efficiency. Finally, tying may guarantee the safe operation of the tying good by ensuring that the complementary products needed to operate that good are fully interoperable.

3. Product tying can have anticompetitive effects

Despite its typical benefits, product tying can be problematic. This makes a rule of *per se* legality inappropriate. Three concerns warrant discussion.

---

12 Second-degree price discrimination involves selling at different prices depending on quantities purchased. The third-degree variant entails charging different consumer groups different prices for the same product.
13 *See, e.g.,* Erik N. Hovenkamp and Herbert Hovenkamp, 'Tying arrangements and antitrust harm' (2010) 52 Ariz L Rev 925. But *see* Einer Elhauge, 'Tying, bundled discounts, and the death of the single monopoly profit theory' (2009) 123 Harv L Rev 397.

First, the practice can harm competition where a monopolist in the tying market imposes a variable proportions tie-in to gain a dominant share of a tied market subject to significant scale economies. For anticompetitive effects to arise in this case, the tying product must not be essential to the use of the tied product (which is an implicit assumption of the single-monopoly-profit theorem).

By using its monopoly to capture sufficient share in the tied market, a tying firm can deny its rivals the requisite scale to compete in the tied market. The tying firm can then increase price in the tied market above the competitive level. An important point here is that a firm that employs a tie-in to deny its rivals sufficient scale in the tied market suffers lost profits for the duration of competitors' presence in the tied market. Once the tying company has forced its rivals from the tied market, however, it may be able to recoup those lost profits through increased prices *ex post*. Observe, however, that this possibility is subject to several demanding assumptions.

A second possibility is that a monopolist may want to acquire a dominant share of a tied market to foreclose competition in the tying market. This theory underlay the US government's 1998 action against Microsoft, which alleged that the software giant tied its dominant Windows operating system to its internet-browsing software to foreclose its rival software producer, Netscape. The government's theory was not that monopolisation of the internet browsing software market permitted Microsoft to earn a second monopoly profit. Rather, it was that Microsoft viewed web browsers as a threat because they exposed application program interfaces ("APIs"), which programmers could conceivably use to write applications that would run regardless of the underlying operating system. The government alleged that Microsoft used product tying (among other practices) to foreclose that nascent competition, which threatened the firm's network effect-protected monopoly in operating systems.

A third case in which product tying may be anticompetitive is where a price-regulated company employs tie-ins to evade rate-of-return, price-cap, or other regulatory price constraints. Even if the single-monopoly-profit theorem holds, a regulated entity might be able to use its dominant position in the tying market to charge monopoly prices over an unregulated tied product.

An important closing observation is that the economic models in which tying reduces efficiency are demanding in their assumptions, such that harmful tie-ins are likely be the exception rather than the rule. Presently, US and EU competition rules on product tying are too restrictive.

C. Anticompetitive Pricing

If competition law fosters lower prices, it is odd that it might condemn a firm for not charging enough. Nevertheless, there are two conflicting reasons why the law might call a dominant firm to task for charging too low a price.

The first is directly at odds with economics, namely that the law should not permit large, efficient companies to price their smaller, neighbourhood, family-owned counterparts out of business. Antitrust rejects this approach, instead respecting consumers' preferences, as revealed through their purchasing decisions. If people would rather pay more from businesses with which they have an affinity, they are free to do so. If they do not, it is because they prefer lower prices and greater choice. Were antitrust to forbid larger-scale or better-run companies from undercutting their less-efficient rivals' prices, it would do violence to consumers' wishes and hence to efficiency.

The second reason to be concerned with low prices is not that the prices themselves are objectionable; it is the possibility that the prices may be a conduit to a larger, nefarious end. This section explores two potentially exclusionary practices: predatory pricing and limit pricing. Although each may be a rational strategy for foreclosing competition, the law should generally approach claims of exclusionary pricing with a sceptical eye.

1. Predatory pricing

Predatory pricing occurs when a monopolist sets price below cost to eliminate consumer demand for its rivals' products, thus forcing its competition from the market. Although the account has a superficial appeal, "predatory pricing schemes are rarely tried, and even more rarely successful".[14] In the first place, it is almost never a realistic basis for monopolising an industry from a fringe position. To force its competitors to exit, a company would have to produce sufficient output to meet all demand for the relevant product at below cost price. In other words, it has to suffer per-unit losses over the entire industry's range of output (which will exceed even the competitive level of output due to below-marginal cost pricing). Even for a pre-existing monopolist, this requires a significant, short-term increase in output, which will be costly in the absence of excess capacity. For a would-be monopolist presently occupying an insignificant share of the market, however, the expansion in output would have to be dramatic and, in most cases, prohibitively expensive.[15]

Generally, if the strategy is to succeed, the predatory firm must be dominant and more efficient than its targeted competitors. To maintain its lucrative monopoly against companies seeking to avail of supracompetitive profits, an incumbent may threaten any aspiring entrant with a below-cost selling campaign. If the potential competitor believes that the threat is genuine, it would be unlikely to enter the market, thus leaving the incumbent's monopoly intact.

In most circumstances, however, the threat of pricing below cost is not credible. The reason is not just that the monopolist would have to sustain losses over a large range of sales; it is also that it must later recoup those losses to make the predatory campaign worthwhile. During the period of recoupment, price would necessarily have to be at monopoly levels, which will again entice entry. A subsequent entrant would reason that the incumbent may not be able to afford a second round of below-cost sales, and thus enter securely for that reason. Ultimately, the monopolist's rational, short-term reaction to entry is almost always to share the market rather than to price below cost. In the terminology of game theory, a threat of predatory pricing is non-credible. To illustrate the hypothetical, we can appeal once more to the extensive-form game that we encountered in Part 1 see Figure 8.11.

The Nash equilibrium in this game is for the competitor, C, to enter the market and for the incumbent monopolist, M, to accommodate entry. Note, however, that this model does not look beyond the period of predation, and thus implicitly assumes that the monopolist cannot recoup its losses through *ex post* supracompetitive pricing. This is a reasonable assumption if entry barriers are limited, but this will not always be the case.

Might predatory pricing ever be a rational strategy and hence a credible threat? The answer is yes. Game theory suggests that dominant companies may be able to use information asymmetries or superior access to capital to foreclose competition, thus insulating their monopolies. For example, suppose that a prospective entrant cannot determine whether the monopolist is a low-cost or high-cost firm. If it believes the latter, the competitor will enter, knowing that the monopolist's productive inefficiency will prevent the incumbent from pricing the entrant out of the market. If the would-be competitor supposes that the incumbent is a low-cost operator, however, it will not enter because of the danger of being priced out of the market. Game theory demonstrates that an incumbent may rationally signal that it is a low-cost company, even though it operates with high costs, by deliberately cutting prices below the short-term, profit-maximising level. This result is more likely if the incumbent possesses superior access to capital than the prospective entrant, as such low-cost financing can sustain the low-price signalling mechanism.

---

14 *Matsushita Elec Indus C. v Zenith Radio Corp*, 475 US 574, 587 (1986).
15 A possible exception could involve a large, well-financed conglomerate with the ability to cross-subsidise a campaign by its wing who wanted to acquire a monopoly in its market.

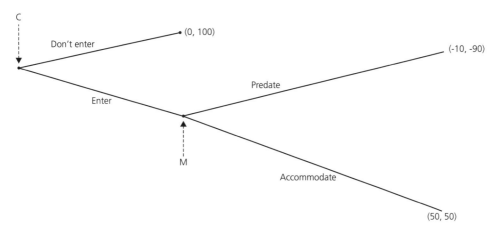

Figure 8.11

The fact that predatory pricing may sometimes be a rational strategy counsels against *per se* legality. Nevertheless, courts should hesitate before equating low prices with an abuse of a dominant position. Error costs may be especially severe in this setting. As low costs are almost invariably desirable in the short term, and only rarely destructive of long-term competition, courts and enforcers would do well to greet predatory-pricing claims coolly. This is all the more so when one realises that inefficient firms out-competed in the market have an incentive to file suit alleging below-cost predation. In short, aggressive enforcement against low pricing by dominant firms is likely to produce Type I errors that suppress price competition. That is a concern that courts and enforcers should take seriously.

United States and EU law differ in their treatment of predatory pricing. Unsurprisingly, both require that the accused dominant firm have priced below a measure of cost, which is most usually average variable cost (a proxy for marginal cost). The major distinction is that, in the United States, a plaintiff must establish that the firm pricing below cost has a dangerous probability of recouping its losses. This requirement reflects the economic insight that pricing at a loss is irrational when unaccompanied by an ability to win back the profits lost during the predatory campaign. The fact of irrationality is pertinent to the disposition of a case for two reasons. First, if low prices are an irrational means of predation, they are more likely to reflect a distinct, pro-competitive purpose. Second, absent the *ex post* acquisition of market power, consumers will reap the benefit of low prices in the short term at no long-term cost.

In Europe, by contrast, a firm abuses its dominant position if it prices below cost. There is no requirement that the undertaking enjoy a likelihood of regaining its losses. Interestingly, this aspect of EU law is consistent with an aggregate-welfare perspective on competition policy, as below-cost pricing is generally inefficient at the allocative level – some people who value the good below the incremental expense of its production will nevertheless get them. Regardless, EU law is likely incorrect not to require a showing of probable recoupment. The reason lies in error costs. It is difficult to determine whether a firm is, in fact, pricing below cost. Requiring a demonstration of exclusionary effect is an important limitation on Type I errors.

An important issue in predatory pricing concerns the appropriate measure of cost. Marginal cost is the relevant benchmark, but it is an academic construct and not something that appears in a financial statement or that can be readily calculated. Instead, the law uses different proxies for marginal cost. EU law typically uses average variable cost as a proxy, and deems any price below that level as presumptively unlawful when charged by a dominant undertaking.[16] The European Commission has also relied on long-term average incremental cost, which is generally a superior proxy for marginal cost.[17] It has also endorsed the use of average avoidable cost.[18]

2. Limit pricing

We conclude our discussion of exclusionary pricing with an example of *above*-cost pricing. This can, nevertheless, foreclose competition. If an incumbent monopolist charges a price equal to (or just below) an entrant's break-even price (i.e. the entrant's short-term average cost) and if the monopolist threatens to maintain that price should the competitor enter, it may be able to exclude competition. This is a limit-pricing strategy.

The problem with limit pricing is that, generally speaking, it is irrational and hence not credible. First, the limit price is less than the monopoly price, so in charging the limit price to deter entry, an incumbent by definition loses money in the short term. Second, it is rarely credible to threaten not to reduce output in the event of entry. The short-term, profit-maximising action in that case is to accommodate the new competition.

Separately, limit pricing is ineffective against prospective entrants that are equally, or more, efficient than the incumbent. A qualification to this last point is that, when scale economies are present, an entrant that would be more efficient than the incumbent at a comparable level of output might nevertheless operate with higher average cost when it first enters the market, possessing only modest market share. In that case, limit pricing could deter entry only if the entrant lacked access to sufficient capital to finance the acquisition of large-scale entry.

Still, limiting pricing can be rational. One solution to make the threat of exclusion rational is to build excess capacity, which pre-commits the monopolist not to reduce output in the event of entry. Creating such extra production capacity is, of course, expensive to the incumbent, but if the expected future profits of maintaining a monopoly are sufficiently lucrative when discounted to present value, the cost may be worth incurring.

An interesting question is whether the law has any place regulating limit pricing specifically and above-cost price reductions generally. Courts are not well placed to distinguish competitive from limit from monopoly prices, particularly in dynamic markets. Absent an ability reliably to demarcate pricing classifications, courts should adopt the insights of error analysis, which counsels *per se* legality. No less problematically, enunciating a prohibitory rule would invite perverse behaviour on the part of dominant firms, spurring them to raise prices to avoid monopolisation claims founded on limit pricing. Cognisant of these perils, US law generally rejects above-cost-price monopolisation claims, though there is some precedent to the contrary.[19] EU competition law takes a harder line. For instance, it is possible in Europe to abuse a dominant position by charging a price above average variable cost, as long as it is below average total cost.[20] Furthermore, in the European Commission's view, even price cuts above average total cost can be abusive in "exceptional" cases.[21]

Although unilateral limit pricing should be lawful, the prospect of such pricing could be an appropriate concern, for instance, in reviewing the propriety of a merger likely to result in a concentrated industry structure.

---

16 *AKZO Chemie BV* v *Commission of the European Communities*, C-62/86, [1991] ECR I-03359.
17 Commission Decision of 20 March 2001, Case COMP/35.141, OJ L 125/27, 5.5.2001.
18 DG Competition Discussion Paper on the Application of Article 82 of the Treaty to Exclusionary Abuses, para. 64 (December 2005). Available at: http://ec.europa.eu/competition/antitrust/art82/discpaper2005.pdf.
19 Compare, e.g., *Virgin Atl Airways Ltd* v *British Airways PLC*, 257 F3d 256, 269 (2d Cir 2001) and *Barry Wright Corp* v *ITT Grinnell Corp*, 724 F2d 227, 235–36 (1st Cir 1983) with *Transam Computer* v *IBM*, 698 F2d 1377, 1387 (9th Cir 1983). *See also LePage's* v *3M*, 324 F3d 141 (3rd Cir 2002) (en banc).
20 *AKZO Chemie BV* v *Commission of the European Communities*, C-62/86, [1991] ECR I-03359.
21 DG Competition Discussion Paper: 'The Application of Article 82 of the Treaty to Exclusionary Abuses', paras 127–129 (December 2005). Available at: http://ec.europa.eu/competition/antitrust/art82/discpaper2005.pdf.

D. Refusals to Deal

The most contentious question in monopolisation law is whether dominant firms must deal with their rivals. Competition rules have sometimes required monopolists to share their networks, infrastructure, or intellectual property with their rivals when such access is a requisite of competition in the market. For instance, in *Sealink*, the European Commission required a ferry company that owned the only port in Holyhead, Wales, to make that facility available to rival ferry lines at reasonable rates.[22] More recently, the European Court of First Instance (CFI) affirmed that Microsoft had abused its dominant position by refusing to share certain of its proprietary protocols necessary to allow Sun Microsystem's Solaris operating system to achieve inter-operability with Microsoft's work-group-server software.[23]

1. The economics of refusals to deal

Imposing a duty to deal can bypass this problem. A bottleneck arises when a private entity controls a facility without which one cannot compete in the market. The question is whether antitrust should require owners of infrastructures that are indispensable to, or even simply facilitative of competition to share them.

Forcing a monopolist to cooperate with its rivals implicates off-setting short- and long-term considerations. The immediate effect is to enhance competition; rivals access the assets they need to compete on comparable terms. As a result, consumers enjoy lower prices and access to a more eclectic range of goods. A duty to deal thus promotes static efficiency, and in that sense, would seem to be a desirable tool of antitrust policy.

There are potentially larger issues at play, however, and these counsel against imposing sharing obligations on dominant undertakings. In particular, denying successful firms the exclusive use of their property invites free riding and dilutes the value of *ex ante* investment in technology or infrastructure. In the presence of a mandatory sharing rule, competitors have obvious reason to sit on the sidelines. If the benefit of mandatory sharing is enhanced static efficiency, the potential cost is reduced dynamic efficiency. As Part VIII explored, however, dynamic efficiency is the greater source of social welfare, which suggests that competition law should require licensing only where the potential for error is slight.

The problem, however, is that the potential for error is usually significant. The long-term consequences of forced sharing are almost impossible to quantify, which means that the relevant short- and long-term factors are incommensurate. Worse, even if a court correctly imposes a duty to deal in a particular case, unless it enunciates a clear limiting principle, the precedential value of the mandatory access order may chill future third-party investment.

The attentive reader will recognise, however, that the under-compensation issue is a concern only if courts or regulators err in setting an appropriate access fee. After all, liability rules induce an efficient use of resources if the relevant price is calculated properly. There are compelling reasons to doubt courts' ability, however, to determine the optimal fee. In antitrust cases in which mandatory-sharing questions arise, transaction costs are rarely preclusive: there is just one monopolist, and presumably a small number of fringe competitors that seek to use the essential facility. If the dominant undertaking refuses to share at any price that its rivals offer, it follows within law and economics theory that the monopolist derives a greater return on its investment in the facility by not licensing at that price. In other words, the proffered licence fees under-compensate the owner. No other entity – neither rivals, nor the antitrust-enforcement agencies, and certainly not

22 *Sealink Containers v Stena Sealink* [1994] OJ L015.
23 Case T-201/04, Microsoft v Commission 2004 ECR II-4463.

the judiciary – has superior information about the value of the relevant infrastructure than the dominant owner itself. Should the courts require the company to deal at a price at which it would not have freely contracted, they deprive the firm of the exclusive use of its property in circumstances where there is no *à priori* basis for presuming that deprivation to be efficient.

There are thus good reasons to favour property rules in the "refusal-to-deal" setting. Exceptions may be appropriate in narrow circumstances. For instance, if a non-innovating monopolist's position has endured for an extended period, the dynamic inefficiency potential of a narrowly tailored duty to deal may be modest, yet the static-efficiency benefits may be large. Similarly, if powerful network effects are present, interoperability requirements may produce greater-than-typical benefits to both static and dynamic efficiency by fostering competition and follow-on innovation. For such reasons, the optimal antitrust rule is that duties to deal should attach only in extreme circumstances. In any other situation, the law should allow private enterprise to use their private property as they see fit.

2. US and EU law governing refusals to deal

US law follows this approach, recognising sharing obligations only in narrow circumstances. The US Supreme Court made this clear in 2007, explaining that "[w]e have been very cautious in recognising such exceptions, because of the uncertain virtue of forced sharing and the difficulty of identifying and remedying anticompetitive conduct by a single firm".[24] It characterised its *Aspen Skiing* decision as lying "at or near the outer boundary of § 2 liability". In that case, the Court had found that a skiing company which owned three mountains had committed unlawful monopolisation by unilaterally terminating a profitable joint venture with the owner of the fourth mountain in the ski resort with the intent of suppressing competition.[25] It seems that, under US law, a rival cannot demand access to a dominant firm's proprietary infrastructure if the owner had not granted such access previously.

EU law is more aggressive in foisting duties to deal on dominant firms. A host of Commission and judicial decisions have found companies to have abused their dominant undertakings when they failed to provide access sufficient to enable the emergence of competition.[26] For instance, in *Magill*, the Court of First Instance upheld a Commission decision that three television companies had collectively abused their dominant position by refusing to licence their copyrighted television listings, which prevented the emergence of a new product: a television guide.[27]

In 2007, the CFI's high-profile decision in *Microsoft* expanded the scope of a dominant firm's duty to deal under EU law.[28] The court (i) viewed a refusal to deal that excluded "effective" competition as being problematic, (ii) equated the state of effectiveness with "viability", and (iii) concluded that Microsoft had impaired a competitive market structure by acquiring a significant market share. Collectively, these elements suggest a broad obligation on dominant firms' part to share their property with competitors when access is indispensable to viable competition. Most problematically, the CFI dismissed Microsoft's claimed objective justification that compulsory licensing would depress incentives to innovate, characterising the argument as "vague, general, and theoretical". The CFI missed that the dynamic-inefficiency effects of forced sharing are unquantifiable and hence cannot be proved in a concrete sense. Yet, those effects are of potentially crucial importance. By requiring tangible proof, the CFI effectively discarded dynamic effects as a limiting

---

24 *Verizon Comm'cns v Law Offices of Curtis v Trinko LLP* (2004) 540 US 398.
25 *Aspen Skiing Co v Aspen Highlands Skiing Corp* (1985) 472 US 585.
26 *See, e.g.,* Case T-184/01, *IMS Health, Inc v Commission* (2002) 4 CMLR 1; Case C-7/97 *Oscar Bronner GmbH v Mediaprint Zeitungs- und Zeitschriftenverlag GmbH* (1998) ECR I-7791.
27 Case C-241/91, *RTE v Commission* (1995) ECR 743.
28 Case T-201/04, *Microsoft v Commission* (2004) ECR II-4463.

principle on duties to deal. Creating such precedent was an economic mistake, even if imposing the duty to deal was the right result on the facts of the case.

E. Loyalty Rebates

Vendors often reward consumers who purchase large quantities of product by charging them a lower average price than they do small-volume buyers. The discount can range from traditional quantity or volume discounts that apply to all prospective consumers to loyalty discounts available to purchasers who meet a minimum-quantity requirement. Loyalty schemes are now pervasive, appearing in the airline, fashion, supermarket, and café industries, and beyond. Given their ubiquity in competitive industries, there is a strong ground for considering the practice to be efficient.

Nevertheless, competition law has occasionally looked on volume discounts and loyalty rebates with a jaundiced eye. The fear is that such arrangements encourage customers to buy from just a single vendor, thus potentially foreclosing its rivals. Of course, this risk cannot be material in a general sense, given the prevalence of loyalty schemes throughout the economy. A dominant firm, however, may use the practice to deny smaller rivals the sales opportunities necessary to achieve sufficient scale economies.

Loyalty schemes can have important efficiency justifications. Most obviously, they may help a seller to realise scale economies and to reduce transaction costs. Manufacturers can use such rebates to induce advertising and pre-sales service among their downstream retailers. Such rebates may also eliminate double-marginalisation problems by inducing their retailers to charge the optimal downstream price. Perhaps most importantly, though, loyalty schemes generally lead to lower prices, even when dominant firms employ them.[29] In addition, they have less exclusionary potential than exclusive contracts. In the presence of such rebates, competitors can always lure consumers away from the dominant firm by offering a lower average price. This fact suggests that loyalty schemes will rarely foreclose equally or more-efficient competitors.

In sum, single-product loyalty rebates often increase output and reduce price. Although there is no basis for presupposing them to be inefficient, EU law has taken a hard line against the practice.[30] In doing so, it has created a transatlantic gulf in the antitrust treatment of loyalty discounting. US law deems above-cost price discounts to be presumptively lawful, even when undertaken by monopolists. The US Supreme Court recently noted that it is "particularly wary of allowing recovery for above-cost price cutting because such claims could, perversely, 'chill legitimate price cutting', which directly benefits consumers".[31] US antitrust law thus provides a "safe harbour" for single-product loyalty rebates that do not result in below-cost prices.

The same immunity does not apply to multi-product or "bundled" rebates, to which the judiciary has reacted with greater hostility. The concern with bundled rebates is that a dominant company may be able to foreclose competitors that do not operate in the same complementary markets as the rebate-offering monopolist, since consumers would not see rivals' offerings as equivalent.[32] The Third Circuit has recognised a cause of action based on above-cost bundled rebates. Economists have criticised this holding, and other US Circuits have rejected it.[33]

European authorities take a different tack, viewing single-product rebates as being inconsistent with "the normal operation of competition".[34] This aspect of EU competition law conflicts with

---

29 See, e.g., Hans Zenger, 'Loyalty rebates and the competitive process' (2012) 8 J Competition L & Econ 717.

30 See, e.g., C-549/10, Tomra Sys ASA v European Commission (2012).

31 Weyerhaeuser Co v Ross-Simmons Hardwood Lumber Co, 127 S Ct 1069, 1074 (2007) (citing Brooke Grp Ltd v Brown & Williamson Tobacco Corp, 509 US 209, 222–23 (1993)).

32 See, e.g., LePage's, Inc v 3M, 324 F3d 141 (3rd Cir 2003).

33 Compare, e.g., Cascade Health Solutions v PeaceHealth, 502 F3d 895, 910 (9th Cir 2007).

34 Case T-219/99 British Airways v Comm'n (BA/Virgin) (2003) ECR II–5917, para. 291.

economics. Indeed, under current EU jurisprudence, non-cost-justified, single-product loyalty rebates are unlawful if a dominant undertaking employs them. This rule would seem to hold true regardless of whether the rebates actually lead to higher levels of competition, and hence lower prices, in the market. Nevertheless, more recent views from the European Commission display greater nuance for the relevant economic principles, focusing in particular on whether single-product rebates could foreclose an equally or more efficient competitor.[35]

Interestingly, a certain convergence recently occurred as both the Federal Trade Commission and the European Commission pursued antitrust actions in the late 2000s against Intel Corporation for its loyalty and bundled discounting. The actions accused Intel of maintaining its dominance over its microprocessor competitor, AMD. These enforcement proceedings attracted academic criticism from economists who argued that the rebates reduced prices to consumers, and only harmed Intel's competitors. Nevertheless, there was an economic basis for concluding that Intel's practices excluded AMD from the market on a basis other than efficiency. The division among economists reveals the complexity of the effects that loyalty rebates have on social welfare, which further justifies a rule-of-reason-style approach that determines legality on case-specific circumstances.

F. Vertical Integration

A firm vertically integrates when it absorbs various functions of the supply chain into its in-house operations. For example, a manufacturer may jettison the distributors and retailers with which it had previously contracted, and instead develop its own distribution network.

Every business is vertically integrated to some degree. The depth of such integration reflects Ronald Coase's insight that firms exist to minimise the transaction costs incurred in contracting to a sought end. There is, therefore, an overwhelming efficiency benefit to vertical integration. Profit-maximising firms will generally handle product distribution and retail itself if it can do so better and/or more cheaply than third parties. Moreover, when separately owned firms perform different elements of the supply chain, double-marginalisation problems ensue. Vertical integration eliminates such Cournot-complements problems. Thus, to outlaw vertical integration would be to forbid a ubiquitous practice that enhances efficiency in almost all circumstances. This is not to say that the practice cannot harm individual companies, for it most certainly injures companies jettisoned in favour of in-house performance. Such effects are of no moment to competition policy, however, which promotes efficiency for consumers' benefit.

Given the benefits of vertical integration, how could the practice injure the competitive process? We shall consider three discrete possibilities. First, a monopolist may be able to "price squeeze" through vertical integration. Second, a dominant firm may attempt to eliminate a non-integrated rival by acquiring monopoly control of an essential input and then asphyxiating its competitor by denying it access. Third, a monopolist may attempt to secure its dominant position against supply-side substitution by vertically integrating, thus requiring potential competitors to enter both the downstream and upstream markets. None of these threats to competition is acute, though there may be circumstances in which vertical integration can be predatory. We shall conclude our discussion with the topical example of alleged search bias on the part of internet search providers, which bias, if true, would be a form of vertical integration.

---

35 European Commission, *Roundtable on Bundled and Loyalty Discounts and Rebates*, 19 May 2008. Available at: http://ec.europa.eu/competition/international/multilateral/2008_june_rebates.pdf.

1. Price squeezes and vertically integrating to control an essential input

A price squeeze can occur where a vertically integrated firm controls a bottleneck to essential upstream inputs that its downstream competitors require to manufacture their end products. To squeeze its rivals, the upstream monopolist can increase the price of the relevant input and then use its ensuing cost advantage profitably to undercut its competitors in the downstream retail market. By reducing its rivals' profit margins, the upstream monopolist may extend its dominance downstream, even forcing its competitors from the market entirely. A company imposing a price squeeze would not necessarily need to reduce thee downstream price below its marginal cost to force its rivals out.

Economic analysis of price squeezes dovetails with that applying to refusals to deal. If the law should generally not require forced sharing, it should be equally hesitant to impose liability for charging too much for an input. After all, if a firm can refuse to deal, surely it can offer to deal at whatever price it deems fit.

To subject a firm to a monopolisation charge for charging too much for an upstream input and too little for its downstream product would be to deter two valuable activities. First, it would undermine the incentive to develop the relevant input. Second, it would deter retail competition because the price-cutting by the integrated firm would later be perceived as monopolisation. Suppressing investment and price-competition incentives makes for poor policy. Note, however, that this analysis would not immunise a firm that monopolises an upstream input market to squeeze a downstream rival. The act of upstream monopolisation would itself be unlawful if it were achieved on a basis other than competition on the merits.

This discussion, of course, does not imply that price squeezes are categorically efficient. Rather, the problem is regulatory in nature, creating preclusive administrative difficulties for the judiciary. To solve the problem of upstream control of an essential resource, the courts would have to employ a liability rule with a suitable access price. As the next chapter explains, however, regulatory agencies with vast expertise in the industries for which they are responsible have long struggled to craft optimal access prices for essential facilities. To expect a court to accomplish what has long eluded such regulators is to ask too much.

Consistent with these insights, the US Supreme Court effectively closed the door on price squeezes as a theory of antitrust liability in 2009, holding that no "price-squeeze claim may be brought under § 2 of the Sherman Act when the defendant is under noantitrust obligation to sell the inputs to the plaintiff in the first place".[36] Given the exceedingly narrow circumstances in which US law imposes a duty to deal, using vertical integration to foreclose retail-market rivals by narrowing their profit margins will not support a viable claim absent below-cost pricing downstream or discontinuation of a previous course of upstream dealing.

Once more, EU competition rules demand more, reflecting a goal beyond efficiency to maintaining competitive market structures. The ECJ's 2010 opinion in *Deutsche Telekom* made clear just how sharply EU antitrust jurisprudence differs from its US equivalent on vertical integration. The court focused on "equality of opportunity" – a non-economic concept – which, combined with dominant undertakings' broad obligation "not to allow [their] conduct to impair genuine undistorted competition on the common market", the court used to fashion a broad prohibition on price squeezes by vertically integrated firms.[37]

---

36 Pacific Bell Tel Co v linkLine Comm'cns, Inc, 555 US 438, 442 (2009).
37 Case C-280/08 P Deutsche Telekom v Commission 14 October 2010 (ECJ).

2. Entry barriers

Can vertical integration bolster a dominant position by making entry more difficult? Suppose that a vertically integrated monopolist controls the only then-existing source of upstream inputs into the manufacturing process for the product line it sells downstream. Some competition agencies worry that potential competitors would be unwilling to enter the retail market to avail of the supra-competitive profit opportunities awaiting there because, without guaranteed access to the requisite input, such entrants could quickly find themselves starved of essential resources. To enter the retail market free of this concern, companies would also have to enter the upstream market, thus securing their own guaranteed supply of necessary inputs.

Whether vertical integration enhances entry barriers is a matter of some dispute, though the risk of its so doing increases when powerful network effects are present in the upstream market. Even if such integration does increase the cost of capital that a firm experiences in entering an industry, though, this fact in itself would not seem to be an adequate economic basis for forbidding the integration. Given the plethora of efficiency benefits associated with the practice, the fact that creating an entire private chain of distribution encumbers the arrival of potential competition would seem to be an ancillary consequence of actions that generally carry larger benefits. Independent of conduct carried out by the monopolist, such as improperly refusing to deal in the narrow circumstances explored above, the fact of vertical integration is itself an insufficient ground of antitrust condemnation.

G. Anticompetitive Mergers: Unilateral and Coordinated Effects

The law rightly condemns naked cartel agreements and monopolisation. Those rules would be without meaning, however, if it allowed competitors to merge into a collective whole. For that reason, antitrust has long forbidden mergers to monopoly, and other combinations that yield anticompetitive effects.

1. Mergers to monopoly, and unilateral effects

It should be no surprise that mergers to monopoly are unlawful. The danger is that, when a combination substantially lessens competition in a market not subject to free entry, the ensuing entity may be able to exercise significant market power. Competition enforcers object to such mergers on the ground of "unilateral effects".

A complication, however, arises in industries subject to scale economies over a large volume of output. Such markets inherently tend toward concentration because productive efficiency requires a small number of competitors to meet all industry demand. In the extreme case of natural monopoly, which is the subject of the next chapter, scale economies are such that a single firm can most efficiently serve the market. Where firms operate on downward-sloping portions of their long-term average-cost curves, each will have an incentive to expand output to reduce its average costs. Although such companies will grow internally to avail of potential efficiencies, mergers may allow quicker and easier means by which to attain those benefits. The problem, of course, is that such combinations will hasten the arrival of allocative inefficiency associated with monopoly pricing.

Scale and scope efficiencies are an important driver of merger activity, and should thus form a central part of the relevant antitrust analysis. Indeed, Oliver Williamson famously demonstrated that combinations generating productive efficiency gains are likely to enhance social welfare, even if they create relatively large allocative efficiency losses through the acquisition of market power.[38] He showed that, in an initially competitive market in which price, P_C, equals marginal cost, a merger that provided the merging company with power sufficient to raise price to a supracompetitive level, P_M, could nevertheless increase net efficiency if it reduced the ensuing firm's marginal cost from P_C[39] to M_C':

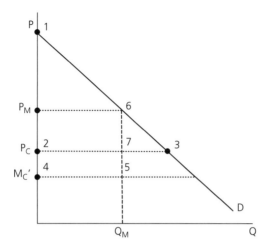

Figure 8.12

Williamson did not merely show that productive efficiency gains could outweigh allocative efficiency losses. He demonstrated that, starting with a competitive equilibrium, even a relatively small reduction in marginal cost could swamp seemingly disproportionate reductions in allocative efficiency caused by monopoly pricing. In the preceding figure, the 1–2–3 triangle represents the pre-merger level of social welfare. After the merger, this results in a deadweight loss represented by the 6–7–3 triangle, but there is also a productive efficiency gain in the form of the 2–4–5–7 rectangle. Whether the merger promotes or restricts efficiency depends on which effect outweighs the other. Intuitively, as the volume in a rectangle grows more quickly than that in a triangle, mergers that simultaneously reduce marginal cost and enhance market power are likely to enhance net welfare. Note, however, that this conclusion is dependent on the assumption that the pre-merger price equals the competitive level.

Notwithstanding this economic insight, however, neither the US nor the EU merger guidelines currently permit such "Williamson mergers". The reason for this omission is not necessarily ideological; it is practical. It is infuriatingly difficult to determine *ex post* whether cost savings resulted from, or had nothing to do with, the preceding merger. Competition agencies have limited access to information about the prospective merging firms' business models, yet those companies' assertions of realisable efficiencies are not credible, particularly when the merger threatens to suppress competition and increase prices to consumers.

As a result, efficiencies play a rather modest role in contemporary merger review in the United States and in Europe. The focus, instead, is on whether the proposed combination is apt to produce unilateral effects in the form of higher prices and reduced output. In particular, competition enforcers analyse whether supply-side substitution limits unilateral effects on account of timely, likely, and sufficient entry, and determine whether demand-side substitution forecloses post-merger market power. Antitrust agencies also use sophisticated econometric studies to determine whether

---

38 Oliver Williamson, 'Economics as an antitrust defense: The welfare trade-offs' (1968) 58 Am Econ Rev 18.
39 Recall that, under perfect competition, price equals marginal cost.

a target firm in fact constrains the acquiring company's pricing power. Direct empirical evidence of such a constraint suggests that the proposed acquisition would yield negative unilateral effects, thus suggesting, in the presence of entry barriers, that the agencies should forbid the combination on the basis of unilateral effects.[40]

2. Horizontal mergers and coordinated effects

Relatively few proposed mergers result in economic monopolies, if only because companies know that such combinations have little chance of obtaining regulatory approval. The horizontal acquisitions that create the most difficult questions are typically those that increase concentration in the relevant industry, though not to the point where the emerging entity has power unilaterally and significantly to depress market output. Such mergers may be problematic when they decrease the number of rivals in an oligopolistic industry, thus enhancing the danger of post-acquisition tacit collusion. Antitrust authorities refer to proposed mergers that create this danger as threatening "coordinated effects".

According to US and EU competition authorities, the primary determinant of whether an acquisition threatens coordinated effects is the level of market concentration. The Herfindahl-Hirschman Index ("HHI") is an important measure of concentration. It sums the squares of each individual firm's market share. Thus, a perfectly concentrated industry – a monopoly – would bear a HHI of 10,000, while if there are 100 identical firms – which would constitute an non-concentrated and nearly perfectly competitive market – the HHI would be 100. United States' agencies regard industries having a HHI of less than 1,500 as "unconcentrated", between 1,500 and 2,500 as "moderately concentrated", and above 2,500 as "highly concentrated". The European Commission generally considers mergers producing a HHI of less than 1,000 to be unlikely to raise competitive concerns. The same is true of mergers creating a HHI between 1,000 and 2,000 with a change of less than 250, or a HHI of more than 2,000 with a change of less than 150.

If the relevant market is "unconcentrated", there is minimal danger of ex post tacit collusion. If the HHI index is greater than 1,500 (2,000 in Europe), however, the agencies will be concerned about possible coordinated effects. In such a situation, competition authorities will look at the history of competitive behaviour in the industry, including whether industry participants have previously engaged in express or tacit campaigns of price fixing, whether industry pricing is transparent, and whether sales are small and frequent or large and sporadic. Another important consideration is whether the scrutinised merger would eliminate a "maverick" firm, which may have been a source of instability in the market, thus frustrating sustainable periods of barometric price leadership.

3. Vertical and conglomerate mergers

Horizontal mergers and acquisitions raise antitrust concerns because they eliminate competition between direct rivals. By contrast, vertical mergers do not extinguish competition because they involve the coming together of two or more firms that operate at different levels of the supply chain. The same is true of conglomerate acquisitions, where the companies neither compete nor lie in a purchaser-supplier relationship. For that reason, vertical and conglomerate mergers are of less concern to the competitive process.

As a general matter, non-horizontal combinations carry few competitive risks and can create overriding efficiencies. Vertical mergers carry the benefits of vertical integration: they can eliminate

---

40 For a classic example, see FTC v *Staples*, 970 F Supp 1066 (DDC 1997).

double marginalisation problems, lower transaction costs, and enhance inter-brand competition. Conglomerate mergers can realise scope efficiencies and eliminate double marginalisation problems associated with separate ownership of complementary goods. Mergers of this nature can thus potentially generate lower prices and superior quality for consumers.

The competitive dangers of vertical acquisitions relate to possible foreclosure – such as cutting off rival access to essential inputs or to consumers – raising barriers to entry, and potentially facilitating upstream collusion. Nevertheless, although economists recognise that vertical mergers can entail anticompetitive effects in some cases, they consider such combinations generally to be innocuous or efficient. Conglomerate mergers rarely create anticompetitive dangers for they neither eliminate a competitive constraint (as occurs with horizontal acquisitions) nor affect rival access to an input or to consumers within the chain of distribution (as may occur with vertical mergers). Conglomerate acquisitions typically involve complementary markets and, by eliminating the Cournot-complements problem, they tend to enhance output and to reduce price.

Nevertheless, a controversial and economically suspect theory of anticompetitive harm holds that "range effects" flowing from a conglomerate merger can entrench an acquiring company's dominance in certain markets. This ground of opposition is weak because it rests on the premise that a merging firm's greater size and enhanced efficiency – achieved through magnified scale and scope economies – will compromise rivals' ability to compete. To condemn an arrangement on the ground that it is efficient, however, is to turn antitrust on its head. Not only should society encourage the attainment of productive-side efficiencies for its own sake, but facilitating such gains magnifies rivals' incentives to enhance their own productivity and innovation.

Although the US Supreme Court historically viewed vertical and conglomerate mergers with hostility, particularly during the Warren Court era of the 1960s, modern US antitrust policy is permissive. EU authorities, however, are more suspicious about such arrangements. This asymmetry has led to a number of high-profile transatlantic divergences. A notable case involved the proposed GE/Honeywell merger, which the US Justice Department approved in 2001, but which the European Commission subsequently vetoed. The EU decision attracted much criticism, because it was not obviously consistent with economic analysis focused on consumer welfare. United States enforcers predicted that the conglomerate merger would reduce prices and expand output by combining the production of complementary goods – jet engines and avionics systems – under one roof. The European Commission, however, concluded that the merger would compromise GE/Honeywell's rivals' ability to compete because they would not enjoy comparable scope economies. This marked an acute point of divergence between US and European antitrust authorities.

Key Points

- While the economic case for condemning cartels between horizontal competitors is iron clad, the question when to intervene to challenge unilateral conduct by dominant firms is hard to answer. Monopolisation cases are protracted and expensive; whether alleged exclusionary practices harm efficiency is often disputed; and industry developments can render a remedy defunct before a court imposes it.
- Although monopoly is generally undesirable, competition law does not condemn it. The reason is that the prospect of attaining a dominant position is the engine underlying capitalist economies, driving firms to innovate and achieve efficiency gains. Removing the prize would undercut the incentive to compete.
- Antitrust has long been concerned about tying arrangements imposed by dominant firms. The fear is that tie-ins allow firms to leverage pricing power to otherwise-competitive tied markets, whilst depriving consumers of choice and creating entry barriers. Economic analysis of this

business practice reveals them to be significantly more complicated. Tying often realises efficiencies, both on the selling and buying side, and can leverage market power only in certain circumstances. Although economic models show that product tying can be anticompetitive, current rules in both the US and EU are too restrictive.

- Predatory pricing occurs when a firm sells below a measure of cost in the hope of forcing its rivals from the market or denying them scale economies. Economic models suggest that it is often an irrational strategy because a predator-firm must suffer losses over a large volume of sales, and its threat to price below cost against subsequent entrants is non-credible. Simultaneously, condemning predatory pricing carries a large Type I error cost. Erroneous condemnation would blunt the most important incentive in competition law: to compete on price to consumers' benefit. EU law is quicker to outlaw below-cost pricing. Unlike US law, it does not require a plaintiff to show a dangerous probability of recoupment.

- One of the most controversial antitrust questions is whether the law should require dominant firms to share their physical infrastructure or proprietary technology with rivals. Imposing a duty to deal increases market competition, and hence static efficiency, but potentially undermines long-term incentives to invest in networks and technology, thus harming dynamic efficiency. The duty to deal in US law is minimal, though more expansive in Europe.

- Loyalty rebates are one dimension on which firms routinely compete. Their ubiquity in competitive markets implies efficiency. Nevertheless, dominant firms could conceivably use them to exclude their rivals. The economic literature suggests that single-product, above-cost rebates are unlikely to be exclusionary save in rare circumstances.

- Vertical integration occurs when a firm absorbs certain or all elements of the distribution chain. By eliminating Cournot complements effects, this process generally increases output and reduces price. In certain settings, though, a firm may vertically integrate to obtain exclusive control over an upstream input that its downstream competitors need to compete. The law scrutinises such situations for anticompetitive "price squeezes", though, under current US law, liability is unlikely where no duty to deal is present.

- It would make little sense to condemn exclusionary conduct and cartel agreements if competitors were free to merge to monopoly. For that reason, the law scrutinises mergers and acquisitions to determine whether they will produce "unilateral effects" (i.e. significant market power) or "coordinated effects" (a sufficiently concentrated industry bearing characteristics making tacit collusion likely).

  ○ Although economics shows that mergers enhancing market power may be desirable on account of achieving productive efficiencies – "Williamson mergers" – the law does not presently permit them. The reasons are a focus on consumer, rather than aggregate, welfare, and the difficulty of verifying the attainment of merger-specific efficiencies.

 ## References and Further Reading

Books and Reports
Elhauge, Einer (ed.), *Research Handbook on the Economics of Antitrust Law* (2013) Chs. 1, 5–6.
European Commission, 'Guidance on the Commission's Enforcement Priorities in Applying Article 82 of the EC Treaty to Abusive Exclusionary Conduct by Dominant Undertakings' (2009).
Guidelines on the Assessment of Horizontal Mergers under the Council Regulation on the Control of Concentrations between Undertakings (2004) OJ (C 31) 5.
Posner, Richard A., *Antitrust Law Part III*, 2nd edn (2001).
Posner, Richard A., *Economic Analysis of Law* (2011) §§ 10.4, 10.8, 10.10.
US Department of Justice and Federal Trade Commission, 'Horizontal Merger Guidelines' (2010).

US Department of Justice, 'Competition and Monopoly: Single-Firm Conduct under Section 2 of the Sherman Act' (2008) (withdrawn 11 May 2009).

Articles:
Areeda, Phillip E. and Turner, Donald F., 'Predatory pricing and related practices under section 2 of the Sherman Act' (1975) 88 Harv L Rev 697.

Areeda, Phillip E. and Turner, Donald F., 'Williamson on predatory pricing' (1977) 87 Yale LJ 1337.

Blair, Roger D. and Kaserman, David. L., 'Vertical integration, tying and antitrust' (1978) 68 Am Econ Rev 397.

Bowman, Jr, Ward, 'Tying arrangements and the leverage problem' (1957) 67 Yale LJ 19.

Cass, Ronald A. and Hylton, Keith N., 'Preserving competition: Economic analysis, legal standards and Microsoft' (1999) 8 Geo Mason L Rev 1.

Coate, Malcolm B. and Fischer, Jeffrey H., 'A practical guide to the hypothetical monopolist test for market definition' (2008) 4 J Competition L & Econ 1031.

Craig, Peter, 'Evaluating the performance of merger simulation' (2006) 49 JL & Econ 627.

Crane, Daniel A., 'Mixed bundling, profit sacrifice, and consumer welfare' (2006) 55 Emory LJ 423.

Crane, Daniel A., 'Rethinking merger efficiencies' (2011) 110 Mich L Rev 347.

Easterbrook, Frank H., 'The limits of antitrust' (1984) 63 Tex L Rev 1.

Easterbrook, Frank H., 'When is it worthwhile to use courts to search for exclusionary conduct?' (2003) Columbus L Rev 345.

Elhauge, Einer, 'Tying, bundled discounts, and the death of the single monopoly profit theory' (2009) 123 Harv L Rev 397

Faella, Gianluca, 'The antitrust assessment of loyalty discounts and rebates' (2008) 4 J Competition L & Econ 375.

Farrell, Joseph and Shapiro, Carl, 'Horizontal mergers: An equilibrium analysis' (1990) 80 Am Econ Rev 107.

Gilbert, Richard J. and Katz, Michael L., 'An economist's guide to *US* v. *Microsoft*' (2001) 15 J Econ Persp 25.

Hovenkamp, Erik and Hovenkamp, Herbert, 'Tying arrangements and antitrust harm' (2010) 52 Ariz L Rev 925.

Hovenkamp, Herbert, 'Exclusion and the Sherman Act' (2005) 72 U Chi L Rev 147.

Kattan, Joseph, 'Efficiencies and merger analysis' (1994) 62 Antitrust LJ 513.

Krattenmaker, Thomas G. and Salop, Steven C., 'Anticompetitive exclusion: Raising rivals' costs to achieve power over price' (1986) 96 Yale LJ 209.

Landes, William M. and Posner, Richard A., 'Market power in antitrust cases' (1981) 94 Harv L Rev 937.

Meese, Alan J., 'Monopolization, exclusion, and the theory of the firm' (2005) 89 Minn L Rev 743.

Posner, Richard A., 'Exclusionary practices and the antitrust laws' (1974) 41 U Chi L. Rev 506.

Posner, Richard A., 'Antitrust policy and the Supreme Court: An analysis of the restricted distribution, horizontal merger and potential competition decisions' (1975) 75 Colum L Rev 282.

Posner, Richard A., 'Antitrust and the new economy' (2001) 68 Antitrust LJ 925.

Salop, Steven C. and Scheffman, David T., 'Raising rivals' costs' (1983) 73 Am Econ Rev 267.

Weinberg, Matthew, 'The price effects of horizontal mergers' (2007) 4 J Competition L & Econ 433.

Williamson, Oliver E., 'Economies as an antitrust defense: The welfare tradeoffs' (1968) 58 Am Econ Rev 18.

Williamson, Oliver E., 'Predatory pricing: A strategic and welfare analysis' (1977) 87 Yale LJ 284, 305.

Chapter 4

The Regulation of Natural Monopoly

Chapter Contents

A.	The Economics of Natural Monopoly	371
B.	Containing Monopoly Power: Regulation of Price and Entry	373
C.	Restoring Competition: The Deregulatory Movement	381
D.	The Limits of Competition: The Case of the Financial Services Industry	389
E.	Conclusion	390
Key Points		391
References and Further Reading		392

A. The Economics of Natural Monopoly

Antitrust law's essential premise is that markets uncorrupted by restrictions on competition tend toward efficiency. That postulate, however, does not universally hold true. In industries bearing natural monopoly characteristics, competition may be antithetical to efficiency. This situation creates a public policy dilemma, as competition law may be an inadequate means of protecting social welfare. To understand these problems, one must first appreciate the economics of natural monopoly and how they differ from those applicable to traditional industries.

Competition is generally desirable because, in regular markets, each firm has an average cost curve that rises at output levels insufficient to satisfy consumer demand. Such curves are typically U-shaped, dropping rapidly as companies achieve scale economies in availing of free productive capacity, but rising once they approach their capacity constraints. Further output increases require firms to extract greater productivity from their available resources, which becomes costly. Where firms experience diseconomies of scale at modest production levels, competition will have two effects: (i) many firms will produce at or near the minimum point of their average-cost curves, thus creating enough output to meet consumer demand while still achieving productive efficiency; and (ii) those competitors will outbid one another until their prices approach marginal cost, thus yielding allocative efficiency.

Natural monopolies are different, being defined by average-cost curves that are still declining when they intersect with the demand curve. More formally, economists define a natural monopoly as an industry in which the production function is sub-additive, meaning that one company can produce all goods in a market at less cost than two or more firms. This phenomenon arises because of a high ratio of fixed-to-marginal cost. Classic examples are utilities, such as electricity transmission grids and telecommunications networks, and common carriers, such as railways and airport infrastructures. In such settings, initial set-up costs are often enormous, but the expense of operating the infrastructure once created is modest. As a result, a company will experience scale economies over the full range of output that would satisfy all demand. It is not difficult to see the problem with competition. If each additional entrant into the market must build a duplicative network at vast expense, every new facility thus created is money wasted. The inputs used to build superfluous installations could have been used for other, more valuable projects.

Figure 8.13 illustrates a natural monopoly. In this example, marginal cost is constant, which ensures in the presence of fixed cost that the average-cost curve will never rise. As that curve slopes downward where it meets the demand curve, productive efficiency requires that just one firm produce the full industry's output. Note, however, that there is no requirement that the marginal-cost curve be flat. A U-shaped, average-cost curve is consistent with natural monopoly, as long as the curve does not begin to slop upward until after it passes the demand curve.

Note in the preceding graph that the average-cost curve, "AC" is still sloping downward as it crosses the industry demand curve. This shows that a single firm can minimise productive inefficiency. Note, however, that a monopolist will restrict output to Q_M, thus creating deadweight loss. Finally, observe that a firm forced to charge a competitive price equal to marginal cost, "MC", would be unable to cover its average cost.

In natural monopolies, society uses the least resources when just a single company produces all the goods in the market. Nevertheless, even in this setting, competition carries important benefits. Once rival infrastructures are in place, their owners would compete with one another to offer more attractive terms to their prospective customers, thus lowering price. In other words, competition carries the same static efficiency advantages that justified it over monopoly in the previous chapters. For that reason, productive and allocative efficiency operate in opposite directions in natural monopolies.

The theoretical solution is clear: build just one network, and then facilitate competition in its operation. In that manner, a lack of duplication would ensure productive efficiency, while

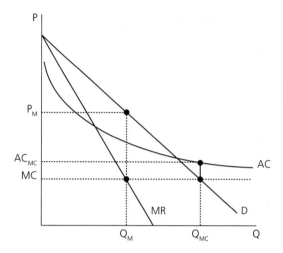

Figure 8.13

price competition would drive the market toward static efficiency. Yet, this approach is no-less problematic. What private company would ever devote the massive capital resources necessary to build electricity, gas, or telecommunications grids, if its competitors were free to avail themselves of the infrastructure without having to pay for its construction? Marginal cost pricing in the presence of unrecovered fixed costs leads to insolvency. For that reason, free entry into a privately constructed network market would deter future investment, with serious, negative results for social welfare.

Of course, if the government were to recognise exclusive property rights in the network, its owner would refuse to grant rivals access at competitive rates. Indeed, it would accept no less than what would compensate it for the loss of monopoly pricing occasioned by the competitor's arrival. To avoid this bottleneck problem, the state might adopt a liability rule, requiring the network owner to grant access at a price sufficient to allow it to recover its fixed costs. This approach would not be a panacea, however, as information asymmetries would hinder the government's ability to identify an optimal access price.

The natural monopoly problem lends itself to one of three solutions, none of which is satisfactory. The problem is that state intervention cannot successfully mimic the desirable incentives associated with Darwinian competition in an open market.

First, the government could grant a single company a lawful monopoly, limit entry and exit into and out of the market, and regulate the firm's pricing. That solves the problem of inefficient duplication. The regulator's challenge, however, is to permit the regulated entity to recoup its fixed costs, while creating incentives for efficient, ongoing investment in infrastructure and limiting pricing to minimise allocative inefficiency.

Second, the state could nationalise the industry, building the grid with public funds and pricing optimally. Unlike private enterprise, the public sector will presumably not price at the profit-maximising level. The absence of competitive pressures, however, handicaps the long-term tendency of state-owned enterprises to operate efficiently. Furthermore, as governments typically impose budgets that limit the expenditures of public companies, such enterprises may have an incentive to charge greater than optimal prices notwithstanding their mandate. More generally, bureaucracy, principal–agent problems, and dull incentives are hallmarks of public administration.

Finally, the government could impose an interconnection duty on a monopolist, requiring it to grant its competitors access to the network at a reasonable price. Ensuring optimal access pricing is, of course, indispensable to the success of this approach. This is no easy task: the network owner's private incentive is to set monopoly access prices, while the state has limited information about the grid operator's cost structure. Nevertheless, regulators have experience grappling with this problem. In recent times, governments have deregulated industry components that are conducive of competition and have imposed unbundling and mandatory access obligations on the owners of bottleneck network components that still display natural monopoly characteristics.

This chapter focuses on the first solution, which has long been the principal US approach to problems of natural monopoly and has been applied in the United Kingdom following the privatisation of state-run enterprises in the 1980s. It is prohibitively difficult to recreate the full panoply of desirable incentives associated with free market competition. This shortcoming means that both regulation and competition are imperfect, making the case for the former over the latter ambiguous in many natural-monopoly settings.

Since the 1970s, economists have come to doubt the severity of the natural-monopoly problem, which has led to deregulation and privatisation. This movement has produced many desirable results, efficiently restructuring some industries and often – but not always – producing consumer savings on account of greater efficiencies. Nevertheless, the deregulatory movement was excessively broad, easing regulatory oversight of the financial industry with grave repercussions that crystallised in the great recession of 2008–2009.

This chapter explores the techniques of price regulation that regulators use to foster efficient pricing, and discusses the various difficulties and shortcomings associated with those efforts. Not the least of these is the inability to define a socially optimal price, which subject is our first port of call. Having both addressed that problem and explored the two leading forms of profit regulation designed to induce desirable pricing, the chapter explores the deregulatory movement. It traces the liberalisation of four representative industries: aviation, natural gas, telecommunications, and electricity. The chapter concludes with a brief word on the banking industry. Although it is not a natural monopoly, the systemic instability and unique economic position of the industry necessitate a high level of regulatory oversight.

B. Containing Monopoly Power: Regulation of Price and Entry

An industry may be a natural monopoly, but it does not follow that only a single firm will serve the market. Depending on scale economies and network effects,[1] the industry may tend irrevocably toward monopoly or it may support an oligopolistic market structure. In the latter event, free entry generates productive inefficiency. To prevent that problem, the government may bestow a lawful monopoly on a single firm pursuant to "a certificate of public convenience and necessity". By forbidding entry, the state solves the inefficient competition problem. This was the approach that the US government historically took over utilities (e.g. electricity, natural gas, and telecommunications) and common carriers (e.g. railroads and airlines).

The prohibition on entry serves a function beyond avoiding duplicative facility based competition. For political reasons, regulators often require common carriers to limit the price differential between their various consumers. This requires cross-subsidisation because the cost of service for some customers is greater than for others. If entry were unregulated, private companies would have

---

1 "Network effects" refers to the phenomenon in which the value of joining a network increases with the number of consumers who have already joined. The classic example is a telephone grid, the value of which rises exponentially as the number of subscribers to the network increases beyond one. Many industries traditionally considered to be natural monopolies display network effects (otherwise known as "positive externalities in consumption").

an incentive to "skim" by entering low-cost parts of the market, while leaving the regulated firm to service the low-volume/high-cost routes.

By foreclosing entry, however, the state invites monopoly pricing. To protect the public against allocative inefficiency, governments appoint regulators to control pricing. This section explores the traditional method of controlling price, which is rate-of-return regulation, as well as the more modern approach of incentive regulation. First, however, it discusses the difficulty of identifying an optimal pricing regimen. Unless it can identify the ideal pricing that it wishes to induce, a regulator is akin to a ship without a rudder. Fortunately, it is possible to identify a number of guiding principles.

1. Optimal pricing in natural monopolies

Only marginal cost pricing ensures the efficient allocation of goods. In dictating or circumscribing a firm's prices, however, a regulator cannot limit revenue to the cost of production of the utility or common carrier. So constrained, a regulated entity could not recoup the fixed costs that it incurred in building and maintaining (a mixed cost) the network. Only a price equal to the regulated firm's average cost will enable it to remain solvent and thus be a going concern.

The problem, however, is that average-cost pricing is allocatively inefficient. A possible solution is to require the regulated firm to price at marginal cost, and for the government to provide a subsidy equal to the company's fixed costs. This is no panacea, however, for the state's collection of the pertinent revenue through taxation or borrowing distorts economic activity elsewhere in the economy. It follows that, although marginal-cost pricing is ideal in an abstract sense, in reality, revenue must cover a firm's costs. Revenue reflecting average-cost pricing is a minimum condition of sustainable operations.

Two issues, however, follow. First, not all methods of recouping fixed costs will be equally destructive of allocative efficiency. Second, price-regulation mechanisms can create perverse incentives for utilities and common carriers to fail desirably to cut costs. If regulators allow their overseen companies to charge prices equal to average cost, those firms will have little need to remedy inefficient operations. We shall discuss each issue in turn.

We begin by acknowledging that marginal cost pricing is unattainable (at least until the regulated company recoups its fixed costs). The question thus facing a regulator is how best to allow the utility or common carrier to break even while minimising the harm of supracompetitive pricing. We consider three forms of pricing other than the simple (and unrealistic) case of requiring a regulated monopolist to charge a single, uniform price equal to average cost.

(a) Ramsey pricing

One possibility is for regulators to permit reverse-elasticity or "Ramsey" pricing. This entails charging high prices to customers whose demand is inelastic (typically due to a lack of substitutes for the regulated service) and low prices to consumers possessing elastic demand (because they enjoy a choice). The firm can charge the former group above marginal-cost prices without triggering a significant drop in output, while charging the latter group closer-to-competitive prices, thus maintaining higher levels of allocative efficiency. The following graphs demonstrate how the deadweight loss of a given supracompetitive price depends on the elasticity of demand see Figure 8.14.

The deadweight loss triangle, 1–2–3 in the market with elastic demand is more severe than the one in which demand is inelastic. The inverse-elasticity principle states that regulators can permit utilities and common carriers to recoup fixed costs by imposing the lion's share of supracompetitive pricing on consumers possessing inelastic demand. The following graphs illustrate the idea of Ramsey pricing see Figure 8.15.

Although it is a valuable regulatory tool, Ramsey pricing puts efficiency and equity in tension because inelastic demand often signals a lack of consumer choice. For that reason, regulators rarely permit its use on an unqualified basis.

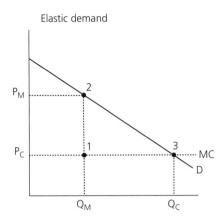 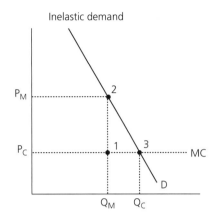

Figure 8.14

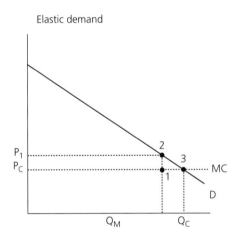 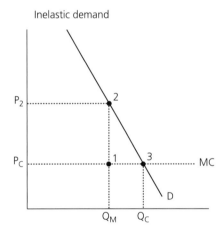

Figure 8.15

Suppose that a railway company builds a track from a major city to two suburban towns, one of which is affluent and the other is economically deprived. Many residents of both towns wish to travel to the city. If a developed road network connects the affluent town to the major city, the rail operator would be subject to competition from private transport by car and from public transport by bus. For the less-well-off town further down the line, however, suppose that the roads are poorly paved, bus services are infrequent, and fewer people own cars. Residents of the town wishing to travel to the city have less choice in transportation, and may thus, on average, pay a higher premium for rail services. Inverse-elasticity pricing would enable the regulated railway operator to recoup its investment with a lower deadweight loss than a single-price mechanism. Nevertheless, residents of the less-affluent town would correctly point out that the regulated company was price discriminating, charging them prices not justified by the differential cost of service. Many observers would find fault with a pricing system in which less-well-off consumers cross-subsidise their relatively wealthy counterparts.

(b) Two-part tariffs

Two-part pricing entails an up-front, access fee, which may cover the regulated firm's fixed costs when aggregated over the relevant consumer population, followed by subsequent use fees equal to marginal cost. This method ensures efficient allocation of the regulated company's product or service among those consumers who pay the initial fee. Regulated firms often employ two-part tariffs to cover their fixed costs (e.g. telecommunications companies may charge a fixed fee for a line rental and a separate amount based on usage).

If a utility knew enough about its consumers, it might discriminate in such a way that it covers its fixed costs without creating allocative efficiency. Suppose that a company has two kinds of consumers: those who value the sold product greatly and marginally, respectively. If the firm must recoup a fixed cost less than the high-value consumers' surplus, it can charge those consumers an upfront fee equal to its fixed costs. The firm can then charge lower-value users no fixed fee, and set usage price for all users at marginal cost. Such an approach may allow the regulated company to achieve revenue equal to its total costs without generating deadweight loss. Consider the following diagram:

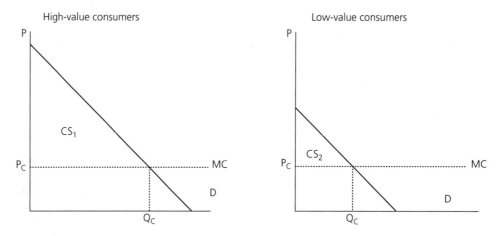

Figure 8.16

If its average-cost curve lies above its marginal-cost curve at the competitive output level, a company forced to charge a price equal to marginal cost will not remain a going concern. If it faced two discernible sets of consumers as illustrated above, however, it may be able to break even without creating allocative inefficiency. CS_1, the high-value consumers' surplus, exceeds CS_2, the welfare that low-value consumers derive from consuming the regulated product. Whether allocative efficiency is possible depends on the magnitude of the firm's fixed costs relative to consumer surplus. If it has sufficient information and its fixed costs are less than CS_1, the regulated firm could charge high-value consumers an upfront fee equal to those costs and then price at marginal cost. Employed in this manner, two-part tariffs can permit first-best outcomes.

In practice, however, it is rarely possible to distinguish consumers in this manner. Should price discrimination be infeasible, the utility would have to charge a single access fee to all consumers. If the firm's fixed costs exceed CS_2, allocative inefficiency would result as low-value consumers are priced out of the market. This result is, of course, undesirable because, as the diagram illustrates, certain low-value consumers value the relevant product at a level exceeding the marginal cost of production.

For that reason, two-part pricing does not always, or even often, solve the problem of the marginal consumer, who would pay an amount equal to or more than marginal cost, but not as much as the upfront fee demands.

(c) Peak-load pricing

In many networks traditionally subject to regulation, such as electricity, natural gas, or aviation, there can be dramatic fluctuations in demand for the regulated and non-storable good at predictable times. For example, demand for electricity in the middle of the night is less than in the morning. Similarly, demand for flights peaks during holiday seasons and at certain times of the week. Problems emerge due to capacity constraints, as the relevant provider may be unable to meet all demand during peak times. To satisfy such demand, a utility or common carrier would have to build an infrastructure that would entail costly excess capacity during off-peak times. In such circumstances, it is inefficient for a regulated company to charge just a single price. Uniform pricing creates no incentive for customers to substitute their consumption away from high-demand times in favour of low-use ones.

A regulated company can expand industrial output, as well as its own profits, by charging higher prices during peak times than during low-demand periods, thus reducing peak demand to a level that does not exceed the firm's capacity constraint. Industry capacity may actually rise in the presence of such "peak-load" or "seasonal" pricing, as net consumer demand rises on account of lower overall cost. In its most simple usage, such pricing involves charging off-peak customers a price equal to marginal cost, and charging peak customers an amount just sufficient to cover its fixed (and associated incremental) costs.

More-sophisticated forms of peak-load pricing, however, may cause prices in both the peak and off-peak periods to drop below the uniform price level. The reason for this seemingly odd result is that, depending on consumers' elasticity of substitution, peak-load pricing may permit a regulated entity to sell its entire capacity multiple times instead of just once. If the regulator requires zero economic profit, the break-even price under a single-price regime may exceed the optimal price under peak demand.

2. Rate-of-return regulation

As we have just seen, identifying the optimal pricing regimen in a natural monopoly poses formidable difficulties. If a regulator concludes that the only realistic solution is to try to constrain a utility's pricing to the point that it approaches the firm's average cost of operation, how might the regulator accomplish this goal? This segment addresses the historically dominant form of profit control: rate-of-return regulation. First, however, we address specific challenges that regulators face in overseeing a common carrier or utility's conduct.

In instilling incentives, a regulator must concern itself with three objectives. First, it must prevent the regulated company from exercising market power to extract monopoly prices. Second, it must spur the utility to achieve productive efficiency gains through superior management policies, more-efficient operations, and greater added value at the level of the individual employee. Third, it must encourage the firm to continue investing efficiently in the relevant network.

A private company, left to its own devices, has an incentive to act in opposition to the first goal because it will maximise profit by charging monopoly prices. Interestingly, though, a profit-maximising monopolist will not necessarily flout the second public-policy objective because productive efficiency gains translate into greater returns. Nevertheless, the incentive to make more productive use of inputs is more acute under competition than under monopoly. In the former case, a failure to achieve efficiency may lead to bankruptcy, while in the latter, it would merely lead to a reduced bottom line. Economists sometimes refer to the tendency of monopolists to fail to maximise the productivity of their resources as "X-inefficiency".

For these reasons, a regulator must force a firm to act contrary to its interests. The regulator's unenviable task is to induce the utility or common carrier to behave as it would if subject to free-market competition, subject only not to driving revenue below cost.

(a) Rate-of-return regulation in practice

The classic solution is rate-of-return, or "cost-of-service", price regulation. Its rationale is straight-forward: prevent the regulated firm from securing excessive profits by tying its permitted revenue to its costs. It works as follows: first, determine the minimum revenue that would allow the regulated firm to attract sufficient capital for ongoing operations and asset investment; then, calculate the maximum rates that the utility can charge such that, when multiplied by the expected number of sales, they will yield revenue equal to the required level. This approach permits the regulated firm to earn a reasonable return on top of its cost of service, but no more. It allows the utility to remain solvent, but stops the company from enjoying an excessive return through monopoly pricing. Getting the balance right, however, is as important as it is difficult. If regulators systemically under-value the appropriate rate of return, the utility or common carrier may have difficulty attracting capital and, in extreme cases, may become insolvent. If regulators allow the firms they oversee to exceed that return, the result is unnecessary allocative inefficiency.

To understand how rate-of-return regulation works, one must appreciate how regulators quantify "cost of service" and "reasonable return on invested capital", the sum of which equals the firm's revenue requirement. Determining cost of service is relatively simple: one looks at a test period – typically, the preceding year – identifies the firm's total costs during that time frame, and then subtracts the company's capital costs, including interest, on long-term debt. "Cost of service" thus includes operational and maintenance costs (such as salaries and raw materials), depreciation, and taxes, but not interest on long-term debt, which instead goes into calculating a reasonable rate of return.

The more challenging task is to calculate an appropriate return on invested capital (equity and long-term debt), which should mimic the return that the firm would earn under competition. To do this, regulators multiply the utility's "rate base" by a reasonable rate of return. The rate base is the value of capital employed to provide the relevant product or service. In turn, the reasonable rate of return is the weighted average cost of the firm's cost of capital, which is the long-term interest rate plus an appropriate return on equity. Equivalently, it is the interest on debt and return on equity necessary to attract sufficient capital to provide the regulated product or service. A simple representation of this calculation follows:

Rev. = CS + RB*RoR[2]

As noted, calculating the cost of service rarely poses intractable difficulties. Valuing the rate base and reasonable rate of return, however, entail significant problems. Three are particularly noteworthy. First, should regulators value the capital investment underlying the rate base on a depreciated original-cost basis or by replacement value? The difference can be vast. Economists favour the latter valuation method because it induces the regulated firm to make efficient invest-ment decisions.

Second, what infrastructure should regulators include in the rate base? This is no trivial detail, for the absence or inclusion of a significant asset can dramatically alter the utility's calculated revenue requirements. The question is most problematic in the presence of "stranded costs", as when an infrastructure must be abandoned in light of deregulation or the emergence of superior technology before the asset has fully depreciated. From the perspective of efficiency, the question is whether the boon to consumers of lower prices associated with writing off the earlier investment outweighs the suppression of future incentives to invest. Equitable considerations, however, suggest that the regulator should permit the utility to recover its investment in the now-defunct facility as long as the original investment was prudent. In such situations, should the government force the

---

2 Where "Rev." = permitted revenue; "CS" = cost of service; "RB" = rate base; and RoR = reasonable rate of return.

firm to suffer the relevant loss or allow it to recoup all or part of the costs from consumers? The easiest cases arise when a regulated firm's investment was negligent. In that setting, regulators' best move is to force the monopolist to internalise the full cost of the mistaken investment subject to not bankrupting the entity, which punishment mimics the operation of the free market.

The third problem lies in devising proper methods of depreciation, which simultaneously reduces the rate base and increases the cost of service, and in identifying an optimal rate of return. Regulators typically look to imperfect benchmarks in calculating the rate of return. More specifically, they may look at the rates that unregulated or regulated firms bearing similar risk profiles command, as well as at the interest on safe investments such as (certain countries') sovereign debt. None is apt to be an accurate proxy.

(b) Shortcomings in cost-of-service regulation

How effective is rate-of-return regulation? The answer is "not very" as this form of regulatory oversight is beset with problems. First, regulators determine the firm's revenue requirement based on industry conditions in the test year, such that the regulator implicitly assumes a static market environment or at least one in which changes over time are predictable. The calculated revenue target is, therefore, vulnerable to fluctuations in demand or inflation between the test period and the current year. Market factors having nothing to do with the regulated entity's efficiency or performance may therefore bestow a windfall, or unjustified loss, on the firm. Second, given the difficulties recounted above in calculating the appropriate rate base and rate of return, the calculated revenue requirement will probably depart from the optimal amount. As a result, the approved set of tariffs may differ significantly from the level that would equate price with average cost.

A third problem is known as the "Averch-Johnson effect". If regulators inadvertently permit utilities to earn an excessive rate of return, those firms can further enhance profit by making unnecessary (i.e. non-cost-justified) investments in capital. This is known as "gold plating". Doing so enables regulated firms artificially to enhance the value of their rate base, thus magnifying the return that regulators permit them to enjoy on top of their cost of service. The result may be an inefficient substitution of capital for labour.

The most significant problem with rate-of-return regulation, however, comes from the fact that it is cost rather than price based. As a result, the regulated firm has limited incentive to reduce costs and to enhance productive efficiency. For instance, if regulators fail to account for unproductive employees, unjustified costs in operating the network, supracompetitive salaries, and the like, the utility may have little incentive to remedy those deficiencies because it will be permitted to charge rates sufficient to meet its revenue requirements anyway.

The failure to cut costs would not be severe if regulators were able to oversee their charges with sufficient accuracy. After all, regulators try not to include unreasonable or unnecessary expenditure for ratemaking purposes, and enforce a prudent investment rule that would exclude unjustified capital investments from inclusion in the rate base. Serious principal–agent problems arise, however, due to information asymmetries that frustrate regulators' ability to monitor utilities' productive efficiency.

It is not the case, of course, that utilities and common carriers subject to this form of regulation have no incentive at all to cut costs. Regulatory lag means that a firm could use productive-efficiency gains in the current year over the test period to achieve a profit by obtaining revenue in excess of its costs. Furthermore, a high elasticity of demand for the regulated product may spur the utility to reduce costs to avoid a shortfall in sales. Moreover, to the extent that they are meaningful, efficiency audits may spur cost cutting on the part of the regulated entity.

Nevertheless, the overall incentive to cut cost is dull, and so regulated firms will not achieve marginal costs of production comparable to what they would reach under competition. For that reason, cost-of-service regulation has long been the subject of economic criticism. We now consider an alternative method of profit control that seeks to remedy these deficiencies.

3. Price caps as a form of incentive regulation

Rate-of-return regulation fails because it links input costs to permissible revenues, thus blunting incentives to achieve productive efficiency. Recognising this and other shortcomings addressed above, the UK Government rejected rate-of-return regulation when it privatised British Telecommunications (BT) in 1984. Instead, it opted for a new form of profit control, known as "price-cap" or "RPI −N X" regulation. This form of incentive regulation is now widely used in the United States, Europe, and elsewhere.

The idea behind price-cap regulation is to sever the link between the regulated firm's input costs and output prices. By limiting how much the utility or common carrier can charge and by committing to reduce that limit in the future, a regulator incentivises a profit-maximising company to reduce its costs. The reason is that profit depends on the gulf between price and cost. As the firm cannot raise the former, to increase profit it must reduce the latter. Should the utility or common carrier fail to achieve sufficient efficiencies, of course, the ensuing price-cap reduction may force it to suffer losses. In theory, this form of regulation should pressure regulated firms to achieve productive efficiency, thus introducing incentives that are sorely lacking under rate-of-return regulation.

Price-cap regulation follows a simple calculus. The regulator sets a maximum price that the firm can charge in the following period, and allows that price to change over time according to a formula known as "RPI − X". The initial price-cap determination is like the revenue-requirement calculation periodically undertaken under the rate-of-return regulation. The approach differs in its pre-commitment to lower the maximum price at a specific time in the future, regardless of the utility's or common carrier's costs at that moment.

The first element of the formula, RPI or "retail price index" measures inflation, reflecting the common sense notion that a regulated entity's price should rise in conjunction with broader upward price movements in the economy. The "X" figure is important. It represents the efficiency savings that the firm should be able to achieve in the relevant period vis-à-vis the larger economy. Calculated properly, the price cap subject to RPI − X adjustment will result in the utility or common carrier's achieving productive efficiency and earning zero economic profit.

Upon superficial examination, this form of incentive regulation has much to commend it. By spurring regulated firms to cut costs in the pursuit of profit, price-cap regulation instils an important incentive associated with competition. It also capitalises on regulated firms' private information. Information asymmetry, of course, hinders agencies' ability to conduct meaningful efficiency audits under cost-of-service regulation.

Nevertheless, price caps are difficult to employ effectively. For this form of incentive regulation to work, the agency must (i) calculate the X-factor correctly; (ii) set a time for the subsequent rate review that is sufficiently far away to spur efforts to achieve productive efficiency, but not so far away as to bestow a windfall on the firm; and (iii) credibly commit not to raise the cap should the firm fail to achieve envisioned cost savings. None of these tasks is straightforward.

First, determining the proper X-factor is difficult, for regulators must calculate the rate at which the relevant firms' inflation-adjusted output prices should fall. To make this determination, a regulator must estimate both the current productive inefficiency of the firm and how quickly incentivised management could eliminate those inefficiencies. If a regulator calculates too low an X-factor, the firm will enjoy excessive profits. Too high an X-factor may threaten the utility or common carrier's commercial viability. In either event, the agency will come under political pressure to alter the cap to eliminate windfalls or to ensure the regulated company's viability. Should the regulator succumb to this pressure, it would adjust output prices based on the input costs of the utility or common carrier, which process would, of course, resemble traditional rate-of-return regulation.

Second, even if the regulator identifies the appropriate X-factor, it must set an appropriate duration for the first gap. The length of time that passes before the agency revisits the appropriate price cap affects the power of the incentive to cut costs. If the regulator divorces input costs from output prices for an extended period, the utility or common carrier can secure enviable profit opportunities by cutting costs and enjoying significant mark-ups over time. Yet, prolonged supra-competitive profits come at the expense of consumers, whose interests the regulators are supposed to protect. Conversely, if the regulator adjusts the price cap too often, there will be little incentive to cut costs.

Third, price caps will spur efficiency gains only if the regulated firm believes that its failure to cut costs will have real consequences. In reality, regulators must ensure the commercial viability of their charges. Thus, they are likely to increase a cap should costs exceed revenues. Knowing this *ex ante*, regulated firms experience cost-cutting pressures that are less acute than those of Darwinian competition.

There is a more general shortcoming, however, which concerns how a regulated firm achieves the cost savings necessary to achieve profitability while subject to a price cap. It is far easier to sacrifice the quality of one's services, thus providing them at lower cost, than it is to endure the painful process of achieving heightened productive efficiency. A concern with price-cap regulation, therefore, is that it will produce inferior services. Thus, price-cap regulation may lead to degraded service quality and infrastructure development vis-à-vis cost-plus regulation.

Although price caps are widely used, and display attractive theoretical benefits over traditional, cost-plus profit control, in practice they are imperfect. Regulation's inability fully to mimic the incentive effects of free competition has been a major driving force behind deregulation, which is addressed in the next section.

4. Yardstick competition as an alternative form of incentive regulation

Incentive regulation seeks to sever the link between production costs and output prices. We conclude our discussion by briefly considering an alternative to price-cap regulation: yardstick competition.

A regulator can use yardstick competition to estimate a utility or common carrier's realisable productive efficiency by comparing the regulated firm's costs to those of a similarly situated company. Ideally, the "benchmark" firm would be identical to the regulated company, differing only in its being run efficiently, thus allowing the regulator to set the price by reference to the otherwise-identical costs of the firm. In such an event, the regulated firm will experience an incentive to achieve efficiency gains, which will be as acute as the regulator's commitment not to raise prices to prevent losses is credible. Unfortunately, a model company will rarely be the efficient twin of the state-regulated firm, and regulators will not always be able perfectly to control for the heterogeneous qualities and factors accompanying the two companies. Furthermore, and as with price-cap regulation, yardstick competition spurs cost cutting, which regulated firms can most easily achieve by sacrificing quality. Moreover, regulators are more forgiving than markets, which dilute the incentive to achieve efficiency. Should a regulated company remain poorly run and thus fail to achieve comparable operational efficiency with the model company, the regulator would probably allow the firm to raise price to ensure solvency. In this event, the link between production costs and output prices is re-established, and "incentive" regulation ceases to be.

C. Restoring Competition: The Deregulatory Movement

The theory of natural monopoly held sway for the first three-quarters of the twentieth century. Economists and policymakers adhered to a deep-rooted conviction that competition in infrastructure-heavy industries would inefficiently cause network duplication, anaemic investment, and insolvency. That ideology begat vast swathes of regulatory oversight in the United States, encompassing the electricity, gas, aviation, trucking, rail, and telecommunications industries, as well as pervasive state ownership of those sectors in Europe. By the 1970s, however, scepticism was growing: not only about the efficacy of profit control, but about the perceived severity of natural-monopoly conditions. Furthermore, economists increasingly came to see regulation as a product that industry demanded and that the state provided at the expense of consumers. Many such commentators believed in "regulatory capture", whereby agencies, who were supposed to force utilities and common carries to behave as they would under competition, became agents of their charges.

The result was a broad deregulatory movement on both sides of the Atlantic that began in the 1970s and picked up steam during the 1980s. Policymakers concluded that many regulated-industry components were not subject to sufficient scale economies to render them natural monopolies. States thus opened up various markets to competition for the first time, with dramatic results. In more complicated settings, governments divided industries into their natural- and non-natural monopoly components, inviting competition over the latter and imposing stringent "duty to deal" requirements on monopoly operators of the former. The idea was to foster competition in network operation where possible, while regulating bottleneck access points to the network still subject to the natural monopoly conditions.

This section explores the deregulatory movement in the illustrative spheres of aviation, natural gas, telecommunications, and electricity. Given the scale of US deregulation and its transformation of industry, this section focuses on the US experience. Before engaging in this account, however, three broad observations are appropriate.

First, the central premise underlying deregulation is not that competition is infallible. It is rather that the benefits of liberalisation are likely to swamp the problems with regulation explored above. Second, privatisation is not the same as liberalisation. In the absence of effective incentive regulation, transferring ownership of an entrenched monopolist from the state to the private sector is unlikely to accomplish much in the way of allocative efficiency gains without competition. Liberalisation, by contrast, opens formerly state-owned or regulated monopolists to competition, which if done properly and in the right setting, promises to yield great benefits for consumers.

Finally, deregulation will be more valuable the less closely the economics of the liberalised industry approximate the natural monopoly theory introduced above. Much governmental regulation is founded not on promoting productive efficiency, but on protectionism that promotes special interests at the expense of larger society. Where state-imposed impediments to competition do not have an efficiency foundation, deregulation will probably produce dramatic benefits (e.g. liberalisation of the US trucking and railroad industries brought vast social gains).

A more recent, though smaller-scale, example entails taxi deregulation in Ireland. Here, the government had long capped the number of cabs at a level far below consumer demand at peak periods. The taxi industry, of course, bears no discernible characteristics indicative of natural monopoly, so the consumer welfare case for such restrictions on competition was non-existent. The regulatory cap fell away in late 2000 and the number of cabs rose precipitously. In 2000, there were almost 4,000 taxi licences in Ireland – two years later, there were more than 8,000. A 2009 study by Goodbody Economic Consultants estimated that market liberalisation yielded consumer benefits of €780 million.[3]

The taxi industry, of course, is straightforward. The economics of the aviation, gas, telecommunications, and electricity sectors are more complex.

---

3 Goodbody Economic Consultants, *Economic Review of the Small Public Service Vehicle Industry* (2009). Available at: www.nationaltransport. ie/downloads/taxi-reg/economic-review-spsv-industry.pdf.

1. The aviation industry

For many decades, the US Government treated the aviation industry as a public utility, The Civil Aeronautics Board ("CAB") regulated airlines' pricing and routing. The economic theory for treating it as a natural monopoly was superficially attractive – it is a network industry the underlying infrastructure of which requires great capital investment. Runways, airport facilities, and aircraft, after all, are fantastically expensive. That a unitary regulator would coordinate the network seemed desirable, not least because of the importance of network investment and minimising duplication. In reality, though, the capacity and per-passenger cost of more modern aircraft are such that competition between airlines using rival fleets is both feasible and efficient. Furthermore, modern airports can handle sufficient capacity to facilitate airline competition.

Long oblivious to these economic facts, the CAB subjected the industry to stringent rules on fares and routes, and controlled entry and exit. Unable to compete on the basis of price, airlines competed the only way they could: quality of service. Knowing that they could pass high operating costs onto consumers with the CAB's blessing, airlines offered outlandish services (culminating in American Airlines' famous piano bars on jumbo jets in the mid-1970s) and lavished their employees with enviable benefits. Air travel was a glamorous activity, and the exclusive purview of the wealthy.

Events in the 1970s, however, culminated in wholesale deregulation. In the first place, academic criticism by economists undermined the conventional wisdom that the aviation industry is a natural monopoly. Second, the combination of higher costs post the 1973 oil crisis and greater capacity associated with the introduction of wide body aircraft (such as the Boeing 747) led the CAB sharply to increase fares so that the regulated carriers could recover their costs. The upward price trends were not popular. Third, and unusually, the regulator itself came to recognise the case for deregulation. The CAB chairman and economist, Alfred Khan, was especially influential in liberalising price and route restrictions on airlines.

In 1978, Congress passed the Airline Deregulation Act, abolishing regulatory control of rates, schedules, routes, entry, and exit. The result was transformational. The industry left the artificial confines of regulatory protection to encounter competition. A new-found consumer focus revealed vast sources of untapped demand. Perhaps the most dramatic changes were structural, as the industry evolved from direct, point-to-point routes across the country to consolidated "hub and spoke" networks that enhanced operational efficiency. The consequences, however, were not uniformly positive. Many hubs became oligopolistic as certain airlines grew to account for a large percentage of flights out of their major centres. This effect permitted, and continues to allow, the dominant airline in certain hubs to exercise market power in that locus. Counteracting this effect, however, was greater productive efficiency and fierce competition on segments served by more than one hub. For that reason, deregulation produced conflicting price effects: small-scale, predominantly local routes became more expensive (and received cutbacks in service), as such cities were less likely to be subject to multiple spokes, while long-distance flights and major destinations in the country were subject to greater competition that produced lower prices.

Despite the asymmetric change in fares, the overall price effect of deregulation was strongly downward. Market demand revealed that consumers valued lower prices over quality of service, which resulted in the introduction of narrower, more-confined seats as airlines increased the number of customers on each flight. Pricing also became more efficient in allocating consumer demand. Peak-load pricing became commonplace, as airlines used asymmetric fares to induce utilisation of capacity during off-peak periods and to offset demand during times of high volume. Load factors (the percentage of filled seats on each plane) grew following deregulation.

Not all established airlines survived. Three major carriers – Pan Am, TWA, and Eastern – had collapsed by 1991, unable to survive the fare wars launched by new, low-cost, no-frills airlines. Such displacement is a common result of opening long-regulated industries to competitive entry. Notwithstanding the aviation industry's greater efficiency today, however, the sector remains somewhat unstable, as low margins induced by competition and high fixed costs leave airlines vulnerable to fluctuations in input prices, especially in the cost of jet fuel, and in consumer demand. Bankruptcy is unusually common in the industry.

Some commentators express nostalgic memories for the glamorous era of air travel in which large seats, high-quality meals, top-shelf drink service, and little crowding reigned supreme. Still, deregulation has produced vast consumer savings and is widely considered to have been a tremendous success. The number of people flying each year has increased, the cross-section of the community availing of air transport is far broader, and net prices have fallen sharply. A 1997 study estimated that aviation deregulation had saved US consumers $19.4 billion per year.[4]

Although this discussion has focused on the US experience, deregulation in Europe has been no less fruitful. The European aviation industry was long subject to fragmented regulatory oversight that protected national carriers from competition. In the years leading up to 1997, however, the EU implemented an "open skies" programme, which reduced fares and increased traffic. Ryanair and easyJet mimicked the US budget airline model that Southwest Airlines and ValuJet typified, launching low-fares and no-frills service and expanding the number of passengers flying annually. A 2007 agreement between the United States and the European Union followed the 1997 liberalisation in Europe, deregulating air traffic over the Atlantic.

The aviation industry's experience illustrates the danger of subjecting markets conducive of competition to regulatory control. Shielded from market forces, and sheltered from consumer demand, regulated companies tend to promote their own interests instead of those of society. By liberalising sectors not subject to powerful scale economies and exposing them to competition, governments can affect vast gains in consumer welfare.

Notwithstanding these benefits, complete deregulation may be undesirable. For example, airports are still natural monopolies, for it would be both inefficient and indeed cost prohibitive for each airline to construct its own airport capable of handling modern airliners in every market that it wished to serve. If airports are privately owned – and many are – they may become bottlenecks subject to monopoly pricing that both eviscerate the efficacy of airline competition and harm consumers. For that reason, today, privately run airports are typically subject to incentive regulation (most often, in the form of price caps).[5] Of course, such regulatory oversight remains fraught with difficulty as agencies seek simultaneously to limit airports' pricing power and to ensure efficient investment in infrastructure. For the time being, however, that approach remains necessary in the absence of a competitive alternative.

2. Natural gas

Few industries traditionally subject to regulatory control were entirely devoid of diseconomies of scale. More often, particular components of a network can accommodate competition, even if certain segments of the larger grid remain natural monopolies. The policy challenge in this setting is to realise the benefits of free-market competition over those elements of the industry conducive of entry, while regulating bottleneck points in the network to prevent monopolist controllers of those segments from charging monopoly access fees. Regulators have sought to accomplish this goal by imposing unbundling and equal access obligations on network owners. We shall discuss three industries in which governments have attempted this difficult balancing act: gas, electricity, and telecommunications.

---

4 Robert Crandall and Jerry Ellig, *Economic Deregulation and Customer Choice: Lessons for the Electric Industry* (1997).
5 One should not exaggerate, however, the natural monopoly traits of airports themselves. In certain, high-profile locations such as London and New York, multiple airports compete with one another within the same geographic vicinity, thus indicating that some form of facilities-based competition may be both feasible and efficient in areas with sufficiently high demand.

The simplest example is the natural gas industry. That sector displays many hallmarks of a classic natural monopoly. Constructing and installing a nationwide distribution pipeline is phenomenally expensive, and not efficiently duplicated. Network-based competition in the transportation of natural gas would therefore see competitors operating on sharply downward-sloping portions of their average-cost curves, which would not only be productively inefficient, but would be unstable. In particular, rivalry would drive price toward marginal cost, thus depriving competitors of the pricing power necessary to recoup the capital investment required to build a gas-distribution network.

Although gas pipelines constitute a natural monopoly, other aspects of the natural-gas industry are susceptible to efficient competition. This is especially true of production, as there are thousands of US gas producers whose price competition inures to consumers' benefit. It is also partially true of gas distribution at the local level. For competition to work, however, rivals must be able to bypass the transportation bottleneck. Otherwise, owners of gas-distribution pipelines, by charging monopoly prices, would be able to commandeer the surplus generated by price wars between gas producers.

From the mid-1980s to the early 1990s, US regulators and Congress addressed the bottleneck problem. They required vertically integrated utilities that produced, transported, stored, and locally distributed natural gas to unbundle their operations, obliging them to sell each of those goods or services separately. By unbundling non-natural monopoly activities from their natural monopoly counterparts, policymakers were able to spur competition. Pipeline owners were then subject to equal-access obligations, being required to provide all comers with identical rights of use in transportation. Ensuing competition resulted in greater choice and lower gas prices for consumers. One study found that deregulation of natural gas led to a 10-year real price reduction in the range of 27–57%.[6]

3. Telecommunications

Policymakers have long viewed the telecommunications industry as a classic natural monopoly because of the cost of building the requisite network of telephone wires, switching equipment, input/output devices, and control centres. Given the fixed costs involved in building this infrastructure, and the slight marginal cost that transferring data between users once the platform is in place entails, powerful scale economies exist in operating a telecommunications grid. Traditional US policy was therefore to regulate a single purveyor of telecommunications services.

There is perhaps no more-famous monopolist than the telecommunications behemoth, American Telephone and Telegraph (AT&T), which the US government first regulated as a state-sanctioned monopoly in 1913. For the next seven decades, AT&T controlled the industry, being comprised of Bell Operating Companies (BOCs) that provided local telephone service, a "Long Lines" department that offered long-distance telephone services, and Bell Laboratories, its famous R&D centre responsible for a series of ground-breaking inventions. For a time, AT&T was the world's largest company.

The emergence of new technologies in the 1960s made limited competition feasible for the first time, as small entrants marketed new network equipment. Microwave Communications, Inc. (MCI) availed of microwave and satellite technology to bypass AT&T's wire grid to offer a limited long-distance service. AT&T fiercely opposed this, refusing to permit its customers to connect non-AT&T telephone equipment to its network. The telecommunications giant also excluded competition in long-distance telephony. Although MCI could bypass AT&T's cross-country wires through its microwave network, doing so would be for naught if it could not connect to the "last mile" or local

---

6 See Crandall and Ellig, *supra* note 4.

loops, which AT&T's BOCs controlled. AT&T denied MCI access to those loops, thus preventing its nascent rival from connecting to end users.

Two major events revolutionised the industry, ushering in an era of competition in what was formerly deemed a natural monopoly. In 1968, the Federal Communications Commission (FCC) issued its "Carterfone" order. This allowed users to connect devices to AT&T's network as long as doing so did not harm the platform. This decision led to rapid innovation in end-user devices, such as answering machines, fax devices, and, later, modems. The transformative moment, however, came in 1984, when, following an antitrust action by the US Department of Justice, AT&T was broken up pursuant to a consent decree. The decree required AT&T to divest its regional BOCs into seven Regional Bell Operating Companies, known as "RBOCs" or "Baby Bells", and to continue in business only as a long-distance service provider. The idea was to separate long-distance telephone service, which was conducive to competition, from local service, which remained a natural monopoly. To facilitate long-distance competition, the consent decree imposed an equal-access obligation on the RBOCs, which were not permitted to enter or otherwise to compete in the long-distance market. These restrictions were necessary because, were the RBOCs to offer a long-distance service, they could use their bottleneck local-loop infrastructure to disadvantage their long-distance competitors. One danger would be a "price squeeze" in which the RBOCs would undercut their rivals' long-distance prices, while charging those competitors higher access fees for accessing the local loop than they effectively charged themselves.

Competition in the long-distance market increased following the 1984 breakup, with MCI, Sprint, and others constructing their own long-distance networks using fibre-optic lines, thus engaging in facilities-based competition, which saw AT&T's market share drop precipitously from monopoly levels in 1984 to 50% by 1998. Competition caused prices to fall dramatically. Economists agree that the deregulation of the long-distance telecommunications market was tremendously successful, but problems continued to afflict local service, which unlike long-distance service, used copper-wire loops that are uneconomical to recreate. Furthermore, the RBOCs lobbied Congress intensively to allow them to compete in the long-distance market, which appeared ever-more lucrative in light of their control of bottleneck access points to end users.

Congress passed the ambitious 1996 Telecommunications Act, overhauling the industry and seeking to spur competition for the first time in local telephony. To accomplish this difficult task, the Act created a quid pro quo. Recognising that RBOCs wished to enter the long-distance market, the legislation allowed them to do so once they had abandoned their local-exchange monopolies by opening their networks to competition. To enable competitive entry, the Act required incumbent local-exchange carriers (RBOCs or ILECs) to unbundle certain of their network elements – specifically those the absence of which the FCC determined would impair CLECs' ability to compete – and to lend the same to entrants, known as competitive local-exchange carriers (CLECs), on a just, reasonable, and non-discriminatory basis. Alternatively, companies could enter the retail market by purchasing ILECs' retail services at wholesale prices or by connecting their own facilities to ILECs' networks.

The Act was not effective in spurring local-service competition. The ILECs opposed the FCC's attempts to implement the statutory provisions, preferring to maintain their local monopolies rather than to proceed swiftly into the long-distance market. The ILECs launched protracted lawsuits challenging the FCC's interpretations of key provisions of the statute. They successfully challenged the FCC's broad interpretation of the key term, "impaired", in 1999, as well as the FCC's line-sharing rules that had allowed CLECs to use the high-frequency portion of ILECs' local loop in 2002.[7] Furthermore, stakeholders contested the price at which RBOCs had to make their

---

7 AT&T Corp v Iowa Utils Bd, 525 US 366 (1999); US Telecom Assoc v FCC, 290 F3d 415 (DC Cir. 2002).

unbundled network elements available to CLECs. The FCC defined the appropriate access price as being equal to the relevant network element's "total element long-run incremental cost" or TELRIC, which problematically failed to provide for ILECs' having to recover fixed investment costs.[8] Nevertheless, the Supreme Court ultimately upheld them in 2002.[9] The RBOCs secured another victory against the FCC in 2004, when the DC Circuit held that the FCC's sub-delegation of authority to state regulators to determine impairment as to CLECs' access to ILEC mass-market switches, and other of the FCC's impairment determinations, was unlawful.[10]

The FCC's inability to give effect to the 1996 Telecommunications Act in the face of the ILECs' opposition stymied a key rationale of the Act, which was to introduce competition in the local loop. Notwithstanding this failure, the FCC liberally interpreted the Act's condition that it not permit ILECs to enter the long-distance market until these had become sufficiently competitive. The agency authorised most ILECs' entry into the long-distance market between 2000 and 2003. The failure to spur competition in the local market spurred a wave of consolidation in the industry, as long-distance providers acquired companies with access to the local market and RBOCs combined to strengthen their positions. In the years since then, exponential growth in broadband, satellite, and other telecommunications technologies have rendered important components of the 1996 Act outdated. The legislation's failure highlights the difficulty of partially exposing an industry to competition when certain aspects of it remain natural monopoly bottlenecks. In the case of tele-communications, the high pace of technological advance rendered partial deregulation in this complex field especially difficult.

4. Electricity

For most of the twentieth century in the US electricity industry, a single, vertically integrated utility would sell a single service combining electricity generation, transportation, and local distribution. Each monopolist operated its own power plants, high-voltage lines for long-distance transmission, and local grids that distributed electricity to consumers. The capital-intensive nature of this infra-structure justified regulating the electricity industry as a natural monopoly, subjecting utilities to cost-of-service profit control. This state of affairs saw different monopolists serving distinct geographical regions throughout the country, presenting consumers with no choice and depriving them of the benefits of competition.

Over time, it became clear that some components of the electricity industry could support competition. Electricity generation, in particular, is not a natural monopoly function, though facilities-based competition in long-distance transportation and local distribution are not feasible on account of inefficient duplication. As in the natural gas industry, unbundling and compulsory access can allow downstream consumers to realise the benefits of upstream competition in network components not subject to powerful scale economies. They do so by preventing owners of bottle-neck segments of the network from extracting monopoly rents.

The United States engaged in a deregulatory campaign stretching from the Public Utility Regulatory Policies Act of 1978, which required utilities to purchase power from independent electricity producers, through the Federal Energy Regulatory Commission's Order 888 in 1996, pursuant to the Energy Policy Act of 1992, and the Energy Policy Act 1996. This process broke up vertically integrated utilities, requiring them to divest their power plants by selling them to third parties. Collectively, these measures required utilities owning transmission lines to grant equal access to all third parties. The combination of unbundling and mandatory access opened electricity

---

8 See Thomas M. Jorde, J. Gregory Sidak, and David J. Teece, *Innovation, Investment, and Unbundling* (2000) 17 Yale J on Reg 1.

9 *Verizon Comm'cns, Inc v FCC*, 535 US 467 (2002).

10 *US Telecom Assoc v FCC*, 359 F3d 554 (DC Cir 2004).

wholesale markets (and, in some cases, retail markets), to competition, though long-distance transmission and local distribution remain subject to regulation because they are natural monopolies. Today's post-restructuring, US electricity industry operates as follows:

Generation rests at the top of the vertical supply chain in the electricity industry. Owners of power plants generate electricity, which is a commodity that ultimately makes its way to end users. The path from generators to consumers, however, is not direct. The wholesale market lies right below generation in the vertical chain, in which entities connected to the grid sell and purchase power on the open market. Companies competing to make sales in the wholesale market typically include independent power producers (IPPs), utility affiliates, and vertically integrated entities that generate excess power. Not all market participants are electricity generators, as electricity is routinely sold and re-sold numerous times before making its way to end users.

The physics of electricity complicates competition in the wholesale market. The inability to store electricity makes it difficult to coordinate an electricity transmission network subject to fluctuating demand and to congestion when demand exceeds supply. In particular, divided ownership of an electricity grid can produce undesirable consequences due to the externalities that accompany individual segment owners' pricing decisions. This problem creates a powerful efficiency justification for an independent system operator (ISO) or regional transmission organisation (RTO) to run the network on behalf of the relevant owners. Most, though not all, regional wholesale electricity markets in the United States operate under an ISO or RTO, which allocates grid capacity on the basis of bids using price auctions. Ensuing contracts vary from real-time, or "spot", arrangements to long-term agreements.

Below the wholesale market is the retail sale of electricity to end users, who run the spectrum from individual consumers and small businesses to large-scale manufacturers. In the US states in which regulators have introduced competition in the retail market, consumers wishing to purchase power enjoy a choice between the incumbent utility (known as the "provider of last resort") and other suppliers. Each competitor in the retail market purchases the electricity that it sells to end users from the wholesale market, the competitiveness of which directly affects how much end users pay downstream.

How well has deregulation worked in this industry? It has not been a smooth process; nor has it produced uniform gains. In the years during and following deregulation, US consumers experienced sharply rising prices. Higher electricity rates following the removal of regulatory pricing constraints. This angered customers, leading some commentators to question the efficacy of liberalisation and to call for the reintroduction of cost-of-service or price-cap regulation.

Consumers may have drawn unjustified inferences from those higher prices, however, for restructuring eliminated price caps that had prevented utilities from selling at market rates. Furthermore, gas prices on which generation, and hence, wholesale-market prices depend rose sharply following deregulation. Separating the effects of (i) rising input prices into electricity generation and (ii) removing the artificial suppression of market rates by transitional price caps from (iii) competition-induced increases in productive efficiency and downward pressure on price is complex. Evidence suggests that, although retail prices rose everywhere, they rose more in deregulated states than those that had remained subject to traditional regulation.[11] This observation, of course, does not control for potentially material distinctions between liberalised and non-liberalised states. Having reviewed the evidence, some economists deem US deregulation of the electricity industry to be a net success, resulting in lower "but for" wholesale and retail prices, and efficient incentive-producing shifts in investment risk from consumers to generators.[12]

---

11 Susan F. Tierney, *Decoding developments in today's electric industry – Ten points in the prism* (2007). Available at: www.epsa.org/analysisgroupstudy. pdf.
12 *See, e.g.* Adam Swadley and Mine Yücel, 'Did residential electricity rates fall after retail competition? A dynamic panel analysis' (2011) 39 Energy Policy 7702; Howard J. Axelrod *et al.* (2006) 'The fallacy of high prices', Public Utilities Fortnightly 55.

No account of deregulation of the US electricity industry would be complete, however, without referencing the process's most dramatic failure, which was the California energy crisis of 2000–2001. As in states across the nation, Californian utilities divested their power generation stations, so that independent power producers and other non-utilities produced electricity. In 2000, the regulator liberalised wholesale prices, though retail prices remained regulated and fixed at a level meant to permit utilities to recover the stranded costs that they had experienced from deregulation. Unfortunately, the wholesale electricity market in California did not become competitive, as power generators, freed from regulatory constraint, began charging monopoly prices. Forced to pay ever-higher input prices on the wholesale market, but forbidden to pass those costs onto consumers in the retail market, the incumbent utilities began to experience financial distress. Electricity generators created artificial scarcity through such strategic behaviour as bringing power plants offline for "maintenance" during periods of peak demand. This forced utilities to go to the spot market to secure critically needed electricity, on which market suppliers were able to command prodigious rates. Resulting shortages caused rolling blackouts in northern California throughout 2000 and resulted in a major utility, Pacific Gas and Electric Company (PG&E), going bankrupt in 2001.

Properly understood, this crisis is not an indictment of deregulation itself, but of the flawed manner in which California partially liberalised its energy industry. Liberalisation is no guarantee to overnight price reductions in wholesale and retail energy markets. Partial deregulation of the kind undertaken in the electricity industry can only work if competition in wholesale markets actually emerges. Should viable competition fail to materialise, unregulated sellers of electricity will do what they could not under rate-of-return regulation: charge monopoly prices. For the duration between liberalisation and the emergence of competition, price spikes and strategic behaviour are likely. The state must plan accordingly.

D. The Limits of Competition: The Case of the Financial Services Industry

The US experience in deregulating industries has generally been positive. Regulated firms, freed of the disciplinary incentives of competition, tend toward productive and allocative inefficiency, as none of cost-of-service regulation, yardstick competition, and price-cap incentive regulation mimics market forces. By lifting the protective arm of the state and subjecting utilities or common carriers to entry and thus to consumer demand, liberalisation can usher forth more efficient industry structures and lower overall prices. In many cases, the transformation can be dramatic, as the aviation industry made plain. The deregulatory process, however, is more complicated for industries in which certain sub-components of the relevant network remain subject to powerful scale economies. Liberalisation can still produce efficiency benefits, though addressing bottleneck access points complicates the state's task. Overall, in comparing the modern aviation, natural gas, telecommunications, and electricity industries to their heavily regulated 1960s counterparts, deregulation has produced significant gains. This holds true even if liberalisation has not always been a smooth process, as the energy and telecommunications industries have illustrated.

Deregulation had calamitous results, however, in one important field: financial services. The deregulatory movement that swept through the United States and elsewhere in the 1970s and 1980s resulted in the liberalisation of myriad rules governing financial institutions. This chapter only briefly references this form of deregulation, for financial services regulation is not based on natural monopoly characteristics. Instead, it reflects the instability of financial services markets, as well as the crucial economic role that financial institutions play as intermediaries in the economy, facilitating business transactions through the provision of credit.

As financial markets have a well-evidenced instability, pursuant to which unfettered competition founded on short-term profit maximisation leads to successive "boom-and-bust" cycles, state supervision is critical. In particular, a bank in an unregulated environment has an incentive excessively to increase its leverage – its debt-to-equity ratio – to increase profit. This strategy can be dangerous, however, because heightened leverage magnifies losses, as well as gains. As we have seen throughout this book, externalities lead to undesirable behaviour, which the law can correct by aligning private and social costs. The losses that a systemically important institution can visit upon society, however, far exceed the private costs to the bank of insolvency. For that reason, neither the market nor the law can itself instil optimal incentives, so regulation designed to induce proper behaviour is crucial. This is all-the-more true because, given the state's need to bail out a bank that is "too big to fail", such financial institutions face skewed incentives. Specifically, they will experience the full benefits of profitable investments, but can pass major losses onto society.

The global banking crisis of 2008 and 2009 revealed that preceding deregulatory measures had been misplaced. The 1999 Gramm-Leach-Bliley Act, for instance, repealed the Glass-Steagall Act, which had prevented commercial banks, investment banks, and insurance companies from combining. Ensuing consolidation produced financial services companies that would bring the economy down with them were they to fail. The 2000 Commodity Futures Modernization Act left over-the-counter derivatives, such as credit-default swaps, unregulated. The opacity of those swaps, which were supposed to serve an insurance/hedging function, created much confusion as to liabilities throughout the crisis, adding to its severity. In 2004, the SEC permitted investment banks to increase leverage and to hold less capital, thus allowing them to achieve greater profitability, but with greater risk of insolvency.

These and other deregulatory measures led to disaster when, in 2007, a US crisis in sub-prime loans triggered a recession, culminating in the March 2008 collapse of Bear Stearns. That bankruptcy spurred unprecedented central bank and government action to prevent the onset of a depression. At the time of writing, US, European, and other western economies have yet fully to recover. In light of this deregulatory failure, it is no surprise that governments have passed stringent new regulatory legislation, such as the Dodd-Frank Wall Street Reform and Consumer Protection Act in the United States, while the European Union continues to debate measures aimed at addressing the myriad problems that the crisis highlighted, including the "too-big-to-fail" issue.

Although competition tends to produce overriding gains, this fact is not universally true. In light of technological advancements, natural monopolies are much less prevalent and severe than in the mid-twentieth century, thus making competition the policy of choice for most industries. Nevertheless, well-designed regulation remains critical in many settings.

E. Conclusion

Policymakers typically trust competition to produce socially desirable market outcomes, relying on antitrust laws to police the marketplace to ensure that renegade firms do not corrupt market forces. This chapter has explored the problems that emerge when certain industries cannot host competition. The historical reaction in the United States was to subject a single monopolist to profit control meant to mimic the effects of free-market competition. For reasons discussed above, rate-of-return regulation, price-cap regulation, and yardstick competition all fail in this regard. The traditional European reaction to natural monopoly – nationalisation – creates similar problems, as in both cases the company is not subject to market incentives. Scepticism concerning the efficacy of regulation has led governments increasingly to deregulate industries, again exposing them to competition. This process has generally, but not universally, produced fruitful results.

Competition is not a cure-all for every circumstance, however, so ongoing regulation will remain necessary for the foreseeable future. A knowledge of economics and incentives is critical for the effective application of regulatory oversight.

Key Points

- Natural monopolies are industries in which one firm can satisfy market demand more cheaply than two or more companies.

  - Competition in such industries creates allocative efficiency, but also generates productive inefficiency due to needless network duplication.
  - Where scale economies are sufficiently powerful, competition may cause insolvency because firms cannot recoup their capital investments in network or infrastructure when forced to price at marginal cost.

- To promote social welfare in natural monopolies, governments should try to spur productive efficiency by eliminating needless replication. They should also minimise allocative inefficiency by limiting supracompetitive pricing to the point necessary to cover a common carrier's or utility's average costs in efficiently investing in the network.

  - The traditional US solution was to grant one company a lawful monopoly and then to regulate its pricing and service.
  - In Europe, the conventional measure was to nationalise the industry.
  - Neither solution is ideal because neither can replicate the incentives of Darwinian competition.

- As marginal-cost pricing leads to insolvency, no optimal pricing regimen exists. Nonetheless, regulators have tools with which to limit the harm caused by allowing regulated utilities to cover their average costs.

  - "Ramsey", or inverse-elasticity pricing, is a form of price discrimination in which price increases with the inelasticity of each consumer's demand. By increasing price more for price-inelastic customers, utilities and common carries can reduce deadweight loss. Such pricing can create equitable issues, though, by forcing people with limited choice to subsidise others.
  - Two-part tariffs consist of an upfront access fee, and subsequent per-use charges. If a utility sets the latter fee equal to marginal cost, and uses upfront fees to cover its fixed costs, it facilitates efficient use of its network for those whose demand exceeds the initial access price.
  - Peak-load pricing adjusts price to smooth consumption between high- and low-demand periods. By charging less for electricity consumed during the night vis-à-vis the morning, for instance, a utility incentivises its customers to shift their usage away from the times of greatest demand, thus reducing congestion. Such pricing facilitates more-efficient usage of the network, and can increase social welfare.

- The leading forms of profit regulation are (1) rate-of-return regulation and (2) price-cap regulation. The goal is to limit supracompetitive pricing while both facilitating a sufficient return to attract capital for ongoing investment and incentivising productive efficiency.

  - Rate-of-return regulation calculates the utility's revenue needs, and then sets the price that over the anticipated volume of sales will generate the targeted sum.

- ■ The revenue requirement equals the rate base (the capital that the utility devotes to providing its product or service) by a reasonable rate of return (calibrated to allow the utility to attract sufficient capital) plus the cost of service, which is the sum of operating and depreciation expenses.

- ■ The problem with rate-of-return regulation is that it links costs and price, thus suppressing the utility's incentive to cut costs and achieve productive efficiency. If the regulator allows an excessive rate of return, it may induce the Averch-Johnson effect, leading the utility to overcapitalise (in order to boost its rate base and hence its authorised revenue).

- ○ Price-cap regulation identifies an authorised revenue target for a utility, sets a price cap designed to facilitate that level of revenue, and then adjusts that cap upward based on inflation and downward based on the utility's perceived ability to achieve productive-efficiency gains. By committing to reduce the cap regardless of whether the utility achieves cost savings, the regulator mimics market incentives to cut costs. Similarly, by delaying the price-cap decrease for a time, the regulator encourages cost-cutting so that the utility can increase profit.

  - ■ In practice, however, a regulator's threat to reduce the cap is non-credible if doing so would threaten the utility's solvency. By adjusting the cap to keep it a going concern, a regulator would re-establish the link between costs and price, thus transforming incentive regulation back into rate-of-return regulation.

- • Since the 1970s, deregulation has taken place in the aviation, natural gas, telecommunications, and electricity industries, and elsewhere. Economists realised that natural monopoly conditions were not as pervasive as once thought, and some argued that regulatory capture had led the state to champion the interests of regulated utilities and common carriers rather than those of consumers. Liberalisation produced overriding consumer benefits in many industries, though the US experience in partially deregulating the telecommunications and electricity was successful only in part.

 ## References and Further Reading

Books

Benjamin, Stuart Minor, Lichtman, Douglas Gary, Shelanski, Howard A., Weiser, Philip J., *Telecommunications Law and Policy*, 3rd edn (2012).

Griffin, James M. and Puller, Steven L. (eds.), *Electricity Deregulation: Choices and Challenges* (2005).

MacAvoy, Paul W. *The Natural Gas Market: Sixty Years of Regulation and Deregulation* (2001).

Miceli, Thomas J., *The Economic Approach to Law*, 2nd edn (2008) pp. 330–32.

Pierce, Richard J. and Ernest Gellhorn, *Regulated Industries*, 4th edn (1999).

Posner, Richard A., *Natural Monopoly and its Regulation*, 30th edn (1999).

Posner, Richard A., *Economic Analysis of Law*, 8th edn (2011) Ch. 12.

Tomain, Joseph P. and Cudahy, Richard D., *Energy Law* (2004).

Articles

Bailey, Elizabeth 'Airline deregulation: Confronting the paradoxes' (1992) 15 Regulation 3.

Kearney, Joseph D. and Merrill, Thomas W. 'The great transformation of regulated industries law' (1998) 98 Colum L Rev 1323.

Part 9

Behavioural Law and Economics

1   Behavioural Law and Economics   395

Chapter 1

Behavioural Law and Economics

Chapter Contents

A.	Introduction	396
B.	Revisiting Expected-Value Theory: Cognitive Psychology, Systemic Biases, and Prospect Theory	397
C.	Behavioural Law and Economics: Applications	404
D.	Normative Dimensions to Rationality: Paternalism and Behavioural Economics	407
E.	The Continuing Importance of Neoclassical Law and Economics	409
Key Points		411
References and Further Reading		412

A. Introduction

Traditional law and economics analysis is steeped in the neoclassical tradition, which ties welfare to the satisfaction of revealed preferences and posits that actors will maximise their utility by making rational decisions based on available information. The rationality assumption underlying this analytic approach is, by design, stylised. In its purest form, it attributes decision-making prowess that few people in the real world possess: consistent preferences, indifference to sunk costs, non-altruism, stable maximum-buy and minimum-sell prices, and disinterest in fairness. Such simplifying assumptions, however, serve an important purpose: they permit economists to construct models using mathematical methods of constrained optimisation to predict conduct. The goal is to identify explanatory variables that affect behaviour, which relationship econometricians then attempt to measure empirically. The concept of rational choice has pervaded this book's discussion of tort, crime, property, contract, litigation, competition, and regulation, which account relies on price theory to predict how the law can affect conduct by changing the shadow price of various behaviours ranging from criminal offences and negligent conduct to the decision whether or not to file a lawsuit.

The neoclassical paradigm carries both positive and normative implications. In the former respect, economists construct models that, using rational-choice theory, predict how proposed changes in law will affect behaviour. Legislators, judges, and other policymakers can use such predictions to inform their decision making, attaching whatever weight to the consequential impact of the proposed rules that they see fit. Neoclassical economics, however, also possesses a strong normative component. The criterion it uses to evaluate welfare is the preference that an economic actor reveals through her purchase and sell decisions. In prescribing laws designed to satisfy people's revealed preferences, neoclassical economics ties well-being to each person's autonomous determination as to his best course. It rejects the proclamations of third parties, such as those of the government, that purport to know an individual's interests better than the individual himself. It also eschews preferences to which people proclaim to adhere in the abstract, such as in surveys, but fail to embrace in the market. When push comes to shove, what people do matters more than what they say.

Focusing momentarily on the positive wing of neoclassical law and economics, many of the assumptions that rational-choice models ascribe to decision makers are unrealistic. They do not comport with the process by which individuals actually make choices. People enjoy various orders of intelligence; some are prone to bouts of anger that overwhelm their reasoning processes; others aspire to a particular long-term goal, but cannot resist immediate temptation antithetical to that objective; and few make decisions in a dispassionate manner divorced from thoughts of regret over bygones or over fairness as to how choices allocate benefits among stakeholders. Uncritical observers jump from the fact that *homus economicus* bears little resemblance to everyday people to reject neoclassical analysis as unrealistic.

Such commentators, however, miss the point, which is that this form of analysis is a theory of behaviour meant to predict large-scale conduct, rather than the subjective experience of individual choice. Empirical work generally supports the predictions of neoclassical welfare economics, which result suggests that, even if many people act irrationally, often their departures from rational choice are random and thus may cancel out. Nevertheless, two important questions arise: First, might there be other economic theories that predict behaviour more accurately than the neoclassical paradigm? Second, might neoclassical analysis produce systemically incorrect predictions in identifiable scenarios? The answer to both queries is a qualified yes.

An exciting development of recent years has been the emergence of a new school of thought aimed at enriching neoclassical analysis. Cognitive psychologists, who study the subjective process by which people make decisions, have contributed to traditional economic analysis by showing that economic actors often depart from the predictions of rational-choice theory. By infusing economics with this branch of psychology, academics have given birth to behavioural economics. This field explores the many ways in which human reasoning is defective, such that people often fail to act in a manner that promotes their preferences. Importantly, behavioural economists have shown not just that people act irrationally, for as just emphasised the fact that some, or even many, people do so has been long known, and is in itself irrelevant if such departures are randomly distributed. Instead, they have produced theoretical and empirical evidence that people tend to err in a particular direction, which, if true, means that large-scale behaviour will not gravitate toward the predictions of neoclassical models.

Applied to law, behavioural economics similarly possesses positive and normative qualities. In enriching the assumptions underlying economic models to render them more realistic, the field can in some (and perhaps in many) circumstances enhance those models' predictive power.

Likely the most influential aspect of the behavioural movement, however, is normative. By demonstrating how cognitive defects lead people to make decisions that run contrary to their best interests, behavioural economics undermines the argument that people are the best determinants of their welfare, such that the state should regard their choices as sacrosanct. Coupled with the fact that people's preferences are contingent, manipulable, and sometimes arbitrary, it suggests that the law may have a legitimate role in protecting people from themselves. Application of this principle need not take the form of an authoritarian regime in which individual liberty is subjugated to the superior mind of the government. Instead, leading behavioural economists have advocated a policy of "libertarian paternalism".[1] The idea is to use default rules to induce people to act in a manner more beneficial to their welfare, but without depriving them of the right to follow another course should they so choose.

This Part discusses the key features of behavioural law and economics, including prospect theory and the various biases that lead people systemically to make irrational decisions. Having addressed the field's underlying theory, it explores some illuminative applications of that theory to legal doctrine, demonstrating how the optimal rules that behavioural economics identifies may differ significantly from more traditional neoclassical analysis.

B. Revisiting Expected-Value Theory: Cognitive Psychology, Systemic Biases, and Prospect Theory

1. Risk aversion and expected-value theory

Much of the analysis undertaken in this book has assumed risk neutrality. Doing so simplifies analysis because it makes expected value the basis for choice. Thus, for example, it is easy to model a rational prospective criminal's election to commit a crime: he will do so if the sum of all possible outcomes in committing the crime multiplied by the corresponding probabilities exceeds his opportunity cost. Suppose that he derives 100 utils from committing the crime and has no opportunity cost, but faces a 25% chance of being caught and punished in the amount of -200 utils, a 10% probability of being caught and punished in the amount of -300 utils, and a 65% of getting away scot free. Assuming risk neutrality makes it simple to calculate the rational decision: he will commit the crime because its expected value is positive: $100 + 0.25*(-200) + 0.1(-300) = 20$.

In reality, though, few people are risk neutral. They may, on occasion, prefer risk, particularly when all of their options are unpalatable. More often, though, they are risk averse, especially where they face a choice implicating a significant share of their total wealth. Thus, when presented with an option between a 10% chance of obtaining £11,000 and a sure thing of £1,000, most people

1 Richard Thaler and Cass Sunstein, 'Libertarian paternalism is not an oxymoron' (2003) 70 U Chi L Rev 1159.

would prefer the latter, which means that they would not choose the option with the highest expected value. Risk-averse actors weigh losses more heavily than equivalent gains. Economic models predicting the effect of a change in the expected cost of tortious conduct, breaching a contract, committing a crime, or copying a patentee's technology may therefore produce erroneous results if the actors whom they study either dislike or embrace risk.

Fortunately, economists have long been aware of this fact, and for almost three centuries have relied on a model of rational decision making that incorporates risk aversion. This model employs the concept of expected utility or "moral expectation". Developed by Daniel Bournelli in 1738, the theory relies on diminishing marginal utility of wealth to explain that a given unit of money confers different subjective value depending on how much wealth the actor already possesses.[2] Under this theory, a person's utility increases with greater wealth, but does so on a logarithmic (i.e. reducing) scale. This effect means that a person's utility function is concave.

As an example, suppose that a person's utility function is given by $U(w) = \sqrt{w}$, where "w" is the individual's wealth. In this case, our subject experiences 1 util from possessing £1, 2 utils from holding £4, 10 utils from owning £100, and 20 utils from having £400. Evidently, this individual experiences sharply diminishing marginal utility of income. Suppose that someone offers him the same choice referenced above: (i) a gamble bearing a 10% probability of £11,000 or (ii) a guaranteed £1,000. Assume also that the decision maker lacks any pre-existing wealth. Were he to act according to expected-value theory, he would choose the first option because $0.1*(£11,000) + 0.9(£0) = £1,100$, which exceeds $1.0*(£1,000)$ or £1,000. Our person will not act in this manner, however, because the expected utility of the sure thing exceeds the expected utility of the gamble. Specifically, $0.1*(\sqrt{£11,000}) + 0.9(\sqrt{£0}) = 10.49$ utils, which is less than $1.0*(\sqrt{£1,000}) = 31.62$ utils.

The reason that £11,000 in our hypothetical are less attractive than the guaranteed £1,000 is that the £1,000 confers a disproportionate amount of utility per pound than the £11,000 do. In fact, our decision maker's utility function means that £11,000 bestow only slightly more than three times the utility of £1,000, but the chance that he will get the former figure is only one in ten, while the latter figure is guaranteed.

By modelling risk aversion, expected utility theory permits more accurate predictions of behaviour in the presence of risk than simple expected-value maximisation. Given its simplicity, this theory has long been the principal tool of neoclassical law and economics, lying at the heart of rational-choice theory. Nevertheless, it has important shortcomings, which are the subject of the discussion that immediately follows.

2. Prospect theory

Bernoulli recognised that a person's utility is not a linear function of wealth, for which reason rational choice in the presence of risk maximises expected utility rather than expected value. Expected utility theory provides a more robust theory of choice with respect to probabilistic payoffs than the maximisation of expected value, and provides reasonably accurate predictions across a broad array of circumstances. The theory is incomplete, however, in that it fails to account for important psychological constituents of utility. In particular, satisfaction is not firmly tied to total wealth. The same amount of money may be variously delightful or crushing to different people depending on the circumstances in which they arrived at that sum.

Suppose that an indigent goes from having nothing to £500,000, while a millionaire sees his wealth cut in half to that same figure. The first person will be overjoyed, while the former million-

---

2 For a detailed discussion of expected-value and expected-utility theories, see Part 1, Chapter 2.

aire will be bitterly disappointed. Yet, because each of them now possesses the same amount of money, expected-utility theory would say that each is equally satisfied. Here, the theory sharply diverges from everyday experience, leading to potentially inaccurate predictions when the context in which a person arrives at a particular state of wealth matters to how she weighs her options. It may matter often.

In a famous paper, cognitive psychologists Daniel Kahneman and Amos Tversky introduced a model of choice aimed at addressing this deficiency.[3] Their model, known as "prospect theory", identifies a reference point as a key determinant of the satisfaction or unhappiness that a person experiences from a certain level of wealth. Under this theory, an outcome that produces a more favourable result than one's reference point is desirable, while a result less than that point is a loss. The theory embraces loss aversion, which is a psychological condition that most people display: losses of a particular amount are worse than financially equivalent gains. It also incorporates diminishing marginal effects in wealth changes.

A defining characteristic of prospect theory is that decision makers are risk averse in the realm of gains, but prefer risk when all options involve losses. So, for instance, people generally prefer (i) an 80% probability of a £10,000 loss with a 20% chance of no loss over (ii) a guaranteed £8,000 loss. Relative to the status quo (i.e. the reference point) of no losses, losing either £10,000 or £8,000 is most undesirable, compared to which the chance of no loss is attractive. This tenet of prospect theory enjoys a strong evidentiary foundation. When confronted with a range of uniformly unpalatable options (i.e. each one falls below the operative reference point) people are willing to take a long shot that, if it pays off, would minimise or eliminate their losses. This phenomenon explains the tendency of people and companies to throw good money after bad, as well as the long-documented propensity of investors to hold onto losing stocks when they should sell to minimise their losses. These effects demonstrate that, in contravention of rational-choice theory, people care about sunk costs.

A graphical representation of prospect theory is shown in Figure 9.1.

This graph displays several material features. First, what matters is not the absolute change in wealth, but the change relative to a reference point, such as the status quo. Second, the curve is S-shaped, which condition reflects diminishing marginal utility of income gains and diminishing marginal disutility of income losses. A corollary of this insight is that people are risk averse in the "gain" quadrant and risk preferring in the "loss" quadrant. Third, the slope of the curve is steeper in the loss quadrant than it is for gains, which effect is due to loss aversion. This phenomenon arises from the "endowment effect", which reflects the fact that people tend to value what they have more than equivalent items or things that they do not yet possess.

Prospect theory is purely descriptive, seeking to explain real-world behaviour. It possesses no normative content. Furthermore, the reference point by which an actor judges the desirability of a change in wealth obviously lies at the heart of prospect theory. Unfortunately, no general theory yet exists as to the identity of this point. In general, the reference point may be the status quo, but it may also be a past choice, a goal, or average behaviour in society. In practice, behavioural economists often match a free-floating "reference point" to observed behaviour. In other words, economists typically determine the reference point exogenously. As a result, prospect theory is not susceptible of generalised application predictive of conduct in the way that rational-choice theory is. Thus, the behavioural literature' major shortcoming is that there is, as yet, no organising principle allowing one to construct predictive models of general application.

Prospect theory, however, comports with real-life experience. After all, we tend to define the intensity of our experiences by reference to expectations rather than on a stand-alone basis. A

---

3 Daniel Kahneman and Amos Tversky, 'Prospect theory: An analysis of decision under risk' (1979) 47 Econometrica 263.

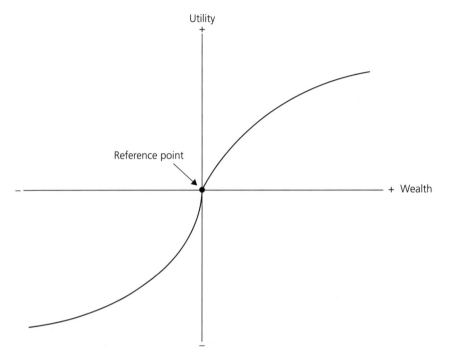

Figure 9.1

certain income might make the same person happy or miserable depending on whether he had been promised a large raise. Although temperatures are objective measures of energy, the sensation of hot and cold depends greatly on context. Entering a building maintained at 20C/68F would feel marvellously warm to a person coming inside from a blizzard, but would be delightfully cool to an individual walking in from a heat wave. Working 10-hour days feels like a respite to someone coming off sustained, 15-hour work days, but an awful lot to someone entering the workforce for the first time. The examples are endless, but the point is simple: reference points matter.

In conjunction with the cognitive defects discussed immediately below that bias choice, the fact that reference points determine perceived losses and gains has important applications to legal problems.

3. Cognitive biases

Psychology has contributed to economic analysis, not by showing that people behave irrationally, but by demonstrating that they err predictably. Cognitive imperfections afflict human reasoning, distorting behaviour in an identifiable direction. While rational-choice theory has many attractive features discussed at the close of this chapter, it can yield misleading or flatly erroneous predictions in the presence of powerful biases. Behavioural law and economics can enhance explanatory power by identifying cognitive defects that influence decision making, thus inducing people to act contrary to the predictions of conventional analysis.

This section explores three significant contributions of the behavioural literature in explaining how people choose to act. These concern bounded rationality, willpower, and self-interest.

(a) Bounded rationality

The purest neoclassical models impose demanding standards of rationality, specifically that people have complete, transitive, and strongly monotonic preferences, ignore sunk costs and fairness, do not engage in hyperbolic discounting, care only for themselves, and process all relevant information pursuant to a cost–benefit calculus. These assumptions permit economists to generate testable predictions using mathematical tools of constrained optimisation. Nevertheless, given their outlandish nature – particularly where opportunities for learning are limited – rational-actor models will sometimes yield erroneous implications.

The reason is that a variety of defects undermines people's capacity for rational choice. Of course, neoclassical economics has not slavishly bound itself to the stringent assumptions identified in the prior paragraph: it routinely uses models incorporating high information costs and altruism, for instance. Nevertheless, cognitive psychology identifies assumptions that more closely mirror real-life decision making. The behavioural-economics literature has identified and explored the imperfections that fetter our mental processes, leading us to err.

The most important insight concerning bounded rationality is that limitations on time and mental acuity prevent us from processing available information to make decisions fully informed as to operative costs and benefits. Interestingly, people react rationally to their limited intelligence, memory, and free time by adopting mental shortcuts and rules of thumb meant to economise on their decision making. By definition, because people generate and apply such heuristics without incorporating the full information attendant on a given choice, these mental shortcuts give rise to imperfect decisions, even if they generally work well.

Heuristics typically reside in people's subconscious, yielding near-immediate responses even to complex problems, which trait carries axiomatic evolutionary benefits. There are countless examples. Lacking any basis to choose between two options, one may pick the one that is most popular with others. Asked to identify which of two unfamiliar cities is the more populous, one might employ a stopping rule, using the first learned fact about the cities that is indicative of size to decide.[4] More controversially, people routinely draw inferences on others' characters based on such immutable characteristics as age, religion, sex, race, and socioeconomic status.

The fact that heuristics guide most of our decisions bears important repercussions for explaining behaviour. Rational-choice theory leaves little room for mental shortcuts, but instead presupposes action consistent with an informed cost-benefit calculation. Although heuristics typically work well, cognitive psychologists have demonstrated that they lead to systemically biased choices in particular circumstances. We shall now consider four important mental shortcuts that lead to skewed conclusions:

(i) Representativeness heuristic

If cognitive psychology shows one thing, it is that people are not natural statisticians. For example, humans discount statistical probabilities and draw unwarranted inferences from the degree to which choice possibilities resemble people's *ex ante* expectations. Put more simply, we calculate likelihoods based on the typicality of the relevant event based on our pre-existing experiences. This leads to trouble if the situation at hand does not align closely with those experiences.

An example makes this point more clear. Imagine that someone asks you to determine whether a given person in a group of 100 is a lawyer or an artist. He instructs you that 90 members of the ensemble are lawyers, and that the remaining 10 are artists. Finally, he says that the specific person whose profession he wants you to identify possesses a Type B personality, being a relaxed individual bestowed with creative prowess.

---

4 For instance, one city may have a premier football club, while the other does not. *See, e.g.,* Gerd Gigerenzer and Peter M. Todd, 'Betting on One Good Reason: The Take the Best Heuristics' in *Simple Heuristics that Make Us Smart* (1999).

Presented with those facts, the majority of us would jump to the conclusion that the person is an artist because lawyers do not conjure forth images of being laid back, easy going, or creative. In so concluding, however, we would err, ignoring or discounting the fact that, character traits aside, the statistical probability that the randomly drawn member of the group was an artist was merely 10%. In other words, we draw conclusions based on relatively unimportant but intuitively attractive details, and overlook the operative base rate (i.e., the underlying statistical probability).

A classic example of the representative heuristic in action is the "gambler's fallacy". Walking through a casino and happening upon a roulette table that has hit black five times in a row, many punters would be strongly inclined to put money on black rather than red because they wrongly ascribe a causal connection based on perceived representativeness. They believe that another black would be typical of the previous results, thus erroneously concluding that black is a better gamble than red. Of course, the odds of either result are identical. Another well-known cognitive error that the representative heuristic explains is that people overlook regression toward the mean, which is a statistical phenomenon that extreme values (such as an extraordinary run of play in sports) are likely to be followed by average values.

The problem in both of the preceding examples is that humans draw unwarranted inferences from small sample sizes. In other words, they apply "the law of large numbers" to small numbers, often with misleading or inaccurate results.

(ii) Anchoring heuristic

The manner in which a choice is presented can affect one's decision. In particular, the initial value that a person perceives can alter his estimate of the relevant parameter, even if the first number has no statistical relationship with the parameter of interest. For example, an empirical study asked participants to determine within five seconds the answer of $8 \times 7 \times 6 \times 5 \times 4 \times 3 \times 2 \times 1$, and then $1 \times 2 \times 3 \times 4 \times 5 \times 6 \times 7 \times 8$. Both calculations yield a result of 40,320. The average answer for the first was 2,250 and the second was 512.[5] In another study, researchers asked people to estimate the percentage of African countries that are members of the United Nations. They spun a wheel, which returned a number between 0 and 100, and then asked participants whether the percentage of those countries exceeded or was lower than the returned numbers. Even though the wheel-generated number obviously had nothing to do with the posed question, it had a large effect on the estimates subsequently obtained. Presented with the number 65, participants in the study reported a median estimate of 45%, while those who first saw the number 10 returned a median estimate of 25%.[6]

(iii) Availability heuristic

The availability heuristic judges the probability of an event by how readily examples of the event come to mind. This mental shortcut uses illustrations as proxies for statistical information, as people assign probabilities based on how closely the objects that they are evaluating resemble other objects with which they are familiar. For example, if asked about the likelihood of one's house burning down, the fact that a neighbour's building recently went up in flames would lead one to conclude that the odds are higher than they actually are.

Although it is often effective, the heuristic can produce skewed results. For instance, demand for earthquake insurance spikes after a bad temblor, but then diminishes over time as the memory becomes less poignant, even though the underlying probability does not change (at least proportionally).[7] Another well-known illustration asked people how many words in a four-page book

---

5 Amos Tversky and Daniel Kahneman, 'Judgment under uncertainty: Heuristics and biases' (1974) 185 Science 1124.

6 David Laibson and Richard Zeckhauser, 'Amos Tversky and the ascent of behavioral economics' (1998) 16 J Risk and Uncertainty 7.

7 Cass R. Sunstein, 'Hazardous Heuristics', John M. Olin Law and Economics Working Paper No. 165, University of Chicago (October 2002) pp. 7–8. Available at: www.law.uchicago.edu/files/files/165.crs_.heuristics.pdf.

ended in "ing" and how many had "n" as the second-last letter. The subjects returned a higher number for the former, which answer even superficial thought reveals to be preposterous.[8]

A particular problem with the availability heuristic is that it leads people to overestimate low-probability events and to understate high-probability occurrences, with potentially serious consequences. For example, many individuals display an irrational fear of flying because they exaggerate the chance that they could die in a plane crash. A principal cause of this cognitive error is the fact that, in the rare case in which such an accident occurs, it invariably receives sensational treatment in the press, often in horrifying detail. Conversely, pervasive causes of death that are far-more likely to lead to one's demise receive too little attention. People routinely discount the risk of cancer, stroke, and diabetes by more than they should.

(iv) Optimism bias

The final bias we discuss is that people are selectively optimistic, believing that beneficial events are more likely than average to happen to them, while negative events are less likely than average to occur. The effect appears to be most powerful with adolescents, and is stronger for events over which actors have some control. For instance, drivers underestimate the risk that they will be in an accident, which is a perception fed by the sense of self-determination associated with controlling one's car. Overconfidence bias has problematic effects on people's ability to make decisions to promote their own welfare. If a smoker thinks that the odds of her getting cancer is less than the average probability, for instance, she will undertake a suboptimal amount of effort to kick the habit.

(b) Bounded willpower

A normative underpinning of neoclassical economics is that satisfying preferences promotes welfare. This assumes that one has and obeys stable preferences that do not conflict. In reality, though, people's psychological decision-making processes are more complicated than rational-choice theory suggests. Here, we discuss an important limitation on tying preference satisfaction to utility: bounded willpower.

Almost everyone's preferences come into conflict. We wish to be fit, but sometimes we feel lazy or otherwise disinclined to exercise. We know that eating unhealthily harms our well-being and possibly our appearance, but we often find fatty foods too delectable to resist. We want to save for the future, but wish to enjoy ourselves today. Many people start and keep smoking, notwithstanding the well-known dangers. In all of these cases, and in many others, we experience conflicting preferences.

Bounded willpower complicates the question of rational decision making. If a person is subject to competing preferences, which one should he seek to fulfil, and is he irrational in choosing one over another? Is it irrational to forego purchasing chocolate in the supermarket while on a diet because, if you buy it, you know you will end up eating it because you want it?

A possible answer is that a person is not a unitary whole, but comprises multiple separate selves possessing distinct preferences. From this perspective, a person today who wants to splurge on a new car is a different economic actor than the same person in three years' time who wishes to have saved enough for a deposit on a house. Each individual cares somewhat for the other, but is primarily interested in maximising his own utility. From this perspective, one can be rational in splurging today and deriving pleasure from doing so, even if one comes to regret it in the future. Each separate self competes with the other for supremacy. Interesting as it is, however, whether this "separate selves" approach is workable and legitimate remains a matter of debate.

---

8 Amos Tversky and Daniel Kahneman, 'Extensional versus Intuitive Reasoning: The Conjunction Fallacy' in Thomas Gilovich, Dale Griffin and Daniel Kahneman (eds.) *Probability Judgment in Heuristics and Biases: The Psychology of Intuitive Judgment* (1998) p. 21.

(b) Bounded self-interest

The final manner in which people act "irrationally" concerns bounded self-interest. Price-theoretic models typically assume perfect selfishness, and indifference to fairness. In real life, however, most people care about these matters. Humans often fail to maximise their financial wealth, often because they care about others and take offence at *ex post* distributions that strike them as unjust. It is for this reason that the famous ultimatum game produces markedly different results in practice than rational-choice theory predicts.[9]

C. Behavioural Law and Economics: Applications

Behavioural law and economics is a burgeoning field, such that a comprehensive account of its many insights would command a book in itself. Nevertheless, this section explores some of the subject's notable contributions to the economic analysis of law. It begins with the endowment effect, or "status quo bias", which is a particularised instance of loss aversion. As people typically dislike losing a unit of certain value more than acquiring an identical unit, they often place a value premium on products they own over equivalent ones that they do not possess. This effect has interesting repercussions for law and economics.

1. The endowment effect and the Coase Theorem

The Coase Theorem holds that, when bargaining is free, the market will efficiently allocate resources regardless of their initial assignment. We have seen that it applies to all manner of legal settings, including tort, crime, contract, litigation, and competition. The overarching theme has been that the law plays a modest role where transaction costs are low, but where bargaining is costly or difficult, it can spur people to act as they would have agreed to behave in a hypothetical environment of zero transaction costs.

The endowment effect, however, complicates matters because it upsets the Coase Theorem's implicit assumption that people's preferences are stable. For instance, if the question of interest is whether A or B should obtain a fine bottle of wine, it is efficient for A to get the bottle if her maximum purchase price is £100 and if B's is only £80. Psychologists have shown, however, that the value that a person places on an object may increase sharply once they own it. Suppose, then, that the bottle is initially assigned to B, and there are no transaction costs or wealth effects. The Coase Theorem would therefore predict that A would purchase the bottle from B for a price between £100 and £80. Yet, if B experiences a powerful endowment effect, he may refuse to sell for anything less than, say, £130. In that event, the initial, seemingly inefficient allocation is final.

The fact that people value items that they possess more than ones they do not is a widespread phenomenon. For instance, most ticket holders for high-profile concerts and sports events refuse to sell their spots even at many multiples of the price for which they purchased them, and even if they would have refused to have bought their tickets at the now going-rate. Gaps often emerge between people's maximum willingness-to-buy and minimum willingness-to-sell prices.

There are, however, two important observations. First, the endowment effect is neither ubiquitous nor constant across individuals. The effect is non-existent, for instance, over goods or items that people hold for the purpose of exchange (such as inventory or cash). Illustratively, one study found that the effect applied to mugs but not tokens that participants could exchange for mugs.[10] Furthermore, the effect appears to be stronger in the United States than in the United Kingdom,

9 *See* Part 1, Chapter 2, Section C *supra*.
10 Daniel Kahneman, *Thinking, Fast and Slow* (2011) 295–97.

suggesting that cultural norms may underlie the phenomenon.[11] Second, even where the effect applies, it merely hinders market transactions – it does not necessarily prevent them. The endowment effect makes initial market allocations "sticky".

For positive analysis, the role of the endowment effect is unclear because the effect various tremendously from person to person. As a normative matter, the phenomenon raises interesting questions concerning efficiency and welfare. Is an initial allocation that becomes permanent by virtue of the endowment effect inefficient? Or is it, by definition, efficient because the owner's minimum-sell price now exceeds others' maximum-buy prices? If endowment increases a person's utility, should the government attempt to identify which first acquirer of an entitlement would experience the greatest total utility, as measured by each person's post-allocation minimum sell price? The state has little means by which to accomplish this task, however, which is what justifies a market system in the first place.

2. Positive and normative implications

Understood from the perspective of economics, law is a tool with which government induces socially desirable behaviour. The core narrative underlying law and economics is that people respond to incentives. Economics provides lawmakers with theoretical and empirical means by which to predict how specific laws will affect conduct. The principal tools that economists have used to forecast the positive effect of law is neoclassical price theory and game theory.

Yet, because biases distort decision making – biases such as representativeness, anchoring, availability, and overconfidence – two consequences follow. First, heuristics may induce people systemically to act irrationally. This implicates positive analysis aimed at forecasting the effects of a proposed law. Second, the fact that biases consistently lead people to make imperfect decisions has normative implications. Specifically, the government cannot rely on revealed preferences as a determinative measure of welfare if biases cause people to harm themselves. If policymakers can detect biases, they may be able to pass laws that induce or require people to act in a better way. For these reasons, observers generally view behavioural economics as being more paternalistic than neoclassical economics.

The biases explored above have numerous applications to law, as people subject to law routinely make probabilistic calculations. Tortfeasors and potential victims implicitly compare the costs of taking care to the corresponding expected liability and accident costs; criminals, to at least some degree, weigh the expected benefits and costs of committing an offence; and parties to a contract include cost-justified terms in their agreement. Consider a small subset of the normative implications of behavioural law and economics:

In the domain of tort, overconfidence bias may lead actors to overestimate their ability to avoid an accident. Similarly, bounded rationality in the form of information-processing limitations may cause injurers and victims alike to conclude that the odds of an accident are lower than they actually are. Both such effects would cause a price schedule in tort that imposes a cost equal to the average or actual social cost of accidents to under-deter. This suggests that courts should increase expected-liability costs above the social costs of the accident. Separately, due to optimism bias, the law might wisely require manufacturers to include safety features upon which over-confident drivers may not insist in the market. Meanwhile, bounded self-interest leads many tortfeasors to take more care than unmodified rational-actor models would suggest in the absence of expected liability. The availability heuristic also suggests that publicity campaigns aimed at informing the public of the dangers of careless driving may be effective, especially if they are graphic or otherwise salient.

---

11 *Ibid.* at 298–99.

These insights are potentially valuable, but unfortunately may not be robust. For instance, some potential tortfeasors may experience pessimism bias or engage in probability neglect (overweighing small probabilities), either of which would lead to excessive precautions. Given the great many cognitive biases that the behavioural literature has identified, and the fact that many of these defects operate in conflicting directions, the net effect on choice at the market level is often unclear. This shortcoming afflicts much of the behavioural movement's application to law. Ongoing research is necessary to craft an overarching theory with which to predict when one set of biases will dominate others.

With respect to litigation, overconfidence bias may be problematic, leading clients, as well as their lawyers, to overstate their chances of success, thus scuttling settlement. Furthermore, given the central role that jurors play in resolving facts and computing damages in uncertain environments, anchoring biases may be a serious concern. For instance, the heuristics explored above suggest that jurors may use a plaintiff's outlandish demand for damages as an anchor that skews their subsequent damages determination upward. This possibility counsels evidentiary rules that limit parties' ability to skew jurors' fact-finding by putting extreme figures in front of them.

Behavioural economics has obvious applications to contract law. The conventional account assumes that competent, informed adults contract only if the agreement is mutually beneficial. The behavioural literature, however, shows that people err all the time, which raises interesting questions whether misconceptions are valid bases for rescinding otherwise valid contracts. From a policy perspective, if sellers are able to identify and manipulate biases such as overconfidence, bounded self-control, and hyperbolic discounting to induce consumers to make poor decisions, such as with respect to credit cards, contracts of adhesion, usurious lending, or price-gouging, consumer-protection regulation may be necessary. Inevitably, that protection takes the form of limiting choice.

In the realm of criminal law, behavioural economics can go a long way to explaining criminal activity. Optimism bias may afflict offenders, leading them to believe that they have a greater chance of getting away with their planned acts than they actually do. As with tort law, to the extent this bias arises, it is necessary to increase their expected punishment cost to maintain a desired level of deterrence. The same holds true for hyperbolic discounting, in which criminals are especially likely to engage. Such a policy reaction, however, is problematic to the extent it calls for sentences disproportionate to the social harm of the crime. In terms of preventing crime, the availability heuristic suggests that visible, salient forms of policing are likely to lead prospective criminals to believe that the chance of their being apprehended is higher than it actually is.

More generally, behavioural economics is relevant to the positive account of law. A mystery for neoclassical economics is why the law bans certain forms of voluntary market transactions such as usurious lending. A possible answer from the behavioural literature is that such practices involve exchanges taking place far from the operative reference point, which causes voters to decry them as unfair. Prohibitions on such "efficient" transactions – efficient if one assumes that the actors are competent and informed – are thus simply a manifestation of social consensus on norms of fairness. Of course, one can accept the fairness critique, but still object to the policy conclusion that unfair contracts should be banned. This objection would point out that one-sided contracts, which provide promisees with performance that is more valuable to them than the amount they paid, are better than no contract at all. An important question, then, concerns the price of a ban on unfair contracts – will parties still reach terms, though more-even terms, or will many promisors simply refuse to deal at all?

All of this raises questions about how the law should respond to systemic departures from rationality by those in whom it attempts to inculpate desirable behaviour. Recent scholarship has progressed from how best to calibrate rules to achieve a certain level of deterrence to the idea of "debiasing through law" – using the law to minimise or even to eliminate bounded rationality.[12]

---

12 Christine Jolls and Cass R. Sunstein, 'Debiasing through law' (2006) 35 J Legal Stud 199.

D. Normative Dimensions to Rationality: Paternalism and Behavioural Economics

1. The neoclassical approach to law and economics, individual liberty, and negative externalities

Behavioural economics suggests a broader case for paternalistic intervention by the state than neoclassical analysis, which emphasises individuals' right to construct, identify, and act pursuant to their own preferences, subject only to their not violating the preferences of others. In light of observed departures from rational choice, much of the behavioural literature advocates policies circumscribing liberty. Indeed, a prominent academic has noted that the bounded-rationality literature "has been used to support the restriction of individual choice, almost without exception".[13] This section first addresses the neoclassical account, to which the next compares the behavioural movement.

The neoclassical economics tradition reflects a qualified form of libertarianism, which emphasises the sanctity of personal freedom. From this perspective, people have a right to make up their own minds as to how they comport themselves, which decisions other people may legitimately criticise, but not prohibit n the absence of third-party harm. In celebrating autonomy, this philosophy rejects those who presume to exercise superior judgment over others' well-being. It thus lies in sharpest contradistinction to autocratic regimes that subjugate individual choice to the whim of the sovereign.

Even accepting the sacrosanct quality that libertarian thought places on individual choice, there is no strong argument in favour of unabridged freedom of action. Few acts of volition bear consequences unique to the decision maker. Even choices that seem localised to the actor produce externalities. A person's decision not to wear a seatbelt, for instance, increases the expected social cost – not just the private cost – of his driving. In the event that the state pays for or subsidises hospitalisation and related healthcare, taxpayers foot part of the bill flowing from the driver's decision. Should the driver have insurance, his insurer will have to raise premia to pool higher coverage costs (a standard repercussion of moral hazard if insurers cannot perfectly monitor the behaviour of their insureds). Should the driver's injury detract from his work, his employer and the larger economy will pay a price. Of course, the driver's family and loved ones pay a heavy emotional toll in being privy to his suffering. In electing to eschew the risk of an accident and in declining to wear a belt, a person enhances the likelihood, and hence expected cost, of such negative effects.

The ubiquity of negative externalities challenges those who champion autonomy. John Rawls' famous principle that "each person is to have an equal right to the most extensive system of equal basic liberty compatible with a similar system for all" encapsulates the operative tension nicely. Compatibility is the problem. The challenge for those of a classic liberal persuasion is that, when even the most prosaic and everyday choices bear some latent risk, the exception built into the harm principle threatens to swallow the rule.

Resolving the tension between liberty and third-party harm depends both on the significance that one ascribes to freedom of choice and on the perceived magnitude of the externality at issue. That weighing process is not only context specific; it involves attributing subjective import to these counterweighing factors. It is, therefore, unsurprising that public policy initiatives aimed at limiting choice to prevent third-party harm are controversial. Contemporary examples abound.

The most prominent at the time of writing is "Obamacare", the so-called "individual mandate" of which requires people to purchase health insurance. To some critics, the mandate is an unprecedented, governmental violation of positive liberty. From this perspective, it is one thing for the

---

state to limit freedom of action (a restraint on negative liberty). It is another thing altogether to order a person to do something. The thinking goes that, if the government can legitimately invade positive liberty, its mandate becomes limitless. At the most fundamental level, if autonomy means anything, it must encapsulate the right not to engage in a form of commerce.

Other commentators, however, laud the legislation as an important first step in both reflecting a universal human right to health care and improving the economics of the healthcare industry, which is a paradigm of inefficiency and waste. In the latter respect, a person's decision not to purchase health insurance carries deleterious effects for others. Save for those who die prematurely and suddenly, almost everyone will consume healthcare services at some point in their lives. To eschew insurance in circumstances where one cannot afford to pay the full costs privately is to offload risk onto the taxpayer. The ensuing inefficiency is severe, as healthy, young adults who are on relatively tight budgets are most likely to shun insurance, while elderly or sick people are most likely to purchase it. If insurers cannot engage in sufficiently precise price discrimination – a practice that some observers consider to be wrong – they will set a price that is unattractive for healthy individuals and attractive for their less-healthy counterparts. Such pricing accelerates low-cost insureds' departure from the market, thus increasing insurers' breakeven price and further feeding a race to the bottom. This is the problem of adverse selection, against which the individual mandate is an important weapon.

The healthcare debate is not readily susceptible to resolution because, for many people, it is a question of principle. Many commentators agree that the contemporary US healthcare system is dysfunctional, but fewer are willing to accept that an individual mandate is the answer. This illustrates the practical difficulty of reconciling individual autonomy with the reality of pervasive externalities. There are, of course, many other examples, such as San Francisco's 2011 ban on McDonald's "Happy Meals", which the city hoped would help to curtail childhood obesity, to New York's 2012 prohibition on soft drinks larger than 16 ounces (subsequently struck down by the courts), which had a comparable purpose. To some observers, such bans smack of governmental paternalism, while to others, they soundly limit the harm that obesity imposes on others, predominantly through higher healthcare costs and reduced work productivity over the long term.

Where does the neoclassical branch of law and economics fit into this debate? The first point is that the field, in focusing on individual preference, respects autonomy. Neoclassical economics applied to law treats people's preferences as exogenous and immutable, thus providing no basis for governmental intervention aimed at altering those preferences. The neoclassical law and economics framework is thus not a conduit for paternalistic policies designed to help people make better choices. The field will regard as efficient any contract into which people enter voluntarily and knowingly and that carries no negative externalities. Others may regard the arrangement as foolish, but while they are free not to enter into such accords themselves and to counsel others accordingly, it is not their place to dictate preferences to others.

The autonomy respecting feature of neoclassical law and economics is all well and good, but what should the discipline make of the externality problem addressed above? After all, if one respects all people's preferences, it is as much an affront to individual liberty for a person to harm another without the latter's permission as it is to prevent someone from conducting himself in a particular way.

Law and economics addresses the problem of inconsistent preferences by focusing on hypothetical bargains. The preceding chapters have explored how legal rules can cure bargaining failures by creating incentives for behaviour consistent with that upon which stakeholders would have agreed, but for transaction costs. Neoclassical economics theory can, therefore, justify a broad swathe of government intervention, but it limits the case for such involvement in an important way. Specifically, the law may impose prices designed to align the social and private costs of behaviour, but it may not intrude upon people's right to choose for themselves. As we shall now see, a potentially important basis for that prohibition lies in the neoclassical assumption of rational choice.

2. Irrational choice, behavioural economics, and paternalism

The framework of neoclassical economics fits comfortably with governmental deference to individual autonomy. If people reliably determine their own welfare, we should respect their decisions. It is hard to argue, in the absence of third-party effects, that the government can legitimately dictate the behaviour of people possessing stable preferences who can access and analyse information pertinent to their choices, and who reliably identify courses of action that best serve their wants.

The problem is that this idealistic view is sharply at odds with actual conduct. The behavioural literature casts doubt on people's ability correctly to analyse complex choices, particularly those involving inter-temporal consequences or risk. Psychologists have documented many instances in which seemingly informed people make choices at variance with their own interests. Moreover, the assumption of perfect information that often accompanies neoclassical analysis has little counterpart in the real world, where circumstances routinely force people to make decisions ignorant of material facts. Cognitive biases induce people to make bad decisions. Furthermore, the case for treating people's preferences as hallowed is not obvious when abundant evidence showcases the contingency of those wants. Influences, from family and school to marketing and religion, continuously buffet people's perception of the world, shaping individual preferences. Why should something which can be easily manipulated be an object of unbending deference?

People fiercely debate the normative implications of "bounded rationality" for public policy. If libertarians ground their philosophy on the positive ground that people make better choices on average than third parties, including the government, their position is subject to empirical falsification. Conversely, if they believe that a society built on individual freedom is more just than one in which the state constrains behaviour, this principle is not contingent on individuals being superior determinants of their own welfare. Even if one accepts the propriety of paternalistic intervention by the state, however, it is unclear that the human actors comprising the government are free of the biases that might justify intervention to "correct" others' revealed preferences.

Such debates ensure that the normative implications of behavioural law and economics will remain controversial. Nevertheless, the behavioural literature has already proven influential. For example, Cass Sunstein, a leading academic who believes that default rules can improve people's decision making without eliminating freedom of choice, led the US Office of Information and Regulatory Affairs. He ran that office, which oversees federal legislation, from 2009 to 2012 using cost–benefit analysis that some believe to have been informed by behavioural economics. There seems little question that this branch of economics will remain pertinent to law for the foreseeable future.

E. The Continuing Importance of Neoclassical Law and Economics

Rational choice theory is an easy target for detractors in light of its stylised and often unrealistic assumptions. Critics misrepresent the role of rationality in neoclassical analysis, suggesting that it purports to describe actual behaviour. Of course, it does not. Understanding its function is important to appreciating the contributions and limitations of behavioural economics to the conventional account. For reasons now to be explained, rational choice theory should, and probably will, long remain the central tool of law and economics.

First, return to first principles. Rational choice theory does not purport to articulate inviolable rules in a manner comparable to physicists' identifying universal laws of nature. Its object is more modest, seeking instead to predict the broad contours of large-scale behaviour. It does so by identifying explanatory variables that it expects to be important determinants of decision making. Rational choice theory could never aspire to precision in predicting actions at the individual level.

This modesty comes from necessity, for human decision making is far-too complex to encapsulate within a workable model.

The challenge for economists – and for social scientists generally – is to develop models that incorporate sufficient information relevant to choice to enable accurate predictions, but that remain simple enough that they are workable. This is an important tension. If a theory fails to account for important explanatory variables that correlate with the dependent variable of interest (e.g. a person driving negligently), the ensuing model will be misspecified and, thus, unreliable. The more complex the model, the greater the amount of information it can take into account in predicting behaviour and the more accurate its ensuing predictions are likely to be. The price of accuracy, however, is complexity.

Rational choice theory has long been economists' principal analytical tool, and it has served the economics profession well. Obeisance to tradition, of course, does not justify adhering to an outdated mode of analysis when superior alternatives are available. Behavioural economics is an important development for the economic analysis of law, but it plays a complementary role alongside conventional analysis. There are numerous reasons why this is the case.

First, the behavioural law and economics literature thus far lacks a unifying theory capable of generalised application. For that reason, it is principally descriptive, rather than predictive.

Second, even if one can identify all operative biases *ex ante* – which is a tall order – behavioural economists cannot always, or even generally, predict the direction in which conduct will depart from what rational choice theory implies. People experience a wide variety of biases, which operate in opposing directions. This makes the ultimate effect ambiguous as a predictive matter. For example, following a sustained and graphic governmental campaign aimed at highlighting the dangers of driving, the availability heuristic may lead people to overestimate the chance that they will be in a car accident. Yet, overconfidence bias suggests that each person would consider the odds of his being in such an accident to be less than average. The net effect is, as a theoretical matter, unclear. *Ex post*, however, one can explain an observed outcome by reference to the heuristics that likely accounted for the deviation from "rational" behaviour. This can be useful, but it is not the principal concern of positive law and economics, which hypothesises the future effects of proposed laws to inform policymakers.

Third, in some market settings, systemic departures from rationality are unlikely to be sustainable due to a combination of learning effects by repeat players and education efforts by sellers. Biases can be unlearned through education and experience, and in any event differ in degree and kind from person to person, and culture to culture.

Fourth, people with specific skills who make relatively calculated and dispassionate decisions are likely to gravitate to positions where those skills are most useful (e.g. actuaries for insurers). Thus, rational choice theory will yield accurate predictions more often than the prevalence of bias might suggest due to self-selection.

Fifth, even if heuristics induce people to act irrationally, such as by favouring driving over flying due to perceived concerns of dying in a plane crash, rational choice theory remains ready to serve a predictive function because the operative biases are subsumed within the revealed preference. Economists can, therefore, employ conventional price theory to predict the effect of price changes on behaviour. Finally, there is still some uncertainty whether the laboratory results upon which behavioural economics is largely dependent are robust, given that people are apt to behave differently when acting in real markets.[14]

In short, although behavioural economics has much to offer the field of economic analysis of law, it is not yet in a position to supplant traditional theory.

---

14 *See, e.g.,* John A. List, 'Neoclassical theory versus prospect theory: Evidence from the marketplace' (2006) 72 Econometrica 615.

Key Points

- Behavioural law and economics adopts cognitive psychology to infuse economic analysis of legal problems with more realistic assumptions.
- Neoclassical price theory assumes that actors are rational, possessing stable preferences that are complete, transitive, and strongly monotonic, and choose among alternatives using informed cost–benefit analysis based on self-interest. Studies reveal that real-world behaviour violates these assumptions.
- Departures from rational behaviour would not compromise rational choice theory if irrationality were randomly distributed. In that event, departures from the mean would cancel each other out, such that neoclassical predictions would be accurate. Research in behavioural economics shows, however, that people depart from rational choice in a systemically biased manner.
- Due to their limitations, people rely on heuristics (i.e. mental shortcuts) to make decisions in complex environments. Although these techniques are often effective, they can produce erroneous conclusions.

  - As a result, people are imperfectly rational, displaying "bounded rationality".
  - Actors also experience bounded willpower and bounded self-interest. Contrary to the assumptions of rational-choice theory, preferences are not stable and can conflict. Furthermore, many people care about fairness and are partially altruistic.

- Behavioural economists have identified numerous "cognitive biases" that afflict human reasoning, leading to departures from rational choice. A small subset of those biases include the following:

  - *Representativeness heuristic*: people judge probabilities based on how well the event being evaluated resembles their existing prototypes of that event.
  - *Anchoring heuristic*: individuals decide based on a reference point, which they use as an anchor and iteratively adjust based on available information. When the anchor has little or no relevance to the choice being made, it can materially bias decisions.
  - *Availability heuristic*: people choose based on readily available information, rather than by scrutinising the larger universe of available evidence.
  - *Optimism bias*: humans tend to conclude that the odds that they will experience a negative event are lower than that of the larger population.

- Prospect theory is the leading behavioural account of choice. It contends that people define their satisfaction by how an outcome compares to a reference point. It posits that individuals are risk-averse in measuring gains relative to that reference point, and risk-preferring when all options entail losses.
- Behavioural economics unsettles previously accepted principles of law and economics.

  - It shows that, due to the endowment effect, people value an item that they possess more than they would if they had yet to acquire it. That drives a wedge between maximum-buy and minimum-sell prices, causing property assignments to become "sticky". The fact that entitlements can alter valuations means that initial assignments may matter, even in zero-transaction cost environments, thus raising interesting questions about efficiency under the Coase Theorem.
  - Biases can affect economic analysis of rules. For instance, if overconfidence bias afflicts potential tortfeasors, setting liability equal to the expected social cost of an accident will inadequately deter.
  - Behavioural economics has much to say about public policy. Due to people's reliance on the availability heuristic, society should promote its goals by making key information

salient. Shocking advertisements concerning car crashes may counteract overconfidence bias, while visible police presence may deter crime more effectively than ramping up prison sentences.

o Normative behavioural economics generally recommends limiting choice, due to people's tendency to err and to make decisions injurious to their own welfare. Thus, unlike neoclassical welfare economics, the field advocates paternalistic policies. Some leading behavioural scholars seek to reconcile autonomy and paternalism by introducing default rules that lead people to make better decisions, but allowing individuals to opt out if they so choose.

 ## References and Further Reading

Books
Ariely, Dan, *Predictably Irrational: The Hidden Forces That Shape Our Decisions* (2010).
Camerer, Colin F., Loewenstein, George and Rabin, Matthew (eds.), *Advances in Behavioral Economics* (2004).
Cartwright, Edward, *Behavioral Economics* (2011).
Jolls, Christine, 'Behavioral Law and Economics' in *Behavioral Economics and its Applications* (2007) pp. 115–44.
Kahneman, Daniel, *Thinking, Fast and Slow* (2011).
Kahneman, Daniel, Knetsch, Jack L. and Thaler, Richard, 'Experimental Tests of the Endowment Effect and the Coase Theorem' in *Advances in Behavioral Economics* (2003) p. 55.
Rachlinski, Jeffrey J., *Behavioral Law and Economics* (2009).
Sunstein, Cass R., *Behavioral Law and Economics* (2000).
Thaler, Richard H. and Sunstein, Cass R., *Nudge: Improving Decisions about Health, Wealth, and Happiness* (2009).

Articles
Bar-Gill, Oren, 'The behavioral economics of consumer contracts' (2008) 92 Minn L Rev 749.
Hayden, Grant M. and Ellis, Stephen E., 'Law and economics after behavioral economics' (2007) 55 U Kan L Rev 629.
Jolls, Christine, 'Behavioral economics analysis of redistributive legal rules' (1998) 51 Vand L Rev 1653.
Jolls, Christine, Sunstein, Cass R., and Thaler, Richard, 'A behavioral approach to law and economics' (1998) 50 Stan L Rev 1471.
Korobkin, Russell B. and Ulen, Thomas S., 'Law and behavioral science: Removing the rationality assumption from law and economics' (2000) 88 Cal L Rev 1051.
Posner, Richard A., 'Rational choice, behavioral economics, and the law' (1998) 50 Stan L Rev 1551.
Teitelbaum, Joshua C., 'A unilateral accident model under ambiguity' (2007) 37 J Legal Stud 431.
Wright, Joshua D. and Ginsburg, Douglas H., 'Behavioral law and economics: Its origins, fatal flaws, and implications for liberty' (2012) 106 Nw U L Rev 1033.

Conclusion

Law and economics has transformed legal doctrine and scholarship. There is no secret as to why the field has been so influential. Out of a morass of seemingly unconnected doctrine, economic analysis yields an elegant analytical framework that binds all law into an interrelated and largely harmonious whole. The conviction that people respond to incentives, which the law can manipulate to achieve desired ends, makes economics an indispensable tool for those who conceive of law in forward-looking terms. We have seen that price theory yields insights into the law of contract, tort, crime, litigation, competition, innovation, property, and beyond. The positive arm of law and economics thus informs the decision making of judges and legislatures by predicting the consequences of proposed rules. Separately, normativity underlying law and economics reflects autonomy and peoples' associated rights to determine their own preferences. Employing a hypothetical bargain consistent with the Coase Theorem as a foundation for efficient outcomes, law and economics can issue prescriptive guidance on a panoply of legal questions. This approach leaves policy makers free to weigh concerns of efficiency against other goals that they deem relevant to the larger question of justice.

Notwithstanding its status as the most influential movement in jurisprudence of the latter half of the twentieth century, the discipline faces challenges. Its first problem is, in many respects, enviable. In the United States, its near-hegemonic position implicates the problem of success: where to go from here? Judge Posner, the individual who is perhaps most responsible for the law and economics revolution, has expressed concern that the field may be becoming excessively mathematical, abstract, and divorced from the real-life application of law. To counter concerns of this nature, to reinvigorate the discipline, and to promote the field's insights on a more global platform, the University of Chicago launched "Law and Economics 2.0" in late 2011. That initiative should form but a single component of law and economics scholars' efforts to magnify the influence of the field.

If the problem in the United States is that economic analysis of law has become a victim of its own success, however, the difficulty elsewhere lies in achieving mainstream legitimacy and ultimately in becoming a compelling force in jurisprudential thought. An entrenched scepticism exists in some jurisdictions. That is particularly true of the United Kingdom and Ireland, where scholars largely conceive of law in doctrinal, rather than in interdisciplinary, terms. Furthermore, rights-based traditions react coolly to the utilitarian foundation of law and economics. To overcome such resistance, proponents of the field should present the theoretical power and illuminative quality of their discipline.

In particular, adherents to law and economics should showcase the subject's power to generate useful insights into the relationship between law and real-world behaviour. Those working in the law and economics movement have already succeeded in making this show in the commercial realm. Today, few dispute that economics is indispensable to the study and practice of competition, regulation, corporate, and financial services law. Thus, even in jurisdictions where the larger field of law and economics has not been embraced, most agree that economics provides the dominant methodology for approaching problems implicating explicit markets. In such settings, many view rational choice theory's focus on profit maximisation to be a reasonable simplification of reality. The most challenging case for advocates of law and economics lies in such fields as criminal and family law, where the rationality assumptions associated with neoclassical welfare economics seem fanciful. More empirical work exploring the accuracy of the predictions of law and economics theory is important to the theory's advance in these settings. Behavioural economics may have much to add in magnifying the explanatory power of economics in these fields.

Second, it is critical that advocates of economic analysis of law refrain from casting their discipline in a manner that excludes other theories of justice. Law and economics yields compelling answers to many vexing problems; in some circumstances, efficiency is indeed co-terminous with justice. Yet, this will not always be the case. Law and economics is most fruitfully understood both as a helpful tool in analysing legal problems and as a complement to other theories of jurisprudence that collectively explore the nature of law.

Finally, given the forbidding mathematical complexity of cutting-edge scholarship in the field, academics specialising in law and economics must take care not to present the discipline as an esoteric subject, the insights of which are comprehensible only to a select few. If the field is to thrive and to gain mainstream acceptance outside the United States and other enclaves of contemporary influence, academics must present it as an accessible theory that yields rich insights into real-life legal problems.

Index

accidents *see* liability and accidents
Akerlof, George 152–3
alcohol addiction 138–9
antitrust approach
  behavioural antitrust 309
  cartels *see* cartels
  competition, policy 304–5
  competition/monopoly, distinction 309–14
  economic role/limits 304–5
  enforcement 341–2
  marginal cost 310
  markets *see* market's role
  monopoly 311–14
  oligopoly *see* oligopoly models
  perfect competition 310–11
  schools of economics 305–9, 331
  summary 330–2
  see also concerted behaviour; monopoly
Appert, Nicolas 276
Arrow, Kenneth 243–4
assumption of risk *see under* tort law
attempts, punishment 130, 143
autonomy 407–8

Bain, Joe 320, 321
bankruptcy laws 246–7
behavioural movement
  applications 404–6
  background 396–7
  cognition *see* cognitive biases
  criminal law 406
  endowment effect 404–5
  heuristics *see* heuristics
  key issues 397, 411–12
  libertarianism 407–8
  negative externalities 407–8
  paternalism 407–9
  positive/normative implications 405–8
  prospect theory 398–400, 411
  risk aversion 397–8

tort 405–6
  see also irrational choice; rational choice
Bentham, Jeremy 44, 48–50, 106
Bertrand competition 316, 331
bilateral-care scenarios
  fixed activity levels 71–6
  no perfect rule 82
  variable activity levels 78–82
biotechnology 259, 262, 270–2
Blackstone, William 158
bounded rationality *see* irrational choice
bounded self-interest 404
bounded willpower 403
Bournelli, Daniel 398
breach of contract remedies
  consequential damages 204–5
  damages effect 199–204
  efficient breach 198–9
  expectation damages 199, 201, 205
  imperfections 203–4
  incentive effects 200–3
  mitigation 203–4
  optimal outcome 199–201
  reliance damages 199, 202–3, 205
  restitution damages 200, 205
  see also contract law
bundled rebates *see under* monopoly

cannabis 139–40
canned food 276
cannibalism 53, 107
Carlton, DW 322
cartels
  as artificial monopolies 336
  lawful restrictions 339–40
  monopsony 340–1, 345
  permissibility 336–8, 345
  tacit collusion 338–9
Chicago Schools 305–8, 414
  neo-Chicago 309

post-Chicago 308–9
Coase, Ronald 29
Coase Theorem 3, 29–31, 414
    behavioural movement 404–5
    concerted behaviour 335
    contract law 176–9, 194–5
    copyright law 291, 297
    criminal behaviour 107
    criminal law 129
    efficiency 32
    externalities 30–1
    law and economics 51, 52, 60
    litigation 211, 227, 229
    meaning 29, 40
    numerical example 29–30
    patent system 252, 266
    property rights/entitlements 158, 165
    scarce resources, allocation 151–2
    strong/weak versions 31, 40–1
cocaine 138–40
cognitive biases
    bounded rationality 401–3
    bounded self-interest 404
    bounded willpower 403
    heuristics see heuristics
    key issues 400, 411
    optimism bias 403
Cohen, Alma 86
competition
    innovation 243–4
    see also antitrust approach
computer software 258–9
concerted behaviour
    cartels see cartels
    exclusive dealerships/territories 343
    horizontal agreements 335–42
    inter/intra-brand competition 342–3
    key issues/conclusion 335–6, 344–5
    lawful restrictions 339–40
    maximum resale prices 343–4
    minimum resale prices 344
    monopsony 340–1, 345
    permissibility 336–8, 345
    vertical restraints 342–5
    see also antitrust approach; breach of trust
        remedies; contract law
conglomerates 366–7
consent 129–30
consequential damages see under breach of
    contract remedies

consumer choice 13–18
    demand 17–18
    price effect 15–17
    rationality as organising principle 13–15
consumer protection 245
contract law
    duress 187, 195
    economic benefits 176
    ex ante bargaining/ex post litigation 189–90, 195
    frustration of purpose 180–1, 195
    impossibility 180, 182–4, 195
    impracticability 180–2, 195
    incentive mechanism 178–9
    interpretation issues 188–90
    key insights 6–7
    misrepresentation/omissions 187–8
    mistake 184–6, 195
    monopoly remedy, enforcement as 176–7, 192
    mutual mistake 185
    oppressive terms 191–3
    procedural unconscionability 191
    public policy, contracts against 194
    remedies see breach of contract remedies
    risk-shifting device 177–8, 180
    substantive unconscionability 191–3
    third-party effects 194
    unconscionable agreements 190–4, 195
    undue influence 186–7
    unfair terms, Directive 193–4
    unilateral mistake 186
    voluntary exchange 184, 195
    see also breach of contract remedies;
        concerted behaviour
copyright law
    artistic creation in public domain 286
    background 284
    copyright system 285
    copyright terms 294–5
    digital copying see digital copying
    expansion of scope 290–1
    expressive works as public goods 286–90
    fair use/fair dealing 291–3
    key issues/conclusion 284–5, 297
    moral rights view 292–4
    optimal scope 290–4
    registration requirements 293
    terms 294–5
    see also innovation policy; intellectual
        property; patent system

corporal punishment 121–2
costs *see under* litigation
Cournet competition 157, 273, 306, 314–16, 317, 319–20, 331
crack cocaine 138, 140
credit crisis 2008–2009 154
crime
    conviction probability 114–16
    desirable crime 108–11
    incentives 106
    inefficient crime 106–8
    key insights 4–5
    law *see* criminal law
    and market equilibrium 20–3
    minor infractions 109
    necessity 108–9
    price elasticity 117–18
    property crimes, low transaction cost settings 107–8
    regulating level 113
    risk preference/price effects 116
    sanctions *see* criminal sanctions
    suffering inflicted on others 106–7
    unilateral acts, private costs 110–11
    voluntary contracts, modest third-party costs 109–10
criminal law
    behavioural movement 406
    consent 129–30
    deterrence *see* deterrence issues
    diminished capacity 131–2
    econometric research 133–4, 136–7
    intent issues 128–30, 143
    irrationality and realism 132
    key issues 128
    non-deliberative crime 128–9
    price discrimination 130–2
    strict liability 129
    unsuccessful attempts, punishment 130, 143
criminal sanctions
    alternative mechanisms 121–2
    corporal punishment 121–2
    deterrence *see* deterrence issues
    fines *see* fines
    imprisonment *see* imprisonment
    key issues 113, 125
    marginal deterrence 124–6
    optimal price 113, 122–3
    premeditated crimes 131
    rehabilitation 131

shaming devices 121
social welfare harm 123–4
cross-price elasticity of demand (CPED) 325–6

death penalty 121
decision making
    risk 37–9
    uncertainty 39–40
    see also rational choice
defective products 101
    background 96
    contributory negligence 99
    Directive on 98–100
    fair apportionment of risk 99
    necessity for tort 96–7
    prevalence of suit 99–100
    strict liability 97, 98
Dehejia, Rajeev 86
demand
    consumer choice 17–18
    cross-price elasticity of demand (CPED) 325–6
    demand-side substitution 324–6
    price elasticity of 323–4
Demsetz, Harold 322
deregulatory movement *see under* natural monopoly
deterrence issues 123–5, 132–7
    econometric difficulties 133–4, 136–7
    imprisonment scale 134–5
    magnitude/probability of punishment 132–3
    marginal deterrence 124–6
    police, increase in numbers 136
    punishment, severity magnification 135
digital copying 289, 290, 292, 295–8
    copyright law 295–6
    digital rights management (DRM) 297
    file sharing 296
    piracy 296–7
    see also copyright law
diminished capacity *see under* criminal law
distribution of resources 12–13
dominant position *see* monopoly
Drago, F. 135
drivers (of vehicles)
    levels of care 69–71
    substantive unconscionability 191–3
drug policy 137–42
    contract law 194

deferential account 137–8
demand, and price elasticity 139–41
key issues 137, 143
legalisation issues 137–9, 141–2
minimum sentences 139–40
third party effects 138
duress see under contract law
dynamic games 25–7

economic analysis of law 2–4
conclusions 414–15
key insights 4–7
economic schools 305–9, 331
ecstasy 140
education 240–2
efficiency 3, 31–3
benchmarks 32–3
and law 32
egg-shell-skull rule 95–6
electricity 387–9
employment agreements 179
employment law 248–9
endowment effect 404–5
equality issues 58–9
ethical dimensions 44
ethics of markets
contracts 53–4
efficiency 54
fairness issues 55–8
market transactions 54
unconscionable prices 56–8
utility/willingness to pay 55–6
wealth distribution 54–5
Evans, W. 136
exclusive dealerships/territories 343
expectation damages 199, 201, 205
externalities 30–1
negative externalities 407–8

financial services 389–90
fines
calibration to social cost 120
and imprisonment, relative superiority
118–20, 125–6
limitations 119–20
firm's behaviour 18–20
Fletcher, George 66
Ford-Pinto case 46–7
frustration of purpose see under
contract law

Galbiati, R. 135
gambler's fallacy 402
gambling 110, 194
game theory 23–7, 318–20
background 318
infinitely repeated game 319–20
static game 319
Greenspan, Alan 154

Harvard School 306
health-care debate 407–8
Herfindahl-Hirschman Index (HHI) 366
heroin 138
heuristics 411
anchoring heuristic 402
available heuristic 402–3
representative heuristic 401–2
horizontal agreements see under concerted
behaviour

immigration rules 248
impossibility/impracticability see under contract
law
imprisonment
and fines, relative superiority 118–20, 125–6
limitations 119–20
income, marginal utility 33–4
information technology industry 274–5
innovation policy
background 236
bankruptcy laws 246–7
capital-market efficiency 242–3
competition 243–4
education 240–2
employment law 248–9
government 238–9
immigration rules 248
inventors 239
key issues/conclusion 236, 249
legal system 242
political stability 240
private sector 237–40
public investment 249
R&D 239–40, 242, 246
regulation 244–6
technological progress 236–7
universities 238
intellectual property 256–7, 279, 297
see also copyright law; innovation policy;
patent system

inter/intra-brand competition 342–3
interdisciplinary study, value 3–4
internet 290–1
inventors/invention *see* copyright law;
      innovation policy; patent system
irrational choice 409
  bounded rationality 401–3, 409
  see also rational choice

Kahneman, Daniel 399
Kaldor-Hicks efficiency benchmark 29, 33, 60
Keynes, J.ML 40
Kitch, Edmund 266
Knightian uncertainty 39–40, 240

Landes, Elisabeth 85
latent defects 188
law and economics *see* economic analysis of law
Lerner Index 323–4
liability and accidents
  basic issues 66–8
  bilateral care *see* bilateral-care scenarios
  drivers, levels of care 69–71
  economic factors 66
  empirical literature 85–6
  insurance 83–4
  multiple liability 68
  negligence *see* negligence
  no liability 70, 73, 77, 80
  optimal standard 66–8
  precaution payoffs 72
  realism of economic account 84–5
  risk aversion 82–3
  strict liability *see* strict liability
  unilateral care *see* unilateral-care scenarios
  see also tort law
libertarianism 407–8
litigation
  agreement on expected outcome 211–13
  appeal decision 220
  bargaining range 213
  costs, English/American comparison 222–6,
    231
  discovery, role 217
  divergent expectations 213–14
  efficiency 228–9
  excessive litigation 225–6
  explanation of process 211–16
  filing complaint 221–2
  full cost 229

  key issues/conclusions 229–30
  lawyers' role 216–17
  legal uncertainty 211
  loser pays regime 224–5
  low probability/high probability 223–4
  magnitude of amount in controversy 215–16
  motion to dismiss 221
  negative-value lawsuits 217, 220–2
  optimal level 226–9
  outcomes 218–19
  parties' expectations 211–13
  policy prescription 230
  post-discovery settlement 220–1
  public good 229
  risk appetite 214–15
  rule of law 210
  social/private costs 227–8
  summary judgment 221
logging industry 150
Lopatka, Sharon 107

Mann, Michael 321
marginal cost/revenue 19
marginal-cost pricing, natural monopoly 391
marijuana 138–9
market equilibrium, and crime 20–3
market's role 323–30
  in antitrust case 323
  entry barriers 326–8
  judicial error 328–9
  market power
    measurement 323–4
    without economics 328–9
  market share as proxy 324–6
  small but significant non-transitory increase
    in price (SSNIP) 326, 330
Marshallian demand 17
Mason, Edward 320
maximum resale prices 343–4
Meiwes, Armin 53, 107
mergers
  conglomerates 366–7
  coordinated effects 366
  unilateral effects 364–6
  see also monopoly
Merges, Robert 169–70
Mill, John Stuart 49–50
minimum resale prices 344
misrepresentation/omissions *see under* contract
    law

mistake *see under* contract law
monopoly
    anticompetitive effects 354–5
    background 349
    bundled rebates 361
    coercion 352
    double marginalisation 354
    efficiencies 353–4
    entry barriers 364
    error analysis 351
    exclusionary behaviour 350–2, 368
    hands-off approach 349–50, 367–8
    limit pricing 358
    loyalty rebates 361–2
    mergers *see* mergers
    predatory pricing 356–8, 368
    price squeezes 363
    pricing issues 355–8
    product tying 352–5
    refusals to deal 359–61
    single monopoly profit theorem 352–3
    US/EU law 360–1
    vertical integration 362–4
    see also antitrust approach; natural monopoly
monopsony 340–1, 345

Nash equilibrium 26, 29, 319
Nash, John 23
natural gas 384–5
natural monopoly
    deregulatory movement 381–9, 392
    economic problems 371–2
    key issues/conclusion 373, 390–1
    limits of competition 389–90
    marginal-cost pricing 391
    optimal pricing 374–7
    peak-load pricing 377
    price caps 380–1, 392
    Ramsey pricing 374–5, 391
    rate of return regulation 377–80
    regulation 373–81
    solutions 372–3, 391–2
    two-part tariffs 376
    yardstick competition 381
    see also antitrust approach; monopoly
negligence
    basic regime 81–2
    bilateral-care scenario 74–5
    comparative negligence 76
    contributory negligence 75–6

professional 94–5
    unilateral-care scenario 70–1, 77–8
normative analysis 2

Obamacare 407–8
oligopoly models
    Bertrand competition 316
    Cournet competition 157, 273, 306,
        314–17, 319–20
    empirical literature 320–2, 331
    game theory *see* game theory
    key issues 314
    SCP *see* Structure-Conduct-Performance
        (SCP) model
    Stackelberg leadership model 316–18, 320
    tacit collusion 338–9
omissions *see under* contract law
Owens, E. 136

Pareto improvement/superiority/optimality 3,
        29, 32–3, 41
    contract law 178
    law and economics 51, 55, 60
patent system
    alternatives to 276–80
    background 252
    buy-outs 278–9
    capital investment 267–8
    claim protection 263–4
    clean room defence 263
    disclosure 262
    economic cost 254–6, 281
    economic foundation 252–4
    economic monopoly 265
    exclusions 258
    failure risk 268
    first-mover advantage 268–9
    fundamental traits 262–5, 281
    immoral patents 259
    independent incentives 266–9
    industrial application 261–2
    industry-specific profiles 269–75
    and innovation 257
    intellectual property 256–7
    inventive step 261
    justification 280
    as lawful monopoly 253–4
    maintenance system 264–5
    non-obviousness 261, 282
    novelty 260, 281

obsolescence 269
overlapping claims 254
parsimony 256–7
prizes 276–8, 281–2
property system 264
public goods theory 252–7
R&D costs 254–7, 268
regulatory exclusivity 279–80
reverse engineering 266–7
right to practice 263
scope 265–6
subject matter 258–60
tax patents 259
time limits 264
utility 281
see also copyright law; innovation policy;
    intellectual property
peak-load pricing 377
pedestrian's compensation right 228
Perloff, J.ML 322
pharmaceutical industry 269–70
concerted behaviour 339
photocopying 289
Pigouvian tax/subsidy 29–30, 41, 141, 201,
    256–7, 276
police, increase in numbers *see under* deterrence
    issues
political stability 240
positive analysis 2
premeditated crimes *see under* criminal sanctions
price
minimum resale prices 344
small but significant non-transitory increase
    in price (SSNIP) 326, 330
see also under monopoly; natural monopoly
price effect 15–17
price elasticity of demand 323–4
prizes 276–8, 281–2
property entitlements, protection
bilateral monopoly 167
damages awards/appropriator's purchase
    price, comparison 164–5
high-transaction-cost settings, proprietary
    interests 169–70
information asymmetries 166
judicial error 162, 165, 167–9
key issues 161–2
property rules/liability 161–9
strategic bargaining 166–7
supporting entitlements 165–9

transaction costs, circumstances 166–7
zero-transaction-cost environments 162–5
property rights 12
absolute/restrictive 158
appropriate scope 156–7
clarification 154–5
design of 154–7, 159
dynamic efficiency 159
dynamic inefficiency 150–1
efficient utilisation 149–51
ex post transactions 155–6
information asymmetry 152–4
key issues 7, 149
mortgage-backed securities 154
ownership 148
preclusive transaction costs 157
static efficiency 158
static inefficiency 149–50
property rules *see under* property entitlements,
    protection
prospect theory 398–400, 411
prostitution 110, 194
public investment 249

R&D 239–40, 242, 246
industry-specific 269–75
patent system 254–6, 257, 268, 277, 280
Ramsey pricing 374–5, 391
rape 129
rational choice
assumptions 34
completeness/transitivity 35–6
constrained optimisation 36
cost–benefit inquiry 35–6
descriptive function 34–5
elusive concept 34–5
expected value of outcomes 36, 41
expected-value theory 397–8
heuristics *see* heuristics
models 34
neoclassical paradigm 396
organising principle 13–15
predictive nature 37, 410–11
price theory 35–7
rationale 409–10
uncertainty 39–40
welfare over time 35
see also behavioural movement; decision
    making; irrational choice
Rawls, John 51–2, 407

rehabilitation *see under* criminal sanctions
reliance damages 199, 202–3, 205
remedies *see* breach of contract remedies
resource distribution 12–13
restitution damages 200, 205
retail price maintenance (index) 344, 380
risk
    assumption of risk *see under* tort law
    expected value/utility 37–9
    marginal utility of income 33–4
risk aversion 397–8

scarce resources
    allocation 151–2
    distribution 12–13
schools of economics 305–9, 331
Schumpeter, Joseph 243
SCP *see* Structure-Conduct-Performance (SCP) model
semiconductor industry 273–4
shaming devices 121
single monopoly profit theorem 352–3
single-shot (static) games 23–5
small but significant non-transitory increase in price (SSNIP) 326
Smith, Adam 339
Sprigman, Christopher 292
Stackelberg leadership model 316–18, 320, 331
Stigler, George 307, 327
strict liability
    bilateral-care scenarios 71, 73–4, 80–1
    comparative negligence 76, 82
    contributory negligence 75–6, 82
    tort law 92
    unilateral-care scenarios 70, 78
Structure-Conduct-Performance (SCP) model 306, 309, 320–2, 351
    critique 321–2, 331
    studies 320–1
substitution effect 16–17

tacit collusion 338–9
tax patents 259
technological progress 236–7
telecommunications 385–7
tort law
    assumption of risk 95, 101
    behavioural movement 405–6
    custom's role 94–5, 101
    defective products *see* defective products
    egg-shell-skull rule 95–6

foreseeability 90–4, 101
    injury requirement 90
    intentional torts 100–1
    key insights 5–6
    marginal deterrence 90, 101
    necessity 67–8
    no liability 92–3
    proximity 93–4
    reasonable person 89–90, 101
    unforeseeability 93–4
    see also liability and accidents
tragedy of the commons 158
TRIPS 279–80
Tversky, Amos 399
two-part tariffs 376

unconscionable agreements *see under* contract law
undue influence *see under* contract law
unilateral-care scenarios
    fixed activity levels 68–71
    variable activity levels 76–8
universities 238
unsuccessful attempts, punishment 130, 143
used cars 153–4
utilitarianism
    actions/omissions, distinction 48
    consequentialist nature 44–5, 48–9
    measurement/comparison issues 45–7
    morality issues 47–50
    rule-based approach 49–50
    social welfare calculus 50
    unpalatable options 48
    value-of-life issues 46–7
utility
    function 12, 14, 26
    willingness to pay 55–6

value-of-life issues 46–7
vehicle drivers *see* drivers (of vehicles)
vertical restraints *see under* concerted behaviour
Vertova, P. 135

wealth effect 15–16
welfare economics 50–3
    conflicting claims, resolution 51
    criminal acts 52
    equality issues 58–9
    key issues 50
    limitations 53
    welfare maximisation 51–2, 60
Williamson, Oliver 365